This book property of

Marshall Beachboard

B270   Animalia by Graeme Base   © Harry N. Abrams, Inc. 1986.

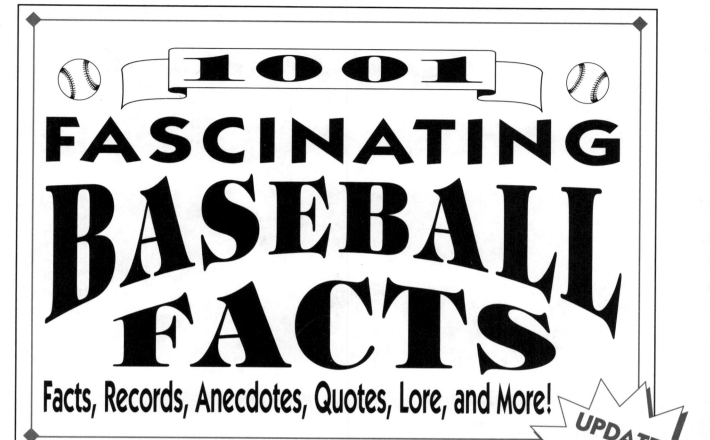

1001
FASCINATING
BASEBALL
FACTS

Facts, Records, Anecdotes, Quotes, Lore, and More!

UPDATED 1994 EDITION

David Nemec & Pete Palmer

LONGMEADOW
P R E S S

David Nemec is a baseball historian and author. He is the author of *Great Baseball Feats, Facts & Firsts* and a co-author of *The Ultimate Baseball Book* and *20th Century Baseball Chronicle.* He has written numerous baseball history, quiz, and memorabilia books as well as franchise histories for major league team yearbooks.

Pete Palmer edited both *Total Baseball* and *The Hidden Game of Baseball* with John Thorn. Palmer was the statistician for *1994 Baseball Almanac* and *1993-94 Basketball Almanac.* Palmer, a renowned sports statistician, is a member of the Society for American Baseball Research (SABR).

Photo Credits: National Baseball Library, Cooperstown, N.Y.; Photo File

ISBN: 0-681-00449-5

Printed in the United States of America

First Longmeadow Press Edition

0 9 8 7 6 5 4 3 2 1

Details of the Game

Since baseball's legacy is made up of thousands of details, only a book that sorts the game's components can complete the picture. With *1001 Fascinating Baseball Facts,* you get these particulars in the order that they happened, giving you a diehard's understanding of baseball's essence.

Some of the facts that you will find reveal a little about the time in which the game was played. For example, the world champion St. Louis Cardinals in 1934 drew only 350,000 fans in home attendance. In 1924, Freddy Lindstrom of the New York Giants, at age 18, was the youngest participant in World Series history. The song "Take Me Out to the Ball Game" was first introduced to the public in 1908. The last team to go through an entire season without using a single relief pitcher was the 1883 New York Metropolitans of the American Association. And Bobby Richardson in 1962 and Tony Oliva in 1964 were the only American Leaguers to enjoy 200-hit seasons during the 1960s.

The only player to collect 400 total bases in a season during the 1950s was Hank Aaron, who had exactly 400 in 1959. As this fact and others reveal, there are many things to discover about the legends who played the game. Did you know that the first World Series pinch homer was slugged by a Yankee rookie named Yogi Berra in 1947? Babe Ruth led the decade of the 1920s with 1,331 RBI. After pounding out 1,153 RBI, Rogers Hornsby was second during that decade only to Ruth. In 1916, while still a pitcher with the Boston Red Sox, Babe Ruth hurled nine shutouts, an AL southpaw record. Lefty Grove was the last southpaw to win 30 games in a season, as he took 31 in 1931.

Quotes from some of the men who played the game help enliven and illustrate any baseball discussion. Dizzy Dean, famed good ol' boy, once commented on his mangled English: "A lot of folks that ain't saying 'ain't' ain't eating." Manager Dave Bristol addressed his Giants team after a loss: "There'll be two buses leaving the hotel for the park tomorrow. The 2 o'clock bus will be for those of you who need a little extra work. The empty bus will leave at 5 o'clock." "Lots of people look up to Billy Martin," according to Jim Bouton.

Above: *Hank Aaron had 100 RBI in a record 13 straight seasons.*

Above: *Harmon Killebrew's 573 career homers is a record for AL righty batters.*

"That's because he just knocked them down."

Each chapter is jammed with decade-long (or era-long) batting, pitching, fielding, and managing and team leaders. The leader boxes reveal some surprising things. Harmon Killebrew was the top home run hitter in the 1960s with 393 dingers. You also may not know that he led the '60s with 970 walks. Who was the top home run hitter of the 1970s? Willie Stargell with 296. Which pitcher had the most shutouts in the

1920s? Walter Johnson with 24. Many fans could probably guess that Whitey Ford had the best winning percentage in the 1950s (.708). What they might not know is that Ford also compiled the best earned run average (2.66) in that decade. These inclusive, up-to-date records inform you of each era's top performers.

A few of the statistical categories included for the records, both in the decades and the all-time lists in the back of the book, may be unfamiliar to

some fans. The categories for batters are games played, runs, hits, total bases, doubles, triples, homers, runs batted in, stolen bases, walks, strikeouts, batting average, slugging average, on-base average, on-base average plus slugging average, and extra-base hits. Slugging percentage is the total number of bases divided by at bats. On-base average is the total number of times a batter reaches safely divided by the total number of plate appearances. On-base average plus slugging average simply adds those two numbers together to measure the effectiveness of a batter each time he makes a plate appearance.

The categories for pitchers are games pitched, games started, complete games, saves, shutouts, wins, innings pitched, strikeouts, winning percentage, earned run average, fewest walks per nine innings, and ratio. Ratio is the number of hits and walks a pitcher allows in nine innings. For fielders, the categories are putouts, assists, chances accepted, and fielding average.

For batters, the minimum for decade-long averages is 700 games played; the minimum for all-time averages is 1,000 games played. The minimum for pitchers decade-long averages is 1,000 innings pitched, all-time is 1,500 innings pitched. Fielding minimums are 500 games or 700 innings pitched for a decade, 700 games or 1,000 innings all time. For managers, the decade-long minimum for winning percentage was 500 games, with 700 for the all-time records.

The records and highlights establish baseball's heritage. Packed with information, *1001 Fascinating Baseball Facts* is a must for any sports library.

Chapter 1
The Early Years

1871-1892 GAMES	
1. Cap Anson	1,993
2. Jim O'Rourke	1,869
3. Paul Hines	1,659
4. Deacon White	1,560
5. Monte Ward	1,554
6. Jack Glasscock	1,493
7. Roger Connor	1,490
8. King Kelly	1,435
9. Harry Stovey	1,430
10. Dan Brouthers	1,385
11. Hardy Richardson	1,331
12. Bid McPhee	1,325
13. George Gore	1,310
14. Fred Pfeffer	1,300
15. George Wood	1,280
16. Ned Hanlon	1,267
17. John Morrill	1,265
Charlie Comiskey	1,265
19. Ezra Sutton	1,263
20. Tom Burns	1,251
21. Arlie Latham	1,241
22. Ned Williamson	1,201
23. Jimmy Wolf	1,198
24. Jack Burdock	1,187
25. Tom Brown	1,170

Ned Williamson of the Chicago White Stockings set the single-season record for home runs in 1884 when he hit 27. Babe Ruth broke Williamson's mark in 1919 by knocking 29 homers.

Buck Ewing of the New York Giants was the first player whose season home run output was in double digits. He hit exactly 10 in 1883, becoming the first catcher in major league history to be a league leader in home runs.

In 1884, when the Chicago White Stockings hit a record 142 home runs, the Columbus Buckeyes of the American Association were the only other major league team to have as many as 40 circuit blows.

Second baseman Fred Pfeffer collected 1,019 RBI during his career and is the only pre-1893 middle infielder who amassed 1,000 ribbies.

Baseball's first home run king was George Hall, who hit five home runs in 1876, the National League's inaugural season; a year later Hall was banned from the game.

Worcester first baseman Chub Sullivan in 1880 failed to collect a single RBI all season in 166 at bats.

Sam Thompson averaged 2.12 career home runs for every 100 at bats, making him the only 19th-century player to average over two home runs per 100 at bats.

Trying to Keep Up With the Joneses

On June 10, 1880, outfielder Charley Jones of the Boston Red Stockings set a new standard for sluggers when he became the first player in major league history to hammer two home runs in an inning. The previous year Jones had led the National League with nine circuit clouts, a record mark that stood until 1883. Jones's reward for his prowess was to be blackballed from the game by

Boston owner Arthur Soden soon after his two-homer feat. Soden held back Jones's paycheck in an effort to extract a pledge from Jones to give up drinking. When Jones objected, he was released for what Soden deemed conduct unbecoming to baseball and the citizens of Boston. Because the National League was the lone major circuit at the time and its owners had the final say as to whether

players should be allowed to play in other professional leagues as well, Jones was unable to earn his living at the game until the rebel American Association was formed in 1882 and began hiring blacklisted NL players a year later. Despite his lengthy absence from the big leagues, Jones quickly regained his stature as one of the game's top sluggers upon his return in 1883.

Foulest Batting Champ: Ross Barnes

Most baseball historians consider the first major league season to have been 1876, when the National League was formed. That year the Chicago White Stockings, owned by loop president William Hulbert, romped to an easy pennant after pilfering several stars from other teams. Among them was crack second baseman Ross Barnes, who became the first NL batting champion when he stroked .429 and scored an amazing 126 runs in just 66 games. Barnes took full advantage of a difference in the rules at the time which counted any batted ball that struck first in fair territory as a fair ball regardless of where it ultimately settled. His specialty was chopping at a pitched ball so that it hit in front of the plate and then caromed into foul territory. Barnes's craftily honed talent forced first basemen and third basemen to play outside the foul lines in order to corral his devious blows. When the rule was changed the following year, requiring a batted ball to pass a base before it could be judged fairly struck, Barnes was never again an offensive force in the game.

Dave Orr set a record for the highest batting average by a player in his final major league season when he hit .373 in 1890 for Brooklyn in the Players' League; that fall his career was ended when he suffered a stroke in an exhibition game.

In 1876, the inaugural National League season, the Chicago White Stockings set a team record that still stands when they hit .337.

◆◆◆

On May 30, 1884, third baseman Ned Williamson of the Chicago White Stockings became the first player to hit three home runs in a major league game.

After blasting a 19th-century record 27 home runs in 1884, Chicago's Ned Williamson hit just three four-baggers the following year.

◆◆◆

On April 16, 1887, rookie outfielder Mike Griffin of the Baltimore Orioles became the first player ever to homer in his first major league at bat.

1871-1892 RUNS	
1. Jim O'Rourke	1,657
2. Cap Anson	1,618
3. Harry Stovey	1,445
4. King Kelly	1,348
5. George Gore	1,327
6. Dan Brouthers	1,272
7. Roger Connor	1,254
8. Paul Hines	1,218
9. Monte Ward	1,179
10. Arlie Latham	1,150
11. Deacon White	1,140
12. Hardy Richardson	1,120
13. Bid McPhee	1,105
14. Tom Brown	1,012
15. Jack Glasscock	1,007
16. Ezra Sutton	992
17. George Wood	965
18. Ned Hanlon	930
Charlie Comiskey	930
20. Pete Browning	914
21. Curt Welch	910
22. John Reilly	898
23. Tip O'Neill	880
24. Fred Pfeffer	877
25. Henry Larkin	871

Above: *The 1880 Troy Trojans finished fourth in the National League with a 41-42 record, despite having Hall of Fame hurlers Mickey Welch and Tim Keefe. Even though they threw most of Troy's innings, the Trojans had an ERA higher than the league's average.*

Original Louisville Slugger

The Hillerich & Bradsby Company, makers of Louisville Slugger bats, long the staple of the vast majority of major league hitters, might never have gone into the business of bat manufacturing were it not for Pete Browning. In 1884, the company still specialized in wagon tongues and butter churns, but that spring Browning, a lifelong resident of Louisville and already recognized as the top hitter in the American Association, prevailed upon young Bud Hillerich to begin custom-making bats for him. In an era when most players used only one bat all season, Browning had several dozen. Each was given a name, usually after a Biblical character. Browning's bats worked such magic for him that he earned four hitting titles and posted a .341 career batting average, second only to Dan Brouthers's .342 figure among players who performed in the pre-1893 era.

In 1892, Dan Brouthers became the only player ever to top two different leagues in batting in consecutive years when he paced the National League with a .335 mark.

After losing a record 48 games to go with his 12 wins for the Philadelphia Quakers in 1883 (a team that won only 17 games), John Coleman became an outfielder and a good one; he led Pittsburgh in hits and RBI in 1887.

Above: *If the designated hitter had been established from baseball's beginnings, Pete Browning would have been among the first to fill the position. He compiled a lifetime .883 fielding percentage in the outfield. Though not a glove man, Browning played 44 games at shortstop.*

Pete Browning leads all performers who played at least four seasons in the American Association with a .345 batting average in AA competition.

Pete Browning led the American Association in batting average three times, in 1882, 1885, and 1886. He also led the Players' League in batting its only year of existence, 1890.

Pete Browning was the uncle of filmmaker and director Tod Browning, creator of Freaks, *the bleak cinema classic about life in a carnival sideshow.*

Second baseman Fred Pfeffer of the Chicago White Stockings in 1884 slugged 24 homers, at the time an amazing total for a middle infielder. Lake Front Park, Pfeffer's home ballpark (as well as the home park for NL home run leader Ned Williamson) had the shortest foul lines in major league history: 180 feet down the left field line and 196 down the right field line.

In 1880, Worcester of the National League hit just eight home runs all season but had the loop coleader in circuit blows, Harry Stovey, who clubbed six of the team's eight homers.

1871-1892 HITS	
1. Cap Anson	2,743
2. Jim O'Rourke	2,490
3. Paul Hines	2,131
4. Deacon White	2,067
5. Dan Brouthers	1,908
6. Roger Connor	1,878
7. King Kelly	1,795
8. Monte Ward	1,769
9. Jack Glasscock	1,743
10. Harry Stovey	1,721
11. Hardy Richardson	1,688
12. George Gore	1,612
13. Ezra Sutton	1,575
14. Pete Browning	1,565
15. George Wood	1,467
16. Jimmy Wolf	1,440
17. Charlie Comiskey	1,416
18. Joe Start	1,411
19. Bid McPhee	1,397
20. Tip O'Neill	1,386
21. Arlie Latham	1,368
22. John Reilly	1,352
23. Henry Larkin	1,329
24. Ned Hanlon	1,317
25. Tom Brown	1,307

1871-1892 DOUBLES	
1. Cap Anson	472
2. Jim O'Rourke	445
3. Paul Hines	405
4. Dan Brouthers	375
5. King Kelly	358
6. Harry Stovey	339
7. Roger Connor	328
8. Hardy Richardson	303
9. Pete Browning	284
10. Jack Glasscock	283
11. Deacon White	270
12. George Gore	262
13. John Morrill	239
Henry Larkin	239
15. Tom Burns	236
16. Ezra Sutton	229
17. George Wood	228
Ned Williamson	228
19. Fred Dunlap	224
20. Tip O'Neill	222
Jerry Denny	222
22. Abner Dalrymple	217
23. Tom York	216
24. John Reilly	215
25. Curt Welch	214
Bill Phillips	214

Bill Kuehne retired in 1892 with a .232 career batting average but had 115 triples, at the time a record for third basemen.

When the Boston Red Stockings won the National League pennant in 1878, they had no players among the top five in any major batting department and had the second-lowest batting average in the loop at .241.

The last player to hit four triples in a nine-inning game was Bill Joyce, who did it with the New York Giants on May 18, 1897.

In 1886, Milt Scott hit .190 for Baltimore of the American Association, the lowest average in history by a first baseman with over 400 at bats.

Ed McKean and Cupid Childs, the Cleveland Spiders' keystone combo in the 1890s, each has the highest career batting average for a player at his position who is not in the Hall of Fame.

"You can't tell the players without a scorecard."
—Harry Stevens, the first ballpark concessionaire

1871-1892 TRIPLES	
1. Roger Connor	181
2. Harry Stovey	168
3. Dan Brouthers	167
4. Jim O'Rourke	144
5. Buck Ewing	142
6. John Reilly	139
7. George Wood	132
8. Hardy Richardson	126
Bid McPhee	126
Cap Anson	126
11. Bill Kuehne	115
12. Henry Larkin	111
13. Jimmy Wolf	109
14. Dave Orr	108
15. Oyster Burns	103
16. King Kelly	102
Charley Jones	102
Tom Brown	102
19. Deacon White	99
20. Bill Phillips	98
21. Ezra Sutton	97
22. Sam Wise	95
23. George Gore	94
24. Tip O'Neill	92
Paul Hines	92

Low, Lower, Lowest Batting Averages

In 1885, while Roger Connor was hitting .371 for the New York Giants to lead the National League in batting, Giants second baseman "Move Up Joe" Gerhardt posted a batting average more than 200 points lower. Gerhardt's .155 figure is the all-time record low for a regular player other than a catcher. A year later, Gerhardt could hike his average only as high as .190 but nevertheless managed to stay in the majors for four more years. He was able to accumulate 3,770 at bats in his career. Another abysmal hitter in 1886, Jim Lillie of the Kansas City Cowboys, then in the National League, was history after he batted a meager .175, the lowest mark ever for a regular outfielder. Shockingly low batting averages were common for several years in the mid-1880s, owing largely to a rule instituted in 1884 allowing pitchers to throw overhand. The increased velocity made possible by an overhand delivery also caused strikeout totals to jump astronomically during that period.

When Dave Orr hit .338 for the New York Metropolitans in 1886, his average was 97 points higher than the club's second-best hitting regular, Frank Hankinson (.241).

Outfielder Dummy Hoy, with a .274 average, was the only regular on the Washington National League team to hit above .225.

When Walks Equaled Hits

In 1887, for one season only, baseball officials decided to credit a batter with a hit each time he received a base on balls or was struck by a pitch. Their generosity enabled outfielder Tip O'Neill of the American Association champion St. Louis Browns to register a .492 batting average. Statisticians have since deducted O'Neill's free passes from his hit total that season, thereupon reducing his average to a mere .435. In addition, O'Neill led or tied for the Association lead in every significant batting department in 1887 except walks. Although O'Neill's RBI figures for the 1887 season are incomplete, it is almost an absolute certainty that he knocked home more runs than any other Association hitter. Most historians consequently award him a Triple Crown—for a number of years he was even regarded as the first Triple Crown winner in major league history. O'Neill never again had a season remotely close to his 1887 campaign but did finish with a .326 career batting average for his ten years of work.

Above: *King Kelly was one of the most daring baserunners of his era. He once stole six bases in a single game, had 84 in one season, and his sliding even inspired a song: Slide, Kelly, Slide.*

Dick Higham, the only umpire ever banned for taking a bribe, tied for the National League lead in doubles in 1876 with 21.

Long Game
King Kelly, asked by a reporter if he drank while playing, responded: "It depends on the length of the game."

1871-1892 TOTAL BASES	
1. Cap Anson	3,725
2. Jim O'Rourke	3,403
3. Paul Hines	2,894
4. Dan Brouthers	2,893
5. Roger Connor	2,865
6. Harry Stovey	2,759
7. Deacon White	2,604
8. King Kelly	2,564
9. Hardy Richardson	2,453
10. Jack Glasscock	2,251
11. George Gore	2,200
12. Monte Ward	2,197
13. George Wood	2,163
14. Pete Browning	2,148
15. Ezra Sutton	2,076
16. John Reilly	2,052
17. Tip O'Neill	1,948
18. Henry Larkin	1,937
19. Bid McPhee	1,936
20. Jimmy Wolf	1,925
21. Fred Pfeffer	1,882
22. Charlie Comiskey	1,823
23. Buck Ewing	1,816
24. John Morrill	1,803
25. Tom Burns	1,790

Hines Wins First Triple Crown

Upon the finish of the 1878 season, the National League batting crown was awarded to rookie Abner Dalrymple of Milwaukee. Not until nearly a century later did it emerge that calculation errors had been made in determining the NL bat leader in 1878. The true winner is now recognized to have been Paul Hines of Providence with a .358 mark, four points above Dalrymple's .354 figure. Dalrymple was originally credited with having outhit Hines .356 to .351. RBI totals for the 1878 season, another recent discovery, reveal that Hines also led in that department. Hines went to his grave in 1935 believing he had topped the NL only in home runs in 1878. Historians now know him to have been the first Triple Crown winner in major league history—and also the National League's first repeat batting champion. After allegedly finishing second to Dalrymple in 1878, Hines won the crown beyond all dispute the following year when he hit .357 for the pennant-winning Providence club.

The first Triple Crown winner in major league history was outfielder Paul Hines of Providence, who did it in 1878. Sixteen years later, Hugh Duffy became the second to turn the trick.

In 1892, catcher Wilbert Robinson led the Baltimore Orioles in RBI with 57—with 11 of them coming in the June 10, 1892, game.

Above: *The first batting champion in the first modern professional baseball league, third baseman Levi Meyerle of the Philadelphia Athletics, won the 1881 National Association's first hit crown with a .492 batting average.*

1871-1892 HOME RUNS

1.	Harry Stovey	121
2.	Roger Connor	99
3.	Dan Brouthers	92
4.	Cap Anson	86
5.	Fred Pfeffer	84
6.	Jimmy Ryan	73
	Jerry Denny	73
8.	Sam Thompson	72
9.	Hardy Richardson	70
10.	John Reilly	69
	King Kelly	69
12.	George Wood	68
13.	Ned Williamson	64
14.	Mike Tiernan	63
15.	Jim O'Rourke	60
16.	Paul Hines	58
17.	Buck Ewing	57
18.	Charley Jones	56
19.	Tip O'Neill	52
	Oyster Burns	52
21.	Charlie Bennett	51
22.	Henry Larkin	49
23.	Jocko Milligan	47
	Denny Lyons	47
25.	George Gore	46

1871-1892 RUNS BATTED IN

1.	Cap Anson	1,449
2.	Dan Brouthers	1,048
3.	Roger Connor	963
4.	King Kelly	935
5.	Jim O'Rourke	915
6.	Hardy Richardson	822
7.	Fred Pfeffer	813
8.	Deacon White	777
9.	Paul Hines	751
10.	Sam Thompson	746
11.	Monte Ward	713
12.	Tom Burns	683
13.	Ned Williamson	667
14.	Jack Glasscock	646
15.	Jack Rowe	644
16.	John Morrill	643
17.	George Gore	618
18.	Jerry Denny	613
19.	Sam Wise	595
20.	Buck Ewing	590
21.	Billy Nash	581
22.	George Wood	565
23.	Joe Hornung	564
24.	Ezra Sutton	541
25.	Ned Hanlon	517

The 1878 Providence Grays had an all-.300 hitting outfield, featuring Triple Crown winner Paul Hines, but had no infielders who could hit above .239.

On June 10, 1892, catcher Wilbert Robinson of the last-place Baltimore Orioles went 7-for-7 and had 11 RBI in a nine-inning game against St. Louis.

Three years after he became the American Association's first home run champion in 1882, Oscar Walker was out of baseball and working as a groundskeeper.

Above: *George Wright was the star shortstop of the 1869 Cincinnati Red Stockings, who went undefeated in 130 consecutive games. Wright later helped establish a successful sporting goods business. In 1884, he helped start the Union Association, a rival major league to the NL. Wright also was instrumental in the start of baseball's Hall of Fame.*

1871-1892 WALKS	
1. Roger Connor	724
2. George Gore	717
3. Cap Anson	712
4. Dan Brouthers	665
5. Yank Robinson	664
6. Paul Radford	621
7. Harry Stovey	609
8. King Kelly	543
9. Jim McTamany	535
10. Bid.McPhee	532
11. Ned Williamson	506
12. George Pinkney	475
13. Emmett Seery	471
Ned Hanlon	471
15. Jim O'Rourke	462
16. Tom Brown	451
17. Billy Nash	448
18. Dummy Hoy	443
19. Charlie Bennett	438
20. Henry Larkin	434
21. Tip O'Neill	421
Pete Browning	421
23. Arlie Latham	420
24. George Wood	418
25. Fred Pfeffer	405

In 1876, Cincinnati outfielder Charley Jones hit all of his team's four home runs and was second in the National League in four-baggers.

The Cincinnati Enquirer reported on Harry Wright: "He is a base ball Edison. He eats base ball, breathes base ball, thinks base ball, and incorporates base ball in his prayers."

The 1869 Cincinnati Red Stockings—the first openly professional team—had payroll expenses totaling about $9,400. That is about what the average contemporary player makes per game.

The 1869 Cincinnati Red Stockings were run by the aptly named Aaron Champion.

1871-1892 STOLEN BASES	
1. Arlie Latham	572
2. Harry Stovey	486
3. Monte Ward	455
4. Curt Welch	452
5. Tom Brown	427
6. Billy Hamilton	400
Charlie Comiskey	400
8. Bid McPhee	384
9. Hugh Nicol	383
10. King Kelly	365
11. Tommy McCarthy	339
12. Hub Collins	335
13. Ned Hanlon	329
14. Jim Fogarty	325
15. Mike Griffin	323
16. Darby O'Brien	321
17. Jack Glasscock	314
18. Paul Radford	290
Fred Pfeffer	290
20. George Pinkney	284
21. Tommy Tucker	282
22. Hugh Duffy	279
23. Dummy Hoy	275
24. Cub Stricker	274
25. Yank Robinson	272

1869 Cincinnati Club Best Ever?

Ten years before he managed and shortstopped the Providence Grays to the National League flag in 1879, George Wright played under his brother Harry for arguably the most formidable team in history—the 1869 Cincinnati Red Stockings. The Queen City nine ran off a record 130 straight victories before being stopped on June 14, 1870, by the Atlantics of Brooklyn. So dominant was the Cincinnati outfit that its games seldom went a full nine innings.

Occasionally the opposition was blown out by over 100 runs. George Wright customarily did the brunt of the damage. His estimated batting average for all games in 1869 was around .629, and in a typical game he would score about five runs. As a team, the Red Stockings are believed to have hit well over .400 in 1869. Oddly, when the club's streak was derailed by the Atlantics, it was not a hitting failure but a muffed double-play ball that settled the issue.

1871-1892 STRIKEOUTS	
1. John Morrill	656
2. Jim Galvin	630
3. Sam Wise	616
4. Jerry Denny	575
5. George Wood	547
6. Charlie Bennett	536
7. Ned Williamson	532
8. Joe Hornung	498
9. Tom Brown	463
10. Silver Flint	461
11. Tom Burns	454
12. Hardy Richardson	445
13. Fred Pfeffer	442
14. Emmett Seery	426
15. King Kelly	412
16. Tim Keefe	387
17. Roger Connor	382
18. Arthur Irwin	378
19. Abner Dalrymple	359
20. Ned Hanlon	357
21. John Clarkson	354
22. Pop Smith	345
23. George Gore	332
24. Mark Baldwin	330
25. Mickey Welch	329
Harry Stovey	329

When he averaged 1.58 runs per game in 1884, second baseman Fred Dunlap of the St. Louis Maroons in the Union Association set an all-time record for players in 100 games, minimum.

Above: *Jack Glasscock led the NL in hits in 1889 with Indianapolis and in 1890 with New York. He replaced Monte Ward at shortstop for the '90 Giants after Ward formed the Players' League.*

'Pebbly' Dominates Early Shortstops

Fred Dunlap of the Union Association St. Louis Maroons set a record with a 1.58 runs per game average in 1884. Only a cut below Dunlap as both a fielder and a hitter in 1884 was Jack Glasscock. Nicknamed "Pebbly" because of his penchant for keeping his shortstop area free of small stones that might cause bad hops, Glasscock began the 1884 season with Cleveland of the National League but jumped in midcampaign to the Cincinnati Outlaw Reds of the Union Association. In 38 games with the Cincinnati club, Glasscock hit .419 and first showed evidence that he was more than a deft fielder. Six years later, back in the National League with the New York Giants, Glasscock became the first shortstop in major league history to win a batting crown when he hit .336. Until the end of his career Glasscock continued to be highly valued. Many analysts rate him the best shortstop of the game's first era.

McTamany On Base

Only in recent years have players who are not particularly good hitters but are nonetheless proficient at the game's primary offensive task—getting on base and scoring runs—begun to receive their due. One such player in the game's early days was Jim McTamany, an outfielder who performed for seven years in the American Association. McTamany might be recognized as a star if he were playing now, but in his time he was so lightly regarded that he was squeezed out of the major leagues after the 1891 season at the early age of 28 when the American Association disbanded and the National League would take on board only four of its eight teams. Baseball moguls considered only McTamany's .239 batting average in 1891.

What they failed to take into account were the 116 runs he scored and his 101 walks. He also compiled a .370 on-base percentage for both Columbus and Philadelphia of the AA. McTamany's departure after what has since come to be viewed as a banner season left him the only player ever to collect both 100 or more walks and runs in his final big league campaign.

Jim McTamany of Columbus led the American Association in both walks and runs in 1890 despite hitting just .258.

Ed Swartwood, who led the American Association in 1883 with a .356 batting average, was the only Pittsburgh performer prior to Honus Wagner to be a batting leader.

Cap Anson was credited with being originator of spring training. In 1886, he took his defending champion White Stockings to Hot Springs, Arkansas to "boil out all the beer and booze they had swilled over the winter."

In 1887, playing in 127 games, Sam Thompson netted 166 RBI to set a pre-1893 record. Thompson also holds the mark for the second-most RBI in the last century—165 in 1895.

Sam Thompson (above) in 1887 catapulted the Detroit Wolverines to an NL pennant and a subsequent World Series triumph over the AA champion St. Louis Browns. In 1888, Thompson was idled much of the season by an injury; Detroit disbanded after plummeting to fifth place. The 1889 NL remained an eight-team circuit by putting a team in Cleveland. Instead of moving the Wolverines franchise to Cleveland, the NL enticed the AA team already in Cleveland to jump to the NL.

Despite his slugging stats, Sam Thompson was overshadowed much of his career by more famous teammates, such as Dan Brouthers and Ed Delahanty.

1871-1892 ON-BASE AVERAGE	
1. Dan Brouthers	.422
2. Denny Lyons	.406
3. Pete Browning	.399
4. Roger Connor	.398
5. Tip O'Neill	.392
6. Cap Anson	.387
7. George Gore	.386
8. Mike Tiernan	.386
9. Ed Swartwood	.378
10. Henry Larkin	.377
11. Yank Robinson	.375
12. Jimmy Ryan	.375
13. Jim McTamany	.373
14. Tommy Tucker	.372
15. Fred Carroll	.370
16. Sam Thompson	.369
17. King Kelly	.368
18. Oyster Burns	.368
19. Dave Orr	.366
20. Mike Griffin	.364
21. Harry Stovey	.359
22. Ed McKean	.359
23. Billy Nash	.355
24. Jim O'Rourke	.353
25. Tommy McCarthy	.348

The major league record for the most career at bats without an extra base hit is held by Herman Pitz, who collected just 47 singles in 284 at bats for two American Association teams in 1890.

In 1887, Tom Poorman of the Philadelphia Athletics in the American Association reached base just 190 times via hits and walks but nevertheless scored 140 runs.

In 1884, the three players who shared the Detroit Wolverines' shortstop job—Frank Meinke, Harry Buker and Frank Cox— hit .164, .150, and .127, respectively.

1871-1892 BATTING AVERAGE	
1. Dan Brouthers	.343
2. Dave Orr	.342
3. Pete Browning	.341
4. Cap Anson	.333
5. Tip O'Neill	.326
6. Roger Connor	.321
7. Denny Lyons	.316
8. Jim O'Rourke	.313
9. Sam Thompson	.312
10. Deacon White	.312
11. King Kelly	.308
12. Jimmy Ryan	.306
13. Mike Tiernan	.303
14. Henry Larkin	.302
15. Paul Hines	.302
16. George Gore	.301
17. Buck Ewing	.301
18. Ed Swartwood	.299
19. Hardy Richardson	.299
20. Charley Jones	.298
21. Joe Start	.298
22. Oyster Burns	.297
23. Tommy Tucker	.297
24. Ezra Sutton	.294
25. Fred Dunlap	.292

Lyons Early Offensive Threat at Third

Like Jim McTamany, Denny Lyons was an unrecognized offensive star from the pre-1893 period. Lyons was the leading hitter of his day at his position. The position was third base, a station that for reasons which are no longer entirely clear became the province in the last century of players with strong arms and weak bats. Lyons was one of the few exceptions. In his 13 big league campaigns he registered a .310 batting average, the highest of any third sacker who played prior to the advent of the lively ball era in 1920. He was often among league leaders in batting and fielding. Lyons's pinnacle came in 1887, his first full season, when he clubbed .367 for Philadelphia of the American Association and netted 209 hits; the latter figure for many years stood as a record for third basemen.

On June 27, 1876, Davy Force of Philadelphia became the first player to make six hits in a nine-inning game; Force went on to bat just .230 that year.

Monte Ward is the only player in major league history to win more than 150 games as a pitcher and accumulate more than 2,000 hits.

In 1876, Mike McGeary of St. Louis in the NL set an all-time record when he fanned just once all season in 276 at bats.

1871-1892 SLUGGING AVERAGE	
1. Dan Brouthers	.520
2. Dave Orr	.502
3. Roger Connor	.489
4. Pete Browning	.468
5. Sam Thompson	.467
6. Harry Stovey	.465
7. Mike Tiernan	.464
8. Jimmy Ryan	.462
9. Buck Ewing	.459
10. Tip O'Neill	.458
11. Denny Lyons	.454
12. Cap Anson	.452
13. Oyster Burns	.447
14. Charley Jones	.444
15. Henry Larkin	.440
16. King Kelly	.440
17. Jocko Milligan	.439
18. John Reilly	.438
19. Hardy Richardson	.435
20. Jim O'Rourke	.428
21. George Gore	.411
22. Abner Dalrymple	.410
23. Paul Hines	.410
24. Fred Carroll	.408
25. Fred Dunlap	.406

Above: *Dan Brouthers played on flag-winning teams in three different major leagues. Among his championship squads were the 1894 Baltimore Orioles, for whom he last saw regular duty. In his final full season Brouthers stroked .347 and drove home 128 runs.*

Bad-Luck Year for Pitchers

The 1884 season—featuring three major leagues and numerous rule changes that altered the game's complexion—was rife with bizarre occurrences and odd achievements. High among them were the contributions made to the game's lore by several pitchers who disappeared from the major leagues at the season's close. Pitching for the Baltimore Union Association entry, Bill Sweeney topped the UA in wins with 40. His 40 victories instead of meriting an encore appearance in the majors became the record for the most wins by a pitcher in his last season, for Sweeney never again participated in a major league game after 1884. Fleury Sullivan served the season as the rookie pitching ace of lowly AA Pittsburgh and then was never seen again, leaving behind a record for the most innings (441) by a hurler in his lone big league season. Hugh Daily was the Jim Abbott of the last century. Despite losing the lower half of his left arm in an explosion at the fireworks factory where he worked as a teenager, Daily fashioned a six-year career in the majors. He reached his apex in 1884, notching 28 wins and 483 strikeouts. After leaving the majors three years later, Daily dropped into oblivion. His whereabouts after baseball is a mystery that haunts present-day baseball researchers.

Pud Galvin won a 19th-century record 361 games but was never a league leader in either wins, strikeouts, or ERA.

On June 7, 1884, Charlie Sweeney of the Providence Grays struck out 19 batters during a game against the Boston Beaneaters. His single-game total of 19 was matched several times, but it was not broken until 1986.

In 1891, Pittsburgh finished last in the National League with a mound staff that featured Hall of Famer Pud Galvin, plus Silver King, and Mark Baldwin, the two top hurlers in the Players' League the previous year.

In 1876, Pud Galvin (above) joined the Allegheny baseball club of Pittsburgh, which was in the International Association, the first minor league in history. Galvin was with Allegheny for two seasons. One of Galvin's wins for Allegheny in 1877 was a 1-0 shutout over Tommy Bond, who was the star pitcher for the Boston Red Stockings of the National League. Bond was 40-17 that year and led the NL with 170 strikeouts. The only run scored that day was a homer by none other than Pud Galvin.

1871-1892 GAMES PITCHED	
1. Pud Galvin	705
2. Bobby Mathews	578
Tim Keefe	578
4. Mickey Welch	564
5. Old Hoss Radbourn	528
6. Jim McCormick	492
7. Tony Mullane	481
8. John Clarkson	473
9. Tommy Bond	417
10. Charlie Buffinton	414
11. Jim Whitney	413
12. Will White	403
13. Al Spalding	347
George Bradley	347
15. Bob Caruthers	340
16. Guy Hecker	334
17. Silver King	329
18. Adonis Terry	321
19. Gus Weyhing	316
20. Ed Morris	311
21. Mark Baldwin	301
22. Charlie Getzien	296
23. Monte Ward	292
24. Stump Weidman	279
25. Matt Kilroy	277
Larry Corcoran	277

In 1887, Bob Caruthers of the St. Louis Browns not only topped all American Association pitchers in winning percentage but finished fourth in the loop in batting.

In 1890, Chicago of the Players' League had the loop's two top individual leaders in games won in Mark Baldwin and Silver King but managed to finish just third.

On August 4, 1882, Pud Galvin of Buffalo pitched the most lopsided no-hitter in history when he beat Detroit 18-0.

As a rookie with Cincinnati in 1889, Jesse Duryea won 32 games and was second in the American Association with a 2.56 ERA; he collected only 27 more career victories.

In 1889, John Clarkson of Boston won 21 more games and hurled 200 more innings than any other pitcher in the National League.

When the American Association first allowed overhand pitching in 1885, batting averages throughout the circuit plummeted so sharply that the top hitting regular for the pennant-winning St. Louis Browns, Curt Welch, batted just .271.

1871-1892 COMPLETE GAMES	
1. Pud Galvin	646
2. Tim Keefe	537
3. Mickey Welch	525
Bobby Mathews	525
5. Old Hoss Radbourn	489
6. Jim McCormick	466
7. John Clarkson	441
8. Tony Mullane	422
9. Will White	394
10. Tommy Bond	386
11. Jim Whitney	377
12. Charlie Buffinton	351
13. Guy Hecker	310
14. George Bradley	302
15. Bob Caruthers	298
16. Ed Morris	297
17. Silver King	293
18. Gus Weyhing	283
19. Al Spalding	281
20. Adonis Terry	280
21. Charlie Getzien	277
22. Mark Baldwin	263
23. Larry Corcoran	256
24. Stump Weidman	249
25. Matt Kilroy	246

Old Hoss Radbourn of National League Providence set an all-time record in 1884 when he won 60 games; that same year Guy Hecker won 52 for Louisville to break the American Association record and Bill Sweeney won 40 for Baltimore to set the Union Association mark.

By today's rule for determining the winning pitcher in a game, Old Hoss Radbourn would have had only 59 victories in 1884 rather than 60.

CHARLES RADBOURN.

Old Hoss Radbourn (above) played outfield in the minors. He was not impressive until he pitched in the bigs.

You Can Take the Boy Outta Jersey

During his 14-year career, Tim Keefe pitched in three major leagues and won games in an all-time record 47 different major league parks. One of Keefe's contemporaries went him one better. Between 1883 and 1891, Jersey Bakely toiled in four different major leagues and had at least one season in each of them in which he won in double figures. No other pitcher before or since has spread his work so widely. Bakely's trouble was that his work was seldom effective. He won just 76 of 201 decisions for a dismal .378 career winning percentage. The fault was not completely his, however, as only in his first season, when he appeared in a handful of games with the American Association champion Philadelphia Athletics, was he with a team that had a winning record. Bakely's best year was 1888 when he won 25 games for Cleveland, a sixth-place finisher in the American Association. His nickname, like those of many early day players, stemmed from the location where he was born.

Beginning in 1890, Kid Nichols won 26 or more games for nine consecutive years. He was the top winning pitcher in any decade, winning 297 in the 1890s.

Monte Ward is the only player in major league history to win more than 150 games as a pitcher and accumulate more than 2,000 hits.

In 1888, pitcher Tim Keefe of the New York Giants won 19 straight games, a single-season record that was tied in 1912 by Rube Marquard, also of the Giants.

During his 14-year career Tim Keefe pitched in three major leagues and won games in an all-time record 47 different major league parks.

1871-1892 SAVES

1.	Jack Manning	13
2.	Harry Wright	12
3.	Al Spalding	10
4.	Tony Mullane	9
5.	Adonis Terry	6
6.	Cal McVey	5
	John Clarkson	5
8.	George Hemming	4
	Herb Goodall	4
	Bill Daley	4
	Oyster Burns	4
	Mickey Welch	4
	George Van Haltren	4
	Billy Taylor	4
	Hank O'Day	4
	Kid Gleason	4
	Dave Foutz	4
	Charlie Ferguson	4
19.	Ned Williamson	3
	John Morrill	3
	Gus Weyhing	3
	Monte Ward	3
	Jack Stivetts	3
	Lee Richmond	3
	Kid Nichols	3
	Sadie McMahon	3
	Bobby Mathews	3
	Pat Luby	3
	Silver King	3
	Bill Hutchinson	3
	Cherokee Fisher	3
	Jesse Duryea	3
	Bob Caruthers	3
	Charlie Buffinton	3

Above: Tim Keefe racked up 342 wins between 1880 and 1893. Known for his control and his ability to pitch from varying mound distances, the beloved "Sir Timothy" led his league in ERA three times, guided the New York Giants to their first pennant, and helped establish the Players' League in 1890. His 1888 season, in which he led the NL in wins, ERA, strikeouts, and shutouts, made him the highest-paid Giant at a king-sized salary of $4,500.

The first team to have two 30-game winners was the 1884 New York Metropolitans, which featured Tim Keefe (37-17) and Jack Lynch (37-15).

Caruthers Delivers Double-Duty

The St. Louis Browns in 1887 showcased rookie sensation Silver King, and the club had two other fine hurlers, Bob Caruthers and Dave Foutz. The trio of 20-game winners gave the Browns the game's first outstanding three-man pitching rotation. King was the youngest at 19, but Caruthers was by far the exceptional all-around talent. In 1885, his first full season, Caruthers paced the American Association with 40 wins, a .755 winning percentage, and a 2.07 ERA. The following year he slipped to 30 victories but part of the reason was because he was too busy elsewhere to devote full attention to his pitching. When not in the box Caruthers was playing right field for the Browns and leading the club in hitting. His .334 average was in fact the fourth-best in the Association that season. Caruthers continued to do double-duty until his pitching arm went in 1892 but not before he compiled a .688 career winning percentage, the highest by any hurler in the game's first era. After his playing days were over, he became a major league umpire for a brief while.

The 1882 Detroit Wolverines were the first major league team to have two 20-game losers.

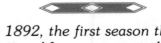

In 1892, the first season the National League operated as a 12-team circuit, every club but St. Louis had at least one 20-game winner.

Hecker's Triple Threat: Hurling, Hitting, and Homers

A pitcher who took his regular turn in the box and hit .334 as an everyday player would stand as one of a kind in baseball history but for one small hitch. In 1886, Bob Caruthers was not the only hurler who was also a great hitter; he was not even the best of his time. That season, Guy Hecker of the Louisville Colonels won 26 games while working 420 innings and also found time to lead the American Association in hitting with a .341 mark. Hecker's arm was on the wane in 1886; two years earlier he had won 52 games for Louisville to establish an American Association single-season record. But if his arm was deserting him, the rest of his game was only just beginning to accelerate. In 1886, Hecker not only became the only pitcher ever to cop a batting crown, he also scored an all-time record seven runs in a game and in the same contest became the first pitcher to blast three home runs. Nicknamed "The Big Blond," Hecker finished with a .283 career batting average and 173 wins, most of them packed into his first four full seasons.

When Guy Hecker hit three homers in one game in 1886, all were inside-the-park dingers.

Guy Hecker was the only AA player to hit three homers in one game.

On July 28, 1875, Joe Borden of Philadelphia, a National Association entry, became the first pitcher to throw a no-hitter in a professional game when he topped Chicago 4-0.

1871-1892 SHUTOUTS	
1. Pud Galvin	57
2. Tommy Bond	42
3. Mickey Welch	41
4. Tim Keefe	39
5. Will White	36
John Clarkson	36
7. Old Hoss Radbourn	35
8. Jim McCormick	33
9. George Bradley	32
10. Tony Mullane	30
Charlie Buffinton	30
12. Ed Morris	29
13. Jim Whitney	26
14. Monte Ward	24
Al Spalding	24
Bob Caruthers	24
17. Larry Corcoran	22
18. Gus Weyhing	21
19. Bobby Mathews	19
Candy Cummings	19
21. Jumbo McGinnis	18
Silver King	18
Matt Kilroy	18
24. Kid Nichols	17
Bill Hutchinson	17

Larry Corcoran debuted in 1880 with 43 wins for Chicago and bagged 170 wins in his first five seasons but then won just seven more games before a lame arm forced him to quit.

In 1890, Sadie McMahon became the first pitcher to top his loop in wins despite pitching for a second-division team when he paced the American Association with 36 victories.

In 1890, Chicago of the Players' League had the loop's two top individual leaders in games won in Mark Baldwin and Silver King but managed to finish just third.

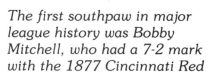

The first southpaw in major league history was Bobby Mitchell, who had a 7-2 mark with the 1877 Cincinnati Red Stockings.

After winning 24 games and topping the National League with an .800 winning percentage as a rookie in 1886, Jocko Flynn of Chicago never pitched another inning in the majors.

1871-1892 WINS	
1. Pud Galvin	364
2. Tim Keefe	332
3. Old Hoss Radbourn	309
4. Mickey Welch	307
5. John Clarkson	304
6. Bobby Mathews	297
7. Jim McCormick	265
8. Tony Mullane	259
9. Al Spalding	253
10. Tommy Bond	234
11. Charlie Buffinton	233
12. Will White	229
13. Bob Caruthers	218
14. Jim Whitney	191
15. Silver King	180
16. Gus Weyhing	177
Larry Corcoran	177
18. Guy Hecker	173
19. Ed Morris	171
George Bradley	171
21. Monte Ward	164
22. Dick McBride	149
23. Dave Foutz	147
24. Charlie Getzien	145
Candy Cummings	145

Cummings, Others Father New Deliveries

To Candy Cummings is attributed the invention of the curveball. Whether or not Cummings really did originate the curve will probably always be a matter of dispute, but the Hall of Fame nonetheless beckoned him inside its doors long ago. Along with curveball practioners like Cummings, the early game offered a panoply of bizarre and contrasting pitching styles. Among the more interesting were the deliveries employed by Stooping Jack Gorman, so-called because he bent so low that his knuckles often scraped the ground when he released the ball. Another who collected a nickname for his unusual pitching style was Peek-a-Boo Veach, who reportedly kept his back to the batter and did not allow him even a peek at the ball until it actually left his hand. Gorman and Veach were never more than sporadically effective hurlers, however, nor was Billy Hart, who brought another dimension to the pitching art in the late 1890s when he began employing a spitball. Hart's spitter in 1897 got him just nine wins to go with his 27 losses for the last-place St. Louis Browns.

In 1892, Bill Hutchinson of Chicago became the last hurler to work over 600 innings when he logged 627 frames.

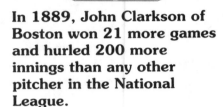

When he won 47 games for Chicago in 1876, Al Spalding logged just 39 strikeouts in 529 innings pitched.

Above: *Amos Rusie, "The Hoosier Cannonball," won 234 games with the Giants in the 1890s. A renowned curveballer, Rusie still holds the single-season record for walks (289). After holding out in 1896, he led the league in ERA the next year. At the end of his career, Rusie was traded for a young Christy Mathewson.*

First Curve

Candy Cummings described how he invented the curve: "A number of my chums and I were throwing shells one day in Brooklyn. When seeing a shell take a wide curve I said, 'Now if only I could make a ball do that I think the other clubs won't be in it.'"

In 1876, George Bradley pitched every inning of every one of the 64 games played by his team, the St. Louis Brown Stockings; Bradley's 45-19 mark brought the club home second.

Amos Rusie of the New York Giants and Bill Hutchinson of the Chicago White Stockings in 1892 were the last two hurlers to both win and lose 30 games in the same season.

In 1886, Matty Kilroy, a rookie lefthander with the Baltimore Orioles of the American Association, fanned an all-time record 513 batters. He never again struck out more than 217 in a season.

In 1889, John Clarkson of Boston won 21 more games and hurled 200 more innings than any other pitcher in the National League.

1871-1892 INNINGS	
1. Pud Galvin	6,003.1
2. Bobby Mathews	4,956.0
3. Tim Keefe	4,883.1
4. Mickey Welch	4,802.0
5. Old Hoss Radbourn	4,535.1
6. Jim McCormick	4,275.2
7. John Clarkson	4,090.2
8. Tony Mullane	4,008.2
9. Tommy Bond	3,628.2
10. Will White	3,542.2
11. Jim Whitney	3,496.1
12. Charlie Buffinton	3,404.0
13. George Bradley	2,940.0
14. Guy Hecker	2,906.0
15. Al Spalding	2,893.2
16. Bob Caruthers	2,828.2
17. Silver King	2,737.1
18. Ed Morris	2,678.0
19. Gus Weyhing	2,629.0
20. Adonis Terry	2,625.1
21. Charlie Getzien	2,539.2
22. Mark Baldwin	2,477.2
23. Monte Ward	2,461.2
24. Larry Corcoran	2,392.1
25. Stump Weidman	2,318.1

Whitney Tops and Bottoms

When Phil Niekro led National League pitchers in both wins and losses in 1979, statisticians had to go back 98 years to find a comparable achievement. In 1881, rookie Jim Whitney of the Boston Red Stockings posted a 31-33 mark to pace the National League in both victories and defeats. He also led the loop with 552⅓ innings pitched. Two years later, Whitney had his best season when he logged 37 triumphs for the champion Bostons, but the club released him after he registered 32 setbacks in 1885. Whitney was nicknamed "Grasshopper" because he had a small head and an elongated body. In addition to being a fine pitcher for a few years, he was an outstanding hitter and the first hurler ever to lead his team in home runs. In 1882, he became the first pitcher ever to finish among his league's top five hitters when he batted .323. The following season Whitney collected 115 hits and 177 total bases along with winning 37 games.

1871-1892 STRIKEOUTS	
1. Tim Keefe	2,474
2. John Clarkson	1,888
3. Mickey Welch	1,850
4. Old Hoss Radbourn	1,830
5. Pud Galvin	1,799
6. Jim McCormick	1,704
7. Charlie Buffinton	1,700
8. Tony Mullane	1,662
9. Jim Whitney	1,571
10. Toad Ramsey	1,515
11. Adonis Terry	1,298
12. Mark Baldwin	1,254
13. Ed Morris	1,217
14. Bobby Mathews	1,216
15. Gus Weyhing	1,208
16. Matt Kilroy	1,137
17. Silver King	1,119
18. Larry Corcoran	1,103
19. Guy Hecker	1,099
20. Amos Rusie	1,075
21. Charlie Getzien	1,070
22. Will White	1,041
23. Elton Chamberlain	1,015
24. Bill Hutchinson	1,007
25. Dupee Shaw	950

Francis Richter, in a eulogy to John Clarkson upon the great pitcher's death, said: "On all counts the deceased will always rank in history as one of the few great masters of the art of pitching."

Left: *Durable and talented, pitcher John Clarkson helped the Chicago White Stockings and Boston Beaneaters win multiple National League pennants in the 1880s and 1890s. Possessing both an intimidating presence and dominating ability, Clarkson was a headliner whenever he pitched. He led his league in strikeouts four times, wins three times, and innings pitched three seasons in a row. Chicago manager Cap Anson, while wary of Clarkson's sensitive demeanor, deigned to title him "one of the greatest of pitchers," an honor seconded by the Hall of Fame in 1963.*

Above: "Smiling" Mickey Welch, a diminutive and crafty righthander, teamed with fellow Hall-of-Famer Tim Keefe to give the New York Giants a strong pitching duo in the 1880s. Mickey often pitched in Keefe's shadow, but still managed to win 308 games in a 13-year career. The durable Brooklynite completed his first 105 major league starts, and won both ends of a doubleheader against Buffalo July 4, 1881. He ranks sixth on the all-time list with 525 complete games.

Tony Mullane won 202 games in the American Association, making him the only pitcher to win 200 games in a loop other than the National League or the American League.

In 1884, the Toledo Blue Stockings were 36-16 when Tony Mullane pitched, but only 10-32 when the club turned to another hurler.

◆◆◆

The first pitcher to win 20 games for a last-place team was Lee Richmond, who notched 25 victories with Worcester in 1881.

When the Boston Red Stockings cruised to the NL pennant in 1878, right-hander Tommy Bond had 40 of the club's 41 wins.

Including his 41 wins during his two years in the National Association, Tommy Bond bagged 221 victories before he was 25 and only 13 thereafter.

◆◆◆

Frequent Mound Climbers

Even poor teams in baseball's first era would sometimes stumble on a potentially great pitcher. If the hurler was lucky, he would be passed on to a quality organization early in his career. For those not so fortunate their careers were often at least mercifully short, owing to overuse. Take the case of Larry McKeon, an 18-year-old rookie with Indianapolis of the American Association in 1884 who set a frosh record when he went down to defeat 41 times. He started 60 games, completed 59, and hurled 512 innings. A scant two years later McKeon's wing was shot. But even as McKeon was departing the scene the lowly Baltimore Orioles of the American Association were unveiling another amazing rookie workhorse in Matt Kilroy. Kilroy celebrated his yearling season in 1886 by notching an all-time record 513 strikeouts for the last-place Orioles and working a total of 583 innings. After being similarly abused by the Orioles for four years, Kilroy had 121 career wins. He collected only 20 more victories before his arm collapsed from overwork.

When rookie Cannonball Morris won 34 games for Columbus of the American Association in 1884, he set a victory record for a southpaw.

The NL record for the most wins in a season by a southpaw is held by Lady Baldwin of the Detroit Wolverines, who notched 42 victories in 1886.

◆◆◆

In 1884, Ed Cushman had a perfect 4-0 record for Milwaukee of the Union Association after starting the year with a 23-1 mark for the club while it was a member of the Northwestern League.

1871-1892 WINNING PERCENTAGE	
1. Al Spalding	.796
2. Dave Foutz	.690
3. Bob Caruthers	.688
4. John Clarkson	.668
5. Larry Corcoran	.665
6. Dick McBride	.656
7. Lady Baldwin	.640
8. Kid Nichols	.639
9. Cy Young	.637
10. Fred Goldsmith	.622
11. Jack Stivetts	.618
12. Monte Ward	.617
13. Tom Lovett	.616
14. Old Hoss Radbourn	.613
15. Charlie Ferguson	.607
16. Candy Cummings	.607
17. Charlie Buffinton	.605
18. Tim Keefe	.604
19. Mickey Welch	.594
20. Tommy Bond	.589
21. Bill Hutchinson	.588
22. Gus Weyhing	.588
23. Silver King	.586
24. Ed Morris	.584
25. Ad Gumbert	.583

Pitching Rotations Take Root

In 1879, the Chicago White Stockings, under manager Cap Anson, became the first major league team to try to develop a pitching rotation of sorts. Previously teams had relied almost exclusively on one pitcher. Chicago's experiment was a success, but it took a year to pay dividends. In 1880, the White Stockings replaced their two boxmen from the previous season, Terry Larkin and Frank Hankinson, with a pair of rookies, Larry Corcoran and Fred Goldsmith. Corcoran proceeded to bag 43 wins and Goldsmith 21 to make the White Stockings the first team in history with two 20-game winners. By 1884, however, both had fallen prey to arm trouble, making it apparent that even a two-man rotation could create problems. That same season the Cincinnati Outlaw Reds of the Union Association found a partial solution when they spread the work among three pitchers. The Outlaw Reds became the first team in history with three 20-game winners— Dick Burns, George Bradley, and Jim McCormick.

In 1890, George Haddock led the Players' League with 26 losses; the following season his 34 wins topped the American Association.

Henry Boyle, Perry Werden, and Charlie Hodnett, three second-line pitchers for the St. Louis Maroons of the Union Association, had a composite record of 39-6 in 1884.

1871-1892 EARNED RUN AVERAGE	
1. Jim Devlin	2.05
2. Monte Ward	2.10
3. Al Spalding	2.22
4. Will White	2.28
5. Tommy Bond	2.31
6. Larry Corcoran	2.36
7. George Bradley	2.42
8. Jim McCormick	2.43
9. Terry Larkin	2.43
10. Kid Nichols	2.49
11. Candy Cummings	2.51
12. Cy Young	2.53
13. Tim Keefe	2.56
14. John Clarkson	2.63
15. Charlie Ferguson	2.67
16. Old Hoss Radbourn	2.67
17. Mickey Welch	2.71
18. Fred Goldsmith	2.73
19. Tony Mullane	2.79
20. Dave Foutz	2.79
21. Dick McBride	2.81
22. George Zettlein	2.81
23. Ed Morris	2.82
24. Bob Caruthers	2.83
25. Lady Baldwin	2.85

"The only thing Abner Doubleday ever started was the Civil War."
—Branch Rickey

In 1892, Baltimore finished last in the National League with a 4.28 team ERA; two years later, with the mound now at 60'6", Baltimore won the NL pennant with a 5.00 ERA.

In 1892, Louisville pitchers posted the fewest strikeouts in the National League with 430; the following year, when the mound was moved from 50' to 60'6", Louisville's 1892 total would have topped the NL.

The last team to go through an entire season without using a single relief pitcher was the 1883 New York Metropolitans of the American Association.

In 1890, the Pittsburgh Innocents won just 23 of 136 decisions and were led in victories by Billy Gumbert with four.

In 1886, "Cannon Ball" Bill Stemmeyer of the Boston Red Stockings won 22 games and had a respectable 3.02 ERA despite committing an all-time record 64 wild pitches.

In 1892, George Cobb of Baltimore set a record for the most losses by a pitcher in his only major league season when he was beaten 37 times.

Larry McKeon of the Indianapolis Hoosiers of the American Association set an all-time rookie record when he suffered 41 losses in 1884.

Asa Brainard, the pitching ace for the undefeated 1869 Cincinnati Red Stockings, was 24-56 during his four seasons in the National Association.

1871-1892 PITCHER FIELDING AVERAGE	
1. Harry Staley	.942
2. Jim Devlin	.937
3. Pat Luby	.937
4. Guy Hecker	.935
5. John Ewing	.935

On May 10, 1884, catcher Alex Gardner of Washington in the American Association committed a major league record 12 passed balls while playing in his only major league game.

The first catcher to collect 500 at bats in a season was Connie Mack of the 1890 Buffalo Players' League club.

In 1886, Doc Bushong became the first player to catch 100 games in a season when he went behind the bat in 106 contests for the St. Louis Browns.

Charlie Bennett, considered by many to have been the game's finest defensive catcher during the 1880s, lost both legs when he slipped under the wheels of a moving train after the 1893 season.

1871-1892 CATCHER GAMES	
1. Charlie Bennett	894
2. Pop Snyder	876
3. Silver Flint	742
4. Doc Bushong	668
5. Jack Clements	646

"Baseball is a peculiar profession, perhaps the only one which capitalized a boyhood pleasure, unfits the athlete for any other career, keeps him young in mind and spirit, and then rejects him as too old before he has yet attained the prime of life."
—*Gerald Beaumont, writer*

Above: *Buck Ewing, whose 18-year career began in 1880, was one of the first men elected to the Hall of Fame. A catcher with a feared throwing arm, a powerful batting stroke, and speed on the basepaths, Ewing was generally considered the best player of his time.*

Buck Ewing hit 10 or more triples in a season 11 times. He paced the NL with 20 triples in 1884 despite playing in only 94 of his team's games.

1871-1892 CATCHER FIELDING AVERAGE	
1. Charlie Bennett	.942
2. Buck Ewing	.931
3. Chief Zimmer	.931
4. Jocko Milligan	.930
5. Wilbert Robinson	.928

Walking Arbiter

In the early days of baseball the man appointed to umpire a game was so much a gentleman that he would not even consider taking payment for his services. When baseball became a business and players began commanding regular salaries, however, umpires too thought to create a profession of their avocation. The first to make a full-time job of umpiring was probably Billy McLean, a former prizefighter. McLean earned the nickname "The King of Umpires" for the assertive way in which he took charge of games while officiating in the National Association in the early 1870s. When the National League was formed in 1876, McLean became one of its charter arbiters. A resident of Providence, he would sometimes rise at 4:00 A.M. and walk from his home in the Rhode Island city to Boston, where he would officiate a game that afternoon. McLean served as a National League umpire until 1884.

1871-1892 CATCHER ASSISTS	
1. Pop Snyder	1,295
2. Silver Flint	1,052
3. Buck Ewing	1,017
4. Bill Holbert	1,013
5. Charlie Bennett	1,008

Catchers in the 1800s were not expected to carry the heavy workload expected of their modern counterparts. Even Charlie Bennett, who caught more games than anyone else between 1871 and 1892, never played in more than 92 games in a single season.

In 1882, a second major league, the American Association, was established to offer baseball fans lower admission prices (25 cents instead of 50 cents), beer and whiskey sales, and Sunday baseball.

Above: *Cap Anson, the first player to get 3,000 hits, manned first base for the Chicago White Stockings from 1876 to 1897, and managed them from 1879 on as well. The fiery Anson directed Chicago to five pennants in the 1880s while leading the NL in runs batted in four times. One of Anson's lasting monuments is the invention of spring training.*

1871-1892 FIRST BASE GAMES	
1. Cap Anson	1,642
2. Dan Brouthers	1,346
3. Roger Connor	1,252
4. Charlie Comiskey	1,239
5. John Reilly	1,075

The 1892 Boston Beaneaters with a 102-48 record were the first major league team to win 100 games in a season.

The Chicago Cubs hold the major league record for the highest, the second highest, the third highest, and the fourth highest single-season winning percentages; the Cubs' four golden years came in 1880, 1876, 1885, and 1906.

1871-1892 FIRST BASE PUTOUTS	
1. Cap Anson	16,069
2. Dan Brouthers	13,619
3. Roger Connor	12,686
4. Charlie Comiskey	12,610
5. John Reilly	10,875

In 1883, their first year of existence, the Philadelphia Quakers, ancestors of the present-day Phillies, made 639 errors in just 98 games, an average of more than six per contest.

In 1887, the New York Metropolitans of the American Association made a record 643 errors.

Bob "Death to Flying Things" Ferguson was the game's first switch-hitter of note and also one of the first players to turn to umpiring.

Most of Cap Anson's 16,069 putouts at first base between 1871 and 1892 were made without the benefit of a glove.

The Sporting News, discussing John Montgomery Ward, called him: "The St. George of base ball, for he has slain the dragon of oppression."

1871-1892 FIRST BASE FIELDING AVERAGE	
1. Jake Beckley	.979
2. Roger Connor	.977
3. Sid Farrar	.974
4. Tommy Tucker	.974
5. Dave Orr	.973

American Association Pushes Umpiring as a Profession

Among the many innovations the American Association brought to the game during its ten-year sojourn as a major league was to make umpiring a reasonably well-paid and respectable profession. Whereas the stodgy National League had only one official working a game, the AA sometimes used as many as three. The loop's most famous arbiter was Ben Young, who was instrumental in forming a code of ethics for umpires before he was killed in a railway accident en route to work an AA game. Young also helped his fellow AA umpires to receive a regular salary during the baseball season, plus a per diem payment for travel expenses. While umpires in other circuits continued to officiate in street clothes, AA arbiters by the mid-1880s wore blue coats and caps issued them by the league office. The National League, the AA's rival major league, meanwhile continued to use only one umpire in a game until the early part of the 20th century.

Moses and Welday Walker

To Moses Fleetwood Walker is accorded the honor of being the first American black player in major league history. A graduate of Oberlin College, "Fleet" joined the Toledo Blue Stockings in 1883 as a catcher. The Blue Stockings were then members of the Northwestern League, a minor league circuit. When the Blue Stockings were invited to join the major league American Association the following year, Fleet accompanied them and served as the club's regular backstopper for most of the season. His brother Welday also played a few games for the club, giving the Walkers the dual distinction of being both the first official black major leaguers and the first black siblings. Following the 1884 season, the Walkers were clandestinely barred from the majors when the owners bowed to a threatened rebellion by Cap Anson and several other leading white players if blacks were continued to be allowed to compete for major league jobs.

Above: *It is impossible to predict what kind of career Fleet Walker could have assembled if given the chance, but he did leave a legacy of another kind. The well-educated Walker published* Our Home Colony *in 1908, an early call for black emigration to Africa as a response to American racial intolerance.*

Fleet Walker and pitcher George Stovey formed baseball's first black battery, playing for Newark in 1887.

Disgrace

Moses Walker's brother Welday, in a letter to president George McDermott of the Tri-State League after the loop adopted a color ban, wrote: "The rule that you have passed is a public disgrace."

The first documented black player to appear in a major league game was Fleet Walker, a catcher for the Toledo Blue Stockings of the American Association in 1884. His brother Welday also played on that team. Fleet, a catcher, played 42 games and scored 23 runs while hitting .263; he was good enough to have the fifth highest batting average among the 24 catchers listed in the AA that season, but he never played another major league game.

1871-1892 SECOND BASE GAMES	
1. Bid McPhee	1,325
2. Fred Pfeffer	1,189
3. Cub Stricker	1,106
4. Jack Burdock	1,084
5. Fred Dunlap	963

1871-1892 SECOND BASE FIELDING AVERAGE	
1. Danny Richardson	.939
2. Bid McPhee	.938
3. Charley Bassett	.932
4. Lou Bierbauer	.929
5. Sam Barkley	.929

1871-1892 THIRD BASE GAMES	
1. Arlie Latham	1,201
2. Hick Carpenter	1,059
3. Jerry Denny	1,047
4. George Pinkney	943
5. Joe Mulvey	915

Dude Esterbrook, a star third baseman during the 1880s, committed suicide in 1901 by jumping off a moving train while being transported to a mental institution.

◆ ◆ ◆

Billy Nash's greatest accomplishment came after he retired in 1896 when he scouted and signed a young Nap Lajoie.

The Pittsburgh NL team first became known as the Pirates in 1891 when the club "pirated" second baseman Lou Bierbauer from Philadelphia of the American Association.

◆ ◆ ◆

Ross Barnes not only won the first National League batting title in 1876, he also set a record for second basemen when he had a .910 fielding average.

Parson Nicholson, Toledo's second baseman during the 1890 American Association season, was the tallest 19th century middle infielder at 6'6".

Other Blacks Who Played Early Pro Ball

Although the Walkers are considered now to have been the only black major leaguers prior to Jackie Robinson's arrival in 1947, the probability is strong that there were a number of other black players who broke the color barrier in the majors, particularly in the last century, by successfully passing as white. One may have been Sandy Nava, a backup catcher with the Providence Grays for three years in the early 1880s. Nava claimed to be Cuban to account for his dark complexion. Other great players of that time who were obviously black were barred from the majors but permitted to perform in the minors until the mid-1890s when the color ban was enforced throughout professional baseball. Perhaps the two best black performers of the last century were George Stovey, the top pitcher in the International League in the mid-1880s, and Frank Grant, a second baseman who was known as the "Black Fred Dunlap." In 1887, Grant hit .353 for Buffalo of the International League and led the loop in homers with 11 while Stovey set the IL record for wins when he posted 34 victories for Newark.

From 1884 to 1898, the durable Billy Nash (above, tagging out Old Hoss Radbourn) played a consistent third base for four clubs. He was an integral part of the dominating Boston Beaneater teams of the early 1890s, and played on five consecutive pennant winners. While not a star, Nash had good line-drive power, batting in 90 or more runs six times.

1871-1892 THIRD BASE FIELDING AVERAGE	
1. George Pinkney	.894
2. Art Whitney	.888
3. Billy Nash	.887
4. Tom Burns	.886
5. Billy Shindle	.882

Chicago White Stockings Are NL's First Powerhouse

The first team to claim as many as three consecutive pennants after the National League opened its doors (in 1876) was the 1880 to 1882 Chicago White Stockings. In those three years, the White Stockings won more than 70 percent of their games. The club featured manager-first baseman Cap Anson, shortstop Fred Pfeffer, third baseman Ned Williamson, outfielders George Gore and Abner Dalrymple, and all-around star King Kelly. When arm woes beset the team's twin pitching aces, Larry Corcoran and Fred Goldsmith, Chicago slipped to second place in 1883 and fourth the following year. The acquisition of hurler John Clarkson, though, rocketed the club back to the top in 1885. When the White Stockings triumphed again in 1886, it gave them five pennants in seven seasons. The 1885 and '86 minidynasty was to be the team's last taste of pennant spoils, however, for a full 20 years. Anson's powerhouse was ended by the team's unpopular sale first of King Kelly and then John Clarkson to the Boston Red Stockings.

In 1894, Sam Thompson's .404 average wasn't even the best on his own team—Ed Delahanty hit .416.

Sam Thompson signed his first professional contract in 1884, making $2.50 a game.

Shortstop Frank Fennelly of Cincinnati in 1886 became the first player to make 100 errors in a season when he committed 117 miscues. In 1889, rookie shortstop Herman Long tied the record 117 errors while playing for Kansas City of the American Association.

Joe Tinker called Monte Ward, "a star outfielder, a brilliant infielder, and a better pitcher than Radbourn. And he was one of the best baserunners who ever lived."

1871-1892 SHORTSTOP GAMES	
1. Jack Glasscock	1,391
2. Germany Smith	998
3. Arthur Irwin	946
4. Monte Ward	826
5. Bill Gleason	796

Above: A fearsome lefthanded-hitting slugger, "Big Sam" Thompson battled injuries throughout a 15-year career. He won two homer crowns, hit over .370 three straight years, and led Detroit to its only NL pennant in 1887 by pacing the league in batting average and RBI.

1871-1892 SHORTSTOP FIELDING AVERAGE	
1. Jack Glasscock	.908
2. Davy Force	.908
3. Germany Smith	.891
4. Herman Long	.890
5. Ed McKean	.885

The first organized league of baseball teams was formed in 1857 and called itself the National Association of Base Ball Clubs.

The 1889 season in the National League was the first time in history that a major league pennant race was decided on the final day of the campaign.

Charlie Comiskey, Arlie Latham, Tip O'Neill, and Yank Robinson were the only players who were members of all four of the St. Louis Browns' pennant winners from 1885 to 1888.

In 1866, Dickey Pearce used to "butt" a pitched ball in order to get on base. Over the years, the term was repeatedly mispronounced until it became "bunt."

In 1886, Washington of the National League won just 28 games all season—and four of them were by forfeit!

In 1888, the total number of strikes allowed a batter before he was out was reduced from four to three, the present number.

Above: *The first man to record a hit in the National League, Jim O'Rourke served as a player, manager, umpire, and minor league president in addition to his 22 years of playing time in the National Association, National League, and Players' League. "Orator Jim" (so named for his endless wordiness) hit .300 13 times and played the outfield for seven pennant-winning clubs.*

In 1892, Brooklyn center fielder Mike Griffin set a record for outfielders that stood until 1904 when he had a .986 fielding average.

1871-1892 OUTFIELD GAMES	
1. Paul Hines	1,374
2. Jim O'Rourke	1,355
3. George Gore	1,297
4. Ned Hanlon	1,251
5. George Wood	1,232
6. Tom Brown	1,169
7. Curt Welch	1,061
8. Joe Hornung	1,054
9. Jimmy Wolf	1,042
10. Pop Corkhill	1,041
11. Tip O'Neill	1,024
12. Blondie Purcell	995
13. Tom York	959
14. Abner Dalrymple	951
15. Pete Browning	938

Von der Ahe Assembles, Dismantles Browns Dynasty

Even as the Chicago White Stockings' dynasty was winding down in the mid-1880s, the St. Louis Browns were emerging as the most powerful dynasty in the last century. Between 1885 and 1888 the Browns swept four consecutive American Association pennants under beer-baron owner Chris Von der Ahe and manager-first baseman Charlie Comiskey. Von der Ahe built his juggernaut by paying his players well, outfitting them in tailor-made uniforms, and organizing parades and other gala events to fete them and bolster their morale through constant adulation. When the Browns lost the 1887 World Series between the National League and the American Association to the Detroit Wolverines, Von der Ahe angrily began to dismantle his team. Prior to the 1888 season the club's two highest paid pitchers, Dave Foutz and Bob Caruthers, were shipped to Brooklyn. The Browns held on to their throne for one last hurrah in 1888 but then gave way to Brooklyn the following year and never again regained the top spot. Von der Ahe too fell on hard times, dying impoverished and forgotten.

In 1876, the Cincinnati Red Stockings opened the inaugural National League season by winning their first two games; the club then lost 56 of its remaining 63 games to finish last with a 9-56 record.

1871-1892 OUTFIELD FIELDING AVERAGE	
1. Pop Corkhill	.947
2. Mike Griffin	.946
3. Jim Fogarty	.940
4. Bug Holliday	.935
5. Darby O'Brien	.934
6. Curt Welch	.933
7. Farmer Weaver	.928
8. Hardy Richardson	.928
9. Sam Thompson	.922
10. Joe Hornung	.922
11. Hugh Duffy	.918
12. Jimmy Wolf	.918
13. Tip O'Neill	.917
14. Oyster Burns	.913
15. Jim McTamany	.913

This is an excerpt from the Brotherhood Manifesto denouncing owners, issued by players seceding in 1890 to the Players' League: "Players have been bought, sold and exchanged as though they were sheep instead of American citizens."

Hall of Fame outfielder Ed Delahanty served at shortstop for the Cleveland Players' League entry in 1890 and fielded a horrible .830.

On June 2, 1892, Benjamin Harrison became the first president to attend a major league game while in office when he saw Washington lose 7-4 to Cincinnati.

The 1885 to 1888 St. Louis Browns of the American Association were the first team to win four consecutive major league pennants.

Fans Beware

Many of the major injuries incurred during a baseball game when the sport was in its infancy did not take place on the field of play. Being a spectator at that time could be a risky business. Until Providence of the National League installed a wire screen behind home plate in its park in the late 1870s, an innovation that other clubs quickly adopted, the stands back of the plate were known as "The Slaughter Pens" because so many fans who sat there were felled by foul balls. Fires and shoddy workmanship of the old wooden stands were other dangers that confronted early spectators. On Opening Day in 1884, in the very first official game the American Association Cincinnati Red Stockings played in their new American Park, a section of the right field grandstand collapsed as fans were hastening out of the park moments after the last out was made. One man in attendance was killed and scores more were badly hurt. Improvements in park construction and design eventually eliminated similar mishaps. Fire remained an ever-present peril until 1920, however, when the St. Louis Cardinals abandoned Robison Field, the last all-wood park in the majors.

Short Spans of Attention

"Two hours is about as long as an American can wait for the close of a base ball game—or anything else, for that matter."
—Albert Spalding

Above: Alexander Cartwright is credited with the development of the modern game of baseball. He and his upper-class banking friends organized a ball club in 1845 and codified the fledgling game's rules. Among other innovations, they measured 90-foot basepaths, created fair and foul territory, and limited the number of players to nine a side. Cartwright spread this more gentlemanly game while he traveled the country in the 1840s, and established baseball as far West as Hawaii.

During the 1880s, Frank Bancroft managed a 19th-century record five different teams in the National League and one in the American Association.

Pat Powers, the manager of the Rochester American Association club in 1890, later became a doctor and took time out from his medical practice to promote the first six-day bike races at Madison Square Garden.

The 1891 season was the first in which teams were allowed to substitute for a player at any time in the game.

Alexander Cartwright's Knickerbocker club abolished the established practice of throwing a hit ball at a runner to retire him. This meant that a harder, faster-traveling baseball could be used.

1871-1892 MANAGER WINS	
1. Harry Wright	1,153
2. Cap Anson	972
3. Charlie Comiskey	719
4. Jim Mutrie	658
5. Billy Barnie	470
6. Gus Schmelz	469
7. Bob Ferguson	417
8. Frank Bancroft	366
9. Jack Chapman	351
10. John Morrill	348

1871-1892 MANAGER WINNING PERCENTAGE	
1. Charlie Comiskey	.640
2. Cap Anson	.618
3. Jim Mutrie	.611
4. Harry Wright	.582
5. Bill Watkins	.532
6. Frank Bancroft	.529
7. Gus Schmelz	.520
8. John Morrill	.510
9. Billy Barnie	.461
10. Horace Phillips	.449

Above: *After leaving baseball in 1898, Cap Anson dabbled in different businesses, but did not do well in any of them. Upon hearing of his financial problems, the NL attempted to establish a pension for him. True to character, the proud Anson refused to accept this charitable contribution.*

Chicken Wolf was the only player to perform in the American Association in all ten seasons that it was a major league.

In 1859, the Brooklyn Excelsiors became the first baseball team to go on a national tour.

In 1877, the Hartford Dark Blues of the National League played all their home games at Union Grounds in Brooklyn.

◆◆◆

The smallest city to have a major league team is Altoona, Pennsylvania, a member of the Union Association for the first month of the 1884 season.

The St. Paul White Caps, members of the Union Association in 1884 for just eight contests, are the only major league team that never played a home game.

◆◆◆

Richmond, a member of the American Association for the last half of the 1884 season, is the only city south of the Mason-Dixon line to field a major league team prior to 1966.

When Boston paid Chicago $10,000 to obtain King Kelly prior to the 1887 season, it was the first five-figure transaction in major league history.

◆◆◆

The Kansas City Union Association entry played just 79 games in 1884 but nevertheless contrived to finish 61 games behind the pennant-winning St. Louis Maroons.

By George
"Baseball has the great advantage over cricket of being sooner ended."
—George Bernard Shaw

First Famous Fans

Baseball spectators were originally called kranks. Around 1883, St. Louis Browns manager Ted Sullivan coined the term "fan" when team owner Chris Von der Ahe referred to the Browns rooters as fanatics. The most well-known fan at the time was Arthur Dixwell of Boston. Independently wealthy, Dixwell bestowed cash and other forms of reward upon Boston players who did something that pleased him. Dixwell was nicknamed "Hi! Hi!" because he shouted Hi! Hi! whenever he was stirred by the action on the field. Another early fan, Harry Stevens, spotted an unfilled need at ballparks and began hawking scorecards and even eventually food to fellow fans. Known as "The Scorecard Man" and also as "Hustling Harry," Stevens soon nailed down exclusive concession rights at most major league parks, a privilege that his heirs still hold. To promote the sale of his scorecards, Stevens encouraged club owners to assign their players uniform numbers, but his plea fell on deaf ears. Not until the early 1930s would players throughout the majors begin wearing numbered uniforms.

Previous to the 1887 season, batters were allowed to call for either high or low pitches; a high strike was a pitch between the belt and the tops of the shoulders while a low strike was a pitch between the belt and the bottoms of the kneecaps.

Chapter 2
The Turn of the Century

In 1895, outfielder Algie McBride hit .444 for Austin of the Texas League while playing in 94 of the club's 95 games.

Arlie Pond, after winning 18 games for Baltimore in 1897, quit the club the following year to serve as a doctor in the Spanish-American war and later became an assistant army surgeon general.

1893-1899 GAMES		
1.	George Van Haltren	961
2.	Hugh Duffy	950
3.	Jesse Burkett	932
4.	Tommy Dowd	922
5.	Joe Kelley	914
	Dummy Hoy	914
7.	Ed Delahanty	904
8.	Tommy Corcoran	902
9.	Patsy Donovan	889
10.	Herman Long	872
11.	Ed McKean	862
	Jake Beckley	862
13.	Tommy Tucker	860
14.	Bobby Lowe	853
15.	George Davis	848
16.	Cupid Childs	842
17.	Bones Ely	835
18.	Elmer Smith	832
	Jimmy Ryan	832
20.	Bill Dahlen	829
21.	Lave Cross	826
	Steve Brodie	826
23.	Willie Keeler	812
24.	Bill Lange	811
25.	Bid McPhee	810

The record for the highest season batting average belongs to Hugh Duffy, who hit .438 for the Boston Beaneaters in 1894.

Hugh Duffy was the only player to win two National League home run crowns between 1893 and 1899 (he did it in '94 and '97).

Long after his stellar career, Hugh Duffy was a batting coach with the Boston Red Sox in the 1940s. His top student was a young outfielder whom Duffy promised would be a legend. The protege's name was Ted Williams.

Above: *Hugh Duffy was a small, speedy center fielder who starred for the Boston Beaneater teams of the 1890s. An excellent and popular player, he won the second Triple Crown in history in 1894 when he hit .438 with 18 homers and 145 RBI. This was by far his best year, but he hit over .300 10 times and played on five pennant winners.*

NL Moves Pitcher's Mound to 60'6"

Following the 1891 season, the American Association gave up its struggle to compete with the entrenched National League for major league status and allowed four of its teams to be absorbed by the older circuit. Where there had been 24 major league teams just two years earlier, there were but half that number in 1892. The cutback enabled the 12 still-existing clubs to weed out the weaker pitchers and resulted in a sharp drop in hitting. Alarmed when the NL as a whole batted just .245 in 1892, loop moguls ordered the distance from the pitcher's box to home plate to be lengthened 10 feet and the box to be made circular and elevated. Reportedly a printer's error caused the new pitcher's mounds to be installed at a 60'6" distance rather than the proscribed 60 feet, but in any case the conversion immediately had the desired effect on the game. In 1893, NL hitters averaged .280 and the next season the loop batting mark climbed to an all-time record .309 as hitters feasted while hurlers struggled to adapt to the increased distance.

Perry Werden First Fence Buster

As has happened throughout the game's history, trends in the majors were almost exactly paralleled in the minors during the mid-1890s. In 1895, the Western League, the forerunner of the present-day American League, saw all eight of its teams top the .300 mark, led by the champion Indianapolis Hoosiers with a .354 batting average. Second to the Indiana club was Minneapolis, which hit .350 and scored a loop-leading 1,282 runs in 123 games, an average of more than 10 runs per contest. Minneapolis was spearheaded by first baseman Perry Werden, who paced the WL in batting with a .438 mark and clouted 45 home runs, the pre-Babe Ruth professional record. Werden preferred life in the minors, particularly when he was allowed to wield his bat in a tiny park like the one in Minneapolis, but he also left his mark on the major league game. Just two years before he embarked on his slugging spree in the WL, Werden clubbed 29 triples for St. Louis of the National League to establish a senior loop record that was broken a year later by Baltimore's Heinie Reitz.

1893-1899 HITS	
1. Jesse Burkett	1,462
2. Ed Delahanty	1,431
3. Willie Keeler	1,346
4. Hugh Duffy	1,305
5. George Van Haltren	1,297
6. Joe Kelley	1,237
7. Patsy Donovan	1,169
8. Billy Hamilton	1,167
9. Ed McKean	1,140
10. George Davis	1,139
11. Herman Long	1,108
12. Elmer Smith	1,085
13. Jake Beckley	1,080
14. Steve Brodie	1,074
15. Tommy Dowd	1,070
16. Jimmy Ryan	1,060
17. Bill Lange	1,055
18. Dummy Hoy	1,053
19. Bobby Lowe	1,047
20. Fred Clarke	1,034
21. Cupid Childs	1,029
22. Tommy Corcoran	1,027
23. Lave Cross	1,023
24. Jake Stenzel	1,013
25. Hughie Jennings	1,005

Above: *Hughie Jennings, a combative, excitable Baltimore Orioles shortstop, was an all-around star. He hit over .350 three straight years, he stole 359 bases, and his fielding was often spectacular and always steady.*

In 1896, Hughie Jennings of Baltimore set a record for the most RBI (121) by a player who hit no home runs all season.

Hughie Jennings became the last player in National League history to hit .400 (.401) and fail to win the batting title in 1896.

Perry Werden might never have hit 45 home runs if not for an arm injury. Originally a pitcher, he compiled a 12-1 record in 1884. Fortunately for opposing batters, Werden's wing went bad and he shifted to first base.

1893-1899 RUNS	
1. Jesse Burkett	955
2. Billy Hamilton	945
3. Ed Delahanty	931
4. Willie Keeler	910
5. Joe Kelley	873
6. George Van Haltren	850
7. Hugh Duffy	844
8. John McGraw	782
9. Herman Long	778
10. Patsy Donovan	762
11. Cupid Childs	758
12. Bill Dahlen	755
13. Hughie Jennings	742
14. Dummy Hoy	740
15. Elmer Smith	701
16. George Davis	698
17. Jimmy Ryan	696
18. Bill Lange	689
19. Mike Tiernan	687
20. Bobby Lowe	681
21. Mike Griffin	672
22. Jake Beckley	671
23. Ed McKean	662
24. Jake Stenzel	659
25. Tommy Dowd	638

While not collecting as many hits as some other players of the era, "Sliding" Billy Hamilton stole 915 bases in his career, which helped him score 945 runs in a seven-year stretch.

The 1898 season was the only campaign between 1894 and 1899 that the National League failed to have at least one .400 hitter.

Louisville outfielder Tom Brown's .254 batting average in 1894 was the lowest among all National League regulars with at least 400 at bats.

In 1894, Louisville was the only National League team that failed to hit at least .286, finishing at .269.

1893-1899 DOUBLES	
1. Ed Delahanty	298
2. Joe Kelley	202
3. Jake Stenzel	189
Jimmy Ryan	189
5. Hugh Duffy	187
6. Bill Dahlen	184
7. Herman Long	182
8. George Davis	181
9. Jake Beckley	180
10. Ed McKean	171
11. Jesse Burkett	168
12. Lave Cross	164
13. Jack Doyle	158
14. Mike Griffin	157
15. Hughie Jennings	153
16. George Van Haltren	148
17. Elmer Smith	147
18. Sam Thompson	144
19. Kip Selbach	139
20. Tommy Tucker	138
21. Deacon McGuire	137
22. Bid McPhee	136
23. Steve Brodie	135
24. Dummy Hoy	134
25. Mike Tiernan	133
Dusty Miller	133
Bill Lange	133
Billy Hamilton	133
Tommy Corcoran	133

1893-1899 TRIPLES	
1. Joe Kelley	112
2. Jake Beckley	105
3. Elmer Smith	101
4. Ed Delahanty	96
5. Kip Selbach	90
6. George Davis	87
7. Ed McKean	86
Willie Keeler	86
9. Mike Tiernan	85
10. George Van Haltren	83
11. Jesse Burkett	82
12. Bill Dahlen	81
13. Bill Lange	80
14. Tommy Corcoran	75
John Anderson	75
16. Dummy Hoy	73
17. Sam Thompson	72
Jimmy Ryan	72
19. Jake Stenzel	71
20. Heinie Reitz	65
21. Hughie Jennings	64
Duff Cooley	64
Fred Clarke	64
24. Harry Davis	63
25. Bid McPhee	62
Candy LaChance	62

Count Campau led the American Association in home runs in 1890. He hit 10 in only 75 games.

After hitting .325 for Chicago in 1899, Bill Lange quit baseball, departing with a .330 career batting average for seven seasons of work.

◆ ◆ ◆

Sam Crawford commented on Wee Willie Keeler: "He choked up on the bat so far he only used about half of it, and then he'd just peck at the ball. Just a little snap swing and he'd punch the ball over the infield."

Major Talents in Minor Leagues

Perry Werden was by no means the only minor league star who was content to perform at a lower competitive level than his talents seemingly would have warranted. With all the major league cities located either in the East or the Midwest, many players from other parts of the country chose to stay close to home rather than uproot themselves. Count Campau, a native of Detroit, dropped down to the minors in 1889 after Detroit was jettisoned from the National League. He compiled 2,286 hits and 136 home runs in a string of lower leagues before retiring in 1905. Connecticut-born Hi Ladd played only two games in the majors in a career that spanned 20 seasons, the last 10 of them with Bridgeport of the Connecticut League. Ladd twice led the circuit in batting, in 1900 and again in 1905. Other fine players of the era who hailed from below the Mason-Dixon Line starred in the Southern League and the Texas League and were never seen at all by major league fans.

Bill Dahlen held the consecutive hitting streak record for three years before Wee Willie Keeler broke it. In 1894, Dahlen had a 42-game hitting streak. The day after it was snapped, he started a 28-game hitting streak.

Willie Keeler tied an all-time major league record when he amassed 17 hits over a four-game span in 1897.

Above: Although only 5'4", Willie Keeler was well respected as a stellar bunter and contact hitter during his 19-year career. As leadoff man and right fielder on the rough-and-tumble Oriole squads of the 1890s, Keeler won back-to-back batting titles and scored 150 runs four consecutive times. His lifetime .343 batting mark is ninth best on the all-time list.

1893-1899 HOME RUNS		
1.	Ed Delahanty	65
2.	Hugh Duffy	62
3.	Bill Joyce	60
4.	Sam Thompson	55
5.	Bobby Lowe	53
6.	Herman Long	48
7.	Jack Clements	47
	Bill Dahlen	47
9.	Joe Kelley	46
10.	Mike Tiernan	43
	George Davis	43
12.	Ed McKean	41
13.	Jake Beckley	40
14.	Bill Lange	39
	Roger Connor	39
16.	Jimmy Collins	34
	Fred Clarke	34
	Jesse Burkett	34
19.	Jake Stenzel	32
20.	Billy Nash	31
21.	George Van Haltren	30
	Candy LaChance	30
23.	Kip Selbach	29
24.	Buck Freeman	28
	Elmer Smith	28
	John Anderson	28

According to legend, Big Ed Delahanty once smacked a baseball so hard that he broke it in two pieces.

Joyce Victimized by Contract Disputes

In all of major league history precious few rookies have ever led a league in walks. Ted Williams was one who did. Another was Bill Joyce, whose 123 free passes paced the Players' League in 1890. Joyce was not on a par with Williams as an all-around hitter, but he may not have been far from it. In a career marred by injuries and bitter holdout battles, Joyce was nevertheless one of the game's top offensive performers in the 1890s. He even tripled four times in one game, in 1897. His high mark, though, came in 1894 when he batted .355 for Washington and knocked home 89 runs in just 99 games. Two years later Joyce tied for the National League lead in home runs with 13 and was second with 101 walks. Playing by then for the New York Giants, Joyce quit after the 1898 season rather than continue to deal with Andrew Freedman, the club's universally despised owner. Freedman's penuriousness had earlier wrecked the career of star pitcher Amos Rusie. Joyce also quit the game, albeit temporarily, back in 1893 when he was traded by Brooklyn to Washington, which immediately tried to cut his salary.

On the science of batting, Wee Willie Keeler explained, "Keep your eye on the ball and hit 'em where they ain't."

Outfielder Jesse Burkett (above) shares a distinction with Ty Cobb and Rogers Hornsby: They are the only three players to hit .400 three times. Burkett hit for high average and drew many walks, which helped him score almost 1,800 runs in a 16-year career. Nicknamed "Crab" due to his continuous griping, Jesse was a colorful and important part of the excellent Cleveland Spider teams of the late 1890s. He led the NL in hits four times and scored 160 runs in 1896.

In 1896, Jesse "Crab" Burkett became the first post-1893 player to be a league pace-setter in both batting average and times at bat.

Jake Stenzel Typifies Shooting Star '90s

The decade of the 1890s was rife with players who had one or two great seasons and then rapidly, and in some cases inexplicably, descended to mediocrity. Among them was Tuck Turner, one of only two players in history with a .380-plus career batting average after their first 700 at bats in the majors (the other was Shoeless Joe Jackson). Considerably more enduring than Turner, who played only 377 games in the majors, was Jake Stenzel. After flopping in two brief earlier trials, Stenzel cracked .362 for Pittsburgh in 1893 when the Pirates gave him a late-season look. Stenzel followed his first prolonged test by hitting .354, .374, .361, and .353 over the next four seasons and also ranking among the National League's RBI and slugging leaders. In 1898, Stenzel slumped to .275. When he started slowly again in 1899, he was traded to his home-town team, the Cincinnati Reds, and then released after getting into just nine games with the Queen City entrant. Less is known about Stenzel than any other great hitter of the 1890s, and no explanation at all has ever been put forward for his sudden decline from stardom.

Tuck Turner finished second in the NL in batting in 1894, ripping out a .416 mark bested only by Hugh Duffy's .438. Turner's mark ranks 10th on the all-time single-season list.

In 1897, Jesse Burkett poked a 19th-century record 240 hits in just 133 games en route to claiming his second straight batting title with a .410 average.

On July 13, 1896, Ed Delahanty of Philadelphia became the only player other than Atlanta's Bob Horner to hit four home runs in a losing cause, as his Phillies bowed to Chicago 9-8.

◆ ◆ ◆

In 1893, Tom Brown of Louisville topped the National League with 66 stolen bases while hitting .240, the lowest average of any player that season with 500 or more at bats.

1893-1899 RUNS BATTED IN	
1. Ed Delahanty	834
2. Hugh Duffy	815
3. Joe Kelley	742
4. Ed McKean	704
5. George Davis	689
6. Jake Beckley	664
7. Steve Brodie	612
8. Bobby Lowe	602
9. Lave Cross	591
10. Herman Long	580
11. Bill Lange	578
Hughie Jennings	578
13. Sam Thompson	550
George Van Haltren	550
Jack Doyle	550
16. Jake Stenzel	530
17. Tommy Corcoran	517
18. Jesse Burkett	504
19. Bill Dahlen	502
20. Tommy Tucker	495
21. Elmer Smith	494
22. Patsy Tebeau	485
23. Bid McPhee	482
24. Mike Tiernan	466
25. Heinie Reitz	462

1893-1899 STOLEN BASES	
1. Billy Hamilton	460
2. Bill Lange	399
3. John McGraw	350
4. Joe Kelley	319
5. Jack Doyle	310
6. George Davis	298
7. Jake Stenzel	291
8. Willie Keeler	288
9. Dummy Hoy	281
10. Patsy Donovan	272
11. Hugh Duffy	269
12. George Van Haltren	268
13. Hughie Jennings	266
14. Ed Delahanty	255
15. Tommy Dowd	245
Fred Clarke	245
17. Bill Dahlen	233
18. Tom Brown	230
19. Jesse Burkett	214
20. Kip Selbach	210
21. Dusty Miller	199
22. Eddie Burke	196
23. Herman Long	195
24. Steve Brodie	187
25. Mike Tiernan	186

Nap Lajoie, later one of the greatest second basemen ever, set an era record for first basemen in 1897 when he hit .361 for Philadelphia.

In 1894, the Baltimore Orioles had a 19th-century record five players who compiled 100 or more RBI, led by Dan Brouthers with 128.

In 1894, the Baltimore Orioles hit just 33 home runs but collected a 19th-century record 150 triples.

In 1899, John McGraw of Baltimore hit .391 and led the National League in runs scored with 140 but had just 33 RBI.

Who's On First?

During the 1890s—while George Davis was setting RBI marks for shortstops, second baseman Heinie Reitz hammered 31 triples, and the Phillies had a .400-hitting outfield and .394-hitting catcher Jack Clements—the lone position that was notably lacking in outstanding offensive performers was first base. By the middle of the decade, with Cap Anson, Roger Connor, and Dan Brouthers all on the decline, Jake Beckley and Jack Doyle were the top two first sackers in the NL, and neither was on a par with the standout players at other positions. Part of the reason for the sudden dearth in talented first basemen lay in the disdain with which the position was viewed by analysts of the time. No player with solid overall skills wanted to be stationed there. By 1897, however, the position was on the upswing again with the arrival of Fred Tenney, one of the most graceful first sackers ever, and Nap Lajoie, who was placed at the initial hassock by the Phillies in his first full major league season. Lajoie promptly set several period batting records for first basemen when he collected 127 RBI and topped the NL with a .578 slugging average.

When outfielder Buck Freeman of Washington led the National League with 25 home runs in 1899, St. Louis shortstop Bobby Wallace (12) was the only other NL player to post a double-figure home run total.

In 1894, the Boston Beaneaters hit 103 home runs to become the first team other than the 1884 Chicago White Stockings to reach triple figures in four-baggers.

The poorest-hitting regular on the champion 1894 Baltimore Orioles was second baseman Heinie Reitz, whose .303 batting average was 40 points below the team average.

Roger Connor retired in 1897 with the career record for both the most home runs (136) and the most triples (233).

1893-1899 STRIKEOUTS	
1. Tom Brown	245
2. Tom Daly	184
3. Bill Dahlen	150
4. Ed Cartwright	128
Joe Kelley	128
6. Chief Zimmer	124
Candy LaChance	124
8. Bill Joyce	121
9. Eddie Burke	119
10. George Treadway	115
11. George Van Haltren	112
12. Tommy Tucker	110
13. Chippy McGarr	107
Jimmy McAleer	107
15. Tommy Dowd	106
16. Charlie Abbey	105
17. Jimmy Bannon	101
18. Jesse Burkett	100
19. Heinie Reitz	99
20. Bones Ely	97
Jake Beckley	97
22. Germany Smith	94
Billy Clingman	94
24. Kid Nichols	92
Jack Crooks	92
Billy Nash	92

Above: *George Davis played in the majors from 1890 through 1909. A star shortstop for the New York Giants most of his career, he hit for an excellent average, played good defense, and was respected enough to play regularly until he was 38. Over his career he collected over 2,600 hits and stole 615 bases.*

At the finish of the 1895 season, his third in the majors, Tuck Turner of Philadelphia had a .380-plus career batting average; he never again hit .300.

On April 21, 1898, Phillies hurler Bill Duggleby became the only player ever to hit a grand slam home run in his first major league at bat.

George Davis has offensive numbers better than most Hall-of-Fame shortstops. His achievements include a 6-for-6 game, and two extra-inning games in which he hit three triples. Davis hit 47 triples in a two-year period.

George Davis Hammers from Both Sides of Plate

Switch-hitters are relatively common now, but for many years they were something of a rarity. Before Mickey Mantle, in fact, only one player who hit from both sides of the plate, Tommy Tucker of the 1889 Baltimore Orioles, had ever copped a batting title. The game's first great switch-hitter was not Tucker, however, but George Davis. In addition, Davis was the most potent offensive force among the infielders of his time. Operating first at third base and then moving to shortstop, he compiled 2,660 career hits, a record for switch-stickers that lasted until Pete Rose came along. Davis also set a single-season RBI record for National League shortstops that still stands when he brought home 136 New York Giants teammates in 1897. At the time, he was regarded as not only the NL's best-hitting shortstop but also as the finest fielder at the position and perhaps the best all-around player in the game.

1893-1899 BATTING AVERAGE	
1. Willie Keeler	.385
2. Ed Delahanty	.384
3. Jesse Burkett	.378
4. Billy Hamilton	.369
5. Joe Kelley	.348
6. Hughie Jennings	.348
7. John McGraw	.346
8. Jake Stenzel	.341
9. George Davis	.338
10. Hugh Duffy	.338
11. Fred Clarke	.334
12. Elmer Smith	.333
13. Bill Lange	.330
14. George Van Haltren	.328
15. Jack Doyle	.327
16. Steve Brodie	.322
17. Mike Tiernan	.318
18. Cupid Childs	.317
19. Mike Griffin	.317
20. Jake Beckley	.317
21. Jimmy Ryan	.316
22. Ed McKean	.313
23. Patsy Donovan	.309
24. Kip Selbach	.307
25. Deacon McGuire	.306

Clements Left Other Backstoppers Behind

When Mike Squires went behind the bat for the Chicago White Sox in 1980, it marked the first time in many years that a lefthander had caught in a major league game. Until the early part of the 20th century, southpaw backstoppers were not uncommon. None had a career of much distinction, however, except for Jack Clements. In a 17-year career spanning from 1884 to 1900, Clements not only established the record for the most games caught by a lefthander (1,073) but he posted the highest single-season batting average by a major league receiver when he hit .394 in 1895 for the Philadelphia Phillies. That same season, Clements tagged 13 circuit clouts in 322 at bats to pace the National League in home run percentage. A short (5'8"), powerfully built man (205 pounds), he retired with a .421 slugging percentage. During his career Clements also on occasion played shortstop and third base, two other positions that are now regarded as anathema to lefthanders.

Besides being a lefthanded backstop, Jack Clements also has claim to preserving every modern catcher's safety. Early in his career, Clements began to wear a chest protector while behind the plate. His "sheepskin" was mocked, but it soon became common equipment.

1893-1899 SLUGGING AVERAGE	
1. Ed Delahanty	.569
2. Joe Kelley	.507
3. Jesse Burkett	.490
4. Jake Stenzel	.484
5. Willie Keeler	.483
6. George Davis	.481
7. Billy Hamilton	.466
8. Jake Beckley	.466
9. Elmer Smith	.465
10. Hugh Duffy	.464
11. Mike Tiernan	.461
12. Bill Lange	.459
13. Hughie Jennings	.457
14. Bill Dahlen	.457
15. Fred Clarke	.448
16. Kip Selbach	.447
17. Ed McKean	.441
18. Jimmy Ryan	.439
19. George Van Haltren	.430
20. Mike Griffin	.427
21. Herman Long	.422
22. Jack Doyle	.420
23. John McGraw	.419
24. Bobby Lowe	.410
25. Steve Brodie	.409

Doggie Miller of Louisville set a new major league record when he collected six pinch hits in 1896.

At the close of the 19th century the record for the most pinch hits in a season was held by Duke Farrell, who had eight for Washington in 1897.

In 1894, Billy Hamilton of the Philadelphia Phillies scored at least one run in an all-time record 24 consecutive games.

Billy Hamilton set the single-season record for runs scored when he totaled 196 in 1894; he totaled 19 more than Tom Brown's record 177 set in 1891.

In 1894, Sam Thompson of the Philadelphia Phillies set an all-time record when he averaged 1.38 RBI per game—the next year he broke his own record!

Billy Hamilton, who led the National League in walks six times, only drew four bases on balls in 35 games in his rookie season with Kansas City in 1888. The next year, he walked 87 times and scored 144 runs.

1893-1899 ON-BASE AVERAGE	
1. Billy Hamilton	.484
2. John McGraw	.474
3. Ed Delahanty	.457
4. Jesse Burkett	.456
5. Joe Kelley	.442
6. Hughie Jennings	.436
7. Willie Keeler	.431
8. Cupid Childs	.430
9. Elmer Smith	.420
10. Mike Griffin	.413
11. Jake Stenzel	.411
12. Bill Lange	.401
13. George Davis	.400
14. Hugh Duffy	.400
15. Bill Dahlen	.398
16. Mike Tiernan	.398
17. Fred Clarke	.397
18. Kip Selbach	.397
19. George Van Haltren	.394
20. Jimmy Ryan	.388
21. Bid McPhee	.388
22. Jake Beckley	.380
23. Jack Doyle	.377
24. Dummy Hoy	.375
25. Steve Brodie	.375

Beaneaters Almost Have Four 20-Game Winners

Moving the pitching mound 10½ feet farther from the plate in 1893 put an immediate end to the days when a team could get by for a full season with just two strong hurlers. By the middle of the decade most clubs had gone to a three-man rotation, and several even used four starters on a regular basis. In 1898, the Boston Beaneaters, en route to their second consecutive National League flag, nearly became the first team in history to have four 20-game winners. Staff leader Kid Nichols posted 31 wins, Ted Lewis followed with 26 victories, and rookie ace Vic Willis kicked in 25 wins. Fred Klobedanz, the previous year's rookie star, narrowly missed joining the charmed circle when he finished with 19 triumphs. The four stalwarts accounted for all but one of Boston's 102 victories. Win No. 102 was claimed by Piano Legs Hickman, who took some turns on the mound before he became a slugging utility player. In 1899, the Brooklyn Superbas also just missed having four 20-game winners as three members of the club's staff reached the charmed circle and Doc McJames fell one victory short of it.

Of the four Boston Beaneater pitchers who compiled 101 wins between them in 1898, only Vic Willis duplicated his victory total in another season. None of the other three ever again won as many games during a single season as they did in 1898.

Above: *Kid Nichols pitched 11 years with the Boston Beaneaters from 1890 to 1901. He led the NL in wins three straight years from 1896 to 1898 as the Beaneaters won two NL crowns. The versatile righthander also led the league in saves four times. In 1900, Nichols became the youngest pitcher ever to win 300 games, a distinction he still holds.*

The 1898 season was the first in National League history that no pitcher won as many as 30 games; Kid Nichols led the loop with 29 victories.

The only rookie to debut with 30 or more wins since the mound was moved to its present distance from home plate in 1893 was Bill Hoffer, who bagged 31 victories for the Baltimore Orioles in 1895.

When Bert Cunningham bagged 28 victories for Louisville in 1898, he became the club's first pitcher to win 20 games since the mound was moved to 60'6".

The only pitcher to cop a league ERA crown both before and after the mound was moved to its present distance is Billy Rhines of the Cincinnati Reds.

In 1897, Nixey Callahan of Chicago became the last player in National League history to pitch enough innings to qualify for the ERA crown and collect enough at bats to qualify for the hitting title.

Jim Hughey, who pitched in the majors from 1891 through 1900, is the only hurler ever to notch 100 complete games without ever tossing a shutout.

1893-1899 GAMES PITCHED	
1. Cy Young	339
2. Kid Nichols	336
3. Ted Breitenstein	307
4. Pink Hawley	306
5. Brickyard Kennedy	299
6. Jack Taylor	266
7. Jouett Meekin	260
8. Frank Killen	244
9. Win Mercer	240
10. Clark Griffith	235
11. Amos Rusie	234
12. Frank Dwyer	228
13. Nig Cuppy	225
14. Gus Weyhing	204
15. Red Ehret	202
16. Kid Carsey	195
17. Jack Stivetts	190
18. Bert Cunningham	170
19. Doc McJames	165
20. Red Donahue	151
21. George Hemming	150
22. Duke Esper	149
23. Bill Hoffer	145
Chick Fraser	145
25. Billy Rhines	143

In 1899, the Cleveland Spiders won only 20 of 154 decisions and were led in victories by Jim Hughey and Charlie Knepper with four apiece.

Nig Cuppy of Cleveland set a National League record for pitchers when he tallied five runs in a game on August 9, 1895.

1893-1899 COMPLETE GAMES	
1. Cy Young	279
2. Kid Nichols	276
3. Ted Breitenstein	252
4. Brickyard Kennedy	229
5. Pink Hawley	228
6. Jouett Meekin	214
7. Clark Griffith	213
8. Jack Taylor	205
Amos Rusie	205
10. Frank Killen	190
11. Win Mercer	179
12. Nig Cuppy	168
13. Frank Dwyer	163
14. Gus Weyhing	158
15. Kid Carsey	142
16. Bert Cunningham	140
17. Jack Stivetts	134
18. Doc McJames	131
19. Red Ehret	130
20. Red Donahue	127
21. Chick Fraser	123
22. George Hemming	122
23. Bill Hoffer	115
24. Bill Hart	105
25. Cy Seymour	102

Gus Weyhing was the only pitcher to appear in as many as 40 games in both 1889 and 1899.

Frank Bates was the only pitcher to register a win for the Cleveland Spiders in both 1898 and 1899.

Spiders Use Cuppy as a Reliever

In the 1890s starting pitchers were expected to finish what they began. Many teams, regardless of the score, stubbornly refused to lift a starter, and in consequence relief pitching was still for the most part an undiscovered art. The Cleveland Spiders were one of the few clubs that broke precedent after manager Patsy Tebeau realized he had something of a find in Nig Cuppy. In 1894, Cuppy won 24 games altogether but only 16 came as a starter. The remaining eight victories were the result of relief stints. Cuppy's eight wins as a fireman set a post-1893 record for relief triumphs that lasted until 1925 when Elam Vangilder of the St. Louis Browns bagged 11 verdicts while working out of the bullpen. What made Cuppy's feat even more spectacular is that he was unbeaten as a reliever in 1894 and at one point in his career was a perfect 14-0 in mop-up roles.

The 1894 season saw a record-low 32 shutout games in the National League; Cleveland topped the circuit with six whitewashes, three of them by Nig Cuppy.

Frank Bates, Crazy Schmit, and Harry Colliflower, three second-line pitchers for the Spiders in 1899, had a composite 4-46 record.

In 1895, Washington pitcher Win Mercer tied for the NL lead in pinch hits with two.

Above: *Clark Griffith, "The Old Fox," won 20 games six straight years for the Chicago Cubs in the 1890s using six different pitches.*

1893-1899 SAVES	
1. Kid Nichols	13
2. Jack Taylor	9
3. Win Mercer	8
Brickyard Kennedy	8
5. Tony Mullane	6
Cy Young	6
7. Jesse Tannehill	5
8. Charlie Hickman	4
Mike Sullivan	4
Tom Parrott	4
Doc McJames	4
Frank Dwyer	4
13. Jim Sullivan	3
Bill Phillips	3
Sam Leever	3
Silver King	3
Bill Hawke	3
Chauncey Fisher	3
Bill Dammann	3
Ernie Beam	3
Amos Rusie	3
Ted Lewis	3
Bill Hill	3
Pink Hawley	3
Duke Esper	3
Nig Cuppy	3
Dad Clarke	3

Above: *Wild but overpowering Amos Rusie starred for the New York Giants in the 1890s, five times leading the NL in strikeouts.*

1893-1899 SHUTOUTS	
1. Cy Young	19
Kid Nichols	19
3. Amos Rusie	17
4. Jack Powell	10
Bill Hoffer	10
6. Jesse Tannehill	9
Frank Killen	9
Brickyard Kennedy	9
Pink Hawley	9
Ted Breitenstein	9
11. Jim Hughes	8
Wiley Piatt	8
Nig Cuppy	8
14. Gus Weyhing	7
Jack Taylor	7
Red Ehret	7
Frank Dwyer	7
18. Vic Willis	6
Cy Seymour	6
Billy Rhines	6
Al Orth	6
Jouett Meekin	6
Doc McJames	6
George Hemming	6
Red Donahue	6
Nixey Callahan	6

O.P. Caylor of the **New York Herald** *wrote about Amos Rusie: "The Giants without Rusie would be like* Hamlet *without the melancholy Dane."*

Amos Rusie of the New York Giants, with a 2.78 ERA, was the only National League hurler in 1894 with an ERA below 3.70.

◆◇◆

In 1894, Amos Rusie and Jouett Meekin had a combined 69-22 record for New York, but the club finished second because its other pitchers were only 19-22.

In 1894, the Giants' twin mound aces, Amos Rusie and Jouett Meekin, were the only two National League hurlers to allow less than one hit per inning.

Cy Seymour in 1898 led the NL with 239 strikeouts pitching; after his pitching career was over, he went on to become an outfielder. Cy almost won the NL's batting Triple Crown in 1905.

◆◇◆

In 1893, Amos Rusie, with 208 strikeouts, was the only National League pitcher able to collect more than 107 Ks.

After winning 23 games for the New York Giants in 1895, Amos Rusie held out for the entire 1896 season.

Seymour Collects Strikeout and Batting Crowns

Even casual students of the game in the 1890s naturally assume that all the period single-season strikeout records were set by Amos Rusie. Nicknamed "The Hoosier Thunderbolt," Rusie indeed was the most prolific K artist during the game's second era. The era's highest season strikeout total, however, was registered by a teammate of Rusie's on the New York Giants. In 1898, while Rusie was notching just 114 strikeouts, southpaw Cy Seymour mowed down 239 National League hitters. He also paced the NL in Ks the previous year when he fanned 157 batters in his first full season. After notching 142 whiffs in 1899, second only to Cincinnati rookie whiz Noodles Hahn, Seymour fell prey to arm problems, but his career was far from over. By 1901, he had completed the transition from the mound to an every-day player and emerged as one of the game's premier hitters—so good that he remains to this day the only player since 1893 to claim a pitching strikeout crown and a batting title.

Amos Rusie won his 243rd and final major league game in 1898 when he was just 27 years old.

When Ted Breitenstein of Cincinnati and Jim Hughes of Baltimore both hurled no-hitters on April 22, 1898, it was the first time two no-nos had occurred on the same day.

1893-1899 INNINGS	
1. Cy Young	2,696.2
2. Kid Nichols	2,683.1
3. Ted Breitenstein	2,446.0
4. Pink Hawley	2,334.2
5. Brickyard Kennedy	2,288.2
6. Jouett Meekin	2,094.0
7. Jack Taylor	2,045.0
8. Amos Rusie	1,941.2
9. Clark Griffith	1,940.2
10. Frank Killen	1,901.0
11. Win Mercer	1,763.0
12. Frank Dwyer	1,724.1
13. Nig Cuppy	1,709.2
14. Gus Weyhing	1,580.1
15. Kid Carsey	1,482.1
16. Red Ehret	1,442.2
17. Jack Stivetts	1,421.0
18. Bert Cunningham	1,340.2
19. Doc McJames	1,270.1
20. George Hemming	1,203.0
21. Red Donahue	1,191.1
22. Bill Hoffer	1,155.1
23. Chick Fraser	1,151.1
24. Duke Esper	1,058.2
25. Billy Rhines	1,042.1

Above: *Cy Young only led the AL in innings pitched twice, but holds the all-time record.*

Jack Dunn, later the owner and manager of the Baltimore Orioles' International League dynasty, led the pennant-winning 1899 Brooklyn Superbas in innings pitched with 299.

Brewery Jack Taylor, winner of 120 games during the 1890s, died of Bright's Disease in 1900 at age 26.

Put It In the 'L' Column

For a pitcher the quality of the team behind him can mean nearly everything. When Bill Hoffer logged a rookie-record 31 wins in 1895, he was hurling for the National League champion Baltimore Orioles. In 1896, another rookie named Bill—Still Bill Hill—set the reverse frosh record when he was beaten 28 times while working for the cellar-dwelling Louisville Colonels. That same season Billy Hart set a post-1893 record by suffering 29 defeats with St. Louis, which finished a notch above Louisville in 11th place. In 1897, Louisville swapped places with St. Louis in the standings, helping Hill to cut his losses to just 17. Hart meanwhile lost 27 more games for St. Louis in 1897, but his moundmate Red Donahue fared even worse. With his St. Louis club able to win only 29 of 131 contests, Donahue dropped a post-1893 record 35 games. Traded to Philadelphia in 1898, Donahue went on to fashion a productive career, but Hill and Hart never recovered from their early stints with abysmal teams.

While losing 33 games (the most of any pitcher since 1893) for St. Louis in 1897, Red Donahue tied for the National League lead in complete games with 38.

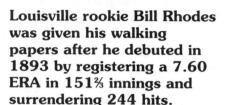

Louisville rookie Bill Rhodes was given his walking papers after he debuted in 1893 by registering a 7.60 ERA in 151⅔ innings and surrendering 244 hits.

On June 14, 1893, Bill Rhodes of the Louisville Colonels, making his second major league start, was allowed to go the route by manager Billy Barnie despite surrendering an all-time record 55 total bases.

1893-1899 WINS	
1. Kid Nichols	205
2. Cy Young	195
3. Brickyard Kennedy	141
4. Amos Rusie	140
5. Ted Breitenstein	139
6. Clark Griffith	138
7. Pink Hawley	136
8. Jouett Meekin	133
9. Frank Killen	125
10. Nig Cuppy	122
11. Jack Taylor	119
12. Frank Dwyer	113
13. Jack Stivetts	96
14. Win Mercer	94
15. Bill Hoffer	89
16. Kid Carsey	82
17. Gus Weyhing	81
18. Bert Cunningham	77
19. Doc McJames	74
20. George Hemming	73
21. Red Ehret	72
22. Sadie McMahon	69
23. Al Orth	66
24. Billy Rhines	65
Ted Lewis	65

Colonel Bert Saves Louisville Baseball

Accepted into the National League when the American Association collapsed after the 1891 season, the Louisville Colonels finished ninth in 1892, their first campaign in the new 12-team circuit, but then became the loop's perennial doormat, finishing either last or next to last for each of the next five seasons. The club's most glaring weakness was pitching. While most of the other NL clubs had at least one 20-game winner, Louisville entered the 1898 season not having had a hurler attain the charmed circle since Scott Stratton won 21 games in 1892. Among the club's mound hopefuls that spring was Bert Cunningham, then 32 years old and the owner of a lackluster career record of 93 wins and 131 defeats. To the dismay of the entire baseball community, Cunningham snared 28 victories in 1898 and helped save the Louisville franchise from extinction. Part-owner Barney Dreyfus had been ready to dispose of his interest in the team before Cunningham brought it credibility. Dreyfus instead held on to his piece of the club until the finish of the 1899 season when he took its best players to Pittsburgh, which he also owned, and formed the team that would soon become the NL's strongest.

Starting pitchers were so seldom relieved in the 1890s, regardless of the score, that in 1899 Cleveland hurlers, despite losing 134 of 154 contests, logged 138 complete games.

In 1895, the Cincinnati Reds and the Louisville Colonels became the first two teams to employ a four-man pitching rotation for the entire season.

In 1899, rookie lefthander Noodles Hahn debuted with a 23-7 record for Cincinnati and topped the National League with 145 strikeouts.

In 1893, the first year the mound was set at its present distance, Cy Young (2.19) was the only National League hurler to surrender fewer than 2.5 walks per nine innings.

1893-1899 STRIKEOUTS	
1. Amos Rusie	853
2. Kid Nichols	822
3. Cy Young	771
4. Ted Breitenstein	708
5. Pink Hawley	675
6. Jouett Meekin	628
7. Cy Seymour	563
8. Doc McJames	551
9. Brickyard Kennedy	538
10. Frank Killen	536
11. Jack Taylor	518
12. Clark Griffith	512
13. Gus Weyhing	440
14. Win Mercer	415
15. Nig Cuppy	356
16. Jack Stivetts	352
17. Red Ehret	350
18. Chick Fraser	306
19. Ed Doheny	296
20. Bill Hoffer	295
21. Vic Willis	280
Bill Hill	280
23. Frank Dwyer	277
24. Adonis Terry	254
25. Willie McGill	248

Clark Griffith of Chicago posted the only sub-2.00 ERA between 1893 and 1899 when he finished at 1.88 in 1898.

In 1894, Washington pitchers fanned only 190 enemy hitters and were led by rookie Win Mercer with 69 Ks.

While Philadelphia hitters were hitting a record .349 in 1894, Phillies pitchers were busy posting a 5.63 ERA and allowing 966 runs.

Rookie hurler Frank Donnelly in 1893 had a 3-1 record for Chicago, hit .444, and led the National League in saves but never again played in the majors.

In 1896, Les German had a 2-20 record for Washington; the club's other pitchers had a composite 56-53 mark.

Cy Young was the staff ace and leading winner for the Cleveland Spiders each year from 1891 to 1898, when he was traded to St. Louis. During that span, Young led the NL in such diverse categories as wins, strikeouts, ERA, saves, and relief wins.

Endurance
Cy Young said to a reporter: "I won more games than you ever saw."

1893-1899 PITCHER FIELDING AVERAGE	
1. Kid Nichols	.962
2. Jack Stivetts	.954
3. Nig Cuppy	.953
4. Zeke Wilson	.947
5. Ad Gumbert	.947

The last southpaw to win 30 games for an NL team was Frank Killen, who bagged exactly 30 victories for the 1896 Pittsburgh Pirates.

Led by Ted Breitenstein with a league-best 3.18 ERA, the 10th place St. Louis Browns paced the National League in 1893 with a 4.06 ERA.

1893-1899 WINNING PERCENTAGE	
1. Bill Hoffer	.701
2. Kid Nichols	.674
3. Amos Rusie	.642
4. Cy Young	.639
5. Clark Griffith	.624
6. Nig Cuppy	.619
7. Jack Stivetts	.593
8. Jouett Meekin	.583
9. Ed Stein	.561
10. Frank Killen	.561
11. Frank Dwyer	.554
12. George Hemming	.553
13. Billy Rhines	.542
14. Brickyard Kennedy	.534
15. Bert Cunningham	.507
16. Jack Taylor	.506
17. Pink Hawley	.506
18. Ted Breitenstein	.502
19. Doc McJames	.500
20. Kid Carsey	.491
21. Win Mercer	.448
22. Red Ehret	.447
23. Duke Esper	.447
24. Gus Weyhing	.445
25. Chick Fraser	.422

1893-1899 EARNED RUN AVERAGE	
1. Amos Rusie	3.08
2. Kid Nichols	3.21
3. Cy Young	3.25
4. Doc McJames	3.34
5. Clark Griffith	3.44
6. Bill Hoffer	3.68
7. Nig Cuppy	3.68
8. Frank Killen	3.97
9. Frank Dwyer	4.00
10. Ted Breitenstein	4.00
11. Pink Hawley	4.03
12. Brickyard Kennedy	4.03
13. Bert Cunningham	4.04
14. Jouett Meekin	4.06
15. Win Mercer	4.09
16. Billy Rhines	4.14
17. Jack Taylor	4.27
18. Ed Stein	4.41
19. Chick Fraser	4.42
20. Jack Stivetts	4.48
21. George Hemming	4.50
22. Red Ehret	4.57
23. Duke Esper	4.74
24. Red Donahue	4.81
25. Gus Weyhing	5.03

Above: *Jake Beckley played more games at first base than anyone in baseball history. The powerful Beckley, an excellent contact hitter, collected 2,930 lifetime hits in a 20-year career.*

Stay West

Between 1892 and 1900 the National League was considered to be the only major league in operation—by those who lived east of the Mississippi anyway. Baseball players in the far West thought the caliber of competition on the Pacific Coast was every bit as strong as the NL offered. Since the weather there was considerably better, making it possible to play year round, and railway travel was still hazardous, many chose to play close to the Pacific. Among them were two pitchers of considerable skill: Joe Corbett and Jim Hughes. The brother of heavyweight champion Gentleman Jim, Joe Corbett balked at returning to Baltimore after posting 24 wins for the Orioles in 1897 and, except for a brief spell with St. Louis in 1904, remained on the West Coast for the rest of his career. Hughes lasted four seasons in the National League and bagged 83 wins before moving his game to the West Coast after his new bride refused to go East with him. In 1924, his body was found below a railroad bridge in Sacramento, California; it was never established whether he fell from the bridge or was pushed to his death.

Despite leading the National League only once in triples, Jake Beckley's 243 three-base hits ranks fourth on the all-time list.

Jake Beckley scored over 100 runs five times during the 1890s, including a high of 121 in 1894.

Crooks Robbed of Career

Beginning in 1893, when the pitcher's mound was stationed at its present distance and batting averages jumped by some 50 points, even middle infielders were expected to hit close to .300. The St. Louis Browns released Jack Crooks after he batted a meager .237 that season, disregarding his .408 on-base percentage and National League leading total of 121 walks (the third consecutive season he had more than 100 walks in a season). Crooks returned to the NL with Washington in 1895 but was soon jettisoned again, as much a victim of his times as outfielder Jim McTamany had been in the game's previous era. His low batting averages notwithstanding, Crooks was possibly the best pure leadoff hitter of his day, skilled both at coaxing walks and moving runners along with sacrifice bunts. Crooks also ranked among the top defensive second basemen of his era. In 1891, he set a new standard for the position when he posted a .957 fielding average. He died in a St. Louis mental hospital in 1918.

The current infield fly rule was first adopted by the National League in 1895.

1893-1899 CATCHER GAMES	
1. Deacon McGuire	652
2. Wilbert Robinson	574
3. Heinie Peitz	514
4. Duke Farrell	505
5. Chief Zimmer	501

1893-1899 CATCHER FIELDING AVERAGE	
1. Chief Zimmer	.972
2. Heinie Peitz	.956
3. Wilbert Robinson	.954
4. Deacon McGuire	.941
5. Duke Farrell	.937

To curb pesky hitters like Willie Keeler, who kept bunting pitches foul until they got one they liked, in 1894 a rule was put in making a foul bunt a strike.

In 1896, the Philadelphia Phillies featured both the last southpaw to be a regular catcher, Jack Clements, and the last lefthander to be a regular shortstop, Billy Hulen.

Cheaters Sometime Prosper

Heywood Broun wrote about the old Baltimore Orioles: "The tradition of professional baseball always has been agreeably free of chivalry. The rule is: Do anything you can get away with."

In 1899, Sport McAllister of Cleveland became the first player to serve at all nine positions in the same season.

The 1894 Washington Nationals, with a .908 fielding average, were the last team to post a fielding average below .910.

Chief Zimmer, just a few weeks shy of his 39th birthday, was the oldest regular catcher prior to 1900 when he served as Louisville's first-string backstopper in 1899.

When he topped the National League with 77 stolen bases in 1899, Baltimore's Jimmy Sheckard set a modern theft mark that endured until 1910.

1893-1899 FIRST BASE GAMES	
1. Tommy Tucker	860
2. Jake Beckley	858
3. Candy LaChance	595
4. Patsy Tebeau	591
5. Jack Doyle	565

Joe Quinn, a member of both the 1884 St. Louis Maroons and the 1899 Cleveland Spiders, had the distinction of playing for the clubs with both the best and the worst records in the 19th century.

The Cleveland Spiders were the only National League team between 1893 and 1899 without a player who stole as many as 50 bases in a season.

Eddie Abbaticchio, who broke in with the Phillies in 1897, was the first Italian player of note in major league history.

In 1896, a Princeton professor named Hinton invented the first mechanical pitching machine.

Phillies Lose Allen, 1894 Pennant

Another middle infielder whose skills were undervalued during the 1890s was Bob Allen. As a rookie with the Philadelphia Phillies in 1890, Allen quickly made a case that he was the best defensive shortstop in the game at the time. Despite batting averages that generally hovered in the .220s, Allen provided the glue for the Phillies infield during the next four seasons. Loaded with offensive talent in its three future Hall of Fame outfielders—Billy Hamilton, Sam Thompson, and Ed Delahanty—Philadelphia seemed poised to make its first serious pennant bid in 1894, only to have its chances short-circuited when Allen was sidelined early in the season by a beaning. Without Allen the club sagged from the NL's top fielding unit in 1893 to no better than average and wound up a distant fourth. Allen's head injury prevented him from playing in the majors again until 1897, and even then he never fully recovered his early form. After his retirement as a player, he later owned the Little Rock club in the Southern Association.

1893-1899 FIRST BASE FIELDING AVERAGE	
1. Patsy Tebeau	.984
2. Candy LaChance	.983
3. Cap Anson	.983
4. Jake Beckley	.982
5. Tommy Tucker	.981

Probably the worst trade during the 1890s came prior to the 1894 season when Brooklyn swapped Willie Keeler to Baltimore for George Treadway.

Hall of Fame first baseman Jake Beckley was released by the New York Giants early in the 1897 season but went on to play ten more years after he was picked up by Cincinnati.

On September 3, 1894, the Baltimore Orioles made an all-time record 21 extra-base hits in a doubleheader with Cleveland.

Above: *The 1898 Cleveland Spiders— with Cy Young (in striped shirt)— contended during the 1890s, but couldn't win a crown.*

Cleveland's Jesse Burkett led the NL in 1896 with 160 runs scored, 240 hits, and a .410 batting average.

Despite a reputation as a poor hitter, infielder Bobby Wallace led the Spiders in 1898 with 99 RBI.

In 1893, three Spiders players had 100 RBI with six or fewer home runs each.

Gotta Be Tough to Play in Cleveland

Cleveland player-manager Patsy Tebeau said about his band of Spiders: "A milk-and-water goody-goody player can't wear a Cleveland uniform."

1893-1899 SECOND BASE GAMES	
1. Cupid Childs	841
2. Bobby Lowe	839
3. Bid McPhee	801
4. Bill Hallman	713
5. Heinie Reitz	687

Pictured above, clockwise from far left, are: Willie Keeler, John McGraw, Hughie Jennings, and Joe Kelley. These four key members of the 1890s Orioles helped to bring winning baseball to the Chesapeake Bay under manager Ned Hanlon.

Hanlon Teaches Orioles Winning Rowdy Style

To alter its fortunes after finishing last in the 12-team National League in 1892, the Baltimore club hired Ned Hanlon as manager. Hanlon steered the Orioles to an eighth-place finish in 1893, then lifted Baltimore to three straight pennants. A series of shrewd trades that brought Hall of Famers Joe Kelley, Wee Willie Keeler, and Hughie Jennings to Baltimore helped put the club over the top, but equally instrumental were two members of the Orioles' original NL cast in 1892: third baseman John McGraw and catcher Wilbert Robinson. Perhaps more than any other player, McGraw exemplified the guileful, spikes-flying brand of play that proliferated during the 1890s. Among McGraw's specialties were tripping runners as they passed his third base station or holding them by the belt when they attempted to tag up on fly balls. When a base-runner himself, McGraw would cut across the diamond if an umpire had his back to the infield and score from second base without bothering with the formality of touching third. The Orioles' practice of winning ugly was soon embraced by other teams. By the mid-1890s the game had become an arena for the rough-house, umpire-baiting style of play that would become the hallmark of the era.

The Washington Nationals and the Philadelphia Phillies set off their own fireworks when they combined to collect an all-time record 73 hits in a doubleheader on Independence Day in 1896.

A New York World-Telegram reader, informing reporter Joe Williams in the 1920s, wrote: "Individually, you haven't lost much in having missed seeing the Old Orioles. But collectively, oh, my dear scribbler, could you have seen them, your whole life might have been different."

The Baltimore Orioles and the Boston Beaneaters were the only teams that did not have at least one 20-game loser between 1893 and 1899.

The 1894 to 1897 Baltimore Orioles are the only major league team to win more than two-thirds of its games for four consecutive years.

1893-1899 SECOND BASE FIELDING AVERAGE	
1. Bid McPhee	.957
2. Heinie Reitz	.955
3. Joe Quinn	.952
4. Bobby Lowe	.949
5. Bill Hallman	.943

All seven National League pennants between 1893 and 1899 were claimed by two managers, Ned Hanlon and Frank Selee.

Selee Directs 1890s Best Club

Although the Baltimore Orioles emerged as the most famous team of the 1890s, they were not the era's best club. The Boston Beaneaters, under manager Frank Selee, had a better overall record during the decade than the Orioles. While Ned Hanlon built his Baltimore dynasty via the trade route, Selee's forte was recognizing, signing, and nurturing young talent. Among Selee's finds were Hall of Famers Kid Nichols and Jimmy Collins, and Vic Willis, regarded by many as the best pitcher not in the Hall of Fame. He managed the Boston National League club from 1890 to 1901, going 1,004-649 and winning five pennants. When his Boston dynasty began to falter in the early 1900s, Selee took over the operation of the Chicago Cubs in 1902. A franchise in disarray, the Cubs had not been a contender since the late 1880s. With Selee at the helm, Chicago quickly rebounded and was only a year away from its first pennant since 1886 when tuberculosis forced Selee to surrender control of the team to Frank Chance.

1893-1899 THIRD BASE GAMES	
1. Billy Shindle	742
2. Lave Cross	653
3. Jimmy Collins	594
4. John McGraw	590
5. Billy Nash	556

In 1898, the Boston Beaneaters won a franchise-record 102 games while cruising to the National League pennant.

1893-1899 THIRD BASE FIELDING AVERAGE	
1. Lave Cross	.939
2. Jimmy Collins	.927
3. Charlie Irwin	.919
4. Billy Nash	.915
5. Billy Shindle	.901

In 1897, eight of the 12 National League teams finished 23½ or more games behind the pennant-winning Boston club.

The 1897 Boston Beaneaters, which tallied 1,025 runs, were the last team prior to 1930 to top 1,000 runs.

George Davis of New York posted a .945 fielding average in 1899 to set a new mark for shortstops in a season when teams played a minimum of 100 games.

In 1893, shortstop Joe Sullivan of Washington collected 102 miscues and became the last major league player to tabulate 100 or more errors in a season.

The Cincinnati Reds became the first team to post a .950 or better fielding average when they finished at .951 in 1896.

In their season finale against the Cincinnati Reds, the hapless 1899 Cleveland Spiders named Eddie Kolb, a Cincinnati cigar store clerk, their starting pitcher.

The 1899 Cleveland Spiders, then in the National League, won only 20 of 154 games and had an all-time record low .130 win percentage.

1893-1899 SHORTSTOP GAMES	
1. Herman Long	855
2. Tommy Corcoran	842
3. Ed McKean	837
4. Bones Ely	828
5. Bill Dahlen	735

In a game on May 9, 1896, Washington and Pittsburgh pitchers combined to hit an all-time record eight batters.

1893-1899 SHORTSTOP FIELDING AVERAGE	
1. Hughie Jennings	.928
2. Bones Ely	.923
3. Tommy Corcoran	.921
4. Germany Smith	.919
5. Bill Dahlen	.915

Mike Griffin of Brooklyn led all National League outfielders in fielding average three times between 1893 and 1899.

1893-1899 OUTFIELD GAMES	
1. George Van Haltren	948
2. Hugh Duffy	933
3. Jesse Burkett	931
4. Dummy Hoy	913
5. Joe Kelley	911
6. Patsy Donovan	888
7. Elmer Smith	831
8. Steve Brodie	826
9. Ed Delahanty	823
10. Jimmy Ryan	822
11. Willie Keeler	794
12. Tommy Dowd	791
13. Billy Hamilton	782
14. Fred Clarke	758
15. Mike Tiernan	753

Tommy Leach remembered Dummy Hoy, the deaf-mute outfielder: "He was a real fine ballplayer. When you played with him in the outfield, the thing was you never called for a ball. You listened for him, and if he made this little squeaky sound, that meant he was going to take it."

To convey ball-and-strike calls to the deaf Dummy Hoy, 1890s plate umpires began using hand signals.

1893-1899 OUTFIELD FIELDING AVERAGE	
1. Mike Griffin	.965
2. Steve Brodie	.964
3. Willie Keeler	.961
4. Joe Kelley	.957
5. Ed Delahanty	.954
6. Hugh Duffy	.954
7. Harry Blake	.948
8. Jimmy McAleer	.947
9. Mike Tiernan	.944
10. Patsy Donovan	.942
11. Bill Lange	.942
12. Kip Selbach	.940
13. Billy Hamilton	.939
14. Duff Cooley	.936
15. Tommy Dowd	.934

Above: William "Dummy" Hoy, the first deaf player in the major leagues, starred in center field for the Cincinnati Reds in the 1890s. Hoy was a solid hitter with great speed and a powerful throwing arm, once nailing three men at home plate in one game.

Soden's Stubbornness Surrenders Beaneaters Reign

A large part of the reason that Frank Selee abandoned Boston for Chicago was Beaneaters owner Arthur Soden. Always intransigent, reactionary, and tight-fisted in his mode of operation, Soden by the early 1900s had become so aloof from his players that he did not even know the names of many of them. During the 1890s when there was only one major league and his players were bound to him like chattels, Soden's intractability had been masked by Selee's genius as a manager. After the American League formed in 1901 as a rival major circuit, though, Soden swiftly began to lose most of his star players to aggressive owners from the other loop who were willing and ready to pay them what they were worth. From the best team in the 1890s, Soden's club descended so far in the following decade that it ranked as the game's worst at its end.

In 1895, the New York Giants came in ninth in the 12-club NL with a .504 winning percentage, the lowest finish ever by a team able to win more than half its games.

In 1894, the pitching staff of the Washington Senators, then in the NL, struck out just 190 batters in 132 games and allowed opponents to hit a pre-1930 major league record .331.

Handsome Tony Mullane Helps Create 'Ladies Day'

Times were hard in the 1890s. Throughout most of the decade the country was suffering from an economic depression, and baseball was not spared the effects of it. In an effort to spark dwindling attendance National League club owners turned to several ploys devised by the American Association in the 1880s after previously being disdainful of them. One of the most popular was "Ladies Day" games in which females were allowed into the park for free. Among the first AA moguls to institute Ladies Days was Cincinnati owner Aaron Stern, who observed that women would flock to his club's games on days that handsome Tony Mullane was slated to pitch. From then on, whenever Mullane worked against weak teams that normally drew poorly, Stern advertised the contest as a special "Ladies Day" event. Other AA owners, like Brooklyn's Charles Byrne, soon adopted the innovation. With the help of Ladies Days, Byrne's 1889 Brooklyn Bridegrooms set a 19th century season attendance record.

1893-1899 MANAGER WINNING PERCENTAGE	
1. Ned Hanlon	.649
2. Frank Selee	.632
3. Buck Ewing	.570
4. Patsy Tebeau	.570
5. Dave Foutz	.507
6. Cap Anson	.483
7. Arthur Irwin	.471

In 1894, the Philadelphia Phillies hit .349 as a team, had three outfielders who batted over .400 and another who hit .399, and finished in fourth place, 18 games off the pace.

Above are the 1892 Phillies, including Hall-of-Famers Ed Delahanty (seated, second from left), Tim Keefe (seated, third from right), Billy Hamilton (seated, far right), and manager Harry Wright (in dark coat).

1893-1899 MANAGER WINS	
1. Ned Hanlon	613
2. Frank Selee	604
3. Patsy Tebeau	539
4. Buck Ewing	394
5. Cap Anson	324
6. Dave Foutz	264
7. Arthur Irwin	249
8. Fred Clarke	180
9. Bill Joyce	179
10. Billy Barnie	162

1893-1899 TEAM WINS	WON	LOST
1. Boston-NL	604	352
2. Baltimore-NL	598	346
3. Cincinnati-NL	514	435
4. Philadelphia-NL	510	441
5. New York-NL	506	451
6. Pittsburgh-NL	491	457
7. Brooklyn-NL	480	466
8. Chicago-NL	475	472
Cleveland-NL	475	474
10. Louisville-NL	356	594
11. Washington-NL	352	604
12. St. Louis-NL	344	613

1893-1899 TEAM WINNING PERCENTAGE	
1. Baltimore-NL	.633
2. Boston-NL	.632
3. Cincinnati-NL	.542
4. Philadelphia-NL	.536
5. New York-NL	.529
6. Pittsburgh-NL	.518
7. Brooklyn-NL	.507
8. Chicago-NL	.502
9. Cleveland-NL	.501
10. Louisville-NL	.375
11. Washington-NL	.368
12. St. Louis-NL	.359

Chapter 3
The 1900s

The only player to average at least two home runs per every 100 at bats prior to 1900 was Sam Thompson, who finished with a 2.12 home run percentage.

In 1906, rookie catcher Branch Rickey, who hit just three home runs in his entire career, became the first player from the St. Louis Browns to hit two dingers in one game.

1900s GAMES PLAYED	
1. Sam Crawford	1,410
2. Honus Wagner	1,391
3. Bobby Wallace	1,362
4. Bill Dahlen	1,332
5. Fred Tenney	1,329
6. Jimmy Sheckard	1,312
7. Jimmy Williams	1,304
8. Harry Steinfeldt	1,303
9. Bill Bradley	1,292
10. Fielder Jones	1,289
11. Hobe Ferris	1,287
12. Willie Keeler	1,278
13. Roy Thomas	1,276
Ginger Beaumont	1,276
15. Tommy Leach	1,273
16. Claude Ritchey	1,272
17. Freddy Parent	1,241
18. Fred Clarke	1,234
19. Cy Seymour	1,224
Nap Lajoie	1,224
21. Elmer Flick	1,198
Harry Davis	1,198
23. Topsy Hartsel	1,189
24. Kitty Bransfield	1,176
25. Wid Conroy	1,165

1900s RUNS	
1. Honus Wagner	1,014
2. Fred Clarke	885
3. Roy Thomas	862
4. Ginger Beaumont	835
5. Tommy Leach	828
6. Sam Crawford	813
7. Jimmy Sheckard	807
8. Nap Lajoie	806
9. Fielder Jones	799
10. Willie Keeler	797
11. Elmer Flick	761
12. Fred Tenney	758
13. Topsy Hartsel	754
14. Harry Davis	721
15. Bill Bradley	700
16. Jimmy Slagle	687
17. Jimmy Williams	655
18. Frank Chance	646
19. Jimmy Collins	624
20. Cy Seymour	622
21. Bobby Wallace	612
22. Freddy Parent	608
23. Bill Dahlen	606
24. Dan McGann	604
25. George Browne	595

Harry Davis of the Philadelphia Athletics led the AL in homers from 1904 to 1907, becoming the first man in major league history to win his circuit's homer crown four years in a row.

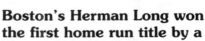

Boston's Herman Long won the first home run title by a shortstop in major league history when he clouted 12 to lead the 1900 National League.

Dahlen, Other Loop Leaders Low

In 1894, Bill Dahlen in 121 games collected 107 runs batted in, a total that barely placed him among the top 20 RBI men in the National League that year. Exactly a decade later Dahlen notched 80 RBI in 145 games, seemingly an indication that his offensive production had declined. In actuality, however, it was not Dahlen that declined but offensive production in general. By 1904, the game was so deeply in the throes of the dead-ball era that Dahlen's modest total of 80 RBI topped the National League. Second to Dahlen with 78 ribbies was his New York Giants teammate Sam Mertes, and another Giant, outfielder George Browne, paced the loop in runs with just 99. Over in the American League hitters had a slightly better time of it in 1904. Nap Lajoie bagged 102 RBI and Patsy Dougherty tallied 113 runs, but the following year A's first sacker Harry Davis led the loop in both departments with just 83 ribbies and 92 tallies.

Bill Dahlen played an NL-record 20 years at shortstop, collected a major league record 13,325 total chances and an NL-record 7,500 assists, while making 972 errors, the most by a player at any position in a single league.

Dead-Ball Clobbers Minors

1900s HITS	
1. Honus Wagner	1,847
2. Sam Crawford	1,677
3. Nap Lajoie	1,660
4. Willie Keeler	1,566
5. Ginger Beaumont	1,559
6. Cy Seymour	1,460
7. Elmer Flick	1,431
8. Fred Clarke	1,396
9. Fred Tenney	1,387
10. Bobby Wallace	1,373
11. Bill Bradley	1,348
12. Jimmy Sheckard	1,343
13. Roy Thomas	1,341
14. Harry Davis	1,332
15. Tommy Leach	1,325
16. Fielder Jones	1,322
17. Jimmy Williams	1,288
18. Harry Steinfeldt	1,262
19. Freddy Parent	1,255
20. Jimmy Collins	1,253
21. Kitty Bransfield	1,232
22. Topsy Hartsel	1,223
23. Claude Ritchey	1,222
24. Jimmy Slagle	1,177
25. Bill Dahlen	1,170

Pittsburgh's Tommy Leach led the NL with six homers in 1902, the fewest by a loop leader in this century.

Tommy Leach, who once won a home run crown largely by hitting inside-the-park homers, remarked: "Today they seem to think that the most exciting play in baseball is the home run. But in my book the most exciting play in baseball is a three-bagger, or an inside-the-park home run."

Cub Jimmy Sheckard collected an NL record 46 sacrifice hits in 1909.

The dead-ball era impacted not just on the two major leagues. In some ways it had an even more pervasive effect on the game in the minors. In 1906, a year after Elmer Flick had won the American League bat title with a .306 average, the lowest ever to that point by a major league leader, outfielder George Whiteman of Cleburne led the Texas League with a .281 figure. A year earlier, Scott Ragsdale of Waco had reigned as the Texas League batting king with a .292 mark. Ragsdale and Whiteman were far from the only minor league leaders to post sub-.300 batting averages during that era. In 1906, Jack Thoney topped the International League with a .294 average. Three years later, both the Southern Association and the American Association lacked for a .300 hitter. In 1909, Bill McGilvray's .291 batting average led the Southern Association, while Minneapolis' Mike O'Neill topped the American Association by hitting .296.

Above: *As Pittsburgh's third baseman in the first World Series in 1903 against the Boston Pilgrims, speedster Tommy Leach hit a Series-record four triples, including two in one game.*

Drought Grips West Coast

Nowhere in organized baseball was the offensive drought more deeply felt during the dead-ball era than in the Pacific Coast League. While all of the other top minor circuits of that time experienced at least one season without a .300 hitter, the Pacific Coast League lacked for a .300 average by a regular player a record three years in a row. In 1908, Babe Danzig of Los Angeles paced the PCL with a .298 mark, and the following year San Francisco's Harry Melchior hit a slightly lower .298 to take the bat crown. In 1910, Hunky Shaw of San Francisco won the honor by finishing with a .281 figure. By 1910, hits and runs were so hard to come by in the Coast loop that the Portland Beavers pitching staff was able to compile a record 88 consecutive shutout innings at one point in the season, and Kid Mohler was voted to the circuit's All-Star Team at second base despite hitting a paltry .191.

Sam Crawford, an outfielder for the Reds and the Tigers from 1899 to 1917, was the first player to be both an NL and an AL leader in home runs.

A former barber from Nebraska, "Wahoo Sam" Crawford tallied an all time-best 312 triples in his 19-year career, 15 more than former teammate Ty Cobb, who collected 297 three baggers.

1900s TOTAL BASES	
1. Honus Wagner	2,668
2. Sam Crawford	2,445
3. Nap Lajoie	2,339
4. Elmer Flick	2,048
5. Harry Davis	1,978
6. Ginger Beaumont	1,969
7. Cy Seymour	1,968
8. Fred Clarke	1,931
9. Bill Bradley	1,861
10. Jimmy Sheckard	1,851
11. Willie Keeler	1,848
12. Jimmy Williams	1,844
13. Tommy Leach	1,829
14. Bobby Wallace	1,804
15. Jimmy Collins	1,724
16. Harry Steinfeldt	1,709
17. Charlie Hickman	1,691
18. Fred Tenney	1,674
19. Topsy Hartsel	1,658
20. Hobe Ferris	1,636
21. Freddy Parent	1,631
22. Fielder Jones	1,614
23. Kitty Bransfield	1,605
24. Danny Murphy	1,555
25. Buck Freeman	1,550

Cincinnati's Fred Odwell led the National League with nine homers in 1905, and never hit another homer in the majors.

Philadelphia Athletic outfielder Socks Seybold led the AL with 16 homers, tying Sam Crawford's one-year-old 20th century record.

Socks Seybold, considered a liability in the field but a threat at the plate, nonetheless made two unassisted double plays from the outfield while roaming the pastures for the Philadelphia Athletics in 1907.

The pennant-winning Detroit Tigers had just 11 home runs in 1907 as six of the team's regulars failed to hit a single four-bagger.

Jimmy Sebring of Pittsburgh hit the first home run in a modern World Series, taking Boston's Cy Young deep in the opening contest of the 1903 fall classic.

After leading the National League with 10 home runs in 1907, Boston third baseman Dave Brain never hit another four-bagger in the majors.

1900s DOUBLES	
1. Honus Wagner	372
2. Nap Lajoie	361
3. Harry Davis	291
4. Sam Crawford	263
5. Bill Bradley	256
6. Bobby Wallace	243
7. Jimmy Sheckard	238
8. Jimmy Collins	232
9. Elmer Flick	228
10. Harry Steinfeldt	225
11. Jimmy Williams	214
Danny Murphy	214
John Anderson	214
14. Socks Seybold	213
Charlie Hickman	213
16. Cy Seymour	205
Kitty Bransfield	205
18. Hobe Ferris	192
19. Fred Clarke	189
20. Bill Dahlen	188
21. George Davis	186
Lave Cross	186
23. Claude Ritchey	178
24. Buck Freeman	177
25. Jake Beckley	175

Cobb Cloaks Dead-Ball Scoring Dearth

The first half of the 20th century's initial decade was the only period in history when the dominant hitter in each league was a middle infielder. The American League's top offensive performer was second baseman Nap Lajoie, while shortstop Honus Wagner copped the majority of the hitting honors in the National League. Wagner's dominance continued until the end of the decade but Lajoie by 1907 had given way to Detroit outfielder Ty Cobb. Then in his third major league season, the rising Tigers star won his first of a record 11 batting titles (some books still say 12, crediting him with the controversial 1910 AL hitting crown) as he hit .350—103 points above the American League average. In 1908, Cobb slipped to .324 but still led the AL by a comfortable 13-point margin. With the exception of the 1910 season, when he lost the hitting title to Nap Lajoie by one point, Cobb not only paced the AL in batting every year between 1907 and 1916 but he customarily topped the average hitter in the game by between 120 and 140 points. Cobb's phenomenal offensive feats for years obscured how little offense most of the other players in the dead-ball era were able to generate.

Above: *If not for his rookie campaign of 41 games and 150 at bats in 1905, Detroit Tiger outfielder Ty Cobb would have played his entire 24 year-career without hitting under .320, while collecting a major league-record 12 batting titles, including a major league-record nine in a row, from 1907 to 1915.*

White Sox shortstop George Davis in 1902 became the first switch-hitter in baseball history to collect 2,000 hits.

1900s TRIPLES		
1. Sam Crawford		167
2. Honus Wagner		148
3. Elmer Flick		139
4. Fred Clarke		134
5. Tommy Leach		123
6. Jimmy Williams		111
7. Buck Freeman		103
8. Hobe Ferris		89
9. Topsy Hartsel		88
10. Cy Seymour		87
Nap Lajoie		87
12. Charlie Hickman		85
13. Jimmy Sheckard		84
14. Bill Bradley		82
15. Mike Donlin		81
16. Sam Mertes		80
17. Sherry Magee		79
18. Chick Stahl		78
19. Harry Davis		77
20. Harry Steinfeldt		75
Wid Conroy		75
22. Joe Kelley		74
23. Bobby Wallace		73
Freddy Parent		73
Dan McGann		73
Jimmy Collins		73
Ginger Beaumont		73

Seymour Misses Hat Trick by Homer

Since 1967, when Carl Yastrzemski led the American League in batting and RBI and tied for the top spot in homers, no one has come close to claiming a Triple Crown. Prior to 1967, no player came closer to winning a Triple Crown without achieving it than Cy Seymour. After converting to the outfield when his pitching arm failed him, Seymour bounced around for several years in the early 1900s before landing in Cincinnati, where he soon began to challenge Honus Wagner for National League hitting honors. The 1905 season was Seymour's apex; he paced the senior circuit in batting average, RBI, hits, total bases, doubles, triples, and slugging average. Missing, however, from his trophy case at the end of the season was the loop home run crown, which was won by his Cincinnati teammate Fred Odwell. In 1905, Odwell tagged nine round-trippers and Seymour finished as the loop runner-up with eight. One more circuit clout would have tied Seymour for the lead and meant a Triple Crown. Ironically, Fred Odwell never hit another home run in the majors after the 1905 season.

Boston's Jimmy Collins led NL third sackers in putouts five times, in assists four times, and in double plays twice, while posting the second most putouts at third base with 2,372.

1900s HOME RUNS		
1.	Harry Davis	67
2.	Charlie Hickman	58
3.	Sam Crawford	57
4.	Buck Freeman	54
5.	Honus Wagner	51
	Socks Seybold	51
7.	Nap Lajoie	48
8.	Cy Seymour	43
9.	Jimmy Williams	40
	Hobe Ferris	40
11.	Mike Donlin	39
12.	Harry Lumley	38
13.	Elmer Flick	37
14.	Tommy Leach	36
15.	Jimmy Sheckard	34
	Ginger Beaumont	34
17.	Tim Jordan	31
	Jimmy Collins	31
	Jesse Burkett	31
	Bill Bradley	31
21.	Sam Mertes	30
	Topsy Hartsel	30
23.	Danny Murphy	28
	Dan McGann	28
25.	Dave Brain	27

Above: *Future Hall of Famer Jimmy Collins in 1903 hit .296 with five home runs and 72 RBI, as well as pacing the Boston Pilgrims in putouts, double plays, and fielding average. He did this while managing the club to a 91-47 record, an AL pennant, and the first World Series crown.*

Nig Clarke of the Texas League's Corsicana went 8-for-8 with eight homers during a game in 1902.

The leading hitter for the first American League flag winner, the 1901 Chicago White Sox, was third baseman Fred Hartman with a .309 batting average.

Before pounding pitchers with his heavy hitting, Cy Seymour was a hard throwing southpaw with the Giants, notching 20 and 25 wins in 1897 and '98 as well as pacing the NL in strikeouts and walks.

1900s RUNS BATTED IN		
1.	Honus Wagner	956
2.	Sam Crawford	808
3.	Nap Lajoie	793
4.	Harry Davis	688
5.	Cy Seymour	685
6.	Jimmy Williams	680
7.	Bobby Wallace	638
8.	Harry Steinfeldt	610
9.	Bill Dahlen	597
10.	Charlie Hickman	590
11.	Kitty Bransfield	581
12.	Sam Mertes	579
13.	Elmer Flick	570
14.	Buck Freeman	569
15.	Ginger Beaumont	557
	John Anderson	557
17.	Hobe Ferris	550
18.	Socks Seybold	548
	Lave Cross	548
20.	Jimmy Collins	545
21.	Danny Murphy	514
22.	Claude Ritchey	510
	Fred Clarke	510
	Bill Bradley	510
25.	Tommy Leach	507

Donlin Makes Dramatic Exit

In 1905, outfielder Mike Donlin of the New York Giants ranked right behind Cy Seymour and Honus Wagner among the National League's premier offensive performers. That season Donlin paced the majors with 124 runs and was second only to Seymour in total bases and hits. At the time, Donlin was 27 years old and had put together four strong offensive seasons, broken only by a jail stint in the summer of 1902 stemming from an altercation he precipitated with the police while playing for Baltimore of the American League. After the 1905 campaign, however, he played regularly in the majors only one more season. That came in 1908, when "Turkey Mike" returned to the Giants after missing all but a fraction of the previous two seasons and promptly hit .334 to lead the club in batting. His protracted absences from the game were the result of suspensions owing either to alcoholism or holdouts and his dramatic ambitions. Early in his career, Donlin married Mabel Hite, a prominent actress, and the two starred together in several stage and vaudeville productions. After Hite died of cancer, Donlin returned briefly to the game and then tried, with some success, to break into the fledgling film industry in Hollywood.

Had Mike Donlin collected the 146 more at bats to reach the qualifying 4,000, his lifetime .333 batting average would have placed him with the 21st highest average.

In his 12 year-career, Mike Donlin (above) played with seven different teams, topped the .300 mark 10 times, the 100 run plateau three times, and paced the NL with 124 runs scored in 1905, the year he hit .316 in the World Series to lead the New York Giants to their first championship.

Shortstop Joe Cassidy of Washington set an American League rookie record when he bagged 19 triples in 1904.

The New York Giants collected a record 31 hits on June 9, 1901; six of them were notched by Kip Selbach.

Ginger Beaumont set an NL record when he led the loop in hits for the three straight years, from 1902 to 1904.

Wee Willie Keeler collected at least 200 hits for eight straight years from 1894 to 1901 to set the National League record.

1900s WALKS	
1. Roy Thomas	912
2. Topsy Hartsel	749
3. Jimmy Sheckard	616
4. Fred Tenney	607
Fielder Jones	607
6. Jimmy Slagle	564
7. Bill Dahlen	525
8. Fred Clarke	524
9. Honus Wagner	518
10. Roger Bresnahan	500
11. Claude Ritchey	470
12. Elmer Flick	459
Frank Chance	459
14. Sammy Strang	458
15. Miller Huggins	431
16. Bobby Wallace	422
Jimmy Barrett	422
18. Jimmy Williams	414
19. Tommy Leach	401
20. Art Devlin	392
21. Sam Crawford	390
22. Jesse Burkett	389
23. George Davis	383
24. John Titus	378
25. Kip Selbach	373

In 1908, Detroit outfielder Matty McIntyre paced the American League with a .385 on-base percentage, the lowest ever by a loop leader.

Phillies center fielder Roy Thomas collected 100 or more walks six times between 1900 and 1909, something no other National League player could do more than once during that period.

Sherry Magee Outshines Top NL Outfielders

For the 10-year period between 1905 and 1914, Sherry Magee was the National League's most potent offensive force apart from Honus Wagner. Magee led the NL three times during that span in RBI, twice in slugging average, and once in batting. In addition, he consistently finished among the stolen base leaders. Despite his speed, he was only a fair defensive outfielder; he nonetheless ranked as the senior loop's top gardener while he was in his prime. After serving the Phillies for 11 seasons without yet being on a pennant winner, Magee was traded after the 1914 campaign to the reigning National League champion Boston Braves. It seemed a great break for him at first but proved otherwise when the Phillies captured their first pennant in franchise history in 1915 while the Braves finished second. Magee's 1,176 career RBI put him second only to Sam Crawford among 20th century outfielders who retired prior to 1920, the end of the dead-ball era.

Nap Lajoie (above) used a split-hands grip on the bat in order to maintain outstanding bat control. The lower portion of Lajoie's bat was specially designed by the J.F. Hillerich Company with two knobs, so he could still generate some power. The double-knobbed bats worked well enough to allow Lajoie to lead his league in slugging percentage in four different seasons.

Ed Walsh said about Nap Lajoie: "If you pitched inside to him, he'd tear the hand off the third baseman, and if you pitched outside he'd knock down the second baseman."

On May 23, 1901, Nap Lajoie was the first player in baseball history to be intentionally walked with the bases full.

When Ty Cobb won his first hitting title in 1907 with a .350 batting average in 605 at bats, he collected just 24 walks.

In 1901, Philadelphia's Nap Lajoie set a 20th century record when he hit .426 to lead the AL; he also won the Triple Crown.

In 1901, Jimmy Sheckard of Brooklyn became the first major league player to hit a grand slam home run in two consecutive games.

In 1901, Irv Waldron led the American League in at bats (598) while batting .311 in his lone season in the major leagues.

Jim Dunleavy of Pacific Coast League Oakland·in 1905 played in an organized baseball record 227 games.

Shortstop Monte Cross of the Philadelphia A's set an all-time record for the lowest batting average by a player in over 500 at bats when he hit .189 in 1904.

1900s STOLEN BASES	
1. Honus Wagner	487
2. Frank Chance	357
3. Sam Mertes	305
4. Jimmy Sheckard	295
5. Elmer Flick	275
6. Jimmy Slagle	251
7. Frank Isbell	250
8. Fielder Jones	239
Wid Conroy	239
Fred Clarke	239
11. Sherry Magee	238
12. Topsy Hartsel	233
Bill Dahlen	233
14. Johnny Evers	230
15. Joe Tinker	229
Art Devlin	229
17. Tommy Leach	226
18. Dan McGann	220
Patsy Dougherty	220
20. Ginger Beaumont	219
21. George Davis	218
22. Sammy Strang	212
23. Harry Davis	204
24. Nap Lajoie	202
25. Willie Keeler	201

Topsy Hartsel, who hit .294, was the lone Philadelphia A's regular to top .200 in the 1905 World Series as the A's scored a Series record-low three runs and batted .161.

When he logged 121 walks in 1905, Topsy Hartsel of the Philadelphia A's became the first American League player to collect 100 or more free passes in a season.

1900s BATTING AVERAGE	
1. Honus Wagner	.352
2. Nap Lajoie	.346
3. Mike Donlin	.338
4. Elmer Flick	.312
5. Jesse Burkett	.312
6. Willie Keeler	.311
7. Cy Seymour	.311
8. Jake Beckley	.309
9. Ginger Beaumont	.309
10. Sam Crawford	.307
11. Fred Clarke	.301
12. Frank Chance	.299
13. Socks Seybold	.296
14. Charlie Hickman	.294
15. Danny Green	.291
16. Lave Cross	.291
17. Chick Stahl	.291
18. Sherry Magee	.291
19. Joe Kelley	.289
20. Jimmy Barrett	.289
21. Roy Thomas	.289
22. Patsy Dougherty	.288
23. Jimmy Collins	.288
24. Buck Freeman	.288
25. Harry Davis	.286

The Phillies' keystone combo of Bill Hallman and Monte Cross hit .184 and .197, respectively (so to speak), in 1901.

In 1901, Philadelphia's Nap Lajoie led the AL in batting average, home runs, RBI, runs scored, hits, doubles, total bases, on-base percentage, and slugging average.

Davis Wins Four Straight Homer Crowns

Improbable as it might seem, the first player to claim four consecutive league home run crowns is not in the Hall of Fame. More than that, Harry Davis has never even been seriously considered for enshrinement. Much of the reason is that during the span when he reigned as the American League four-bagger king (1904 to 1907), Davis collected just 38 home runs, an average of less than 10 per season. Indeed, the paucity of four-base blows during the dead-ball era made the home run crown of little consequence. While many observers took no particular notice of Davis's home run stats, they did recognize the Philadelphia first baseman's stature as an all-around slugger and run producer. The circuit clout was only one dimension of Davis's game. He also paced the American League twice in RBI and three times in doubles. Playing in the dead-ball era rendered Davis's career home run and RBI totals comparatively modest, but he nevertheless ranks as the game's leading slugger during the first decade of the 20th century.

In 1909, Brooklyn catcher Bill Bergen hit .139 in 112 games, the lowest average in history by a regular.

Only Home Run Baker, Babe Ruth, and Ralph Kiner have matched Philadelphia slugger Harry Davis's accomplishment of four straight home run crowns.

1900s SLUGGING AVERAGE	
1. Honus Wagner	.508
2. Nap Lajoie	.488
3. Mike Donlin	.474
4. Sam Crawford	.447
5. Elmer Flick	.446
6. Buck Freeman	.443
7. Charlie Hickman	.438
8. Socks Seybold	.427
9. Harry Davis	.424
10. Cy Seymour	.419
11. Sherry Magee	.418
12. Fred Clarke	.417
13. Jesse Burkett	.412
14. Harry Lumley	.410
15. Jake Beckley	.405
16. Joe Kelley	.400
17. Frank Chance	.398
18. Jimmy Collins	.396
19. Chick Stahl	.394
20. Sam Mertes	.393
21. Danny Murphy	.391
22. Ginger Beaumont	.390
23. Jimmy Sheckard	.386
24. Danny Green	.386
25. Roger Bresnahan	.383

Second baseman Pete Childs of the Phillies possessed a .206 slugging average in 1902, the lowest ever by a player with more than 400 at bats.

Bobby Byrne of the St. Louis Cardinals had just 14 RBI in 1908, the all-time record low by a third baseman in 400 or more at bats.

In 1908, the New York Giants led the majors in runs with 652 and in hitting with a .267 batting average as offense was so skimpy that both loops averaged an identical .239.

Only Seven Bat Over .300 in 1908

In 1898, some 33 regular players in the National League hit above .300. Ten years later the game had changed so much that just seven regulars in the major leagues were able to bat .300 and a mere four managed to hit above .308. Offensive production was so dismal that the National League and the American League each hit a composite .239, a figure that still stands as the record low for the senior loop and has been topped only in 1968 by the AL. In 1908, just two teams, one in each league, succeeded in hitting above .250. Detroit topped the AL with a .263 mark, thanks in large part to Ty Cobb and Sam Crawford, the loop's two top hitters that season, while the New York Giants rapped .267 to lead the majors. The Giants had just one hitter among the top five in the NL, the .334-batting Mike Donlin, but were also blessed with two part-time regulars, Larry Doyle and Moose McCormick, who cracked the .300 barrier. This trio combined with shortstop Al Bridwell, center fielder Cy Seymour, and catcher Roger Bresnahan to give the Giants an offense that led the majors with 652 runs, produced in 157 games.

In 1906, Honus Wagner led the National League in total bases with just 237, the fewest since 1893 by a league leader in a season when a full schedule was played.

In 1906, Frank Chance (above) hit .319 and led the NL with 103 runs scored, 57 stolen bases, and a .406 on-base percentage, all while managing the team to a major league-best 116-36 record.

Cub Frank Chance was hit by pitches a record five times in a 1905 double-header.

Swing, Batter, Swing

Bill Byron, the singing umpire, serenaded a batter who took a called third strike: "Let me tell you something, son/ Before you get much older/ You cannot hit the ball, my friend/ With the bat upon your shoulder."

1900s ON-BASE AVERAGE

1.	Honus Wagner	.412
2.	Roy Thomas	.408
3.	Mike Donlin	.388
4.	Topsy Hartsel	.385
5.	Jesse Burkett	.384
6.	Frank Chance	.384
7.	Nap Lajoie	.384
8.	Roger Bresnahan	.381
9.	Elmer Flick	.378
10.	Fred Clarke	.377
11.	Jimmy Barrett	.374
12.	Sammy Strang	.371
13.	Jimmy Sheckard	.364
14.	Fred Tenney	.360
15.	Miller Huggins	.359
16.	Joe Kelley	.359
17.	John Titus	.358
18.	Danny Green	.357
19.	Fielder Jones	.356
20.	Art Devlin	.355
21.	Ginger Beaumont	.355
22.	Kip Selbach	.355
23.	Cy Seymour	.354
24.	Sam Crawford	.353
25.	Willie Keeler	.352

Future Hall of Famer Ed Delahanty (above) was swept over Niagara Falls to his death after getting kicked off a train for being drunk and disorderly, leaving his .346 lifetime average the fourth highest ever.

1900s EXTRA-BASE HITS

1.	Honus Wagner	571
2.	Nap Lajoie	496
3.	Sam Crawford	487
4.	Harry Davis	435
5.	Elmer Flick	404
6.	Bill Bradley	369
7.	Jimmy Williams	365
8.	Jimmy Sheckard	356
	Charlie Hickman	356
10.	Fred Clarke	349
11.	Jimmy Collins	336
12.	Cy Seymour	335
13.	Buck Freeman	334
14.	Bobby Wallace	330
15.	Harry Steinfeldt	324
16.	Hobe Ferris	321
17.	Socks Seybold	317
18.	Danny Murphy	312
19.	Tommy Leach	309
20.	Topsy Hartsel	287
21.	Kitty Bransfield	284
	John Anderson	284
23.	Sam Mertes	277
24.	Ginger Beaumont	269
25.	Sherry Magee	267

Ed Delahanty in 1902 became the first player to win batting titles in both the National League and the American League. He won the NL title in 1899 with a .410 average and won the AL batting title in 1902 with a .376 average.

On April 12, 1906, Johnny Bates became the first player in the century to homer in his first major league at bat.

With the dead-ball era underway, the Pittsburgh Pirates led the National League with a .254 team batting average, the lowest ever by an NL leader.

Cards, Others Average Deuce Per Game

While the New York Giants were scoring runs at the "heady" rate of over four a game in 1908, the Brooklyn Superbas and the St. Louis Cardinals averaged little more than two tallies per contest. In 1908, the Cardinals crossed the plate just 371 times in 154 games, and Brooklyn collected a mere 377 tallies. Brooklyn moreover had only one player, Tim Jordan, who notched more than 41 RBI. Jordan not only led the club in ribbies with 60 but his .247 average paced it in batting as the club posted 20th century National League record lows for both batting average and slugging average with figures of .213 and .277, respectively. With all that, Brooklyn avoided the cellar, leaving that ignominy to the Cardinals. Two years later, the Chicago White Sox also dodged the American League basement when they registered 20th-century record lows with a .211 batting average and a .261 slugging average. Pitching was much of the reason that Brooklyn and Chicago survived with so little firepower. The Superbas had a 2.47 staff ERA in 1908, while the White Sox in 1910 posted a 2.01 staff ERA and allowed the second-fewest runs in the majors that season.

In 1904, 10 years after he became the first player to hit four home runs in a game, Bobby Lowe hit .207 for Detroit, the lowest average in history by a second baseman with 500 or more at bats.

Big Ed Supplies Own Attack

No pitcher profited more from the style of play during the dead-ball era than Big Ed Walsh. At the same time no pitcher suffered more as a result of it. Allowed to throw a spitball, Walsh became the reigning master of the wet delivery. What made the pitch even more effective was the fact that when he was on the mound the same ball was sometimes used for the entire game. By the late innings, the sphere was so soggy and lopsided that batters found it virtually impossible to hit out of the infield. But the benefits Walsh accrued during the dead-ball era were on occasion severely outweighed by the impact it had on his own team, the Chicago White Sox. Labeled "The Hitless Wonders" in 1906, when they won their only pennant while Walsh was with the club despite posting the lowest team batting average in the American League, the White Sox carried that tag all during his career. In 1908, while becoming the last pitcher to win 40 games in a season, Walsh was supported by a crew that hit .224 and scored just 537 runs. Two years later he contrived to lose 20 games in the process of leading the American League with a 1.27 ERA as the Sox set 20th century records for both the lowest batting average and the lowest slugging average. Walsh was given so little offensive help by his team that he at times had to shoulder the hitting load as well as the pitching burden. When he won 40 games in 1908, Walsh also tied for the Sox lead in home runs— with a grand total of one!

In 1908, when Ed Walsh (above) posted a 40-15 record, he won 44.5 percent of the White Sox' 88 games, the highest percentage of an AL team's wins in history.

Ed Walsh set an American League record in 1908 when he hurled 139 more innings and collected 16 more wins than any other pitcher in the loop.

Ed Walsh's 464 innings in 1908 set a 20th century record, breaking Jack Chesbro's old mark.

What Did You Expectorate?

About Ed Walsh's spitter, Sam Crawford said: "I think that the ball disintegrated on the way to the plate and the catcher put it back together again. I swear, when it went past the plate it was just the spit that went by."

On October 2, 1908, with a pennant hanging in the balance, Cleveland's Addie Joss dueled Big Ed Walsh of the White Sox. When Walsh allowed a run on a wild pitch, that was all Addie needed. He shut the White Sox down cold without a single baserunner and thus registered only the fourth perfect game in major league history and the first in a pennant race.

Lefty Tex Neuer started six games for the New York Yankees in the last month of the 1907 season and won four of them, three by shutouts, but then never pitched again in the majors.

1900s GAMES PITCHED		
1.	Joe McGinnity	417
2.	Cy Young	403
3.	Vic Willis	398
4.	Christy Mathewson	388
5.	Rube Waddell	385
6.	Jack Powell	377
7.	Jack Chesbro	373
8.	Eddie Plank	334
9.	George Mullin	330
10.	Bill Dinneen	325
11.	Al Orth	315
12.	Doc White	309
	Harry Howell	309
14.	Sam Leever	306
15.	Tom Hughes	298
16.	Deacon Phillippe	296
17.	Bill Donovan	295
18.	Chick Fraser	288
19.	Tully Sparks	281
20.	Dummy Taylor	274
21.	Addie Joss	273
22.	Case Patten	270
23.	Jack Taylor	264
24.	Togie Pittinger	262
25.	Bob Ewing	252

In his 13-year career, Vic Willis (above) completed 388 of the 471 games in which he started.

1900s GAMES STARTED

1.	Vic Willis	372
2.	Cy Young	366
3.	Christy Mathewson	344
4.	Joe McGinnity	340
5.	Jack Powell	334
6.	Rube Waddell	328
7.	Jack Chesbro	315
8.	Eddie Plank	314
9.	George Mullin	298
10.	Bill Dinneen	290
11.	Al Orth	284
12.	Doc White	278
13.	Bill Donovan	273
14.	Harry Howell	255
15.	Chick Fraser	252
16.	Sam Leever	249
17.	Tully Sparks	248
	Addie Joss	248
	Tom Hughes	248
20.	Jack Taylor	242
	Deacon Phillippe	242
22.	Case Patten	238
23.	Dummy Taylor	237
24.	Jesse Tannehill	229
25.	Togie Pittinger	228
	Bob Ewing	228

Hub Quartet Drop Score

In 1905, Vic Willis's final season with the Boston Braves, the Beantown club became the first in major league history with four pitchers who lost 20 or more games. In addition to Willis, who was tagged with a record 29 defeats, Chick Fraser and Kaiser Wilhelm both sustained 22 setbacks and rookie Irv Young was bested 21 times. Young that season at least had the distinction of being the only modern hurler to both win and lose 20 games in his yearling season as he also collected 20 victories, but the following year the bottom dropped out for the entire Boston mound staff. In 1906, the Braves again had four 20-game losers as they finished a 20th century major league record 66½ games out of first place. Leading the club in losses were Young and Gus Dorner with 25 apiece, while Viv Lindaman absorbed 23 setbacks, and Jeff Pfeffer 22. Bad as the quartet was, it was just about all the Braves had. The foursome accounted for all 49 of the Braves victories and for 95 of the team's 102 defeats.

Dode Criss, a rookie hurler with the St. Louis Browns, collected 12 pinch hits in 1908 to break Howard Wakefield's old major league mark.

Cy Young pitched the first perfect game of the 20th century on May 5, 1904, notching a 3-0 victory over the Philadelphia A's and Rube Waddell.

1900s COMPLETE GAMES

1.	Cy Young	337
2.	Vic Willis	312
3.	Christy Mathewson	281
4.	Jack Powell	277
5.	Joe McGinnity	276
6.	Eddie Plank	263
7.	George Mullin	258
8.	Bill Dinneen	254
9.	Rube Waddell	251
10.	Bill Donovan	246
	Jack Chesbro	246
12.	Jack Taylor	234
13.	Al Orth	229
14.	Addie Joss	225
15.	Harry Howell	221
16.	Chick Fraser	219
17.	Doc White	215
18.	Case Patten	206
19.	Deacon Phillippe	204
20.	Sam Leever	200
21.	Tom Hughes	195
22.	Tully Sparks	193
23.	Togie Pittinger	187
24.	Red Donahue	186
25.	Jesse Tannehill	185

Boston's Vic Willis notched an NL record 45 complete games in 1902.

Washington hurler Cy Falkenberg in 1906 became the first AL pitcher to hit a grand slam.

Henry Schmidt snagged 22 wins as a rookie with Brooklyn in 1903 but then never pitched another game in the major leagues.

In 1909, Babe Adams of the Pirates became the first rookie to start the opening game of a World Series.

1900s SAVES

1.	Joe McGinnity	22
2.	Hooks Wiltse	20
3.	Mordecai Brown	19
4.	Christy Mathewson	15
5.	Ed Walsh	14
	Jack Powell	14
7.	Orval Overall	11
8.	Tom Hughes	10
9.	Cy Young	9
10.	Frank Arellanes	8
	Tully Sparks	8
	Sam Leever	8
	Frank Kitson	8
	George Ferguson	8
	Chief Bender	8
16.	Deacon Phillippe	7
	Harry McIntire	7
	Bill Donovan	7
	Bill Dinneen	7
	Red Ames	7
21.	Claude Elliott	6
	Doc Crandall	6
	Vic Willis	6
	Elmer Stricklett	6
	George Mullin	6
	Carl Lundgren	6
	Ed Killian	6
	Bill Duggleby	6
	Howie Camnitz	6
	Nick Altrock	6

New York Giant hurler Hooks Wiltse won the first 12 decisions of his major league career.

In 1909, Walter Johnson lost an AL record ten games in which his team (the Washington Senators) was shut out— five of them to Chicago.

Pirates pitchers blanked foes for a record 57 consecutive innings in 1903.

Although Orval Overall (above) pitched for only seven big league seasons, his career 2.24 ERA is the eighth lowest in history.

1900s SHUTOUTS

1.	Christy Mathewson	61
2.	Rube Waddell	49
3.	Cy Young	45
4.	Addie Joss	44
5.	Vic Willis	43
6.	Mordecai Brown	41
7.	Doc White	38
8.	Ed Walsh	36
	Eddie Plank	36
10.	Sam Leever	35
	Jack Chesbro	35
12.	Jack Powell	32
13.	Bill Donovan	31
14.	Ed Reulbach	28
	Joe McGinnity	28
16.	Jesse Tannehill	25
	Orval Overall	25
	Al Orth	25
	George Mullin	25
20.	Deacon Phillippe	24
21.	Togie Pittinger	23
	Lefty Leifield	23
	Bill Dinneen	23
24.	Frank Smith	22
	Tom Hughes	22

1906 Cub Staff Best Ever?

At the opposite end of the spectrum from the 1906 Boston Braves' four 20-game losers was the Chicago Cubs' hill staff, which laid claim to being the deepest of its time and arguably the best in history. Led by Three Finger Brown's loop-leading 26 wins and 1.04 ERA, the Cubs that season bagged a record 116 victories and posted a record 1.75 staff ERA. Brown's supporting cast numbered Jack Pfiester, Ed Reulbach, Carl Lundren, Jack Taylor, and Orval Overall. The six Bruins hurlers combined for 106 wins and just 30 defeats. All but Lundgren had an ERA of 1.88 or less and Pfiester was the only staff member to lose as many as eight games. In 1906, the Cubs led the majors in runs with 704 while surrendering the fewest tallies, 381. Nevertheless, the Bruins lost the first inter-city World Series in history four games to two to the crosstown Chicago White Sox in the biggest sports upset to that time. The Cubs were made to wait until the following autumn to garner their first 20th century world championship.

In game five of the 1908 World Series, Cub hurler Orval Overall struck out four Detroit batters in one inning.

Cub pitcher Three Finger Brown was 13-9 in head-to-head matchups against Giants hurler Christy Mathewson.

After tallying 31 wins in the regular season, Giants hurler Christy Mathewson (above) shut out the Philadelphia Athletics in games one, three, and five of the 1905 World Series, allowing only 14 hits and leading New York to the Series crown.

Coombs Gives Philly Straight A's

In 1906, with the Cubs in the process of setting a major league ERA record, the Philadelphia Athletics collected the last key ingredient to the mound staff that would set the American League ERA record four years later when Jack Coombs joined the club. In 1910, Coombs led all hurlers in the game with 31 wins and chipped in a 1.30 ERA, second in the AL only to Ed Walsh's 1.27 mark. As a unit, the A's registered a 1.79 ERA, shattering their own year-old loop mark of 1.92. Teaming with Coombs for the record-breaking A's were Hall of Famers Chief Bender and Eddie Plank, along with secondary contributors Cy Morgan and Harry Krause. The same quintet, plus Jimmy Dygert, had formed the nucleus of the 1909 hill staff. Coombs was the difference in 1910, upping his win total from 12 to 31 and enabling the A's to romp to the AL flag by a 14½-game margin and thus end the Tigers' three-year lock on the loop's top spot.

"Matty was the greatest pitcher I ever saw. He was the greatest anybody ever saw. Let them name all the others. I don't care how good they were. Matty was better."
—John Kieran, sportswriter

Easy Livin'
Roger Bresnahan remarked about Christy Mathewson: "I could have caught him sitting in a rocking chair."

Judge Landis, on the death of Christy Mathewson, said: "Why should God wish to take a thoroughbred like Matty so soon, and leave some others down here that could well be spared?"

1900s WINS	
1. Christy Mathewson	236
2. Cy Young	230
3. Joe McGinnity	218
4. Jack Chesbro	192
5. Vic Willis	188
6. Eddie Plank	186
7. Rube Waddell	183
8. Sam Leever	166
9. Jack Powell	160
10. George Mullin	157
11. Addie Joss	155
Bill Donovan	155
13. Doc White	154
Deacon Phillippe	154
15. Bill Dinneen	147
16. Mordecai Brown	144
17. Jesse Tannehill	138
Al Orth	138
19. Jack Taylor	129
20. Chick Fraser	118
21. Dummy Taylor	116
Harry Howell	116
23. Togie Pittinger	115
24. Tully Sparks	113
25. Red Donahue	111

In 1904, Joe McGinnity won 35 games and Christy Mathewson won 33 for the Giants, setting a modern teammates tandem record.

Christy Mathewson (24 in 1907) was the only pitcher to top his league in wins between 1900 and 1909 with fewer than 25.

ChiSox Find Cleveland 'Joss Perfect'

When the Chicago White Sox arrived at Cleveland's League Park on Friday afternoon, October 2, 1908, to begin a do-or-die series for the American League pennant, a crowd of 10,598 was on hand. No ballpark in the world, however, would have been large enough had the baseball-going public known what was in the offing. That day in Cleveland, Addie Joss dueled Ed Walsh in the greatest pitchers' battle in history considering the stakes and the outcome. Walsh allowed just one unearned run in the contest, it coming on a third-inning wild pitch, but Joss was even more brilliant. Not a single White Sox batter reached first base safely the entire game, as Cleveland prevailed 1-0 and moved into first place. Cleveland ultimately lost the pennant to Detroit by a one-half game margin, but it was no fault of Joss's. Working against one of the greatest pitchers of his time in a game that potentially could mean everything, Joss authored the only perfect game in major league history under such auspicious circumstances.

Cleveland's Addie Joss (above left, with Dusty Rhoads) *completed 234 of his 260 starts and notched an ERA of 1.88 in nine years, which convinced the Veterans Committee to waive the 10-year career minimum rule and allow him in the Hall of Fame.*

Cub Three Finger Brown in 1906 led the NL with a 1.04 ERA, lowest ever by a pitcher with more than 250 innings.

Between June 20, 1901, and August 9, 1906, Jack Taylor started 187 games in the NL and completed every one of them.

In 1906, en route to a 2-21 record, Joe Harris of the Boston Red Sox hurled the longest complete-game loss in American League history, a 24-inning setback at the hands of Philadelphia.

George McQuillan debuted in 1907 with the Phillies by registering a perfect 4-0 record, including three shutouts.

When he won the opener of the 1908 fall classic, Three Finger Brown of the Cubs became the first pitcher to bag a World Series victory in a relief role.

Chick Fraser lost 20 or more games for three consecutive seasons with three different National League teams between 1904 and 1906.

Two Shutouts All in Day's Work For Reulbach

The 1908 season was made for pitchers. With scoring at an all-time low and both pennant races destined to go down to the wire, conditions were ideal for monumental hill feats. Ed Walsh's 40 wins and Addie Joss's perfect game were the two most enduringly famous achievements, but Ed Reulbach's performance on September 26 of that season was only a notch behind. That day, Reulbach pitched two complete-game victories for the Chicago Cubs over Brooklyn. Many other hurlers prior to Reulbach had posted doubleheader wins and several would do it after him, but none would match his excellence. Reulbach not only logged two complete-game triumphs in the thick of the 1908 pennant race—he hurled two shutouts, winning the first game 5-0 and the second contest 3-0. He allowed just eight Brooklyn safeties in the twin bill. For the season, Reulbach posted a 24-7 record and topped the National League with a .774 winning percentage.

Harry "Rube" Vickers in 1906 pitched an organized baseball record 526 innings with Seattle in the Pacific Coast League.

Ogden Nash penned this poem:

Y is for Young
The Magnificent Cy
People batted against him
But I never knew why.

1900s STRIKEOUTS	
1. Rube Waddell	2,251
2. Christy Mathewson	1,794
3. Cy Young	1,565
4. Eddie Plank	1,342
5. Vic Willis	1,304
6. Bill Donovan	1,293
7. Jack Chesbro	1,237
8. Jack Powell	1,209
9. Tom Hughes	1,115
10. Doc White	1,105
11. George Mullin	1,091
12. Joe McGinnity	994
13. Bill Dinneen	953
14. Chief Bender	935
15. Harry Howell	925
16. Ed Walsh	901
17. Bob Ewing	884
18. Addie Joss	871
19. Red Ames	844
20. Earl Moore	833
21. Togie Pittinger	832
22. Deacon Phillippe	828
23. Orval Overall	813
24. Mordecai Brown	799
25. Chick Fraser	792

Above: Chicago Cubs pitcher Ed Reulbach's eyesight was so poor that his catchers used gloves that were painted white, making his career 182-106 record, 2.28 ERA, and a NL-record three consecutive years of league-leading winning percentages, all the more astonishing.

Three Finger Brown, asked if his curve was helped by his missing index finger, responded: "To know for sure, I'd have to throw with a normal hand, and I've never tried it."

The 1908 World Series— won by the Cubs 4-0 over Detroit after an opening game tie—is the only one in history in which four different pitchers on the same team hurled complete-game victories on four consecutive days.

1900s INNINGS	
1. Cy Young	3,344.2
2. Vic Willis	3,130.1
3. Joe McGinnity	3,074.2
4. Christy Mathewson	2,967.0
5. Jack Powell	2,876.2
6. Rube Waddell	2,835.1
7. Jack Chesbro	2,748.0
8. Eddie Plank	2,666.0
9. George Mullin	2,592.1
10. Bill Dinneen	2,565.1
11. Bill Donovan	2,426.0
12. Al Orth	2,393.2
13. Harry Howell	2,337.0
14. Doc White	2,315.0
15. Jack Taylor	2,221.1
16. Addie Joss	2,219.2
17. Chick Fraser	2,204.1
18. Deacon Phillippe	2,158.1
19. Tully Sparks	2,143.0
20. Sam Leever	2,138.0
21. Tom Hughes	2,095.1
22. Case Patten	2,062.1
23. Togie Pittinger	2,040.1
24. Bob Ewing	2,020.2
25. Jesse Tannehill	1,935.1

On September 26, 1908, Ed Reulbach of the Cubs notched two shutouts in one day.

Branch Rickey, who played against Rube Waddell, recalled: "When Waddell had control—and some sleep—he was unbeatable."

In 1905, eccentric Philadelphia southpaw Rube Waddell (above) topped the AL with 27 victories, a .730 winning percentage, 46 games pitched, 287 strikeouts, and a 1.48 ERA, only to hurt his shoulder while rough housing with a teammate to keep him out of the '05 fall classic.

In 1900, Rube Waddell of Pittsburgh led the NL in strikeouts with just 130 and was the only hurler to average more than four whiffs per game.

Rube Waddell of the Athletics fanned 349, a post-1893 record and the best mark for a 154-game season. He broke his one-year-old record of 302 strikeouts.

Rube Waddell won his record seventh AL strikeout crown in 1907; it was the sixth season in a row that he led the loop in strikeouts.

When Eddie Plank and Rube Waddell won 51 games between them in 1904, they made the Philadelphia A's the only team in this century to have two southpaw 25-game winners.

Rube Waddell beat Cy Young in a 20-inning game on July 4, 1905.

Brooklyn's Joe McGinnity led the NL with 28 wins in 1900, while no other pitcher won more than 20.

1900s WINNING PERCENTAGE	
1. Ed Reulbach	.713
2. Sam Leever	.697
3. Mordecai Brown	.689
4. Christy Mathewson	.678
5. Hooks Wiltse	.637
6. Ed Walsh	.636
7. Joe McGinnity	.634
8. Jesse Tannehill	.633
9. Deacon Phillippe	.631
10. Addie Joss	.628
11. Carl Lundgren	.623
12. Cy Young	.612
13. Clark Griffith	.612
14. Jack Chesbro	.610
15. Eddie Plank	.606
16. Orval Overall	.605
17. Frank Smith	.594
18. Lefty Leifield	.592
19. Bill Bernhard	.591
20. Red Ames	.590
21. Chief Bender	.590
22. Jake Weimer	.584
23. Bill Donovan	.581
24. Doc White	.572
25. Jack Harper	.568

Early Aces Render Relief

In the early 1900s, starting pitchers still were seldom relieved no matter how one-sided the game. As late as 1906, the Boston Braves notched a major league top 137 complete games even though the club claimed only 49 victories. By the end of the decade, however, a change in philosophy was occurring. In 1909, the Boston Red Sox finished third in the American League despite registering only 75 complete games, the lowest total in post-1893 major league history to that point. The Red Sox featured a combination starter-reliever in Frank Arellanes, who headed the majors with eight saves, but most clubs preferred to use their ace starter in a fireman role if the game was on the line. The National League save leader in 1909 hence was Cubs star Three Finger Brown, who also topped the loop that year in wins and innings pitched. Brown led the NL in saves several times, as did White Sox ace Ed Walsh in the AL. In 1908, while bagging 40 wins, Walsh also paced the AL with six saves.

In 1906, the year before he became the only pitcher in this century to lose 20 games for a pennant winner, Detroit's George Mullin was 21-18 for a sixth-place team.

In his lone game with the Boston Red Sox, King Brady flipped a complete-game shutout in 1908.

On April 28, 1901, rookie Bock Baker, making his first and only start for Cleveland, was touched for 23 hits, all of them singles.

In 1908, the only team in the majors with a staff ERA above 2.64 was the New York Highlanders at 3.16.

In 1901, Noodles Hahn won a 20th century record 22 games for a last-place team—the 52-87 Reds. He was the last lefthander to have won 20 for a last-place club until Steve Carlton did it in 1972. Hahn also had 41 complete games in '01, a record for a 20th century lefty.

Noodles Hahn fanned 16 Boston Braves on May 22, setting a post-1893 record.

When he bagged 27 wins in 1907, Doc White of the White Sox set a 20th century southpaw record that stood until 1930.

Head West
Henry Schmidt, a Californian who went 22-13 as a rookie pitcher with Brooklyn in 1903, returned his unsigned contract the following spring with this comment: "I do not like playing in the East and will not report." Schmidt never again pitched a single inning in the major leagues

Crandall Forerunner to Relief Specialists

Saves by relief pitchers were not kept, even unofficially, in the early part of the century. Team and individual save totals during the days of Three Finger Brown, Christy Mathewson, and Ed Walsh are therefore the result of recent research efforts and are still the subject of some controversy. What has been clearly established, however, is that John McGraw was probably the first manager who played with the notion of developing relief specialists. As a result, his Giants teams had a string of pitchers like Claude Elliott and George Ferguson who did little but work in relief of faltering starters, and the Giants accordingly paced the majors in saves. In 1908, McGraw stumbled on Doc Crandall, a rookie righthander whom he soon decided was perfectly suited to relief roles. Crandall didn't necessarily agree with McGraw—he fancied himself a starter—but for several years he went along with the Giants skipper. When the Federal League formed as a rival major league, though, Crandall jumped to the St. Louis Terriers in 1914 on the promise that he would be given a crack at a starting job. The following year he made good on his boast by winning 21 games for the Terriers.

In September 1904, Doc White of the Chicago White Sox became the first pitcher in major league history to win six shutout games in a single month.

1900s EARNED RUN AVERAGE	
1. Mordecai Brown	1.63
2. Ed Walsh	1.68
3. Ed Reulbach	1.72
4. Addie Joss	1.87
5. Christy Mathewson	1.98
6. Rube Waddell	2.11
7. Cy Young	2.12
8. Orval Overall	2.13
9. Frank Smith	2.19
10. Doc White	2.20
11. Lefty Leifield	2.20
12. Jake Weimer	2.23
13. Hooks Wiltse	2.29
14. Andy Coakley	2.32
15. Sam Leever	2.33
16. Ed Killian	2.35
17. Bob Ewing	2.37
18. Barney Pelty	2.39
19. Eddie Plank	2.42
20. Carl Lundgren	2.42
21. Chief Bender	2.43
22. Red Ames	2.45
23. Jack Taylor	2.50
24. Deacon Phillippe	2.50
25. Earl Moore	2.51

A mainstay with the 1906 "Hitless Wonders" Chicago White Sox, Doc White (above) paced the AL with a 1.52 ERA while going 18-6, allowing only 38 bases on balls in 219 innings, helping him to allow a league-lowest .244 on-base percentage.

Above: *Spitballer Jack Chesbro starred for the Pittsburgh Pirates and New York Highlanders in the early 1900s. He won 70 games between 1901 and 1903 before reeling off 41 victories in 1904, thus becoming the last pitcher to win 40 in a season.*

In 1904, Jack Chesbro and Jack Powell between them started 97 of the 155 games played by the New York Highlanders and completed 86 of them. Chesbro set the major league record with 454⅔ innings pitched.

1900s CATCHER GAMES	
1. Billy Sullivan	923
2. Johnny Kling	849
3. Red Dooin	811
4. Bill Bergen	768
5. Lou Criger	761

"It was more fun to play ball then. The players were more colorful, you know, drawn from every walk of life, and the whole thing was sort of chaotic most of the time, not highly organized in every detail like it is nowadays."
—Davy Jones, on the game in the early 1900s

Tigers Take Title by One-Half Game

The tightest finish in American League or National League history occurred in 1908 when the Detroit Tigers claimed the AL flag by a mere four percentage points by dint of finishing half a game ahead of Cleveland. Just one and one-half games behind Detroit were the Chicago White Sox, and the St. Louis Browns were also in the race until the last week of the season. Going into the season's final day on October 6, Cleveland was actually mathematically eliminated from the race, having split a doubleheader with St. Louis the previous afternoon. The White Sox and Tigers meanwhile squared off in Detroit with the Sox just half a game back and the pennant slated to go to the winner. When Detroit beat Chicago ace Ed Walsh on October 6, it vaulted Cleveland ahead of Chicago into second place and gave the Motor City club the flag. Anger in Cleveland over the fact that the local team might have tied for the pennant if the Tigers had been forced to make up a postponed game resulted in a rule change that required all unplayed games to be rescheduled if they had a potential bearing on a pennant race.

In 1900, the National League contracted from 12 teams to eight teams. The Pirates gained more than other teams. Pittsburgh absorbed Honus Wagner, Fred Clarke, Rube Waddell, Tommy Leach, Deacon Phillippe, and others from the defunct Louisville team.

1900s CATCHER CHANCES ACCEPTED	
1. Johnny Kling	5,148
2. Ossee Schreckengost	4,965
3. Billy Sullivan	4,848
4. Red Dooin	4,841
5. Bill Bergen	4,686

In 1909, Pittsburgh's George Gibson became the first backstopper to catch 150 games in a season.

The Cardinals committed a record 17 errors in a double-header on July 3, 1909.

1900s CATCHER FIELDING AVERAGE	
1. Billy Sullivan	.976
2. John Warner	.975
3. George Gibson	.974
4. Lou Criger	.974
5. Pat Moran	.974

The Tigers committed an AL record 12 errors in one game on May 1, 1901. Two years later, the White Sox tied the AL single-game record with 12 errors on May 6; in the same game, the Tigers made six errors.

In 1906, despite winning 96 games and posting a .632 winning percentage, the New York Giants finished 20 games out of first place.

Dave Fultz, with 44 steals for the 1905 New York Highlanders, set a 20th century record for the most thefts by a player in his final season.

Cobb In Cleveland? Thought Flick-ers Out

The most significant trade during the first decade of the current century was one that was not made. In the spring of 1908, Cleveland trained in Macon, Georgia, while Detroit drilled in Augusta. Both teams had a morale problem. Cleveland consistently contended for the American League pennant but had yet to win one, and Detroit manager Hugh Jennings was tired of having to cope with the dissension aroused on the team by its fiery and irascible new star, Ty Cobb. One evening Cleveland owner Charley Somers received a phone call in Macon from Jennings offering Cobb to Cleveland for outfielder Elmer Flick, even up. Knowing Cobb's reputation as a scrapper and his penchant for creating team disharmony, Somers opted to keep Flick. It quickly proved to be a disastrous misjudgment. Illness idled Flick for most of the 1908 campaign, and he was never again able to play regularly. Cobb, on the other hand, went on to play for two more decades at a level that almost undoubtedly would have meant several pennants for Cleveland had the trade been made.

The modern infield fly rule was adopted in 1901. The rule was developed to thwart the fly-ball trap play, during which a fielder would trap pop-ups instead of catching them to throw out the lead runner of a double play. The fly-ball trap was developed by Hall of Fame outfielder Tommy McCarthy.

Honus Wagner (above, left) and Ty Cobb were the two greatest players of the early 1900s, and they faced off in the 1909 World Series. From 1907 to 1909, each player led his respective league in batting average and RBI.

1900s FIRST BASE GAMES	
1. Fred Tenney	1,318
2. Harry Davis	1,191
3. Kitty Bransfield	1,169
4. Dan McGann	1,094
5. Jake Beckley	921

In 1903, the Los Angeles Angels of the Pacific Coast League won an all-time organized baseball record 133 games.

"Baseball is in its infancy."
—Brooklyn owner Charlie Ebbets in 1909

1900s FIRST BASE FIELDING AVERAGE	
1. Dan McGann	.989
2. John Ganzel	.987
3. Jiggs Donahue	.987
4. Frank Chance	.986
5. Frank Isbell	.986

Pirates Swap, Shuffle Deck

Before the turn of the century, player deals were relatively uncommon, but in the early 1900s a number of teams suddenly became quite active in the trade mart. At the forefront was Pittsburgh. On December 15, 1905, the Pirates swapped three players to the Boston Braves for mound ace Vic Willis. Almost exactly a year later Pittsburgh dealt three more players, including former batting king Ginger Beaumont, to the Braves for infielder Ed Abbaticchio. Both trades ultimately helped the Pirates in their bid to dethrone the Chicago Cubs as the reigning National League champion. A swap engineered with the Philadelphia Phillies a year before the Willis trade made Pittsburgh's task considerably harder, though. On December 20, 1904, the Pirates sent first baseman Kitty Bransfield and two other players to the Quaker City entry for first sacker Del Howard. Howard played just one season for the Pirates before going to Boston in the Willis deal. His departure left Pittsburgh with a gaping first base hole that remained until the mid-1910s. Bransfield meanwhile gave the Phillies six years of solid service at the initial hassock.

Hugh Fullerton, sportswriter, called Johnny Evers, "a bundle of nerves with the best brain in baseball."

Franklin P. Adams, a journalist for the **New York World,** *penned this poem in 1908:*

These are the saddest of possible words:
"Tinker to Evers to Chance."
Trio of bear cubs, and fleeter than birds,
Tinker and Evers and Chance.
Ruthlessly pricking our gonfalon bubble,
Making a Giant hit into a double—
Words that are heavy with nothing but trouble:
"Tinker to Evers to Chance."

Above: *Second baseman Johnny Evers played on four NL championship teams over an 18-year career. Nicknamed "The Crab" for his peculiar way of charging grounders, he played stellar defense for the Cubs and Braves while making a solid offensive contribution. Evers scored over 80 runs in five seasons.*

1900s SECOND BASE GAMES	
1. Claude Ritchey	1,262
2. Jimmy Williams	1,176
3. Nap Lajoie	1,118
4. Hobe Ferris	1,019
5. Kid Gleason	935

In 1907, Claude Ritchey led NL second basemen in fielding average for a record sixth consecutive year.

The Giants' .928 team fielding average in 1900 was the poorest by any team since 1896 and the last team fielding average under .930. New York's corner men contributed the most to this inauspicious honor. Piano Legs Hickman that year committed a modern record 86 errors by a third baseman, while first baseman Jack Doyle committed a modern record 41 errors.

1900s SECOND BASE FIELDING AVERAGE	
1. Nap Lajoie	.965
2. Claude Ritchey	.960
3. Jimmy Williams	.955
4. Germany Schaefer	.955
5. Hobe Ferris	.954

When they garnered just 99 stolen bases in 1906, the Boston Red Sox became the first American League team to collect fewer than 100 thefts in a season.

In 1902, the Pittsburgh Pirates won the National League pennant by a record 27½ games. The Pirates compiled a 56-15 home record, the best home record ever in the NL.

The 1906 to 1908 Chicago Cubs won three NL pennants with an infield of (above, from left) Harry Steinfeldt at third, Joe Tinker at short, Johnny Evers at second, and first baseman-manager Frank Chance. Each of them was a star in the dead-ball era, and all but Steinfeldt are in the Hall of Fame.

Gloves Preserve McBride and Wallace

The dead-ball era put runs at such a premium that most teams relied on a strong defense to keep them in the game. Accordingly, there was always a place on the major league scene for a good-field no-hit middle infielder or catcher. In 1906, Brooklyn backstopper Bill Bergen hit .159 while working 103 games but nonetheless held his job. That season, the St. Louis Cardinals released shortstop George McBride after he batted .169 in 90 contests, but McBride's glovework was so sturdy that the Washington Senators handed him their shortstop post two years later and left him there for nearly a decade—even though he never hit above .234 in his 16-year career. Hall of Fame shortstop Bobby Wallace was another whose defensive skill kept him in the game long after the dead-ball era had undermined his offensive talent. Early in his career, Wallace customarily hit around .300, but after batting .324 for the St. Louis Cardinals in 1901, he jumped to the American League St. Louis Browns and played 17 more seasons while just once hitting above .280.

Washington's George McBride led AL shortstops in fielding percentage every year from 1912 to 1915.

Despite his poor batting totals, George McBride was known as "Pinch" for his ability to deliver in the clutch.

1900s THIRD BASE GAMES	
1. Bill Bradley	1,238
2. Harry Steinfeldt	1,158
3. Jimmy Collins	1,089
4. Lave Cross	979
5. Bill Coughlin	977

In 1906, the Chicago White Sox won an AL-record 19 straight games. When the streak began on August 2, the Sox were nine games out, in fourth place; 11 days later they were in first by a half-game.

1900s THIRD BASE FIELDING AVERAGE	
1. Lave Cross	.941
2. Lee Tannehill	.939
3. Art Devlin	.935
4. Bill Bradley	.933
5. Wid Conroy	.932

After a spring training game in 1904, New York Giants players, fomented by manager John McGraw (who was a notorious ump-baiter), beat an umpire unconscious. McGraw was suspended in 1905 for 15 days and fined $150 by the NL for abusing umpires. Then, in 1906, he got into a savage fight with Phils rookie infielder Paul Sentell.

Alibi Ike

"You must have an alibi to show why you lost. If you haven't one, you must fake one. Your self-confidence must be maintained. Always have that alibi. But keep it to yourself. That's where it belongs."
—Christy Mathewson

1900s Hurlers Truly Fifth Infielders

A typical big inning in the dead-ball era consisted of a bunt single, a stolen base, a sacrifice bunt to put the runner on third, and a wild pitch or a passed ball that enabled him to score. Owing to the frequency of bunt attempts, a pitcher in the early 1900s truly did function as a fifth infielder, and as a result the vast majority of single-season records for fielding chances handled by a moundsman were set between 1901 and 1910. In 1904, for instance, southpaw Nick Altrock of the Chicago White Sox registered a 20th-century record 49 putouts by a pitcher. That season, Vic Willis logged 39 putouts to set the modern National League record. Three years later, White Sox ace Ed Walsh established all-time major league single-season marks for both assists (227) and total chances (262). In 1905, Harry Howell, good enough with a glove to play second base on days when he wasn't on the mound, set the all-time hurlers mark for the most chances handled per game when he averaged 5.24 chances each time he toed the rubber for the St. Louis Browns.

Ted Turner, the owner of the Atlanta Braves who took over the managing reins for one game in 1977, was not the first owner to pull such a maneuver. In 1905, Stanley Robison, the owner of the St. Louis Cardinals, became the on-field manager and brought the team home sixth.

M. BROWN.   J. PFEISTER   A. HOFMAN   C. G. WILLIAMS   O. OVERALL   E. REULBACH.   J. KLING.
I GESSLER .   J. TAYLOR.   H. STEINFELDT.   J. McCORMICK.   F. CHANCE.   J. SHECKARD.   P. MORAN.   F. SCHULT
C. LUNDGREN.   T. WALSH.   J. EVERS.   J. SLAGLE.   J. TINKER.

CHICAGO NATIONAL LEAGUE BALL CLUB 1906

The 1906 Chicago Cubs (above) scored 705 runs and allowed 381 runs, a difference of 324 runs. That is an average of 2.09 runs a game more than the opposition. Chicago led the National League in batting average (.262), ERA (1.75), and fielding average (.969). The Cubs won the NL pennant by 20 games over the New York Giants, and the Giants in 1906 were 95-56 for a .632 winning percentage.

"You can learn little from victory. You can learn everything from defeat."
—Christy Mathewson

Cleveland shortstop John Gochnauer in 1903 made a 20th-century record 98 errors, and he batted only .185.

Cincinnati shortstop Tommy Corcoran made a record 14 assists in a game on August 7, 1903.

1900s SHORTSTOP GAMES	
1. Bobby Wallace	1,330
2. Bill Dahlen	1,309
3. Freddy Parent	1,125
4. Joe Tinker	1,080
5. Honus Wagner	1,044

The 1906 Chicago Cubs won the National League pennant and may have been the best club of all time. Manager and first baseman Frank Chance's team won 116 games, still a record, and lost only 36 for a record .763 winning percentage. The Cubs had a record 60-15 road mark. A 50-7 stretch drive included a 26-3 run in August.

1900s SHORTSTOP FIELDING AVERAGE	
1. Terry Turner	.950
2. George Davis	.944
3. Bobby Wallace	.940
4. Bill Dahlen	.937
5. Tommy Corcoran	.936

1900s OUTFIELD PUTOUTS	
1. Roy Thomas	2,926
2. Fielder Jones	2,747
3. Cy Seymour	2,617
4. Jimmy Sheckard	2,582
5. Fred Clarke	2,552
6. Ginger Beaumont	2,503
7. Sam Crawford	2,292
8. Jimmy Slagle	2,285
9. Topsy Hartsel	1,928
10. Elmer Flick	1,878
11. Chick Stahl	1,819
12. Jimmy Barrett	1,772
13. Willie Keeler	1,764
14. Jesse Burkett	1,716
15. Charlie Hemphill	1,705

Outfielder Jack McCarthy of the Chicago Cubs threw a record three runners out at the plate during a game against Pittsburgh on April 26, 1905.

Wildfire Schulte of the Chicago Cubs set a record for outfielders that stood until 1928 when he had a .994 fielding average in 1908.

1900s OUTFIELD FIELDING AVERAGE	
1. Frank Schulte	.976
2. Spike Shannon	.974
3. Roy Thomas	.974
4. Fred Clarke	.972
5. Fielder Jones	.971
6. Ed Hahn	.970
7. Harry Bay	.968
8. Matty McIntyre	.967
9. Sherry Magee	.967
10. Davy Jones	.964
11. Socks Seybold	.963
12. Chick Stahl	.962
13. Bob Ganley	.962
14. Patsy Donovan	.962
15. Willie Keeler	.960

Above: Cub shortstop Joe Tinker's defense made him invaluable in the 1900s. He led the NL four times in fielding percentage, three times in total chances, and twice in putouts and assists. In addition, he swiped 336 career bases.

1900s OUTFIELD GAMES	
1. Jimmy Sheckard	1,289
Fielder Jones	1,289
3. Sam Crawford	1,285
4. Roy Thomas	1,268
5. Ginger Beaumont	1,251
6. Willie Keeler	1,243
7. Fred Clarke	1,209
8. Cy Seymour	1,189
9. Elmer Flick	1,180
10. Topsy Hartsel	1,177
11. Jimmy Slagle	1,146
12. George Browne	1,041
13. Patsy Dougherty	1,004
14. Charlie Hemphill	962
15. John Titus	941

Bill Klem was the first umpire to be elected to the baseball Hall of Fame.

In the 1900s, only two umpires, instead of today's four, were assigned to oversee each game.

Umpire O'Day Makes Tough Call on Merkle

To plate umpire Hank O'Day fell the responsibility of calling Fred Merkle out for failing to touch second base when base arbiter Bob Emslie claimed he had not seen the play in the historic 1908 game at the Polo Grounds. O'Day had been watching for the play after having been alerted to its potential significance several days earlier by Cubs second baseman Johnny Evers in a game with Pittsburgh. Belatedly, O'Day realized Evers had been correct in asserting that Warren Gill of the Pirates should be declared out for neglecting to tag second base as another Pirate scored the game-winning run. O'Day's decision in the Merkle game earned the eternal wrath of Giants manager John McGraw but made him one of the most well-known umpires of his time. A former big league pitcher, O'Day had first turned to umpiring back in the late 1880s while still an active player. Emslie, O'Day's co-worker in the Merkle game, also had pitched in the majors.

Take That
When threatened by John McGraw that McGraw would have umpire Bill Klem stripped of his job after he rendered an unpopular decision against the Giants, Klem responded: "Mr. Manager, if it's possible for you to take my job away from me, I don't want it."

Pennsylvania Launches Two Permanent Ballparks

In 1909, Shibe Park and Forbes Field, the first two all concrete-and-steel major league baseball stadiums, first opened their doors. Shibe was home to the Philadelphia Athletics while Forbes housed the Pittsburgh Pirates. When Pittsburgh joined with Detroit in co-hosting the World Series that autumn, sportswriters across the land found themselves pounding their typewriters in the first fully modern park in the majors. Forbes had triple-decker stands, elevators, electric lights, telephones, inclined ramps instead of stairs, and maids in the ladies' restrooms. It also shared with Shibe the distinction of having the first visitors' dressing room, ending the practice of visiting teams dressing at their hotels and then riding to the park in uniform. Shibe Park later became the home not only of the Philadelphia A's but also the Phillies, who continued to play in it through the 1970 season. Forbes Field also closed in 1970 after the Pirates moved to Three Rivers Stadium.

Both the Philadelphia Phillies and Athletics played at Shibe Park (above), named for Athletics stockholder Ben Shibe. In the new stadium's first seven seasons, five Philadelphia teams played World Series games there.

1900s MANAGER WINS	
1. Fred Clarke	938
2. John McGraw	782
3. Connie Mack	734
4. Clark Griffith	653
5. Jimmy McAleer	606
6. Ned Hanlon	540
7. Frank Chance	481
8. Jimmy Collins	455
9. Fielder Jones	426
10. Frank Selee	415

In 1903, foul balls were counted as strikes by both leagues for the first time. The National League first counted foul balls as strikes in 1901, but the American League did not comply with the rule until two years later.

In 1901, John McGraw tried to sign Charlie Grant, a black second baseman, to a contract with the Baltimore Orioles by claiming that Grant was a Cherokee Indian.

New York Giant backstop Roger Bresnahan experimented with the first "batting helmet" after being beaned in a game in 1905.

In 1907, the Detroit Tigers and the Pittsburgh Pirates were the only two teams in the majors to average more than four runs per game.

In 1902, the Chicago Daily News *coined the nickname "Cubs" for the Chicago National League team.*

Winning Is Everything

"In playing or managing, the game of ball is only fun for me when I'm out in front and winning. I don't care a bag of peanuts for the rest of the game."
—John McGraw

1900s MANAGER WINNING PERCENTAGE	
1. Frank Chance	.688
2. Fred Clarke	.636
3. John McGraw	.597
4. Fielder Jones	.592
5. Connie Mack	.564
6. Nap Lajoie	.550
7. Jimmy Collins	.548
8. Frank Selee	.540
9. Clark Griffith	.539
10. Bill Armour	.524

The 1908 Detroit Tigers won the AL pennant by one-half game, the smallest margin of victory in AL or NL history. Detroit had .004 percentage points better than Cleveland. Cleveland led by 2½ games with less than two weeks to go, when the Tigers started a string of ten victories in a row to put them ½ game up. On the final day of the season, Detroit beat Chicago and Cleveland beat St. Louis to bring Cleveland's record to 90-64 and the Tigers to 90-63. Since Detroit had lost a game due to a rain-out (that under the rules of the time did not have to be made up), the Tigers won the pennant by a raindrop.

1900s TEAM WINNING PERCENTAGE

1.	Pittsburgh-NL	.636
2.	Chicago-NL	.598
3.	Chicago-AL	.564
4.	Philadelphia-AL	.564
5.	New York-NL	.561
6.	Cleveland-AL	.525
7.	Boston-AL	.522
8.	Detroit-AL	.519
9.	New York-AL	.501
10.	Philadelphia-NL	.485
11.	Cincinnati-NL	.478
12.	St. Louis-AL	.466
13.	Brooklyn-NL	.445
14.	Baltimore-AL	.435
15.	Boston-NL	.401
16.	St. Louis-NL	.395
17.	Washington-AL	.365
18.	Milwaukee-AL	.350

The first game in American League history was played on April 24, 1901, at the Chicago Cricket Club. The score was Chicago 6, Cleveland 2. Chicago went on to win the first AL pennant.

First Modern Series—Phillippe Completes Five Games

During the 1903 season, flag-winners Pittsburgh of the National League and Boston of the AL agreed to play a best five-of-nine postseason series. Pittsburgh was 91-49 in 1903, while Boston was 91-47 that year. There were a number of late-season injuries to two of the Pirate pitchers, including Sam Leever, who had hurt his shoulder. Nevertheless, the Pirates beat Cy Young 7-3 in game one, as Deacon Phillippe struck out 10 and walked none on a six-hitter. After Boston evened matters behind Bill Dinneen in game two, Phillippe returned on a day's rest to win again in game three, 4-2. Phillippe started again in game four, played three days later. Though his arm was showing signs of strain (he struck out only one), he won again, beating Dinneen 5-4. The Series stood at Boston one game, Phillippe three. The tide turned in games five and six; Young shut down the Pirates 11-2 and Dinneen beat Leever 6-3. Young then beat Phillippe 7-3 in game seven, and Dinneen beat Phillippe 3-0 in game eight. The BoSox won four straight to win the first modern World Series, although Phillippe hurled five complete games in eight contests.

Mike Donlin, on hearing night baseball was now played in the minors, exclaimed: "Jesus! Think of taking a ballplayer's nights away from him."

Above: *Charles "Deacon" Phillippe won 20 games five seasons in a row and six times total in his career, all but one year of which was spent with the Pirates. Blessed with outstanding control, Phillippe five times led the NL in fewest walks per game.*

Cardinals Jack and Mike O'Neill formed the NL's first brother battery in 1902.

1900s TEAM WINS

		WON	LOST
1.	Pittsburgh-NL	938	538
2.	Chicago-NL	879	592
3.	New York-NL	823	645
4.	Chicago-AL	744	575
5.	Philadelphia-AL	734	568
6.	Philadelphia-NL	709	752
7.	Cincinnati-NL	705	769
8.	Cleveland-AL	698	632
9.	Boston-AL	691	634
10.	Detroit-AL	683	632
11.	Brooklyn-NL	649	809
12.	Boston-NL	587	877
13.	St. Louis-NL	580	888
14.	St. Louis-AL	551	632
15.	New York-AL	520	518
16.	Washington-AL	480	834
17.	Baltimore-AL	118	153
18.	Milwaukee-AL	48	89

Chapter 4
The 1910s

Oldster Cravath Masters 1910s

Gavvy Cravath was nearly as dominant a slugger during the 1910s as Babe Ruth would be in the following decade. Beginning in 1913, Cravath won six National League home run crowns over the next seven seasons and twice led the circuit in RBI and slugging average. Cravath's slugging peak came in 1915 when he hammered 24 home runs to spark the Phillies to their first pennant and set a post-1900 major league record. His two finest all-around seasons, though, were probably his first and last as the NL four-bagger champ. In 1913, Cravath pounded home 128 teammates to go with his 19 home runs and .341 batting average. Six years later, reduced by age to part-time status, he nonetheless topped the NL with 12 round-trippers despite accumulating only 214 at bats. Cravath's performance was made all the more extraordinary by the fact that he did not arrive in the majors to stay until he was past 32 years old.

Fear

"Every great batter works on the theory that the pitcher is more afraid of him than he is of the pitcher."

—Ty Cobb

Above: *Gavvy Cravath starred in the high minors before arriving for good with Philadelphia in 1912. The stocky outfielder's home run stroke made him the dominant power hitter before Babe Ruth.*

Gavvy Cravath of the Philadelphia Phillies slugged 24 homers in 1915, a 20th-century major league record.

Gavvy Cravath, who paced the National League in 1918 with eight homers, was the last four-bagger leader to total less than 10.

Joe Jackson of the Cleveland Indians in 1912 smacked an AL record 26 triples. Sam Crawford of the Tigers tied the record in 1914.

Cleveland's Shoeless Joe Jackson gathered a .408 batting average in 1911 to set a major league rookie record.

Ed Walsh in 1910 topped the AL with a 1.26 ERA; nonetheless he lost 20 games, as the Sox hit a record-low .211 as a team. The 1910 White Sox compiled a major league record-low .261 slugging percentage.

1910s GAMES	
1. Donie Bush	1,450
2. Eddie Collins	1,441
3. Tris Speaker	1,438
4. Ed Konetchy	1,430
5. Harry Hooper	1,427
6. Fred Merkle	1,406
7. Clyde Milan	1,393
8. Larry Gardner	1,367
9. Jake Daubert	1,353
10. Zack Wheat	1,348
11. Heinie Zimmerman	1,340
12. Ty Cobb	1,334
13. Duffy Lewis	1,325
14. Fred Luderus	1,319
15. Jimmy Austin	1,315
16. Dode Paskert	1,312
17. Larry Doyle	1,309
18. Buck Herzog	1,296
19. Hal Chase	1,291
20. Stuffy McInnis	1,260
21. Sherry Magee	1,257
22. Dots Miller	1,256
23. Frank Baker	1,255
24. Art Fletcher	1,247
25. Burt Shotton	1,236

New Ball Core Uncorks Offense

Following the 1910 season, the increasing imbalance between pitchers and hitters finally induced baseball moguls to take steps to pep up the game. In 1911, a cork-and-rubber center ball replaced the dead-as-duck-feathers rubber-core ball, and the results were immediately heartening. Joe Jackson of Cleveland hit a rookie-record .408 but failed to win the American League batting title. Ty Cobb batted .420, collected 248 hits and 367 total bases, and posted a .621 slugging average. All of Cobb's figures were major league records since the adoption of a 154-game schedule in 1904. But Cobb's totals, astonishing as they were, could have been more or less anticipated. The real surprise was the 21 home runs Wildfire Schulte slammed to lead the National League and set a 20th-century record. Adding juice to the ball pumped up offensive stats across the board. The American League as a whole tallied 5,658 runs, a whopping 20-percent increase over its 1910 total, and the National League run total jumped 10 percent.

1910s RUNS	
1. Ty Cobb	1,050
2. Eddie Collins	991
3. Tris Speaker	967
4. Donie Bush	958
5. Harry Hooper	868
6. Joe Jackson	765
7. Clyde Milan	758
8. Larry Doyle	745
9. Frank Baker	733
10. Jake Daubert	727
Max Carey	727
12. Dode Paskert	704
13. Burt Shotton	698
14. Ed Konetchy	679
15. Sherry Magee	670
16. Fred Merkle	662
17. Bob Bescher	660
18. Heinie Zimmerman	655
19. Hal Chase	654
20. George Burns	651
21. Jack Graney	650
22. Zack Wheat	620
23. Buck Herzog	612
24. Larry Gardner	605
25. Frank Schulte	603

Above: *"Shoeless" Joe Jackson may not have been able to write his name, but he left his mark on plenty of American League baseballs over a 13-year career ended by his 1920 expulsion by commissioner Kenesaw Mountain Landis. A lefty-swinging outfielder, Jackson three times led the AL in home runs. He blossomed with the Cleveland Indians in the early 1910s and played in two World Series with the 1917 and 1919 Chicago White Sox. Jackson never won a batting title, but his lifetime mark of .356 is the third best of all time.*

Shoeless Joe Jackson led all batters in the 1919 World Series with 12 hits and a .375 batting average. He was later thrown out of baseball by commissioner Kenesaw Mountain Landis for conspiring to throw the Series.

Doyle At Second Is First in Batting

In 1915, the New York Giants finished in the cellar for the first and only time under manager John McGraw, but the club was far from a typical last-place team. First and foremost, it posted a .454 winning percentage and finished just 21 games behind the pennant-winning Phillies; both figures are record highs for a basement dweller. Furthermore, the National League teams were so tightly packed that year that the Giants would have finished in the first division if they had lost just four less games. Last, but far from least, McGraw's 1915 Giants were the first cellar-finisher in major league history to showcase a batting titlist. New York second sacker Larry Doyle paced all senior loop hitters, albeit with a .320 average, the lowest prior to 1988 by an NL leader. Doyle was also in the top five in runs, hits, doubles, total bases, on-base percentage, and slugging percentage. Doyle became the first second sacker since 1876 to cop a senior loop batting title.

New York Giants second baseman "Laughing" Larry Doyle (above) quickly became one of manager John McGraw's favorites due to his quick bat, strong defense, and baserunning speed. Doyle hit .300 five times and played in three World Series for New York.

In 1914, Brooklyn outfielder Casey Stengel was fifth in the National League in batting and topped the circuit with a .404 on-base percentage.

Ernie "Crazy Snake" Calbert set a new 20th-century organized baseball record in 1917 when he slugged 43 home runs for Muskogee of the Western Association.

Third baseman Buck Herzog of the New York Giants set a World Series record in 1912 when he totaled 12 base hits in the tournament.

Ed Konetchy of Brooklyn set a 20th-century NL record in 1919 with 10 consecutive hits. Doc Johnston of Cleveland set an AL record that year when he collected nine consecutive hits.

Joe Wilhoit of Wichita in the Western League in 1919 had a base hit in an organized baseball record 69 consecutive games.

Thou Shalt Not Steal
Sportswriter Bugs Baer, commenting on slewfooted Ping Bodie, wrote: "He had larceny in his heart but his feet were honest."

In Two Stretches, Giants Go 43-0

1910s HITS	
1. Ty Cobb	1,949
2. Tris Speaker	1,821
3. Eddie Collins	1,682
4. Clyde Milan	1,556
5. Joe Jackson	1,548
6. Jake Daubert	1,535
7. Zack Wheat	1,516
8. Frank Baker	1,502
9. Heinie Zimmerman	1,481
10. Ed Konetchy	1,475
11. Harry Hooper	1,468
Hal Chase	1,468
13. Stuffy McInnis	1,430
14. Fred Merkle	1,413
15. Larry Doyle	1,406
16. Duffy Lewis	1,400
17. Larry Gardner	1,381
18. Donie Bush	1,334
19. Fred Luderus	1,328
20. Max Carey	1,284
21. Sherry Magee	1,279
22. Dode Paskert	1,270
23. Burt Shotton	1,263
24. Art Fletcher	1,246
25. Sam Crawford	1,245

In 1914, Sherry Magee of the Phils led the NL with just 171 hits, the fewest ever by a leader in a season when the schedule called for a minimum of 154 games.

Shortly after Fenway Park first opened its doors in 1912, substitute Red Sox first baseman Hugh Bradley hit the first home run over Fenway's "Green Monster" (short but towering left field wall).

In 1912, all of the five top hitters in the National League were second basemen, shortstops, or third basemen.

Incensed by his Giants' last-place finish in 1915, John McGraw made two key lineup changes the following season, replacing aging Fred Snodgrass in center field with Federal League star Benny Kauff and installing another Federal League refugee, Bill McKechnie, at third base in place of Hans Lobert. McGraw's Giants responded by rattling off a record 17 consecutive victories on the road in May, the first full month of the 1916 season. In September, the last full month of the season, McGraw's crew embarked on a 26-game winning streak, the longest victory skein since the National League was formed in 1876. For nearly two full months of the 1916 season, then, the New York Giants had an incredible 43-0 record. During the other five months of the campaign, however, McGraw's team also won 43 games—but against 66 losses. Overall, the Giants ended with an 86-66 mark, good only for fourth place, and an advance of just 17 games over their 1915 finish despite the two record winning streaks.

Above: *Strong-armed outfielder Sherry Magee played in the Philadelphia Phillies outfield between 1904 and 1914. He led the NL in RBI four times as well as winning the 1910 bat crown. Magee also stole 441 bases in his 16-year career.*

1910s DOUBLES	
1. Tris Speaker	367
2. Ty Cobb	313
3. Duffy Lewis	277
4. Joe Jackson	265
5. Heinie Zimmerman	261
6. Sherry Magee	259
7. Fred Merkle	257
Frank Baker	257
9. Fred Luderus	248
10. Ed Konetchy	246
11. Zack Wheat	244
12. Larry Doyle	232
Hal Chase	232
14. Dode Paskert	231
15. Del Pratt	225
16. Gavvy Cravath	217
17. Bobby Veach	216
18. Harry Hooper	213
19. Shano Collins	209
20. Red Smith	208
21. Jack Graney	205
22. George Burns	204
23. Frank Schulte	201
24. Larry Gardner	200
25. Sam Crawford	192

On June 9, 1914, Honus Wagner became the first player in major league history to collect 3,000 hits.

1910s HOME RUNS	
1. Gavvy Cravath	116
2. Fred Luderus	83
3. Frank Baker	76
4. Frank Schulte	75
5. Larry Doyle	64
6. Sherry Magee	61
7. Heinie Zimmerman	58
8. Fred Merkle	56
9. Vic Saier	55
10. Chief Wilson	52
11. Zack Wheat	51
12. Babe Ruth	49
Cy Williams	49
14. Ed Konetchy	47
Ty Cobb	47
Hal Chase	47
17. Benny Kauff	46
18. Joe Jackson	42
19. Tilly Walker	39
Sam Crawford	39
Beals Becker	39
22. Tris Speaker	38
23. Ping Bodie	36
24. Dode Paskert	35
Jake Daubert	35

Above: Benny Kauff, a previously obscure New York Yankee outfielder from Pomeroy, Ohio, rose to prominence when given an opportunity to play in the new Federal League. He won batting titles for Indianapolis in 1914 and Brooklyn in 1915, and was the unqualified marquee player for the short-lived Federal League.

"I was like a steel spring with a growing and dangerous flaw in it. If it is wound too tight or has the slightest weak point, the spring will fly apart and then it is done for."
—Ty Cobb

Ex-Fed Star Kauff Romps in NL

Rival National League owners and managers winced at first when the New York Giants signed center fielder Benny Kauff prior to the 1916 season. In each of his two previous campaigns, he had led the rebel Federal League in both batting and stolen bases and become known as "The Ty Cobb of the Feds." Most observers felt that

Kauff was no more than an average player whose stats were inflated by the uneven quality of play in the Federal League. Kauff's first season with the Giants seemed to confirm this gloomy assessment when he hit just .264. In 1917, however, he hiked his average to .308 and finished fourth in the National League in batting and third in

runs. Although he never approached his towering achievements in the Federal League, Kauff proved to be a much more productive player than Federal League critics had predicted. He was still in his prime when he was banned from the game by Commissioner Kenesaw Mountain Landis in 1920 after he was implicated in a stolen-car ring.

Edd Roush Best Ex-Fed

Benny Kauff was far and away the most coveted Federal League star when the Feds closed up shop after 1915. Several other players who first cut their major league teeth in the outlaw circuit, however, had a much greater impact on the game over the fullness of time. Easily the most famous Federal League alumnus was Edd Roush. A .298 hitter for the Newark

Feds in 1915, Roush, like Kauff, was signed by the New York Giants for the 1916 season. But since both of them played center field, Roush saw little action in New York and was included as a throw-in player in a midseason trade that sent Christy Mathewson to Cincinnati to manage the Reds. It was the deal that Giants manager John McGraw would live to regret above all others.

For the next decade, while Roush twice led the National League in batting and was the loop's best all-around center fielder, McGraw worked to reacquire him. Finally, in 1927 McGraw met with success, but by then Roush was on the wane. Prior to his death in 1988 (he lived to be 94), Roush was both the most famous and the last surviving FL participant.

Above: *Edd Roush parlayed an aggressive batting style and good defense into an 18-year career as the National League's top center fielder. After establishing himself in the Federal League, Roush played 10 seasons with Cincinnati. He hit over .320 11 straight years and won two bat crowns, and he was elected to the Hall of Fame in 1962.*

In 1910, the American League had a composite .243 batting average; the following year, after the ball was juiced up, the St. Louis Browns were the only AL team to hit below .250.

	1910s TRIPLES	
1.	Ty Cobb	161
2.	Joe Jackson	148
3.	Sam Crawford	135
4.	Tris Speaker	133
5.	Ed Konetchy	126
6.	Eddie Collins	114
7.	Harry Hooper	109
8.	Zack Wheat	104
9.	Heinie Zimmerman	102
10.	Larry Doyle	101
11.	Jake Daubert	99
	Hal Chase	99
13.	Larry Gardner	98
14.	Chief Wilson	95
15.	Shano Collins	94
16.	Bobby Veach	92
17.	Dots Miller	90
18.	Sherry Magee	87
19.	Del Pratt	86
20.	Honus Wagner	84
21.	Max Carey	82
22.	Frank Baker	79
23.	Amos Strunk	78
	Jack Graney	78
	Chick Gandil	78

Zimmerman Sizzles At Bat, Hot Corner

In 1912, Heinie Zimmerman of the Chicago Cubs had the greatest offensive season to that point by a third baseman when he hit .372 and collected 14 home runs and 103 RBI. Since all three figures topped the National League, Zimmerman was voted the loop's Most Valuable Player and awarded the Triple Crown. The MVP prize was entirely deserved, but the Triple Crown now seems to have been tainted. In recent years, a close scrutiny of 1912 box scores and game reports revealed that Zimmerman accumulated only 99 RBI that season and the real leader was Honus Wagner with 102. Baseball officials, preferring not to tamper with records that many feel have already been etched in stone, continue to recognize Zimmerman as a Triple Crown winner, but many current encyclopedias list Wagner as the 1912 RBI king. In any event, Zimmerman's 1912 season stands unchallenged in one very important respect. His .372 batting average made him the first third baseman in major league history to bag a hitting crown.

After beginning his career as a utility infielder, Henry "Heinie" Zimmerman (above) was given a chance to play regular third base for the Chicago Cubs and New York Giants in the 1910s. Aside from his disputed Triple Crown of 1912, Zimmerman led the NL in RBI in 1916 and 1917 and reached double figures in triples six times.

1910s RUNS BATTED IN	
1. Ty Cobb	828
2. Frank Baker	793
3. Heinie Zimmerman	765
4. Sherry Magee	746
5. Tris Speaker	718
Duffy Lewis	718
7. Sam Crawford	697
8. Ed Konetchy	687
9. Eddie Collins	682
10. Gavvy Cravath	665
11. Fred Merkle	662
12. Joe Jackson	658
13. Hal Chase	649
14. Larry Doyle	645
15. Stuffy McInnis	642
16. Zack Wheat	636
Bobby Veach	636
18. Fred Luderus	629
19. Larry Gardner	606
20. Dots Miller	578
21. Del Pratt	566
22. Chick Gandil	557
23. Art Fletcher	554
24. Frank Schulte	537
25. Honus Wagner	519

Athletics third baseman Frank Baker received the nickname "Home Run" because of two clutch homers that he hit during the 1911 World Series against the Giants.

McGraw Wises Up, Chase, Zimmerman Out of Game

After his remarkable season in 1912, Heinie Zimmerman remained a potent offensive force until the end of the decade, although he never again challenged for a batting crown. It remains unclear, however, whether his hitting dropped off because pitchers got on to him or because he was not always giving his best. Zimmerman was a member of the game's unsavory element during the 1910s, a faction that included Lee Magee, Claude Hendrix, Hal Chase, and a number of other players who were strongly suspected of entering into collusion with gamblers to dump games when the price was right. In 1919, Zimmerman teamed with Chase on the New York Giants. By having substandard years, both helped cripple the club, a preseason favorite to win the National League pennant. Giants manager John McGraw then heeded rumors that certain team members were not always playing to win. Although never formally banned from the game, Zimmerman and Chase were released at the close of the 1919 season and never again given the opportunity to hold major league jobs.

Even without the benefit of flashy home run totals, Ty Cobb (above) still led the American League in slugging percentage eight times (including six years consecutively) and won four RBI crowns.

Ty Cobb in 1911 had a base hit in 40 straight games, an AL record.

In 1911, the Chalmers Award was established as the first modern Most Valuable Player honor. That year, Cub Wildfire Schulte won the NL's Chalmers Award, while Ty Cobb received the AL Chalmers.

Gen. Douglas MacArthur commented about Ty Cobb: "This great athlete seems to have understood early in his professional career that in the competition of baseball, just as in war, defensive strategy never has produced ultimate victory, and as a consequence, he maintained an offensive posture to the end of his baseball days."

Nap Lajoie edged Ty Cobb by a single point to win the 1910 bat crown. Nap made eight hits in a season-ending doubleheader. Seven of those safeties were bunts that Lajoie was able to beat out because St. Louis Browns third baseman Red Corriden was playing deep on orders from his manager, Jack O'Connor. The title is still in dispute.

The only Chalmers Award recipient to be a unanimous selection was Ty Cobb, who received all 64 first-place votes in 1911.

In 1915, Detroit's three regular outfielders—Bobby Veach, Sam Crawford, and Ty Cobb—finished 1-2-3 in the American League in RBI.

When he departed from the majors in 1917, Sam Crawford held the records for the most career triples (309) and the most games played by an outfielder (2,297).

Tris Speaker pounded out an AL single-season record 53 doubles in 1912.

Jackson's Early Records Would Have Been Shoo-Ins

Most record books do not recognize Joe Jackson's .408 batting average in 1911 as a record for the highest mark by a rookie, because Jackson was not considered a yearling player at the time, since he had played a handful of games in the majors prior to 1911. By today's rule for what constitutes a frosh player, however, Jackson was still a rookie during the 1911 campaign. If the modern standard is accepted, then Jackson also set a second mark when he hit .395 in 1912, his second full big league season. No other player has ever averaged over .400 when his freshman and sophomore years are combined. Oddly, even though Jackson remained a steady .300 hitter throughout his career, his lifetime batting mark dipped every year after 1912 until his last season in 1920. That year Shoeless Joe cracked .386, hiking his overall average to .356. When he was banished from the game at the season's close, he took with him the highest career batting mark of any man to that point who was no longer an active player.

When he paced the National League with 263 total bases in 1917, Rogers Hornsby of the St. Louis Cardinals became the first shortstop other than Honus Wagner to lead a major league in that department.

Above: *Pop Lloyd played 26 years as a shortstop in the Negro Leagues. Called by Babe Ruth the greatest player ever, Lloyd batted .321 in recorded exhibitions against major leaguers.*

1910s BATTING AVERAGE

1.	Ty Cobb	.387
2.	Joe Jackson	.354
3.	Tris Speaker	.344
4.	Eddie Collins	.326
5.	Nap Lajoie	.321
6.	Edd Roush	.314
7.	Sam Crawford	.313
8.	Benny Kauff	.313
9.	Frank Baker	.310
10.	Stuffy McInnis	.309
11.	Bobby Veach	.304
12.	Jake Daubert	.302
13.	Zack Wheat	.299
14.	Honus Wagner	.296
15.	Heinie Zimmerman	.296
16.	Hal Chase	.295
17.	Heinie Groh	.294
18.	Clyde Milan	.293
19.	Chief Meyers	.293
20.	Sherry Magee	.292
21.	Steve Evans	.291
22.	Gavvy Cravath	.291
23.	George Burns	.289
24.	Larry Doyle	.289
25.	George Burns	.287

1910s STOLEN BASES

1.	Ty Cobb	576
2.	Eddie Collins	489
3.	Clyde Milan	434
4.	Max Carey	392
5.	Bob Bescher	363
6.	Tris Speaker	336
7.	Donie Bush	322
8.	George Burns	293
9.	Buck Herzog	286
10.	Burt Shotton	285
11.	Harry Hooper	269
12.	Fred Merkle	260
13.	Larry Doyle	236
14.	Benny Kauff	231
15.	Hal Chase	229
16.	Dode Paskert	227
	George Cutshaw	227
18.	Rollie Zeider	223
19.	Ray Chapman	220
20.	Jimmy Austin	209
21.	Del Pratt	208
22.	Frank Baker	206
23.	Fred Snodgrass	204
24.	Sherry Magee	203
25.	Jake Daubert	198

"I am honored to have John Lloyd called the Black Wagner. It is a privilege to have been compared with him."
—Honus Wagner

The record for the fewest career home runs by a first baseman in over 500 games belongs to Fritz Mollwitz, who hit just one four-bagger in 1,740 at bats during the 1910s.

In 1919, the last year of the dead-ball era, Hy Myers of Brooklyn led the NL with a .438 slugging average and 223 total bases.

Above: *Chief Meyers was the catcher for the New York Giants' 1911 to 1913 pennant winners. He was as known for his guidance of hurlers Christy Mathewson and Joe McGinnity as for his hitting.*

1910s SLUGGING AVERAGE

1.	Ty Cobb	.541
2.	Joe Jackson	.511
3.	Gavvy Cravath	.490
4.	Tris Speaker	.485
5.	Sam Crawford	.459
6.	Benny Kauff	.450
7.	Frank Baker	.442
8.	Sherry Magee	.433
9.	Bobby Veach	.424
10.	Heinie Zimmerman	.424
11.	Edd Roush	.423
12.	Steve Evans	.421
13.	Eddie Collins	.419
14.	Zack Wheat	.419
15.	Larry Doyle	.418
16.	Honus Wagner	.413
17.	Frank Schulte	.410
18.	Hal Chase	.410
19.	Chief Wilson	.410
20.	Vic Saier	.409
21.	Nap Lajoie	.405
22.	Ed Konetchy	.404
23.	Fred Luderus	.404
24.	George Burns	.396
25.	Tilly Walker	.395

In 1911, Chief Meyers of the Giants fell one hit short of being the first catcher to win a batting title.

1910s ON-BASE AVERAGE

1.	Ty Cobb	.457
2.	Tris Speaker	.428
3.	Eddie Collins	.424
4.	Joe Jackson	.422
5.	Miller Huggins	.402
6.	Benny Kauff	.389
7.	Wally Schang	.384
8.	Johnny Evers	.382
9.	Gavvy Cravath	.381
10.	Ward Miller	.380
11.	Heinie Groh	.377
12.	Steve Evans	.376
13.	Sam Crawford	.372
14.	Sherry Magee	.371
15.	Nap Lajoie	.370
16.	Bobby Veach	.368
17.	Burt Shotton	.368
18.	Frank Baker	.368
19.	Chief Meyers	.367
20.	Fred Snodgrass	.366
21.	Bill Sweeney	.366
22.	George Burns	.366
23.	Clyde Milan	.365
24.	Honus Wagner	.363
25.	Jake Daubert	.360

In 1919, Brooklyn outfielder Hy Myers's 73 RBI topped the National League, which played an abbreviated 140-game schedule that year.

The Philadelphia A's set a dead-ball era record in 1911 when they compiled a .296 team batting average.

Second sacker Morrie Rath of the White Sox had just 19 RBI in 157 games and 591 at bats in 1912, a record low for a player with over 550 at bats.

Hollocher Leads NL in Total Bases as Rookie

Joe Jackson was far from the only hitter during the 1910s to enjoy a great rookie season. In 1913, his first full season, second baseman, Jim Viox hit .317 for the Pirates and finished third in the National League batting race. Viox soon proved to be a flash in the pan, but another National League rookie middle infield star later in the decade failed to match his superb frosh campaign for a very different reason. In 1918, Charlie Hollocher, the Cubs yearling shortstop, hit .316 and topped the senior loop in total bases. Unlike Viox, Hollocher subsequently had several other fine seasons, but mental problems kept him continually on the brink between having to quit the game and blossoming into a full-fledged star. Hollocher managed to stick it out until 1924 when his disturbances overcame him. Then just age 28, he returned to his home in Missouri, where he continued to struggle with his internal demons until he committed suicide in 1940.

Detroit catcher Oscar Stanage set a record for the fewest runs by a player in 400 or more at bats when he collected just 16 tallies in 1914.

Marty Kavanagh of Cleveland hit the first pinch grand slam in American League history on September 24, 1916, when his blow skipped through a hole in the fence.

Wood Blazes to 30 Wins

Smokey Joe Wood pitched his first game in the majors for the Boston Red Sox in 1908 when he was just 18 years old. The following year he stuck with the Sox, and at the finish of the 1911 season, although just 21 years old, he already had 47 career wins. Great as Wood's achievements at such a tender age were, they did little to prepare the baseball world for his 1912 campaign. That season Wood became the youngest 30-game winner since 1893. Wood fashioned a 34-5 mark that included 35 complete games, 10 shutouts, and an .872 winning percentage. In 1912, Wood topped the American League in every major mound category except strikeouts and in addition launched a loop-record 16-game winning streak. But Wood was not done. In the World Series that fall against the New York Giants, he won three more games, including the deciding 10-inning clash that is considered to have been the most exciting postseason game in the dead-ball era.

Above: *Smokey Joe Wood, star pitcher of the Boston Red Sox, set baseball on its ear in 1916 with a 34-5 record and a 16-game winning streak that riveted the country. Wood threw an incomparable fastball with outstanding control before arm miseries sidetracked him.*

"Can I throw harder than Joe Wood? Listen, my friend, there's no man alive can throw harder than Joe Wood."
—Walter Johnson

In 1914, Boston Red Sox lefthander Dutch Leonard posted a 20th-century record-low 0.96 ERA. He had seven shutouts in 25 starts.

In 1916, lefthander Ferdie Schupp of the New York Giants racked up an 0.90 ERA in 140⅓ innings and was tagged for just 79 hits.

On August 1, 1918, Braves hurler Art Nehf pitched 20 scoreless innings before losing 2-0 in the 21st inning against the Pirates.

Chicago Cub pitcher King Cole in 1910 compiled a 20-4 mark, setting a National League rookie record with an .833 winning percentage.

Phillies righthander Pete Alexander hurled an incredible 16 shutouts in 1916, an all-time major league record.

Smokey Joe Cultivates New Career as Gardener

The toast of the baseball world and a winner of 81 career games before he turned 23, Joe Wood was fated to win only 39 more games before his arm betrayed him. Unlike many other great pitchers whose careers were ended prematurely by arm and shoulder problems, though, Wood had an option. A pretty good hitter for a pitcher, he believed he could make a comeback as an outfielder. By 1918, Wood's conversion was so successful that he held down the regular left field post for Cleveland. He had a .366 batting average in 1921 in 194 at bats. At the close of the 1922 season, he retired to become a college coach after notching 92 RBI, prior to 1986 a record for a player in his final major league season who retired of his own volition. Interestingly, another converted pitcher had an equally noteworthy season in 1922. Reb Russell, a former 20-game winner with the White Sox, hit .368 and knocked home 75 runs in just 60 games as a utility outfielder with the Pittsburgh Pirates.

In 1910, the Portland Beavers of the Pacific Coast League held their opponents scoreless for an all-time organized baseball record 88 consecutive innings.

The last pitcher to lose 20 games with an ERA below 2.00 was Jim Scott, 20-20 in 1913 with a 1.90 ERA.

When he defeated the Red Sox in game three of the 1916 World Series, Jack Coombs became the first pitcher to win a game for both a National League and an American League club in the fall classic.

The 1910 Philadelphia A's pitching staff set an AL record when it compiled a 1.79 ERA. The principal members of that staff were Jack Coombs, Chief Bender, Cy Morgan, and Eddie Plank.

Above: *Jack Coombs won 59 games in the 1910 and '11 seasons for Connie Mack's Philadelphia Athletics. Coombs won five World Series games without a loss, threw 13 shutouts in 1910, and was good enough on offense to hit 10 career homers.*

1910s GAMES PITCHED	
1. Walter Johnson	454
2. Eddie Cicotte	396
3. Pete Alexander	362
4. Red Ames	359
5. Slim Sallee	356
6. Claude Hendrix	333
7. Hippo Vaughn	331
8. Rube Marquard	330
9. Bob Groom	323
10. Larry Cheney	313
11. Bob Harmon	300
12. Eddie Plank	289
13. Rube Benton	288
14. Lefty Tyler	286
15. Jim Scott	281
16. Pat Ragan	278
Babe Adams	278
18. Willie Mitchell	273
19. Earl Hamilton	272
Ray Caldwell	272
21. Hooks Dauss	269
Wilbur Cooper	269
23. Dave Davenport	259
24. Dick Rudolph	253
25. Joe Benz	251
Doc Ayers	251

Philadelphia's Jack Coombs in 1910 set an AL record when he totaled 13 shutouts.

The 1917 Chicago White Sox are the only world championship team to be victimized twice during the season by no-hitters.

How Do You Spell Relief?

Eddie Collins described his pitching teammate Eddie Plank: "His motion was enough to give a batter nervous indigestion."

Perry Wins 20 in Abbreviated Campaign

Very few pitchers since 1900 have won 20 games while toiling for a last-place team, which makes Scott Perry's 20 victories in 1918 for the cellar-dwelling Philadelphia A's a remarkable feat in any season. But 1918 was not a normal season. With the country involved in World War I, a "Work or Fight" order called a halt to the campaign on Labor Day. At that time the A's had played just 128 of their scheduled 154 games. Had the complete slate been played Perry was on course to make another seven or eight starts. He almost certainly would have shattered the record for the most wins by a hurler on a tail-ender prior to 1961—when expansion lengthened the schedule to the current 162-game mark. Perry won 38.5 percent of the A's 52 victories. He also led the league with 30 complete games and 332⅓ innings. The 1918 season in any case was to be Perry's lone moment in the limelight. The following year he slipped to a 4-17 record, then was quickly gone after he led the American League with 25 losses in 1920.

1910s COMPLETE GAMES	
1. Walter Johnson	327
2. Pete Alexander	243
3. Eddie Cicotte	193
4. Hippo Vaughn	184
5. Claude Hendrix	172
6. Dick Rudolph	167
7. Slim Sallee	163
8. Lefty Tyler	160
Ray Caldwell	160
10. Hooks Dauss	156
11. Christy Mathewson	153
12. Eddie Plank	147
13. Rube Marquard	142
14. Bob Groom	140
Babe Adams	140
16. Jack Coombs	136
17. Jeff Pfeffer	135
18. Bob Harmon	133
19. Larry Cheney	132
20. Wilbur Cooper	128
21. Russ Ford	126
22. Jeff Tesreau	123
23. Red Ames	118
24. Dutch Leonard	114
25. Ed Walsh	112
George Suggs	112

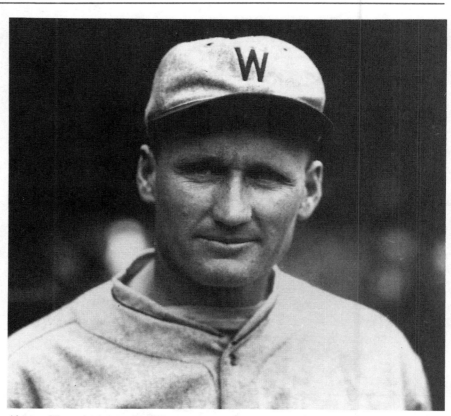

Above: *Thought by some the greatest pitcher ever, Walter Johnson was a durable and overpowering righthander who won six ERA titles and led the American League in strikeouts every year of the 1910s except one. In a 21-year career spent entirely with Washington, "The Big Train" won 20 games in a season 12 times and is second all time with 416 victories.*

Blinded

Ping Bodie explained what it was like to bat against Walter Johnson by saying: "You can't hit what you can't see."

Washington's Walter Johnson pitched a record fifth Opening Day shutout in 1919, winning 1-0 over the A's in 13 innings.

Walter Johnson became the first Washington Senator pitcher to win 20 in a season in 1910 when he won 25.

1910s SAVES

1.	Slim Sallee	32
2.	Mordecai Brown	30
3.	Red Ames	29
4.	Chief Bender	26
5.	Eddie Plank	22
6.	Jim Bagby	21
7.	Ed Walsh	20
	Walter Johnson	20
9.	Eddie Cicotte	19
	Larry Cheney	19
	Hugh Bedient	19
12.	Allan Russell	17
	Gene Packard	17
	Rube Marquard	17
	Claude Hendrix	17
16.	Hooks Dauss	16
	Rube Benton	16
	Pete Alexander	16
19.	George Suggs	15
	Bob Shawkey	15
	Tom Hughes	15
	Dave Danforth	15
23.	Hooks Wiltse	14
	Doc Ayers	14
25.	Jim Shaw	13
	Reb Russell	13
	Christy Mathewson	13
	Bob Groom	13
	Doc Crandall	13

Righthanded pitcher Christy Mathewson (above right, with Joe Wood) helped John McGraw's Giants win four NL titles. Universally admired as a gentleman, Matty relied on stellar control and an unhittable screwball, which he parlayed into 373 wins, five ERA titles, and five strikeout crowns.

Christy Mathewson in 1913 pitched an NL record 68 consecutive innings without giving up a walk.

The first pitcher to collect 300 wins in the 20th century was Christy Mathewson; Walter Johnson was the second.

A letter-writer, informing the Washington club of Walter Johnson's talent as an Idaho semi-pro, reported: "He knows where he's throwing because if he didn't there would be dead bodies strewn all over the place."

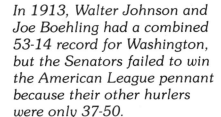

In 1913, Walter Johnson and Joe Boehling had a combined 53-14 record for Washington, but the Senators failed to win the American League pennant because their other hurlers were only 37-50.

Nabors Goes 1-20 for A's

After Connie Mack broke up his early 1910s Philadelphia Athletics dynasty, the team in the latter half of the 1910 decade provided a graveyard for promising young pitchers, like Scott Perry. Between 1915 and 1921 Connie Mack's club finished in the cellar a major league record seven straight seasons. Along the way, fireballer Elmer Myers set a rookie mark in 1916 when he issued 168 walks. Three years later Myers escaped the A's when he was traded to Cleveland, but other hurlers, such as Jack Nabors, were not so fortunate.

After losing all five of his decisions in his 1915 debut with the A's, Nabors suffered the worst season ever by a pitcher the following season when he sustained 20 losses while garnering just one win. His ERA was 3.47, just 0.65 above the league average of 2.82. At one point, Nabors reportedly grew so frustrated with his team that he deliberately threw a wild pitch to allow the winning run to score in the ninth inning of a tie game, preferring to end the contest then and there rather than labor on to an almost certain defeat in overtime.

1910s SHUTOUTS	
1. Walter Johnson	74
2. Pete Alexander	70
3. Hippo Vaughn	37
4. Eddie Plank	33
5. Dutch Leonard	29
6. Lefty Tyler	28
Eddie Cicotte	28
8. Jeff Tesreau	27
Claude Hendrix	27
Babe Adams	27
11. Dick Rudolph	26
12. Reb Russell	24
Rube Marquard	24
14. Joe Wood	23
Slim Sallee	23
Jeff Pfeffer	23
Pol Perritt	23
18. Fred Toney	22
Jim Scott	22
Nap Rucker	22
Jack Coombs	22
Joe Bush	22
23. Ed Walsh	21
Bob Groom	21
25. Bill Doak	20
Larry Cheney	20

Larry Gardner reminiscing about Babe Ruth said: "That's the first thing I can remember about him— the sound when he'd get a hold of one. It was just different, that's all."

Above: *Rabbit Maranville (left) and Ernie Shore (right) both starred for Boston, but the Rabbit played an acrobatic shortstop for the NL Braves while Shore practiced his excellent control with the AL Red Sox. Shore's career with the Red Sox and Yankees was good but relatively brief, but Hall-of-Famer Maranville played for 23 seasons in the senior circuit. The diminutive Rabbit still rates as one of the game's all-time great defensive shortstops.*

Ernie Shores Up Perfectly for Ruth

On June 23, 1917, the Boston Red Sox sent Babe Ruth to the mound in a game against the Washington Senators. After walking Ray Morgan, the Senators leadoff hitter, Ruth got into an argument with the home plate umpire and was heaved out of the game. His replacement in the box, Ernie Shore, watched as Morgan was thrown out trying to steal second base. Shore then retired the next two Senators to end the first inning. He proceeded to set down the side one-two-three for the next eight innings to earn a 4-0 verdict. Since, technically, he retired 27 Senators in a row, Shore was judged to have hurled a perfect game even though he was not the starting pitcher.

Many analysts have since argued that Shore's effort cannot be considered perfect since he pitched neither a complete game nor one in which there were no enemy base runners. Sound as their complaints would seem, the contest is still listed in many record books as the lone perfect game in the majors between 1908 and 1922.

Pitchers Lead BoSox to Four Crowns in Seven Seasons

After winning a World Championship in 1912, the Boston Red Sox surrendered the American League's top rung to the Philadelphia A's for the next two seasons when Joe Wood and several other young Hub pitchers stumbled. Babe Ruth's arrival in 1914, however, heralded a return to the head of the AL and the making of the game's leading dynasty during the 1910s. Between 1912 and 1918, the Red Sox snagged four pennants and on each occasion were victorious in the World Series. Ruth's pitching was an important reason for the Sox ascendancy, but the club also had several other moundsmen nearly as good. Among them were Bullet Joe Bush, Dutch Leonard, and Carl Mays. In 1918, when the Sox claimed their fourth world title during the decade, Mays led them with 21 victories. On September 11, he bested the Chicago Cubs 2-1 to win the sixth and final game of the World Series. No one could possibly have predicted then that Mays's triumph would be the last time to date that a Red Sox hurler ended a fall classic with a victory.

Cy Young, on why he retired in 1912, said: "I guess it was about time. I was 45 years old. I never had a trainer rub my arm the whole time I was in baseball."

1910s WINS	
1. Walter Johnson	265
2. Pete Alexander	208
3. Eddie Cicotte	162
4. Hippo Vaughn	156
5. Slim Sallee	149
6. Rube Marquard	144
7. Eddie Plank	140
8. Christy Mathewson	137
9. Claude Hendrix	135
10. Hooks Dauss	125
11. Jack Coombs	123
12. Babe Adams	119
13. Dick Rudolph	117
14. Larry Cheney	116
15. Jeff Tesreau	115
16. Lefty Tyler	113
17. Bob Groom	112
18. Red Ames	111
19. Chief Bender	110
20. Ray Caldwell	107
21. Rube Benton	106
22. Joe Wood	104
Dutch Leonard	104
24. Bob Harmon	101
25. Russ Ford	99

Above: *Submarining righthander Carl Mays won 20 games five times. He also led the AL in shutouts, saves, and complete games twice. He pitched in four World Series, but he is most remembered for his role in Cleveland shortstop Ray Chapman's death on August 16, 1920. One of Mays's patented underhanded rising fastballs fractured Chapman's skull, for which the pitcher endured constant public criticism.*

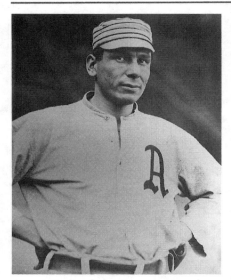

Above: *Perhaps the best of Connie Mack's Philadelphia Athletics mound stars, Charles "Chief" Bender led the American League three times in winning percentage. Relying on excellent control, Bender won 191 AL games in 12 seasons and tagged on six more wins in five World Series with the Athletics.*

Chief Bender of the Philadelphia Athletics in 1913 saved an American League record 13 games.

After leading the American League in 1914 with an .850 winning percentage, Chief Bender jumped to the Federal League the following season and went 4-16 with a .200 winning percentage, the lowest in that loop.

Money
Connie Mack described Chief Bender: "If I had all the pitchers I ever handled, with one game coming up that I simply had to win, I would call on the Chief. He was my greatest money pitcher."

Reb Russell of the Chicago White Sox tied the all-time rookie record when he bagged eight shutouts in 1913.

Grover Cleveland Alexander was the second pitcher in the 20th century to win 30 games for three consecutive years, when he notched at least 30 from 1915 to 1917. The first hurler to achieve the mark was Christy Mathewson from 1903 to 1905.

The 1919 Philadelphia Phillies had seven pitchers who won at least five games and none who won more than eight.

1910s INNINGS	
1. Walter Johnson	3,434.0
2. Pete Alexander	2,752.1
3. Eddie Cicotte	2,535.0
4. Hippo Vaughn	2,317.1
5. Slim Sallee	2,244.2
6. Claude Hendrix	2,167.2
7. Rube Marquard	2,128.1
8. Bob Groom	2,075.2
9. Red Ames	2,011.1
10. Lefty Tyler	1,987.0
11. Dick Rudolph	1,923.1
12. Babe Adams	1,908.2
13. Bob Harmon	1,895.0
14. Larry Cheney	1,881.1
15. Hooks Dauss	1,869.0
16. Ray Caldwell	1,857.1
17. Eddie Plank	1,829.2
18. Christy Mathewson	1,814.0
19. Rube Benton	1,723.2
20. Wilbur Cooper	1,687.0
21. Jeff Tesreau	1,679.0
22. Jack Coombs	1,650.0
23. Jim Scott	1,641.2
24. Willie Mitchell	1,609.0
25. Pat Ragan	1,593.2

Cicotte Polishes Delivery, Shines as Pitcher

During the 1910s, the spitball continued to be the "out" pitch for many hurlers. None threw it more often than Bill Doak, thus explaining his nickname of "Spittin' Bill." Other pitchers, finding the spitter too hard to control, became masters of trick deliveries like the shine ball or the emery ball. To Russ Ford is credited the invention of the latter. Ford would abrade a spot on a ball with an emery board he secreted in his glove, causing his pitches to dip unpredictably. The shine ball was the creation of Dave Danforth, but Eddie Cicotte became its most infamous practitioner. By rubbing powder on a portion of the dirty, spit-laden ball that was customarily in play when he was on the mound, Cicotte added both an extra bit of weight and a glint of shininess to the horsehide, making its path to the plate all the more difficult for a batter to follow. The shine ball and the emery ball were among the pitches that were banned when a rule was instituted barring the application of any foreign substance to a ball.

Despite debuting at age 21, Ed Cicotte never led the AL in any pitching category before he reached age 33.

Ed Cicotte led the AL in wins in 1917, losses in 1918, and wins again in 1919. In 1917 and 1919, his White Sox won the pennant.

Above: *Rube Marquard led the NL in strikeouts in 1911, but his real forte was the off-speed pitch. He won 73 games in a three-year period with McGraw's Giants and became a vaudeville star during the winter. Despite injuries, the Hall-of-Famer won 201 games.*

Grover Cleveland Alexander of Philadelphia led the 1911 National League with 28 wins, which set the 20th-century major league rookie record. He also fanned 227 batters, another rookie record.

Walter Johnson of the Senators in 1912 won an AL single-season record 16 straight games. Smokey Joe Wood began his AL single-year record-tying skein of 16 straight wins even while Johnson's streak was still going.

Hurlers Streak, but Wrong Way

More significant mound winning and losing streaks were manufactured during the 1910s than any other decade in the game's history. Not only did Rube Marquard establish the all-time record for most consecutive victories with 19 and Walter Johnson and Smokey Joe Wood both fashion 16-game win skeins to set an American League record, but several monumental losing streaks also occurred during the period. In 1916, Jack Nabors of the A's dropped 19 straight games to tie the all-time single-season record. Two years earlier, Cleveland's Guy Morton lost his first 13 decisions in the majors, a record that stood until it was broken in 1980 by Terry Felton. And in 1910, after starting off the season with six wins in his first 11 decisions, Boston Braves hurler Cliff Curtis embarked on an all-time record losing streak that carried over into the following season. Curtis dropped his last 18 verdicts in 1910 and his first five decisions in 1911, giving him 23 straight defeats before he finally beat Brooklyn to end his tailspin.

Eddie Plank became the first southpaw to win 300 career games in 1915.

On May 6, 1917, Bob Groom of the Browns no-hit the White Sox in the second game of a doubleheader after earning a save in the first game.

Rube Marquard in 1912 set a major league single-season record by winning 19 straight games for the New York Giants.

According to today's rules for determining the winning pitcher in a game, the Giants' Rube Marquard would have had 20 consecutive wins in 1912 rather than 19.

The only pitcher to hurl a no-hitter in the majors but never register a shutout is Ed LaFitte, who tossed a 6-2 no-no for the Brooklyn Tip Tops of the Federal League on September 19, 1914.

1910s STRIKEOUTS		
1.	Walter Johnson	2,219
2.	Pete Alexander	1,539
3.	Hippo Vaughn	1,253
4.	Rube Marquard	1,141
5.	Eddie Cicotte	1,104
6.	Bob Groom	1,028
7.	Claude Hendrix	1,020
8.	Lefty Tyler	938
9.	Larry Cheney	926
10.	Willie Mitchell	913
11.	Eddie Plank	904
12.	Joe Wood	889
13.	Jeff Tesreau	880
14.	Dutch Leonard	873
15.	Red Ames	858
16.	Ray Caldwell	850
17.	Ed Walsh	835
18.	Jim Scott	810
19.	Chief Bender	776
20.	Dick Rudolph	756
21.	Rube Benton	750
22.	Hooks Dauss	739
23.	Dave Davenport	719
24.	Babe Adams	714
25.	Jack Coombs	711

Leonard's Sub-1.00 ERA Dutch Treat

Earned run averages were first made an official statistic in 1912. Two years later, Dutch Leonard of the Boston Red Sox paced the American League with an ERA that was calculated at the time as being 1.01. When a decision was made during the 1980s to round off fractions of an inning pitched to the next full inning, either higher or lower, Leonard's 222⅔ innings worked became 223 and his ERA was altered to 1.00. Researchers have since determined that Leonard was charged with a run that ought to have been viewed as unearned, reducing his ERA to 0.96. The baseball powers have not yet officially accepted Leonard's 0.96 figure, but most historians now recognize his mark to be the best single-season ERA in history by a hurler since the early 1880s, when the schedule was first lengthened to over 100 games. Tim Keefe in 1880 had the best ERA with an 0.86 mark, which he accumulated in 105 innings (in 12 games).

Three Finger Brown of the Chicago Cubs notched 13 saves in 1911, setting a National League record.

On May 2, 1917, neither Reds pitcher Fred Toney nor Cubs hurler Hippo Vaughn allowed a hit through nine innings. It was major league history's only double no-hit game. Cincinnati won on one hit in the 10th inning, 1-0.

The unsung workhorse of John McGraw's Giants in 1912 to 1916 was "Big Jeff" Tesreau (above), a 6'2" righthander who threw a hard spitter. Tesreau led the NL in starts twice and shutouts in 1914 as well as topping the league in ERA in his 1912 rookie year.

John McGraw chose rookie Jeff Tesreau over Christy Mathewson and Rube Marquard to pitch game one of the 1912 World Series.

Maybe Not
About Babe Ruth becoming an outfielder, Tris Speaker said: "Ruth made a grave mistake when he gave up pitching. Working once a week, he might have lasted a long time and become a great star."

Jeff Tesreau's 1912 season is one of the best ever for a first-year pitcher. He won 17 games for the pennant-winning Giants, tossed a no-hitter, and won the league ERA crown with a 1.96 mark.

New York Yankee hurler Russ Ford notched 26 wins in 1910, setting an AL rookie record. Ford introduced the "emery ball" delivery to the majors, and he beat the A's 1-0 in his debut on April 21 of that year.

1910s EARNED RUN AVERAGE	
1. Walter Johnson	1.60
2. Joe Wood	1.97
3. Ed Walsh	1.98
4. Pete Alexander	2.09
5. Carl Mays	2.15
6. Babe Ruth	2.19
7. Jeff Pfeffer	2.20
8. Dutch Leonard	2.22
9. Eddie Plank	2.25
10. Fred Toney	2.28
11. Eddie Cicotte	2.29
12. Jim Scott	2.30
13. Hippo Vaughn	2.31
14. Reb Russell	2.33
15. Stan Coveleski	2.37
16. Christy Mathewson	2.39
17. Wilbur Cooper	2.40
18. Carl Weilman	2.42
19. Jeff Tesreau	2.43
20. Joe Benz	2.43
21. Red Faber	2.43
22. Harry Coveleski	2.45
23. Slim Sallee	2.47
24. Chief Bender	2.47
25. Jim Bagby	2.49

In 1910, Bill Bailey of the St. Louis Browns was 0-17 as a starting pitcher and 2-18 overall.

Joe Oeschger of the Phils and Burleigh Grimes of Brooklyn battled to a 9-9, 20-inning tie on April 30, 1919.

Burleigh Grimes described Pete Alexander: "If anybody was ever a better pitcher than that guy, I wouldn't know what his name was. It was just a pleasure to watch him work, even though he was beating your brains out most of the time."

Above: *Stan Coveleski won 20 games four seasons in a row for the Cleveland Indians. He threw a spitball with great control and won 215 games with a career ERA of 2.88.*

1910s WINNING PERCENTAGE	
1. Joe Wood	.680
2. Pete Alexander	.675
3. Chief Bender	.663
4. Babe Ruth	.659
5. Eddie Plank	.657
6. Walter Johnson	.650
7. Doc Crandall	.646
8. Christy Mathewson	.643
9. Jack Coombs	.621
10. Jeff Tesreau	.615
11. Harry Coveleski	.614
12. Stan Coveleski	.607
13. Carl Mays	.600
14. Red Faber	.599
15. Vean Gregg	.596
16. Mordecai Brown	.594
17. Jeff Pfeffer	.593
18. Tom Seaton	.589
19. Bernie Boland	.588
20. Hippo Vaughn	.586
21. Rube Marquard	.583
22. Russ Ford	.582
23. Reb Russell	.579
24. Dutch Leonard	.578
25. Hooks Dauss	.576

Gregg Beset by Tribe Luck

A good case can be made that the Cleveland American League franchise has been jinxed ever since its inception. Addie Joss, the club's first great pitcher, died of meningitis on the eve of the 1911 season. That same year Cleveland fans first thrilled to Joss's heir apparent, Vean Gregg. The rookie southpaw won 23 games in 1911 and paced the American League with a 1.81 ERA. Gregg followed his stunning debut by winning 20 games in 1912 and again reaching the charmed circle in 1913. He then fell prey to the ill luck that has been visited on so many Cleveland rookie stars over the years and in particular southpaw pitchers. After winning 63 games in his first three seasons, Gregg had only 28 more major league wins left in his arm. His final two triumphs came with Washington in 1925 when he was past age 40. Prior to that season, Gregg had labored for six years in the minors to receive his final big league chance.

Babe Ruth made his major league debut on July 1, 1914, pitching seven innings for the Boston Red Sox to beat Cleveland.

In 1915, Jack Quinn and George Suggs combined to win 51 of the Federal League Baltimore Terrapins' 84 victories and make the Terrapins one of only three teams to feature two 25-game winners that did not win a flag in this century.

Square Deal

"In the old days, you know, a shake of your hand was your word and your honor. In those days, if anything was honest and upright, we'd say it was 'on the square.' Nowadays, they've even turned that word around. Now it means you don't belong, you're nothing. You're a 'square.' Where do they get that stuff, anyhow?"

—Chief Meyers,
Giants catcher

The 1912 World Series was the first to go the limit and be won by a team in its final at bat in the final game.

The all-time career record for most fielding chances received per game (11.4) is held by first sacker Tom Jones, who played last with Detroit in 1910.

1910s CATCHER GAMES	
1. Oscar Stanage	916
2. Ray Schalk	905
3. Bill Rariden	898
4. Bill Killefer	891
5. Chief Meyers	847

Tris Speaker in 1918 made a major league season record two unassisted double plays by an outfielder.

Tris Speaker led the American League in total chances by an outfielder for a record eighth straight season in 1919.

On July 19, 1911, center fielder Walter Carlisle of the Vernon Villagers in the Pacific Coast League performed an assisted triple play, the only one in history by an outfielder.

Cleveland's Terry Turner broke the season fielding average record at shortstop with a .973 mark in 1910. He was such a versatile player that the next year, 1911, he broke the season fielding average mark at third base with a .970 average.

The 1914 "Miracle Braves" were in last place on July 4, but went on to win the franchise's first flag of the century. The Braves won it even though they got out of the gate by winning only four of their first 22.

Peerless center fielder Tris Speaker (above) combined a strong arm with great range. He hit a career .344, led the AL in doubles eight times, stole 433 bases, and collected more than 3,500 total hits.

Czar Landis Cleans House

Many close to the game in the late 1910s felt the Black Sox Scandal was merely the tip of the iceberg and that there were a sizeable number of players who were not averse to dumping games for a cash inducement. Baseball moguls, without a clue how to clean their own house, hired United States District Judge Kenesaw Mountain Landis to be the game's first commissioner. Among his first acts as the new baseball czar, Landis barred the eight accused 1919 World Series fixers from the game even in the absence of conclusive evidence of their guilt. Few criticized Landis for this move or for any of his numerous subsequent lifetime expulsions over the next few years, for the game had entered the period of its greatest prosperity to date. Only years later did it emerge that several players barred by Landis, most notably pitcher Ray Fisher, were guilty of little more than insubordination.

The "Miracle Braves" of 1914 had one of the best defenses in the NL, led by such players as shortstop Rabbit Maranville. He set an NL record for putouts and the major league record for total chances at shortstop that year.

1910s CATCHER FIELDING AVERAGE	
1. George Gibson	.980
2. Ray Schalk	.979
3. John Henry	.978
4. Bill Killefer	.978
5. Frank Snyder	.977

Eight is Too Many?

When the heavily favored Chicago White Sox lost the 1919 World Series to the Cincinnati Reds, many who had seen the fall classic smelled something foul in the air. Not until late in the following campaign did it emerge that eight members of the Pale Hose had indeed taken money from gamblers to dump the Series. The eight included star hurlers Eddie Cicotte and Lefty Williams, shortstop Swede Risberg, first sacker Chick Gandil, third baseman Buck Weaver, outfielders Joe Jackson and Happy Felsch, and utility player Fred McMullin. Their sellout resulted in their wholesale expulsion from the game by commissioner Kenesaw Mountain Landis and the team being dubbed the Black Sox. Evidence has since been presented that several of the eight conspirators, most prominently Weaver, took no money from gamblers and may have been guilty of no more than failing to divulge they knew the Series was rigged. Jackson's role also remains a mystery. Although reputedly in on the fix, he led all Series participants in batting with a .375 average and 12 hits.

Above, left to right: *Honus Wagner, Tommy Leach, and Fred Clarke came together with the 1900 Pittsburgh Pirates and remained a trio until 1911. Wagner was easily the game's greatest shortstop ever; Leach was a speedy jack-of-all trades; and Clarke was a .300-hitting player-manager.*

"For over half a century I've had to live with the fact that I dropped a ball in the World Series. But nevertheless, those were wonderful years, and if I had the chance I'd gladly do it all over again, every bit of it."

—Fred Snodgrass

Major League owners first encountered Judge Landis in 1915 when he disallowed the Federal League's antitrust lawsuit.

At one point in his "cleaning up" of baseball, Judge Landis had banished 53 players from further competition.

1910s FIRST BASE FIELDING AVERAGE	
1. Ed Konetchy	.993
2. Chick Gandil	.992
3. Jake Daubert	.991
4. Stuffy McInnis	.991
5. Wally Pipp	.991

Bill Dahlen retired in 1911 with the records (since broken) for both the most games played (2,132) and the most assists (7,500) by a shortstop.

Cardinal second baseman Miller Huggins was caught stealing 36 times in 1914, an NL record. He successfully swiped 32 bases that season.

1910s FIRST BASE GAMES	
1. Ed Konetchy	1,421
2. Fred Merkle	1,360
3. Jake Daubert	1,347
4. Fred Luderus	1,308
5. Hal Chase	1,204

First sacker Ed Konetchy posted the top fielding average in his league eight times between 1910 and 1919.

Magee Suspends RBI Title Fight

Billy Evans was not the only umpire in the early 1900s to engage in fisticuffs with a player, but he was among the last. By the time Judge Landis took office as baseball's first commissioner in 1920, umpires were no longer fair game for irate players whenever they rendered an unpopular decision. Had Landis been made to review an incident like the one in July of 1911 involving Phillies outfielder Sherry Magee and rookie National League umpire Bill Finneran, he might well have banished Magee for life. Magee slugged Finneran after he was thrown out of the game for disputing a call. For what was described as his "brutal and unprovoked assault," Magee was suspended for the season and fined $200. However, league president Tom Lynch, himself a former umpire, lifted the suspension after Magee had been out of uniform just 36 days. Brief as the suspension was, however, considering the seriousness of Magee's offense, it probably cost him the NL RBI crown that year. He finished with 94 ribbies, just 13 behind the leader, Honus Wagner.

Charlie Comiskey made two of the greatest acquisitions in baseball history in 1915 while building the White Sox dynasty. Prior to the season, he bought Eddie Collins from Connie Mack's Philadelphia A's for $50,000. During the season, The Old Roman traded Braggo Roth and cash to Cleveland for Shoeless Joe Jackson.

1910s SECOND BASE GAMES	
1. Eddie Collins	1,440
2. Larry Doyle	1,280
3. Del Pratt	1,121
4. George Cutshaw	1,098
5. Otto Knabe	857

Ty Cobb in 1915 stole 96 bases, the major league record for a 154-game season.

New York's Fritz Maisel led the 1914 American League with 74 steals, setting a major league record for third basemen.

Giant Attitude

"Oh it's great to be young and a Giant."
—Larry Doyle, the Giants second baseman for more than 10 seasons

In 1914, Frank Crossin of the St. Louis Browns became the only catcher ever to perform two unassisted double plays in a season despite the fact that he was behind the plate in only 41 games.

The Giants' 347 steals in 1911 set a 20th-century major league record for a team.

1910s SECOND BASE FIELDING AVERAGE	
1. Eddie Collins	.969
2. Nap Lajoie	.965
3. George Cutshaw	.964
4. Johnny Evers	.962
5. Miller Huggins	.961

Twice in an 11-day period, Eddie Collins stole a major league single-game record six bases, on September 11 and again on September 22, 1912.

Above: *Eddie Collins played 25 years in the American League as its premier offensive and defensive second baseman. He led the league in runs scored from 1912 to 1914, led in steals four times, and starred in six World Series with the Athletics and White Sox.*

As a manager, John McGraw (above) taught his teams the same feisty style he used as a player. He was almost universally respected by his players. McGraw won nine league championships and three World Series in his 31 years managing the Giants.

John McGraw said to Connie Mack after the 1911 Series: "You have one of the greatest teams I've ever seen. It must be. I have a great team too, but you beat us."

After winning the AL pennant in 1918 for the third time in four seasons, the Boston Red Sox did not finish in the first division again until 1934.

In 1914, the New York Yankees became the last major league team to post a sub-.300 slugging average (.287); 13 years later the Yankees set a major league record with a .489 slugging average.

Cobb Trounces Umpire

Even though the rowdyism brought to the game by John McGraw and others of his type was curbed to a large extent by the 1910s, there were still isolated incidents. In 1912, Ty Cobb was suspended after he went into the stands in New York to fight with a fan. Cobb's pugnacious temperament got him into a multitude of fistfights with fellow players both on the field of play and off and even on at least one occasion with an umpire. Billy Evans, the most fastidious and also generally the most mild-mannered arbiter of his day, nevertheless locked horns with Cobb during a contest he was officiating. The argument grew so heated that Cobb challenged Evans to meet him under the stands after the game. To Cobb's surprise and pleasure, Evans accepted. The few witnesses to the bout later characterized it as quick and brutal, with Cobb as expected administering a sound thrashing to Evans. Following the custom of the times, Evans chose not to report the incident to the American League office.

The New York Giants began their game with St. Louis on May 13, 1911, by scoring a major league record 10 runs before the Cardinals could get the first out.

1910s THIRD BASE GAMES	
1. Frank Baker	1,250
2. Jimmy Austin	1,231
3. Larry Gardner	1,184
4. Red Smith	1,050
5. Mike Mowrey	967

1910s THIRD BASE FIELDING AVERAGE	
1. Heinie Groh	.966
2. Terry Turner	.961
3. Ossie Vitt	.958
4. Hans Lobert	.953
5. Charlie Deal	.952

The 1911 Boston Braves posted a home record of 19-54, the worst in this century by an NL team.

On July 19, 1915, catcher Steve O'Neill of Cleveland suffered in silence as a record eight Washington Senators stole bases against him in the first inning. On July 7, 1919, Giant catcher Mike Gonzalez allowed eight stolen bases in a single inning.

First sacker George Burns was dropped by Detroit after he hit .226 in 1917; the following year he batted .352 for Philadelphia to finish second in the American League in batting.

In an effort to produce more scoring, both leagues introduced a new "jack-rabbit" ball during the 1910 season.

In 1918, owing to schedule inequities created by the war-shortened season, Cleveland played 11 more games on the road than Boston did and lost the AL pennant to the Red Sox by 1½ games.

Early Black Stars Excel Against Major League Competition

Above: *Everett Scott was a fine-fielding shortstop for the Red Sox and the Yankees. He was able to keep his job with five pennant-winning clubs despite compiling batting averages as low as .201 (in 1915) and .232 (in 1916).*

Although the first organized black league, the Negro National League, was not founded until 1920, there were a number of loosely organized black federations during the early part of the century. In the main, though, black players and teams most enjoyed the head-on-head competition with their all-white major league peers. It was in these exhibition contests that black stars earned their greatest recognition. John Lloyd, for one, became known as "The Black Honus Wagner" after white audiences saw him perform at shortstop during the 1910s with the New York Lincoln Giants and the Chicago American Giants. In a like vein, Joe Rogan, a hard-throwing black righthander, was nicknamed "Bullet Joe" after Bullet Joe Bush, a hard-throwing white major league righthander. Other great black pitchers of the era, particularly those of Cuban heritage such as Cristobel Torriente, were seldom seen, however, by white fans. Of those who faced major league hitters with some frequency, Smokey Joe Williams, who was nicknamed after Smokey Joe Wood, was rated by many observers as the best pre-1920 black hurler. Already 35 years old when the first organized black circuit formed in 1920, Williams nevertheless put in 13 seasons in the Black National League and its descendants.

Brooklyn owner Charlie Ebbets announced why he built Ebbets Field: "Brooklyn has supported a losing team better than any other city on Earth. Such a patronage deserves every convenience and comfort that can be provided at a baseball park, and that is what I hope to provide."

Owing to World War I, the 1918 season was ended on Labor Day, September 2. The Red Sox triumphed in the six-game World Series that year, which began on September 5 and ended on September 11. The 1919 season was abbreviated to 140 games because of the war.

1910s SHORTSTOP FIELDING AVERAGE	
1. Everett Scott	.963
2. George McBride	.951
3. Honus Wagner	.948
4. Joe Tinker	.945
5. Mickey Doolan	.944

Babe Ruth, still a part-time pitcher, tied for the AL homer lead with 11 in 1918. In 1919, the Boston Red Sox finished sixth in Ruth's last year with the club as Ruth hit 29 of the team's 33 home runs.

1910s SHORTSTOP GAMES	
1. Donie Bush	1,448
2. Art Fletcher	1,177
3. George McBride	1,121
4. Roger Peckinpaugh	1,010
5. Mickey Doolan	915

Earl Mack of the A's in 1910 was the first son to play in the major leagues for his father (manager Connie Mack).

1910s OUTFIELD FIELDING AVERAGE	
1. Amos Strunk	.981
2. Max Flack	.973
3. Tommy Leach	.973
4. Happy Felsch	.973
5. Sam Crawford	.973
6. Sherry Magee	.972
7. Chief Wilson	.972
8. Dode Paskert	.972
9. Possum Whitted	.972
10. Edd Roush	.971
11. Hy Myers	.971
12. Max Carey	.970
13. Cy Williams	.970
14. Lee Magee	.969
15. Rube Oldring	.969

Pirates Plunder Glove Mark

As late as 1911, it was a rare team that made fewer than 250 errors in a season, and many clubs still averaged more than two errors a game. In 1911, the St. Louis Browns committed 358 bobbles, six other teams also topped 300 miscues, and the record for the fewest errors (194) and the best fielding average (.969) was held by the 1906 Chicago Cubs. But in 1912, the Pittsburgh Pirates shattered all then-existing team fielding marks when they collected just 169 errors and posted a .972 fielding average. As an illustration of just how much better the Pirates were defensively than the game's other 15 clubs, the New York Yankees made 382 errors in 1912, the Philadelphia A's led the American League in fewest miscues with 263, and only one team, the Philadelphia Phillies (.963), finished within 12 points of Pittsburgh in fielding average. Even individually, the Pirates were so superior that only two regulars, second baseman Alex McCarthy (.962) and left fielder Max Carey (.961), had lower fielding averages than the Phillies' fielding average, which was the second best in the majors that year.

The Philadelphia Athletics suffered the worst fall from first place by any club in baseball history. In 1914, Philadelphia won the AL flag with a 99-53 record. In 1915, Connie Mack's charges fell to last place with a 43-109 record—down an all-time record 56 games.

Above: *The Philadelphia A's star "$100,000" infield of (left to right) Stuffy McInnis, Frank "Home Run" Baker, Jack Barry, and Eddie Collins. After winning three World Series between 1910 to 1914, Connie Mack traded or sold all but McInnis, precipitating the team's fall to last place.*

The last major league team to make more than 300 errors in a season was the 1916 Philadelphia Athletics, who committed 314 miscues in 154 games.

The only player who amassed the most career assists at his position yet failed to make the Hall of Fame is Deacon McGuire, whose 1,859 assists lead all catchers. McGuire played from 1884 to 1912.

1910s OUTFIELD GAMES	
1. Tris Speaker	1,430
2. Harry Hooper	1,424
3. Clyde Milan	1,380
4. Zack Wheat	1,324
5. Ty Cobb	1,307
6. Duffy Lewis	1,306
7. Dode Paskert	1,258
8. Max Carey	1,217
9. Burt Shotton	1,198
10. Jack Graney	1,190
11. Joe Jackson	1,135
12. Frank Schulte	1,114
13. George Burns	1,053
14. Bob Bescher	1,039
15. Sherry Magee	1,034

William Taft started the custom of the President of the United States throwing out the first ball at the 1910 Washington home opener.

*Heywood Broun wrote in **The New York Times** in 1914 that "it may be true that a person can do only one thing at a time but this rule does not hold true for Larry Doyle on his good days."*

Above: *Pitchers Harry (left) and Stan Coveleski's careers dovetailed nicely. Harry won 20 games for Detroit in 1914, 1915, and 1916 while younger brother Stan won 20 in four consecutive seasons with Cleveland starting in 1918. They were often asked to pitch against each other, but never would.*

Miscues Still Abound

The Pirates' watershed fielding performance in 1912 proved to be a quirk rather than a harbinger of a general improvement in fielding stats. For several years afterward, teams regularly continued to make upwards of 300 errors a season. In 1914, the Cubs had not one but two infielders, shortstop Red Corriden and Heinie Zimmerman, who had fielding averages below .900. Two years earlier, right fielder Guy Zinn of the Yankees registered an .893 fielding average, the last sub-.900 fielding average in history by a regular outfielder. In 1916, A's third sacker Charlie Pick became the last regular until Butch Hobson in 1978 to fall below the .900 mark when he finished with an .899 fielding average. In 1916, Pick's club became the last to make over 300 errors in a season as improvements in the construction of gloves during the latter part of the decade resulted in a sharp drop in both runs and miscues as the dead-ball era wound to a close.

By mutual agreement the Coveleski brothers, Stan and Harry, never pitched against each other in a major league game.

1910s MANAGER WINS	
1. John McGraw	889
2. Hughie Jennings	790
3. Clark Griffith	770
4. Connie Mack	710
5. George Stallings	595
6. Miller Huggins	486
7. Fred Clarke	484
8. Wilbert Robinson	445
9. Pat Moran	419
10. Frank Chance	404

The Polo Grounds—the home of the New York Giants—was ravaged by fire before the 1911 season and was rebuilt by Giants owner John Brush. It was New York's first steel-and-concrete ballpark.

Cincinnati outfielder Edd Roush said about the 1919 World Series and the Black Sox: "One thing that's always overlooked in the whole mess is that we could have beaten them no matter what the circumstances!"

1910s MANAGER WINNING PERCENTAGE	
1. Bill Carrigan	.612
2. John McGraw	.598
3. Pat Moran	.582
4. Pants Rowland	.578
5. Frank Chance	.544
6. Fred Clarke	.529
7. Hughie Jennings	.529
8. Clark Griffith	.515
9. Red Dooin	.514
10. Lee Fohl	.513

The majority of the minor leagues shut down in mid-1918 due to World War I.

The 1912 New York Yankees featured the first brother battery, catcher Homer Thompson (who appeared in only one major league game) and his brother, hurler Tommy Thompson.

Helen Britton became the first woman to own a major league team when she took control of the St. Louis Cardinals in 1911.

Comiskey Conducts Experiment Under Light

The first baseball game under artificial light was played on September 2, 1880, between two Boston department store teams barely a year after Thomas Edison invented the incandescent lamp, but the illumination was still too rudimentary for any major league team to consider adopting the idea of installing lights in its home park. By the early 1900s, however, George Cahill had devised a portable lighting system that was both good enough and economic enough to entice White Sox owner Charlie Comiskey to stage an exhibition game under artificial glare at his new stadium, Comiskey Park. Some 20,000 Chicagoans watched two local amateur teams play a full nine innings under 20 different 137,000-candlepower arc lights on a summer night in 1910, but Comiskey remained unconvinced that Cahill's contrivance had any future. Hence it would be another 25 years before Cahill's dream became a reality on the major league front.

A rule giving a runner three bases if a fielder stops a ball with a thrown glove or cap was adopted by organized baseball in 1914.

The 1919 World Series was extended to a best-of-nine affair for extra revenue, and the Reds triumphed in eight games.

Above, left to right: *Ty Cobb, Joe Jackson, and Sam Crawford. Crawford hit more triples than any player in history (317); Cobb is second on the list with 297. Jackson ranks 26th with 168, though he did lead the AL three times in three-baggers.*

1910s TEAM WINS		
	WON	LOST
1. New York-NL	889	597
2. Boston-AL	857	624
3. Chicago-NL	826	668
4. Chicago-AL	798	692
5. Detroit-AL	790	704
6. Philadelphia-NL	762	717
7. Washington-AL	755	737
8. Cleveland-AL	742	747
9. Pittsburgh-NL	736	751
10. Cincinnati-NL	717	779
11. Philadelphia-AL	710	774
12. New York-AL	701	780
13. Brooklyn-NL	696	787
14. Boston-NL	666	815
15. St. Louis-NL	652	830
16. St. Louis-AL	597	892
17. Chicago-FL	173	133
18. Buffalo-FL	154	149
19. Pittsburgh-FL	150	153
20. St. Louis-FL	149	156
21. Kansas City-FL	148	156
22. Brooklyn-FL	147	159
23. Baltimore-FL	131	177
24. Indianapolis-FL	88	65
25. Newark-FL	80	72

1910s TEAM WINNING PERCENTAGE	
1. New York-NL	.598
2. Boston-AL	.579
3. Indianapolis-FL	.575
4. Chicago-FL	.565
5. Chicago-NL	.553
6. Chicago-AL	.536
7. Detroit-AL	.529
8. Newark-FL	.526
9. Philadelphia-NL	.515
10. Buffalo-FL	.508
11. Washington-AL	.506
12. Cleveland-AL	.498
13. Pittsburgh-FL	.495
14. Pittsburgh-NL	.495
15. St. Louis-FL	.489
16. Kansas City-FL	.487
17. Brooklyn-FL	.480
18. Cincinnati-NL	.479
19. Philadelphia-AL	.478
20. New York-AL	.473
21. Brooklyn-NL	.469
22. Boston-NL	.450
23. St. Louis-NL	.440
24. Baltimore-FL	.425
25. St. Louis-AL	.401

Chapter 5
The 1920s

Williams Pulls Weight for Phillies

For the first decade of Babe Ruth's reign as the game's home run king, his closest counterpart in the National League was Cy Williams, an outfielder with the Chicago Cubs and Philadelphia Phillies. Williams won his first NL four-bagger crown in 1916 and his fourth and last in 1927 when he was just two months shy of his 40th birthday. Three years later, he became the first player to retire with more than 250 career home runs. A sinewy lefthanded pull-hitter, Williams benefitted from playing in the Baker Bowl for much of his career. The Phillies' home park had the shortest right field porch in the majors. For at least half his games every year, Williams had a target that was only 280 feet from the plate. Other Phillies hitters, though, could not seem to take nearly the same advantage from it. In 1927, Williams's league-leading total of 30 home runs represented more than half of the Phillies' total of 57.

During the 1920s, both leagues had at least one 200-hit man in every season, although the National League just barely met the standard in 1926 when Eddie Brown topped the loop with 201 safeties.

Above: In 1923, 35-year-old Cy Williams of Philadelphia surprised baseball by smacking 41 home runs when the next nearest competitor in the home run race, Jack Fournier of Brooklyn, was only able to clear the fences 22 times.

In 1927, Phillies outfielder Cy Williams had 30 homers but just 98 ribbies to become the first 30-homer man to notch fewer than 100 RBI.

Philadelphia's Cy Williams topped the NL in 1920 with 15 homers, 39 fewer than Babe Ruth socked as the AL leader.

Cy Williams, an outfielder for the Cubs and Phillies from 1912 to 1930, collected just 41 pinch hits in his career but 11 of them were home runs, making him the first player to notch 10 or more pinch dingers.

Lee Allen explained Rogers Hornsby: "He was frank to the point of being cruel, and subtle as a belch."

1920s GAMES	
1. Sam Rice	1,496
2. Charlie Grimm	1,458
3. Rogers Hornsby	1,430
4. Harry Heilmann	1,417
5. Joe Sewell	1,404
6. Babe Ruth	1,399
7. Frankie Frisch	1,378
8. Joe Judge	1,359
9. George Kelly	1,351
10. George Sisler	1,326
11. Charlie Jamieson	1,310
12. Bob Meusel	1,294
13. Dave Bancroft	1,264
14. Marty McManus	1,257
15. Bucky Harris	1,251
16. Ken Williams	1,249
17. Jimmy Dykes	1,247
18. Max Carey	1,244
19. Cy Williams	1,239
Wally Gerber	1,239
21. Lu Blue	1,230
22. Curt Walker	1,224
23. Bibb Falk	1,192
24. Wally Pipp	1,189
25. Pie Traynor	1,186

Above: *Rogers Hornsby batted over .360 for three teams during three straight years: .361 for the '27 Giants, .387 for the '28 Braves, and .380 for the '29 Cubs. He also had at least 20 homers and 90 RBI for each of the three clubs.*

In 1925, Rogers Hornsby set a National League record with a .756 slugging average.

In 1925, Rogers Hornsby won his sixth straight National League batting crown (.403). He was also the first Triple Crown winner of the decade, leading the loop in homers (39) and RBI (143).

In 1921, three members of the St. Louis Cardinals— Rogers Hornsby, Austin McHenry, and Jack Fournier—finished 1-2-3 in the NL batting title race.

Glenn Wright Man for Buc Shortstop Job

In the 20th century, only three shortstops have claimed a National League batting title— Honus Wagner, Arky Vaughan, and Dick Groat—and all three did it while playing for the Pittsburgh Pirates. In the 1920s, the Pirates had another offensive-minded shortstop, Glenn Wright, who was never a batting leader but for many years held the record for the most home runs by a National League shortfielder. In addition, Wright was the first player in senior loop history to compile 100 or more RBI in each of his first two seasons. As a rookie in 1924, Wright registered 111 ribbies and the following year he hiked his total to 121. Early in his career, Wright was also a fine defensive shortstop, but a shoulder injury suffered while playing handball idled him for almost the entire 1929 season and permanently impaired his throwing. Nonetheless Wright rebounded in 1930 to club 22 home runs, the pre-Ernie Banks NL mark for shortstops.

Fetch
Rogers Hornsby revealed why he preferred baseball to golf: "When I hit a ball I want someone else to go chase it."

In 1922, Rogers Hornsby set NL records with 42 homers, 152 RBI, and .722 slugging average. His .401 batting average made him the first National League player since 1901 to top the .400 mark.

Rogers Hornsby has the two top on-base percentages in NL history: .507 in 1924 for St. Louis and .498 in 1928 for Boston.

In mid-1925, Rogers Hornsby became the player-manager of the Cardinals. He managed the Redbirds to the franchise's first championship in 1926. Hornsby's personality was such, nevertheless, that he still was traded before the '27 season.

Pirate shortstop Glenn Wright missed getting 100 RBI in his third consecutive season, in 1926, when he had 77, but he rebounded in 1927 with 105 RBI.

1920s RUNS		
1.	Babe Ruth	1,365
2.	Rogers Hornsby	1,195
3.	Sam Rice	1,001
4.	Frankie Frisch	992
5.	Harry Heilmann	962
6.	Lu Blue	896
7.	George Sisler	894
8.	Charlie Jamieson	868
9.	Tris Speaker	830
	Ty Cobb	830
11.	Max Carey	818
12.	Joe Sewell	813
13.	Ken Williams	805
14.	Joe Judge	765
15.	Pie Traynor	764
	Bob Meusel	764
17.	Marty McManus	741
18.	Dave Bancroft	740
19.	George Kelly	736
20.	Cy Williams	721
	Bucky Harris	721
22.	Goose Goslin	717
23.	Jim Bottomley	711
24.	Edd Roush	698
25.	Eddie Collins	682

In 1922, when Browns outfielder Ken Williams (above) led the American League in home runs with 39, he was able to slug 32 round-trippers in Sportsman's Park in St. Louis. Williams also stole 30 bases that year to become a "30-30" man. He finished second to Babe Ruth in home runs during three different seasons.

1920s HITS		
1.	Rogers Hornsby	2,085
2.	Sam Rice	2,010
3.	Harry Heilmann	1,924
4.	George Sisler	1,900
5.	Frankie Frisch	1,808
6.	Babe Ruth	1,734
7.	Joe Sewell	1,698
8.	Charlie Jamieson	1,623
9.	Charlie Grimm	1,570
10.	George Kelly	1,569
11.	Joe Judge	1,567
12.	Bob Meusel	1,565
13.	Pie Traynor	1,496
	Tris Speaker	1,496
15.	Edd Roush	1,479
16.	Ty Cobb	1,476
17.	Goose Goslin	1,436
18.	Ken Williams	1,428
19.	Dave Bancroft	1,420
20.	Baby Doll Jacobson	1,398
21.	Bing Miller	1,387
22.	Max Carey	1,381
23.	Marty McManus	1,360
24.	Jim Bottomley	1,354
25.	Bibb Falk	1,352

Bill Klem, one of the greatest umpires in history, said to a green pitcher protesting a ball call: "Young man, when you pitch a strike, Mr. Hornsby will let you know."

Williams Shifts Into High Gear

When Cleveland manager Lou Boudreau devised the "Williams Shift" in 1946 to combat Ted Williams's lefty pull-hitting prowess, he was not inventing something new. Boudreau was actually resurrecting a version of the first Williams shift, which had been employed in the early 1920s to thwart Ken Williams. In 1922, the lefty-swinging outfielder nearly spearheaded the St. Louis Browns to their first pennant when he topped the American League with 39 home runs and 155 RBI. Both figures will always stand as a Browns' club record now that the team has moved from St. Louis to Baltimore. Like his contemporary namesake, Cy Williams, the National League slugging star, the Browns' bomber played most of his career in the enormous shadow of Babe Ruth. Even in his peak year of 1922, Williams emerged from Ruth's umbra largely because the Babe started the season under suspension for an illegal barnstorming trip the previous fall. Despite not becoming a full-time regular until he was 30 years old, Williams amassed 1,552 hits and a .319 career batting average.

The St. Louis Browns in 1922 became the first team in major league history to have four 100-RBI men. Outfielder Ken Williams led the AL with 155 RBI, second baseman Marty McManus had 109, first baseman George Sisler had 105, and outfielder Baby Doll Jacobson had 102.

Above: *Lefty O'Doul was another in a line of 1920s position players who started as pitchers. O'Doul pitched in the Pacific Coast League, gathering a 25-win season before his arm went dead. He moved to the outfield in 1925, and by 1929 was setting the single-season NL hit record (254) for the Phillies.*

Philadelphia Foursome Fashions 200 Hits

In 1929, the first of three successive seasons that would constitute the greatest offensive deluge ever, the Philadelphia Phillies led the majors with a .309 batting average. The Phils were paced by left fielder Lefty O'Doul, who topped the National League in batting with a .398 figure and compiled 254 hits to set a new loop record. Three other Phils also had 200 or more hits, making the club the only one in history with four 200-hit men. Right fielder Chuck Klein collected 219 safe blows, third baseman Pinky Whitney had 207, and second sacker Fresco Thompson notched 202. Thompson was the least likely member of the quartet. O'Doul, Klein, and Whitney all had several more fine seasons after 1929, but Thompson amassed just 762 hits in his career and only 183 after 1929. Despite their wealth of offensive punch in 1929, the Phillies finished fifth in the NL, mostly because the Philadelphia pitching staff gave up a National League-high 6.13 team ERA.

Baseball Magazine *reviewed Ken Williams in 1922: "The seeming miracle has happened. Another player rose to the occasion, and did as well as Ruth had ever done in the first weeks of the season. Kenneth Williams was the stalwart figure who picked up the king's idle bludgeon in the true kingly fashion."*

In 1929, second baseman George Grantham of the Pirates collected 90 RBI and 93 walks in just 349 at bats.

In 1929, Philadelphia A's second baseman Max Bishop hit just .232 but led the majors in walks with 128.

Smokey Joe Wood set a record in 1921 for the most RBI by a player with under 200 at bats when he totaled 60 ribbies in 194 at bats.

1920s DOUBLES	
1. Rogers Hornsby	405
2. Tris Speaker	397
Harry Heilmann	397
4. Joe Sewell	358
5. Sam Rice	346
6. Bob Meusel	338
7. George Burns	317
8. Babe Ruth	314
9. George Kelly	304
10. George Sisler	297
11. Ty Cobb	293
12. Joe Judge	290
13. Frankie Frisch	277
14. Jimmy Dykes	276
15. Bibb Falk	275
16. Marty McManus	273
17. Charlie Jamieson	269
18. Ken Williams	265
19. Bing Miller	264
20. Baby Doll Jacobson	262
21. Jim Bottomley	261
22. Charlie Grimm	257
23. Lu Blue	248
24. Joe Dugan	241
25. Goose Goslin	240

The 1925 St. Louis Browns were the first team to have six players who each hit 10 or more home runs.

Bengal Bats Blast AL

In Harry Heilmann (.394) and Ty Cobb (.389), the Detroit Tigers had the American League's two top hitters in 1921. The Bengals third outfielder, Bobby Veach, hit .338. Catcher Johnny Bassler finished at .307, first sacker Lu Blue at .308, and third baseman Bob Jones at .303. Second baseman Ralph Young (.299) and shortstop Donie Bush (.281) were the only regulars who fell below .300 as the club hit .316 as a unit to set an all-time American League record. For all the offense the Tigers generated, though, they could finish no better than sixth, 11 games below .500. Indifferent pitching and fielding were the easy culprits to cite, but the St. Louis Browns, who had an even higher staff ERA—4.62 to the Tigers 4.40—and stood only a point higher in fielding average, finished in third place, 9½ games ahead of Detroit. The more likely cause for the team's poor showing was Ty Cobb, then still finding his way in his first year as a player-manager after replacing the popular Hughie Jennings at the reins.

In 1922, first baseman Ray Grimes of the Cubs set an all-time record when he collected at least one RBI in 17 consecutive games played by him.

The Pirates could finish no better than fourth in 1928 despite leading the majors in batting by a 13-point margin with a .309 average.

From 1921 to 1927, Detroit's Harry Heilmann (above) hit a composite .380, capturing four batting titles, with averages of .394, .403, .393, and .398. He also topped 200 hits four times, helping him to retire with the 11th highest career batting average, at .342.

Rogers Hornsby as a player and a manager had many detractors, but as Clyde Sukeforth said of Hornsby: "When he had a bat in his hands, he had nothing but admirers."

In 1926, all three of Detroit's regular outfielders—Heinie Manush, Harry Heilmann, and Bob Fothergill—hit .367 or better.

Harry Heilmann was waived out of the American League after he hit .344 for Detroit in 1929.

Jim Murray wrote about Babe Ruth's gargantuan appetite: "His stomach used to rumble in the outfield if the other team had a big inning."

Paul Strand of Salt Lake City in the Pacific Coast League collected an organized baseball single-season record 325 hits in 1923.

Ty Cobb took over first place on the career runs scored list for the first time when he tallied his 1,741st run on May 25, 1923, to put him one ahead of Honus Wagner.

1920s TRIPLES	
1. Sam Rice	133
2. Rogers Hornsby	115
3. George Sisler	111
Edd Roush	111
5. Goose Goslin	110
6. Pie Traynor	109
7. Frankie Frisch	107
8. Curt Walker	106
9. Jim Bottomley	104
10. Joe Judge	101
Harry Heilmann	101
12. Rabbit Maranville	99
13. Wally Pipp	87
Bob Meusel	87
Charlie Grimm	87
Lu Blue	87
17. Ty Cobb	85
18. Earle Combs	84
19. Babe Ruth	82
20. Kiki Cuyler	81
21. Johnny Mostil	80
Irish Meusel	80
23. Max Carey	77
24. Baby Doll Jacobson	76
25. Ross Youngs	75
Bing Miller	75

1920s HOME RUNS

1.	Babe Ruth	467
2.	Rogers Hornsby	250
3.	Cy Williams	202
4.	Ken Williams	190
5.	Bob Meusel	146
	Lou Gehrig	146
	Jim Bottomley	146
8.	Harry Heilmann	142
9.	Hack Wilson	137
10.	George Kelly	134
11.	Jack Fournier	121
12.	Al Simmons	115
13.	Goose Goslin	108
14.	Irish Meusel	97
15.	Marty McManus	91
	George Harper	91
17.	Bing Miller	85
	Chick Hafey	85
19.	Zack Wheat	81
	Travis Jackson	81
	Gabby Hartnett	81
22.	Joe Hauser	80
23.	Tilly Walker	79
24.	George Sisler	78
25.	Frankie Frisch	77

When Tigers rookie Al Wingo hit .370 in 1925, he had the lowest average in the Detroit outfield, trailing Harry Heilmann's .393 and Ty Cobb's .378.

Although Ty Cobb (above) failed to win a batting title in the 1920s, from 1920 to 1928 he never fell below .323, topping at .401 in 1922, 19 points behind league-leader George Sisler's .420.

Wingo, Others Explode On and Off Scene

The 1920s were loaded with odd feats and performers. There was Dick Spalding, a soccer player who didn't turn to professional baseball until he was nearly 34 years old and hit .296 for the Philadelphia Phillies in 1927, his first pro season. A year earlier it had been Cuckoo Christensen, who hit .350 and nearly won the National League batting title as a rookie only to find himself back in the minors before the following season was out. In 1925, Dick Burrus was the story in the National League after he came out of nowhere to hit .340 and notch 200 hits, nearly half of his career total. (Burrus had batted .185 the year before.) The oddest note of all was struck by Al Wingo, likewise in 1925, when he batted .370 in his first season as a regular outfielder with the Tigers. It was also to be Wingo's only campaign of regular duty, gaining him the record for the highest batting average by a one-year regular.

Reliable Lou Replaces Merkle

Legend would have it that Lou Gehrig's record consecutive games played streak began one day when Wally Pipp, the New York Yankees regular first baseman at the time, had a headache and Larrupin' Lou replaced him. The truth, however, is that the streak had its inception a day earlier when Gehrig pinch hit for Yankees shortstop Pee Wee Wanninger. Pipp's replacement on the afternoon he came down with a headache was not Lou, but it was Fred Merkle, who was in turn replaced by Gehrig after the heat got to Merkle. At one point in Gehrig's streak he played left field, freeing Babe Ruth to pitch, and on another occasion Lou, while suffering from a back injury, was penciled in the lineup at shortstop and leadoff hitter to keep his streak alive and then replaced by a pinch runner after he started off the game with a single. In all, Gehrig played in 2,130 straight games.

On May 1, 1920, Babe Ruth hit his first homer as a Yankee off Boston's Herb Pennock, who was the Babe's teammate with the Red Sox. The two would become teammates two years later with the Yankees.

714 × 4
"I have only one superstition. I make sure to touch all the bases when I hit a home run."
—Babe Ruth

Above: *In 1927, Yankees Babe Ruth (right) and Lou Gehrig finished as the top two in the major leagues in home runs, runs batted in, slugging average, and runs scored.*

In 1923, Babe Ruth collected a record 170 walks.

The 1920 New York Yankees were the first team in history to collect more home runs than stolen bases.

Lou Gehrig's 175 RBI in 1927 set an American League record.

In 1921, Babe Ruth hit his 137th career homer, breaking Roger Connor's mark of 136.

In 1921, Babe Ruth set a major league RBI record with 171, breaking Sam Thompson's mark of 166 set back in 1887. The Bambino also set records that year with 59 homers, 457 total bases, and 177 runs scored.

Lee Allen, baseball historian, wrote about Babe Ruth: "For almost two decades he battered fences with such regularity that baseball's basic structure was eventually pounded into a different shape."

In 1920, Babe Ruth set major league records with 54 homers, 158 runs scored, an .847 slugging average, and 241 runs produced.

The New York Yankees set a 20th-century major league record in 1927 with 975 runs scored.

1920s RUNS BATTED IN	
1. Babe Ruth	1,331
2. Rogers Hornsby	1,153
3. Harry Heilmann	1,133
4. Bob Meusel	1,005
5. George Kelly	923
6. Jim Bottomley	885
7. Ken Williams	860
8. George Sisler	827
9. Joe Sewell	821
Goose Goslin	821
11. Pie Traynor	804
12. Charlie Grimm	748
13. Joe Judge	739
14. Marty McManus	738
Frankie Frisch	738
16. Ty Cobb	726
17. Tris Speaker	724
Sam Rice	724
19. Bibb Falk	720
20. Cy Williams	715
21. Al Simmons	712
22. Baby Doll Jacobson	700
23. Irish Meusel	698
24. Bing Miller	684
25. Wally Pipp	674

Bombers Blossom at First

When the 1920s opened, most of the leading sluggers and hit makers, as in the previous three decades, were outfielders. With the exception of George Sisler there remained a notable lack of first basemen who could both hit for average and produce an occasional long ball. During the 1910s, Wally Pipp of the Yankees had been the only first baseman to win an undisputed home run crown in either the American League or National League, and neither of the two gateway guardians who won hitting crowns, Hal Chase and Jake Daubert, were power hitters. By the end of the 1920s, however, first base was the position with the greatest representation on the batting and slugging charts in both leagues. The senior loop featured Jim Bottomley and Bill Terry while the junior circuit had Jimmie Foxx and Lou Gehrig; only a cut behind these four were Dale Alexander, who set a rookie record in 1929 when he amassed 137 RBI; Lew Fonseca, the 1929 AL batting champ; Don Hurst (31 home runs and 125 RBI); and George Kelly, earlier in the decade both a home run and an RBI leader.

First baseman George Sisler broke into the bigs as a southpaw hurler, notching two complete-game victories over hall-of-famer Walter Johnson.

In his only season as a regular at one position, Lew Fonseca paced the AL with a .369 average, while collecting 209 hits.

1920s STOLEN BASES	
1. Max Carey	346
2. Frankie Frisch	310
3. Sam Rice	254
4. George Sisler	214
5. Kiki Cuyler	210
6. Eddie Collins	180
7. Johnny Mostil	175
8. Bucky Harris	166
9. Cliff Heathcote	145
10. Jack Smith	144
11. Ken Williams	142
Edd Roush	142
13. Bob Meusel	130
14. Pie Traynor	129
15. Ty Cobb	126
Sparky Adams	126
17. Rabbit Maranville	124
18. Ross Youngs	118
19. Joe Judge	114
George Grantham	114
21. Goose Goslin	108
Lu Blue	108
23. Carson Bigbee	105
24. Charlie Jamieson	100
25. Bing Miller	98

Giants first baseman George Kelly (above), respected more for his fielding talents than his hitting, nonetheless set two NL offensive records in 1924, including a power binge in which he hit seven home runs in six games, with at least one in each game.

Bubbles Pops .353 for Crown

Before 1926 every position on the diamond, including pitcher, had furnished at least one batting titlist with a single exception. As yet there had never been a catcher who reigned as batting king. The closest to it had been King Kelly, who had won two hitting crowns in the 1880s while shuttling between catcher and several other positions. But 1926 saw the first full-blooded catcher triumph in a batting race when Cincinnati backstopper Bubbles Hargrave hit .353 to edge out rookie teammate Cuckoo Christensen's .350 mark and top the National League. Purists were anguished by the fact that Hargrave had only 326 at bats—for that matter, Christensen had just 329—but the rule at the time required only that a player participate in two-thirds of his team's games to be eligible, and Hargrave qualified since he appeared in 105 of the Reds' 157 contests. A steady .300 hitter throughout his career, Hargrave was the first backstopper to play 10 or more seasons and finish with a .300-plus career average (.310).

The Detroit Tigers set an AL record in 1921 when they posted a .316 team batting average; remarkably the Tigers finished in sixth place that year.

In 1925, Kiki Cuyler of Pittsburgh became the last player to rap as many as 26 triples in a season.

Tell It Like It Is

When asked by team owner Judge Fuchs whether his club could win the pennant, Braves player-manager Rogers Hornsby responded: "Not with these humpty-dumpties."

In 1926, Bill Diester of Salina in the Southwestern League hit .444, the highest average in this century by a batting title winner with 400 at bats in an American-based minor league.

The American League compiled a record .292 batting average in 1921.

Above: *Kiki Cuyler captured four stolen base titles in his 18-year career, winning three titles in a row from 1928 to 1930, to become the first major league player since Max Carey to win as many as three in a row.*

1920s STRIKEOUTS

1.	Babe Ruth	795
2.	George Kelly	571
3.	Bob Meusel	556
4.	Jimmy Dykes	497
5.	Aaron Ward	439
6.	Rogers Hornsby	431
7.	Marty McManus	414
8.	Bernie Friberg	412
9.	Cy Williams	401
10.	Hack Wilson	388
11.	Lou Gehrig	351
12.	George Grantham	343
13.	Kiki Cuyler	341
14.	Heinie Sand	340
15.	Jim Bottomley	337
16.	Johnny Mostil	330
17.	Harry Heilmann	324
18.	Joe Dugan	314
19.	Lu Blue	311
20.	Bucky Harris	306
21.	Travis Jackson	299
22.	Ray Powell	298
	Rabbit Maranville	298
24.	Hod Ford	297
25.	Ross Youngs	289

When catcher Bubbles Hargrave was awarded the National League batting title in 1926 despite having only 326 at bats, Pittsburgh backstopper Earl Smith ranked third in hitting with a .346 average in just 292 at bats.

George Sisler, wrote Robert Smith, "spent 10 years building up the fiction that he could not hit a high inside pitch. He used to strike out on such pitches occasionally, just so he could count on having pitchers throw them to him in tight spots."

Young Cy Warmoth Rings Up Sewell Twice

In 1923, Cy Warmoth won just seven games for the Washington Senators and collected an unimposing total of 45 strikeouts before disappearing from the majors. But among his strikeout victims was Cleveland shortstop Joe Sewell. Moreover, Warmoth managed to whiff Sewell twice in the same game. It was the first time that Sewell had ever been rung up twice on the same afternoon, and it happened on only one other occasion in his 14-year career. On May 26, 1930, White Sox rookie Pat Caraway, nearly as obscure as Warmoth, zapped the game's greatest contact hitter twice. The second K swelled Sewell's total for the season to three. He then played the rest of the 1930 campaign without fanning again, but his real apex came in 1925 when he went down on strikes a mere four times in 608 at bats. For his career, Sewell in his 7,132 at bats collected 114 whiffs, about the number that the typical free-swinger nowadays posts in a single season.

1920s BATTING AVERAGE	
1. Rogers Hornsby	.382
2. Harry Heilmann	.364
3. Ty Cobb	.357
4. Al Simmons	.356
5. Babe Ruth	.355
6. Tris Speaker	.354
7. George Sisler	.347
8. Eddie Collins	.346
9. Bob Fothergill	.342
10. Riggs Stephenson	.340
11. Zack Wheat	.339
12. Heinie Manush	.338
13. Lou Gehrig	.335
14. Edd Roush	.332
15. Kiki Cuyler	.331
16. Earle Combs	.331
17. Goose Goslin	.330
18. Jim Bottomley	.328
19. Ross Youngs	.326
20. Bill Terry	.326
21. Frankie Frisch	.326
22. Ken Williams	.325
23. Sam Rice	.325
24. Jack Fournier	.324
25. Lew Fonseca	.323

Hall of Fame member Joe Sewell (above left) *played 14 years in the big leagues and was joined by brothers Luke* (above right), *who toiled for 18 seasons as a catcher with four teams, and Tommy, who had one at bat.*

On August 2, 1925, Joe Hauser of the A's set an AL record with 14 total bases in a single game.

In 1920, Tris Speaker found a comfort zone, setting a major league record with 11 consecutive base hits.

Phillie flycatcher Lefty O'Doul's 254 hits in 1929 set a major league record for outfielders.

In 1925, Joe Sewell of Cleveland fanned just four times in 608 at bats, the fewest in a full season by a regular player.

Sunny Jim Bottomley of the St. Louis Cards collected a major league record 12 runs batted in against Brooklyn on September 16, 1924.

Al Simmons amassed 253 base hits in 1925, setting an American League record for outfielders.

Cudgel-Wielding Trio Dons Tools of Ignorance

By the late 1920s, the majors were stocked for the first time with a wealth of outstanding offensive catchers, including the three who would establish the vast majority of the then-existing career batting records for receivers before they retired. Gabby Hartnett was the first to arrive, joining the Chicago Cubs in 1922; 19 years later he would be the first catcher to leave the game with over 200 career homers and more than 1,000 RBI. In 1925, Mickey Cochrane appeared on the scene with the Philadelphia A's and hit .331 as a rookie; when he quit in 1937 he held the record for the highest career batting average (.320) and on-base percentage (.419) by a catcher. The last of the dynamic trio, Bill Dickey, joined the Yankees in 1928 and immediately served notice that he would offer a blend of Hartnett's slugging prowess and Cochrane's bat control. A .313 hitter for his career, Dickey batted .362 in 1936, the highest single-season average in history by a catcher with 400 or more at bats.

Not Exactly the Science of Hitting

Babe Ruth said about hitting: "All I can tell you is I pick a good one and sock it. I get back to the dugout and they ask me what it was I hit and I tell 'em I don't know except it looked good."

Above: *George Sisler at age 16 signed a contract that would have made him a Pirate, but the National Commission ruled that the pact was nonbinding.*

George Sisler led the 1922 American League with a .420 batting average, a 20th-century record for first basemen.

In 1920, George Sisler of the St. Louis Browns set an all-time major league record with 257 base hits. He won the 1920 American League batting title with a .407 average.

In 1922, George Sisler won the first Most Valuable Player Award that was given out by the American League.

In 1921, Browns teammates George Sisler, Baby Doll Jacobson, and Jack Tobin collected more than 200 hits.

1920s SLUGGING AVERAGE	
1. Babe Ruth	.740
2. Rogers Hornsby	.637
3. Lou Gehrig	.622
4. Al Simmons	.570
5. Harry Heilmann	.558
6. Hack Wilson	.557
7. Jim Bottomley	.547
8. Ken Williams	.547
9. Tris Speaker	.534
10. Cy Williams	.521
11. Goose Goslin	.511
12. Kiki Cuyler	.509
13. Jack Fournier	.507
14. Ty Cobb	.505
15. Bob Meusel	.500
16. Bill Terry	.499
17. Heinie Manush	.498
18. Riggs Stephenson	.495
19. Zack Wheat	.491
20. Gabby Hartnett	.490
21. Bob Fothergill	.486
22. George Sisler	.484
23. Joe Harris	.484
24. George Harper	.482
25. Irish Meusel	.482

George Sisler in 1922 had an American League record 41-game hitting streak.

When he notched 205 hits for the Braves in 1929, George Sisler became the first player to have a 200-hit season in both the National League and the American League.

Johnny Frederick of Brooklyn in 1929 set an all-time rookie record with 52 doubles.

Pittsburgh's Charlie Grimm set an NL record in 1923 by hitting in 23 consecutive games to begin the season.

According to the current rule for determining a batting champion, Paul Waner would have won the National League hitting crown in 1926 with a .336 average and Fred Leach would have been second at .329.

On July 3, 1925, Brooklyn's Milt Stock accumulated four hits for a record fourth day in a row.

Lyman Lamb of Tulsa in the Western League in 1924 compiled an organized baseball record 100 doubles.

1920s ON-BASE AVERAGE

1.	Babe Ruth	.488
2.	Rogers Hornsby	.460
3.	Tris Speaker	.441
4.	Lou Gehrig	.436
5.	Eddie Collins	.435
6.	Harry Heilmann	.433
7.	Ty Cobb	.431
8.	Johnny Bassler	.420
9.	Riggs Stephenson	.413
10.	Lu Blue	.405
11.	Ross Youngs	.405
12.	Wally Schang	.404
13.	Jack Fournier	.401
14.	Ken Williams	.400
15.	Joe Harris	.399
16.	Kiki Cuyler	.399
17.	Joe Sewell	.399
18.	George Grantham	.399
19.	Hack Wilson	.397
20.	Earle Combs	.397
21.	Al Simmons	.396
22.	Goose Goslin	.394
23.	Steve O'Neill	.393
24.	George Harper	.392
25.	Rube Bressler	.392

Above: *Lloyd Waner was a high-average hitter in the major leagues, but in 1925, the San Francisco Seals of the Pacific Coast League used him as a defensive replacement. The Seals thought so little of him that they waived him before the 1926 season.*

In 1929, Pie Traynor of Pittsburgh hit .356, drove in 108 runs, and fanned just seven times in 540 at bats.

In 1920, third sacker Sammy Hale of the Detroit Tigers set a still-extant American League rookie mark when he snared 17 pinch hits.

Cleveland's George Burns set a major league record with 64 doubles in 1926.

On May 11, 1923, right fielder Pete Schneider, a former major league pitcher, clouted five home runs and a double for Vernon of the Pacific Coast League in a 35-11 win over Salt Lake City.

Siblings Toxin for NL Hurlers

The 1927 season was the first that a pair of siblings finished one-two on their team in batting. Moreover, the Waner brothers, Paul and Lloyd, ranked first and third among their loop's hitting leaders. What made the feat even more remarkable was that the elder of the two Waners, Paul, was then only in his second major league season and Lloyd, his younger sib, was just a rookie. Playing side by side in the outfield for the Pittsburgh Pirates, the Waners hit a combined .367, Paul topping the National League with a .380 mark, and Lloyd hitting .355 and collecting a rookie-record 223 hits and a 20th-century frosh-record 133 runs. Between them the fabulous Waners also compiled a single-season brother-record 460 hits. Never again did they scale such heights, individually or collectively, but they nonetheless finished with career records for the most hits, the most runs, and the highest combined batting average by a pair of brothers.

Lloyd Waner in 1927 collected a rookie-record 223 hits; he set another record by hitting 198 singles in a season.

Tim-ber!
Zack Wheat, after playing in the 26-inning game between the Braves and the Dodgers in 1920, said: "I carried up enough lumber to the plate to build a house today."

Wachtel Moistens Way to 317 Farm Wins

In 1920, as part of the effort to rid the game of its undesirable element, baseball moguls abolished all types of pitches in which a foreign substance was applied to the ball and most especially the unseemly spitball. A total of 17 designated spitball pitchers who were in the majors at the time the spitter was outlawed were permitted to ply their salivary trade until the finish of their careers, but any spitball pitcher then in the minor leagues was barred from throwing a spitter should he happen to reach the majors in the future. Enormous inequities resulted. Several of the chosen 17 spitballers were marginal hurlers whose major league careers were destined for an early end anyway, while many talented minor league hurlers who had made the spitball the fulcrum of their repertoire were forced either to drop the spitter or remain in the bush leagues. Among the leading victims when the spitball prohibition was put into effect was Paul Wachtel. Unable to give up the wet one, Wachtel was relegated to a 19-year career in the minors, where he won 317 games.

Seventeen-year-old Mel Ott in 1926 was the youngest player to get a pinch hit in NL history.

Giants outfielder Mel Ott was the youngest player ever to hit 40 homers in a season when, at the age of 20, he smacked 42 in 1929.

From 1920 to 1930, no one pitched in more ballgames than Philadelphia Athletic Eddie Rommel (above), who topped the AL in appearances in back-to-back years (1922 and '23) while twice leading the league in wins with 27 in 1922 and with 21 in 1925.

The only NL player in this century to have more than 100 at bats per strikeout in a season is Charlie Hollocher, who fanned just five times in 592 at bats for the 1922 Chicago Cubs.

Southpaw Eppa "Jephtha" Rixey finished second in games pitched, wins, and innings pitched in the 1920s, third in complete games, sixth in ERA, and ninth in shutouts, ending his Hall of Fame career with 266-251 record, all while hurling in the National League.

Carl Mays in 1971, just prior to his death, said: "I think I belong in the Hall of Fame. I know I earned it. What's wrong with me?"

In 1922, Eddie Rommel led the majors in victories when he won 27 for the seventh-place Philadelphia A's.

Ike Boone of the Mission Reds in the Pacific Coast League collected 553 total bases in 1929.

Bob Fothergill of Detroit set a new American League record when he garnered 19 pinch hits in 1929.

In 1926, Hack Wilson's 69 walks topped the NL and were the fewest ever to lead a league.

1920s GAMES PITCHED	
1. Eddie Rommel	423
2. Eppa Rixey	386
3. Waite Hoyt	379
4. Bill Sherdel	378
5. Burleigh Grimes	373
6. Jack Quinn	368
7. Elam Vangilder	364
8. Sam Jones	363
9. George Uhle	356
10. Dolf Luque	353
11. Herb Pennock	352
12. Slim Harriss	349
13. Jesse Haines	346
14. Tom Zachary	336
15. Firpo Marberry	333
Howard Ehmke	333
17. Urban Shocker	330
18. Jack Scott	329
19. Pete Alexander	325
20. Red Faber	316
21. Jimmy Ring	312
Art Nehf	312
23. Hal Carlson	310
24. Pete Donohue	308
25. Carl Mays	304

1920s COMPLETE GAMES

1.	Burleigh Grimes	234
2.	Pete Alexander	195
3.	Eppa Rixey	185
4.	George Uhle	182
5.	Red Faber	181
6.	Herb Pennock	179
7.	Dazzy Vance	171
8.	Urban Shocker	168
	Dolf Luque	168
	Jesse Haines	168
11.	Howard Ehmke	162
12.	Waite Hoyt	160
13.	Wilbur Cooper	151
14.	Sam Jones	150
15.	Lee Meadows	146
16.	Walter Johnson	143
17.	Stan Coveleski	138
18.	Eddie Rommel	134
19.	Dutch Ruether	132
	Carl Mays	132
21.	Pete Donohue	131
22.	Joe Bush	129
23.	Tom Zachary	127
	Bill Sherdel	127
	Ted Lyons	127

In 1928, his only year as a regular, Cleveland's Carl Lind topped the American League in at bats with 650 and also led all AL second basemen in assists and double plays.

Spitball artist Burleigh Grimes earned his nickname "Ol' Stubblebeard" because he didn't shave on the days he pitched, citing that the slippery elm he chewed to increase saliva irritated his skin.

Good Company
"The secret of success as a pitcher lies in getting a job with the Yankees."
—Waite Hoyt

Righthander Burleigh Grimes (above) *led all pitchers in wins and innings pitched during the 1920s, pacing the league twice in wins and five times posting 20 or more, while working 300 innings five seasons.*

Grimes Hurls Final Legal Spitball

Stan Coveleski, Burleigh Grimes, and Red Faber all might have suffered the same fate as Paul Wachtel if they had not had the fortune to be established major leaguers by the time the spitball was abolished. Allowed to continue to water his deliveries, each of the trio went on to win over 200 games in the majors and make the Hall of Fame. Coveleski had the most dazzling career stats of any spitballer who remained active in the lively ball era, but Grimes posted the most victories of the 17 designated spitballers—270. Active in the majors from 1916 until 1934, he hurled for seven different teams in both leagues. A starting pitcher throughout most of his career, he was relegated to the bullpen in his last few seasons. In 1934, pitching in relief for the New York Yankees, Grimes posted the final win in major league history by a pitcher legally permitted to employ a spitball.

ChiSox Quartet Wins 20, ChiSox Lose Trio

All summer long in 1920, the Chicago White Sox played under a dark cloud as several key members of the club were suspected of having thrown the 1919 World Series. The Sox nevertheless held tough in a heated pennant race with the Cleveland Indians and the New York Yankees, and much of the reason was the quality of their starting pitchers. In 1920, the Pale Hose became the first team in history to feature four 20-game winners: Red Faber, Lefty Williams, Dickie Kerr, and Eddie Cicotte. Among them the four figured in all but 21 of the club's 154 decisions. When the scandal broke late in the campaign and implicated Cicotte and Williams, both were promptly suspended by Sox owner Charlie Comiskey and never pitched another inning. Kerr was suspended by Comiskey when he demanded more money after winning 19 games the following year and his holdout lasted so long that it ruined his major league career. Indeed, by the commencement of the 1922 season only Faber remained of the foursome that had made the Sox the envy of every club in the game just two short years before.

In 1929, Tom Zachary of the Yankees set the current major league single-season record for the most wins without a loss when he compiled a 12-0 mark for the Yankees.

In 15 of the 20 years that Red Faber (above) pitched for the White Sox, the team finished in the second division, while Faber posted only six losing seasons and retired with 254 wins.

Notching 31 wins, hurler Jim Bagby of the Cleveland Indians was the last AL righty until 1968 to win 30 games in a season.

In 1924, Sloppy Thurston won 20 games for the last-place Chicago White Sox and topped the American League with 28 complete games.

Cardinals third baseman Les Bell, after the seventh game of the 1926 World Series in which Pete Alexander fanned Tony Lazzeri in relief to end a Yankees threat: "Doggone, there wasn't another man in the world I would rather have seen out there at that moment than Grover Cleveland Alexander."

In 1921, Red Faber had an AL-leading 2.47 ERA; it was the only ERA figure below 3.00 in that circuit.

Red Faber and Dickie Kerr in 1921 won 44 of the White Sox' 62 victories.

Former major league pitcher Danny Boone, brother of minor league star Ike Boone, won the Piedmont League Triple Crown in 1928 when he hit .419 with 38 home runs and 131 RBI.

1920s SAVES	
1. Firpo Marberry	75
2. Waite Hoyt	29
3. Allan Russell	25
Sarge Connally	25
Garland Braxton	25
6. Bill Sherdel	24
Eddie Rommel	24
Lefty Grove	24
Hooks Dauss	24
10. Wilcy Moore	23
Sam Jones	23
12. Urban Shocker	22
Jack Quinn	22
Johnny Morrison	22
15. Herb Pennock	20
16. Elam Vangilder	19
Carl Mays	19
18. Rube Walberg	18
Jack Scott	18
Ted Lyons	18
Hal Carlson	18
Guy Bush	18
23. Rosy Ryan	17
Claude Jonnard	17
25. Jakie May	16
Ken Holloway	16
Slim Harriss	16
Pete Alexander	16

Chapman's Death Prompts Rule Changes

On August 16, 1920, the Cleveland Indians were in first place, albeit by just a few percentage points, and making their third and final visit of the season to the Polo Grounds, then the cavernous home of both the New York Giants and the New York Yankees. Facing Cleveland on that day was Yankees ace Carl Mays. An ethereal fog that hung over the Polo Grounds had been complicated by a drizzle by the time shortstop Ray Chapman led off the fifth inning for Cleveland. Mays's best pitch was delivered with an underhand sweep. Down went his body and out shot his arm from the blur of white shirts and dark suits in the open bleachers in the deep background behind him. The pitch struck Chapman in the temple and killed him—from all indications he never saw it. As a consequence of the only on-the-field fatality in major league history, dirty or scuffed balls thereafter were discarded immediately from play and patrons were no longer allowed to sit in the center field bleachers. Mays was quickly exonerated from any wrong doing but the following season fell under suspicion of throwing the 1921 World Series. This, more than the Chapman incident, would haunt him the rest of his days.

Above: *Tribe shortstop Ray Chapman, left, takes the toss from second baseman Bill Wambsganss. In game five of the 1920 World Series, Wambsganss completed the only postseason unassisted triple play in history.*

Yankee hurler Carl Mays liked pitching against Philadelphia; in August of 1923, he beat the A's for a record 23rd consecutive time.

1920s SHUTOUTS		
1.	Walter Johnson	24
2.	Dazzy Vance	22
	Urban Shocker	22
4.	Herb Pennock	21
	Dolf Luque	21
	Sam Jones	21
	Jesse Haines	21
	Stan Coveleski	21
9.	Eppa Rixey	20
	Burleigh Grimes	20
	Pete Alexander	20
12.	Jack Quinn	19
13.	Eddie Rommel	17
	Waite Hoyt	17
	Red Faber	17
16.	George Uhle	16
	Pete Donohue	16
	Wilbur Cooper	16
19.	Tom Zachary	15
	Bob Shawkey	15
	Lee Meadows	15
	Hal Carlson	15
	Jesse Barnes	15
24.	Dutch Ruether	14
	Carl Mays	14
	Howard Ehmke	14
	Bill Doak	14
	Rip Collins	14
	Babe Adams	14

Rookie southpaw Emil Yde of Pittsburgh had a dazzling 16-3 record in 1924 and paced the National League with an .842 winning percentage.

Trouble In Mind

"The pressure never lets up. Doesn't matter what you did yesterday. That's history. It's tomorrow that counts. So you worry all the time. It never ends. Lord, baseball is a worrying thing."
—Stan Coveleski

Bagby's Improvement Gives Tribe Flag

Despite the loss of Ray Chapman, probably the best shortstop in the game at the time, Cleveland held on to hoist its first pennant in 1920, thanks in no small part to three pitchers, Jim Bagby, Stan Coveleski, and Ray Caldwell. Caldwell, a reformed alcoholic who had nearly been killed by a lightning bolt while on the mound a few years earlier, won an even 20 games and Coveleski contributed 24 victories. But Bagby was the icing on the cake. A 17-game winner the previous year and scarcely expected to surpass that figure now that he was approaching his 31st birthday, Bagby instead became the last 30-game winner in the American League prior to 1961 when expansion swelled the schedule to 162 games. His 31 victories exactly matched his age after the Indians not only won the pennant but added the 1921 World Series trophy to their spoils. Those 31 wins were also 10 more than Bagby won during the rest of his career in the majors.

Johnny Frederick remarked about Dazzy Vance: "He could throw a cream puff through a battleship."

The 1923 season was the first time that no pitcher in either major league lost 20 games during a campaign in which a full 154-game schedule was played.

On September 13, 1925, Brooklyn fireballer Dazzy Vance (above) *pitched a rare 1920s no-hitter, as he beat Philadelphia 10-1 despite three Dodger errors.*

When he paced the National League in strikeouts with just 134 in 1922, Dazzy Vance set a loop mark for the fewest Ks by a leader.

In 1924, the National League joined the AL in giving a league MVP award; the first NL winner was Brooklyn's Dazzy Vance.

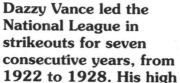

Dazzy Vance led the National League in strikeouts for seven consecutive years, from 1922 to 1928. His high point in the skein was in 1924, when he notched 262 whiffs.

1920s WINS	
1. Burleigh Grimes	190
2. Eppa Rixey	166
3. Pete Alexander	165
4. Herb Pennock	162
5. Waite Hoyt	161
6. Urban Shocker	156
7. Eddie Rommel	154
8. Jesse Haines	153
9. George Uhle	152
10. Red Faber	149
11. Dazzy Vance	147
12. Bill Sherdel	139
13. Dolf Luque	138
14. Sam Jones	137
15. Howard Ehmke	136
16. Stan Coveleski	133
17. Jack Quinn	131
18. Tom Zachary	128
Lee Meadows	128
20. Carl Mays	126
Pete Donohue	126
22. Art Nehf	123
23. Walter Johnson	120
Wilbur Cooper	120
25. Joe Bush	118

1920s INNINGS

1.	Burleigh Grimes	2,797.2
2.	Eppa Rixey	2,678.1
3.	Dolf Luque	2,479.2
4.	Pete Alexander	2,415.1
5.	Red Faber	2,364.0
6.	Waite Hoyt	2,346.0
7.	Jesse Haines	2,328.1
8.	Herb Pennock	2,313.0
9.	George Uhle	2,309.2
10.	Howard Ehmke	2,265.0
11.	Eddie Rommel	2,242.2
12.	Sam Jones	2,230.0
13.	Urban Shocker	2,148.2
14.	Bill Sherdel	2,061.1
15.	Dazzy Vance	2,054.0
16.	Jack Quinn	2,042.0
17.	Tom Zachary	2,018.1
18.	Pete Donohue	1,962.0
19.	Lee Meadows	1,946.1
20.	Jimmy Ring	1,941.0
21.	Stan Coveleski	1,933.2
22.	Walter Johnson	1,825.0
23.	Dutch Ruether	1,800.0
24.	Carl Mays	1,796.1
25.	Wilbur Cooper	1,793.0

Despite posting the majors' best ERA of 3.25 in 1928, the Brooklyn Dodgers could finish no better than sixth in the National League.

In 1923, the Cincinnati Reds' staff ERA of 3.21 was nearly half a run better than that of any other team in the majors.

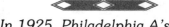

In 1925, Philadelphia A's rookie Lefty Grove topped the American League in strikeouts with just 116.

Athletics hurler Lefty Grove's 2.81 ERA in 1929 was the only one in the major leagues below 3.00.

Ferrell Rebounds, Tribe Holds Bag

Eighteen years after Vean Gregg burst onto the scene, the Cleveland Indians found themselves blessed with another rookie phenom when Wes Ferrell won 21 games in 1929. Like Gregg, Ferrell proceeded to reach the 20-game circle in each of his first three seasons, then went Gregg one better when he bagged 20 or more for the fourth straight time, in 1932. The following year, however, Ferrell seemed to go the way of Gregg and so many other Cleveland rookie stars when he was plagued by arm trouble. Certain he was through, the Tribe dealt him cheap to the Boston Red Sox, only to see him rebound to lead the American League in wins in 1935 and in complete games for three straight years in the mid-1930s. With outfielder Earl Averill, another rookie whiz who joined the club the same year as Ferrell, Cleveland was wiser. The Indians retained Averill until 1939 and saw him set many team career batting marks.

Larry Benton, the National League leader in winning percentage in 1927 and 1928, is the only two-time winning percentage champ to finish with a career winning percentage below .500 (.498).

Excuse Me
Miller Huggins revealed what a player needs when he's in a slump: "A string of alibis."

As a rookie in 1919, Cleveland pitcher George Uhle (above) won a 20-inning shutout and then had a 19-inning complete game in 1929.

George Uhle in 1922 was the first pitcher since 1901 to both win 20 games and have an ERA over 4.00.

George Uhle of Cleveland compiled 52 hits in 1923, a season record for pitchers.

On April 28, 1921, Cleveland pitcher George Uhle collected six RBI in a game.

Cleveland hurler George Uhle in 1926 proved he could pitch, leading the majors with 27 wins.

Fibber Kremer Wins 143 After 30

Wes Ferrell was not even 20 years old when he played in his first major league game and already an established star by the time he was 25, but many pitchers in Ferrell's era who were equally talented found the path to stardom much more arduous. Hall of Famer Dazzy Vance did not reach the majors to stay until he was past 30. Wilcy Moore had already turned 30 when he led the American League in saves and ERA as a rookie with the 1927 Yankees. In the World Series that year, Moore and the Yankees were opposed by a pitcher for the Pirates who may have faced the hardest climb of all to the majors. Remy Kremer toiled in the minors for a full 10 seasons before Pittsburgh gave him his first big-league test in 1924. At that, he might never have received the opportunity if he had not shaved three years off his age, a common practice at the time. Although really 31, Kremer pretended to be 28. Not until his career was over did he reveal that he had been over 40 when he finally retired in 1933 with 143 wins, all of them achieved after his 31st birthday.

From 1910 to 1924, Walter Johnson led the American League in strikeouts in a record 12 different seasons.

Walter Johnson had 110 shutouts in his career, a total that still is a major league record.

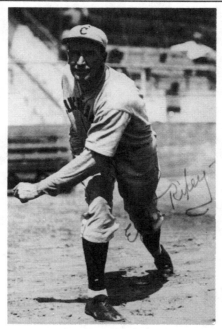

Above: *Eppa Rixey held the record for most wins by a National League lefthander from his retirement in 1933 to 1963, when Warren Spahn broke the record. Rixey was a fine fielder. He compiled 108 chances in 1917 without an error; he also had 1,196 career assists.*

In 1921, Eppa Rixey of the Reds gave up only one home run in 301 innings, a National League record since the end of the dead-ball era.

After the 1927 season, Walter Johnson retired with a major league record 3,506 strikeouts.

Walter Johnson batted .433 in 1925, a single-season record for pitchers with 75-plus at bats.

In 1928, righthander Russ Miller had an 0-12 record for the last-place Phillies.

"I think the reason I pitched so long is that I never wasted my arm throwing over to first to keep runners close to the base. There was a time there, for five years, I never once threw to first base to chase a runner back."
—*Sad Sam Jones, pitcher who spanned the dead-ball era and into the 1930s*

On April 30, 1922, White Sox hurler Charlie Robertson threw a perfect game against Detroit; it was the last perfect game that the major leagues would see until 1956.

1920s STRIKEOUTS	
1. Dazzy Vance	1,464
2. Burleigh Grimes	1,018
3. Dolf Luque	904
4. Walter Johnson	895
5. Lefty Grove	837
6. Howard Ehmke	824
7. George Uhle	808
8. Red Faber	804
9. Bob Shawkey	788
10. Urban Shocker	753
11. Waite Hoyt	748
12. Jesse Haines	742
13. Herb Pennock	731
14. Sam Jones	718
15. Jimmy Ring	715
16. Eppa Rixey	686
17. Bill Sherdel	657
18. Pete Alexander	653
19. Slim Harriss	644
20. Joe Bush	631
21. Jack Scott	588
22. Dutch Ruether	585
23. Wilbur Cooper	577
24. Jack Quinn	575
25. Lee Meadows	574

1920s WINNING PERCENTAGE

1.	Ray Kremer	.660
2.	Carl Mays	.636
3.	Urban Shocker	.627
4.	Freddie Fitzsimmons	.626
5.	Lefty Grove	.626
6.	Dazzy Vance	.620
7.	Art Nehf	.615
8.	Waite Hoyt	.612
9.	Pete Alexander	.611
10.	Stan Coveleski	.599
11.	Burleigh Grimes	.594
12.	Herb Pennock	.591
13.	Eddie Rommel	.588
14.	Firpo Marberry	.582
15.	Sam Gray	.577
16.	Walter Johnson	.577
17.	Rip Collins	.573
18.	Dutch Ruether	.572
19.	Johnny Morrison	.567
20.	Larry Benton	.565
21.	Bill Sherdel	.563
22.	Jesse Haines	.563
23.	Red Faber	.562
24.	Charlie Root	.562
25.	Guy Bush	.561

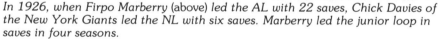
In 1926, when Firpo Marberry (above) led the AL with 22 saves, Chick Davies of the New York Giants led the NL with six saves. Marberry led the junior loop in saves in four seasons.

Firpo Marberry in 1926 pitched in 64 games, setting a 20th-century major league record.

In 1926, Firpo Marberry compiled 22 saves for Washington, setting a major league record.

Cubs manager Joe McCarthy described Pete Alexander: "I like Alec. Nice fellow. But Alec was Alec. Did he live by the rules? Sure. But they were always Alec's rules."

Washington's Firpo Marberry Makes Living Out of the Bullpen

Wilcy Moore in 1927 became the first reliever to win a league ERA crown. That year he also led the American League in saves, but the following season he returned the bullpen mantle to the hurler who was the game's reigning relief king throughout the 1920s, Firpo Marberry of the Washington Senators. Marberry was both the first moundsman to compile 100 career saves and the first to make a living exclusively as a bullpen artist. In 1925, he was the first pitcher to lead his league in mound appearances without making a single start. Subsequently the Senators learned that he could also take his turn as a starter without impairing his relief work and began using him in both roles. Marberry continued to do double duty until the end of his career in 1936. He led the loop in appearances in six seasons. He was the only pitcher to retire prior to the expansion era with over 100 saves and 2,000 innings pitched. He had 101 saves and pitched 2,067 innings.

Ehmke One Dribble Away From Back-to-Back No-Hitters

No-hitters were nearly as rare during the hitting-happy 1920s as perfect games are now. The National League had only four no-hitters the entire decade and the American League had none at all between August 21, 1926, and April 29, 1931. When Howard Ehmke tossed a no-hitter against the Philadelphia A's on September 7, 1923, it was therefore a significant event, made all the more impressive by the fact that he was toiling for the last-place Boston Red Sox. Four days later, Ehmke narrowly missed becoming the first hurler in history to throw two successive no-hitters when a ground ball that was misplayed by his third baseman was deemed a hit by official scorer Fred Lieb. Even though the muffed dribbler turned out to be the only hit that day off Ehmke, Lieb refused after the game to buckle to an adamant attempt to get him to reverse his decision.

Pitcher Howard Ehmke of the Philadelphia A's in 1929 struck out 13 Chicago Cubs to set a World Series record.

The only St. Louis Browns pitcher ever to lead the American League in strikeouts was Urban Shocker with 149 in 1922.

Charlie Root of the Cubs topped the major leagues with 26 victories in 1927.

1920s EARNED RUN AVERAGE	
1. Pete Alexander	3.04
2. Lefty Grove	3.09
3. Dolf Luque	3.09
4. Dazzy Vance	3.10
5. Stan Coveleski	3.20
6. Eppa Rixey	3.24
7. Tommy Thomas	3.24
8. Walter Johnson	3.33
9. Urban Shocker	3.34
10. Red Faber	3.34
11. Wilbur Cooper	3.36
12. Bill Doak	3.38
13. Herb Pennock	3.44
14. Carl Mays	3.44
15. Firpo Marberry	3.44
16. Bob Shawkey	3.45
17. Ray Kremer	3.46
18. Eddie Rommel	3.47
19. Jack Quinn	3.50
20. Waite Hoyt	3.51
21. Burleigh Grimes	3.52
22. Charlie Root	3.53
23. Freddie Fitzsimmons	3.53
24. Jesse Petty	3.54
25. Guy Bush	3.59

In 1921, no fewer than eight pitchers tied for the NL lead in shutouts with the meager total of three.

The 1922 New York Giants were the first team to win a pennant without the benefit of a 20-game winner on their pitching staff.

"When I couldn't get anybody to catch me, I'd throw against a stone wall or barn door. It wasn't always fun, but I kept plugging away because it meant so much to me."
—Herb Pennock, on how he acquired his marvelous control

Bob Smith, the Boston Braves' top pitcher during the late 1920s, was the club's regular shortstop as a rookie in 1923.

New York Giant hurler Bill Walker led the NL in ERA at 3.08 in 1929, the highest mark ever to lead the senior loop.

When he bagged 11 wins in relief for the 1925 St. Louis Browns, Elam Vangilder set a new record for bullpenners.

When Herb Pennock topped the American League with 277 innings pitched in 1925, it was the first time a loop leader worked fewer than 300 innings.

In game three of the 1927 World Series, Yankee ace Herb Pennock retired the first 22 batters he faced, on his way to a three-hitter and 8-1 victory, giving the Bronx Bombers a 2-1 Series lead.

Robertson Routs Tigers

Charlie Robertson had been in the major leagues for only a few weeks when he took the mound on April 30, 1922, for the Chicago White Sox at Detroit's Navin Field. Facing the team that a year earlier had hit .316 to set an American League record, the rookie righthander was expected by Tigers fans to be easy meat. Instead, to their utter dismay, he set the home nine down in order inning after inning. With two out in the bottom of the ninth and Detroit still looking for its first baserunner, Tigers skipper Ty Cobb sent Johnny Bassler up to pinch hit. Among the best-hitting catchers in the game and one of the first to retire with a .300-plus career batting average, Bassler presented a formidable challenge. When Robertson made Bassler his 27th straight victim that afternoon, he tailored the only undisputed perfect game in the majors between 1908 and 1956. It was to be Robertson's lone bright moment in an eight-year career that ended with just 49 wins and a .380 winning percentage.

After winning only 10 games in two years with the Red Sox and 122 in seven years with the New York Yankees, Waite Hoyt (above) was fortunate that Boston had the habit of trading good players to the Yankees.

In 1928, Ed Morris came within one victory of being a rookie 20-game winner for the last-place Red Sox when he finished at 19-15.

On August 28, 1926, Dutch Levsen of the Cleveland Indians was the last pitcher to win two complete games in one day.

In 1924, Wilbur Cooper of the Pirates became the last pitcher in major league history to notch 25 or more complete games five years in a row.

1920s PITCHER FIELDING AVERAGE	
1. Walter Johnson	.988
2. Jakie May	.987
3. Pete Alexander	.986
4. Urban Shocker	.985
5. Hooks Dauss	.985

On May 1, 1920, Joe Oeschger of the Boston Braves and Leon Cadore of the Brooklyn Robins pitched the entire way in a 26-inning 1-1 tie.

In 1926, White Sox hurler Ted Lyons no-hit the Boston Red Sox in one hour and seven minutes.

Yankee pitcher Waite Hoyt won two complete games in the 1928 World Series.

"Wives of ballplayers, when they teach their children their prayers, should instruct them to say: 'God bless mommy, God bless daddy, God bless Babe Ruth.'"
—Waite Hoyt

Cobb, Speaker Accused of Throwing Game

In 1926, memories of the Black Sox Scandal were revived when it surfaced that former big league pitcher Dutch Leonard had incriminating letters from Smokey Joe Wood regarding bets that Leonard, Wood, Tris Speaker, and Ty Cobb had made on a 1919 game between the Tigers and the Indians. In a quandary, commissioner Kenesaw Mountain Landis at first induced both Cobb and Speaker to retire quietly. Landis, though, was forced to recant when Cobb and Speaker reconsidered and demanded a hearing with Leonard, their chief accuser, presenting his evidence. When Leonard chose to avoid the confrontation, Landis decided to let the issue die, but neither Speaker nor Cobb, both player-managers at the time, was ever offered a manager's post in the majors again. The possibility is strong that if Wood's letters had come to light several years earlier when Landis was barring players at the slightest provocation, two of the game's greatest players might not now be in the Hall of Fame.

When describing how Judge Kenesaw Mountain Landis (above) was appointed as commissioner, Will Rogers said: "Somebody said, 'Get that old boy who sits behind first base all the time. He's out there every day anyhow.' So they offered him a season's pass and he jumped at it."

1920s CATCHER GAMES	
1. Muddy Ruel	1,115
2. Bob O'Farrell	937
3. Cy Perkins	917
4. Wally Schang	895
5. Ray Schalk	822

New York Giant Heinie Groh in 1924 set a record with a .983 fielding average for third basemen.

In 1923, the New York Yankees not only won their first world championship but became the first team ever to average less than one error per game.

1920s CATCHER FIELDING AVERAGE	
1. Hank Severeid	.985
2. Frank Snyder	.984
3. Bubbles Hargrave	.984
4. Ray Schalk	.983
5. Muddy Ruel	.983

Dramatics

Heywood Broun said of Judge Kenesaw Mountain Landis: "His career typifies the heights to which dramatic talent may carry a man in America if only he has the foresight not to go on the stage."

Stuffy McInnis of the Boston Red Sox had a .999 fielding average in 1921, a major league record for first basemen.

Connie Mack answered when asked who could provide the most value to a ballclub: "If I could only have nine players named [Al] Simmons."

O'Connell Last to Go

On the closing weekend of the 1924 season, the Giants were facing a stern challenge from the Brooklyn Dodgers in New York's quest for a fourth straight pennant. Giants utility outfielder Jimmy O'Connell approached Phillies shortstop Heinie Sand before a game and told him there was $500 in it for him if he took it easy that day. Sand reported the bribe attempt and both O'Connell and Giants coach Cozy Dolan, who had allegedly given O'Connell his instructions, were called on the carpet by commissioner Kenesaw Mountain Landis. Despite testimony from O'Connell that several other Giants were involved in the incident, including stars like Frankie Frisch and George Kelly, he and Dolan were the only two made to suffer the consequences. O'Connell's banishment marked the last time a player has been barred for life from the game for baseball-related activities. After leaving the Giants, he played for years in outlaw circuits in the Southwest along with Hal Chase and several members of the 1919 Black Sox.

1920s FIRST BASE GAMES	
1. Charlie Grimm	1,455
2. Joe Judge	1,339
3. George Sisler	1,309
4. Lu Blue	1,199
5. George Kelly	1,159

The 1927 Philadelphia A's had a record seven future Hall of Famers on their active roster in 1927: Ty Cobb, Al Simmons, Mickey Cochrane, Eddie Collins, Zack Wheat, Jimmie Foxx, and Lefty Grove.

Doc Johnston of Cleveland opposed his brother, Jimmy, a hurler for Brooklyn, in the 1920 World Series.

In 1922, for the record eighth consecutive season, White Sox Ray Schalk led American League catchers in fielding average.

Playing the outfield in 1928 for the A's with 40-year-old Tris Speaker and 41-year-old Ty Cobb flanking him, Al Simmons said: "If this keeps up, by the end of the season I'll be an old man myself."

1920s FIRST BASE FIELDING AVERAGE	
1. Stuffy McInnis	.995
2. Joe Judge	.995
3. Walter Holke	.993
4. Charlie Grimm	.993
5. George Kelly	.992

The 1925 Pirates were the first team to come back to win a World Series after trailing three games to one.

In the 1924 Series, Frankie Frisch of the Giants hit .333 with four doubles, while Bucky Harris of the Senators also hit .333 and rapped two home runs while managing Washington to its only world championship.

Baltimore, Fort Worth in Seventh Heaven

In 1924, even as the New York Giants were about to become the first team in major league history to win four consecutive pennants, the Baltimore Orioles were wrapping up their sixth consecutive International League pennant and the Fort Worth Panthers were claiming their sixth straight Texas League flag. The Giants fell to second place in 1925, but the twin minor league dynasties continued for yet one more season, giving both clubs seven flags in a row. To the Orioles and the Panthers thus belongs the dual honor of the longest pennant skein in professional baseball history. The Orioles were owned and managed by Jack Dunn, a former major league pitcher, while Jake Atz, an erstwhile second baseman with the White Sox, piloted the Panthers. Both clubs fell from their lofty perch in 1926 when age and the forced sale of several of their star players to major league teams caught up to them.

About the 1929 World Series, Heywood Broun wrote: "When danger beckoned thickest it was always [Lefty] Grove who stood towering on the mound, whipping over strikes against the luckless Chicago batters."

In 1924, Freddy Lindstrom of the New York Giants, at age 18, was the youngest participant in World Series history.

1920s SECOND BASE GAMES	
1. Rogers Hornsby	1,405
2. Bucky Harris	1,242
3. Eddie Collins	1,010
4. Frankie Frisch	1,006
5. Aaron Ward	805

Many accused White Sox owner Charlie Comiskey of being cheap. Before the 1923 season, however, Comiskey bought third baseman Willie Kamm from San Francisco of the Pacific Coast League for $125,000.

On August 15, 1926, Dodger Babe Herman smacked a double and was tagged out on a double play as he was one of three Dodgers who wound up on third base.

1920s SECOND BASE FIELDING AVERAGE	
1. Eddie Collins	.973
2. Frankie Frisch	.973
3. Hod Ford	.973
4. Max Bishop	.971
5. Hughie Critz	.971

Farm Star Arlett Buzzes Bigs

Among the stars of the great Baltimore Orioles dynasty were Lefty Grove and George Earnshaw, two pitchers who graduated to fine careers in the majors after they were purchased by the Philadelphia Athletics. For many other minor league stars of their time, graduation to the majors either occurred too late in their careers or in some instances never occurred at all. Frozen for years in the Pacific Coast League when their teams refused to sell their contracts to major league clubs were such great hitters as Lefty O'Doul, Smead Jolley, Ike Boone, and Buzz Arlett. All but Arlett eventually reached the majors before their skills had begun to erode. By the time Arlett joined the Philadelphia Phillies in 1931 he was already 32 years old and on the downside of his career. Nevertheless he amply proved that he could play in exclusive company. In his lone season up top, Arlett hit .313 and ranked fifth in the National League in slugging average and tied for fourth in home runs.

Pie Traynor (above) *led NL third basemen in putouts for seven seasons, prompting a sportswriter to pen: "He doubled down the left field line, but Traynor threw him out."*

1920s THIRD BASE GAMES	
1. Pie Traynor	1,135
2. Joe Dugan	1,041
3. Willie Kamm	1,035
4. Ossie Bluege	828
5. Milt Stock	750

In 1922, Pittsburgh's Max Carey set a stolen base percentage record of .962 when he swiped 51 bases and was caught stealing only two times.

In 1921, the Giants beat the Yanks in the last best-of-nine World Series and the first "Subway Series."

In 1928, Willie Kamm of the Chicago White Sox became the first third baseman in major league history to handle more than 200 consecutive chances without making an error.

Harry Hooper grumbled about Red Sox owner Harry Frazee: "He sold the whole team down the river to keep his dirty nose above water. What a way to run a ballclub!"

In game five of the 1920 World Series, Brooklyn had Pete Kilduff on second and Otto Miller on first with none out. Clarence Mitchell lined a shot up the middle and both runners took off. Indians second baseman Bill Wambsganss made the catch and let his momentum carry him to second base for the easy second out. Then he turned, saw Miller standing a few feet away, and applied the tag for the third out for the first World Series triple play.

1920s THIRD BASE ASSISTS	
1. Pie Traynor	2,179
2. Willie Kamm	2,124
3. Joe Dugan	1,924
4. Ossie Bluege	1,759
5. Babe Pinelli	1,481

Red Sox owner Harry Frazee was a theatrical producer who often sold his players to raise cash for his shows. In January of 1920, he sold Babe Ruth to the Yankees for $125,000 and a $300,000 loan.

1920s THIRD BASE FIELDING AVERAGE	
1. Willie Kamm	.970
2. Heinie Groh	.968
3. Freddy Lindstrom	.962
4. Joe Dugan	.957
5. Bob Jones	.956

Hornsby-Frisch Swap Biggest Yet

After the St. Louis Cardinals bagged their first pennant in 1926, team owner Sam Breadon judged that player-manager Rogers Hornsby's ego and salary demands would soon be more than he cared to bear. New York Giants manager John McGraw meanwhile began to fear that his star second baseman, Frankie Frisch, would soon begin having managerial aspirations of his own. Between them Breadon and McGraw thus struck the greatest trade in history to that point, a swap of the game's top two second basemen at the time. Since Hornsby was undeniably the better of the two, the Giants agreed to throw in pitcher Jimmy Ring. When Ring quickly demonstrated he was about washed up—he never won a game for the Cardinals—New York at first seemed to have gotten the better of the deal, as Hornsby belted .361 in 1927 to set a modern Giants club record. McGraw, however, found Hornsby's ego and personality no more tolerable than Breadon had and sent Hornsby to the Boston Braves before the 1928 season. Frisch in contrast remained with the Cardinals until the end of his playing career and achieved his managerial ambitions in 1933 when he was named the club's player-pilot. The next year, Frisch's club won the World Series.

Second baseman Frankie Frisch (above) set major league single-season records in 1927 for most assists (641) and total chances (1,059).

George Burns stole home for the 27th time in 1925, setting a National League lifetime record.

In 1920, third baseman Larry Gardner of the Cleveland Indians was caught stealing 20 times in 23 attempts for a miserable .130 success rate.

1920s SHORTSTOP GAMES	
1. Dave Bancroft	1,237
2. Joe Sewell	1,216
3. Wally Gerber	1,201
4. Chick Galloway	976
5. Roger Peckinpaugh	972

The Chicago White Sox were just a game and one-half out of first place in 1920 when news of the 1919 World Series fix broke on September 28 and eight team members were promptly suspended.

1920s SHORTSTOP FIELDING AVERAGE	
1. Everett Scott	.966
2. Charlie Hollocher	.963
3. Rabbit Maranville	.959
4. Hod Ford	.959
5. Roger Peckinpaugh	.955

Hub Heroes Stock Bronx Dynasty

During the 1920s, the St. Louis Cardinals became the first major league organization to develop a minor league farm system. New York Yankees owner Jake Ruppert's fellow American League moguls could be forgiven, however, for feeling that he too had a farm club. Only in Ruppert's case his affiliate was not a minor league team but a rival AL outfit—the Boston Red Sox. Beginning with the sale of Babe Ruth to the Yankees after the 1919 season, the Red Sox furnished the Yankees with so many key members of the cast that made them the game's most formidable team during the 1920s that several important rules regulating trades finally had to be drafted. Among the many stars the Yankees acquired from the Crimson Hose at little or no cost were Ruth, Everett Scott, Joe Dugan, Carl Mays, Joe Bush, Herb Pennock, Sam Jones, and Waite Hoyt. The crowning blow was a deal early in the 1930 season that sent Red Ruffing to New York from Boston for Cedric Durst and cash. So one-sided was the trade that Sox officials seemed to grow sufficiently embarrassed after that to discontinue their generosity.

On September 26, 1926, the New York Yankees and the St. Louis Browns played a doubleheader that was concluded in two hours and seven minutes (excluding the time between games). One of the games was the shortest in AL history—55 minutes.

1920s OUTFIELD GAMES	
1. Sam Rice	1,486
2. Babe Ruth	1,388
3. Charlie Jamieson	1,279
4. Harry Heilmann	1,217
5. Max Carey	1,204
6. Bob Meusel	1,192
7. Curt Walker	1,190
8. Ken Williams	1,163
9. Bibb Falk	1,147
10. Cy Williams	1,122
Goose Goslin	1,122
12. Bing Miller	1,108
13. Edd Roush	1,107
14. Baby Doll Jacobson	1,102
15. Tris Speaker	1,091

The last major leaguer to be banned from the game while still an active player was Jimmy O'Connell of the 1924 New York Giants, who was barred for his role in a bribe offer to Phillies shortstop Heinie Sand.

On the final day of the 1926 season, and trailing Babe Ruth and fellow teammates Harry Heilmann and Bob Fothergill, Detroit center fielder Heinie Manush (above) went 6-for-9 in a doubleheader to overtake Ruth and win the crown at .378.

Chewing gum magnate William Wrigley bought the Chicago Cubs in 1921 and soon thereafter changed the name of the team's home park to Wrigley Field.

Dry

"There is much less drinking now than there was before 1927, because I quit drinking on May 24, 1927."
—Rabbit Maranville

The Indians and Yankees in 1929 were the first teams to put numbers on their uniforms and keep them on.

In 1929, Judge Fuchs of the Boston Braves became the last club owner to manage his team for an entire season.

The Boston Red Sox in 1926 lost a club record 107 games.

1920s OUTFIELD FIELDING AVERAGE	
1. Paul Waner	.979
2. Al Simmons	.978
3. Heinie Manush	.977
4. Earl McNeely	.976
5. Ira Flagstead	.976
6. Les Mann	.976
7. Riggs Stephenson	.975
8. Baby Doll Jacobson	.975
9. Freddy Leach	.975
10. Cy Williams	.975
11. Cliff Heathcote	.974
12. Tris Speaker	.974
13. George Burns	.974
14. Hy Myers	.973
15. Clyde Barnhart	.973

In 1924, Goose Goslin (above) posted a .344 batting average, 199 hits, scored 100 runs, and became the first Washington Senator player to lead the AL in RBI, with 129.

Steady Scott Secures Shortstop with Glove

Lou Gehrig's record of 2,130 consecutive games played is full of ironical twists. Gehrig began the streak when he pinch hit for Pee Wee Wanninger, who in turn had replaced Everett Scott, the consecutive-games record holder prior to Gehrig, as the New York Yankees shortstop. Before losing his post to Wanninger, Scott had played 1,307 straight games. Even if he had not been so durable, though, Scott would have had a meritorious career. In his 11 seasons as a regular, he played on five American League pennant winners, three in Boston and two in New York, and led all AL shortstops in fielding eight years in a row between 1916 and 1923. When he posted a .976 fielding average in 1918 and then tied his own mark the following year, he set a new fielding average standard for shortstops that would endure until 1942. A woefully weak hitter, even for a shortstop, Scott was hampered in his bid for recognition among the game's immortals by his glaring lack of offensive production.

The 1927 Yankees beat the St. Louis Browns 21 times during the season to set the AL record.

In 1924, Cincinnati manager Pat Moran died during spring training and the club's first baseman, Jake Daubert, died after the season was over, following surgery.

Us Versus Them
"I never saw a game without taking sides and never want to see one. That is the soul of the game."
—Warren G. Harding

On July 5, 1929, the New York Giants became the first team to employ a public address system in their home park, the Polo Grounds.

Goose Goslin: "I loved to play against the Yankees, especially in Yankee Stadium. Boy, did I get a kick out of beating those guys. They were so great, you know, it was a thrill to beat them."

1920s MANAGER WINS	
1. Miller Huggins	927
2. John McGraw	836
3. Connie Mack	770
4. Wilbert Robinson	765
5. Tris Speaker	577
6. Bill McKechnie	538
7. Bucky Harris	499
8. Ty Cobb	479
9. Jack Hendricks	469
10. Branch Rickey	404

1920s MANAGER WINNING PERCENTAGE	
1. Miller Huggins	.608
2. Bill McKechnie	.585
3. Joe McCarthy	.581
4. John McGraw	.575
5. Donie Bush	.556
6. Bucky Harris	.544
7. Tris Speaker	.536
8. Pat Moran	.536
9. Ty Cobb	.519
10. Jack Hendricks	.510

As the skipper of the powerful Ruth and Gehrig Yankee teams, Miller Huggins (above) paced all 1920s managers in wins (927) and winning percentage (.608), as he led the Bronx Bombers to three world titles.

The Reading team of the International League in 1926 posted a .194 win percentage, going 31-129.

1920s TEAM WINNING PERCENTAGE

1.	New York-AL	.608
2.	New York-NL	.582
3.	Pittsburgh-NL	.572
4.	St.Louis-NL	.536
5.	Chicago-NL	.526
6.	Cincinnati-NL	.521
7.	Washington-AL	.519
8.	Cleveland-AL	.512
9.	Philadelphia-AL	.505
10.	Brooklyn-NL	.499
11.	St.Louis-AL	.498
12.	Detroit-AL	.494
13.	Chicago-AL	.476
14.	Boston-NL	.394
15.	Boston-AL	.388
16.	Philadelphia-NL	.370

Taylor Douthit Ranges Into Record Books

Many record-breaking performances seem to come from nowhere. Nothing in the careers of Earl Webb or Chief Wilson could possibly have prepared students of the game for their setting all-time single-season records for doubles and triples, respectively. Taylor Douthit's 1928 season is a similar aberration. Playing center field for the St. Louis Cardinals that year, Douthit made 547 putouts, nine more than any other outfielder in history. What's more, Douthit in 1928 collected 123 more putouts than any other outfielder in the majors. That means that on the average he caught nearly one more fly ball per game than his closest peer. He also scored 111 runs with a .295 average that year. In 1930, Douthit again topped NL gardeners in putouts but with just 425, a total much more within reason. His only other flirtation with recognition for his glove work came in 1927, the year before his record feat, when he paced all NL outfielders in errors.

Hall of Fame umpire Bill McGowan, who at one point officiated in a record 2,541 consecutive games, made his American League debut in 1925 after 12 seasons in the minors.

Shortstop Specs Toporcer, the first bespectacled infielder in major league history, hit .324 as the Cardinals' regular shortstop in 1922.

1920s TEAM WINS

		WON	LOST
1.	New York-AL	933	602
2.	New York-NL	890	639
3.	Pittsburgh-NL	877	656
4.	St.Louis-NL	822	712
5.	Chicago-NL	807	728
6.	Cincinnati-NL	798	735
7.	Washington-AL	792	735
8.	Cleveland-AL	786	749
9.	Philadelphia-AL	770	754
10.	Brooklyn-NL	765	768
11.	St.Louis-AL	762	769
12.	Detroit-AL	760	778
13.	Chicago-AL	731	804
14.	Boston-NL	603	928
15.	Boston-AL	595	938
16.	Philadelphia-NL	566	962

On August 5, 1921, Harold Arlen of radio station KDKA in Pittsburgh announced the first broadcast of a baseball game.

In 1926, the Cardinals won the first pennant by either a St. Louis National League or American League team.

On October 2, 1920, in the last tripleheader in major league history, between Pittsburgh and Cincinnati, umpire Peter Harrison was behind the plate in all three games.

"Funny thing, I played in the big leagues for 13 years—1914 through 1926—and the only thing anybody seems to remember is that once I made an unassisted triple play in a World Series.
—Bill Wambsganss

Chapter 6
The 1930s

Klein Clubless as Cubbie

At the conclusion of the 1933 season, Chuck Klein became the only player ever to be traded after a Triple Crown performance, when he was sent to the Chicago Cubs by the Philadelphia Phillies. The Phillies at the time had the worst pitching in the majors, meaning that Klein would now have an opportunity to feast on his former teammates. The Cubs were a much better team, able to surround Klein in the batting order with a corps of strong hitters. Hence it was expected that his slugging would only accelerate in the Windy City. Instead, for reasons that still remain elusive, Klein flopped so egregiously with the Cubs that Chicago returned him gladly to the Phillies early in the 1936 season. Even back in his old haunts, Klein was unable to retrieve his earlier form. He did have one last moment in the sun, though, after his return to the Quaker City club. On July 10, 1936, he slammed four home runs in a 10-inning game at Pittsburgh's Forbes Field, which during the 1930s was the most difficult park in the NL for sluggers to conquer.

The New York Yankees set a 20th-century major league record when they tallied 1,067 runs in 1931.

Above: *Chuck Klein, a powerful and fast outfielder, slugged 300 homers in his 17-year career, 180 of them in a five-year span with the Phillies from 1929 to 1933. Klein took advantage of the 280-foot right field fence of Philadelphia's Baker Bowl to lead the NL in home runs four times.*

The only player to have two seasons in which he collected 420 or more total bases is Chuck Klein, who did it in 1930 and 1932.

◆ ◆

In 1930, the National League set a record when it had three players—Chuck Klein, Hack Wilson, and Babe Herman— with 400 or more total bases.

Buddy Hassett, commenting on Paul Waner's theory of hitting, wrote: "He said he just laid his bat on his shoulder and when he saw a pitch he liked he threw it off."

In 1933, Chuck Klein of Philadelphia set a 20th-century record in the National League when he collected 200 hits for the fifth consecutive year.

1930s GAMES		
1.	Mel Ott	1,473
2.	Jimmie Foxx	1,470
3.	Paul Waner	1,463
4.	Earl Averill	1,445
5.	Charlie Gehringer	1,434
6.	Ben Chapman	1,431
7.	Gus Suhr	1,425
8.	Lou Gehrig	1,397
9.	Joe Cronin	1,391
10.	Dick Bartell	1,358
11.	Chuck Klein	1,344
12.	Leo Durocher	1,339
	Tony Cuccinello	1,339
14.	Wally Berger	1,328
15.	Sam West	1,316
16.	Al Simmons	1,305
17.	Joe Vosmik	1,259
18.	Pinky Whitney	1,234
19.	Lloyd Waner	1,233
20.	Buddy Myer	1,227
21.	Bill Dickey	1,213
	Doc Cramer	1,213
23.	Billy Rogell	1,207
24.	Billy Herman	1,198
25.	Rick Ferrell	1,196

Six players in major league history have collected more than 100 extra-base hits in a season, but the only one to do it more than once was Chuck Klein, in 1930 and again in 1932.

In 1932, Chuck Klein became the only player since the end of the dead-ball era to top his league in both total bases and stolen bases.

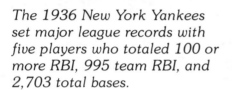

The 1936 New York Yankees set major league records with five players who totaled 100 or more RBI, 995 team RBI, and 2,703 total bases.

1930s RUNS	
1. Lou Gehrig	1,257
2. Jimmie Foxx	1,244
3. Charlie Gehringer	1,179
4. Earl Averill	1,102
5. Mel Ott	1,095
6. Ben Chapman	1,009
7. Paul Waner	973
8. Chuck Klein	955
9. Al Simmons	930
10. Joe Cronin	885
11. Buddy Myer	841
Doc Cramer	841
13. Wally Berger	806
14. Billy Herman	794
15. Sam West	782
16. Dick Bartell	781
17. Joe Vosmik	771
Joe Medwick	771
19. Goose Goslin	766
20. Arky Vaughan	754
21. Lyn Lary	752
22. Frankie Crosetti	738
23. Bob Johnson	728
24. Lloyd Waner	724
25. Joe Kuhel	722
Bill Dickey	722

Durable and consistent, Mel Ott (above) won six National League home run titles in a 22-year career with the New York Giants. He also led the NL in on-base percentage four times, runs scored twice, and outfield assists twice. Ott ranks eighth lifetime in RBI with 1,861.

In the early 1930s, NL pitchers were so stingy with walks that Mel Ott was the only senior loop hitter between 1931 and 1933 to collect as many as 75 walks in a season.

Journalists Thirst For Quotes

Joe DiMaggio related how unsophisticated he was as a rookie: "I can remember a reporter asking for a quote, and I didn't know what a quote was. I thought it was some kind of a soft drink."

Slugger Ott Also Garners Walks

New York Giants star Mel Ott was nicknamed "Master Melvin," largely for his skill at pounding balls over the inviting right field wall in the Polo Grounds, the Giants home field. But Ott could also have merited the nickname for his mastery at working pitchers for walks. Between 1929 and 1944, he led the National League in free passes six times and likewise topped the circuit on four occasions in on-base percentage. During each of those years, he was in the NL's top five in bases on balls. Ott never achieved the monstrous walk totals that Babe Ruth registered, but then no one else did either during Ruth's heyday. Pitchers in the 1930s were quite stingy for the most part with free trips to first base. When Ott paced the NL with 100 walks in 1932, he was the only senior loop performer to garner more than 65 passes. The following year his walk total dropped to 75, but he again led as his closest pursuer could collect only 72. Over his career Ott walked an average of once in every seven trips to the plate.

In 1930, Chuck Klein set a National League record with 158 runs scored.

Joe Hauser became the only player in organized baseball to twice slug 60 homers in a season in 1933, when he blasted 69 for Minneapolis of the American Association. In 1930, he totaled 63 for Baltimore of the International League.

Simmons Starts Strong, Stops Swiftly

Few players have managed to collect 100 RBI as rookies. A mere handful have had 100-RBI campaigns in each of their first two seasons, and only one man, Al Simmons, has commenced his career with more than three straight 100-RBI efforts. Simmons assembled no less than 11 consecutive seasons of 102 or more RBI, beginning with his frosh year of 1924 and ending in 1935 when he fell to just 79 ribbies. Between 1929 and 1933, Bucketfoot Al also became the first player in American League history to collect 200 or more hits for five consecutive years. He almost made it six in a row, as he had 192 safeties in 1934. At the finish of the 1939 season, Simmons had 2,864 hits and seemed within easy range of the coveted 3,000 mark. Age caught up to him abruptly, however, the following year, relegating him to spot duty for the remaining four years of his career. Simmons retired in 1944 with 2,927 hits and 1,827 RBI, good for 10th place on the all-time list.

Paul Waner, who was a drinking man, said about hitting: "I see three baseballs, but I only swing at the middle one."

On June 3, 1932, Lou Gehrig knocked four home runs in a single game, becoming the first major league player in the 20th century to do so.

New York Yankees first baseman Lou Gehrig (above) hit 493 home runs, winning three American League homer crowns while scoring 115 or more runs for 14 straight seasons. He led the AL in RBI five times and played in seven World Series. Gehrig's record of 2,130 consecutive games played was stopped by amyotrophic lateral sclerosis, which took his life in 1941.

Lou Gehrig of the New York Yankees set an AL record in 1931 when he drove home 184 runs.

In 1931, Lou Gehrig slammed a record three grand slams in a four-day period.

Lou Gehrig in 1934 tied an American League record by leading the loop in RBI for a fifth time.

Yankee first baseman Lou Gehrig slugged 14 homers against Cleveland in 1936, setting a record against one opponent in a single season.

Lou Gehrig set a career record with 23 grand slams.

1930s HITS	
1. Paul Waner	1,959
2. Charlie Gehringer	1,865
3. Jimmie Foxx	1,845
4. Lou Gehrig	1,802
5. Earl Averill	1,786
6. Al Simmons	1,700
7. Ben Chapman	1,697
8. Chuck Klein	1,676
9. Mel Ott	1,673
10. Joe Cronin	1,650
11. Lloyd Waner	1,585
12. Doc Cramer	1,557
13. Joe Vosmik	1,550
14. Billy Herman	1,540
15. Wally Berger	1,537
16. Dick Bartell	1,504
17. Sam West	1,502
18. Joe Medwick	1,492
19. Gus Suhr	1,442
20. Bill Dickey	1,431
21. Buddy Myer	1,426
22. Tony Cuccinello	1,424
23. Arky Vaughan	1,413
24. Heinie Manush	1,405
25. Jo-Jo Moore	1,348

Hafey Wins Photo-Finish '31 Batting Crown

Going into the final day of the 1931 season, Al Simmons had his second consecutive American League batting title locked up, but in the National League the crown was still at issue, so much so that mathematicians began calculating whether it was possible that the race could finish in a flat tie. At the end of the afternoon less than one percentage point separated the top three hitters in the senior loop. When their averages were calculated to the fourth decimal point, St. Louis Cardinals outfielder Chick Hafey stood at .3489; New York Giants first baseman Bill Terry, the defending bat titlist, was at .3486; and Hafey's teammate, first sacker Jim Bottomley, came in at .3482. The three were so tightly packed that if Bottomley, the third place finisher, had collected just one fewer at bat, he would have won the crown, and Hafey would have dropped from the top spot to third place if he had batted one more time without a base hit.

Lou Gehrig surpassed Everett Scott's record streak of 1,307 games played in 1933.

Lou Gehrig in 1938 totaled 100 or more RBI for a major league record 13th consecutive season.

Joe DiMaggio scored an AL rookie record 132 runs in 1936.

Above: *Chick Hafey, the first batting champion to wear glasses, suffered from illness much of his career. With the Cardinals and Reds, Hafey hit .329 or better six straight years, a streak that included his 1931 batting title.*

Twice during the 1932 season, Buzz Arlett socked four homers in a game for Baltimore of the International League.

The 1931 New York Yankees set a record with six players who scored 100 or more runs.

2,987 But Who's Counting?
Sam Rice explained why he retired with 2,987 hits: "You must remember, there wasn't much emphasis then on 3,000 hits. And to tell the truth, I didn't know how many hits I had when I quit."

Speak Softly and Carry a Big Stick
Mickey Cochrane said about Charlie Gehringer: "He says hello on opening day and goodbye on closing day, and in between he hits .350."

On June 27, 1932, Goose Goslin became the first major league player in history to hammer three homers in a game three times in his career.

On May 6, 1930, Gene Rye of Waco in the Texas League launched three home runs in one inning.

1930s DOUBLES	
1. Charlie Gehringer	400
2. Joe Cronin	386
3. Paul Waner	372
4. Earl Averill	354
5. Joe Medwick	353
6. Ben Chapman	346
7. Lou Gehrig	328
8. Dick Bartell	325
9. Chuck Klein	323
10. Billy Herman	322
11. Joe Vosmik	319
12. Jimmie Foxx	316
13. Wally Berger	297
14. Al Simmons	292
15. Gus Suhr	288
16. Mel Ott	287
17. Sam West	286
18. Tony Cuccinello	280
19. Heinie Manush	275
20. Gee Walker	269
21. Hank Greenberg	262
22. Goose Goslin	260
23. Babe Herman	258
24. Pepper Martin	251
25. Doc Cramer	248

Vosmik Sits, Plays, Loses Both Ways

The American League also had a batting race during the 1930s that resulted in a photo finish. Cleveland outfielder Joe Vosmik entered the last day of the 1935 season with a seemingly safe lead over second sacker Buddy Myer of the Washington Senators. To protect his batting average Vosmik was told to sit out the Tribe's doubleheader that afternoon. Alarmed when word reached the Cleveland press box that Myer was going wild in his finale, the Indians rushed Vosmik into action in the second half of the twin bill. Vosmik went 1-for-4, lowering his average to .348. Myer meanwhile was 4-for-5 in his finale to hike his average to .349, one point above Vosmik's. Of some consolation to Vosmik was the fact that his lone single on the closing day enabled him to beat Myer out by one hit for the loop lead in safeties; the irony is that if Vosmik had sat out the second game as well, he and Myer would have finished in a dead heat in both hits and batting average.

1930s TRIPLES	
1. Gus Suhr	114
Earl Averill	114
3. Paul Waner	112
4. John Stone	100
Ben Chapman	100
6. Arky Vaughan	94
7. Buddy Myer	92
8. Lou Gehrig	91
9. Joe Cronin	90
10. Al Simmons	89
11. Heinie Manush	88
12. Jimmie Foxx	87
13. Joe Vosmik	86
14. Sam West	84
Carl Reynolds	84
16. Joe Medwick	81
17. Charlie Gehringer	76
Kiki Cuyler	76
19. Lloyd Waner	74
20. Pepper Martin	71
Tony Lazzeri	71
Babe Herman	71
23. Bill Terry	70
Joe Kuhel	70
Ival Goodman	70
Earle Combs	70

Josh Gibson said about Cool Papa Bell: "Cool Papa Bell was so fast he could get out of bed, turn out the lights across the room, and be back in bed under the covers before the lights went out."

Above: *Chicago Cubs center fielder Hack Wilson led the NL in homers four times. Even at 5'6", 190 pounds, Wilson ran well, hit for a high average, and twice led the league in RBI and walks. A popular local favorite, his career declined after 1930 from excessive high living.*

In 1930, Cub outfielder Hack Wilson drove in a major league record 190 runs. He also set an NL record with 56 home runs.

Harry Heilmann, with the Reds after years with Detroit, was the first player to homer in every major league park in use during his career.

New York Giants first baseman Bill Terry in 1930 batted .401, the last .400 average in the league.

Hurler Red Lucas Comes Through in Pinch

The decade of the 1930s saw the emergence of a new phenomenon: the pinch-hitting specialist. For the first time, several teams had at least one player whose main job was to sit patiently in the dugout and await pivotal situations, usually late in the game, when his bat was needed. In 1932 Bill Terry's understudy for the New York Giants' first base job, Sam Leslie, broke Doc Miller's 19-year-old record for the most pinch hits in a season when he garnered 22 pinch blows. Leslie was so much a specialist that he played only two games in the field that season. Four years later, Ed Coleman of the St. Louis Browns was also seldom used in the field when he nabbed 20 pinch hits to set a new American League record.

The game's most consistently productive pinch hitter during the 1930s was Red Lucas, a pitcher who in 1929 had led the National League not only in pinch hits but also in complete games. The first player in major league history to accumulate 100 career pinch hits, Lucas retired in 1938 with 114 and still ranks high on the all-time list.

1930s HOME RUNS	
1. Jimmie Foxx	415
2. Lou Gehrig	347
3. Mel Ott	308
4. Wally Berger	241
5. Chuck Klein	238
6. Earl Averill	218
7. Hank Greenberg	206
8. Babe Ruth	198
9. Al Simmons	190
10. Bob Johnson	186
11. Hal Trosky	180
12. Bill Dickey	168
13. Gabby Hartnett	149
14. Dolph Camilli	148
15. Charlie Gehringer	146
16. Joe Medwick	145
17. Goose Goslin	140
18. Joe DiMaggio	137
19. Ripper Collins	135
20. Harlond Clift	123
21. Babe Herman	122
22. Tony Lazzeri	114
23. Zeke Bonura	112
24. Joe Cronin	108
25. Hack Wilson	107

Tony "Poosh-Em-Up" Lazzeri (above) played second base for the dominating New York Yankees teams of the 1920s and 1930s. Over his 14-year career, he batted .292 with nine seasons of 10 or more home runs. Noted for his fine glovework at second, Lazzeri compiled a Hall of Fame career though suffering from epilepsy.

In 1938, Hank Greenberg cudgeled a record 39 homers at home.

On May 24, 1936, Yankee Tony Lazzeri drove in an AL record 11 runs in a game.

"I had most of my trouble with lefthanded hitters. Charlie Gehringer could hit me in a tunnel at midnight with the lights out."

—Lefty Gomez

Above: *Hall of Fame first baseman Jimmie Foxx played 20 years in the majors. With the Philadelphia A's and Boston Red Sox, "Double X" won four home run crowns, three RBI titles, three batting championships, and the 1933 Triple Crown. Foxx hit 30 or more homers 12 straight seasons and hit 534 overall.*

1930s RUNS BATTED IN	
1. Jimmie Foxx	1,403
2. Lou Gehrig	1,358
3. Mel Ott	1,135
4. Al Simmons	1,081
5. Earl Averill	1,046
6. Joe Cronin	1,036
7. Charlie Gehringer	1,003
8. Chuck Klein	979
9. Bill Dickey	937
10. Wally Berger	893
11. Ben Chapman	880
12. Joe Medwick	873
13. Hank Greenberg	853
14. Joe Vosmik	819
15. Gus Suhr	813
16. Goose Goslin	788
17. Tony Lazzeri	787
18. Gabby Hartnett	777
19. Hal Trosky	767
20. Bob Johnson	750
21. Paul Waner	749
22. Tony Cuccinello	742
23. Pinky Whitney	709
24. John Stone	671
25. Sam West	668

Jimmie Foxx won American League Most Valuable Player honors in 1932 and 1933, becoming the first player to net consecutive awards.

Billy Evans explained why he signed Earl Averill: "There was something about the nonchalant Averill that won you over. I guess it was the easy, steady manner in which he did his work, without any great show."

Frederick Is Pinch Fence-Buster

For most of his six-year career with the Brooklyn Dodgers, Johnny Frederick was a regular outfielder who was used only occasionally as a pinch hitter. Indeed, he collected only 62 career pinch at bats and never more than nine pinch blows in a season. Of those nine pinch hits in 1932, nonetheless, six were home runs, giving Frederick a major league record that has endured since. What makes his achievement still more improbable is that he was never regarded as a slugger. His best home run percentage was 4.2 in that 1932 season. Following his record-breaking season, he collected just seven home runs in 1933 in 556 at bats, and his home run percentage for his career is 2.7. Released by the Dodgers after the 1934 season, Frederick dropped down to the Pacific Coast League. Even there he rapped a mere 35 home runs in his final six seasons of professional ball, averaging less per year as a full-time player in the minors than he had achieved in 1932 exclusively as a pinch hitter.

Philadelphia Athletics first baseman Jimmie Foxx barely lost the Triple Crown in 1932, winning the homer and RBI crowns with 58 home runs and 169 RBI, but losing the batting crown to Dale Alexander .367 to .364. Alexander had 392 at bats and was back in the minors the next season. Foxx's 58 homers that year were the most by anyone other than Babe Ruth.

When he copped the American League hitting crown in 1937 at age 34, Charlie Gehringer set a junior loop record for the oldest player to win his first batting title.

1930s STOLEN BASES

1.	Ben Chapman	269
2.	Billy Werber	176
3.	Gee Walker	158
	Lyn Lary	158
5.	Pepper Martin	136
6.	Kiki Cuyler	118
7.	Roy Johnson	115
8.	Charlie Gehringer	101
9.	Stan Hack	100
	Pete Fox	100
11.	Frankie Frisch	94
12.	Tony Lazzeri	86
	Luke Appling	86
14.	Joe Kuhel	85
15.	Frankie Crosetti	84
16.	Augie Galan	81
17.	Tony Piet	80
18.	Buddy Myer	78
19.	Carl Reynolds	77
20.	Billy Rogell	76
21.	Jo-Jo White	75
22.	Lou Gehrig	72
23.	Chuck Klein	71
24.	Bill Cissell	70
25.	Joe Cronin	69

Catcher Lombardi Cruises to Crown

Some purists were still contending that no catcher had ever legitimately won a major league batting title when Ernie Lombardi put an end to the controversy. In 1938, Lombardi hit .342 to cop the National League hitting crown by five points. More important to the purists, he had 489 at bats, well above the figure of 400 that many in the game felt should be the true minimum standard. Reds backstopper Bubbles Hargrave hit .353 in 1926 to win a crown, but with only 326 at bats. Lombardi was also awarded a second batting crown in 1942 for hitting .330, albeit in only 309 at bats. His latter triumph marked the last time except for the strike-torn 1981 season that a player won recognition as a major league hitting leader with fewer than 400 at bats. It also was the last time that a catcher has finished at the top of the heap in a batting race. If the rule had not been changed subsequent to 1942, requiring 400 at bats, backstopper Smoky Burgess, who hit .368 for the Phillies in 105 games, would have been granted the National League batting crown in 1954.

Chuck Klein won the National League Triple Crown in 1933, batting .368 with 28 homers and 120 RBI. Jimmie Foxx won the AL Triple Crown that year, batting .356 with 48 homers and 163 RBI. This was the only time both leagues had a Triple Crown winner in the same season.

Line-drive-hitting catcher Ernie Lombardi (above) batted .330 or better five times despite his lack of speed. Possessor of a powerful throwing arm, he won the 1938 batting title and helped his Cincinnati Reds win NL crowns in 1939 and 1940.

In 1935, Phil Cavarretta set all-time season records for the most hits, runs, RBI, triples, doubles, and total bases by a teenage major leaguer.

In 1932, Dale Alexander of the Red Sox became the first American League batting champ from a last-place team.

Seventeen years after he hit a record 18 homers in a month, Rudy York in 1954 was earning $150 a month as a fire fighter. In an interview in '54, he said: "I've heard thousands cheer for me, like the time I hit the home run that beat the Cardinals in the first game [of the World Series] in 1946. I've been rich."

Average NL Hitter Bats .303 in 1930

Hitters had the time of their lives in 1930. Four teams in the American League batted over .300, but pitchers were even more ravaged in the National League where the average hitter in 1930 posted a .303 mark. As a result, Bill Terry's .401 figure—the last .400 season to date in the NL—was only 98 points above the league norm, and he needed to go down to the wire before besting Babe Herman (.393) and Chuck Klein (.386) for the batting crown. Terry's New York Giants were similarly hard-pressed before copping the team batting award. New York's .319 figure, though a 20th century record, was only four points better than the runner-up Philadelphia Phillies, who hit .315 as a unit (although the Phillies had a last-place record). Even Cincinnati, the most punchless club in the loop with 665 runs and a .281 batting average, had marks that would have outhit and outscored every team in the National League in 1917, the last year during the dead-ball era that a full schedule was played.

The last time Babe Ruth was a league-leader in a major offensive department was in 1933 when he paced the AL in bases on balls.

First baseman Lu Blue hit just one home run in 155 games with the Chicago White Sox in 1931 but nevertheless set a club record when he walked 127 times.

According to legend, Babe Ruth made his famous "called shot" (above) in the 1932 fall classic. Whether he actually called it, the home run was his last four-bagger in the World Series.

Babe Ruth was the first documented player to fan 1,000 times in his career in 1930.

Babe Ruth slugged the first homer in All-Star competition—a two-run shot in the first game, in 1933.

Wait'll Next Year

"Baseball is like this. Have one good year and you can fool them for five more, because for five more years they expect you to have another good one."
—Frankie Frisch

1930s STRIKEOUTS		
1.	Jimmie Foxx	876
2.	Wally Berger	685
3.	Dolph Camilli	592
4.	Tony Lazzeri	591
5.	Hank Greenberg	556
6.	Frankie Crosetti	542
7.	Ben Chapman	485
8.	Bob Johnson	478
9.	Mel Ott	474
10.	Al Simmons	458
11.	Bruce Campbell	455
12.	Joe Cronin	452
13.	Lyn Lary	448
14.	Earl Averill	447
15.	Lou Gehrig	439
16.	Sam West	435
	Dick Bartell	435
18.	Woody English	432
19.	Gus Suhr	428
20.	Gabby Hartnett	416
21.	Kiki Cuyler	411
22.	Harlond Clift	409
23.	Pepper Martin	401
24.	Pinky Higgins	398
25.	Chuck Klein	395

Tom Oliver, an outfielder with the Red Sox in the early 1930s, holds the post-1900 record for the most career at bats (1,931) without ever hitting a home run.

Doc Cramer of the Red Sox set an American league record in 1938 when he was homerless for the season in 658 at bats.

When shortstop Bunny Griffiths of San Diego in the Pacific Coast League went homerless in 1939, it marked the ninth straight season he had played 110 or more games and failed to hit a home run.

1930s BATTING AVERAGE	
1. Bill Terry	.352
2. Lou Gehrig	.343
3. Joe Medwick	.338
4. Paul Waner	.336
5. Jimmie Foxx	.336
6. Babe Ruth	.331
7. Charlie Gehringer	.331
8. Arky Vaughan	.329
9. Chuck Klein	.326
10. Al Simmons	.325
11. Heinie Manush	.324
12. Mickey Cochrane	.323
13. Hank Greenberg	.323
14. Cecil Travis	.321
15. Babe Herman	.321
16. Bill Dickey	.320
17. Earl Averill	.318
18. Hal Trosky	.317
19. Pie Traynor	.316
20. Chick Hafey	.315
21. Ernie Lombardi	.315
22. Kiki Cuyler	.313
23. Mel Ott	.313
24. Zeke Bonura	.313
25. Gee Walker	.312

Nicknamed "Old Aches and Pains," shortstop Luke Appling (above) won two batting titles for the White Sox. Combining high walk totals and high batting averages, Appling scored 90 runs six times.

Foul

Luke Appling, famed for fouling pitches into stands, was once denied a request for two baseballs to give to admiring fans by a White Sox official because they cost $2.75 apiece. Appling then proceeded to foul ten straight pitches into the stands. He looked toward the official sitting in the club boxes and yelled: "That's $27.50 and I'm not done yet."

Luke Appling of the Chicago White Sox set a 20th-century record for shortstops when he hit .388 in 1936 to cop the American League batting crown.

In 1936, outfielder Woody Jensen of the Pirates totaled 696 at bats, the all-time record for a 154-game season.

High Low Card in '30 With .279 Mark

The St. Louis Cardinals' team batting average of .314 made them merely the National League's third-best hitting club in 1930, but the Redbirds used their hits to bag a 20th-century loop record 1,004 runs. Part of the reason the Cards scored so freely was that their batting order was packed from top to bottom with .300 hitters. In 1930, every Cardinals regular hit at least .300, ranging from rookie George Watkins's .373 figure to Taylor Douthit's .303. To add to the Cards' riches, backup outfielder Showboat Fisher rapped .374, second-string catcher Gus Mancuso finished at .366, and spot performer Ray Blades clubbed 40 hits in just 101 at bats to give him a .396 mark. The only member of the club's cast to have cause for embarrassment was utility infielder Andy High, a mere .279 hitter. Move the calendar up 38 years to 1968, when pitchers reigned supreme, and High's .279 mark would have tied for second place on the Cardinals' team stats.

Outfielder Johnny Cooney hit the only two home runs of his 20-year career in the majors on consecutive days in 1939.

In 1933, eight years before his major league-record 56-game hitting streak, Joe DiMaggio hit safely in 61 consecutive games for San Francisco of the Pacific Coast League.

Medwick Muscles Way to 1937 Triple Crown

Starting in 1933, Cardinals outfielder Ducky Medwick started ringing up impressive statistics, finishing near the top of the league in several offensive categories. After knocking at the door for a few seasons, he finally broke through in 1937 to win the National League batting title. Since Medwick also paced the loop in RBI with 154, and his 31 homers tied Mel Ott for the four-bagger lead, Medwick additionally claimed the Triple Crown. It was to be the last such achievement to date by a National League player. The closest anyone has come in the years since was in 1948 when another Cardinal, Stan Musial, missed the Triple Crown by a margin of one home run. Medwick followed his Triple Crown season by having another good year in 1938, hitting .322, topping the NL in doubles for the third consecutive year, and bagging his second consecutive RBI title. Although just 26 years old that season, he never again was a league leader in a major hitting department.

"Baseball must be a great game to survive the fools who run it."

—Bill Terry

In 1930, the New York Yankees scored a post-1901 major league record 591 runs on the road; nine years later the Yankees scored 585 runs on the road while playing three fewer games away from home than they did in 1930.

Above: *Joe "Ducky" Medwick played left field with the Cardinals' hustling "Gashouse Gang." A 10-time .300 batter, he led the NL in doubles and RBI three times each.*

Lloyd Waner set a record in 1933 for the fewest strikeouts by an outfielder in 500 or more at bats, when he struck out just eight times.

On September 29, 1935, catcher Aubrey Epps of the Pirates went 3-for-4 in his only big league game and knocked home three runs.

In his only taste of big league action, outfielder Tom Hughes hit .373 in 17 games for Detroit in 1930.

1930s SLUGGING AVERAGE	
1. Jimmie Foxx	.652
2. Babe Ruth	.644
3. Lou Gehrig	.638
4. Hank Greenberg	.617
5. Hal Trosky	.563
6. Mel Ott	.560
7. Joe Medwick	.552
8. Chuck Klein	.551
9. Earl Averill	.538
10. Bob Johnson	.537
11. Babe Herman	.533
12. Al Simmons	.524
13. Wally Berger	.522
14. Bill Dickey	.513
15. Bill Terry	.510
16. Charlie Gehringer	.507
17. Chick Hafey	.507
18. Dolph Camilli	.504
19. Zeke Bonura	.504
20. Ripper Collins	.495
21. Gabby Hartnett	.492
22. Mickey Cochrane	.491
23. Goose Goslin	.488
24. Harlond Clift	.482
25. Joe Cronin	.476

Joe "Ducky" Medwick of the Cardinals cracked an NL record 64 doubles in 1936.

On April 19, 1938, Dodger Ernie Koy and Phillie Heinie Mueller each homered in their first major league at bat in the same game.

St. Louis Cardinal outfielder George Watkins set a major league rookie record in 1930 when he batted .373.

"There's no room for sentiment in baseball if you want to win."

—Frankie Frisch

Mize Just Misses Triple Crowns in 1939 and '40

When Stan Musial fell short by one home run in his bid to capture the National League home run crown in 1948, he also missed becoming the Cardinals' first home run leader since 1940 when St. Louis first sacker Johnny Mize snared his second consecutive four-bagger crown. The previous season Mize had topped the senior loop in round trippers with 28 and also copped the batting crown with a .348 mark. RBI, normally Mize's forte, proved to be the lone stumbling block in his quest for a Triple Crown—he finished with 108, 20 behind the leader, Frank McCormick of the Reds. In 1940, Mize easily paced the NL in ribbies with 137 and again took the four-bagger crown with a Cardinals-record 43 round trippers, but this time his quest was thwarted by his .314 batting average, a sizeable 41 points behind Debs Garms's loop-leading figure of .355. If the 400 at bat rule had been in effect in 1940, however, Mize would have missed the Triple Crown by a scant three points. Among National League players with 400 or more at bats, only Stan Hack at .317 ranked ahead of Mize.

First baseman Johnny Mize (above) led the NL in home runs four times. "The Big Cat" is the only player to hit three homers in a game six times. Later, with the Yankees, he led the AL in pinch hits three straight seasons.

1930s ON-BASE AVERAGE	
1. Babe Ruth	.472
2. Lou Gehrig	.453
3. Jimmie Foxx	.440
4. Mickey Cochrane	.434
5. Mel Ott	.420
6. Arky Vaughan	.420
7. Hank Greenberg	.415
8. Charlie Gehringer	.414
9. Harlond Clift	.404
10. Bob Johnson	.401
11. Bill Terry	.399
12. Paul Waner	.399
13. Luke Appling	.399
14. Buddy Myer	.399
15. Earl Averill	.397
16. Joe Cronin	.394
17. Dolph Camilli	.393
18. Bill Dickey	.389
19. Ben Chapman	.389
20. Rick Ferrell	.388
21. Zeke Bonura	.386
22. Stan Hack	.386
23. Chuck Klein	.384
24. Babe Herman	.380
25. Goose Goslin	.380

The St. Louis Cardinals have not had an NL home run king since 1940, when Johnny Mize bagged the crown with 43 taters.

Stan Hack said about his hometown: "It's so small we don't even have a town drunk. Everybody has to take a turn."

The last player to lead the NL in both home runs and batting in the same season was Johnny Mize of the St. Louis Cardinals in 1939.

Despite hitting .355 in a late-season trial in 1938 and becoming the first White Sox player to have a three-homer game in Comiskey Park, Merv Connors was dropped by the Sox and never again played in the majors.

Diz Is All-Around Whiz

Dizzy Dean was one of the last great starting pitchers who was also used frequently in relief roles. When he won 30 games in 1934 to become the most recent National League hurler to reach that figure, four of his victories came as a reliever, and he also notched seven saves. Two years later, in the process of winning 24 games, he became the last pitcher to top his league in both complete games and saves. The colorful Dean was also among the better hitting pitchers during the 1930s and often helped his own cause. In 1931, his last minor league season, he pitched for Houston of the Texas League. One afternoon he hit a solo homer to give his club an early lead. When manager Joe Schultz removed him from the mound after he ran into trouble, Dean stalked out to the scoreboard in center field and took down his marker, arguing that if he wasn't allowed to keep pitching, Houston couldn't have his run.

Above: *Pitcher Jay Hanna "Dizzy" Dean was the biggest star of the Cardinals' "Gashouse Gang." The flamboyant righty.won 58 games in 1934 and '35, led the NL in innings pitched three times, and captured four strikeout titles before a sore arm cut his career short.*

Dizzy Dean, the famed hurler and good ol' boy, commented on his mangled English: "A lot of folks that ain't saying 'ain't' ain't eating."

In 1934, St. Louis Card hurler Dizzy Dean won 30 games, the last National League hurler to garner 30 victories.

St. Louis Cardinal rookie Dizzy Dean led the National League with 191 strikeouts in 1932.

Dizzy Dean in 1936 was the last major league pitcher to lead his league in complete games (28) and saves (11) in the same year.

On July 19, 1933, Dizzy Dean fanned 17 Cubs, setting a modern major league record.

"I may not have been the greatest pitcher ever, but I was amongst 'em."
—*Dizzy Dean*

King Carl
After watching Carl Hubbell in the 1934 All-Star Game fan Babe Ruth, Lou Gehrig, Jimmie Foxx, Al Simmons, and Joe Cronin in a row, Frankie Frisch commented: "I could play second base 15 more years behind this guy. He doesn't need any help."

Carl Hubbell of the Giants won an all-time record 24 straight games in 1936 and 1937.

1930s GAMES PITCHED	
1. Larry French	430
2. Jack Russell	394
3. Mel Harder	385
4. Carl Hubbell	383
5. Charlie Root	377
6. Paul Derringer	375
7. Bump Hadley	374
8. Dick Coffman	366
9. Lefty Grove	351
10. Fred Frankhouse	345
11. Clint Brown	344
12. Willis Hudlin	338
13. Red Ruffing	334
14. Syl Johnson	327
15. Chief Hogsett	323
Wes Ferrell	323
17. Lefty Gomez	322
18. Lon Warneke	318
19. Earl Whitehill	317
20. Guy Bush	316
21. Ed Brandt	314
22. Danny MacFayden	313
23. Tommy Bridges	309
24. Bill Swift	305
Dizzy Dean	305

1930s COMPLETE GAMES	
1. Wes Ferrell	207
2. Red Ruffing	201
3. Carl Hubbell	197
Lefty Grove	197
5. Ted Lyons	168
6. Lefty Gomez	163
Paul Derringer	163
8. Larry French	160
9. Tommy Bridges	156
10. Dizzy Dean	151
11. Lon Warneke	146
12. Red Lucas	136
13. Earl Whitehill	134
Mel Harder	134
15. Bobo Newsom	129
16. Danny MacFayden	128
17. Ed Brandt	125
18. Van Mungo	114
19. Bill Lee	110
20. Freddie Fitzsimmons	109
21. Willis Hudlin	101
22. Hal Schumacher	100
General Crowder	100
24. Guy Bush	99
25. Bump Hadley	98

On August 15, 1932, Tommy Bridges of the Tigers lost a chance at a perfect game when pinch-hitter Dave Harris of the Senators hit a bloop single with two out in the ninth inning.

Above: *"King Carl" Hubbell, ace New York Giants lefty, threw his screwball past hitters for 16 NL seasons. Hubbell led the NL in wins and ERA three times and was the league's Most Valuable Player in 1933 and 1936.*

Carl Hubbell's 1.66 ERA in 1933 (in 308 frames) was the lowest ever by an NL lefty for over 300 innings.

Phillies Hurlers Hit Hard and Often in 1930

In 1930, when the Philadelphia Phillies hit .315 as a unit under manager Burt Shotton to set a 20th century club record, they averaged over six runs a game. Shotton's men nonetheless finished in last place, winning just 52 of 154 contests, as the team's pitchers surrendered nearly seven runs per nine innings. The leading miscreants were Les Sweetland (7.71 ERA), Claude Willoughby (7.59 ERA), and Hal Elliott (7.67 ERA). This trio was instrumental in dooming the 1930 Phillies to a 6.71 staff ERA, the worst in the 20th century. Philadelphia allowed 16.8 baserunners per nine innings. And although the Phils batted .315 and had a .367 on-base percentage, their opponents were able to bat at a .345 clip and get an on-base average of .405. So ghastly was the club's pitching that only one hurler, Phil Collins (4.78) managed to post an ERA below the NL average mark of 4.97. Amid the chaos, Collins even succeeded in fashioning a winning record of 16-11; the rest of the Phils mound corps meanwhile had an aggregate 36-91 record.

Pitcher Red Lucas led the National League in pinch hits four times.

Between 1927 and 1933, Pat Malone of the Chicago Cubs was the only NL hurler to win 20 games in a season more than once.

Detroit's Schoolboy Rowe in 1934 tied Lefty Grove's American League record by notching 16 straight victories.

Lefty Grove, asked whether money was important when he played, responded: "Sure, I looked for as much as I could get. But the truth was, I would have played for nothing. Of course I never told Connie [Mack] that."

Lefty Grove (above) dominated AL hitters for 17 seasons, leading the league in strikeouts his first seven years. Of his 300 lifetime victories, 203 came after he turned age 30.

AL Mound City Mound Staff Roundly Unsound

During the 1930s, the St. Louis Browns hill staff never sank to the depths that the Phillies hurlers had in 1930, but in one vital respect the Browns were even more disgraceful. Between 1935 and 1939, the American League Mound City entry posted the junior loop's worst ERA for five straight years. The low point came in 1936 when the Browns registered a 6.24 ERA and surrendered 1,064 runs; both figures stand as all-time American League negative marks. Poor as St. Louis' pitching was in 1936, the team still managed to dodge the cellar. The following year, however, the Brownies plummeted deep into the AL basement, when the pitching improved throughout the junior circuit while their own mound work remained horrendous. In 1937, the Browns' staff ERA of 6.00 was 1.15 runs per game higher than that of the Philadelphia Athletics, the loop's second-worst pitching crew. As a result, St. Louis had a dismal .299 winning percentage despite a .285 team batting average that ranked second that year in the AL.

Lefty Grove won an AL record 16 straight games in 1931.

On August 23, 1931, Lefty Grove of the A's missed collecting an American league-record 17th straight win when he lost 1-0 to the Browns after his left fielder misplayed a fly ball.

The first pitcher in history to hurl 50 or more games and register fewer than 10 decisions was Orville Jorgens of the 1937 Phillies.

In 1933, National League pitchers had a collective earned run average nearly a full run below American League pitchers, 3.34 to 4.28.

When Johnny Vander Meer tossed back-to-back no-hitters in 1938, it marked the only season between 1917 and 1944 that there were two no-nos in the National League.

1930s SAVES		
1.	Johnny Murphy	54
2.	Clint Brown	49
3.	Jack Russell	37
4.	Chief Hogsett	33
	Joe Heving	33
	Dick Coffman	33
7.	Bob Smith	31
	Lefty Grove	31
9.	Jack Quinn	30
	Syl Johnson	30
	Carl Hubbell	30
	Dizzy Dean	30
13.	Charlie Root	28
14.	Wilcy Moore	26
	Firpo Marberry	26
16.	Willis Hudlin	23
	Waite Hoyt	23
18.	Pat Malone	22
	Mace Brown	22
20.	Mel Harder	21
	Hi Bell	21
22.	Bump Hadley	20
23.	Jack Knott	19
	Curt Davis	19
	Phil Collins	19
	Don Brennan	19

Newsom Wins 20 Despite 5.08 ERA

When Dave Stewart of the Oakland Athletics lost his final decision in 1991, he missed becoming the first pitcher since Bobo Newsom in 1938 to post a winning record in 200 or more innings of work despite having an ERA above 5.00. What made Newsom's performance all the more remarkable was that he was pitching for a seventh-place team. In 1938, while his St. Louis Browns mates were finishing with a 55-97 record, Newsom somehow went 20-16 despite notching a 5.08 ERA, the worst in history by a 20-game winner. He also led the loop in complete games and innings pitched that year. Newsom's achievement was by no means without a precedent, though, during the 1930s. In the high-scoring 1930 season, Pittsburgh's Remy Kremer became the first 20-game winner with a 5.00 plus ERA (5.02), and seven years later Roxie Lawson of the Tigers had a dazzling 18-7 record on a 5.26 ERA. Lawson's .720 winning percentage in 1937 stands as the best ever by a pitcher who gave up more than five earned runs a game.

In 1930, Brooklyn moundsman Dazzy Vance's 2.61 ERA was 1.15 runs better than the next-lowest ERA in the National League, belonging to Carl Hubbell. Lefty Grove's 2.54 ERA in 1930 was 0.76 runs better than the next-lowest ERA in the AL, belonging to Wes Ferrell.

Above: *Cincinnati Reds hurler Johnny Vander Meer, "The Dutch Master," won consecutive strikeout crowns in 1941, 1942, and 1943 with his hard sinking fastball. He compiled 115 victories in an injury-shortened career.*

It's Academic

Dizzy Dean revealed his pitching strategy to sportswriter Red Smith: "I never tried to outsmart nobody. It was easier to outdummy them."

In 1938, Cincinnati's Johnny Vander Meer became the only pitcher in major league history to throw back-to-back no-hitters. He no-hit Boston on June 11 and shut down the Dodgers on June 15.

Cleveland hurler Johnny Allen in 1937 set an American League record with a .938 winning percentage.

In 1933, last-place Cincinnati set a National League record when its pitching staff issued just 257 walks.

1930s SHUTOUTS

1.	Larry French	32
2.	Carl Hubbell	31
3.	Red Ruffing	28
4.	Lefty Grove	26
	Lefty Gomez	26
	Dizzy Dean	26
7.	Tommy Bridges	25
8.	Lon Warneke	24
9.	Bill Lee	23
	Paul Derringer	23
11.	Hal Schumacher	20
12.	Freddie Fitzsimmons	17
	Ed Brandt	17
14.	Van Mungo	16
	Mel Harder	16
	Wes Ferrell	16
17.	Schoolboy Rowe	15
	Tex Carleton	15
19.	Bucky Walters	14
	Bill Walker	14
	Bill Hallahan	14
	Lou Fette	14
23.	Danny MacFayden	13
	Cy Blanton	13
25.	Bobo Newsom	12
	George Earnshaw	12
	Johnny Allen	12

Struggling righthanded pitcher Red Ruffing (above) joined the Yankees in 1931 and reeled off 231 wins in pinstripes over the next 15 years.

Don't Sweat It
When asked if he ever threw a spitter, Lefty Gomez replied: "Not intentionally, but I sweat easy."

In 1937, Giants rookie Cliff Melton won 20 games, tied for the National League lead in saves and was second in the NL in both ERA and winning percentage.

On June 10, 1938, Bill Lefebvre of the Red Sox became the first pitcher in American League history to homer in his first major league at bat.

1930s WINS	
1. Lefty Grove	199
2. Carl Hubbell	188
3. Red Ruffing	175
4. Wes Ferrell	170
5. Lefty Gomez	165
6. Mel Harder	158
7. Larry French	156
8. Tommy Bridges	150
9. Paul Derringer	148
10. Dizzy Dean	147
11. Lon Warneke	144
12. Earl Whitehill	131
13. Bump Hadley	121
14. Freddie Fitzsimmons	120
15. Hal Schumacher	117
Ted Lyons	117
17. General Crowder	115
18. Charlie Root	114
19. Guy Bush	112
20. Johnny Allen	108
21. Bill Lee	106
22. Willis Hudlin	105
23. Ed Brandt	104
24. Van Mungo	101
Danny MacFayden	101

Red Sox Hurlers Not Durable Goods

By the end of the 1930s, the hitting and scoring onslaught that prevailed throughout the decade had so drained pitchers that in 1939 the New York Yankees nearly became the first team to win a pennant without a single hurler capable of working 200 innings. Only Red Ruffing (233 innings) kept the Bronx Bombers from that dubious distinction. The previous year, the Boston Red Sox had become the first team to finish as high as second lacking a pitcher good for at least 200 innings of work. In 1939, the Crimson Hose repeated as the American League runner-up without a true staff leader. Jim Bagby Jr. led the 1938 Crimson Hose with 198⅔ innings, while Lefty Grove topped the '39 club with 191 innings. The BoSox dipped to fourth in 1940, with Bagby (183 innings) the only moundsman who hurled more than 158 frames. When rookie Dick Newsome won 19 games in 214 innings in 1941, he gave the Red Sox their largest hill output since 1937, when Grove, Jack Wilson, and Bobo Newsom all labored over 200 innings.

Above: *Yankee hurler Lefty Gomez collected 189 wins in a 14-year career that included four 20-game win seasons, two ERA titles, and six World Series victories.*

1930s INNINGS	
1. Carl Hubbell	2,596.2
2. Larry French	2,481.2
3. Red Ruffing	2,439.0
4. Lefty Grove	2,399.0
5. Wes Ferrell	2,345.1
6. Paul Derringer	2,343.2
7. Mel Harder	2,326.0
8. Lefty Gomez	2,234.2
9. Earl Whitehill	2,129.1
10. Bump Hadley	2,121.2
11. Tommy Bridges	2,083.0
12. Lon Warneke	2,021.0
13. Danny MacFayden	1,997.0
14. Ted Lyons	1,972.0
15. Freddie Fitzsimmons	1,937.2
16. Dizzy Dean	1,908.1
17. Ed Brandt	1,875.1
18. Charlie Root	1,829.1
19. Hal Schumacher	1,736.2
20. Willis Hudlin	1,736.1
21. Van Mungo	1,715.1
22. Bobo Newsom	1,689.2
23. Guy Bush	1,628.1
24. Red Lucas	1,622.0
25. Fred Frankhouse	1,620.2

Lefty Gomez set an All-Star Game record for the longest pitching stint when he went six innings in 1935 in helping the American League to a 4-1 victory.

The 1937 Boston Braves were the only team in this century to have two rookie 20-game winners, Lou Fette and Jim Turner; both were over age 30.

Roy Mahaffey, who last pitched in the majors in 1936, holds the 20th-century record for the most complete games (45) without ever tossing a shutout.

Murphy Slams Door on Yankee Foes

One important reason that Red Ruffing was the only member of the New York Yankees' hill unit to pitch over 200 innings in 1939 was the mound depth that manager Joe McCarthy enjoyed. McCarthy had seven pitchers who won at least 10 games. Furthermore, the Yankees were equipped with Johnny Murphy, the first hurler to carve an outstanding career while functioning almost exclusively as a relief pitcher. An occasional starter during his early seasons with the Yankees in the mid-1930s (he notched more than 200 innings pitched in 1934, getting 10 complete games), Murphy by 1939 had found a permanent niche in the bullpen. That year he notched a career-high 19 saves, but he had several other seasons nearly as good. Because of the regularity with which he dowsed enemy uprisings, Murphy was nick-named "Fireman Johnny." He finished in 1947 with 73 career relief wins and 107 career saves; both marks at that juncture were all-time records.

"I'd rather be lucky than good."

—Lefty Gomez

In 1931, for the first time in history, no pitcher won 20 games in a major league. Three National League hurlers—Pittsburgh's Heinie Meine, St. Louis' Wild Bill Hallahan, and Philadelphia's Jumbo Jim Elliott—tied for the loop lead with 19 wins.

Brown's Fame Comes with Fog

The National League had no bullpen operatives of Johnny Murphy's quality during the 1930s. Early in the decade, ancient Jack Quinn of the Brooklyn Dodgers was the loop's top fireman, but by the end of the period Pittsburgh's Mace Brown claimed that honor. Like most of the leading relievers in that era, Brown was also used frequently as a starter. In 1938, however, 49 of his league-leading 51 mound appearances were relief assignments. Brown shattered the major league single-season record for relief wins that year when he bagged 15 victories out of the bullpen, two more than Wilcy Moore logged as a Yankees rookie in 1927. But the taste of his magnificent season turned to ashes in his mouth on September 28, 1938, at Wrigley Field in Chicago. With the score tied 5-5 and darkness falling, Brown retired the first two Cubs in the bottom of the ninth but then served up a two-strike four-bagger to catcher Gabby Hartnett that vaulted the Cubs into first place ahead of Brown's Pirates. When the Cubs clinched the flag two days later, Brown earned ever-lasting fame as the man who surrendered "The Homer in the Gloamin'."

In 1934, Dizzy Dean's brother Paul hurled the first no-hitter in the National League since 1929 when he beat Brooklyn 3-0 on September 21. Dizzy shut out the Dodgers in the other game of the double-header.

Above: *Paul, left, and Dizzy Dean were not only teammates but best friends. During the 1934 season, Dizzy staged a short strike so Paul could get a raise on his $3,000 salary.*

1930s STRIKEOUTS

1.	Lefty Gomez	1,337
2.	Lefty Grove	1,313
3.	Carl Hubbell	1,281
4.	Red Ruffing	1,260
5.	Tommy Bridges	1,207
6.	Dizzy Dean	1,144
7.	Van Mungo	1,022
8.	Paul Derringer	1,018
9.	Bump Hadley	1,006
10.	Bobo Newsom	963
11.	Larry French	901
12.	Lon Warneke	877
13.	Wes Ferrell	867
14.	Johnny Allen	838
15.	Charlie Root	818
16.	Mel Harder	812
17.	Earl Whitehill	783
18.	Bill Hallahan	768
19.	Ed Brandt	743
20.	George Earnshaw	736
21.	Tex Carleton	720
22.	Bob Feller	712
23.	Pat Malone	703
24.	Monte Pearson	652
25.	Bill Lee	640

In 1934, Paul Dean's strikeouts per game ratio of 5.79 was the highest in the majors, and his brother Dizzy was second with 5.63.

When he registered a .345 winning percentage in 1938, Larry French of the Cubs set the all-time record for the lowest winning percentage by a full-time starting pitcher on a pennant winner.

Rapid

Bucky Harris, Washington manager, instructed his players before a game in which the Senators were to face Bob Feller: "Go up and hit what you see. And if you don't see it, come on back."

Ferrell Gives Way to Young Feller

In the summer of 1935, the Cleveland brass suffered in silence as Wes Ferrell led the American League in wins after having been traded to the Boston Red Sox the previous year for next to nothing. Much of the abuse heaped on the Tribe's front office turned to praise, however, when the local press got its first look at the 16-year-old pitching phenom Cleveland scout Cy Slapnicka signed. Even at that tender age, Bob Feller's blazing speed was so apparent that it brought instant comparison to Walter Johnson. The problem for Cleveland was that Slapnicka had signed Feller illegally while he was still in high school. When Slapnicka's gaffe came to light, it was expected that Commissioner Kenesaw Mountain Landis would void Feller's contract with Cleveland. Instead Landis elected to accept its validity, thereby averting a potential bidding war for Feller that might have toppled the already shaky financial underpinnings of the game during the last years of the Depression.

On September 23, 1936, 17-year-old Indian Bob Feller set an AL record when he struck out 17 batters in a game. He set the modern major league record in 1938 with 18 Ks in a game.

In 1931, Cleveland hurler Wes Ferrell hit a season record nine home runs while serving as a pitcher.

1930s WINNING PERCENTAGE	
1. Lefty Grove	.724
2. Johnny Allen	.706
3. Firpo Marberry	.686
4. Lefty Gomez	.650
5. Dizzy Dean	.648
6. Carl Hubbell	.644
7. Red Ruffing	.641
8. Monte Pearson	.634
9. Lon Warneke	.629
10. Bill Lee	.602
11. Schoolboy Rowe	.602
12. Wes Ferrell	.596
13. Tommy Bridges	.595
14. General Crowder	.593
15. Hal Schumacher	.591
16. Monte Weaver	.587
17. Eldon Auker	.581
18. Pat Malone	.577
19. Roy Mahaffey	.574
20. Tex Carleton	.573
21. Guy Bush	.566
22. Mel Harder	.562
23. Charlie Root	.562
24. Curt Davis	.558
25. Bill Walker	.556

Bob Feller recounted the game on September 13, 1936, when he fanned 17 Philadelphia A's to set a new American League strikeout record at age 17: "I was pretty excited. I knew I was approaching the record. I was counting those whiffs. And the closer I got to the record, the more I wanted to break it. I just kept pouring them in."

Indian hurler Bob Feller's 240 strikeouts in 1938 led the majors; NL strikeout leader Clay Bryant of Chicago totaled just 135.

In 1932, four-year vet Wes Ferrell of Cleveland won 20-plus games for the fourth straight year.

Above: *After Bob Feller's rookie year (1936) with the Indians, the 17-year-old returned to Iowa to finish high school.*

Feller Blows 18 Bengals Away

By 1938, though just 19 years old, Bob Feller was already the Cleveland hill ace. That season he captured 17 of 28 decisions despite issuing 208 walks to set a new 20th century record. Feller's penchant for giving up free passes was more than outweighed by his strikeout totals. Massive in any era, his K figures in the late 1930s towered over those of his closest competitors. In 1938, while Clay Bryant was leading the National League in whiffs with 135, Feller bagged 240 Ks to pace the junior circuit. Feller's total was the highest in the majors since 1924. The apex of his season came in his final start when he set down 18 Detroit Tigers on strikes to set a new post-1893 single-game K mark. When Feller again topped the AL with 246 whiffs in 1939, he became the first junior loop hurler since Walter Johnson in 1916 to register back-to-back 200-K campaigns.

"The secret to my success was clean living and a fast-moving outfield."
—Lefty Gomez

In 1937, Joe Kohlman had a 25-1 record for Salisbury of the Eastern Shore League and then won a late-season start with Washington, giving him an overall 26-1 mark.

Lefty Grove was the last southpaw to win 30 games in a season, as he took 31 in 1931.

Hall-of-Famer Ted Lyons (above) toiled for poor White Sox clubs, but won 260 games.

1930s EARNED RUN AVERAGE

1.	Carl Hubbell	2.71
2.	Lefty Grove	2.91
3.	Dizzy Dean	2.96
4.	Bill Lee	3.21
5.	Lon Warneke	3.23
6.	Lefty Gomez	3.24
7.	Hal Schumacher	3.38
8.	Larry French	3.42
9.	Van Mungo	3.42
10.	Charlie Root	3.50
11.	Paul Derringer	3.50
12.	Curt Davis	3.50
13.	Freddie Fitzsimmons	3.54
14.	Bill Swift	3.57
15.	Ed Brandt	3.57
16.	Bill Walker	3.57
17.	Red Ruffing	3.59
18.	Johnny Allen	3.73
19.	Ben Cantwell	3.74
20.	Mel Harder	3.74
21.	Tom Zachary	3.74
22.	Tommy Bridges	3.76
23.	Waite Hoyt	3.76
24.	Red Lucas	3.77
25.	Bucky Walters	3.80

1930s FEWEST WALKS

1.	Red Lucas	1.46
2.	Carl Hubbell	1.62
3.	Syl Johnson	1.63
4.	Watty Clark	1.76
5.	Bill Swift	1.79
6.	Paul Derringer	1.85
7.	Curt Davis	1.87
8.	Benny Frey	2.02
9.	Dizzy Dean	2.04
10.	Ben Cantwell	2.08
11.	Waite Hoyt	2.14
12.	Clint Brown	2.16
13.	Larry French	2.21
14.	Charlie Root	2.29
15.	Freddie Fitzsimmons	2.32
16.	Ted Lyons	2.40
17.	Lefty Grove	2.40
18.	Tom Zachary	2.41
19.	Lon Warneke	2.47
20.	Bob Smith	2.51
21.	George Blaeholder	2.56
22.	Guy Bush	2.58
23.	Schoolboy Rowe	2.60
24.	Lefty Stewart	2.63
25.	Ray Benge	2.64

Ted Lyons, a 260-game winner, hurled 21 seasons in the majors without ever having a 100-strikeout campaign; his high was 74 Ks in 1933.

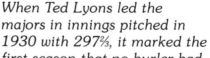

When Ted Lyons led the majors in innings pitched in 1930 with 297⅔, it marked the first season that no hurler had worked at least 300 innings.

Pitcher Russ Van Atta of the Yankees made his major league debut on April 25, 1933, by collecting four hits in the process of shutting out Washington 16-0.

Red Hot

Bill Dickey said about Red Ruffing: "If I were asked to choose the best pitcher I ever caught, I would have to say Ruffing."

As a rookie in 1934, Curt Davis had the best season of any Phillies hurler between 1918 and 1949 when he won 19 games and posted a 2.95 ERA.

The National League's best pitching tandem during the 1930s belonged to the 1939 Reds, which featured Bucky Walters and Paul Derringer with 52 wins between them.

1930s RATIO	
1. Carl Hubbell	10.07
2. Dizzy Dean	10.74
3. Bill Swift	11.03
4. Lefty Grove	11.19
5. Syl Johnson	11.31
6. Lon Warneke	11.35
7. Red Lucas	11.41
8. Charlie Root	11.49
9. Ben Cantwell	11.52
10. Curt Davis	11.61
11. Watty Clark	11.70
12. Freddie Fitzsimmons	11.70
13. Bill Lee	11.72
14. Red Ruffing	11.75
15. Paul Derringer	11.77
16. Lefty Gomez	11.82
17. Firpo Marberry	11.83
18. Van Mungo	11.95
19. Hal Schumacher	11.97
20. Johnny Allen	11.97
21. Ed Brandt	11.99
22. Larry French	12.01
23. Schoolboy Rowe	12.08
24. Waite Hoyt	12.27
25. Tex Carleton	12.37

Above: *"Fat Freddie" Fitzsimmons had a 19-year major league career. A righthanded knuckleball pitcher, Fitzsimmons debuted in 1925 with the Giants and won 173 games for them before being traded to the Dodgers, where he led the NL for the second time in winning percentage with a 16-2 mark in 1940.*

In 1937, Johnny Allen won his first 15 starts of the season, then lost on the season's closing day.

On July 5, 1935, Al and Tony Cuccinello were the first brothers on opposing teams to homer in the same National League game.

Eddie Rommel's last big league victory came on July 10, 1932, when he hurled an American League-record 17 relief innings for the A's and surrendered 29 hits and 14 runs before beating Cleveland 18-17. In that game, Johnny Burnett of Cleveland set a major league record with nine hits.

Fitzsimmons Wins and Zips Four

In the late 1920s and early 1930s, Freddie Fitzsimmons had been one of the New York Giants' mound mainstays and had won in double figures for nine straight seasons. Perhaps as importantly, he had topped 200 innings from 1926 to 1934. In 1935, however, Fitzsimmons was below par physically, working just 94 innings and notching only six complete games in 15 starts. His record at the season's close was a miserable 4-8 with an earned run average over four. His lousy season contributed heavily to the Giants' disappointing third-place finish. Yet Fitzsimmons contrived to top the National League in a major pitching department. All four of his victories were shutouts, tying him with four other hurlers for the loop lead in whitewashes. The following year Fitzsimmons rebounded to bag 10 wins but failed to hurl a single shutout. In fact, his 1935 total of four tied a personal high in a career that spanned 19 seasons and brought him 217 wins, 29 of them by the shutout route.

In 1931, Lefty Grove, George Earnshaw, Roy Mahaffey, and Rube Walberg had a composite 87-27 record for the Philadelphia A's.

1930s PITCHER FIELDING AVERAGE	
1. General Crowder	.990
2. Bob Smith	.988
3. Lon Warneke	.983
4. Huck Betts	.982
5. Red Lucas	.982

Brooklyn Buys, Benches .448 Bopper Boone

In 1930, the action in the minor leagues once again mirrored what fans were seeing on the major league level. All of the top minor circuits were stocked with hitters who produced mammoth stats, but none was more dazzling than Ike Boone's. The property of the Mission Reds in the Pacific Coast League, Boone, a former Boston Red Sox club batting leader, launched the 1930 campaign by hitting at a .448 clip for his first 83 games. Since Boone had hit .407 the previous year with 55 home runs and an all-time professional baseball record 553 total bases, major league magnates began to think that even in an era of superinflated hitting stats Boone might be worth another look in top company. Hence the Brooklyn Dodgers purchased Boone from the Mission club, thereupon depriving him of an opportunity to set a new minor league record for the highest single-season batting average. While it is doubtful that Boone could have maintained his .448 pace over the entire season, in 1930 conditions were such that it was certainly possible. The shame is that the Dodgers didn't really need Boone. After acquiring him, they kept him on the bench for the balance of the season.

John Lardner wrote that the teetotaling, God-fearing Branch Rickey was "a man opposed to Sunday baseball except when the gate receipts exceeded $5,000."

1930s CATCHER FIELDING AVERAGE	
1. Frankie Pytlak	.991
2. Mickey Cochrane	.990
3. Gabby Hartnett	.989
4. Bill Dickey	.988
5. Shanty Hogan	.988

Pirate first baseman Gus Suhr had his NL-record streak of 822 consecutive games snapped in 1937.

In 1931, Bill Dickey of the New York Yankees became the first catcher to work 100 or more games behind the plate in a season without allowing a passed ball.

Ray Hayworth of the Tigers in 1932 became the first catcher to work 100 consecutive errorless games.

On May 17, 1932, Milt Gaston of the Chicago White Sox became the first pitcher in major league history to start four double plays in a game.

1930s CATCHER GAMES	
1. Bill Dickey	1,179
2. Al Lopez	1,172
3. Rick Ferrell	1,162
4. Gabby Hartnett	1,123
5. Spud Davis	958

Above: *Bill Dickey caught nearly 1,800 games with the Yankees from 1928 to 1946. In addition to his defensive skills, Dickey hit 102 homers between 1936 and '39, hit over .300 10 times, and batted in more than 1,200 runs.*

Lee, French Maintain Fine Gloves in Minors

Buried under the welter of massive hitting and slugging feats on both the minor and major league level in the early 1930s were the accomplishments of players who made their way in the game with their gloves. Lost in particular were several fine shortstops such as Dud Lee and Ray French, who were relegated to long careers in the minors because the emphasis was so strongly on offense. Few major league teams could afford to carry a weak-hitting regular regardless of his defensive talent. In a career that lasted from 1914 to 1941, French played a record 2,736 games in the minors at shortstop and also set the minor league mark for the most at bats, 12,174. His total major league experience consisted of only 82 games in the early 1920s. Lee played 253 games in the majors during the 1920s, mostly with the Red Sox, but did not really reach his peak until the following decade. In 1930, despite hitting just .275, one of the lowest marks in the Pacific Coast League, Lee was so highly regarded a fielder that he was voted the Most Valuable Player on the loop champion Hollywood Stars.

Connie Mack (above left, with Ira Thomas) *managed nine pennant-winning Philadelphia Athletic teams, the last champion being the 1931 club. Mack would run the A's until 1950, totaling a record 53 years of service.*

The 1933 Senators won the last pennant by a Washington-based major league team.

Support Squad
Fresco Thompson, Phillies captain, delivered a lineup card to umpire Bill Klem in 1930 with the following notation in the ninth or pitcher's spot in the batting order: "Willoughby and others."

Cleveland third sacker Willie Kamm set a new standard for hot cornermen that lasted until 1948 when he had a .984 fielding average in 1933.

In his first 33 seasons as manager of the Philadelphia A's, Connie Mack won nine pennants (the last in 1931); in his last 17 seasons with the club, he finished in the first division just once, bringing the A's home fourth in 1948.

1930s FIRST BASE GAMES	
1. Gus Suhr	1,399
2. Lou Gehrig	1,394
3. Jimmie Foxx	1,377
4. Joe Kuhel	1,139
5. Bill Terry	930

In 1938, Stan Hack led the NL with 16 steals, an all-time low by an NL leader.

1930s FIRST BASE FIELDING AVERAGE	
1. Charlie Grimm	.994
2. Zeke Bonura	.993
3. Jack Burns	.992
4. Bill Terry	.992
5. Ripper Collins	.992

Browns Shortstops Found Wanting

In the early 1930s, batting averages climbed to their highest level since the mid-1890s, after the pitching distance was increased by 10½ feet. Yet, not all hitters thrived. In 1931, rookie St. Louis Browns shortstop Jim Levey batted just .209. Levey upped his hitting mark the following year to .280 but the bottom fell out on him in 1933. Playing in 141 games, he collected just 103 hits in 529 at bats and clocked a .195 batting average, the lowest of the 1930s decade for a regular. Levey never again appeared in the majors but played for several seasons in the National Football League. In 1934, the Browns gave his shortstop post to rookie Alan Strange, another notoriously weak hitter of the period. After hitting .233 as a frosh, Strange played four more seasons in the majors before departing with a .223 career batting average. He batted .186 in 167 at bats in 1940. Levey's career mark, even including his horrendous 1933 campaign, was seven points higher at .230.

By the time Babe Ruth (above left, with Wally Berger) came to the Braves in 1935, he had already slugged 708 career homers. That season he hit his final six and retired at age 40.

Credits and Debits

"You'd be surprised the amount of guys that were broke after they quit playing. They always thought they were gonna keep making that good money, and as fast as they got the money, they spent it."

—Joe Stripp, third baseman during the 1930s

1930s SECOND BASE GAMES	
1. Charlie Gehringer	1,397
2. Billy Herman	1,194
3. Buddy Myer	1,173
4. Tony Cuccinello	1,136
5. Ski Melillo	958

Released by the Yankees in 1935, Babe Ruth signed a three-year contract with the Boston Braves. On May 25, 1935, Ruth hit three homers at Pittsburgh's Forbes Field, then retired a few days later.

Cleveland is the only team in this century to have two home parks at the same time; between 1932 and 1946 the Indians played in both League Park and Cleveland Municipal Stadium.

1930s SECOND BASE FIELDING AVERAGE	
1. Max Bishop	.981
2. Charlie Gehringer	.978
3. Ski Melillo	.978
4. Hughie Critz	.977
5. Jackie Hayes	.976

Oliver Twists in Wind Without Homer

In 1922, shortstop Rabbit Maranville, then with the Pittsburgh Pirates, set the all-time single-season record for the most at bats without a four-bagger when he went homerless in 672 turns at the plate. Doc Cramer of the Boston Red Sox established the corresponding American League record in 1938 by failing to homer in 658 at bats. Both Cramer and Maranville hit a fair number of round trippers during their careers, however. Center fielder Tom Oliver, on the other hand, played four years with the Boston Red Sox in the early 1930s without ever connecting for the distance. Oliver's career homerless skein of 514 games and 1,914 at bats is a 20th century record, made even more noteworthy by the period in which he was active and the park in which he performed. A righthanded hitter, Oliver played his entire career in Fenway Park without ever being able to clear its inviting left field wall.

Above: *Mickey Cochrane was beaned by Bumb Hadley on May 25, 1937. The pitch fractured Cochrane's skull, ending his career.*

1930s THIRD BASE ASSISTS	
1. Pinky Whitney	2,014
2. Harlond Clift	1,830
3. Pinky Higgins	1,774
4. Marv Owen	1,679
5. Billy Werber	1,645

The Philadelphia A's (58-91 in 1935) sold Jimmie Foxx and Johnny Marcum to the Boston Red Sox for $150,000 after the 1935 season.

The Chicago Cubs won 21 straight games in 1935, setting a record for most consecutive wins without a tie.

The Detroit Tigers won the franchise's first world championship in 1935; Tigers owner Frank Navin died shortly after seeing his club win its first fall classic.

1930s THIRD BASE GAMES	
1. Pinky Whitney	1,055
2. Pinky Higgins	997
3. Marv Owen	912
4. Stan Hack	886
5. Harlond Clift	873

In 1934, Lou Gehrig won the Triple Crown in the AL, batting .363 with 49 homers and 165 RBI. Despite his performance, Detroit player-manager Mickey Cochrane was selected as the AL MVP.

Robert Creamer, on the game in the 1920s and 1930s, wrote: "A man could spend an entire career in the minor leagues, and major league veterans who had seen their best days would come back down and play another half-dozen seasons in the high minors."

Each Detroit Tiger received a $6,544.76 World Series share in 1935, the highest prior to 1948.

The New York Yankees won an AL-record four straight pennants from 1936 to 1939.

The 1936 New York Yankees won the AL pennant by 19½ games, setting a circuit record.

In 1934, the Detroit Tigers won the franchise's first flag since 1909.

The St. Louis Cardinals in 1934 won the World Series with a rowdy club that went down in history as "The Gashouse Gang."

1930s THIRD BASE FIELDING AVERAGE	
1. Ossie Bluege	.963
2. Joe Stripp	.962
3. Willie Kamm	.962
4. Pinky Whitney	.962
5. Jimmy Dykes	.960

Dihigo, Bell, Other Negro Leaguers Play Year-Round

During the Depression years baseball promoters, hoping to appeal to fans of all races and denominations, began to stage more and more games between Negro League all-star teams and white major leaguers. Black stars like Buck Leonard, Josh Gibson, Judy Johnson, Cool Papa Bell, and Martin Dihigo in that way got their only chance to compare their skills to those of the reputedly best players in the land. Because the salaries Negro League players received were far less than their white brethren could earn, many chose to play elsewhere than the United States. Dihigo, for one, spent the bulk of the 1930s playing first in Cuba and then in Mexico. Bell generally stayed stateside during the summer, but the lure of additional money took him south of the border in the winter months. For over two decades he played baseball year around, not retiring until he was well into his 40s.

Above: *Martin Dihigo is the only player to be in the Cuban, Mexican, and American baseball halls of fame.*

1930s SHORTSTOP GAMES

1.	Joe Cronin	1,360
2.	Dick Bartell	1,348
3.	Leo Durocher	1,316
4.	Billy Rogell	1,148
5.	Arky Vaughan	1,129

The Boston Red Sox in 1932 set a club record for losses with 111.

In 1933, total attendance in the majors fell to 6.3 million, the lowest it had been since the early 1900s.

1930s SHORTSTOP FIELDING AVERAGE

1.	Billy Jurges	.963
2.	Leo Durocher	.962
3.	Billy Rogell	.957
4.	Lyn Lary	.955
5.	Bill Knickerbocker	.955

On May 24, 1935, the Reds beat the Philadelphia Phillies 2-1 at Cincinnati's Crosley Field in the first major league night game.

Commenting on playing, traveling, and living conditions in the black leagues which drove him to pursue a career in real estate in 1934, Negro League star Dave Malarcher said: "They were conditions which I could not continue to bear."

A Cincinnati bank took over the bankrupt Reds in 1933, then convinced magnate Powell Crosley to buy the club.

Braves Beaten By the Bushel

In 1934, the Boston Braves finished fourth, rousing hopes in the Hub of their first pennant since 1914. To bolster the club for the 1935 campaign, owner Judge Fuchs made only one significant change; he signed 40-year-old Babe Ruth after the Yankees released the Bambino. Ruth's legs were shot, causing him to retire before the season was barely six weeks old, but by that time the race was over for the Braves anyway. The club went on to lose 115 of 153 decisions and post a .248 winning percentage, the lowest in this century by a senior circuit nine. Boston's opponents scored 277 more runs, an average of 1.8 a game. Center fielder Wally Berger paced the loop with 34 home runs and 130 RBI, but no other Brave was able to collect more than five dingers or 60 ribbies. The pitching staff was equally inept. Frank Frankhouse had a semirespectable 11-15 record, but the rest of the hill corps was an aggregate 27-100. The club finished so far off the pace that it came in 26 games behind the seventh-place Philadelphia Phillies.

"Next to religion, baseball has had a greater impact on the American people than any other institution."
—Herbert Hoover

The New York Yankees in 1934 released two future Hall of Famers, Herb Pennock and Joe Sewell, on the same day.

Above: *Luminaries at the 1939 Centennial Celebration included, left to right: Ford Frick, NL president; Ken Landis, commissioner; Will Harridge, AL president; and William Bramham, president of the National Association.*

1930s OUTFIELD GAMES	
1. Paul Waner	1,418
2. Earl Averill	1,412
3. Wally Berger	1,285
4. Chuck Klein	1,275
5. Al Simmons	1,271
6. Ben Chapman	1,270
7. Mel Ott	1,251
8. Joe Vosmik	1,241
9. Sam West	1,238
10. Doc Cramer	1,185
11. Lloyd Waner	1,174
12. Joe Medwick	1,080
13. John Stone	1,068
14. Goose Goslin	1,066
15. Jo-Jo Moore	1,045

On April 14, 1936, Cardinal Eddie Morgan became the first player to hit a pinch homer in his first major league at bat.

In 1938, the Phillies moved to Shibe Park after 51 years in the Baker Bowl.

The Hall of Fame was established in 1936. In the first vote for enshrinement, the leading vote-getter was Ty Cobb. Other first electees were: Babe Ruth, Honus Wagner, Christy Mathewson, and Walter Johnson.

1930s OUTFIELD FIELDING AVERAGE	
1. Tom Oliver	.986
2. Mule Haas	.985
3. Terry Moore	.985
4. Al Simmons	.985
5. Lloyd Waner	.984
6. Sam West	.983
7. Mel Ott	.982
8. Heinie Manush	.981
9. Augie Galan	.980
10. George Selkirk	.980
11. Pete Fox	.979
12. Joe Vosmik	.979
13. Danny Taylor	.978
14. Fred Schulte	.978
15. Ethan Allen	.978

Above: *Joe McCarthy managed the 1929 Chicago Cubs to the National League pennant. When he skippered the 1932 Yankees to the American League flag, he became the first manager in major league history to win pennants in both the NL and the AL.*

Few Practice Art of Base Thievery

After Sam Rice of Washington stole 63 bases in 1920 to pace the American League, thievery totals began a sharp and steady decline that would continue into the late 1950s. Periodically, however, someone would step forward to remind fans of what the game had been like only a generation earlier. In 1930, it was Yankees outfielder Ben Chapman, whose 61 swipes were the most by any major leaguer between 1920 and World War II. Later in the decade Billy Werber of the Red Sox emerged to challenge Chapman for the AL theft crown while Pepper Martin and Augie Galan were the only two National Leaguers who could consistently garner more than 20 steals in a season. In 1938, the art of basestealing declined in the NL to a point where third sacker Stan Hack led the circuit with just 16 thefts. The AL experienced a sudden resurgence the following year, however, when Washington's George Case bagged 51 steals and claimed the first of what would become at that time a record five consecutive junior loop theft crowns.

The first night game in American League history was played at Philadelphia's Shibe Park on May 16, 1939, with Cleveland beating the A's 8-3 in 10 innings.

In 1934, Mel Harder of Cleveland became the first 20-game winner in American League history to wear glasses.

The world champion St. Louis Cardinals in 1934 drew only 350,000 fans in home attendance.

1930s MANAGER WINNING PERCENTAGE	
1. Joe McCarthy	.638
2. Charlie Grimm	.591
3. Mickey Cochrane	.579
4. Bill Terry	.574
5. Walter Johnson	.566
6. Frankie Frisch	.564
7. Joe Cronin	.540
8. Roger Peckinpaugh	.532
9. Pie Traynor	.530
10. Gabby Street	.519

"Give a boy a bat and a ball and a place to play and you'll have a good citizen."
—Joe McCarthy

1930s MANAGER WINS	
1. Joe McCarthy	970
2. Bill McKechnie	739
3. Bucky Harris	723
4. Connie Mack	678
5. Bill Terry	677
6. Joe Cronin	574
7. Charlie Grimm	534
8. Walter Johnson	458
Frankie Frisch	458
10. Pie Traynor	457

Warstler Rare '30s Defensive Specialist

Any outfielder during the 1930s who could not keep his batting average above .300 was generally without a job the following year. The same held true of first and third basemen, and even catchers and middle infielders were expected to hit somewhere around .280. It was a rare player who was retained even as a substitute if he fell below .250, which made Rabbit Warstler's performance one of a kind. A middle infielder, Warstler played every year during the 1930s and got into over 1,200 games—even though he never once batted over .250. More typically, Warstler hit in the low .220s. His .229 career batting average and .287 slugging average both are the lowest of any player who was active all 10 seasons of the greatest offensive decade in the game's history. For some reason, Warstler was occasionally used as a pinch hitter despite his meager offensive output. In 20 pinch at bats, he never once came through with a hit. Warstler hit just 11 career homers and stole only 42 bases.

Above: *Big Bill Dineen was a former pitcher who, in 1909, retired and immediately became an American League umpire. He was an umpire in the AL until 1937.*

It Ain't Over

"You can't freeze the ball in this game. You have to play till the last man is out."

—Joe McCarthy

1930s TEAM WINS

		WON	LOST
1.	New York-AL	970	554
2.	Chicago-NL	889	646
3.	St.Louis-NL	869	665
4.	New York-NL	868	657
5.	Cleveland-AL	824	708
6.	Detroit-AL	818	716
7.	Pittsburgh-NL	812	718
8.	Washington-AL	806	722
9.	Brooklyn-NL	734	793
10.	Philadelphia-AL	723	795
11.	Boston-AL	705	815
12.	Boston-NL	700	829
13.	Chicago-AL	678	841
14.	Cincinnati-NL	664	866
15.	Philadelphia-NL	581	943
16.	St.Louis-AL	578	951

In 1931, the Baseball Writers Association of America appointed two committees, one in each league, to select the Most Valuable Players. Lefty Grove was the first BBWAA winner in the American League, while Frankie Frisch of the Cards won the NL Award.

The sacrifice fly rule was abolished in 1931 and reinstated in 1939.

In 1934, a few members of the Cincinnati Reds flew to a game in Chicago, the first major league teammates to travel together by air.

1930s TEAM WINNING PERCENTAGE

1.	New York-AL	.636
2.	Chicago-NL	.579
3.	New York-NL	.569
4.	St.Louis-NL	.566
5.	Cleveland-AL	.538
6.	Detroit-AL	.533
7.	Pittsburgh-NL	.531
8.	Washington-AL	.527
9.	Brooklyn-NL	.481
10.	Philadelphia-AL	.476
11.	Boston-AL	.464
12.	Boston-NL	.458
13.	Chicago-AL	.446
14.	Cincinnati-NL	.434
15.	Philadelphia-NL	.381
16.	St.Louis-AL	.378

Chapter 7
The 1940s

1940s GAMES

1.	Bob Elliott	1,455
2.	Lou Boudreau	1,425
3.	Marty Marion	1,396
4.	Bill Nicholson	1,389
5.	Dixie Walker	1,363
6.	Eddie Miller	1,328
7.	Bobby Doerr	1,283
8.	Rudy York	1,259
9.	Frankie Gustine	1,230
10.	Phil Cavarretta	1,217
11.	Wally Moses	1,212
12.	George McQuinn	1,210
13.	Ken Keltner	1,209
14.	Frank McCormick	1,191
15.	Luke Appling	1,188
16.	Joe Gordon	1,169
17.	Johnny Hopp	1,159
18.	Tommy Holmes	1,157
19.	Vern Stephens	1,154
20.	Stan Spence	1,112
21.	Jeff Heath	1,104
22.	Roy Cullenbine	1,081
23.	Stan Musial	1,072
24.	Mickey Vernon	1,044
25.	Ted Williams	1,035

Above: *Young Ralph Kiner (left) and the veteran Johnny Mize tied for the National League lead in home runs in two straight seasons, as they belted 51 each in 1947 and 40 apiece in 1948.*

Dynamic Giants Drive Dingers Downtown

In 1947, Mel Ott, the most prolific home run hitter in New York Giants history, retired as a player and turned his full attention to managing the Polo Grounds tenants. All that summer he watched from the dugout in amazement as his charges, lacking his booming bat for the first time in two decades, nevertheless set off on a home run spree that shattered every then-existing team single-season home run record. When the doors of the Polo Grounds finally closed for the 1947 campaign, the Giants had amassed 221 round-trippers, nearly a quarter of the 886 compiled by the entire National League. Leading the way was first sacker Johnny Mize, whose 51 four-baggers tied Pittsburgh's Ralph Kiner for the National League lead, followed by right fielder Willard Marshall (36), catcher Walker Cooper (35), and center fielder Bobby Thomson (29), who finished third, fourth, and fifth respectively in the NL homer derby. For all the power the Giants packed into their batting order in 1947, they could finish no better than fourth.

When he paced the National League in 1942 with a .521 slugging average, Johnny Mize set a senior-loop mark after the dead-ball era for the lowest slugging average by a leader.

New York Giants teammates Johnny Mize and Willard Marshall in 1947 combined for 87 homers, setting an NL teammate tandem record.

The first National Leaguer to clout 50 or more home runs in a season twice was Ralph Kiner, who accomplished it in 1947 and 1949.

1940s RUNS	
1. Ted Williams	951
2. Stan Musial	815
3. Bob Elliott	803
4. Bobby Doerr	764
5. Lou Boudreau	758
6. Bill Nicholson	743
7. Dom DiMaggio	721
8. Vern Stephens	708
9. Dixie Walker	704
10. Joe DiMaggio	684
11. Joe Gordon	680
12. Tommy Henrich	669
13. Phil Cavarretta	664
14. Johnny Mize	655
15. Rudy York	653
16. Tommy Holmes	651
17. Enos Slaughter	650
18. Stan Hack	639
19. Wally Moses	635
20. George McQuinn	626
21. Charlie Keller	625
22. Johnny Hopp	618
23. Luke Appling	613
24. Pee Wee Reese	609
25. George Case	599

Cardinal outfielder Stan Musial (above) won three MVP awards in the 1940s. He appeared in four World Series, won seven batting titles, and led the National League in doubles eight times.

Stan Musial, with 429 total bases in 1948, is the only player to top 420 total bases in a season since 1930.

Pirate outfielder Ralph Kiner in 1949 slugged 25 homers on the road, an NL record.

Pittsburgh's Ralph Kiner in 1946 became the first rookie to lead the NL in homers, socking just 23.

Lloyd Waner in 1941 played an NL-record 77 straight games without striking out.

Las Vegas Stakes Prospects on 271 Jackpots

As serious devotees of the game would expect, in 1947 there was a parallel in the minors to the New York Giants' home run binge. The Las Vegas team of the Sunset League clubbed a minor league record 271 four-baggers in 140 games and posted a .338 club batting average. Each of the team's eight regulars hit at least .303. All that firepower enabled Las Vegas to tally 1,261 runs, nine a game, but the team surrendered 1,235 markers and finished with a record of 73-67 for a .521 winning percentage, roughly the same as that of the 1947 Giants. The short-lived Sunset League was only one of several Southwestern circuits in the late 1940s that promoted high-scoring contests and provided a haven for hitters whose skills were just a shade below major league standards.

All Business
Robert Smith wrote about Joe DiMaggio: "He never offered the appearance of either gaiety, or anger, or tremendous effort. His smile was self-conscious, his manner withdrawn to the point of a chill."

White Sox outfielder Taffy Wright in 1941 collected at least one RBI in an AL-record 13 straight games.

The 1947 New York Giants swatted an NL-record 221 homers.

Above: *Shortstop Lou Boudreau was named player-manager of the Indians at age 25. He paced the AL in fielding percentage eight times and batted as high as .355. In 1948, Boudreau guided Cleveland to the AL crown and won the MVP Award.*

1940s HITS	
1. Lou Boudreau	1,578
2. Bob Elliott	1,563
3. Dixie Walker	1,512
4. Stan Musial	1,432
5. Bobby Doerr	1,407
6. Tommy Holmes	1,402
7. Luke Appling	1,376
8. Bill Nicholson	1,328
9. Marty Marion	1,310
10. Phil Cavarretta	1,304
11. Ted Williams	1,303
12. Vern Stephens	1,290
13. Rudy York	1,266
14. Frank McCormick	1,261
15. Ken Keltner	1,211
16. Wally Moses	1,205
17. Frankie Gustine	1,198
18. Enos Slaughter	1,190
19. George McQuinn	1,171
20. Joe Gordon	1,165
21. Joe DiMaggio	1,156
22. Stan Hack	1,155
23. Dom DiMaggio	1,154
24. Mickey Vernon	1,149
25. Doc Cramer	1,148

In 1948, Lou Boudreau of Cleveland was the only shortstop in AL history to hit over .350 and drive in more than 100 runs in the same season.

The only team to have three players who accumulated at least 119 walks was the 1949 Philadelphia A's, with Eddie Joost, Ferris Fain, and Elmer Valo.

During Ted Williams's first spring training with the Red Sox, Bobby Doerr told Ted to wait until he'd seen Jimmie Foxx hit. Ever confident, Williams responded: "Wait'll Foxx sees me hit."

Crusher Crues Drives 254 Home in 1948

Prominent among the minor league loops that became a cradle for sluggers in the years immediately after World War II was the West Texas-New Mexico League. Born in 1937, the league suspended operations during the war years and resumed play in 1946. Two years later, Bob Crues, an outfielder with the Amarillo entry, hammered 69 home runs and rang up an all-time professional record 254 RBI. Crues in 1948 was 30 years old and playing his seventh successive season in the circuit, with three years out for military duty during the war. Prior to his service interruption, Crues had been a pitcher and had notched just two home runs and 32 RBI in his first four professional seasons. Crues's mound career was short-circuited by an arm injury after he posted a 20-5 record with Lamesa-Borger of the border loop in 1940. After his record-shattering 1948 season, Crues joined Roswell of the Longhorn League, another federation that was especially suited to offensive-minded performers.

Williams, Stephens Set Duo Ribbie Record

In 1949, Ted Williams and Vern Stephens of the Boston Red Sox collected the most RBI of any pair of teammates since World War II, when they tied for the American League ribbie crown with 159 apiece. Stephens in addition set a still-existing record for the most RBI by a shortstop. His 39 home runs also established a mark for shortfielders that was later broken by Ernie Banks. Although always a slugger of the first order, Stephens did not really emerge as an RBI threat until he joined the Red Sox in 1948 after an off-season trade freed him from the lowly St. Louis Browns. With Dom DiMaggio and Johnny Pesky, solid .300 hitters, batting ahead of him, and the specter of Ted Williams following him in the Red Sox batting order, Stephens was usually assured of both coming to the plate with men on base and seeing good pitches to hit. In 1950, with rookie slugger Walt Dropo added to the Red Sox cast, Stephens again tied for the AL RBI lead with 144.

Hard-hitting Vern "Junior" Stephens (above) *led the Browns to their only pennant in 1944, knocking in an AL-best 109 runs and batting .293. He slugged 20 homers six times, scored more than 110 runs three years in a row, and became a fine-fielding shortstop as his career progressed.*

1940s DOUBLES	
1. Lou Boudreau	339
2. Stan Musial	302
3. Dixie Walker	291
Bob Elliott	291
5. Bobby Doerr	272
6. Ted Williams	270
7. Tommy Holmes	269
8. Wally Moses	252
9. Marty Marion	251
10. Frank McCormick	246
11. Bill Nicholson	241
Phil Cavarretta	241
13. Eddie Miller	240
Ken Keltner	240
15. George McQuinn	233
16. Rudy York	230
17. Mickey Vernon	224
Dom DiMaggio	224
19. Frankie Gustine	218
20. Jeff Heath	213
21. Tommy Henrich	207
Luke Appling	207
23. Vern Stephens	205
24. Enos Slaughter	200
Stan Hack	200

In 1946, Hank Greenberg of the Detroit Tigers became the first player ever to hit more than 40 homers in a season while batting under .280.

When Hank Greenberg hit his 331st and last home run late in the 1947 season, he was the only active player who had more than 300 four-baggers.

Hank Greenberg returned from the service on July 1, 1945, and he slugged a grand slam on the season's final day to clinch a pennant for Detroit.

Ink By the Barrel

John Lardner wrote of Ted Williams: "By the time the press of Boston has completed its daily treatment of Theodore S. Williams, there is no room in the papers for anything but two sticks of agate type about Truman and housing, and one column for the last Boston girl to be murdered on a beach."

First sacker Eddie Robinson was the only member of the Cleveland Indians infield in 1948 who totaled less than 100 RBI.

Chicago Cub third baseman Stan Hack won the 1940 National League batting crown with a .317 batting average, setting a record for the lowest in NL history by the loop leader.

Joltin' Joe Compiles 56-Game Hitting Streak

Joe DiMaggio was the antithesis of a streaky ballplayer, yet he had a aptitude for batting streaks. Immediately after his major league record 56-game hitting streak in 1941, he started on a 16-game streak. In 1933, he put together a 61-game hitting streak in the Pacific Coast League. DiMaggio started his infamous major league streak with a scratch single off the White Sox' Eddie Smith on May 15. By the time DiMaggio tied George Sisler's 1922 American League-record 41, the "Yankee Clipper" was a national sensation. On July 2, DiMaggio homered off Boston's Dick Newsome to move past the major league record of 44 games set by Baltimore's Wee Willie Keeler in 1897. Two weeks later, 67,468 Cleveland fans saw the streak come to an end. Twice, third baseman Ken Keltner made sparkling plays on DiMaggio drives down the line. Joltin' Joe made four hits in a game only four times and 34 times kept the streak alive with a single hit. Overall, he batted .408—dealing 91 hits over the 56 games.

When he collected his 3,000th hit in 1942, Paul Waner was the last player to reach that milestone until 1957.

Chicago's Luke Appling was the only shortstop to win two American League batting crowns, in 1936 and 1943.

Above: *Joe DiMaggio, "The Yankee Clipper," defined an era. His graceful image and mystique were matched by his determination and superior baseball skills. Able to run, throw, and hit as well as any contemporary, DiMaggio won three MVP awards, hit a lifetime .325, and played in 10 World Series in his 13-year career.*

1940s TRIPLES	
1. Stan Musial	108
2. Enos Slaughter	84
3. Bob Elliott	80
4. Jeff Heath	70
Phil Cavarretta	70
6. Johnny Hopp	68
Joe DiMaggio	68
8. Snuffy Stirnweiss	66
Bobby Doerr	66
10. Wally Moses	63
Charlie Keller	63
12. Stan Spence	60
13. Lou Boudreau	59
14. Dixie Walker	56
Mickey Vernon	56
16. Barney McCosky	54
17. Bill Nicholson	51
18. Jim Russell	49
Buddy Lewis	49
Ken Keltner	49
Tommy Henrich	49
22. Frankie Gustine	47
Doc Cramer	47
24. Rudy York	46
Tommy Holmes	46

Fritz Ostermueller explained why teammate Ralph Kiner didn't choke up on the bat with two strikes on him: "Cadillacs are down at the end of the bat."

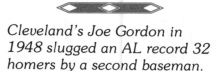

Cleveland's Joe Gordon in 1948 slugged an AL record 32 homers by a second baseman.

Guy Curtwright of the Chicago White Sox in 1943 hit in 26 straight games, setting an AL rookie record.

Reds first baseman Frank McCormick tied an NL record in 1940 when he led the loop in hits (191) for the third consecutive season.

The record for the fewest strikeouts in a season by a righthanded hitter playing 150 or more games is held by Emil Verban, who fanned just eight times in 1947 while playing 155 games for the Philadelphia Phillies.

Joe McCarthy said that Joe DiMaggio was "the best baserunner I ever saw. He could have stolen 50, 60 bases a year if I had let him. He wasn't the fastest man alive. He just knew how to run the bases better than anybody. I don't think in all the years [he] played for me he was ever thrown out stretching."

Seerey's Strikeout Sums Not Endearing

In the 1940s, a hitter who struck out 100 times in a season was still something of a rarity. The emphasis on making contact caused a serious problem for Cleveland outfielder Pat Seerey. After topping the AL in strikeouts for three successive seasons, Seerey was reduced to a part-time role in 1947. When he fanned 66 times in just 216 at bats and hit .171, he was dealt to the White Sox early in '48. Although Seerey got into only 103 games and batted less than 400 times, he still collected 102 Ks to regain his unwanted crown as the game's whiff king. However, on July 18, 1948, some two months after his trade to the White Sox, Seerey became only the second player in AL history to blast four homers in a game (in 11 innings). When his four-bagger binge only resulted in 19 homers for the season to go with his .231 batting average and 102 strikeouts, however, Seerey was released by Chicago early in 1949 and never played in the majors again. As a further indication of how different priorities are now than they were in the 1940s, one might compare Seerey's 1948 stats, which were judged too skimpy to merit continued major league status, to those produced in 1991 by Rob Deer, who retained his job as a regular Detroit gardener for 1992.

	AB	H	R	HR	RBI	SO	BA	SA	OBP
Seerey	363	84	51	19	70	102	.231	.419	.353
Deer	448	80	64	25	64	175	.179	.386	.314

Above: *Brothers Dixie (left) and Harry Walker were slash-hitting outfielders who spent much of the 1940s on rival NL powerhouses Brooklyn and St. Louis, while hitting for consistent .300 averages.*

Dixie Walker topped the National League in hitting in 1944; three years later his brother Harry won the title to make the Walkers the first pair of siblings each to win a batting crown.

In 1941, Brooklyn's outfield trio of Pete Reiser, Joe Medwick, and Dixie Walker all finished among the top-10 hitters in the National League.

1940s HOME RUNS

1.	Ted Williams	234
2.	Johnny Mize	217
3.	Bill Nicholson	211
4.	Rudy York	189
5.	Joe Gordon	181
6.	Joe DiMaggio	180
7.	Vern Stephens	177
8.	Charlie Keller	173
9.	Ralph Kiner	168
10.	Bobby Doerr	164
11.	Jeff Heath	158
12.	Stan Musial	146
13.	Mel Ott	142
14.	Tommy Henrich	138
15.	Hank Greenberg	125
16.	Ken Keltner	124
17.	Sam Chapman	119
18.	Bob Elliott	109
	Walker Cooper	109
20.	Whitey Kurowski	106
21.	Frank McCormick	105
22.	Roy Cullenbine	104
23.	George McQuinn	103
24.	Bob Johnson	102
25.	Danny Litwhiler	99

In mid-1947, Harry Walker was traded by the Cards to the Phils and became the first player traded in midseason to win the NL bat crown.

Vernon Snatches Two Crowns

In 1946, Washington first sacker Mickey Vernon returned from a two-year military hitch to lead the American League in hitting with a .353 batting average. Prior to World War II, Vernon had done nothing in his five seasons with the Senators to suggest that he was a potential .300 hitter, let alone a future batting titlist. So fans in the nation's capital were both pleasantly surprised and naturally hopeful that Vernon had somehow matured unexpectedly as a hitter during his service interruption. Instead, he slipped to a .265 average in 1947 and then hit .242 the following year with just 48 RBI in 558 at bats, embarrassing totals in that era for a first baseman. Vernon's average then hovered around the .290 mark for the next three years before sinking again in 1952 to an ignominious .251. Since he was then approaching his 35th birthday, it seemed certain that his 1946 season had been an inexplicable aberration. Vernon then proceeded to hit .337 in 1953 and snatch his second AL bat crown. He retired in 1960 with a .286 career batting average, the lowest to that point by a two-time bat titlist.

Sportswriter Jimmy Powers penned about Jackie Robinson as a rookie: "Robinson will not make the grade in the major leagues. He is a thousand-to-one shot at best. The Negro players simply don't have the brains or the skills."

Above: *Second baseman Eddie Stanky was respected for his ability to win though possessing few raw skills. Three times he led the NL in walks, twice in on-base percentage, and once in runs scored while playing a gritty brand of baseball for five NL teams.*

In 1945, Brooklyn second baseman Eddie Stanky set a National League record for walks with 148.

Cleveland outfielder Jeff Heath was the first player in AL history to hit at least 20 homers, 20 triples, and 20 doubles in a season.

Dale Mitchell's 23 triples for Cleveland in 1949 are the most by any player in either major league since 1930.

1940s RUNS BATTED IN	
1. Bob Elliott	903
2. Ted Williams	893
3. Bobby Doerr	887
4. Rudy York	854
5. Bill Nicholson	835
6. Vern Stephens	824
7. Joe DiMaggio	786
8. Dixie Walker	759
9. Johnny Mize	744
10. Joe Gordon	710
11. Stan Musial	706
12. Frank McCormick	703
13. Lou Boudreau	692
14. Jeff Heath	690
15. Enos Slaughter	649
16. Charlie Keller	640
17. Ken Keltner	639
18. George McQuinn	605
19. Phil Cavarretta	598
20. Eddie Miller	582
21. Stan Spence	575
22. Tommy Henrich	571
23. Roy Cullenbine	567
24. Marty Marion	565
25. Mickey Vernon	550

Kell Edges Williams's Triple Crown Bid

All during the 1949 campaign, Ted Williams had his sights set on becoming the first player in major league history to bag three Triple Crowns. True, he was being chased hard by teammate Vern Stephens for slugging honors and by Detroit's George Kell for the batting title, but neither Stephens nor Kell was a hitter of Williams's caliber and hence both were expected to fade in the late going. Stephens hung unexpectedly tough, however, finally surrendering the home run crown to Williams 43 to 39, but tying his much more highly regarded Red Sox teammate in RBI with 159. Kell meanwhile proved to be even harder for Williams to shake. When the final batting averages were calculated, both Williams and the Detroit third baseman finished with identical .343 marks, but Kell won out by .00016 of a point. Besides homers and RBI, The Thumper led the AL that year in runs (150), doubles (39), total bases (368), walks (162), on-base percentage (.490), and slugging average (.650).

Above: *George Kell combined outstanding defensive skills at third base with a quick bat that won him the 1949 bat crown, two hit titles, and two doubles titles. Never a slugger, Kell hit a career .306 over 15 AL seasons and paced the league in fielding percentage seven times on his way to the Hall of Fame.*

"If I had my career to play over, one thing I'd do differently is swing more. Those 1,200 walks I got, nobody remembers them."
— *Pee Wee Reese*

The Boston Red Sox in 1949 collected a major league record 835 walks.

The last batter to lead his loop in strikeouts with fewer than 90 was Hank Sauer, who topped the National League with 85 in 1948.

In 1947, Roy Cullenbine of Detroit batted .224 and had just 104 hits yet set an AL record for first basemen when he walked 137 times.

In 1947, Roy Cullenbine of Detroit set an all-time record for the most walks by a player in his final season when he amassed 137 free passes.

1940s STOLEN BASES		
1.	George Case	285
2.	Snuffy Stirnweiss	130
3.	Wally Moses	126
4.	Johnny Hopp	117
5.	Mickey Vernon	108
	Pee Wee Reese	108
7.	Joe Kuhel	93
8.	Luke Appling	91
9.	Bob Dillinger	90
10.	Jackie Robinson	88
11.	Phil Rizzuto	85
12.	Pete Reiser	81
13.	Thurman Tucker	76
14.	Dom DiMaggio	75
15.	Don Kolloway	73
16.	Johnny Barrett	69
17.	Gee Walker	65
	Stan Hack	65
19.	Joe Gordon	63
20.	Lonny Frey	62
21.	Elmer Valo	61
	Don Gutteridge	61
23.	George Myatt	60
	Eddie Miller	60
	Frankie Gustine	60
	Vince DiMaggio	60

Homer Leader Holmes Has Few Fans

At the beginning of the 1945 season, the Boston Braves had possessed just three National League home run champions since 1900 and only one, Wally Berger in 1935, since 1907. When the season closed, the Braves for the only time in this century prior to their move to Milwaukee had the top two home run hitters in the senior loop. Outfielder Tommy Holmes slugged 28 round-trippers and third sacker Chuck Workman was the runner-up with 25. Holmes also led the NL in total bases, slugging average, hits, and doubles, but perhaps the most significant offensive department he headed was the fewest strikeouts by a regular player. By fanning just nine times in 636 at bats, Holmes became the only player since the end of the dead-ball era to lead his league in both home runs and fewest Ks. In 1947, he led the league with 191 hits, and he fanned just 16 times in 618 at bats. Holmes currently stands fourth on the list of the hardest batters in this century for pitchers to strike out; he fanned 122 times in 4,992 at bats, and he compiled a .302 batting average.

In 1948, catcher Ray Lamanno of Cincinnati collected 93 hits in 127 games but just 105 total bases, giving him a .273 slugging average that was only 31 points higher than his .242 batting average.

Besides his exceptional 1945 season, Tommy Holmes (above) was a high-average hitter with little power. He played 11 years in the outfield for the Braves and hit over .300 five times.

In 1949, Cincinnati shortstop Virgil Stallcup received just nine walks in 575 at bats.

Boston's Tommy Holmes safely hit in 37 consecutive games in 1945, setting a modern NL record.

In 1945, Tommy Holmes became the only player ever to lead the National League in homers (28) and fewest batter strikeouts (nine).

Tommy Holmes, whose single won the 1948 World Series opener 1-0, whenever he was asked about the famous pickoff play in the game: "Never mind that; let's talk about who got the hit."

1940s STRIKEOUTS	
1. Bill Nicholson	708
2. Rudy York	688
3. Vince DiMaggio	582
4. Jeff Heath	538
5. Joe Gordon	529
6. George McQuinn	521
7. Eddie Joost	520
8. Vern Stephens	489
9. Pat Seerey	485
10. Marty Marion	465
11. Bobby Doerr	437
12. Charlie Keller	431
13. Jerry Priddy	423
14. Bob Elliott	418
15. Chet Laabs	415
Frankie Gustine	415
17. Eddie Miller	414
18. Pee Wee Reese	413
19. Sam Chapman	403
20. Dom DiMaggio	388
21. Jim Russell	385
22. Frankie Hayes	383
23. Andy Seminick	374
24. Snuffy Stirnweiss	373
Bob Johnson	373

On July 24, 1948, just six days after he hit four home runs in one game, Pat Seerey of the Chicago White Sox became the first player to strike out seven times in a doubleheader.

In 1943, only three major league teams, the Giants, the Yankees, and the Browns, averaged more than 0.5 home runs per game.

Above: *Ted Williams, despite missing three years to the war, captured four homer crowns and six runs scored titles during the decade of the 1940s.*

Boston's Ted Williams was the only player in American League history to win two Triple Crowns; he turned the trick in 1942 and 1947.

When he won the Triple Crown in 1942, Ted Williams also paced the American League in runs, walks, total bases, and slugging average; he led the loop in slugging average by a 135-point margin.

Win One For the Gina

"When you win, you eat better, sleep better, and your beer tastes better. And your wife looks like Gina Lollobrigida."
—Johnny Pesky

There's No 'K' in 'Slugger'

With the exception of his magnificent 1945 season, Tommy Holmes was never among the slugging leaders, but several other home run kings of his era were nearly as difficult to fan. Ted Williams and Mel Ott, both of whom also won home run crowns in the 1940s, are the only two members of the 500-home run club who finished with fewer than 1,000 career strikeouts. Williams fanned just 709 times in 7,706 at bats and never more than 64 times in a season. In 1941, he had 37 home runs and 27 strikeouts. In 9,456 at bats, Ott went down on strikes 896 times with a high of 69 in 1937. In 1929, Ott had 42 homers and 38 Ks. Both Ott and Williams were free-swingers, however, compared to two-time home run champion Joe DiMaggio. When he won his second homer crown in 1948 with 39 round-trippers, The Yankee Clipper fanned a mere 30 times. DiMaggio is the only slugger who has more than 300 career home runs (361) and fewer than 500 career strikeouts (369).

Red Sox outfielder Ted Williams was batting .3995 on the last day of the 1941 season; he finished the year with a 6-for-8 performance in a doubleheader to finish at .406.

Ted Williams smacked a three-run homer with two out in the bottom of the ninth inning to give the AL a 7-5 win in the 1941 All-Star Game.

1940s BATTING AVERAGE	
1. Ted Williams	.356
2. Stan Musial	.346
3. Joe DiMaggio	.325
4. Barney McCosky	.321
5. Johnny Pesky	.316
6. Enos Slaughter	.312
7. Luke Appling	.312
8. Dixie Walker	.311
9. Taffy Wright	.308
10. George Kell	.305
11. Joe Medwick	.305
12. Tommy Holmes	.304
13. Johnny Mize	.304
14. Stan Hack	.303
15. Pete Reiser	.303
16. Harry Walker	.302
17. Phil Cavarretta	.301
18. Lou Boudreau	.300
19. Johnny Hopp	.295
20. Dom DiMaggio	.294
21. Andy Pafko	.294
22. Ernie Lombardi	.294
23. Buddy Lewis	.292
24. Augie Galan	.292
25. Bob Elliott	.292

In 1943, Mel Ott of the Giants was runner-up for the National League home run crown with 18 four-baggers, all of which were hit in his home park, the Polo Grounds.

Mel Ott is now 14th on the career home run list, but when he retired after the first four games in 1947 he stood third, behind Babe Ruth and Jimmie Foxx.

In 1941, when Ted Williams batted .406 and Joe DiMaggio fashioned a 56-game hitting streak, Washington shortstop Cecil Travis led the American League in hits with 218.

Snuffy Stirnweiss, who was a .219 hitter in 1943, led the major leagues in 1944 with 205 hits.

The record for the lowest career batting average by a major league bat crown winner belongs to Snuffy Stirnweiss, who won the AL title in 1945 and retired with a .268 batting average.

Batting champ Snuffy Stirnweiss was the only one of the top five hitters in the American League in 1945 who ever again played a full season in the majors.

Snuffy Stirnweiss in 1945 topped the AL with a .476 slugging percentage, the lowest in AL history by a loop leader.

In 1943, the Boston Braves had three regular infielders—Eddie Joost, Connie Ryan, and Whitey Weitelmann—who had 83 RBI among them and posted batting averages of .185, .212, and .215.

Legs Diamond

"I think the game of baseball is just like any other sport, in that you've got to keep your legs in shape. I was able to play for so many years because I took care of my legs."
—Enos Slaughter

Darned Sox Duo Ditched After Title Try

In 1945, circumstances conspired to produce the oddest batting race in American League history. At the top with a .309 average when the season closed was second baseman Snuffy Stirnweiss of the New York Yankees, a good wartime ballplayer who was hampered afterward by injuries. Behind Stirnweiss were a pair of Chicago White Sox retreads, third baseman Tony Cuccinello and outfielder Johnny Dickshot. The trio were the only three AL batting title qualifiers to hit .300 in 1945, owing to the absence of many of the era's leading stars and the slightly deader brand of ball that was employed during the war years. Stirnweiss was an all-around offensive threat in 1945—he also led the loop in stolen bases, triples, and slugging average—but Cuccinello and Dickshot had little more than their batting averages to recommend them. So little in fact that despite vying all season for the batting title each was released by the White Sox soon after the curtain descended on the last wartime campaign and never played another inning in the majors.

In 1945, the Washington Senators hit only one four-bagger at home all season, an inside-the-park blow by first sacker Joe Kuhel.

The 1943 American League had only three .300 hitters and only five above .290.

Above: *Snuffy Stirnweiss enjoyed two great wartime years at second base for the New York Yankees. After 1945, he hit around .250, drew a lot of walks, and played good defense for the rest of his 10-year AL career.*

1940s SLUGGING AVERAGE	
1. Ted Williams	.647
2. Stan Musial	.578
3. Joe DiMaggio	.568
4. Johnny Mize	.561
5. Charlie Keller	.521
6. Jeff Heath	.499
7. Tommy Henrich	.492
8. Enos Slaughter	.484
9. Mel Ott	.477
10. Bobby Doerr	.468
11. Bob Johnson	.467
12. Bill Nicholson	.467
13. Vern Stephens	.466
14. Walker Cooper	.465
15. Joe Gordon	.459
16. Pete Reiser	.459
17. Rudy York	.457
18. Whitey Kurowski	.455
19. Chet Laabs	.454
20. Wally Judnich	.452
21. Sam Chapman	.448
22. Ron Northey	.446
23. Andy Pafko	.442
24. Ernie Lombardi	.440
25. Joe Medwick	.439

Above: *Cardinals outfielder Enos "Country" Slaughter lost three prime years to World War II but still hit .300 six times during the 1940s. His all-around hustle made him a popular and valuable player.*

In 1946, the New York Giants hit 121 home runs, 40 more than any other National League team, but finished in last place.

The first pinch home run in World Series history was slugged by Yankee rookie Yogi Berra in game three of the 1947 World Series.

In 1945, pitcher-outfielder Rene Monteagudo achieved the highest pinch-hit total during the 1940s by a National Leaguer when he collected 18 pinch singles in 52 at bats.

1940s ON-BASE AVERAGE	
1. Ted Williams	.496
2. Stan Musial	.428
3. Augie Galan	.414
4. Roy Cullenbine	.411
5. Charlie Keller	.406
6. Joe DiMaggio	.404
7. Elbie Fletcher	.404
8. Eddie Stanky	.403
9. Mel Ott	.403
10. Luke Appling	.403
11. Stan Hack	.401
12. Barney McCosky	.396
13. Elmer Valo	.396
14. Johnny Pesky	.394
15. Johnny Mize	.394
16. Enos Slaughter	.392
17. Phil Cavarretta	.390
18. Dixie Walker	.388
19. Lou Boudreau	.385
20. Bob Johnson	.383
21. Pete Reiser	.383
22. Dom DiMaggio	.382
23. Tommy Henrich	.379
24. Taffy Wright	.378
25. Bob Elliott	.377

War Talent Shortage Launches Stars

Snuffy Stirnweiss was far from the only good player who was shot to greatness during the war years largely by dint of not being summoned for military duty. Nick Etten, a 4-F first baseman for the Yankees with no particular slugging credentials prior to the war, led the American League in home runs in 1944 and RBI the following year. Tigers bonus baby Dick Wakefield, a bust after the war, hacked out a .316 batting average and an AL-leading 200 hits as a rookie in 1943 before receiving a service call-up. He then knocked .355 in half a season the following year when he was temporarily released from military duty. Yet many prewar stars, such as Mel Ott, who might have been expected to thrive on pitching staffs that had been diluted by the draft, barely held their own. After leading the NL in home runs in 1942, Ott (then age 34) plummeted to a .234 batting average and just 47 RBI in 1943, the first year that the game was severely impaired by the war effort. He rebounded to 26 and 21 homers in '44 and '45.

Enos Slaughter, when told by a doctor prior to game six of the 1946 World Series that his arm was so badly injured he risked having it amputated if he tried to play that day, responded: "Doc, I guess we'll have to take that gamble."

1940s GAMES PITCHED	
1. Hal Newhouser	377
2. Dizzy Trout	374
3. Kirby Higbe	354
Harry Gumbert	354
5. Rip Sewell	316
6. Clyde Shoun	315
7. Bobo Newsom	302
Ace Adams	302
9. Dutch Leonard	294
10. Hugh Casey	290
11. Bob Muncrief	283
12. Al Benton	280
13. Joe Haynes	277
14. Nels Potter	272
15. Bob Feller	266
16. Hank Borowy	261
17. Claude Passeau	258
Joe Dobson	258
19. Murry Dickson	248
20. Ted Wilks	247
Allie Reynolds	247
22. Bucky Walters	246
Mort Cooper	246
24. Ken Raffensberger	245
25. Red Barrett	244

The last pitcher to win 25 or more games in back-to-back seasons was Hal Newhouser in 1944 and 1945.

Hal Newhouser in 1946 led the major leagues in ERA (1.94), and was second in AL MVP voting.

Hal Newhouser's 29 wins in 1944 were the most since 1931 by a major league lefty.

Give 'Em the Ball
"You don't save a pitcher for tomorrow. Tomorrow it might rain."
—Leo Durocher

In a five-year period from 1944 to 1948, durable Detroit lefthander Hal Newhouser (above) won 118 games, capturing two ERA crowns and two strikeout titles as well as winning consecutive MVP awards in 1944 and 1945.

Newhouser Top Hurler, Wartime or No

Until 1992, Hal Newhouser was judged unworthy of Hall of Fame selection because he was considered by many panelists to be little more than a wartime fluke who won 29 games in 1944, 25 games in 1945, and then subsequently did little to recommend himself once all the other top-flight pitchers of the era returned from military stints. The fact is, Newhouser led the American League in victories twice after the war and went on to win more games during the decade of the 1940s than any other hurler. In addition, Newhouser was second only to Bob Feller among the game's strikeout artists in the years immediately following the war. When he notched 275 strikeouts in 1946, the first postwar season, it was the highest total by a southpaw since 1905. He was 26-9 that year and 21-12 in 1948. Everything points to Newhouser being an outstanding pitcher whose peak seasons happened to dovetail with World War II rather than a wartime fluke.

Reiser Injures Chance at Excellence

No one will ever know how great a player Pete Reiser might have been if he had not had a penchant for bringing his body into bone-shattering contact with pitched balls and outfield walls. The sports pages during the 1940s seemed constantly to be running photos of Reiser either lying in a heap after colliding with a concrete barrier or being hauled off the field on a stretcher after he was decked by an inside fastball. In 1941, though, his only full injury-free season in the majors, Reiser was something extraordinary. At age 22, he became the youngest batting titlist in National League history when he took the loop crown with a .343 average. Reiser also paced the senior circuit that year in doubles (39), triples (17), runs (117), and slugging percentage (.558)— spurring the Brooklyn Dodgers to their first pennant since 1920. Injuries then prevented him from ever again playing more than 125 games in a season.

On September 27, 1940, the last game of the season, Detroit no-name hurler Floyd Giebell beat Cleveland's Bob Feller 2-0 to clinch the flag by a single game for the Tigers over the Tribe.

Floyd Giebell's final major league win was on September 27, 1940, when he clinched a flag for the Detroit Tigers.

Above: *Allie Reynolds toiled with Cleveland before joining the Yankees in 1947. That year he led the AL in winning percentage and garnered 19 victories. For the next five years, the wild but overpowering righthander won at least 16 games and enjoyed a 20-win, 2.07 ERA season in 1952. Overall, Reynolds bagged 182 victories while losing only 107 times in his 13-year career.*

In 1941, Lefty Grove became only the second southpaw in major league history to win 300 games.

In 1941, Lefty Grove became the last hurler until 1963 to win 300 career games.

On May 12, 1941, Lefty Grove of the Red Sox became the only pitcher ever to win 20 consecutive games in his home park.

1940s GAMES STARTED	
1. Hal Newhouser	305
2. Dutch Leonard	274
3. Bobo Newsom	261
4. Dizzy Trout	239
5. Bucky Walters	238
6. Rip Sewell	231
Bob Feller	231
8. Johnny Vander Meer	219
9. Mort Cooper	210
10. Hank Borowy	208
11. Claude Passeau	207
Kirby Higbe	207
13. Tiny Bonham	193
14. Allie Reynolds	192
15. Early Wynn	188
16. Bill Voiselle	183
Sid Hudson	183
Denny Galehouse	183
19. Joe Dobson	182
20. Bill Lee	178
21. Harry Brecheen	172
22. Jack Kramer	171
23. Ed Lopat	170
24. Mickey Haefner	168
25. Jim Tobin	167

Two Years Cement Page's Standing

When Joe Page won 14 games and collected 17 saves in 1947 as the Yankees' bullpen ace, he was nicknamed "Fireman" because he brought to mind Johnny Murphy, the stopper whose job he inherited. But Page's postgame escapades were such that he was soon dubbed "The Gay Reliever." His lax approach to conditioning contributed to a poor season in 1948 and probably cost the Yankees the American League pennant. The following year, though, Page recovered his 1947 wizardry and bagged 27 saves to set a record that lasted until 1961 when expansion lengthened the schedule to 162 games. The Gay Reliever then succumbed to his old ways, stumbling so badly in 1950 (a horrible 5.04 ERA) that he was released by the Yankees at the season's end and left to struggle for the rest of his career in the minors except for a brief and abortive comeback in 1954 with the Pittsburgh Pirates. Page's reputation thus was based almost entirely on his work in two seasons—1947 and 1949—but no other reliever during the 1940s had even one season nearly as good.

Above: *Flamethrowing Yankee lefty Joe Page is shown here during the 1949 season. In helping the underdog Yankees capture the AL flag, "The Fireman" collected an astounding (for the time) 27 saves that season while topping the league in appearances and winning 13 games.*

New York Giant hurler Dave Koslo led the 1949 senior circuit in ERA (2.50)—he became the first loop leader without a shutout.

1940s COMPLETE GAMES	
1. Hal Newhouser	181
2. Bob Feller	155
3. Bucky Walters	153
4. Dutch Leonard	139
5. Dizzy Trout	132
Rip Sewell	132
7. Claude Passeau	130
8. Jim Tobin	127
9. Mort Cooper	120
10. Bobo Newsom	115
11. Tiny Bonham	110
12. Johnny Vander Meer	103
13. Harry Brecheen	101
14. Ed Lopat	99
Tex Hughson	99
16. Early Wynn	97
Thornton Lee	97
18. Hank Borowy	93
19. Johnny Sain	90
20. Spud Chandler	89
21. Mickey Haefner	88
Paul Derringer	88
23. Kirby Higbe	84
24. Howie Pollet	82
Phil Marchildon	82

Young At Heart
"Age is a question of mind over matter. If you don't mind it doesn't matter."
—Satchel Paige

1940s SAVES

1.	Joe Page	63
2.	Hugh Casey	54
3.	Johnny Murphy	53
4.	Al Benton	50
5.	Ace Adams	49
6.	Harry Gumbert	47
7.	Tom Ferrick	41
8.	George Caster	37
9.	Russ Christopher	35
10.	Gordon Maltzberger	33
	Ed Klieman	33
12.	Joe Heving	30
13.	Joe Beggs	29
14.	Ted Wilks	28
15.	Andy Karl	26
	Mace Brown	26
17.	Earl Caldwell	23
18.	Dizzy Trout	22
	Bob Klinger	22
	Kirby Higbe	22
21.	Ken Trinkle	21
22.	Jim Turner	19
	Clyde Shoun	19
	Hank Behrman	19
25.	Joe Berry	18

Adams Aces to 65 Games Per Season

Prior to the early 1940s, relief specialists seldom worked more than once every third day or so, but in 1942 Ace Adams of the New York Giants became the first bullpenner to change the notion of how often a stopper could be used and still maintain his effectiveness. In the four seasons between 1942 and 1945, Adams appeared in 261 games, an average of 65 a season. As Adams's career was winding to a close, Andy Karl of the Phillies in 1945 logged 167 relief innings, a record that lasted until Mike Marshall appeared on the scene. After the war, however, the manner in which relievers were used reverted for a time to the previous standard. In 1949, for example, Ted Wilks of the Cardinals and Jim Konstanty of the Phils were the only two NL firemen to work more than 50 games, and they finished one-two in saves with the rather inauspicious totals of nine and seven respectively.

Between the end of the dead-ball era (1920) and expansion (1961), George Uhle (1922, 1923) and Bob Feller (1941, 1946) were the only two pitchers to start 40 or more games in a season twice during their careers.

Tribe moundsman Bob Feller pitched the only AL Opening Day no-hitter in history on April 16, 1940, against the Chicago White Sox.

Cleveland hurler Bob Feller's 261 strikeouts in 1940 were the most by any pitcher in a major league since 1924.

Above: *Bob Feller used his overpowering fastball to lead the AL in victories six times. Spending his entire career with the Indians, "Rapid Robert" won seven strikeout crowns and tossed three no-hitters.*

Southworth Stays Sain, Whereas Slogan Spahns Story

The Boston Braves' slogan in 1948 of "Spahn and Sain and pray for rain" made for a good story but took some liberties with the facts. One would think the Braves had only two starting pitchers of any worth that year, Warren Spahn and Johnny Sain, and the rest of the mound crew was called on only in desperation. In actuality, rookie righthander Vern Bickford had a fine 11-5 record for the 1948 Braves and Bill Voiselle labored 213 innings and collected 13 wins, only two less than Spahn. And a fifth hurler, Nels Potter, a midseason acquisition from the American League, was nominated by Braves manager Billy Southworth to start the key fifth game of the World Series against Cleveland when a loss would have knocked Boston out of the postseason picture. Closer to the truth perhaps would have been a slogan that began and ended with Sain, who in 1948 led the National League in wins, innings, and complete games, and was third in ERA. Spahn, in contrast, had a 3.71 ERA, the poorest on the club among pitchers in a minimum of 10 decisions or 75 innings.

Above: *Braves pitchers Warren Spahn (left) and Johnny Sain formed a knockout lefty-righty tandem in the late 1940s. Between 1946 and 1950, the two combined for seven 20-win seasons. Each led the league in complete games twice, and Spahn captured four consecutive strikeout titles.*

1940s SHUTOUTS

1.	Hal Newhouser	31
	Mort Cooper	31
3.	Bucky Walters	28
	Bob Feller	28
5.	Dizzy Trout	27
6.	Johnny Vander Meer	26
7.	Dutch Leonard	23
8.	Spud Chandler	22
	Harry Brecheen	22
10.	Claude Passeau	21
	Tiny Bonham	21
12.	Rip Sewell	19
	Bobo Newsom	19
	Tex Hughson	19
15.	Howie Pollet	18
16.	Joe Dobson	17
17.	Allie Reynolds	16
	Max Lanier	16
	Ken Heintzelman	16
	Hank Borowy	16
21.	Whit Wyatt	15
	Ken Raffensberger	15
	Al Javery	15
	Denny Galehouse	15
25.	Virgil Trucks	14
	Warren Spahn	14
	Ed Lopat	14

Bill Dickey, commenting on Hal Newhouser, said: "As far as the Yankees are concerned, we'd rather face anyone else."

McCarthy Maximizes Parnell, Kinder

In 1949, the Boston Red Sox seemed to borrow a page from their fellow Hub entry as they chased the Yankees all season for the American League pennant before succumbing at the wire. During the final weeks of the season, BoSox manager Joe McCarthy started his twin mound aces Mel Parnell and Ellis Kinder at every opportunity and also had no hesitation about calling on them in relief. As a result, Parnell not only led the American League with 25 wins, 295 innings, and a 2.77 ERA, but he notched two saves and came out of the bullpen on several other occasions late in the campaign. Kinder meanwhile won 23 games and topped the AL with a .793 winning percentage at age 35 but still found the strength to relieve in 13 contests and collect four saves. Between them Parnell and Kinder accounted for exactly half of the BoSox 96 wins. Joe Dobson (14) and Chuck Stobbs (11) were the club's only other hurlers to win more than six.

Above: *Paul "Dizzy" Trout enjoyed several excellent seasons with the Tigers during the mid-1940s. A big righthander with excellent control, Trout won 47 games, with 12 shutouts, in 1943 and '44. His 2.12 ERA in 1944 was the AL's best. Over 15 seasons, he captured 170 victories.*

1940s WINS	
1. Hal Newhouser	170
2. Bob Feller	137
3. Rip Sewell	133
4. Dizzy Trout	129
5. Bucky Walters	122
Dutch Leonard	122
7. Mort Cooper	114
8. Claude Passeau	111
9. Bobo Newsom	105
Kirby Higbe	105
Harry Brecheen	105
12. Hank Borowy	104
13. Allie Reynolds	103
Tiny Bonham	103
15. Tex Hughson	96
16. Joe Dobson	94
17. Johnny Vander Meer	93
18. Harry Gumbert	88
19. Virgil Trucks	87
20. Spud Chandler	85
21. Early Wynn	83
Howie Pollet	83
23. Nels Potter	82
Ed Lopat	82
Jack Kramer	82

The 1944 Detroit Tigers are the last team to date to fail to win a pennant despite having two 25-game winners—Hal Newhouser (29) and Dizzy Trout (27). Their tandem record of 56 wins was a record for teammates after the dead-ball era.

Paige Produces More Than Publicity

When Cleveland owner Bill Veeck inked Satchel Paige to an Indians' contract during the 1948 campaign, his fellow magnates thought it was another of his publicity stunts. The Negro League great was then at least 42 years old, and many believed his true age was closer to 50. In any case, Paige was not expected to provide much more than a couple of relief innings here and there, usually in a lost cause. Veeck, though, had another plan. He saw Paige as still having the wherewithal to serve as a starter, and he was right. Facing the Chicago White Sox in his first major league start, Paige became the first black hurler to throw a shutout. That October, in game five of the World Series, he became the first black to pitch in a fall classic when he gave Cleveland manager Lou Boudreau a perfect relief stint. At the close of the 1948 season, the oldest rookie ever to that point had a 6-1 record and two shutouts to go with his snappy 2.48 ERA in 21 mound appearances.

1940s INNINGS	
1. Hal Newhouser	2,453.1
2. Dutch Leonard	2,047.1
3. Dizzy Trout	2,026.1
4. Bobo Newsom	1,961.1
5. Bob Feller	1,897.0
6. Rip Sewell	1,894.0
7. Bucky Walters	1,868.1
8. Claude Passeau	1,693.2
9. Kirby Higbe	1,692.2
10. Hank Borowy	1,607.1
11. Mort Cooper	1,606.1
12. Johnny Vander Meer	1,589.1
13. Tiny Bonham	1,551.0
14. Allie Reynolds	1,484.0
15. Joe Dobson	1,434.2
16. Jim Tobin	1,426.1
17. Early Wynn	1,411.0
18. Bob Muncrief	1,393.1
19. Harry Brecheen	1,388.0
20. Jim Bagby	1,387.2
21. Sid Hudson	1,380.1
Denny Galehouse	1,380.1
23. Nels Potter	1,377.1
24. Tex Hughson	1,375.2
25. Mickey Haefner	1,372.0

Satchel Paige, when asked his age, responded: "How old would you be if you didn't know how old you was?"

In 1940, Ernie Bonham of the Yankees did not come up from the minors until August but nevertheless won the American League ERA crown.

Giant reliever Ace Adams in 1943 appeared in 70 games, setting a modern major league mound record.

Legendary Negro League pitcher Satchel Paige (above) didn't reach the majors until into his 40s. Paige, who many consider the greatest hurler ever, collected 12 wins for the seventh-place 1952 St. Louis Browns at age 46.

Harry Brecheen of St. Louis in 1946 won three World Series games for the Cards.

Newcombe Debuts in '49, Wins Rookie Prize

In 1949, for the second time in three seasons, the Brooklyn Dodgers unveiled a black Rookie of the Year Award winner when Don Newcombe debuted with a 17-8 mark and a National League-leading five shutouts. He had 19 complete games in 31 starts, and he also notched a save. Newk began the 1949 campaign with Montreal, the Dodgers' International League affiliate, before being called up to the parent club in May. Soon after his arrival, he became the mainstay of Brooklyn's mound staff, a role he would continue to serve until the team moved to Los Angeles. Newcombe was on the rubber in most of the key games Brooklyn played during his career. It was he who was relieved by Ralph Branca moments before Bobby Thomson hit "The Shot Heard 'Round the World" in 1951. The previous season, Newcombe had been positioned to win his 20th game and bring the Dodgers into a tie for first place with the Phillies on the final day of the campaign before Richie Ashburn of the Phils cut down the pennant-tying run at the plate.

Ace Adams of the Giants was the first hurler in the 20th century to appear in 60 or more games for three consecutive years.

In 1945, Philadelphia Phillie hurler Andy Karl pitched 167 innings in relief to set an NL record that lasted until 1974.

Above: Ewell "The Whip" Blackwell, so named for his intimidating sidearm delivery, was occasionally overpowering during his 10-year career. Sidetracked by injuries, he still racked up an NL-high 22 victories with the Reds in 1947 and won 33 combined games in 1950 and 1951.

On June 22, 1947, Ewell Blackwell was only two outs away from registering his second consecutive no-hitter when he surrendered a single to Eddie Stanky of the Dodgers.

Howie Krist of the Cardinals set a National League record for the most wins by a pitcher without a loss when he was 10-0 in 1941.

Cardinals reliever Ted Wilks had a perfect 10-0 record over a two-season span (1946 and '47).

The 1944 season was the first since 1915 in which two National League pitchers hurled no-hitters in two different games.

Bullpenner Mike Ryba, whose last major league appearance was a relief inning for the Red Sox in the 1946 World Series, led the Western Association in batting 13 years earlier as a catcher.

Fireman
Casey Stengel said reliever Joe Page "could get the fire out quick. He just came in and blasted the ball in there."

On September 9, 1945, Dick Fowler of the A's notched the first no-hitter in more than five years by an American League hurler.

1940s STRIKEOUTS	
1. Hal Newhouser	1,579
2. Bob Feller	1,396
3. Bobo Newsom	1,070
4. Johnny Vander Meer	972
5. Dizzy Trout	930
6. Kirby Higbe	853
7. Allie Reynolds	791
8. Dutch Leonard	779
9. Mort Cooper	772
10. Virgil Trucks	760
11. Tex Hughson	693
12. Bucky Walters	677
13. Harry Brecheen	666
14. Joe Dobson	665
15. Hank Borowy	650
16. Claude Passeau	646
17. Nels Potter	644
18. Bill Voiselle	620
19. Johnny Niggeling	599
20. Max Lanier	588
21. Denny Galehouse	560
22. Rip Sewell	548
23. Spud Chandler	543
24. Johnny Sain	539
25. Bob Muncrief	522

Pale Hose Procure Experienced Pitchers

Ted Lyons was appointed manager of the Chicago White Sox when he returned to the game in 1946 following a three-year military commitment. The Sox career leader in wins, Lyons rallied his 45-year-old arm to make five starts and post a 2.32 ERA before retiring to strictly a dugout role. His performance, however, convinced him that life in the majors didn't necessarily end at age 40. In 1947, Lyons accordingly designated 42-year-old Earl Caldwell as his bullpen ace and encouraged the Sox to sign 43-year-old Red Ruffing, who had been released by the Yankees after the 1946 season. Joining Caldwell and Ruffing on Lyons's mound staff in 1947 was 41-year-old Thornton Lee. The trio made the Pale Hose the first team in major league history with three hurlers who had passed their 40th birthdays. Lyons himself nearly made a fourth before deciding not to mount a comeback bid in 1947. That season, while Caldwell notched eight saves, Lee was 3-7 and Ruffing was only 3-5.

One of many who gained their chance during World War II, New York Giants rookie pitcher Bill Voiselle (above) led the NL in innings pitched and strikeouts in 1944 and won 21 games. Though he pitched until 1950, Voiselle never again enjoyed a season as good as his first campaign. He did contribute to the Boston Braves' 1948 crown with 13 wins and a 3.63 ERA.

"In USA Today I was voted one of the 21 all-time hardest throwers. But I would trade it all to have had great control. The thing I'll think about all my life—the frustrating thing—is what that lack of control cost me. Bull on that throwing hard."
—Rex Barney, whose wildness cost him what could have been a remarkable career

In 1941, the Chicago White Sox became the last major league team to collect 100 or more complete games when their mound staff notched 106 complete games.

Cincinnati pitcher Bucky Walters led the National League in both innings (302) and complete games (27) for three straight years, from 1939 to 1941.

Giants rookie Bill Voiselle in 1944 was the last rookie in major league history to pitch 300 or more innings, as he worked 313.

White Sox Ted Lyons compiled a 14-6 mark in 1942, as he made just 20 mound appearances, all of them complete games.

1940s WINNING PERCENTAGE

1.	Spud Chandler	.714
2.	Harry Brecheen	.640
3.	Tex Hughson	.640
4.	Howie Pollet	.629
5.	Mort Cooper	.626
6.	Bob Feller	.626
7.	Max Lanier	.621
8.	Schoolboy Rowe	.619
9.	Rip Sewell	.605
10.	Allie Reynolds	.602
11.	Whit Wyatt	.595
12.	Hal Newhouser	.590
13.	Tiny Bonham	.589
14.	Virgil Trucks	.580
15.	Hank Borowy	.578
16.	Joe Dobson	.577
17.	Bucky Walters	.575
18.	Claude Passeau	.566
19.	Hank Wyse	.561
20.	Kirby Higbe	.559
21.	Elmer Riddle	.556
22.	Johnny Sain	.549
23.	Harry Gumbert	.547
24.	Ed Lopat	.539
25.	Al Benton	.539

On August 10, 1944, Red Barrett of the Boston Braves tossed a record low 58 pitches in a complete-game shutout of the Reds.

Harry Brecheen, the winner of three games in the 1946 World Series, had just a 15-15 record for the Cardinals during the regular season.

Orbit

Don Newcombe explained as to the kind of pitch Tommy Henrich hit to beat him 1-0 in the opener of the 1949 World Series, calling it "A change of space."

Bearden Brings Tribe Banner

Going into the final day of the 1948 season, Cleveland needed only to beat Detroit that afternoon to clinch the Tribe's first pennant since 1920. When Tigers ace Hal Newhouser knocked off the Tribe, though, it put Cleveland into a tie with the Boston Red Sox and necessitated the first pennant playoff game in American League history. A coin flip determined that the game would be played in Boston's Fenway Park, the bane of southpaws. When Cleveland player-manager Lou Boudreau named rookie lefty Gene Bearden the Tribe's starter in the do-or-die game, everyone doubted his sanity. Bearden made a genius of Boudreau by taming Boston with his knuckleball and becoming the only pitcher ever to attain his 20th win after the season's regulation closing date. He lost only eight games that year, while giving up 106 walks in 230 innings. A subsequent inability to control his butterfly pitch prevented Bearden from ever again winning more than eight games in a season, but for that one year he was gold.

In 1949, Mel Parnell and Ellis Kinder had a combined 48-13 record for the Red Sox, but the club's other pitchers were only 48-45.

The 1949 season was the last time until 1959 that two New York Yankees pitchers lost as many as 10 games.

Best remembered for throwing a key wild pitch in the 1941 World Series, Dodger reliever Hugh Casey (above) twice led the NL in saves during the 1940s. He served in the military from 1943 to 1945, but returned strong in 1946 with 11 wins and a 1.98 ERA.

1940s EARNED RUN AVERAGE

1.	Spud Chandler	2.67
2.	Max Lanier	2.68
3.	Harry Brecheen	2.74
4.	Hal Newhouser	2.84
5.	Bob Feller	2.90
6.	Mort Cooper	2.93
7.	Claude Passeau	2.94
8.	Tex Hughson	2.94
9.	Bucky Walters	2.97
10.	Howie Pollet	2.99
11.	Dizzy Trout	3.01
12.	Hank Wyse	3.03
13.	Whit Wyatt	3.04
14.	Tiny Bonham	3.06
15.	Johnny Niggeling	3.12
16.	Thornton Lee	3.13
17.	Dutch Leonard	3.14
18.	Al Benton	3.16
19.	Ed Lopat	3.28
20.	Johnny Sain	3.28
21.	Virgil Trucks	3.29
22.	Johnny Vander Meer	3.32
23.	Curt Davis	3.32
24.	Max Butcher	3.33
25.	Preacher Roe	3.35

War Inspires May-December Mound Staffs

Some nine months prior to Joe Nuxhall's major league debut, the Philadelphia A's hired Carl Scheib to finish out the 1943 season in mop-up roles. Scheib, at age 16, was the youngest pitcher ever to appear in an American League game. He lasted 11 seasons in the majors, notching a 45-65 record, before departing in 1954 at age 27. Many other fuzzy-cheeked performers who surfaced during the war years, however, were never seen again. By the end of the war, big league rosters were also dotted with grizzled oldsters such as Detroit's Chuck Hostetler. A career minor leaguer, the 40-year-old Hostetler had been playing semi-pro ball when the Tigers signed him in 1944, making him the oldest rookie in history to that juncture. The pennant-bound St. Louis Browns, meanwhile, solidified their mound staff that same season with Sig Jakucki, out of the majors since 1936. He went 13-9 in '44, helping to secure the Browns flag. The following year, the Yankees activated batting practice pitcher Paul Schreiber, whose last major league appearance had been back in 1923.

Above: *Brothers Walker (left) and Mort Cooper formed a battery for the Cardinals between 1940 and 1945. Walker caught for 18 years in the NL and hit .300 six times; Mort won 20 games in 1942, 1943, and 1944.*

Whit Wyatt, a knockdown artist, revealed how to play the game: "You ought to play it mean. They ought to hate you on the field."

In 1946, Bill Kennedy of Rocky Mount in the Coastal Plains League fanned 456 hitters and had a 28-3 record with a 1.03 ERA.

The 1946 Cincinnati Reds dropped a major league record 41 one-run games.

In 1941, the New York Yankees amassed 101 victories despite having no hurlers who won more than 15 games.

Wes Ferrell retired in 1941 with a career record 38 homers by a pitcher.

The Card's Mort Cooper in 1942 became the first pitcher since Carl Hubbell in '33 to notch at least 10 shutouts. St. Louis' pitching staff that year was the first in the lively ball era to allow fewer than 500 runs in a season.

1940s PITCHER FIELDING AVERAGE	
1. Lon Warneke	1.000
2. Si Johnson	.989
3. Joe Dobson	.987
4. Elmer Riddle	.987
5. Bob Klinger	.984

1940s RATIO	
1. Tiny Bonham	10.38
2. Whit Wyatt	10.49
3. Harry Brecheen	10.50
4. Spud Chandler	10.59
5. Mort Cooper	10.66
6. Tex Hughson	10.74
7. Curt Davis	11.09
8. Paul Derringer	11.12
9. Preacher Roe	11.21
10. Dutch Leonard	11.21
11. Bob Feller	11.23
12. Max Lanier	11.24
13. Claude Passeau	11.32
14. Bucky Walters	11.34
15. Schoolboy Rowe	11.35
16. Virgil Trucks	11.35
17. Red Barrett	11.39
18. Ken Raffensberger	11.55
19. Nels Potter	11.56
20. Jim Tobin	11.59
21. Thornton Lee	11.60
22. Johnny Niggeling	11.60
23. Hank Wyse	11.62
24. Johnny Sain	11.67
25. Howie Pollet	11.70

George Ferrell, the elder brother of Wes and Rick Ferrell, concluded a 20-year career in the minors in 1945 with 2,876 hits and a .321 batting average.

In 1942, outfielder Danny Litwhiler of the Phils became the first player in major league history to field a perfect 1.000 over a full season.

In 1948, some three years after his 11-year major league career came to an end, Jake Powell shot himself to death in a Washington D.C. police station.

In 1946, Buddy Rosar of the A's became the only catcher ever to play more than 100 games behind the plate without making an error.

In 1942, shortstop Eddie Miller of the Braves had a .981 fielding average to break Everett Scott's old mark of .976, which had stood since 1919.

Delinquent Juvenile

Telling William Mead, baseball historian, of his big league debut at age 15, Joe Nuxhall said: "I walked five, gave up two hits and I think a wild pitch. I was just scared to death. Finally, McKechnie just walked out and said, 'Well, son, I think you've had enough.'"

Above: *Johnny Vander Meer captured the NL strikeout crown in 1941, 1942, and 1943. Serving the next two years in the military seemed to sidetrack him, for he never again reached his previous level of effectiveness.*

Gray Bats .218 in Bigs Despite Having One Arm

After Pete Gray was voted Most Valuable Player in the Southern Association in 1944, the St. Louis Browns raised eyebrows by purchasing his contract and announcing that he would compete for an outfield job with the club the following season. Normally a minor leaguer with Gray's credentials would have seemed a fitting addition, but Gray was no ordinary performer. He had only one arm, his left, having lost his right limb in a childhood accident. Gray quickly established that there was a vast difference in the quality of play between the minors and the majors, even in wartime. Because he had little power, swinging with just one arm, outfielders played him so shallow that he was frequently deprived of what would otherwise have been base hits. In the field, Gray needed extra time to remove his glove in order to throw after catching a ball, allowing runners to take liberties. He batted .218 in 77 games, and was returned to the minors during the season.

1940s CATCHER FIELDING AVERAGE

1.	Buddy Rosar	.992
2.	Al Lopez	.989
3.	Jim Hegan	.988
4.	Ray Mueller	.988
5.	Rick Ferrell	.986

Sportswriter Rud Rennie said about Lou Boudreau: "He can't run and his arm's no good, but he's the best shortstop in the game."

Above: *Pete Gray in 1944 batted .333 with five homers in the Southern Association. He tied a loop record that year with 68 stolen bases.*

"Catching a fly ball is a pleasure, but knowing what to do with it after you catch it is a business."
—Tommy Henrich

1940s CATCHER GAMES

1.	Mike Tresh	890
2.	Phil Masi	842
3.	Bob Swift	841
4.	Buddy Rosar	818
5.	Frankie Hayes	816

Snuffy Stirnweiss's .993 fielding average in 1948 set a new standard for second basemen that lasted until 1964.

Lou Boudreau in 1948 led AL shortstops in fielding average for the eighth time to tie a loop record.

In 1944, Ray Mueller set a National League record when he participated in his 217th consecutive game as a catcher.

In 1947, third sacker Hank Majeski of the A's posted a record .988 fielding average that has since been bettered only once.

On August 14, 1942, the New York Yankees generated a record seven double plays against the A's.

Dom DiMaggio of the Boston Red Sox in 1948 set an AL record with 503 outfield putouts.

The last major league player to make as many as 60 errors in a season was Al Brancato, a shortstop with the 1941 Philadelphia Athletics.

The 1942 St. Louis Cardinals were the first team since 1923 to beat the New York Yankees in the World Series.

Bert Shepard Pitches in Majors with Artificial Leg

Pete Gray remains the only one-armed position player in major league history, but there have been two one-armed pitchers—Hugh Daily during the 1880s and Jim Abbott in our own time—as well as numerous other hurlers who have functioned with deformed arms or missing digits. A one-legged player seemed an impossibility, though, at least until 1945. Before then, Monte Stratton, a White Sox pitcher who lost a leg to a hunting accident in the late 1930s, had been the only performer to make a serious attempt to compete in the professional game with an artificial leg. Bert Shepard was a former minor league pitcher turned Army Air Corps pilot who had a leg amputated after his plane was shot down over Germany in World War II; in 1945 he braved the odds to pitch for the Washington Senators in an August 14 game with the Boston Red Sox. In a five-inning relief stint, Shepard gave up only one run. Since the Senators were making one of their rare pennant bids that year, Shepard was not used again, but he later played in the minors.

"Nice guys finish last."
—Leo Durocher

1940s FIRST BASE GAMES	
1. Rudy York	1,241
2. George McQuinn	1,189
3. Frank McCormick	1,119
4. Mickey Vernon	1,034
5. Johnny Mize	927

Bob Considine wrote of Connie Mack in 1948: "When he signals for an obviously wrong move, Al Simmons [A's coach at the time] turns his back on the man . . . and calls for the right move."

1940s FIRST BASE FIELDING AVERAGE	
1. Frank McCormick	.995
2. Elbie Fletcher	.993
3. Johnny Mize	.993
4. Tony Lupien	.993
5. George McQuinn	.992

Joe DiMaggio in 1949 signed the first $100,000 contract in major league history.

New York Yankees second baseman Joe Gordon and shortstop Phil Rizzuto set an AL keystone record in 1942 when they totaled a combined 234 double plays.

The Dodgers lost game four of the 1941 Series when Mickey Owen dropped a third strike in the ninth inning with two out, allowing Tommy Henrich to take first base and giving the Yankees another chance to score.

Lawrence Berra received the nickname "Yogi" as a youngster in St. Louis. One of his boyhood pals thought that Berra walked like a "yogi," who is someone who practices yoga.

Above: *Phil "Scooter" Rizzuto (left) and Joe DiMaggio. Like DiMaggio, Rizzuto spent his entire 13-year career in a Yankee uniform. He played an excellent defensive shortstop, stealing bases, drawing up to 92 walks a season, and hitting a lifetime .273.*

In 1946, Pete Reiser of the Brooklyn Dodgers stole home an NL record seven times during the season.

"Leo Durocher is a man with an infinite capacity for immediately making a bad situation worse."
—Branch Rickey

Washington's George Case won his fifth consecutive American League theft crown in 1943.

The 1949 St. Louis Cardinals tallied only 17 stolen bases, a record low for an NL team.

Opportunities Expand in Postwar Game

Come the spring of 1946 the Joe Nuxhalls, the Paul Schreibers, and the Chuck Hostetlers were all gone from the major league scene now that the war was over. The many missing stars like Joe DiMaggio, Bob Feller, Ted Williams, and Stan Musial had returned from military duty. Owing to the flood of returning vets, major league rosters for the only time in history were expanded from the 25-man limit to 30 so that as many experienced players as possible could be accommodated. The minor leagues too swelled to record proportions, increasing to 43 circuits in the first postwar season after just 10 had been in operation only two years earlier. Given a sudden wealth of openings, many returning war veterans who might otherwise have either chosen to pass up the game or else been denied an opportunity to find their way in it fashioned long and successful careers in professional baseball.

Above: *Shortstop Pee Wee Reese (second from left) and second baseman Jackie Robinson (right) formed a star double-play combo for the powerful Brooklyn Dodgers in the late 1940s and 1950s.*

Dangerous Concoction

Chuck Connors, actor and former Dodgers first baseman, remembered Branch Rickey: "He had both players and money— and just didn't like to see the two mix."

"Prefer the errors of enthusiasm to the complacency of wisdom."
—*Branch Rickey*

1940s SECOND BASE GAMES	
1. Bobby Doerr	1,279
2. Joe Gordon	1,137
3. Eddie Stanky	833
4. Emil Verban	792
5. Ray Mack	752

Jackie Robinson's 37 stolen bases in 1949 were the most since 1930 by a National League performer.

The Cincinnati Reds in 1940 won their first untainted world championship.

When Jackie Robinson topped the National League in steals as a rookie first sacker in 1947, he became the only gateway guardian since 1906 to lead the senior loop in thefts.

And a Game of Feats

"Baseball is a game of inches."
—Branch Rickey

In 1942, the Brooklyn Dodgers tied a major league record for the most victories by an also-ran when they finished second in the NL with 104 wins.

The Brooklyn Dodgers in 1941 won their first pennant since 1920.

1940s SECOND BASE FIELDING AVERAGE	
1. Red Schoendienst	.982
2. Pete Suder	.982
3. Bobby Doerr	.981
4. Snuffy Stirnweiss	.980
5. Eddie Mayo	.978

1940s THIRD BASE FIELDING AVERAGE	
1. George Kell	.968
2. Ken Keltner	.964
3. Pinky May	.963
4. Stan Hack	.960
5. Whitey Kurowski	.957

"If Judy Johnson were white, he could name his price."

—Connie Mack

The New York Yankees clinched the 1941 American League in a loop-record 136 games.

The 1942 to '44 St. Louis Cardinals were the last NL team to win three consecutive pennants and also the last NL team to win 100 or more games three years in a row.

The Philadelphia A's won 84 games in 1948, their best season between 1933 and 1969.

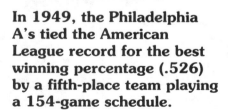

In 1949, the Philadelphia A's tied the American League record for the best winning percentage (.526) by a fifth-place team playing a 154-game schedule.

Prior to the 1949 season, Cleveland traded first sacker Eddie Robinson to Washington for first baseman Mickey Vernon and got Hall of Fame hurler Early Wynn in the same deal.

Above: *Red Sox second baseman Bobby Doerr played excellent defense and starred offensively. Over his 14-year career, Doerr batted .288 with 223 homers and 1,247 RBI.*

In 1940, Gabby Hartnett said: "If managers were given permission, there'd be a mad rush to sign up Negroes."

The Cincinnati Reds won the National League pennant by 12 games in 1940, the largest margin in the NL since 1931.

The 1940 Cincinnati Reds won a major league record 41 one-run games.

On January 5, 1946, the Giants bought Walker Cooper from the Cards for $175,000.

The Red Sox in 1947 got Vern Stephens and Jack Kramer from the Browns for six players and $310,000.

Mexican League Bandit Gardella Sues For Reinstatement

The postwar baseball boom was not without its share of obstacles. In 1946, the two major leagues faced the sternest challenge to their monopoly on the best professional players in the land since the Federal League ceased operation at the finish of the 1915 season. On this occasion the challenge came from south of the border. Mexican League entrepreneur Jorge Pasquel parlayed a chance meeting with New York Giants outfielder Danny Gardella in a Manhattan gym into a raging effort to entice as many major leaguers as possible to play in his loop. Soon not only Gardella but several dozen other performers—such as Mickey Owen, Sal Maglie, and Max Lanier—had been lured to Mexico. To nip the threat, Commissioner Happy Chandler banned all the defectors from the major leagues for five years. The ban was ultimately lifted in 1949 after a series of court battles, led by Gardella, but of all the Mexican League deserters the only one who returned to play in the majors with any great impact was Maglie.

1940s THIRD BASE GAMES	
1. Ken Keltner	1,188
2. Bob Elliott	985
3. Stan Hack	950
4. Whitey Kurowski	868
5. Jim Tabor	821

"Problems are the price you pay for progress."
—Branch Rickey

Masi Ruled Safe in Controversial Series Play

Not many current baseball fans have been alive long enough to remember when Cleveland last won a pennant. They don't realize what they are missing. When the Indians make a postseason appearance something extraordinary inevitably occurs. In 1920, the Tribe's first World Series experience, there was an unassisted triple play. The Indians' last fall outing in 1954 began with Willie Mays's incredible catch, and Cleveland's only other Series exposure, in 1948, opened with a game that was decided by perhaps the most controversial umpire's decision in fall history. In the lid-lifter at Boston's Braves Field, Cleveland hurler Bob Feller seemingly picked Braves catcher Phil Masi off second base on a carefully timed play with Lou Boudreau, only to have Masi ruled safe by umpire Bill Stewart. Moments later the Boston backstopper scored the game's only run on a single by Tommy Holmes. Photographs from every angle later demonstrated that Masi had been out, but by then it was too late for Feller. That 1-0 defeat in the 1948 opener was the closest he ever came to gaining a Series victory.

"A baseball fan has the digestive apparatus of a billy goat. He can—and does—devour any set of statistics with insatiable appetite and then muzzle hungrily for more."
—Arthur Daley, sportswriter

After leading the National League with 26 stolen bases as a rookie in 1945, Red Schoendienst never again swiped more than 12 bases in a season.

Detroit rookie outfielder Chuck Hostetler, age 41, in 1944 batted .298 in 90 games.

In 1947, Spud Chandler of the Yankees was the first 40-year-old hurler to bag a loop ERA crown as he topped the American League with a 2.46 figure.

1940s SHORTSTOP GAMES	
1. Marty Marion	1,383
2. Lou Boudreau	1,372
3. Eddie Miller	1,233
4. Vern Stephens	1,126
5. Luke Appling	1,100

Paul Richards, later a highly successful and innovative manager, caught all seven games for the Tigers in the 1945 World Series at age 36.

The average player's salary in 1942 was down to $6,400.

1940s SHORTSTOP FIELDING AVERAGE	
1. Lou Boudreau	.973
2. Eddie Miller	.972
3. Marty Marion	.968
4. Buddy Kerr	.967
5. Phil Rizzuto	.966

"Baseball is almost the only orderly thing in a very unorderly world. If you get three strikes, even the best lawyer in the world can't get you off."
—Bill Veeck

Above: Cardinals second sacker Red Schoendienst (left) collected 2,449 hits in a 19-year career. Shortstop Marty Marion (right) was a stellar defensive shortstop, and he won the 1944 NL MVP Award.

Above: *Duke Snider was known, affectionately, as "The Lord of Flatbush." He hit a career .295 with 407 home runs. He led the NL in runs scored from 1953 to 1955.*

"For the Washington Senators, the worst time of the year is the baseball season."
—*Roger Kahn*

1940s OUTFIELD FIELDING AVERAGE	
1. Thurman Tucker	.988
2. Tommy Holmes	.988
3. Wally Judnich	.988
4. Joe Medwick	.987
5. Andy Pafko	.987
6. Mike Kreevich	.986
7. Terry Moore	.986
8. Stan Musial	.985
9. Johnny Hopp	.985
10. Stan Spence	.984
11. Peanuts Lowrey	.983
12. Barney McCosky	.983
13. Danny Litwhiler	.983
14. Vince DiMaggio	.983
15. Doc Cramer	.982

Dillinger's Stone Hands Rob Him of Career

Bob Dillinger is the only third baseman since World War II who could not hold a major league job despite being a steady .300 hitter. Probably the best good-hit, no-field third sacker ever, Dillinger is also the only hot corner man in this century to sweep three consecutive stolen base crowns. After struggling at second base in the first few seasons of his professional career, Dillinger was stationed at third in 1942 by the Toledo Mud Hens of the American Association. Returning from a three-year service interruption, Dillinger joined Toledo's parent club, the St. Louis Browns, in 1946 and hit .280 as a rookie. It was to be his lowest batting average in his brief but eventful major league sojourn that saw him finish in 1951 with a .306 career mark, a figure that would have made him the sixth-best hitting third baseman of all-time if he had played four more seasons to acquire the necessary 10-year minimum to qualify for the list.

Passable Average
"A king may be king because his father was, but a ballplayer is a major leaguer only so long as his averages show he is."
—**Jim Murray**

The Philadelphia Phillies won just one pennant in the club's first 67 years of existence and had only one first-division finish between 1917 and 1949.

"I believe in God, but I'm not too clear on the other details."
—*Bill Veeck*

1940s OUTFIELD GAMES	
1. Bill Nicholson	1,325
2. Dixie Walker	1,268
3. Tommy Holmes	1,134
4. Wally Moses	1,083
5. Jeff Heath	1,043
6. Ted Williams	1,021
7. Stan Spence	990
8. Enos Slaughter	985
9. Dom DiMaggio	964
10. Doc Cramer	956
11. George Case	941
12. Joe DiMaggio	921
13. Charlie Keller	899
14. Jim Russell	883
15. Danny Litwhiler	879

On March 8, 1941, Hugh Mulcahy of the Phillies became the first major league player to be drafted for World War II.

On August 20, 1945, Tommy Brown of the Dodgers became the youngest player in this century to hit a home run when he connected at age 17.

Hi Bithorn, the first Puerto Rican player of note, won 18 games for the Cubs in 1943 and led the National League in shutouts.

Here Today, Gone Today
Bill Veeck, when asked what his first act would be if named baseball commissioner, answered: "Resign."

Gordon-Reynolds Swap Helps Both Teams

The number of trades that have made both teams who were party to them into a pennant-winner can be counted on the fingers of one hand. Some analysts even contend the count begins and ends with the deal made prior to the 1947 season that sent Joe Gordon from New York to Cleveland and Allie Reynolds from the Tribe to the Yankees. Gordon immediately shored up a gaping second base hole, brought punch to the middle of the Indians' batting order, and perhaps most important, lent his experience with the Yankees to help Cleveland learn how to win. In 1948, his second season with the Tribe, the Forest City club hoisted its first flag since 1920. Reynolds meanwhile spurred New York to a pennant in his very first season with the Bronx Bombers. Before he finished in 1954 he participated in five more World Series, bagged 182 victories, and also logged 49 saves. Gordon retired in 1950 with 253 career home runs, still the most by an American League second baseman. Many observers consider the pair the best two players from the 1940s not yet in the Hall of Fame.

How 'Bout That Game?

Bruce Caton, historical novelist, remarked: "Say this much for baseball—it is beyond any question the greatest conversation piece ever invented in America."

Those Were the Days

"Looking back, it seemed like it was all good times. Some people don't like to look back, but I don't find the view all that bad."
—Kirby Higbe, reflecting on his baseball days

The St. Louis Browns went a major league-record 42 seasons without winning a pennant, but broke the string in 1944, winning the Browns' first and only flag.

1940s MANAGER WINNING PERCENTAGE	
1. Billy Southworth	.615
2. Joe McCarthy	.607
3. Eddie Dyer	.595
4. Leo Durocher	.555
5. Steve O'Neill	.551
6. Joe Cronin	.539
7. Bill McKechnie	.528
8. Lou Boudreau	.520
9. Luke Sewell	.512
10. Charlie Grimm	.502

In 1946, the St. Louis Cardinals beat the Brooklyn Dodgers two games to none in the first pennant playoff in major league history.

Joe McCarthy and Eddie Sawyer were the only two men to manage in the majors in the 1940s who were not former major league players.

A four-man management group, including John Galbreath and Bing Crosby, bought the Pirates in 1946.

Above: *Reds manager Bill McKechnie won pennants in 1939 and 1940, keeping the team in contention through 1944. The skipper won four pennants and two World Series.*

"I find now at this stage of the game that if I had my life to live over again, I'm inclined to think that I'd have to try and do something that's more fundamental for humanity than a professional athletic career."
—Dick Wakefield, some years after his playing days were over

1940s MANAGER WINS	
1. Billy Southworth	890
2. Joe McCarthy	768
Leo Durocher	768
4. Joe Cronin	662
5. Connie Mack	638
6. Lou Boudreau	636
7. Frankie Frisch	581
8. Bill McKechnie	565
9. Steve O'Neill	509
10. Mel Ott	464

Elmer Gedeon in 1944 was the first former major league player to be killed in action in World War II.

1940s TEAM WINS		
	WON	**LOST**
1. St. Louis-NL	960	580
2. New York-AL	929	609
3. Brooklyn-NL	894	646
4. Boston-AL	854	683
5. Detroit-AL	834	705
6. Cleveland-AL	800	731
7. Cincinnati-NL	767	769
8. Pittsburgh-NL	756	776
9. Chicago-NL	736	802
10. New York-NL	724	808
11. Boston-NL	719	808
12. Chicago-AL	707	820
13. St. Louis-AL	698	833
14. Washington-AL	677	858
15. Philadelphia-AL	638	898
16. Philadelphia-NL	584	951

Frank Graham commented on the 1942 World Series: "The Yankees have finally found a team they can't frighten half to death just by walking out on the field and taking a few swings in batting practice. The Cardinals haven't been around and they don't read the papers; the chances are they don't even know these are the Yankees they are playing."

Above: *Leo Durocher's first managerial job came with the Dodgers, and from 1939 to 1946 they fell lower than third place only once.*

Veeck Early Promotion Developer

In 1948, a Cleveland night watchman named Joe Early wrote a letter to Indians owner Bill Veeck lamenting the numerous special days the Tribe was constantly giving to heap rewards on such players as Bob Feller and Lou Boudreau, who scarcely needed the booty, let alone the recognition. Why not honor an average fan for a change, Early inquired. Why not indeed, responded Veeck, and then promptly scheduled a night for Early at Cleveland Stadium which brought the Tribe rooter an outhouse, a backfiring Model T, some weird animals, a Ford convertible, and plenty more. Joe Early Night was just one of the multitude of promotional gimmicks that Veeck dreamed up to make his product as entertaining as possible. Between them and some good old-fashioned solid baseball from Veeck's players in 1948, the Tribe drew 2,620,627 spectators to its 77 home contests that year and shattered every then-existing attendance record.

Browns manager Luke Sewell said to William Mead, war-time game historian, that Pete Gray "didn't belong in the majors, and he knew he was being exploited."

Starting in 1943, major league teams conducted spring training in northern sectors because of the travel restrictions brought on by World War II.

1940s TEAM WINNING PERCENTAGE	
1. St. Louis-NL	.623
2. New York-AL	.604
3. Brooklyn-NL	.581
4. Boston-AL	.556
5. Detroit-AL	.542
6. Cleveland-AL	.523
7. Cincinnati-NL	.499
8. Pittsburgh-NL	.493
9. Chicago-NL	.479
10. New York-NL	.473
11. Boston-NL	.471
12. Chicago-AL	.463
13. St. Louis-AL	.456
14. Washington-AL	.441
15. Philadelphia-AL	.415
16. Philadelphia-NL	.380

The 1947 Brooklyn Dodgers set an NL attendance record, while attendance everywhere was at an all-time high as the postwar baseball boom was in full swing.

In 1940, the sacrifice fly rule was abolished for the second time.

The only manager to lose two pennants in a row on the last day of the season was Joe McCarthy with the 1948 and '49 Boston Red Sox.

Drop the Ball
On the night after Mickey Owen dropped a third strike to give the Yankees a chance to win game four of the 1941 World Series, Tommy Henrich said about Owen "That was a tough break. I bet he feels like a nickel's worth of dog meat."

Chapter 8
The 1950s

1950s GAMES

1.	Richie Ashburn	1,523
2.	Nellie Fox	1,512
3.	Gil Hodges	1,477
4.	Stan Musial	1,456
5.	Alvin Dark	1,441
6.	Eddie Yost	1,439
7.	Willie Jones	1,419
8.	Duke Snider	1,418
9.	Yogi Berra	1,396
10.	Gus Bell	1,380
11.	Minnie Minoso	1,337
12.	Chico Carrasquel	1,325
13.	Del Ennis	1,317
14.	Whitey Lockman	1,314
15.	Carl Furillo	1,307
16.	Jackie Jensen	1,301
17.	Bobby Thomson	1,286
18.	Hank Bauer	1,284
19.	Mickey Vernon	1,280
20.	Red Schoendienst	1,272
	Ted Kluszewski	1,272
22.	Earl Torgeson	1,271
23.	Bobby Avila	1,269
24.	Dave Philley	1,250
25.	Mickey Mantle	1,246

Beginning in 1956, his first full season, Rocky Colavito (above) hit at least 21 homers for 11 straight years with a high of 42 in 1959.

In 1956, Cincinnati Reds outfielder Frank Robinson clubbed 38 homers to tie the major league rookie record.

No Problem

"All I want out of life is that when I walk down the street people will say, 'There goes the greatest hitter who ever lived.'"
—Ted Williams

From 1946 to 1952, Ralph Kiner won or tied each year for the National League lead in home runs.

In 1954, Ray Jablonski of the Cardinals became the first third sacker in major league history to accumulate 100 or more RBI in each of his first two seasons.

In 1951, each of the New York Giants' eight regular performers had at least 12 home runs, led by Bobby Thomson with 32.

Rocky Creams Quartet, Gets Traded

On June 10, 1959, Cleveland outfielder Rocky Colavito became only the third player in American League history to belt four home runs in a game. Colavito's feat occurred in Baltimore's Memorial Stadium, at the time one of the toughest parks in the majors for sluggers to conquer. In 1959, it housed the team with the second-fewest homers in the majors, as the resident Orioles, awed by its imposing dimensions, reached the seats just 109 times. Enamored of his accomplishment, Colavito began swinging for the fences after the four-homer game, causing his batting average to drop to .257 from his .303 mark the previous year. Although he finished tied with Harmon Killebrew for the American League home run crown in 1959, Colavito's thirst for the long ball helped frustrate the Indians in their bid for the American League flag that year and made them receptive to trade offers. When the Tribe was offered batting titlist Harvey Kuenn by Detroit even up for the Rock, they jumped at the bait and, some think, have been paying dearly for it ever since.

Fain Gains Two Batting Claims

Ferris Fain—a fine-fielding, singles-hitting first baseman—won back-to-back batting titles in 1951 and '52. To find a repeat batting champion as unlikely as Fain, one must go back to 1913 and '14, when Brooklyn first baseman Jake Daubert copped consecutive National League hitting crowns. But in his own way Fain was one of a kind. A first baseman with little power

and not much run production, Fain nevertheless accumulated an inordinate number of walks (136 in 1949 and 133 in 1950). As a result, his on-base percentage was almost always higher than his slugging average, an extreme rarity for a first baseman. Indeed, Fain retired in 1955 with a .425 career on-base percentage, the highest in history by a player with a sub-

.300 career batting average. Fain's first batting championship in 1951 was somewhat tainted because an injury idled him for the last part of the season, freezing his average at .344 after 117 games. In 1952, however, he played in 145 games while posting a .327 batting mark that nipped Cleveland's Dale Mitchell by four points.

Above: *Ferris Fain was the first two-time batting leader to retire with a sub-.300 batting average.*

1950s RUNS		
1.	Mickey Mantle	994
2.	Duke Snider	970
3.	Richie Ashburn	952
4.	Stan Musial	948
5.	Nellie Fox	902
6.	Eddie Yost	898
	Minnie Minoso	898
8.	Gil Hodges	890
9.	Alvin Dark	860
10.	Yogi Berra	848
11.	Eddie Mathews	821
12.	Willie Mays	777
13.	Larry Doby	768
14.	Jackie Jensen	746
15.	Gus Bell	737
16.	Red Schoendienst	732
17.	Hank Bauer	730
18.	Pee Wee Reese	729
19.	Bobby Avila	722
20.	Jim Gilliam	705
21.	Willie Jones	684
22.	Ted Kluszewski	683
23.	Earl Torgeson	672
24.	Billy Goodman	666
	Del Ennis	666

About teammates Whitey Ford and Billy Martin, Mickey Mantle commented: "If I hadn't met those two guys at the start of my career, I would have lasted another five years."

On August 1, 1954, Milwaukee's Joe Adcock hit four homers and a double, collecting a major league-record 18 total bases in one game.

"If somebody came up and hit .450, stole 100 bases, and performed a miracle in the field every day I'd still look you in the eye and say Willie [Mays] was better."

—Leo Durocher

Westrum, Others Amass Free Passes

Ferris Fain was not the only player during the 1950s who was neither a slugger nor a high-average hitter but was nonetheless deft at collecting walks. In 1951, Giants second baseman Eddie Stanky, who had collected a National League-record 148 walks in 1945, garnered exactly the same number of free passes as hits (127) to go with a .247 batting average. Washington third baseman Eddie Yost meanwhile lived up to his nickname of "The Walking Man" by collecting walks in such bunches that in 1962, he retired as the only member of the top-10 list in free passes who registered fewer than 2,000 hits. Shortstop Eddie Joost of the Philadelphia A's on several occasions also totaled more walks than hits. Probably the most striking stats in this genre, nevertheless, belong to Giants catcher Wes Westrum. Notwithstanding his .217 career batting average, Westrum posted a .357 on-base percentage, largely aided by his performance in 1951 when he achieved 104 walks but only 79 hits, the fewest ever by a player who topped 100 free passes.

Brooklyn's Roy Campanella in 1953 pounded 41 homers to set a major league record for catchers.

In 1955, the National League had four catchers—Roy Campanella, Del Crandall, Stan Lopata, and Smoky Burgess—who had 20 or more home runs.

Above: *Roy Campanella claimed the Dodgers' catching job from incumbent Bruce Edwards midway through the 1948 season and held it against all comers until an auto accident crippled him after the 1957 season. In his 10 major league campaigns, Campy caught an average of 118 games per season.*

Brooklyn first baseman Gil Hodges socked four homers in one game, on August 31, 1950.

On September 10, 1950, Joe DiMaggio became the first player to pound three homers in a game in Washington's Griffith Stadium.

Lay One Down
Robin Roberts offered this as his greatest All-Star game thrill: "When Mickey Mantle bunted with the wind blowing out in Crosley Field."

1950s HITS	
1. Richie Ashburn	1,875
2. Nellie Fox	1,837
3. Stan Musial	1,771
4. Alvin Dark	1,675
5. Duke Snider	1,605
6. Gus Bell	1,551
7. Minnie Minoso	1,526
8. Red Schoendienst	1,517
9. Yogi Berra	1,499
10. Gil Hodges	1,491
11. Carl Furillo	1,399
12. Mickey Mantle	1,392
13. Del Ennis	1,390
14. Ted Kluszewski	1,380
15. Harvey Kuenn	1,372
16. Billy Goodman	1,347
17. Jackie Jensen	1,332
18. Eddie Yost	1,312
19. Willie Jones	1,298
20. Bobby Avila	1,293
21. Willie Mays	1,291
22. Pete Runnels	1,280
23. Mickey Vernon	1,274
24. Whitey Lockman	1,258
25. Don Mueller	1,250

Stan Musial in 1957 was the first player since Paul Waner in 1942 to collect a career 3,000 hits.

On May 2, 1954, Cardinal Stan Musial slugged a record five homers in a doubleheader.

In 1956, Yankees center fielder Mickey Mantle won the only Triple Crown of the decade, batting .353 with 52 homers and 130 RBI.

Mickey Mantle in 1956 was the first switch-hitter to lead a major league in batting since 1889.

BoSox Bat .300, Score 1,000

In 1950, the Boston Red Sox became the last team to date to compile a .300 batting average when they hit .302 as a unit and tallied 1,027 runs, only 40 less than the American League record of 1,067, set by the 1931 New York Yankees. The BoSox that year featured Billy Goodman, whose .354 average copped the American League batting crown, and three other regulars—Walt Dropo, Al Zarilla, and Dom DiMaggio—who hit better than .320. So deep was the club in offense that Goodman could not win a regular job and nearly did not acquire enough at bats to qualify for the bat title. Manager Steve O'Neill instead used Goodman to spell tired regulars until Ted Williams was shelved by an All-Star game injury. At that point, Goodman went to left field, where he continued to hit well but never with the power of Williams. In fact, it was the loss of Williams for over two months that for the third straight season prevented the top-scoring team in the major leagues from claiming a pennant.

Above: *Between them, Mickey Mantle and Willie Mays hammered 1,196 regular season home runs and accounted for 3,412 RBI. Strangely, however, the pair produced just one RBI crown. In 1956, Mantle topped the American League with 130 ribbies. Mays, despite 1,903 career RBI, was never a loop leader.*

1950s TOTAL BASES	
1. Stan Musial	3,047
2. Duke Snider	2,971
3. Gil Hodges	2,733
4. Yogi Berra	2,555
5. Mickey Mantle	2,548
6. Gus Bell	2,489
7. Alvin Dark	2,421
8. Willie Mays	2,403
9. Eddie Mathews	2,383
10. Minnie Minoso	2,368
11. Ted Kluszewski	2,363
12. Richie Ashburn	2,348
13. Nellie Fox	2,336
14. Del Ennis	2,310
15. Jackie Jensen	2,214
16. Carl Furillo	2,167
17. Larry Doby	2,144
18. Red Schoendienst	2,110
19. Willie Jones	2,066
20. Bobby Thomson	2,035
21. Ernie Banks	1,987
22. Hank Bauer	1,978
23. Ted Williams	1,975
Mickey Vernon	1,975
25. Hank Aaron	1,971

The last NL player to net as many as 20 triples in a season was Willie Mays, who logged exactly 20 three-baggers in 1957.

The only player since 1939 to hit .360 or better and fail to win a batting title is Mickey Mantle, who was runner-up to Ted Williams for the American League crown in 1957 with a .365 average.

On April 17, 1953, in Washington, Mickey Mantle swatted a 565-feet home run, the longest measured round-tripper in history.

"There have been only two geniuses in the world— Willie Mays and Willie Shakespeare."
—Tallulah Bankhead, *actress and personality*

"Trying to sneak a pitch past Hank Aaron is like trying to sneak the sunrise past a rooster."
—Joe Adcock

In 1950, third baseman Al Rosen of Cleveland set an American League rookie record when he hammered 37 home runs.

After being idled by polio for much of the 1955 campaign, Cleveland slugger Vic Wertz rebounded to have two successive 100-plus RBI seasons before being felled again in 1958 by a knee injury.

1950s DOUBLES

1.	Stan Musial	356
2.	Red Schoendienst	284
3.	Alvin Dark	282
4.	Duke Snider	274
5.	Gus Bell	269
6.	Minnie Minoso	259
7.	Nellie Fox	254
8.	Richie Ashburn	252
9.	Mickey Vernon	251
10.	Harvey Kuenn	244
11.	Jackie Jensen	238
	Gil Hodges	238
13.	Billy Goodman	237
14.	Carl Furillo	235
15.	Eddie Yost	232
16.	George Kell	224
	Del Ennis	224
18.	Yogi Berra	222
19.	Ted Kluszewski	220
20.	Granny Hamner	216
21.	Mickey Mantle	208
	Willie Jones	208
23.	Hank Aaron	205
24.	Willie Mays	204
	Hank Bauer	204

Unable to beat out Kenny Keltner for the Cleveland third base post, Al Rosen (above) remained in the minors till he was 26. Partly owing to his late start, he played just seven full seasons in top company.

Al Rosen of Cleveland in 1953 just missed winning the Triple Crown when he lost the batting title by failing to beat out a ground ball in his final at bat of the season.

Dale Long of the Pittsburgh Pirates in 1956 slugged home runs in a record eight consecutive games.

Take the Santa Fe Railway
Jimmy Dykes commented about Ernie Banks: "Without him the Cubs would finish in Albuquerque."

Rosen Smashes Hot-Corner Records

When he stepped to the plate for his final at bat of the 1953 season, Al Rosen stood to win the Triple Crown if he hit safely. A single would lift his batting average to .33722 and squeeze him in ahead of Washington's Mickey Vernon by .00005 of a point for the American League hitting crown. Rosen already had slugging honors sewed up with 43 home runs and 145 RBI. But, alas, the Cleveland third sacker hit a grounder and then missed beating the throw to first by half a step. Disappointing as his last at bat was, Rosen could only be proud of his overall accomplishments in 1953. He set all-time single-season records for the most total bases (367) and the most RBI (145) by a third baseman. His 43 round trippers also still stand as the AL mark for the most by a hot-corner man. Seemingly just reaching his prime, Rosen began the 1954 season with a bang but then was shelved by a broken finger that severely hampered him for the remainder of his career.

When his 34 doubles led the National League in 1956, Hank Aaron set a loop record for the fewest two-baggers by a league leader since the 154-game schedule was adopted.

The only player to collect 400 total bases in a season during the 1950s was Hank Aaron, who had exactly 400 in 1959.

Mathews Joins Hot-Corner Hit Parade

In 1953, even as Al Rosen was enjoying what is arguably the best season ever by a third baseman, Eddie Mathews helped the Braves celebrate their first campaign in Milwaukee by putting up some of the best numbers of any National League third baseman in history. Mathews swatted 47 home runs (the most ever by a third sacker until 1980 when Mike Schmidt rapped 48) and piled up 135 RBI, still the NL record for a hot-corner performer. The Milwaukee slugger also amassed 363 total bases to set a new NL third sacker's mark and rank second in history only to Rosen's 367 total bases that same season. Mathews also had a slugging percentage of .627, which was even better than Rosen's astounding .613 mark. Rosen was second in the AL with a .422 on-base percentage, while Mathews was fifth in the NL with his .406 on-base mark. Never before and never again would two performers at the same position conjoin in the same campaign to establish so many loop and all-time marks.

1950s TRIPLES	
1. Nellie Fox	82
Richie Ashburn	82
3. Willie Mays	79
4. Minnie Minoso	74
5. Bill Bruton	66
6. Stan Musial	61
7. Mickey Vernon	60
8. Alvin Dark	58
9. Duke Snider	57
Gus Bell	57
11. Bobby Thomson	56
Jim Rivera	56
13. Mickey Mantle	54
Jim Gilliam	54
15. Pete Runnels	53
16. Granny Hamner	52
17. Red Schoendienst	51
18. Enos Slaughter	49
Hank Bauer	49
20. Ernie Banks	48
21. Wally Moon	47
Gil McDougald	47
Dee Fondy	47
24. Hank Aaron	46
25. Pee Wee Reese	45

The 1952 season in the American League marked the only time since the end of the dead-ball era that either major loop failed to have a player with at least 300 total bases for two years in a row.

Above: Eddie Mathews is the only player to perform regularly on the same team in three different cities. After breaking in with the Boston Braves in 1952, he moved with the club to Milwaukee the following year and then to Atlanta in 1966.

Although he made 200 or more hits in a season just once, Nellie Fox led the AL in hits four times and was runner-up on four other occasions.

McDougald, Minoso Surpass Two Other 'M' Rooks

In the spring of 1951, the New York Yankees were laboring to convert an enormously talented but erratic-fielding shortstop named Mickey Mantle to the outfield and the New York Giants were trying to decide whether to install rookie Willie Mays in center field and move incumbent center gardener Bobby Thomson to third base. Mantle eventually opened the campaign in right field for the Yankees while Mays started the season at Minneapolis, the Giants' top farm club. Before the summer was out both would show flashes of the brilliance that would soon establish them as the two best center fielders of their era; Mays would even do enough to gain selection as the National League Rookie of the Year. But both Mays's and Mantle's offensive stats were pallid in comparison to those of two other frosh arrivals in 1951. While Mantle hit .267 and collected 13 home runs as a yearling, his rookie teammate Gil McDougald batted .306 and swatted 14 home runs to bag the American League Rookie of the Year honor. Chicago White Sox frosh Minnie Minoso meanwhile rapped .326 to out-hit all rookies that year; in addition, he paced the majors with 14 triples.

> "You've got to be a man to play baseball, but you've got to have a lot of little boy in you too."
> —Roy Campanella

Prior to Frank Thomas in 1992, Minnie Minoso (above) was the last White Sox player to boast consecutive 100-RBI seasons. Minoso did the trick in 1953 and '54 and finished with 1,023 ribbies.

In 1955, Detroit Tigers outfielder Al Kaline batted .340 to win the American League crown. At age 20, he was the youngest batting titlist in major league history.

Stan Musial in 1957 won his final National League batting title with a .351 mark at age 36.

In 1958 and '59, Boston's Jackie Jensen was the American League RBI champ; he had no triples in either season.

Boston Red Sox utility player Billy Goodman was the 1950 American League batting leader with a .354 average; he was the only player ever to win a hit title without having a regular position.

In 1950, George Kell became the only 20th-century third baseman prior to Wade Boggs to hit .340 or better two years in a row.

In 1951, catcher Wes Westrum of the New York Giants batted just .219 but had a .400 on-base percentage, the sixth highest in the NL, as he walked 104 times despite compiling only 79 hits.

1950s HOME RUNS	
1. Duke Snider	326
2. Gil Hodges	310
3. Eddie Mathews	299
4. Mickey Mantle	280
5. Stan Musial	266
6. Yogi Berra	256
7. Willie Mays	250
8. Ted Kluszewski	239
9. Gus Zernial	232
10. Ernie Banks	228
11. Ted Williams	227
12. Hank Sauer	215
Larry Doby	215
14. Roy Campanella	211
15. Del Ennis	204
16. Ralph Kiner	201
17. Roy Sievers	199
18. Vic Wertz	195
19. Al Rosen	192
20. Jackie Jensen	186
21. Bobby Thomson	185
Gus Bell	185
23. Joe Adcock	181
24. Hank Aaron	179
25. Frank Thomas	175

Robinson Reaches Rookie Round-Tripper Record

Even though he hit just .263 and clouted a mere 12 home runs for Columbia of the Sally League in an injury-marred 1955 season, Frank Robinson demonstrated enough talent to induce several National League clubs to try to pry him away from the Cincinnati Reds. The Reds, though, elected not to listen to trade offers for Robinson, and events could not have proved them more right. As a 21-year-old rookie in 1956, Robinson tied Wally Berger's then-existing frosh record for home runs, when he slammed 38 round-trippers. Equally impressive to many observers was the fact that he tallied 122 runs to set a new 20th-century club record. In addition, Robinson served notice of the give-no-quarter type of batter he would be throughout his career when he was hit by pitches 20 times to pace the National League and also establish a second new Cincinnati record. He batted .290 and had 83 RBI. To no one's surprise, Robinson was named Rookie of the Year, the first of many honors he would win in his Hall of Fame career.

Ted Williams in 1957 led the American League with a .388 batting average, the highest in the major leagues since Williams himself batted .406 in 1941. Williams was age 39 when he won the batting crown. In 1958, Williams again won the AL bat crown (with a .328 average), this time at age 40.

Until his last season, Ted Williams (above) was among the game's top pinch hitters. A 1-for-19 coda shaved his pinch-hit batting average from .390 to .297.

In 1954, Cleveland second baseman Bobby Avila was awarded the AL batting crown with a .341 average; Ted Williams, who had a .345 batting average, had fewer than the required 400 at bats, although he had 115 walks.

Ted Williams of the Boston Red Sox reached base a record 16 times in 16 consecutive plate appearances in 1957.

Yogi Berra, when joshed for his homely appearance, replied: "I hit with a bat, not with my face."

1950s RUNS BATTED IN	
1. Duke Snider	1,031
2. Gil Hodges	1,001
3. Yogi Berra	997
4. Stan Musial	972
5. Del Ennis	925
6. Jackie Jensen	863
7. Mickey Mantle	841
8. Ted Kluszewski	823
9. Larry Doby	817
Gus Bell	817
11. Minnie Minoso	790
12. Carl Furillo	784
13. Eddie Mathews	777
14. Vic Wertz	745
15. Bobby Thomson	740
16. Gus Zernial	738
17. Mickey Vernon	730
18. Ted Williams	729
Roy Campanella	729
20. Al Rosen	712
21. Willie Mays	709
22. Ray Boone	695
23. Willie Jones	689
24. Roy Sievers	682
25. Walt Dropo	680

Banks Bags Tribute Despite Bad Ballclub

It is a rare player who can overcome voter prejudice to win a Most Valuable Player Award while playing for a second-division team. Until Hank Sauer of the Cubs broke through in 1952, no member of a noncontender had bagged the award since the Baseball Writers Association of America had established the honor in 1931.

Six years after Sauer collected his trophy with the fifth-place Cubs, Bruins shortstop Ernie Banks became only the second MVP winner in history from a second-division club. When Banks was accorded the honor again in 1959, it marked the only time a player from an also-ran has been so feted twice during his career. The selectors were lauded for swallowing their bias against players from weak clubs, especially in 1959. That year the Cubs finished fifth with Banks but probably would have finished last without him. His 143 RBI were 91 more than the Cubs' second-most productive run producer collected in 1959. He also batted .304 with 45 round-trippers.

1950s STOLEN BASES	
1. Willie Mays	179
2. Minnie Minoso	167
3. Richie Ashburn	158
4. Jim Rivera	150
5. Jackie Jensen	134
Luis Aparicio	134
7. Jim Gilliam	132
8. Pee Wee Reese	124
9. Bill Bruton	121
10. Jackie Robinson	109
11. Johnny Temple	105
12. Sam Jethroe	98
Earl Torgeson	98
Mickey Mantle	98
15. Jim Busby	93
16. Dee Fondy	84
17. Bobby Avila	78
18. Duke Snider	77
19. Nellie Fox	68
20. Ken Boyer	65
Don Blasingame	65
22. Phil Rizzuto	64
Jim Piersall	64
24. Wally Moon	63
25. Eddie Yost	55

In 1952, Cubs outfielder Frankie Baumholtz played only 103 games but collected 409 at bats, just enough to qualify him as the runner-up to Stan Musial for the National League bat crown with a .325 average.

Above: Ernie Banks clubbed more home runs than he did doubles and triples combined. Mr. Cub accounted for 512 career round-trippers but just 90 triples and 407 two-baggers.

"The space between the white lines—that's my office. That's where I conduct my business."
—Early Wynn

Above: *Gus Zernial came along about 15 years too soon. Through as a regular outfielder at 34, he could probably have been a fine designated hitter for another five or six years.*

In 1958, Richie Ashburn of the Phillies became only the second batting titlist in National League history from a last-place team.

In 1959, Ernie Banks set two National League shortstop records by getting 143 RBI and a .985 fielding average.

Ernie Banks of the Cubs in 1955 set a major league record by whacking six grand slams.

Cub shortstop Ernie Banks set a record of 424 consecutive games played at the start of a career, starting in 1954.

Zernial Slugs For Lowly Clubs

When the names of all the great sluggers during the 1950s who won home run and RBI crowns are bandied about, Gus Zernial's is the one most often forgotten. Much of the reason is that Zernial played most of his career with the Philadelphia-Kansas City Athletics, generally the game's worst team all during the decade. After hammering 29 home runs in 1950 to set a new Chicago White Sox club record, Zernial was dealt to the A's in a gigantic three-club deal at the beginning of the following season. He then promptly became the first player ever to win both a home run and an RBI crown in a campaign divided between two different teams when he pounded 33 taters in 1951 and knocked home 129 runs. Zernial never repeated as a loop home run or RBI leader, although on three occasions he paced the American League in home-run percentage. His nickname of "Ozark Ike," after the comic strip character of the postwar era, was pinned on him in 1948 while a member of the Hollywood Stars by Fred Haney, later a major league manager but then a broadcaster for the Stars.

White Sox second baseman Nellie Fox, with 192 hits, was the only American League player in 1952 to collect more than 179 safe blows.

Nellie Fox of the Chicago White Sox in 1958 played in a major league-record 98 consecutive games without fanning.

Giants outfielder Monte Irvin described the clubhouse scene after Bobby Thomson's "Shot Heard 'Round the World": "When we fell behind in the late innings, the clubhouse people must have lost heart, because they didn't ice the champagne. So when we finally got around to toasting our pennant, we had to do it with warm champagne. Can you imagine that?"

St. Louis Cardinals rookie Rip Repulski collected two or more hits in a major league record 10 consecutive games during the 1954 season.

1950s WALKS	
1. Eddie Yost	1,185
2. Mickey Mantle	892
3. Ted Williams	845
4. Stan Musial	842
5. Richie Ashburn	828
6. Earl Torgeson	772
7. Gil Hodges	751
8. Eddie Mathews	726
9. Larry Doby	725
10. Duke Snider	711
11. Jackie Jensen	684
12. Gene Woodling	663
13. Minnie Minoso	648
14. Willie Jones	647
15. Pee Wee Reese	629
16. Ralph Kiner	610
17. Pete Runnels	595
18. Al Rosen	580
19. Jim Gilliam	579
20. Vic Wertz	567
21. Ferris Fain	560
Bobby Avila	560
23. Ray Boone	554
24. Mickey Vernon	551
25. Yogi Berra	531

Campy, Yogi Load Up on MVPs

For the first two decades the baseball writers' Most Valuable Player awards were given, catchers had been very infrequent recipients. In the 1950s, however, Yogi Berra and Roy Campanella combined to bring an abrupt end to the backstoppers' drought, as both players emerged as perhaps the two best all-around catchers in the game's history. In 1951, each was named his respective league's MVP, marking the first time that receivers had swept the honor. Both Berra and Campanella then proceeded to win two more MVP plaques during the decade, enabling them to become the only receivers to be so often feted. Campanella's other victories came in 1953 and 1955 while Berra's additional triumphs occurred in 1954 and 1955, making him the lone backstopper ever to sweep consecutive honors. Berra furthermore was among the top four finishers for the AL MVP Award in every year between 1950 and 1956, an achievement unmatched by any other player during the era. Campy's 41 home runs and 142 RBI in 1953 set records for backstoppers.

Walt Dropo in 1952 tied a major league record by getting 12 hits in 12 consecutive at bats.

The Brooklyn Dodgers in 1953 tied a major league record with six players scoring 100 runs or more.

Five times during the 1950s, Yogi Berra (above) topped 100 RBI. In 1950, he also tallied 116 runs, ranking him fourth in the American League.

"The game's not over till it's over."

—Yogi Berra

In 1959, Cleveland's Tito Francona set a 20th-century record for the most hits by a player in under 400 at bats when he bagged 145 safeties and hit .363.

Yankees second baseman Billy Martin in 1953 tied a World Series record with 12 hits.

Peanuts Lowrey of the Cardinals collected 22 pinch hits in 1953 to tie a major league record.

1950s STRIKEOUTS		
1.	Mickey Mantle	899
2.	Gil Hodges	882
3.	Duke Snider	851
4.	Larry Doby	833
5.	Gus Zernial	729
6.	Eddie Mathews	678
7.	Eddie Yost	626
8.	Wally Post	585
9.	Bobby Thomson	581
10.	Gil McDougald	578
11.	Walt Dropo	553
12.	Joe Adcock	552
13.	Gus Bell	550
14.	Hank Sauer	541
15.	Hank Bauer	539
16.	Vic Wertz	528
17.	Dee Fondy	526
18.	Roy Sievers	525
19.	Frank Thomas	521
20.	Earl Torgeson	520
21.	Jim Lemon	516
22.	Jim Rivera	506
23.	Joe DeMaestri	489
24.	Del Ennis	484
25.	Pee Wee Reese	477
	Jackie Jensen	477

Better Late . . .

Yogi Berra explained the tough late-inning shadows in left field in Yankee Stadium: "It gets late early out there."

Prior to Pete Rose's 44-game skein in 1978, Red Schoendienst held the major league record for the most consecutive games hitting safely by a switch-hitter, with 28 in 1954.

In a game against Detroit on June 18, 1953, outfielder Gene Stephens of the Boston Red Sox collected three hits in the seventh inning as the Sox put a record 20 men on base during the frame.

In 1950, the Boston Red Sox scored a record 625 runs at home and became the last major league team to tally more than 1,000 runs (1,027) or bat over .300 (.302).

Gene Stephens, who often served as a late-inning defensive replacement for Ted Williams, in 1956 played 104 games with the Red Sox but had only 63 at bats.

Russ Snyder, a major league outfielder from 1959 to '70, made his professional debut in 1953 by batting .432 with 240 hits for McAlester of the Sooner State League.

After debuting as an outfielder in 1945, Red Schoendienst (above) took the Cardinals second base job from Emil Verban the following year and held it for 10 seasons.

1950s BATTING AVERAGE	
1. Ted Williams	.336
2. Stan Musial	.330
3. Hank Aaron	.323
4. Willie Mays	.317
5. Harvey Kuenn	.314
6. Richie Ashburn	.313
7. Jackie Robinson	.311
8. Al Kaline	.311
9. Mickey Mantle	.311
10. George Kell	.308
11. Duke Snider	.308
12. Minnie Minoso	.306
13. Ted Kluszewski	.302
14. Billy Goodman	.302
15. Dale Mitchell	.301
16. Nellie Fox	.300
17. Carl Furillo	.299
18. Smoky Burgess	.298
19. Ferris Fain	.297
20. Red Schoendienst	.297
21. Don Mueller	.296
22. Ernie Banks	.295
23. Monte Irvin	.295
24. Bob Nieman	.293
25. Wally Moon	.293

Solid Backstoppers Develop in 1950s

Although Yogi Berra and Roy Campanella were the only two catchers to bag MVP honors during the 1950s, several other backstoppers put together seasons that caused quite a stir. In 1956, Stan Lopata of the Philadelphia Phillies rocked 32 home runs and notched 95 RBI, figures that were matched by only two other National League receivers, Campanella and Walker Cooper, between the end of World War II and expansion. Two years earlier, another Phils catcher, Smoky Burgess, stroked .368, the highest batting average in this century by a receiver in 100 or more games. Lopata and Burgess were a successful lefty-righty combo the three years that they were teammates. From 1952 to '54, Burgess had five homers and 46 RBI a year, while Lopata had eight homers and 33 RBI a year. Berra had no such rivals in the American League until the late 1950s when Gus Triandos emerged. In 1958, Triandos became only the second catcher in AL history to total 30 home runs when he posted exactly 30 with Baltimore.

In 1959, Gene Freese collected only seven pinch hits for the Phillies but five of them were home runs, just one shy of the single-season major league record.

In 1957, the Kansas City A's set the modern major league record for the fewest men left on base in a season when they stranded just 925 runners.

Also-Ran Reds Benefit from Power Boost

Entering the 1956 season, the Cincinnati Reds had finished in the second division for 11 straight seasons, and few saw much hope for improvement in the near future. Regardless, the arrival of rookie star Frank Robinson and the sudden emergence of catcher Ed Bailey as a bonafide slugger helped the Reds vault all the way up to first place early in the season and remain in contention until the last week of the campaign. The Reds slipped to third, just two games back of the pennant-winning Dodgers. Not even the vaunted Dodgers, though, could match the Reds at smacking balls into the seats. Led by Robinson's 38 home runs, Wally Post's 36, and Ted Kluszewski's 35, Cincinnati tied the 1947 New York Giants' then-existing major league record of 221 round-trippers. One more four-base blow by Gus Bell (29) and two more by Bailey (28) were all that kept the Reds from being the only team in history with five 30-homer men.

In 1953, Tommy Byrne's only hit in 18 pinch at bats was a game-winning grand-slam homer for the White Sox.

Luke Easter finished his major league career in 1954 with the distinction of being the only player to hit 25 or more homers three years in a row yet fail to collect 100 career home runs.

Problems in learning the strike zone hampered Duke Snider (above) in his first two seasons with the Dodgers. By 1956, he had learned it well enough to pace the National League in walks.

Deep Depth
"In 1950, I led the American League in batting with a .354 average, and when I came to spring training the next year, I was considered a utility man. You see, you have to remember what kind of ballclub the Red Sox had in those years— an All-Star at just about every position."

—Billy Goodman

1950s SLUGGING AVERAGE	
1. Ted Williams	.622
2. Willie Mays	.590
3. Duke Snider	.569
4. Mickey Mantle	.569
5. Stan Musial	.568
6. Hank Aaron	.559
7. Ernie Banks	.558
8. Eddie Mathews	.548
9. Ralph Kiner	.533
10. Ted Kluszewski	.518
11. Gil Hodges	.514
12. Roy Campanella	.507
13. Al Rosen	.500
14. Hank Sauer	.496
15. Larry Doby	.495
16. Yogi Berra	.490
17. Al Kaline	.489
18. Vic Wertz	.487
19. Joe Adcock	.486
20. Gus Zernial	.485
21. Sid Gordon	.483
22. Monte Irvin	.480
23. Roy Sievers	.477
24. Jackie Robinson	.476
25. Wally Post	.476

The first major league player to achieve 40 home runs and less than 100 RBI was Duke Snider of the Brooklyn Dodgers in 1957 with 40 four-baggers and 92 ribbies.

In 1956, Ron Northey of the White Sox notched 23 RBI in just 48 at bats and was 15-for-39 as a pinch hitter.

In 1950, the Cubs rapped 161 homers, second in the National League only to the Dodgers' 194, but scored the fewest runs in the loop owing to a .248 team batting average that was the NL's poorest by 11 points.

Klu Last of Low K Sluggers

Ted Kluszewski during the 1950s continued the tradition of such sluggers from the 1940s as Ted Williams, Mel Ott, and Joe DiMaggio by compiling huge home run totals while seldom striking out. In 1954, Big Klu fanned just 35 times when he paced the National League with 49 homers. Other fence-busters, though, such as Mickey Mantle and Duke Snider, regularly led their respective leagues in whiffs, usually with figures well over 100. Kluszewski proved to be the last slugger of his kind as by the end of the decade even lesser hitters thought little of fanning with a frequency that had earned Pat Seerey a ticket to the minors 10 years earlier. During the 1950s, only 22 players whiffed 500 times or more. When he topped the American League in strikeouts in 1957 with 94, Jim Lemon became the last AL player to lead with under 100. The following year Harry Anderson of the Phils became the last leader in either loop with under 100 after his 95 Ks paced the National League.

Above: *Ted Kluszewski was an outstanding two-way end for the Indiana Hoosiers in the mid-1940s, good enough to be an NFL prospect.*

Ted Kluszewski of the Cincinnati Reds in 1954 broke Johnny Mize's National League record by scoring at least one run in 17 consecutive games.

The Eyes Have It
Dan Parker, sportswriter, penned this poem about Johnny Mize, aging Yankees first baseman: "Your arm is gone; your legs likewise/ But not your eyes, Mize, not your eyes."

1950s ON-BASE AVERAGE	
1. Ted Williams	.478
2. Ferris Fain	.432
3. Mickey Mantle	.426
4. Stan Musial	.423
5. Jackie Robinson	.418
6. Eddie Yost	.407
7. Elmer Valo	.405
8. Minnie Minoso	.402
9. Richie Ashburn	.399
10. Ralph Kiner	.399
11. Willie Mays	.394
12. Duke Snider	.392
13. Gene Woodling	.390
14. Solly Hemus	.390
15. Larry Doby	.389
16. Al Rosen	.389
17. Earl Torgeson	.387
18. Eddie Mathews	.385
19. Monte Irvin	.385
20. Sid Gordon	.385
21. Enos Slaughter	.378
22. Al Kaline	.377
23. Billy Goodman	.376
24. George Kell	.375
25. Hank Aaron	.375

First sacker Rocky Nelson won the Triple Crown in the International League in both 1955 and 1958.

The 1953 Dodgers slugged home runs in a record 24 straight games.

Herb Scores Sizable Strikeout Sums

In the fall of 1954, American League hitters everywhere but in Cleveland cringed when they read Indians farmhand Herb Score's stats that season with Indianapolis of the American Association. All Score had done was top the AA in wins (22), winning percentage (.815), and ERA (2.62) while notching 330 strikeouts in just 251 innings.

Since the defending AL champion Indians already had the deepest pitching staff in the game, if Score was anywhere near as formidable as his minor league numbers made him seem, the rest of the AL was in trouble. Score quickly demonstrated that he was the real McCoy. In 1955, his rookie campaign, he set a new modern frosh record when he fanned 245 hitters and in addition became the first hurler in history to average more than a strikeout per inning. His average of 9.7 Ks in 1955 for every nine innings he worked is still a rookie record. Score went 16-10 with a 2.45 ERA, and he held opposing batters to a .194 batting average.

1950s GAMES PITCHED	
1. Hoyt Wilhelm	432
2. Gerry Staley	430
3. Clem Labine	412
4. Robin Roberts	405
5. Johnny Klippstein	400
6. Warren Spahn	389
7. Murry Dickson	376
8. Early Wynn	374
9. Chuck Stobbs	359
10. Turk Lown	358
11. Mike Garcia	355
12. Billy Pierce	353
13. Ellis Kinder	346
14. Jim Konstanty	344
15. Bob Friend	342
16. Lew Burdette	333
17. Bob Rush	327
18. Marv Grissom	325
19. Roy Face	324
20. Bob Lemon	311
21. Jim Hearn	308
22. Virgil Trucks	302
23. Joe Nuxhall	299
24. Carl Erskine	296
25. Herm Wehmeier	292

Above: *Beginning in 1957, Herb Score (right) was joined for three seasons on the Indians by Dick Brown, his battery mate at Florida's Lake Worth High School.*

Dale Mitchell, a .312 hitter who fanned just 120 times in over 4,000 regular and postseason at bats, ended his major league career in 1956 when he took a called third strike to become the final out in Don Larsen's perfect game.

Bob Lennon won the Triple Crown in the Southern Association in 1954 when he hit .345 for Nashville with 64 home runs and 161 RBI.

Billy Goodman assessed the pitching staff of the 1959 White Sox: "What a staff! I'll tell you, if we would have had those guys in Boston during those big years [in the early 1950s], we would have had some fun. We could have closed shop in August and gone fishing."

Score Hit in Face with Line Drive

After winning 16 games as a rookie in 1955 and 20 the following season while leading the major leagues in strikeouts both years, Herb Score earned regard as one of the premier pitchers in the game. In his third campaign, he had a 2-1 record after four starts and once again was on a record-setting strikeout pace. His fifth start came in a night game against the New York Yankees. Score's pitching delivery had long been a source of concern to the Cleveland Indians because he put so much effort behind his fastball that he was often left off balance and unable to field his position after

he released it. Facing Gil McDougald on that fateful night in the spring of 1957, Score paid the full price for his awkward delivery. McDougald's line drive back through the box shattered Score's cheekbone, endangered the vision in his eye, and came within a hair of killing him—nearly resulting in the second on-the-field fatality in major league history. Like Gene Bearden, the great Cleveland rookie southpaw of a few years earlier, albeit for a very different reason, Score was prevented by the fates from delivering on his enormous promise.

1950s GAMES STARTED		
1.	Robin Roberts	370
2.	Warren Spahn	350
3.	Early Wynn	339
4.	Billy Pierce	306
5.	Bob Rush	278
6.	Bob Friend	262
7.	Mike Garcia	261
8.	Bob Lemon	260
9.	Ned Garver	257
10.	Don Newcombe	246
11.	Johnny Antonelli	241
12.	Murry Dickson	230
	Lew Burdette	230
14.	Curt Simmons	223
15.	Sal Maglie	222
	Alex Kellner	222
17.	Harvey Haddix	214
18.	Whitey Ford	208
19.	Carl Erskine	204
20.	Chuck Stobbs	202
21.	Ruben Gomez	198
22.	Jim Wilson	196
23.	Vern Law	192
24.	Jim Hearn	191
25.	Herm Wehmeier	185

Above: *Wily vet Preacher Roe (left) counsels rookie Johnny Podres on pitching. The two Dodger lefties had a combined 20-7 record in 1953, Podres's recruit campaign.*

Dodger hurler Preacher Roe in 1951 notched an .880 winning percentage; it was the highest in history by a 20-game winner in the National League.

Endowed With Deprivation

Dizzy Dean said at his Hall of Fame induction: "The Good Lord was good to me. He gave me a strong body, a good right arm, and a weak mind."

In his only taste of big league action, Jim Baxes, a 31-year-old rookie infielder, hammered 17 homers for Cleveland in 1959 in just 280 at bats.

Don Newcombe Wins First Cy Young Award

At a special meeting on July 9, 1956, the Baseball Writers' Association of America, by a narrow 14-12 vote, approved Commissioner Ford Frick's recommendation to establish an annual Cy Young Award honoring the game's best pitcher. Frick had campaigned hard for the award because he was bothered by pitchers' lack of representation in MVP balloting. It was a problem that had hit particularly hard in 1952, when Robin Roberts won 28 games for the fourth-place Phillies but lost the MVP to Hank Sauer, a .270 hitter with the fifth-place Cubs. Ironically, the first Cy Young Award winner, Don Newcombe of Brooklyn, had a season so overwhelmingly dominant that he also won the MVP Award. Newcombe fashioned a 27-7 mark for the pennant-winning Dodgers, with a 3.06 ERA and 18 complete games. Newk received 10 of the 16 ballots cast; four of the remaining six went to Sal Maglie, who also finished the season with the Dodgers after being released by Cleveland when Tribe manager Al Lopez felt he was washed up.

Roy Smalley of the Cubs set a National League mark for shortstops that still stands when he fanned 114 times in 1950.

Don Mueller finished his major league career in 1959 with 1,292 hits and a .296 batting average but only 167 walks.

Above: *Don Newcombe remains the only hurler to cop a Cy Young, MVP, and Rookie of the Year Award during his career.*

Dodger pitcher Don Newcombe in 1955 knocked 42 hits.

After hitting .283 in 118 games as a Pittsburgh rookie in 1953, Paul Smith spent the following season in the minors with Havana of the International League.

In 1954, their first season in Baltimore, the Orioles were led in both homers and RBI by third sacker Vern Stephens with eight four-baggers and 46 ribbies.

Scooper?
"My best pitch is anything the batter grounds, lines, or pops in the direction of [Phil] Rizzuto."
—Vic Raschi

1950s COMPLETE GAMES	
1. Robin Roberts	237
2. Warren Spahn	215
3. Early Wynn	162
Billy Pierce	162
5. Bob Lemon	139
6. Ned Garver	125
7. Don Newcombe	116
8. Bob Rush	105
9. Lew Burdette	104
10. Mike Garcia	103
11. Murry Dickson	100
12. Curt Simmons	99
13. Johnny Antonelli	98
14. Whitey Ford	94
15. Bob Friend	89
16. Bob Porterfield	87
17. Sal Maglie	86
Harvey Haddix	86
19. Alex Kellner	80
20. Frank Lary	78
21. Bobby Shantz	71
Billy Hoeft	71
23. Bob Turley	70
24. Mel Parnell	69
25. Frank Sullivan	68

1950s SAVES

1.	Ellis Kinder	96
2.	Clem Labine	82
3.	Jim Konstanty	65
4.	Hoyt Wilhelm	58
	Ray Narleski	58
	Marv Grissom	58
7.	Al Brazle	55
8.	Turk Lown	51
	Roy Face	51
10.	Frank Smith	44
11.	Tom Morgan	43
12.	Tom Gorman	42
	Fritz Dorish	42
14.	Gerry Staley	41
	Johnny Sain	41
16.	George Zuverink	40
17.	Jim Hughes	39
18.	Hersh Freeman	37
19.	Allie Reynolds	35
	Ryne Duren	35
21.	Don Mossi	32
	Don McMahon	32
	Bob Grim	32
24.	Don Elston	31
	Ike Delock	31

In 1952, Cardinals farmhand Larry Jackson had a 28-4 record for Fresno of the California League.

After batting .323 with 103 RBI for the Tigers in 1950, outfielder Hoot Evers slumped to .224 the following year.

Baltimore's Dave Philley in 1959 compiled a major league-record nine consecutive pinch hits.

Yankee hurler Vic Raschi in 1950 set a major league record when he retired 32 batters in a row.

Above: *Robin Roberts never started less than 32 games or worked fewer than 249⅔ innings in any season during the 1950s.*

In 1952, when Robin Roberts was 28-7 for the Philadelphia Phillies, the club's other moundsmen were a composite 59-60.

Robin Roberts in 1952 won 28 games for the fourth-place Philadelphia Phillies; his win total was the most in the NL since 1934.

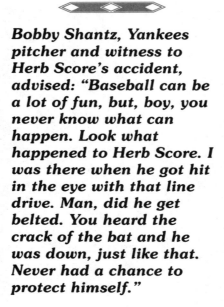

Bobby Shantz, Yankees pitcher and witness to Herb Score's accident, advised: "Baseball can be a lot of fun, but, boy, you never know what can happen. Look what happened to Herb Score. I was there when he got hit in the eye with that line drive. Man, did he get belted. You heard the crack of the bat and he was down, just like that. Never had a chance to protect himself."

In 1956, Robin Roberts of the Phillies was tagged for a National League-record 46 home runs.

Cardinals first baseman Steve Bilko registered the top strikeout total in the National League in the 1950s when he fanned 125 times in 1953.

Floyd Baker finished his big league career in 1955 with just 90 extra-base hits and one home run in 13 seasons and 2,280 at bats.

1950s SHUTOUTS

1.	Early Wynn	33
	Warren Spahn	33
	Billy Pierce	33
4.	Robin Roberts	30
5.	Whitey Ford	24
6.	Johnny Antonelli	23
7.	Bob Porterfield	22
	Sal Maglie	22
	Mike Garcia	22
10.	Bob Turley	21
	Lew Burdette	21
12.	Allie Reynolds	20
13.	Virgil Trucks	19
	Don Newcombe	19
15.	Curt Simmons	18
	Bob Lemon	18
	Harvey Haddix	18
	Murry Dickson	18
19.	Jim Wilson	17
20.	Vic Raschi	16
	Ken Raffensberger	16
	Billy Hoeft	16
	Bob Friend	16
24.	Bob Rush	15
	Johnny Podres	15
	Mel Parnell	15
	Ruben Gomez	15
	Ned Garver	15
	Dick Donovan	15

1950s WINS	
1. Warren Spahn	202
2. Robin Roberts	199
3. Early Wynn	188
4. Billy Pierce	155
5. Bob Lemon	150
6. Mike Garcia	128
7. Don Newcombe	126
Lew Burdette	126
9. Whitey Ford	121
10. Johnny Antonelli	116
11. Sal Maglie	114
12. Bob Rush	110
13. Carl Erskine	108
14. Ned Garver	106
Murry Dickson	106
16. Gerry Staley	104
17. Curt Simmons	103
Bob Friend	103
19. Harvey Haddix	95
20. Virgil Trucks	90
21. Bobby Shantz	88
Jim Hearn	88
23. Frank Sullivan	84
Ed Lopat	84
Bob Buhl	84

Above: *Whitey Ford's 9-1 rookie mark with a .900 winning percentage remained an American League frosh record until it was broken by Kansas City's Jim Nash in 1966.*

"Hitting is timing. Pitching is upsetting timing."
—*Warren Spahn*

'51 Yanks Discover Ford in Their Future

In the spring of 1951, Whitey Ford insisted that he was ready to make the leap from Class-A Binghampton of the Eastern League to the majors. The Yankees instead farmed him out to Kansas City of the American Association, where he remained for the first three months of the season. Short a starting pitcher, Casey Stengel persuaded the team's brass to summon Ford to the Bronx. Despite not making his big league debut until July 1, Ford was voted the top rookie pitcher in the majors at the conclusion of the 1950 season. Used both as a starter and in relief roles, he won his first nine decisions before dropping his final verdict to finish with a glittering 9-1 record. He started 12 games that year, and completed seven of them. In the World Series that fall, Ford added to his awesome rookie stats when he carried a shutout into the ninth inning of the fourth and deciding game against the Philadelphia Phillies, before an error allowed the Phils to tally two unearned runs.

In 1955, for the first time in American League history, no pitcher was able to win as many as 20 games. Cleveland's Bob Lemon, New York's Whitey Ford, and Boston's Frank Sullivan tied for the AL lead in wins with 18.

In 1951, Chet Nichols of the Boston Braves became the first rookie to top the National League in ERA since Jim Turner of the Braves did it in 1937.

Braves Bilk Bronx Bombers Out of Burdette

During the 1950s, rival general managers were loath to talk turkey with Yankees general manager George Weiss because of the Yankees reputation for bilking other teams in the trade mart. One of Weiss's specialties was working out complicated interleague waiver deals with National League clubs that would put aging senior loop stars, like Johnny Mize, in pinstripes just in the nick of time to aid the Yankees in another of their patented stretch drives. Usually these transactions cost the Bombers little in player talent, so no one in the Yankees camp thought much of it when Weiss in late August of 1951 sweetened a cash deal with the Boston Braves for pitcher Johnny Sain by adding minor league hurler Lew Burdette to the $50,000 package. But for once it was the Yankees who were robbed. Sain was a helpful pitcher for several more years, but Burdette was destined to win 203 games after he left the Yankees chain and three more in the 1957 World Series when he faced his original teammates.

In 1957, Bob Riesner had a 20-0 record for Alexandria in the Evangeline League but spoiled his chance for a perfect season when he lost two games for New Orleans of the Southern Association.

In the '58 Series against the Yankees, Brave Lew Burdette went 1-2 with a 5.64 ERA.

Above: *Lew Burdette was a master at working just hard enough to win. Given an eight-run cushion, he'd often allow six or seven tallies. In 1959, Burdette joined a select group of hurlers when he posted 21 wins despite registering an ERA above 4.00 (4.07).*

In 1950, after being sent to the Giants by the Cardinals early in the season, Jim Hearn became the first hurler to win an ERA crown while dividing the campaign between two teams.

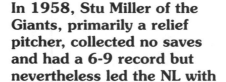

In 1958, Stu Miller of the Giants, primarily a relief pitcher, collected no saves and had a 6-9 record but nevertheless led the NL with a 2.47 ERA.

Jittery

Lew Burdette fidgeted so much on the mound that his Milwaukee manager Fred Haney said: "Lew would make coffee nervous."

1950s INNINGS	
1. Robin Roberts	3,011.2
2. Warren Spahn	2,822.2
3. Early Wynn	2,562.0
4. Billy Pierce	2,383.0
5. Bob Rush	2,047.0
6. Bob Lemon	2,015.1
7. Bob Friend	1,976.0
8. Mike Garcia	1,960.1
9. Murry Dickson	1,918.0
10. Ned Garver	1,904.1
11. Lew Burdette	1,863.2
12. Don Newcombe	1,773.2
13. Johnny Antonelli	1,721.1
14. Sal Maglie	1,638.2
15. Curt Simmons	1,625.1
16. Chuck Stobbs	1,588.1
17. Alex Kellner	1,581.1
18. Carl Erskine	1,575.0
19. Harvey Haddix	1,572.0
20. Whitey Ford	1,561.2
21. Gerry Staley	1,552.1
22. Vern Law	1,441.0
23. Herm Wehmeier	1,436.1
24. Bobby Shantz	1,433.1
25. Bob Porterfield	1,432.0

In the 1957 World Series, Milwaukee Brave hurler Lew Burdette had three complete-game World Series wins, including two shutouts, against the New York Yankees.

The only American League hurler to work 300 innings in a season during the 1950s was Cleveland's Bob Lemon, who toiled 309⅔ frames in 1952.

On May 6, 1953, St. Louis Browns hurler Bobo Holloman became the only pitcher this century to toss a no-hitter in his first major league start.

Cleveland Hoards Heroic Hurlers

Students of the game are still puzzled that the Indians could manage to win only one pennant in the early 1950s. In 1952, Cleveland became the only team in history to come up empty despite having the loop home run and RBI kings as well as three 20-game winners; poor fielding was cited as the culprit. A year earlier, however, the Tribe had paced the American League in fielding, featured their usual three 20-game winners, and fallen short because . . . well, just because. No one really knew why Cleveland didn't win, but pitching was certainly not the reason. When the Indians finally ended the Yankees' five-year monopoly on the AL flag in 1954, their pitching staff had one future 300-game winner (Early Wynn), three 200-game winners (Bob Lemon, Bob Feller, and Hal Newhouser), and in Mike Garcia a fifth hurler who at times was better than any of the other four. In 1954, Garcia had the top ERA in the AL, Lemon and Wynn tied for the loop lead in wins, and Newhouser and Feller contributed stats that gave the quintet an aggregate 85-33 record and a .720 winning percentage.

When he turned 30 in 1950, Early Wynn (above) had just 83 victories. He retired with an even 300 career wins and a .551 winning percentage. Wynn was only the second pitcher in this century to start a game in four different decades.

1950s STRIKEOUTS	
1. Early Wynn	1,544
2. Robin Roberts	1,516
3. Billy Pierce	1,487
4. Warren Spahn	1,464
5. Harvey Haddix	1,093
6. Bob Rush	1,072
7. Johnny Antonelli	1,026
8. Mike Garcia	1,000
9. Sam Jones	994
10. Bob Turley	983
11. Don Newcombe	917
12. Whitey Ford	915
13. Carl Erskine	903
14. Bob Friend	901
15. Bob Lemon	888
16. Curt Simmons	870
17. Sal Maglie	830
18. Billy Hoeft	821
19. Johnny Klippstein	777
20. Virgil Trucks	774
Murry Dickson	774
22. Camilo Pascual	748
23. Vinegar Bend Mizell	747
24. Herb Score	742
25. Chuck Stobbs	729

The 1952 Indians are the only team ever to have three 20-game winners, plus the league home run and RBI leaders, yet fail to win the pennant.

Cleveland Indians pitchers led the American League in complete games for five straight seasons between 1951 and 1955.

Cleveland hurler Early Wynn topped the 1950 American League with a 3.20 ERA, the highest ERA in major league history by a loop leader.

The only American League hurler to work 300 innings in a season during the 1950s was Cleveland's Bob Lemon, who toiled 309⅔ frames in 1952.

Antonelli Eventually Returns Investment

A few days after he graduated from high school in 1948, mound prospect Johnny Antonelli was given a $65,000 bonus to sign with the Boston Braves. Since the rules at that time forbade major league teams from farming out bonus babies to the minors for seasoning, the Braves were forced to keep Antonelli on their roster while he learned his pitching craft. In 1948, the high-priced southpaw got into just four games. The following two seasons he collected only five wins against 10 losses. Antonelli then spent all of the 1951 and 1952 campaigns in the military service, where he apparently matured. Returning to the Braves in 1953, their first season in Milwaukee, he won 12 games and exhibited enough artistry to tempt the New York Giants to trade Bobby Thomson for him. In 1954, Antonelli became the first bonus-baby hurler to make the heavy investment in him seem worth it, when he won 21 games for the Giants and paced the National League with a .750 winning percentage and a 2.29 ERA.

Cleveland pitchers Mike Garcia, Bob Lemon, and Early Wynn in 1954 were the top three AL pitchers in ERA, with Garcia leading at 2.64.

In 1952, Cleveland's "Big Three" of Bob Lemon, Mike Garcia, and Early Wynn ranked 1-2-3 in the AL in innings pitched.

1950s WINNING PERCENTAGE	
1. Whitey Ford	.708
2. Allie Reynolds	.669
3. Ed Lopat	.667
4. Sal Maglie	.663
5. Vic Raschi	.643
6. Don Newcombe	.633
7. Bob Buhl	.618
8. Bob Lemon	.615
9. Early Wynn	.612
10. Warren Spahn	.607
11. Lew Burdette	.606
12. Bob Feller	.597
13. Carl Erskine	.593
14. Mel Parnell	.587
15. Mike Garcia	.584
16. Robin Roberts	.572
17. Bob Turley	.568
18. Frank Sullivan	.568
19. Billy Pierce	.562
20. Billy Loes	.559
21. Dick Donovan	.558
22. Johnny Antonelli	.558
23. Johnny Podres	.557
24. Virgil Trucks	.556
25. Hoyt Wilhelm	.554

Above: *Bullet Bob Turley paced American League hurlers in walks in three of his first five full seasons.*

Bob Turley collected two wins and a save in the last three games of the 1957 World Series as the Yankees became the first American League team to rebound from a 3-1 deficit.

When Bob Turley suffered 13 losses in 1955, he became the only New York Yankees pitcher to lose as many as 10 games in a season between 1952 and 1956.

Robin Roberts discussed why he had such pinpoint control: "I can neither understand it nor explain it. I can't comprehend why other pitchers are wild."

Harvey Haddix described the prelude to his famous perfect game: "I didn't feel good. But about the middle of the afternoon I had a hamburger and a milkshake. I went out to the ballpark, still not feeling good. Yet I intended to pitch, no matter what."

Carl Erskine of the Brooklyn Dodgers in 1953 struck out a World Series record 14 hitters in game three.

Bonus Babies Go Boom-Boom

In the period between World War II and expansion, bonus babies posed the same problem for major league magnates that multiyear player contracts do now. Much as owners knew that the financial risk far exceeded the probable dividend, they were compelled to take the plunge because so many of their fellow moguls were doing it. The bonus baby era officially ended when the present amateur free-agent draft began in 1965; its actual end came some years earlier after too many teams had been stung too often by expensive prospects who never materialized. For every Johnny Antonelli who grew into a bonafide major leaguer, there were a dozen Paul Pettits and Billy Joe Davidsons. After taking the Pirates for $100,000, Pettit won just one game in the majors. At that, he was made to seem like a bargain by Davidson, who never even pitched a single inning at the major league level after looting the Indians of some $125,000.

Above: *Catcher Yogi Berra (left) joins teammate hurler Don Larsen in the fall of 1956, after the Yankees pair formed the battery that registered the only perfect game in World Series history.*

In game five of the 1956 World Series, Yankees hurler Don Larsen pitched the only perfect game in fall classic history against the Brooklyn Dodgers.

On July 1, 1951, Cleveland pitcher Bob Feller became the first hurler in the 20th century to toss three career no-hitters.

When he bagged 20 victories for the last-place Browns in 1951, Ned Garver also topped the American League with 24 complete games.

1950s EARNED RUN AVERAGE	
1. Whitey Ford	2.66
2. Hoyt Wilhelm	2.79
3. Warren Spahn	2.92
4. Billy Pierce	3.06
5. Allie Reynolds	3.07
6. Ed Lopat	3.12
7. Bob Buhl	3.14
8. Johnny Antonelli	3.18
9. Sal Maglie	3.19
10. Early Wynn	3.28
11. Frank Sullivan	3.29
12. Frank Lary	3.32
13. Robin Roberts	3.32
14. Mike Garcia	3.32
15. Bob Lemon	3.34
16. Lew Burdette	3.39
17. Curt Simmons	3.44
18. Bob Turley	3.47
19. Virgil Trucks	3.47
20. Jack Harshman	3.48
21. Dick Donovan	3.48
22. Sam Jones	3.52
23. Bobby Shantz	3.54
24. Don Newcombe	3.54
25. Bob Rush	3.57

Despite leading the National League in both ERA and winning percentage as a yearling in 1952, Hoyt Wilhelm (above) lost the Rookie of the Year Award to Joe Black of the Dodgers.

Reynolds Wraps Up No-Hitter Pair

With the departure of Joe Page after his miserable 1950 season, the Yankees lacked a bullpen ace. In the spring of 1951, manager Casey Stengel toyed with the notion of converting starter Allie Reynolds into a fireman. Reynolds rebelled, though, and he convinced Stengel that his arm was still strong enough to serve both functions. The results certainly bore Reynolds out. In 1951, not only did he lead the Yankees in saves but he topped the American League in shutouts and became the first junior loop hurler to toss two no-hitters in the same season. The first was a 1-0 masterpiece against Cleveland. Reynolds's second gem came against the Boston Red Sox in his final start of the season. With the Yankees ahead 8-0 the verdict was scarcely in doubt when the Red Sox batted in the ninth inning, but Reynolds was nonetheless nervous. The screws tightened in him when Ted Williams stepped to the plate with two out, especially after Yankees catcher Yogi Berra muffed Williams's pop foul. Moments later Reynolds induced Williams to loft another foul fly, and when Berra squeezed it the Yankees double-duty ace had his second no-no.

1950s FEWEST WALKS

1.	Robin Roberts	1.57
2.	Don Newcombe	2.00
3.	Warren Hacker	2.10
4.	Lew Burdette	2.13
5.	Ed Lopat	2.27
6.	Harvey Haddix	2.37
7.	Steve Gromek	2.39
8.	Gerry Staley	2.39
9.	Vern Law	2.44
10.	Warren Spahn	2.52
11.	Dick Donovan	2.58
12.	Paul Minner	2.60
13.	Bob Friend	2.66
14.	Pedro Ramos	2.80
15.	Frank Sullivan	2.82
16.	Frank Lary	2.83
17.	Bobby Shantz	2.88
18.	Bob Rush	2.91
19.	Mike Garcia	2.92
20.	Sal Maglie	2.97
21.	Murry Dickson	2.99
22.	Ned Garver	2.99
23.	Johnny Antonelli	3.00
24.	Curt Simmons	3.01
25.	Russ Meyer	3.05

Hoyt Wilhelm hit a home run in his first major league at bat in 1952 and then played 21 seasons up top without ever hitting another four-bagger.

Aim Low
"Never win 20 games, because then they'll expect you to do it every year."
—Billy Loes, eccentric hurler

In 1954, Bob Grim of the New York Yankees became the first and, to date, only pitcher in major league history to win 20 games in a season while hurling less than 200 innings.

Pittsburgh's Elroy Face in 1959 won a single-season record 17 straight games in relief; he also won 22 games over a two-year period. He finished the season with an 18-1 record.

Trucks Picks Up Two No-Nos

Just one year after Allie Reynolds's double no-hit feat, the first of its kind in the American League, Tigers righthander Virgil "Fire" Trucks matched it. But while Reynolds had won 17 games in 1951, Trucks could post only a 5-19 record for the season. Much of the reason for his poor mark was because he was pitching for the first team in Tigers' franchise history to finish in the cellar, going 50-104. He had a 3.97 ERA that year, while the loop average was a 3.67. In 1952, Detroit had so little bite on offense that Trucks was given just one run to work with on both occasions when he no-hit the opposition. Trucks also tossed a 1-0 one-hit victory that year over Washington that was marred only by leadoff batter Eddie Yost's single on the first pitch of the game. Traded the following year to the Chicago White Sox, Trucks blossomed immediately into a 20-game winner.

In 1954, Karl Spooner of the Dodgers hurled shutouts in his first two major league starts—they were his only two major league games that year.

Cub rookie pitcher Toothpick Sam Jones in 1955 set a National League record by issuing 185 walks.

White Sox reliever Dixie Howell clubbed five home runs in just 44 at bats in 1956 and '57.

Above: *Bobby Shantz was a fine-fielding hurler as well as a good pitcher. He won eight consecutive Gold Gloves, including the first Gold Gloves awarded in 1957.*

The 1957 Kansas City A's were the first club in major league history that did not have a single pitcher who worked enough innings to qualify as an ERA leader.

1950s RATIO	
1. Robin Roberts	10.16
2. Warren Spahn	10.62
3. Don Newcombe	10.73
4. Harvey Haddix	10.92
5. Warren Hacker	11.01
6. Steve Gromek	11.09
7. Billy Pierce	11.13
8. Hoyt Wilhelm	11.18
9. Dick Donovan	11.20
10. Ed Lopat	11.21
11. Lew Burdette	11.24
12. Johnny Antonelli	11.26
13. Sal Maglie	11.31
14. Whitey Ford	11.32
15. Early Wynn	11.40
16. Frank Sullivan	11.41
17. Bob Rush	11.43
18. Bobby Shantz	11.54
19. Curt Simmons	11.56
20. Allie Reynolds	11.74
21. Billy Loes	11.76
22. Frank Lary	11.80
23. Vic Raschi	11.84
24. Mike Garcia	11.85
25. Ned Garver	11.86

1950s PITCHER ASSISTS	
1. Warren Spahn	515
2. Bob Lemon	478
3. Murry Dickson	416
4. Robin Roberts	406
5. Gerry Staley	365
Lew Burdette	365

"I had my bad days on the field, but I didn't take them home with me. I left them in a bar along the way."

—Bob Lemon

Asked if he ever tired of talking about his World Series perfect game, Don Larsen answered, "No. Why should I?"

1950s PITCHER PUTOUTS	
1. Robin Roberts	199
2. Bob Lemon	181
3. Ned Garver	159
4. Murry Dickson	156
5. Bob Rush	149

When Sam Jones of the St. Louis Cardinals racked up 225 strikeouts in 1958, he became the first NL hurler since 1941 to collect 200 or more whiffs in a season.

Sam Jones in 1955 tossed a no-hitter against the Pirates after walking the bases full in the ninth and then fanning the side.

1950s PITCHER CHANCES ACCEPTED	
1. Bob Lemon	659
2. Warren Spahn	645
3. Robin Roberts	605
4. Murry Dickson	572
5. Ned Garver	523

On August 31, 1959, Dodger Sandy Koufax became the first National League hurler in this century to fan 18 batters in a game.

On May 25, 1953, Max Surkont of the Milwaukee Braves became the first player in the 20th century to fan eight batters in a row during a game.

After posting a 6.34 ERA as a rookie reliever with Detroit in 1948, Billy Pierce (above) was dealt to the White Sox for catcher Aaron Robinson. It proved to be one of the worst deals the Tigers ever made, as Pierce was arguably the American League's top southpaw during the 1950s.

When he notched 11 saves in 1953, his last full season in the majors, Satchel Paige came within one save of tying the St. Louis Browns' club record of 12, set in 1944 by George Caster.

In 1957, Pedro Ramos of the Washington Senators set an American League record when he surrendered 43 home runs in 1957.

In 1953, Ben Flowers of the Boston Red Sox became the first relief pitcher to appear in eight consecutive games in an eight-day period.

1950s PITCHER FIELDING AVERAGE	
1. Pedro Ramos	.991
2. Jim Wilson	.990
3. Bob Miller	.990
4. Steve Gromek	.990
5. Don Mossi	.988

Braves Success in Milwaukee Triggers Franchise Shifts

In 1948, just two years after a new ownership group headed by contractor Lou Perini took over the club and hired Billy Southworth as manager, the Boston Braves won their first pennant since 1914. Since the Red Sox were also contenders at the time, the city of Boston had no difficulty supporting two teams. Four years later, however, the Braves plunged to seventh, and home attendance was less than a fifth of what it had been in 1948. The following spring, Perini moved the club to Milwaukee for the 1953 season, marking the National League's first realignment since the close of the 1899 season, when four teams were dropped from the senior loop. It was the first realignment in either major circuit since the Baltimore Orioles moved to New York prior to the 1903 campaign. The move was such a spectacular success—the Braves rebounded to finish second in 1953 and attendance in Milwaukee jumped 649 percent over the last figure in Boston—that it quickly triggered the departure of the weak-sister entry in every city but Chicago that had at least two major league teams.

In '51, the New York Giants beat the Brooklyn Dodgers in a one-game playoff 5-4 on Bobby Thomson's ninth-inning three-run homer, known as "The Shot Heard 'Round the World." It was the third time in six years that the Bums lost the pennant on the last day of the season.

In 1958, Richie Ashburn (above) of the Phillies became the first member of a last-place team since 1915 to top the National League in batting. His .350 mark edged Willie Mays by three points.

1950s CATCHER GAMES	
1. Yogi Berra	1,316
2. Sherm Lollar	1,116
3. Jim Hegan	1,011
4. Roy Campanella	978
5. Sammy White	967

Eddie Mathews described the diving stop he made to end the 1957 World Series: "I'd made better plays, but that big one in the spotlight stamped me the way I wanted to be remembered."

In 1959, Yankee backstopper Yogi Berra's record streak of 148 consecutive errorless games at catcher ended.

The first bespectacled catcher to appear in a major league game was Clint Courtney of the New York Yankees in 1951.

Connie Mack said upon his retirement in 1950: "I'm not quitting because I'm too old. I'm quitting because I think people want me to."

Richie Ashburn in 1958 tied a National League record by leading loop outfielders in chances for a ninth time.

In 1954, Willie Mays made the most famous catch in World Series history in game one, snaring a long line drive by Vic Wertz on a dead run in center field of the Polo Grounds.

The Brooklyn Dodgers set a National League record in 1952 when they fielded .982 and committed just 106 errors.

In 1958, the Cincinnati Reds made just 100 errors to set a major league record.

While at the helm of the St. Louis Browns in 1952, Rogers Hornsby contended that rookie Browns outfielder Jim Rivera was the only major leaguer he would pay to see play.

1950s CATCHER FIELDING AVERAGE	
1. Sherm Lollar	.992
2. Jim Hegan	.990
3. Red Wilson	.990
4. Yogi Berra	.990
5. Roy Campanella	.989

Bums, Jints Flee to California

In 1946, Paul Fagan, part-owner of the San Francisco Seals, spearheaded an attempt to have the Pacific Coast League certified as a third major league. Although the bid ultimately failed, wiser moguls like Brooklyn's Walter O'Malley recognized that it was only a matter of time before big-league ball came to the West Coast. When attendance began slipping at antiquated Ebbets Field in the mid-1950s, and the borough of Brooklyn seemed disinclined to build the Dodgers a new stadium, O'Malley opted to cast his oar westward to Los Angeles at the finish of the 1957 season. To make the venture economically feasible, a second team had to be planted on the West Coast. O'Malley thus persuaded Giants owner Horace Stoneham to abandon the Polo Grounds, which also was in a state of decay, and flee to San Francisco. When the Giants and the Dodgers opened the 1958 season at San Francisco's Seals Stadium, it was the first major league game ever to be played in the Pacific Time Zone.

Above: *Jubilant Dodgers owner Walter O'Malley (left) embraces an equally ecstatic Walter Alston in 1955 after the latter piloted the Dodgers to their first world championship since 1900.*

In 1950, the Chicago White Sox stole just 19 bases, the fewest in the majors; the following year, under manager Paul Richards, they became the "Go-Go White Sox" and topped the majors with 93 thefts.

Modern Management

"The secret of managing a ballclub is to keep the five guys who hate you away from the five guys who are undecided."
—**Casey Stengel**

"Show me a good loser and I'll show you an idiot. Show me a sportsman, and I'll show you a guy I'm looking to trade."
—**Leo Durocher**

1950s FIRST BASE GAMES	
1. Gil Hodges	1,407
2. Ted Kluszewski	1,142
3. Mickey Vernon	1,128
4. Earl Torgeson	1,126
5. Walt Dropo	1,084

1950s FIRST BASE FIELDING AVERAGE	
1. Vic Power	.994
2. Ted Kluszewski	.994
3. Joe Adcock	.994
4. Gil Hodges	.993
5. Eddie Waitkus	.992

On May 18, 1950, Cardinal third sacker Tommy Glaviano made errors on three straight plays, blowing the game against the Dodgers.

A good case can be made that Wes Westrum (above) was the most productive sub-.220 hitter in major league history. In 1951, Westrum hit .219 for the Giants and made just 79 hits, yet collected 20 homers, 79 RBI, and a phenomenal 104 walks.

In 1955, Billy Bruton of the Milwaukee Braves became the first National Leaguer in history to pace the loop in steals in each of his first three major league seasons.

In his only three full seasons in the majors (1950 to 1952), Sam Jethroe topped the National League in steals twice and was second in the loop on the third occasion.

"Most ballgames are lost, not won."
—Casey Stengel

1950s SECOND BASE GAMES	
1. Nellie Fox	1,502
2. Red Schoendienst	1,214
3. Bobby Avila	1,163
4. Johnny Temple	948
5. Jim Gilliam	681

Wes Westrum of the New York Giants is the only catcher in major league history to catch three foul pop-ups in an inning twice during his career.

"Rooting for the New York Yankees is like rooting for U.S. Steel."
—Red Smith, sportswriter

1950s SECOND BASE FIELDING AVERAGE	
1. Red Schoendienst	.985
2. Gil McDougald	.984
3. Billy Martin	.983
4. Nellie Fox	.983
5. Danny O'Connell	.982

In 1957, Gold Glove Awards for fielding excellence were originated. The nine original awards went to: Giant Willie Mays, Tiger Al Kaline, and White Sox Minnie Minoso in the outfield; Red Sox third baseman Frank Malzone, Reds shortstop Roy McMillan, White Sox second baseman Nellie Fox, and Dodger first baseman Gil Hodges in the infield, and White Sox catcher Sherm Lollar and Yankee pitcher Bobby Shantz were the battery.

The last NL contest that ended with a forfeit occurred on July 18, 1954, when the Phils were declared 9-0 victors over the Cardinals after St. Louis was guilty of stalling for darkness at Busch Stadium.

Bauman Blasts 72

By 1954, the number of minor leagues had diminished to 36 from a high of 59 five years earlier, but among the circuits that continued to flourish was the Longhorn League, a bastion in the Southwest for players who lived more than anything else to hit. Making his home in the Longhorn League for the third successive season in 1954 was first sacker Joe Bauman of the Roswell Rockets. The previous two years, Bauman had been with Artesia and had topped the circuit on both occasions in homers with totals of 50 and 53 respectively. In 1954, he racked Longhorn loop hurlers for an all-time organized baseball record 72 home runs. Bauman also netted 224 RBI and tallied 188 runs, all in only 498 at bats. In addition to setting the record for the most four-baggers in a season, he also set the all-time mark for the best home run percentage as he tagged 14.46 round-trippers per every 100 at bats.

Tough Crowd

"All literary men are Red Sox fans. To be a Yankee fan in literary society is to endanger your life."
—John Cheever, novelist and short story writer

After the 1954 season, the New York Yankees and the Baltimore Orioles fashioned a record 18-player swap. The principles included Don Larsen and Bob Turley going to the Yankees, while Gene Woodling and Gus Triandos went to Baltimore.

Three Thump 60 in '56

Beginning in 1925, when Tony Lazzeri clubbed 60 home runs for Salt Lake City of the Pacific Coast League, hitters in the minor leagues began reaching the 60-homer plateau with fair regularity. The spate ended abruptly, however, just two years after Joe Bauman's record-setting achievement. But it ended with an unprecedented bang as no fewer than three minor league sluggers cracked the 60-homer barrier in 1956. The pacesetter was Dick Stuart, an outfielder with Lincoln of the Western League who slammed 66 taters. Most followers of the game better remember Stuart for his later escapades as a first baseman in the majors. Ironically, neither of the other two 60-homer men in 1956 ever again played regularly on the professional level. After hammering 62 dingers and 143 RBI for Shreveport of the Texas League in 1956, Ken Guettler performed for three more seasons as a part-time outfielder and pinch hitter before retiring in 1959. First sacker Frosty Kennedy played just 53 more games professionally following his monster 1956 season of 60 homers and 184 RBI for Plainview of the Southwestern League.

Above: *Gil McDougald was one of the few players in this century to perform regularly at three different positions—second, third, and short. He excelled at all of them.*

Money's Worth

"One thing you learn as a Cubs fan: When you bought your ticket, you could bank on seeing the bottom of the ninth."

—Joe Garagiola

1950s THIRD BASE GAMES	
1. Willie Jones	1,388
2. Eddie Yost	1,380
3. Eddie Mathews	1,157
4. Al Rosen	918
5. George Kell	896

Eddie Robinson from 1942 to 1957 played for every American League franchise except the Boston Red Sox.

Willie Mays in 1956 led the National League with 40 steals, the most in the majors since 1944.

"I don't like them fellas who drive in two runs and let in three."

—*Casey Stengel*

In 1959, Walter Alston of the Dodgers became the only pilot to lead the same franchise to world championships in two different cities.

In 1950, a record-low 258 stolen bases were achieved in the AL as no team swiped more than 42 and Boston's Dom DiMaggio led the loop with just 15 thefts.

1950s THIRD BASE FIELDING AVERAGE	
1. George Kell	.970
2. Willie Jones	.966
3. Billy Cox	.966
4. Don Hoak	.961
5. Al Rosen	.960

Coliseum Suitable for Moon Shots

After moving to Los Angeles in 1958, the Dodgers played their first four seasons on the West Coast in Memorial Coliseum. The Dodgers set an all-time single-game attendance record on May 7, 1959, when they drew 93,103 for an exhibition game against the Yankees honoring Roy Campanella. The Coliseum was built for football, however, and the Dodgers were forced to be inventive in order to make its contours work for a baseball game. Among the innovations was a towering 42-foot high screen in left field, reminiscent of the screen erected in right field of Philadelphia's Baker Bowl in the 1930s, designed to prevent cheap home runs. The distance of 251 feet to the stands in left, nevertheless, remained so tempting that lefthanded hitters began tailoring their swings to loft fly balls off the screen. Wally Moon, a Dodgers outfielder in the late 1950s, gained the most notoriety for his screen shots, but other Dodgers, like Norm Larker, were also adept at nailing the inviting barrier.

Above: *White Sox receiver Sherm Lollar awaits the throw as Dodgers outfielder Wally Moon slides home in this piece of action from the 1959 World Series, won by Los Angeles.*

1950s SHORTSTOP GAMES

1.	Chico Carrasquel	1,241
2.	Johnny Logan	1,192
3.	Roy McMillan	1,186
4.	Alvin Dark	1,134
5.	Pee Wee Reese	1,031

Before the 1954 season, the St. Louis Browns were sold and moved to Baltimore, becoming the first American League franchise to be moved since 1903.

Means To an End

Sportswriter Warren Brown, after Minnie Minoso joined the White Sox, said the team "was off and running, but now, for the first time since 1920, they had a general idea of why and where."

The 1950 Phils clinched their pennant on the last day of the season, as Dick Sisler's 10th-inning homer beat the second-place Dodgers.

In 1952, Tiger pitcher Fred Hutchinson was named team manager, becoming the last pitcher to serve as a player-manager.

"Being traded is like celebrating your 100th birthday. It might not be the happiest occasion in the world, but consider the alternatives."
—*Joe Garagiola*

1950s SHORTSTOP FIELDING AVERAGE

1.	Roy McMillan	.971
2.	Phil Rizzuto	.970
3.	Chico Carrasquel	.969
4.	Ernie Banks	.969
5.	Alex Grammas	.968

On September 13, 1951, the St. Louis Cardinals played a home doubleheader against two different opponents. Because of rainouts, the Cards had to play the Giants in the afternoon and Braves at night.

Two Blue Slew Taboo

For many years, umpires concealed their faulty or failing eyesight either by wearing contact lenses or relying on their fellow arbiters to see what they no longer could. By the mid-1950s, however, the taboo against an umpire wearing glasses to officiate had been broken. Former major league pitcher Ed Rommel became the first arbiter to take the field in specs on April 26, 1956, at Washington in a game between the Senators and the Yankees. Larry Goetz shortly thereafter was the first National League umpire to follow suit. Both could afford to risk criticism because they were well-established in their profession. Goetz in 1956 was working his 21st season in the majors and was only a year away from retirement. Rommel had been an American League umpire since 1939 and would wear blue for only three more years before retiring.

1950s OUTFIELD FIELDING AVERAGE

1.	Gene Woodling	.989
2.	Johnny Groth	.989
3.	Jim Piersall	.989
4.	Jim Delsing	.988
5.	Sam Mele	.988
6.	Jim Busby	.988
7.	Charlie Maxwell	.987
8.	Enos Slaughter	.987
9.	Larry Doby	.987
10.	Hoot Evers	.986
11.	Duke Snider	.986
12.	Sid Gordon	.986
13.	Gus Bell	.985
14.	Richie Ashburn	.984
15.	Al Kaline	.984

Richie Ashburn explained why the 1950 Phillies "Whiz Kids" never won another pennant: "We were all white."

Prove It

"Baseball gives you every chance to be great. Then it puts every pressure on you to prove that you haven't got what it takes. It never takes away the chance, and it never eases up on the pressure."
—Joe Garagiola

In 1950, Cleveland finished fourth in the American League with a better record (92-62) than the Phillies' 91-63 mark, which won the National League pennant.

In 1953, their final season in the Mound City, the St. Louis Browns lost a major league record 20 straight games at home and finished in last place.

In 1950, the St. Louis Cardinals hosted the first "Opening Night" game in major league history.

In 1957, a Cincinnati newspaper printed All-Star ballots and urged readers to stuff the ballot boxes for Reds players. As a result, all the Reds regulars were voted All-Star starters. Commissioner Ford Frick replaced some of the Reds with what he felt were more deserving players.

Unable to displace Pete Suder at second base, Nellie Fox (above) was traded by the A's to the White Sox in 1950 for sub catcher Joe Tipton. Fox debuted in 1947 at age 19.

John Drebinger wrote in The New York Times *after the 1955 World Series: "Far into the night rang shouts of revelry in Flatbush. Brooklyn at long last has won a World Series and now let someone suggest moving the Dodgers elsewhere."*

1950s OUTFIELD GAMES

1.	Richie Ashburn	1,515
2.	Duke Snider	1,372
3.	Gus Bell	1,352
4.	Del Ennis	1,262
5.	Jackie Jensen	1,260
6.	Carl Furillo	1,258
7.	Minnie Minoso	1,251
8.	Hank Bauer	1,238
9.	Mickey Mantle	1,213
10.	Larry Doby	1,179
11.	Jim Busby	1,127
12.	Gene Woodling	1,112
13.	Bobby Thomson	1,069
14.	Willie Mays	1,058
15.	Don Mueller	1,056

Courtney First Backstopper to Wear Specs

Long before the 1950s, there had been bespectacled players at every position but one—catcher. While umpires eschewed wearing glasses on the field of play mostly for psychological and cosmetic reasons, the assumption was that it would be both too cumbersome and too dangerous for a player in spectacles to don a mask and go behind the bat. The first receiver to end the stigma against catchers wearing cheaters was Clint Courtney, when he caught a few innings for the Yankees on September 29, 1951. Courtney's scholarly looking spectacles belied his true demeanor, which was captured by his nickname of "Scrap Iron." He caught nearly 1,000 games in the majors before retiring in 1961. It was nearly three years after Courtney's debut before the NL unveiled a receiver wearing glasses. The first was Tim Thompson of the Brooklyn Dodgers, in April of 1954.

The major league attendance record for a single game was set by 93,103 Los Angeles Dodgers fans on May 7, 1959, when they attended an exhibition game to pay tribute to Roy Campanella.

Weighty

"Ballplayers who are first into the dining room are usually last in the averages."
—Jimmy Cannon, sportswriter

1950s MANAGER WINS	
1. Casey Stengel	955
2. Al Lopez	836
3. Paul Richards	692
4. Walter Alston	526
5. Leo Durocher	523
6. Bucky Harris	510
7. Fred Haney	504
8. Lou Boudreau	472
9. Fred Hutchinson	426
10. Chuck Dressen	414

Above: *Bill Veeck was just following a family tradition when he took over the Indians in 1946. His father, Bill Veeck Sr., had earlier been a successful executive with the Cubs.*

Outfielders Are People, Too

"They had room at the Los Angeles Coliseum for 93,000 people and two outfielders."
—Lindsay Nelson

In 1953, visiting teams in the AL won 312 games and home teams won 301, marking the first season in major league history that visitors won over half the games played.

Pee Wee Reese said about making the transition from a player to a coach: "I felt like a mosquito in a nudist colony. I didn't know where to begin."

All the players who in 1946 jumped to the Mexican League were banned by commissioner Happy Chandler. Following the 1950 season, the players were reinstated after the suit filed by Danny Gardella.

1950s TEAM WINS	WON	LOST
1. New York-AL	955	582
2. Brooklyn-Los Angeles-NL	913	630
Brooklyn-NL	*754*	*479*
Los Angeles-NL	*159*	*151*
3. Cleveland-AL	904	634
4. Boston-Milwaukee-NL	854	687
Boston-NL	*223*	*238*
Milwaukee-NL	*631*	*449*
5. Chicago-AL	847	693
6. New York-San Francisco-NL	822	721
New York-NL	*659*	*576*
San Francisco-NL	*163*	*145*
7. Boston-AL	814	725
8. St.Louis-NL	776	763
9. Philadelphia-NL	767	773
10. Cincinnati-NL	741	798
11. Detroit-AL	738	802
12. Chicago-NL	672	866
13. Washington-AL	640	898
14. St.Louis-Baltimore-AL	632	905
Baltimore-AL	*404*	*517*
St.Louis-AL	*228*	*388*
15. Pittsburgh-NL	616	923
16. Philadelphia-Kansas City-AL	624	915
Philadelphia-AL	*311*	*459*
Kansas City A's-AL	*313*	*456*

Rules Make Game Safer

In 1957, the American League became the first major circuit to make batting helmets mandatory equipment, and the National League quickly followed suit. Prior to then, many players had already begun wearing either helmets or protective liners inside their caps. Also during the 1950s, as another measure to guard against disabling injuries, warning tracks were required for the first time in the outfields of all major league parks. Padded fences, however, would not become mandatory until the 1970s. The rules requiring helmets and warning tracks met with instant approval from the game's fraternity. Another rule that came into effect in 1954 resulted in the passing from the scene of a tradition whose departure is still lamented by many fans with memories that reach back into the early 1950s. The 1954 season was the first in which players were no longer allowed to leave their gloves on the field of play while their team was at bat.

Wes Westrum, Giants catcher and later a manager, said about baseball: "It's like church. Many attend, but few understand."

In 1957, Richie Ashburn of the Phillies hit a fan with a foul ball. While the fan was being taken out of the stadium, Ashburn again fouled the pitch off, and again struck the patron.

America's Pastime

"Whoever wants to know the heart and mind of America had better learn baseball, the rules and realities of the game."
—Jacques Barzun, American historian

Cass Michaels, although just 28 years old, was playing his 12th big league season in 1954 when a beanball brought his career to an abrupt halt.

1950s TEAM WINNING PERCENTAGE	
1. New York-AL	.621
2. Brooklyn-	
Los Angeles-NL	.592
Brooklyn-NL	*.612*
Los Angeles-NL	*.513*
3. Cleveland-AL	.588
4. Boston-	
Milwaukee-NL	.554
Boston-NL	*.484*
Milwaukee-NL	*.584*
5. Chicago-AL	.550
6. New York-	
San Francisco-NL	.533
New York-NL	*.534*
San Francisco-NL	*.529*
7. Boston-AL	.529
8. St. Louis-NL	.504
9. Philadelphia-NL	.498
10. Cincinnati-NL	.481
11. Detroit-AL	.479
12. Chicago-NL	.437
13. Washington-AL	.416
14. St. Louis-	
Baltimore-AL	.411
St. Louis-AL	*.370*
Baltimore-AL	*.439*
15. Philadelphia-	
Kansas City-AL	.405
Philadelphia-AL	*.404*
Kansas City A's-AL	*.407*
16. Pittsburgh-NL	.400

1950s MANAGER WINNING PERCENTAGE	
1. Casey Stengel	.621
2. Al Lopez	.603
3. Steve O'Neill	.581
4. Walter Alston	.569
5. Leo Durocher	.564
6. Charlie Grimm	.545
7. Chuck Dressen	.523
8. Pinky Higgins	.522
9. Birdie Tebbetts	.510
10. Paul Richards	.504

Were it not for Al Lopez (above), the Yankees might have claimed every American League pennant between 1949 and 1965. Lopez-managed clubs broke the Bombers' stranglehold on the American League title by winning in 1954 and again in 1959.

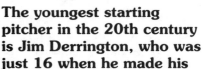

The youngest starting pitcher in the 20th century is Jim Derrington, who was just 16 when he made his lone major league start for the White Sox in 1956.

The Pittsburgh Pirates were the guests in both the last major league game played in Ebbets Field and the last game the New York Giants played in the Polo Grounds.

Chapter 9
The 1960s

'60s Start Stresses Safeties Scarcity

When the New York Yankees broke open a close three-team race in the American League in 1960 by ending the season with 15 straight wins, attention focused on who would be the loop's MVP winner. The baseball writers suddenly realized that there were no especially compelling candidates. None of the loop's pitchers had won more than 18 games, and it was certainly not because hitters had worn out hurlers. In fact, for the first time since the war-abbreviated 1918 season no AL batsman managed to accumulate as many as 190 hits. The pacesetter, Minnie Minoso of the White Sox, notched just 184 base hits, and at that he topped the AL by the fairly wide margin of nine safeties. In the National League, there were also strong indications that the game was about to descend to its lowest offensive ebb since the end of the dead-ball era. Willie Mays of the Giants led both the senior loop and the majors with just 190 safeties.

Quality Control
"It isn't hard to be good from time to time in sports. What's tough is being good every day."
—Willie Mays

In 1965, Willie Mays (above) became the lone National Leaguer to hammer 50 or more homers in a season in two different decades when he logged 52 round-trippers to set a San Francisco club record.

San Francisco Giant slugger Willie Mays pounded four homers in a game on April 30, 1961.

Willie Mays collected 1,903 ribbies in his career, including a high of 141 in 1962, but never was a league leader in RBI.

During the 1960s, Willie Mays and Hank Aaron became the only two players to win home run crowns while playing for the same franchise in two different cities.

Willie Mays in 1965 hammered an NL-record 17 homers in one month.

Giant Willie Mays in 1966 played in 150 or more games for a major league record 13th consecutive year.

Jimmy Wynn of the Astros tied the all-time National League record when he bagged 148 walks in 1969.

1960s GAMES	
1. Brooks Robinson	1,578
2. Hank Aaron	1,540
3. Ron Santo	1,536
4. Vada Pinson	1,516
5. Maury Wills	1,507
6. Willie Mays	1,498
7. Curt Flood	1,496
8. Ernie Banks	1,495
9. Luis Aparicio	1,494
10. Frank Robinson	1,468
11. Roberto Clemente	1,464
12. Billy Williams	1,454
13. Norm Cash	1,442
14. Johnny Callison	1,432
15. Bill Mazeroski	1,431
16. Harmon Killebrew	1,429
17. Orlando Cepeda	1,400
18. Clete Boyer	1,390
Felipe Alou	1,390
20. Carl Yastrzemski	1,383
21. Bill White	1,371
22. Frank Howard	1,370
23. Tony Taylor	1,361
24. Julian Javier	1,349
25. Willie Davis	1,347

Even though he bagged Rookie of the Year honors in 1959, Willie McCovey (above) did not win a regular job until 1963.

In 1969, Willie McCovey of the San Francisco Giants received a major league-record 45 intentional walks.

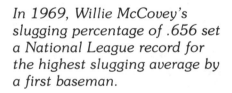

In 1969, Willie McCovey's slugging percentage of .656 set a National League record for the highest slugging average by a first baseman.

The 45-year-old John F. Kennedy remarked to 42-year-old Stan Musial at the 1962 All-Star Game: "A couple of years ago they told me I was too young to be President and you were too old to be playing baseball, but we both fooled them."

1960s RUNS	
1. Hank Aaron	1,091
2. Willie Mays	1,050
3. Frank Robinson	1,013
4. Roberto Clemente	916
5. Vada Pinson	885
6. Maury Wills	874
7. Harmon Killebrew	864
8. Billy Williams	861
9. Ron Santo	816
10. Al Kaline	811
11. Carl Yastrzemski	795
12. Brooks Robinson	787
13. Norm Cash	779
14. Johnny Callison	774
15. Orlando Cepeda	773
16. Curt Flood	771
17. Lou Brock	767
18. Luis Aparicio	765
19. Felipe Alou	742
20. Willie McCovey	728
21. Bob Allison	712
22. Bill White	698
23. Ernie Banks	694
24. Eddie Mathews	688
25. Mickey Mantle	683

Runnels Wins Bat Crown, Makes 169 Hits

Minnie Minoso milked his league-leading 184 hits in 1960 for a .311 batting average, third best in the American League, and also finished second in the loop in RBI and tied for third in total bases. Had the White Sox won the pennant, he probably would have copped the MVP Award, but the prize went instead to Roger Maris, the loop pacesetter in RBI and slugging average. The AL batting leader in 1960 was Pete Runnels of the Red Sox with a .320 average, the lowest to top either major circuit since 1945. Runnels also set a record for the fewest total bases in history (208) by a hitting titlist with 500 or more at bats. He had 169 base hits, and he finished 17th in MVP balloting. Runnels won a second batting crown in 1962 with a .326 mark that seemed low at the time but would not be surpassed again by an AL batsman until 1969.

The Minnesota Twins in 1963 hit 225 home runs, the most homers in history by a team that didn't win a pennant.

In 1961, the American League had a record six players who amassed 40 or more home runs, ranging from Roger Maris's 61 to Norm Cash's 41.

Bobby Richardson of the Yankees in 1964 set a World Series record with 13 hits.

Cash Profits from Expanded Pitching Staffs

By adding two new teams in 1961, the American League also brought some 20 pitchers into the majors who otherwise would have spent the campaign in the minors. Hitters who had suffered in 1960 feasted on the diluted pitching staffs in the junior loop. Mickey Mantle vaulted from a .275 average to .317 and Al Kaline from .278 to .324. No batsman, however, profited more than Norm Cash of the Tigers. After hitting .286 in 1960 while sharing the Tigers' first base job with Steve Bilko, Cash ripped .361 in the first expansion season, adding 41 home runs and 132 RBI. All those figures turned out to be Cash's personal highs by a whopping margin. In 1962, with pitchers once again gaining the upper hand in the junior loop, he sagged to a .243 average. Cash's 118-point drop was the largest in history by a defending batting titlist. Moreover, his .361 mark was 75 points higher than he ever hit before or after 1961.

"When I was 17 years old I realized I was in a form of show business. It's like being an actor on the Broadway stage. He doesn't phrase his part exactly the same way every day. He thinks up new things. So I played for the fans, and I wanted to make sure each fan that came out would see something different I did each day."

—Willie Mays

Above: *Norm Cash tailed off considerably after his glittering performance in 1961, never again hitting .300.*

The '61 Yankees had a major league-record six players who hit 20 or more homers.

Mickey Mantle in 1961 smacked 54 homers, giving the Yankees a teammate record of 115 four-baggers.

Roger Maris broke Babe Ruth's major league single-season home run record in 1961 by swatting 61 homers.

In 1966, Mickey Mantle became the first player in major league history to fan 1,500 times.

1960s TOTAL BASES	
1. Hank Aaron	3,343
2. Willie Mays	3,050
3. Frank Robinson	2,948
4. Roberto Clemente	2,865
5. Billy Williams	2,799
6. Vada Pinson	2,797
7. Harmon Killebrew	2,727
8. Ron Santo	2,706
9. Brooks Robinson	2,647
10. Ernie Banks	2,590
11. Orlando Cepeda	2,588
12. Carl Yastrzemski	2,515
13. Johnny Callison	2,426
14. Frank Howard	2,424
15. Norm Cash	2,401
16. Felipe Alou	2,355
17. Al Kaline	2,338
18. Willie McCovey	2,323
19. Bill White	2,233
20. Curt Flood	2,216
21. Rocky Colavito	2,179
22. Ken Boyer	2,130
23. Lou Brock	2,125
24. Bob Allison	2,065
25. Luis Aparicio	2,057

Above: *The 1961 Yankees' six 20-homer men: (left to right) Roger Maris, Yogi Berra, Mickey Mantle, Elston Howard, Johnny Blanchard, and Bill Skowron.*

Mickey Mantle holds the record for the most home runs in a season by a switch-hitter, with 54 in 1961.

Mickey Mantle holds the record for the highest career slugging average—.557—by a player who failed to post a .300 career batting average.

Bronx Bombers Blast Benchmark

Even with Roger Maris and Mickey Mantle hammering a teammate-record 115 home runs between them in 1961, the Yankees were not the top offensive team that year in the junior circuit. That honor fell to the Tigers, which hit .266 and tallied 841 runs. No team out-homered the Bombers, however, either in 1961 or in any other campaign. Their 240 circuit clouts shattered the old major league team record of 221. Maris and Mantle contributed nearly half the total (115 between them), but four other sluggers joined with them to make the Yankees the only team ever to showcase six players with 20 or more home runs. The other bammers were first sacker Bill Skowron (28), left fielder Yogi Berra (22), catcher Ellie Howard (21), and backup catcher and pinch hitter deluxe Johnny Blanchard (21). Blanchard's home-run percentage of 8.6 was nearly as high as that of the two M&M boys, as Johnny found the seats 21 times in just 243 at bats.

1960s HITS		
1.	Roberto Clemente	1,877
2.	Hank Aaron	1,819
3.	Vada Pinson	1,776
4.	Maury Wills	1,744
5.	Brooks Robinson	1,692
6.	Curt Flood	1,690
7.	Billy Williams	1,651
8.	Willie Mays	1,635
9.	Frank Robinson	1,603
10.	Ron Santo	1,592
11.	Luis Aparicio	1,548
12.	Felipe Alou	1,530
13.	Orlando Cepeda	1,522
14.	Carl Yastrzemski	1,517
15.	Ernie Banks	1,460
16.	Johnny Callison	1,438
17.	Bill White	1,413
18.	Lou Brock	1,406
19.	Al Kaline	1,399
20.	Bill Mazeroski	1,385
21.	Willie Davis	1,363
22.	Tommy Davis	1,350
23.	Harmon Killebrew	1,331
24.	Ken Boyer	1,328
25.	Pete Rose	1,327

RBI Totals Expand Everywhere

Expansion created temporarily inflated offensive statistics in both major leagues during the early 1960s and led to several performances that proved to be nearly as anomalous as Norm Cash's .361 batting average in 1961. When the National League swelled to 10 teams the season following Cash's stunner, Tommy Davis of the Dodgers logged 153 RBI while topping the National League with 230 hits and a .346 batting average. Davis's ribbie total remains the highest in the senior loop since 1937—when Ducky Medwick of the Cardinals drove home 154 mates—and the highest in either major league since 1949. RBI figures were also up in 1961, the year the American League expanded, as both loop leaders, Roger Maris and Orlando Cepeda, posted an identical total of 142. Cepeda's numbers were accomplished on a 154-game schedule, however, and in several respects are a more impressive achievement than Davis's the following year. Baltimore first baseman Jim Gentile in '61 had 141 RBI, the only season that he had more than 100 runs batted in.

Stan Musial is the only player who ranks among the top 20 in career singles, doubles, triples, and home runs.

Milwaukee Braves third baseman Eddie Mathews hit 30 or more homers for an NL record nine consecutive years from 1953 to '61.

Above: Orlando Cepeda produced 100-RBI seasons for three different National League clubs during the 1960s—San Francisco, St. Louis, and Atlanta. After his career seemingly ended by a knee injury, he briefly found a second life in the American League as a designated hitter.

Outfielder Tommy Davis of the Los Angeles Dodgers knocked home 153 runs, the most by anyone in the major leagues since 1949.

The Los Angeles Angels, a first-year expansion team, had five players who had 20 or more home runs in 1961, led by Leon Wagner with 28.

Roger Maris confided to sportswriter Joe Reichler: "It would have been a hell of a lot more fun if I had never hit those 61 home runs. All it brought me was headaches."

In 1965, Boston's Tony Conigliaro led the AL with 32 homers, and at age 20, he was the youngest player to ever win a league homer crown.

Boston's 19-year-old Tony Conigliaro in 1964 knocked 24 homers and notched a .530 slugging average—both records for a teenage player.

Boston's Tony Conigliaro was beaned by Angel Jack Hamilton in 1967. Conigliaro's vision was impaired, and he was out of the game until 1969.

1960s DOUBLES	
1. Carl Yastrzemski	318
2. Vada Pinson	310
3. Frank Robinson	309
Hank Aaron	309
5. Brooks Robinson	297
6. Orlando Cepeda	268
7. Johnny Callison	265
8. Billy Williams	263
9. Felipe Alou	260
10. Willie Mays	259
Roberto Clemente	259
12. Ron Santo	247
Al Kaline	247
Curt Flood	247
15. Lou Brock	243
Ernie Banks	243
17. Bill White	221
18. Luis Aparicio	220
19. Zoilo Versalles	219
20. Pete Rose	218
21. Willie Davis	214
22. Tony Oliva	213
23. Dick Groat	211
24. Tony Gonzalez	209
25. Leo Cardenas	206

'68 AL Batting Averages Hit Bottom

At the beginning of the final week of the 1968 season, it seemed a very real possibility that for the first time in history a major league batting titlist would hit below .300. Only a closing rush by Boston's Carl Yastrzemski that lifted his average to .301 spared the American League its most ignominious moment. Yaz's figure topped runner-up Oakland's Danny Cater by 11 points. Rounding out the top five hitters in the AL in 1968 were Tony Oliva of the Twins (.289), Willie Horton of the Tigers (.285), and Minnesota's Ted Uhlaender (.283). Shortstop Bert Campaneris of Oakland was the sixth-best hitter in the loop at .276, trailed by teammate Rick Monday and Washington's Frank Howard, who finished with identical .274 marks. Six players in the AL with more than 400 at bats had under a .215 batting average. In 1968, Yaz was not only the AL's sole bat title qualifier to hit .300, he was also the lone player in the loop with over 100 at bats to top the .300 figure.

1960s TRIPLES		
1.	Roberto Clemente	99
2.	Vada Pinson	93
3.	Lou Brock	85
4.	Johnny Callison	84
5.	Billy Williams	69
6.	Willie Davis	68
7.	Jim Fregosi	64
8.	Zoilo Versalles	63
9.	Maury Wills	62
10.	Dick Allen	60
11.	Dick McAuliffe	59
	Luis Aparicio	59
13.	Tony Taylor	55
14.	Ron Santo	54
	Donn Clendenon	54
16.	Willie Mays	53
	Tony Gonzalez	53
18.	Pete Rose	52
19.	Brooks Robinson	50
20.	Bill White	49
21.	Julian Javier	48
22.	Chuck Hinton	47
	Ken Boyer	47
24.	Hank Aaron	45
25.	Frank Robinson	44
	Bob Allison	44

In his 23 seasons with the Red Sox, Carl Yastrzemski (above) logged 3,419 hits but batted .300 just six times.

In 1960, for the first time in major league history, both the NL and the AL batting leaders hit under .330.

In 1968, Carl Yastrzemski was not only the lone .300 hitter in the AL but the lone major league player to have an on-base percentage of .400.

Billy Herman, one of Carl Yastrzemski's first managers with the Red Sox, said of Yaz: "How did I get along with Yastrzemski? Like everybody else. By that I mean nobody ever got along with Yastrzemski."

Above: *Zoilo Versalles broke in with the Washington Senators in 1959. Four years after he won the 1965 American League MVP Award, he was released by the expansion Senators at age 29.*

In 1965, Twins shortstop Zoilo Versalles paced the American League in doubles, triples, and total bases.

After Carl Yastrzemski, Zoilo Versalles, and Tony Oliva all bagged 40 or more doubles in 1965, no American Leaguer achieved as many as 40 two-baggers again until 1975.

Cardinal Stan Musial retired after the 1963 season as the holder of the NL record for most hits, with 3,630; games (3,026); and runs (1,949).

1960s HOME RUNS		
1.	Harmon Killebrew	393
2.	Hank Aaron	375
3.	Willie Mays	350
4.	Frank Robinson	316
5.	Willie McCovey	300
6.	Frank Howard	288
7.	Norm Cash	278
8.	Ernie Banks	269
9.	Mickey Mantle	256
10.	Orlando Cepeda	254
11.	Ron Santo	253
12.	Billy Williams	249
13.	Rocky Colavito	245
14.	Bob Allison	225
15.	Roger Maris	217
16.	Eddie Mathews	213
17.	Al Kaline	210
18.	Carl Yastrzemski	202
	Boog Powell	202
20.	Leon Wagner	193
21.	Brooks Robinson	186
22.	Dick Stuart	185
	Johnny Callison	185
24.	Jim Gentile	178
25.	Roberto Clemente	177
	Dick Allen	177

ChiSox Scoring Severely Suffers

As might be expected, with batting averages in the American League so low all across the board in 1968, hit totals were equally meager. The A's Bert Campaneris topped the circuit in safe blows with just 177, 10 ahead of runner-up Cesar Tovar. With Campaneris, Danny Cater, and Rick Monday all placing among the top 10 in hitting, the A's paced the American League with a .240 batting average, the lowest *ever* by a loop leader. Second to the A's with a .237 mark were the Minnesota Twins, who also had three hitters in the top 10—Tony Oliva, Ted Uhlaender, and Tovar. The New York Yankees brought up the rear in batting at .214, the lowest team average since the dead-ball era. The Chicago White Sox, though, got the least mileage from their hits. Despite finishing at .228, some 14 points above the Yankees, the White Sox saw the Bombers outscore them by 73 runs and finished last in the majors with 463 tallies, less than three a game.

Switch-Hitting Pete Rose to NL Top

When Pete Rose hit .335 in 1968 to capture the first of his three National League batting titles, it also represented the first hitting crown in senior loop history won by a switch-hitter. Just 12 years earlier, Mickey Mantle had broken the ice in the American League, becoming the first two-way batsman to be a league leader since Tommy Tucker of Baltimore paced the American Association in 1889. Rose bagged his second consecutive bat crown in 1969 with a .348 mark that tied the then-existing post-1900 NL record for the highest batting average by a switch-hitter, first set in 1923 by Frankie Frisch of the New York Giants. Maury Wills in 1962 had broken the NL record for most at bats by a switch-hitter when he accumulated 695 at bats. The all-time senior loop switch-stickers mark belongs to George Davis, also of the Giants, who slapped .362 in 1893. Mantle holds the post-1893 major league record with his .365 average in 1956. There were three switch-hitters who received 400 at bats for the 16-team majors in 1956, opposed to 10 switch-hitters who received 400 at bats for the 20-team majors in 1966.

When Rocky Colavito led the American League in RBI in 1965 and Fred Whitfield finished fifth, it marked the last time that two Cleveland Indians finished among the American League's top-five RBI men.

A second baseman his first four seasons in the majors, Pete Rose (above) played only 41 more games there in his final 20 campaigns. During his seemingly interminable career, Rose also played first, third, and left and right fields.

Between 1964 and 1968, no National Leaguer collected as many as 100 walks; Joe Morgan of the Astros, with 97 in 1965, had the top figure in that span.

Mr. Clutch of 1962

Discussing Tommy Davis in 1962, Sandy Koufax said: "Every time there was a man on base he'd knock him in, and every time there were two men on base, he'd hit a double and knock them both in."

1960s RUNS BATTED IN	
1. Hank Aaron	1,107
2. Harmon Killebrew	1,013
3. Frank Robinson	1,011
4. Willie Mays	1,003
5. Ron Santo	937
6. Ernie Banks	925
7. Orlando Cepeda	896
8. Roberto Clemente	862
9. Billy Williams	853
10. Brooks Robinson	836
11. Frank Howard	835
12. Norm Cash	830
13. Willie McCovey	821
14. Vada Pinson	792
15. Rocky Colavito	786
16. Al Kaline	773
17. Carl Yastrzemski	767
18. Bill White	735
Ken Boyer	735
20. Bob Allison	704
21. Boog Powell	677
Tommy Davis	677
23. Eddie Mathews	676
24. Mickey Mantle	668
25. Johnny Callison	666

Eddie Yost was the only player in major league history to compile more than 1,500 walks and fewer than 2,000 hits.

The only player during the 1960s to total more than 15 triples in a season was Johnny Callison of the Phillies with 16 in 1965.

Willie Davis of the Dodgers compiled the longest hitting streak during the 1960s when he hit safely in 31 straight games in 1969.

Above: *Frank Robinson hit his first home run in 1956 when he was just 20 and his 586th and last after age 40.*

Matty Alou Bats Over .330 Four Straight Years

After annexing the National League batting title in 1966 with a .342 average, Matty Alou of the Pirates embarked on a run that would make him the last senior looper to date to hit .330 or better for four consecutive years. Alou followed his hit crown by rapping .338 in 1967, .332 in 1968, and .331 in 1969. His four-season skein marked the only time in his 15-year career that he topped .330. Nevertheless, he ended his career in 1974 with a .307 career average, among the highest of the postexpansion, prefree-agency era that encompassed the years from 1961 through 1975. He had 231 base hits and 41 doubles to lead the NL in '69. Prior to Alou, the last NL player to enjoy a comparable stretch of hitting success was Stan Musial. Between 1948 and 1954 Musial belted .330 or better for seven consecutive seasons. Roberto Clemente (1969 to '71) is the only other senior circuit hitter since Musial to reach the .330 figure as many as three years in a row.

In 1965, when he topped the National League with 130 ribbies, Deron Johnson notched 100 RBI for the only time in his 16-year career.

Chuck Hinton holds the expansion Washington Senators' record for the highest batting average with a .310 mark in 1962.

Dave Philley of the Orioles set a record for pinch hitters when he collected 24 pinch singles in 1961.

The 1966 American League had only two hitters with batting averages above .288—Frank Robinson (.317) and Tony Oliva (.307).

In 1968, George Scott of the Red Sox became the only first sacker in American League history to collect fewer than 100 total bases in 350 or more at bats when he hit .171 and had just 83 total bases.

Pinnacle
When asked what was his career high point, Bob Uecker replied: "In 1967 with St. Louis, I walked with the bases loaded to drive in the winning run in an intersquad game in spring training."

Alous Dominate '66 NL Batting Race

When Matty Alou won the National League bat title in 1966, the runner-up to him with a .327 average was his brother Felipe of the Atlanta Braves. It marked the only time in big league history that a pair of brothers finished one-two in a loop batting race. Also playing in the senior circuit in 1966 was a third Alou brother, Jesus of the San Francisco Giants. The youngest of the three Alou siblings, Jesus was also the least prominent, but each member of the trio played at least 15 years in the majors and compiled well over 1,000 hits. Felipe was the only one with power, once slugging 33 homers in a season, more than either Jesus or Matty accumulated in their careers. Their aggregate career stats helped the Alous to lay claim to being the best threesome of brothers in major league history with the sole exception of the DiMaggios. All three broke in with the San Francisco Giants and in 1963 were teammates for one season before Felipe was traded to the Braves.

"During my 18 years I came to bat almost 10,000 times. I struck out about 1,700 times and walked maybe 1,800 times. You figure a ballplayer will average about 500 at bats a season. That means I played seven years in the major leagues without ever hitting the ball."
—Mickey Mantle

Felipe Alou (above) and his brothers Matty and Jesus started a game in late 1963 for the Giants to form the first all-brother outfield.

1960s STOLEN BASES

1.	Maury Wills	535
2.	Lou Brock	387
3.	Luis Aparicio	342
4.	Bert Campaneris	292
5.	Willie Davis	240
6.	Tommy Harper	208
7.	Hank Aaron	204
8.	Vada Pinson	202
9.	Don Buford	161
10.	Tony Taylor	157
11.	Jose Cardenal	149
12.	Frank Robinson	145
13.	Chuck Hinton	130
14.	Willie Mays	126
15.	Julian Javier	123
16.	Cesar Tovar	117
17.	Jim Wynn	115
18.	Joe Morgan	113
19.	Tommy McCraw	107
20.	Dick Howser	105
21.	Sonny Jackson	101
22.	Matty Alou	100
23.	Tommy Davis	98
24.	Tommie Agee	97
25.	Zoilo Versalles	94
	Orlando Cepeda	94

1960s WALKS

1.	Harmon Killebrew	970
2.	Mickey Mantle	841
3.	Frank Robinson	778
	Norm Cash	778
5.	Ron Santo	768
6.	Carl Yastrzemski	751
7.	Bob Allison	719
8.	Eddie Mathews	718
9.	Willie Mays	681
10.	Rocky Colavito	676
11.	Hank Aaron	672
12.	Al Kaline	652
13.	Willie McCovey	650
14.	Norm Siebern	582
15.	Dick McAuliffe	580
16.	Billy Williams	556
17.	Tom Tresh	550
18.	Ron Hansen	519
19.	Ron Fairly	513
	Johnny Callison	513
21.	Bill White	508
22.	Boog Powell	501
23.	Frank Howard	500
24.	Jim Wynn	491
25.	Roger Maris	489

In 1968, Dick McAuliffe of Detroit became the first player in AL history to participate in 150 or more games without grounding into a double play.

First sacker Gordy Coleman left the majors in 1967 with a .333 career average as a pinch hitter, the highest in history among players with a minimum of 100 pinch at bats.

In 1968, the Los Angeles Dodgers had so little punch that they scored a mere 470 runs in 162 games and catcher Tom Haller paced the club in RBI with just 53.

Howard Hammers for Hapless Senators

Had he played in the 1930s, Frank Howard might be nearly as well remembered now as Jimmie Foxx and Hank Greenberg. Because his prime years came in the late 1960s and roughly paralleled the most difficult span of time for hitters since the depths of the dead-ball era, Howard's career totals are dwarfed by Foxx's and seem significantly lesser than Greenberg's. Further hampering Howard's case is the fact that his peak stats were produced for a lackluster Washington Senators team. In 1968, while Howard was blasting an American League-leading 44 homers and knocking home 106 runs for the last place Senators, only one other club member, Ken McMullen with 62, produced more than 40 RBI. A year earlier, Howard's 36 home runs represented nearly a third of Washington's total of 115. In 1970, Howard's last monster season, he became one of a very few sluggers to lead his loop in both homers and RBI while playing for a tail-ender as the Senators finished last in the American League East.

An All-American basketball player at Ohio State, Frank Howard (above) forsook his senior year of college baseball to sign a bonus contract with the Dodgers.

1960s STRIKEOUTS

1.	Frank Howard	1,103
2.	Harmon Killebrew	1,029
3.	Lou Brock	946
4.	Donn Clendenon	934
5.	Bob Allison	916
6.	Ron Santo	896
7.	Johnny Callison	854
8.	Dick Allen	851
9.	Leo Cardenas	824
10.	Mickey Mantle	811
11.	Eddie Mathews	809
12.	Willie McCovey	805
13.	Dick Stuart	796
14.	Roberto Clemente	795
15.	Bill White	789
16.	Clete Boyer	785
17.	Willie Mays	783
18.	Vada Pinson	778
19.	Don Lock	776
20.	Norm Cash	770
21.	Orlando Cepeda	767
22.	Ernie Banks	756
23.	Zoilo Versalles	755
24.	Willie Stargell	751
25.	Frank Robinson	749

On August 5, 1969, Pirate Willie Stargell became the first player to hit a homer out of Dodger Stadium.

On May 9, 1961, Jim Gentile hit grand slams in two consecutive innings for Baltimore.

Gates Brown of Detroit was the first black player to homer in his first at bat in an American League game, on June 19, 1963.

Elmer Valo set a major league record in 1960 when he walked 18 times as a pinch hitter, with the Yankees and Senators.

In 1968, Frank Howard led the majors in total bases with 330 while playing for the Washington Senators, which had the majors' poorest record at 65-96.

Cleveland was the first AL team to hit four consecutive homers, on July 31, 1963.

The Milwaukee Braves hit four consecutive homers on June 8, 1961.

In 1968, the only Yankees player in 400 or more at bats to hit higher than .240 was Roy White at .267.

Double Dip

Ernie Banks, upon arriving at the ballpark each day, would exclaim: "Let's play two!"

Mack Jones of the Milwaukee Braves collected four hits in his first major league game on July 13, 1961.

Williams Works Magic for New Nats

The expansion Washington Senators customarily brought up the rear of either the American League or the AL East in each year of their existence from 1961 until the franchise was moved to Texas. Only once in the club's 11-year sojourn in the nation's capital did it break .500. The watershed season came in 1969, the Senators' first under rookie skipper Ted Williams. After replacing Jim Lemon at the helm following a last-place finish in 1968, Williams seemed at first to be that rare great hitter who could convey his batting genius to his charges. In 1969, the Senators rocketed to an 86-76 finish, aided in large part by the team's .251 batting average, tied for the third-best in the AL. Even slugger Frank Howard seemed to benefit from William's tutelage, cutting his strikeout total below 100 while still managing to hammer 48 home runs. Williams's magic quickly deserted him, however. In 1970, his second season at the Senators' helm, the club fell into the AL East basement and tied for last in hitting.

Above: *Cleveland's Vic Power is the odd man in this picture with two Red Sox batting kings, Ted Williams (center) and Pete Runnels. Despite never hitting above .326 in his 14-year career, Runnels captured two American League bat crowns during the 1960s.*

In 1968, the New York Yankees posted the lowest team batting average since the dead-ball era when they hit just .214.

In 1967, Ron Fairly led the Dodgers in RBI with 55; the following year the club leader, catcher Tom Haller, had just 53 ribbies.

The White Sox finished 16 games over .500 (89-73) in 1967 despite hitting a meager .225 and tallying only 531 runs.

Class
"Most of what I know about style I learned from Roberto Clemente."
—John Sayles

In 1965, Houston shortstop Bob Lillis became the only player to lead his league in both fewest batter strikeouts and lowest batting average.

1960s BATTING AVERAGE

1.	Roberto Clemente	.328
2.	Matty Alou	.312
3.	Pete Rose	.309
4.	Tony Oliva	.308
5.	Hank Aaron	.308
6.	Frank Robinson	.304
7.	Dick Allen	.300
8.	Willie Mays	.300
9.	Manny Mota	.297
10.	Curt Flood	.297
11.	Tommy Davis	.296
12.	Al Kaline	.296
13.	Orlando Cepeda	.295
14.	Felipe Alou	.294
15.	Carl Yastrzemski	.293
16.	Joe Torre	.293
17.	Vada Pinson	.292
18.	Billy Williams	.292
19.	Tony Gonzalez	.290
20.	Smoky Burgess	.290
21.	Bill White	.287
22.	Lou Brock	.287
23.	Maury Wills	.286
24.	Dick Groat	.286
25.	Ken Boyer	.285

Oliva, Allen Top Class of '64

In 1964, Tony Oliva of the Twins became the only rookie since Pete Browning in 1882 to win a major league batting title. Oliva accomplished something nearly as rare when he also paced the American League in total bases. The first frosh total base leader in the AL since George Stone in 1905, Oliva could have expected to have the pedestal all to himself in a normal season. But 1964 was a very unusual year. The National League, for the first time since 1918, also had a yearling player, Dick Allen of the Phillies, garner the total base crown. Oliva in addition tied Hal Trosky's 1934 mark for the most total bases by a frosh (374) and Allen set an all-time NL frosh record with 352. Rather surprisingly, however, neither of the pair was a unanimous Rookie of the Year selection in his loop. Oliva fell one vote short of perfection while Allen missed obtaining two of the 20 ballots cast by NL writers. Rico Carty and Jim Ray Hart received ballots for the NL honor, while Wally Bunker received an American League vote.

In 1963, Houston second sacker Ernie Fazio fanned 70 times in just 228 at bats.

When he went down on strikes 103 times as a rookie with Houston in 1963, John Bateman became the first catcher to compile 100 whiffs in a season.

Above: *Pedro Oliva played under his brother's name of Tony for his entire 15-year career.*

Tony Oliva in '64 set an AL rookie record with 217 base hits.

1960s SLUGGING AVERAGE	
1. Hank Aaron	.565
2. Frank Robinson	.560
3. Willie Mays	.559
4. Dick Allen	.554
5. Harmon Killebrew	.546
6. Willie McCovey	.546
7. Mickey Mantle	.542
8. Frank Howard	.508
9. Orlando Cepeda	.502
10. Willie Stargell	.501
11. Roberto Clemente	.501
12. Tony Oliva	.500
13. Norm Cash	.498
14. Billy Williams	.494
15. Al Kaline	.494
16. Roger Maris	.492
17. Jim Gentile	.489
18. Willie Horton	.486
19. Carl Yastrzemski	.486
20. Joe Adcock	.484
21. Ron Santo	.478
22. Dick Stuart	.478
23. Jim Ray Hart	.477
24. Bob Allison	.474
25. Rocky Colavito	.470

1960s ON-BASE AVERAGE	
1. Mickey Mantle	.418
2. Frank Robinson	.405
3. Harmon Killebrew	.389
4. Carl Yastrzemski	.385
5. Al Kaline	.384
6. Norm Cash	.382
7. Dick Allen	.382
8. Willie McCovey	.381
9. Hank Aaron	.379
10. Albie Pearson	.379
11. Willie Mays	.379
12. Roberto Clemente	.377
13. Norm Siebern	.377
14. Jim Gentile	.373
15. Eddie Mathews	.371
16. Pete Rose	.371
17. Ron Santo	.370
18. Floyd Robinson	.367
19. Bob Allison	.364
20. Jim Wynn	.364
21. Rusty Staub	.363
22. Tony Oliva	.362
23. Rocky Colavito	.360
24. Lenny Green	.360
25. Joe Torre	.359

Tony Oliva led the American League in hits in each of his first three seasons in the majors, 1964 to '66.

Bobby Richardson in 1962 and Tony Oliva in 1964 were the only American Leaguers to enjoy 200-hit seasons during the 1960s.

"I don't think those people at Wrigley Field ever saw but two players they liked—Billy Williams and Ernie Banks. Billy never said anything, and Ernie always said the right thing."

—Fergie Jenkins

Tresh, Other Rookies Swing and Miss

Tony Oliva and Dick Allen both followed their outstanding rookie campaigns in 1964 by fashioning long and noteworthy careers, but numerous other performers in the 1960s, after starring at the plate as rookies, soon fell prey to the home-run-or-bust syndrome that permeated the game all during the decade. Among the leading victims were Pete Ward of the White Sox, Curt Blefary of the Orioles, Tom Tresh of the Yankees, and Jimmie Hall of the Twins. All followed their exceptional freshmen seasons with sophomore campaigns that were in some instances even better before beginning to succumb to the lure of the long ball. Hall hit .260 his rookie year, .254 for his career; Ward hit .295 his first year, .254 for his career; and Blefary hit .260 his rookie season, .237 for his career. Tresh was probably the most talented of the four and also the most disheartening to watch disintegrate at the plate. After hitting .286, .269, .246, and .279 in his first four seasons, he slipped to .233, .219, .195, and .211 in his last four campaigns.

In 1963 and '64, Dave Nicholson of the White Sox fanned 301 times in 743 at bats, including a then-record 175 Ks in 1963 alone.

Howie Goss set a record for the most strikeouts by a player in his final big league season when he fanned 128 times for Houston in 1963.

Above: *Many followers of the game felt Dick Allen had more raw talent than any other player who debuted during the 1960s.*

Harmon Killebrew in 1962 set a major league record when he struck out 142 times.

1960s ON-BASE PLUS SLUGGING	
1. Frank Robinson	.965
2. Mickey Mantle	.960
3. Hank Aaron	.945
4. Willie Mays	.938
5. Dick Allen	.936
6. Harmon Killebrew	.935
7. Willie McCovey	.927
8. Norm Cash	.881
9. Al Kaline	.878
10. Roberto Clemente	.878
11. Carl Yastrzemski	.871
12. Jim Gentile	.862
13. Tony Oliva	.862
14. Orlando Cepeda	.856
15. Frank Howard	.855
16. Billy Williams	.852
17. Ron Santo	.848
18. Willie Stargell	.847
19. Roger Maris	.846
20. Eddie Mathews	.840
21. Bob Allison	.839
22. Rocky Colavito	.830
23. Joe Adcock	.828
24. Jim Ray Hart	.827
25. Jim Wynn	.823

1960s EXTRA-BASE HITS	
1. Hank Aaron	729
2. Frank Robinson	669
3. Willie Mays	662
4. Harmon Killebrew	593
5. Billy Williams	581
6. Vada Pinson	578
7. Carl Yastrzemski	557
8. Ron Santo	554
9. Ernie Banks	552
10. Orlando Cepeda	540
11. Roberto Clemente	535
12. Johnny Callison	534
13. Brooks Robinson	533
14. Frank Howard	503
15. Willie McCovey	501
16. Al Kaline	488
17. Norm Cash	486
18. Bob Allison	461
19. Felipe Alou	460
20. Rocky Colavito	453
21. Bill White	437
22. Lou Brock	430
23. Ken Boyer	419
24. Eddie Mathews	416
25. Mickey Mantle	410

Cleveland shortstop Dick Howser had a mere six RBI in 107 games and 307 at bats in 1965.

White Sox outfielder Dave Nicholson in 1963 fanned 175 times, breaking the major league record by 33.

In 1967, Luis Aparicio of Baltimore became the first player to be a league leader in fewest strikeouts despite fanning over 40 times (44).

Bobby Bonds of the San Francisco Giants set a major league record by striking out 187 times in 1969.

Gibson's Stats Shave Mound, Strike Zone

In 1968, Bob Gibson of the Cardinals notched 13 shutouts, the most by any hurler since 1916. He also registered a 1.12 ERA, which set a new low for the game after the dead-ball era. He led the league in fewest hits per game, strikeouts, opponents batting average, and opponents on-base percentage. Gibson's overwhelming stats earned him both the Cy Young and the MVP awards and in the end helped to earn hitters a reprieve from further seasons like his. Alarmed by how far the balance scale had so obviously tilted in the favor of pitchers, baseball officials shaved the regulation height of pitchers' mounds and also squeezed the size of the strike zone prior to the 1969 season. Gibson's ERA swelled correspondingly to 2.18 in 1969 and his shutout total dipped to four, but he continued to be perhaps the most dominant pitcher in the game. His best season was still a year away. In 1970, toiling for a Cardinals team that had a 76-86 record, Gibson went 23-7 and topped the majors with a .767 winning percentage.

A fine all-around athlete, Bob Gibson (above) would probably have found a home in baseball even if he had failed as a pitcher. Playing in the toughest era ever for hitters, he batted .206 and notched 24 home runs during his 17 years with St. Louis.

Bob Gibson of the St. Louis Cardinals posted a 1.12 ERA in 1968, the lowest in the major leagues since 1914.

1960s GAMES PITCHED	
1. Ron Perranoski	589
2. Lindy McDaniel	558
3. Hoyt Wilhelm	557
4. Don McMahon	547
5. Roy Face	524
6. Ron Kline	519
7. Stu Miller	468
Eddie Fisher	468
9. Bob Miller	450
10. Turk Farrell	445
Jack Baldschun	445
12. Ted Abernathy	444
13. Gary Bell	442
14. John Wyatt	435
15. Phil Regan	434
16. Al McBean	401
17. Al Worthington	393
18. Dick Hall	392
19. Larry Sherry	388
20. Ron Taylor	385
21. Dick Radatz	381
22. Hal Woodeshick	380
23. Jim Bunning	378
24. Jim Perry	377
25. Pedro Ramos	373
Jack Fisher	373

Whatta Break

"Bob Gibson is the luckiest pitcher I ever saw. He always pitches when the other team doesn't score any runs."
—Tim McCarver

Drysdale Pitches Zips for 58 Frames

Don Drysdale began the 1968 season as if he were invincible. He pitched four consecutive shutouts for the Dodgers in May and was on the brink of breaking the record for the most consecutive shutout innings pitched on the final day of the month when he took a 3-0 lead into the ninth inning against the Giants. He proceeded to load the bases with none out, though, then hit Giants catcher Dick Dietz with a pitch to seemingly force home a run. Plate umpire Harry Wendelstadt ruled instead that Dietz hadn't tried to avoid the pitch. Dietz subsequently popped out, and Drysdale retired the next two hitters to preserve his streak and run his record to 58 consecutive scoreless innings before he was stopped. His shutout skein notwithstanding, the 1968 season was not an unqualified success for Drysdale. After his five straight whitewashes, his arm seemed to run out of gas, and he finished with a so-so 14-12 record.

In 1968, Card hurler Bob Gibson notched 13 shutouts, the most in the major leagues since 1916.

In the 1968 World Series, Bob Gibson set a fall classic record by striking out 17 Tigers in one game.

At age 42, Warren Spahn became the oldest 20-game winner in history, in 1963, going 23-7 for the Braves.

The ace of the Dodgers mound staff at age 21 when the club abandoned Brooklyn after the 1957 season, Don Drysdale (above) remained the franchise's most durable hurler for 11 more years before fading in 1969.

In 1961, Warren Spahn of the Milwaukee Braves led the National League in wins a major league record ninth time.

Warren Spahn in '61 became the first NL southpaw to win 300 games.

"Regrets about not winning 300? No, not really. A lot of people thought I was striving for 300 wins. But what I was really striving for was to pitch until I was 44 or 45 years old. I knew if I could do that the wins would take care of themselves."
—Robin Roberts

Prior to the 1966 season, Sandy Koufax and Don Drysdale staged the first dual holdout by teammates in major league history.

Warren Spahn and Lew Burdette of the Milwaukee Braves were the only pair of mound teammates to win as many as 40 games between them in 1960.

Warren Spahn's first win of the season in 1963 gave him 328 career victories, breaking Eddie Plank's career southpaw record.

1960s GAMES STARTED	
1. Jim Bunning	360
2. Don Drysdale	359
3. Larry Jackson	321
4. Juan Marichal	320
5. Jim Kaat	316
6. Dick Ellsworth	308
7. Milt Pappas	302
Bob Gibson	302
9. Claude Osteen	287
10. Earl Wilson	281
11. Camilo Pascual	273
12. Steve Barber	263
13. Ray Sadecki	261
Dean Chance	261
15. Jack Fisher	258
16. Jim Maloney	255
17. Mike McCormick	251
18. Mudcat Grant	246
19. Don Cardwell	243
20. Joe Horlen	240
21. Chris Short	239
22. Bill Monbouquette	238
23. Sandy Koufax	237
24. Bob Friend	235
25. Jim Perry	233

1960s Witness to Three Perfect Games

After Harvey Haddix of the Pirates hurled 12 perfect innings on May 29, 1959, before losing to the Braves in the 13th frame, a door swung ajar that had been sealed shut for nearly 40 years. His effort marked the first time since 1922 that a pitcher had achieved perfection for the first nine innings of a regular-season game. On Father's Day in 1964, the Phillies' Jim Bunning, himself the sire of a multitude of offspring, became the first hurler in 42 years to win a perfect game during the regular season and the first National Leaguer to toss a perfect contest since 1880, when he blanked the Mets 6-0. The following year, Sandy Koufax of the Dodgers was letter-perfect against the Cubs 1-0. That game nearly marked the second double no-hitter in big league history, as Chicago's Bob Hendley surrendered just one hit on the day. In 1968, Catfish Hunter of the Athletics made the 1960s the first decade in history to feature three perfect games, when he bested Minnesota 4-0 on May 8.

Above: *Pittsburgh's Harvey Haddix (left) and Art Ditmar of the Yankees shake hands before facing each other in game five of the 1960 World Series. Making his first fall appearance, Haddix got the decision, 5-2, to give the Pirates a 3-2 lead. Three days later, when the Pirates bagged the classic, Haddix won the game in a relief role.*

1960s COMPLETE GAMES		
1.	Juan Marichal	197
2.	Bob Gibson	164
3.	Don Drysdale	135
4.	Sandy Koufax	122
5.	Larry Jackson	116
6.	Jim Bunning	108
7.	Jim Kaat	102
8.	Warren Spahn	95
9.	Camilo Pascual	93
	Denny McLain	93
11.	Gaylord Perry	88
12.	Dick Ellsworth	87
13.	Mel Stottlemyre	85
14.	Dean Chance	82
15.	Claude Osteen	80
16.	Milt Pappas	79
17.	Chris Short	76
18.	Mike McCormick	74
	Jim Maloney	74
	Bob Friend	74
21.	Bob Veale	73
22.	Ray Sadecki	72
	Mudcat Grant	72
24.	Bill Monbouquette	71
25.	Sam McDowell	70

"They called us 'The Miracle Mets.' Miracle, my eye. What happened was that a lot of good young players suddenly jelled and matured all at once."
—Tom Seaver

Granger Toes Rubber 90 Times

In 1964, John Wyatt of the Kansas City Athletics became the first pitcher to appear in 80 or more games in a season, when he took the mound in 81 of the A's 163 contests. The following year Ted Abernathy of the Cubs upped the record to 84 appearances, a mark that held until 1968, when Wilbur Wood of the White Sox worked in 88 games. Wood's record, which seemed to push the limit beyond the endurance of the human arm, lasted only one year. In 1969, Wayne Granger, then in his second season, came on in relief for the Reds 90 times. Granger was used so often by Cincinnati manager Dave Bristol out of necessity. The Reds in 1969 had one of the most uninspiring crews of starting pitchers in the majors. Largely owing to Granger and Clay Carroll, however, who posted 34 saves and 21 wins between them, Cincinnati topped the majors with 44 saves and finished at 89-73. The following year, with Granger and Carroll again forming a sterling relief tandem, the Reds won the National League pennant.

Dave McNally of the Orioles tied an American League record when he won 17 consecutive games in 1968 and '69.

Righthander Jack Sanford of the San Francisco Giants won 16 straight games in 1962.

Above: *When Elroy Face retired in 1969, he held the major league records for career saves (193), relief wins (96), relief appearances (821), and most appearances for one club (802 with Pittsburgh).*

When Phillie hurler Jim Bunning pitched a perfect game against the Mets on June 21, 1964, it was the first perfect game in the NL in this century.

Jim Bunning was the only pitcher ever to win exactly 19 games for three consecutive years (1964 to '66).

Cleveland's Sam McDowell in 1965 set an AL southpaw record for Ks with 325.

Early Wynn won his 300th game on July 13, 1963.

1960s SAVES		
1.	Hoyt Wilhelm	152
2.	Roy Face	142
3.	Ron Perranoski	138
	Stu Miller	138
5.	Dick Radatz	122
6.	Lindy McDaniel	112
7.	Ted Abernathy	106
8.	John Wyatt	103
	Ron Kline	103
10.	Al Worthington	98
11.	Don McMahon	87
12.	Larry Sherry	79
13.	Frank Linzy	77
14.	Phil Regan	74
15.	Jack Aker	72
16.	Bill Henry	71
17.	Eddie Fisher	65
18.	Fred Gladding	64
19.	Bob Lee	63
20.	Al McBean	62
	Dick Hall	62
22.	Hal Woodeshick	61
23.	Claude Raymond	60
	Joe Hoerner	60
	Jack Baldschun	60

In 1960, Lindy McDaniel of the Cardinals set an NL record with 26 saves, posted a 12-4 record, and had a 2.09 ERA, the best of any hurler in the majors who worked at least 100 innings.

Mickey Lolich said after his Series MVP performance in the 1968 World Series: "All my life somebody else has been the big star and Lolich was No. 2. I figured my day would come."

Minnesota pitcher Jim Kaat in 1962 and '63 won a record 14 consecutive complete games.

1960s SHUTOUTS	
1. Juan Marichal	45
2. Bob Gibson	41
3. Don Drysdale	40
4. Sandy Koufax	37
5. Jim Bunning	35
6. Dean Chance	32
7. Jim Maloney	30
Larry Jackson	30
9. Milt Pappas	28
10. Camilo Pascual	26
Denny McLain	26
12. Claude Osteen	23
13. Mel Stottlemyre	22
14. Luis Tiant	21
Mickey Lolich	21
Whitey Ford	21
Steve Barber	21
18. Chris Short	20
Bob Friend	20
20. Bob Veale	19
Jim Perry	19
Sam McDowell	19
Vern Law	19
24. Curt Simmons	18
Gary Peters	18
Bill Monbouquette	18
Mike McCormick	18
Joe Horlen	18

Above: *Jim Kaat led American League pitchers in hits surrendered for three straight years in the mid-1960s but nevertheless won 59 games during the period, including 25 in 1965.*

Relieving Develops into Laudable Livelihood

A career as a relief pitcher first became a worthy profession during the 1960s. For every failed starter—such as Phil Regan or Ted Abernathy, or Dave Giusti or Stu Miller—who found a second life in the majors as a fireman, there was a Ron Perranoski or a Dick Radatz or a Wayne Granger who began and ended his major league career in the bullpen. Perranoski was the first hurler in history to work in more than 700 contests without ever pitching a complete game. The first pitcher to average more than a strikeout an inning throughout his career, Radatz appeared in 381 games during his seven seasons in the majors without ever making a start. Granger also never received a starting assignment during his nine-year career. Fred Gladding—the National League save leader in 1969—made just one start in his 13 seasons and surprised everyone, most of all himself, by going five innings. Gladding made such a specialty of short relief stints that he labored just 601 career innings in 450 games.

Gibson, Lolich Take Series Trio

Since pitchers reigned supreme during the regular season in the late 1960s, it was only to be expected that they would also dominate the action in World Series play. The 1966 fall classic saw Baltimore hurlers cede the Los Angeles Dodgers two runs in the early innings of the opening game and then shut them out for the remaining 33 frames. In the 1967 Series, Bob Gibson of the Cardinals and Jim Lonborg of the Red Sox paired off in the crucial seventh game with two fall victories apiece and identical 0.50 ERAs. Gibson, working on one more day of rest than Lonborg, prevailed 7-2 to become the last National League hurler to date to post three victories in a World Series. The 1968 fall affair again came down to a game seven that featured two hurlers in search of their third Series wins—Gibson and Mickey Lolich of the Tigers. Like Jim Lonborg, Lolich had one less day of rest than Gibson. On this occasion, nevertheless, it was the Cards ace who faltered, bowing 4-1. Lolich's triumph marked the only time in World Series history that a hurler bagged three wins two years in a row.

In his 16-year career, Mickey Lolich (above) won 217 games but hit just one home run. It came in 1968 when he strode to the plate for his first at bat in World Series competition. Lolich posted a .110 career batting average.

1960s WINS

1.	Juan Marichal	191
2.	Bob Gibson	164
3.	Don Drysdale	158
4.	Jim Bunning	150
5.	Jim Kaat	142
6.	Larry Jackson	141
7.	Sandy Koufax	137
8.	Jim Maloney	134
9.	Milt Pappas	131
10.	Camilo Pascual	127
11.	Earl Wilson	115
	Chris Short	115
	Whitey Ford	115
	Dean Chance	115
15.	Jim Perry	114
	Claude Osteen	114
	Denny McLain	114
18.	Dick Ellsworth	112
19.	Mudcat Grant	111
	Steve Barber	111
21.	Bill Monbouquette	104
22.	Mike McCormick	103
23.	Mickey Lolich	102
24.	Tony Cloninger	101
25.	Bob Veale	100
	Juan Pizarro	100

White Sox pitchers Joe Horlen, Gary Peters, and Tommy John finished 1-2-4 in the American League in ERA.

"Baseball is such a great life that anyone who complains about it, I think, is a little clouded. I could never find the time to complain."

—Jim Lonborg

'Stros Stockpile Strikeouts

Strikeout totals zoomed in the 1960s, culminating in the 1969 expansion season when seven pitching staffs registered 1,000 or more Ks. The previous year, five teams had whiff totals in four figures, led by Cleveland, which topped the majors for the second year in a row and the fourth time in five seasons. In 1967, Tribe hurlers established a new major league record by setting 1,189 enemy hitters down on strikes, then threatened their own mark in 1968 before finishing with 1,157. Sam McDowell and Luis Tiant both pitched more than 200 innings in 1967 and '68, and they contributed a strikeout an inning to the Tribe's mark. Cleveland's record, however, was toppled by Houston in the last year of the decade. The Astros hill staff logged 1,221 Ks in 1969, led by Don Wilson (235), Larry Dierker (232), and Tom Griffin (200). Wilson and Griffin both averaged at least one strikeout per inning, as did Jim Ray, a combination starter-reliever, and two secondary Astros hurlers, Skip Guinn, and none other than Jim Bouton.

Denny McLain in 1968 was the first 30-game winner in the major leagues since 1934.

In 1966, former Tigers starter Phil Regan led the National League with 21 saves and compiled a 14-1 record with a 1.62 ERA for the Dodgers.

Above: *Denny McLain had logged 114 career wins by the time he was 25 and seemed destined for Cooperstown. A lengthy suspension for being involved in a bookmaking operation helped to hold him to just 17 more victories.*

Pirate Elroy Face in 1962 set the NL save record with 28.

In 1960, Art Ditmar led the pennant-winning Yankees in wins with 15 and innings pitched with just 200.

The last team with an ERA below 2.50 was the 1968 St. Louis Cardinals with a 2.49 mark.

"Pitching is the art of instilling fear by making a man flinch."
—Sandy Koufax

1960s INNINGS	
1. Don Drysdale	2,629.2
2. Jim Bunning	2,590.1
3. Juan Marichal	2,550.0
4. Bob Gibson	2,447.0
5. Larry Jackson	2,335.2
6. Jim Kaat	2,223.2
7. Dick Ellsworth	2,079.1
8. Claude Osteen	2,077.0
9. Milt Pappas	2,033.2
10. Dean Chance	1,900.2
11. Jack Fisher	1,887.0
12. Earl Wilson	1,867.0
13. Camilo Pascual	1,864.2
14. Chris Short	1,843.2
15. Mudcat Grant	1,834.2
16. Sandy Koufax	1,807.2
17. Jim Perry	1,806.0
18. Jim Maloney	1,802.0
19. Mike McCormick	1,786.1
20. Ray Sadecki	1,778.0
21. Bill Monbouquette	1,755.2
22. Steve Barber	1,727.0
23. Ken Johnson	1,718.0
24. Gaylord Perry	1,686.0
25. Don Cardwell	1,685.2

Koufax Strikes Out 382 in 1965

After Van Lingle Mungo led the National League with 238 strikeouts in 1936, 21 seasons would pass before another senior loop hurler would collect as many as 225 strikeouts. Once Sam Jones broke the dry spell in 1958, not until the strike-abbreviated 1981 season would an NL whiff leader again bag fewer than 225 Ks. A similar phenomenon occurred in the American League, where only Bob Feller, Herb Score, and Hal Newhouser had prevented an equally long string of seasons with lackluster strikeout totals. In the free-swinging expansion-packed 1960s, however, whiff totals went through the roof. In 1963, Sandy Koufax of the Dodgers became the first NL pitcher since 1892 to score 300 or more Ks in a season. Two years later, Koufax set a new modern record with 382 whiffs, averaging 10.24 Ks per nine innings. Sudden Sam McDowell of Cleveland became only the third hurler in American League history to enjoy a 300-strikeout season in '65, when he amassed 325 strikeouts. Koufax in 1966 enjoyed his third 300-strikeout season by notching 317.

Above: As a youth, Sandy Koufax's best sport appeared to be basketball. He was being groomed for court stardom at the University of Cincinnati before a bonus offer from Brooklyn intervened. Koufax was pitching for the Dodgers at age 19.

Los Angeles Dodgers hurler Sandy Koufax in 1963 was the first unanimous choice for the Cy Young Award.

In his final season in the big leagues, Sandy Koufax led the 1966 National League in ERA a record fifth consecutive time.

Sandy Koufax was a unanimous choice for the Cy Young Award, for the second time in his career, in 1965. In 1966, he won his third unanimous Cy Young Award in four years.

Sandy Koufax in 1963 set a modern National League record with 306 strikeouts. He also set the modern record for southpaws with 11 shutouts that year.

On September 9, 1965, Sandy Koufax pitched a perfect game and his fourth no-hitter in four years, beating Chicago 1-0.

Dodger Sandy Koufax struck out 18 Cubs on April 24, 1964.

In 1960, Detroit's Frank Lary led the American League with 15 complete games, setting a record for the lowest total to lead a major league.

1960s STRIKEOUTS	
1. Bob Gibson	2,071
2. Jim Bunning	2,019
3. Sandy Koufax	1,910
Don Drysdale	1,910
5. Juan Marichal	1,840
6. Sam McDowell	1,663
7. Jim Maloney	1,585
8. Jim Kaat	1,435
9. Bob Veale	1,428
10. Camilo Pascual	1,391
11. Dean Chance	1,361
12. Mickey Lolich	1,336
13. Earl Wilson	1,332
14. Chris Short	1,329
15. Gaylord Perry	1,234
16. Larry Jackson	1,206
17. Milt Pappas	1,201
18. Ray Sadecki	1,174
19. Denny Lemaster	1,161
20. Steve Barber	1,144
21. Gary Bell	1,132
22. Juan Pizarro	1,119
23. Dick Ellsworth	1,108
24. Denny McLain	1,098
25. Gary Peters	1,097

Sandy Koufax explained why he quit so young with an arthritic elbow: "When I'm 40 years old, I'd still like to be able to comb my hair."

Hurlers on Pale Hose Lack Support

Picture a team that had a 2.75 staff ERA, only .09 runs higher than the best mark that year in its league. Add the fact that the club allowed just 527 runs, a fraction more than three a game. Note that the team had the best relief corps in its loop and led the majors with 40 saves. Finally, take a guess where this pitcher-rich crew finished. The answer is next to last in a 10-team circuit—and at 67-95 only one and one-half games out of the cellar. Those who well remember the 1960s will have already recognized that the team being described here is the 1968 Chicago White Sox. That year the Sox had so little punch that any Pale Hose hurler who allowed more than two earned runs a game was virtually guaranteed a losing record. Among pitchers who figured in at least 10 decisions, only Tommy John (1.98 ERA and 10-5) and Wilbur Wood (1.87 ERA and 13-12) won more often than they lost as the Sox finished with a 67-95 mark. Joe Horlan (12-14, 2.37 ERA), Jack Fisher (8-13, 2.98) and Gary Peters (4-13, 3.75 ERA) were other pitchers of note on that club.

Stout Reasoning

Mickey Lolich defended his portly physique: "All the fat guys watch me and say to their wives, 'See? There's a fat guy doing okay. Bring me another beer.'"

Above: *Juan Marichal won 154 games during the seven-year period between 1963 and 1969, including three seasons of 25 or more victories. He finished with 243 triumphs and a career winning percentage of .631 that would have been markedly higher but for an abysmal 6-16 campaign in 1972.*

In 1961, Luis Arroyo of the New York Yankees set a major league record when he notched 29 saves.

Ted Abernathy's 31 saves and 84 pitching appearances for the Cubs in 1965 set major league records.

In 1965, southpaw relief ace Billy McCool of the Reds notched 120 strikeouts in 105⅓ innings and tied for second in the NL in saves with 21.

Boston reliever Dick Radatz in 1963 had 25 saves, a 15-6 record, and 162 Ks in 132⅓ innings for a seventh-place team.

In 1964, Boston's Dick Radatz totaled 16 wins and a major league-best 29 saves for a team that won only 72 games.

Whitey Ford in 1967 retired with a .690 career winning percentage, the best in history among 200-game winners.

Jim Maloney of Cincinnati no-hit Houston on April 30, 1969; the next day, Houston's Don Wilson no-hit Cincinnati.

1960s WINNING PERCENTAGE	
1. Sandy Koufax	.695
2. Juan Marichal	.685
3. Whitey Ford	.673
4. Denny McLain	.667
5. Jim Maloney	.626
6. Dave McNally	.621
7. Bob Gibson	.610
8. Eddie Fisher	.600
9. Ray Culp	.596
10. Bob Purkey	.593
11. Ralph Terry	.582
12. Camilo Pascual	.580
13. Mickey Lolich	.580
14. Jim Perry	.576
15. Jack Sanford	.575
16. Al McBean	.573
17. Mel Stottlemyre	.571
18. Fergie Jenkins	.570
19. Phil Regan	.570
20. Bob Veale	.568
21. Warren Spahn	.568
22. Vern Law	.567
23. Bobby Bolin	.566
24. Sonny Siebert	.564
25. Johnny Podres	.563

Ken Holtzman was 9-0 for the Cubs in 1967 when his season was brought to an end by a military call-up.

Above: *Before Tom Seaver's arrival, few Mets pitchers had ever had a winning season. Seaver called the Shea Stadium mound home for 12 campaigns and never had a losing season in Mets livery until his finale in 1983 when he went 9-14. Of his 311 wins, 188 came with the Mets.*

In 1968, Luis Tiant of the Cleveland Indians struck out 19 batters in a 10-inning game.

On September 12, 1962, Washington's Tom Cheney struck out 21 Orioles in a 16-inning game, winning 2-1.

In 1969, Houston hurlers struck out a major league record 1,221 hitters.

Jim Nash of the Kansas City A's set an American League rookie record in 1966 when he compiled a .923 winning percentage by going 12-1.

'68 Mets Finish Ninth Despite 2.72 ERA

Any who guessed the 1968 New York Mets were the team that fared so poorly despite having a wealth of pitching can easily be forgiven. In 1968, the Mets also finished next to last, a mere one game away from the basement, with an even better staff ERA than the White Sox (2.72) and also surrendered fewer runs than the Hose (499). The Mets had a 73-89 record, however, substantially better than the White Sox managed to piece together, and two young pitchers, Jerry Koosman and Tom Seaver, who fashioned winning records of 19-12 and 16-12 respectively with ERAs above 2.00. Also on that club was a young hurler named Nolan Ryan, who was 6-9 with a 3.09 ERA in 134 innings pitched. Unlike the White Sox, who suffered a mound collapse the following year and again finished near the bottom, the Mets maintained their stellar hill work in 1969 and added just enough offensive zip to improve to a 100-62 mark, good enough for their first NL pennant.

In 1962, Ralph Terry of the Yankees became the first hurler to win the seventh and deciding game of a World Series 1-0.

In 1969, Hoyt Wilhelm, then with the Angels, became the first pitcher in major league history to log 200 saves.

"There are only two places in this league: first place and no place."
—Tom Seaver

Orioles manager Paul Richards in 1960 designed a catcher's mitt that was 50 inches in circumference to handle Hoyt Wilhelm's knucklers.

After going hitless in 47 at bats as a Giants rookie hurler in 1964, Ron Herbel went on to compile an .029 career batting average, the lowest ever by a player with 200 or more career at bats.

1960s EARNED RUN AVERAGE	
1. Hoyt Wilhelm	2.16
2. Sandy Koufax	2.36
3. Juan Marichal	2.57
4. Bob Gibson	2.74
5. Mike Cuellar	2.76
6. Dean Chance	2.77
7. Tommy John	2.81
8. Joe Horlen	2.83
9. Bob Veale	2.83
10. Don Drysdale	2.83
11. Whitey Ford	2.83
12. Luis Tiant	2.84
13. Mel Stottlemyre	2.86
14. Sonny Siebert	2.91
15. Gary Peters	2.92
16. Gaylord Perry	2.95
17. Fergie Jenkins	2.95
18. Sam McDowell	2.95
19. Jim Bunning	3.01
20. Denny McLain	3.04
21. Jim Maloney	3.08
22. Al McBean	3.09
23. Claude Osteen	3.13
24. Hank Aguirre	3.15
25. Eddie Fisher	3.17

Chance Ensures Cy Young

Juan Marichal, arguably the most consistently outstanding pitcher during the 1960s, never won a Cy Young Award, the honor often going instead to a hurler like Mike McCormick or Vern Law who had only one truly exceptional season. Dean Chance was another hurler in the McCormick and Law mold, a good pitcher throughout his career but never brilliant except in the one season when he copped his lone Cy Young Award. Chance's year of destiny was 1964. Toiling for a mediocre Los Angeles Angels team that barely broke .500, Chance tailored a magnificent 20-9 record and a 1.65 ERA, tops in the majors. He led the league with 287⅓ innings pitched, and had 207 strikeouts opposed to 86 bases on balls. The frosting on the cake, however, was his 11 shutouts, the most since 1913 by an American League pitcher. At the finish of the 1964 season, Chance, although just 23, already had 47 career victories and seemed headed for Coop-erstown. He won only 81 more games, however, before depart-ing in 1971.

"First thing I do when I wake up in the morning is breathe on a mirror and hope it fogs."
—Early Wynn

When he posted a 1.65 ERA in 1964, Dean Chance recorded the lowest ERA in the American League since World War II.

Above: *Lew Burdette in the 1957 World Series against the Yankees was the first hurler since Christy Mathewson in 1905 to toss two shutouts in one fall classic.*

In 1968, Wilbur Wood of the White Sox set a major league record by pitching in 88 games.

At the finish of the 1960s, the record for the most saves in a season was held by Jack Aker, with 32 for the Kansas City A's in 1966.

In 1964, Bill Wakefield set a record for the most mound appearances by a pitcher in his only big league season when he toed the rubber in 62 contests for the Mets.

1960s FEWEST WALKS	
1. Lew Burdette	1.39
2. Vern Law	1.51
3. Robin Roberts	1.66
4. Bob Friend	1.70
5. Juan Marichal	1.78
6. Ralph Terry	1.88
7. Don Drysdale	2.05
8. Larry Jackson	2.06
9. Bob Purkey	2.09
10. Bill Monbouquette	2.10
11. Ken Johnson	2.12
12. Jim Bunning	2.16
13. Ray Herbert	2.18
14. Warren Spahn	2.20
15. Fergie Jenkins	2.22
16. Turk Farrell	2.23
17. Curt Simmons	2.24
18. Jim Kaat	2.27
19. Gaylord Perry	2.30
20. Claude Osteen	2.31
21. Eddie Fisher	2.33
22. Jack Kralick	2.33
23. Whitey Ford	2.36
24. Ray Washburn	2.41
25. Dick Ellsworth	2.46

Above: *When Jim Bunning retired, his 2,855 strikeouts ranked him second all time to Walter Johnson. Bunning was the first to K more than 1,000 in the NL and AL since Cy Young.*

In 1964, Johnny Wyatt of Kansas City was the first pitcher in major league history to appear in at least half of his team's games (81 of 162).

Pack a Lunch

Early Wynn, asked about his retirement plans when he was still pitching in his 40s, responded: "Somebody will have to come out and take the uniform off me, and the guy who comes after it better bring help."

1960s RATIO	
1. Hoyt Wilhelm	8.94
2. Sandy Koufax	9.04
3. Juan Marichal	9.40
4. Fergie Jenkins	9.76
5. Denny McLain	9.85
6. Don Drysdale	10.06
7. Eddie Fisher	10.12
8. Sonny Siebert	10.13
9. Ralph Terry	10.16
10. Jim Bunning	10.28
11. Luis Tiant	10.28
12. Bob Gibson	10.32
13. Mike Cuellar	10.32
14. Gaylord Perry	10.38
15. Joe Horlen	10.46
16. Dean Chance	10.54
17. Whitey Ford	10.56
18. Gary Peters	10.69
19. Ken Johnson	10.73
20. Dave McNally	10.75
21. Tommy John	10.77
22. Hank Aguirre	10.77
23. Mel Stottlemyre	10.78
24. Larry Jackson	10.79
25. Catfish Hunter	10.79

Jackson Misses Chance for Cy Young

The National League's top hurler in 1964 was the antithesis of Cy Young winner Dean Chance. Larry Jackson was in his 10th major league season that year and had never been more than a steady workmanlike performer, good for around 14 or 15 wins a season. But in 1964, then in his second campaign with the Cubs after coming from St. Louis in a trade the previous year, Jackson snared 24 wins to lead the majors. He pitched almost 300 innings that year, and completed 19 of his 38 starts. Since only one Cy Young Award was given in 1964 and Chance was the popular choice by virtue of his dazzling ERA and shutout total, Jackson was doomed to disappointment in his lone brush with stardom. For the remaining four years of his career, Larry reverted to his earlier form, winning in double figures but losing as often as he won. Minus his snazzy 24-11 season in 1964, Jackson's career record was two games below .500 (170-172).

In 1965, Arnold Earley appeared in 57 games in relief for the Boston Red Sox without earning a single save and figuring in just one decision, a loss.

Joe Niekro of the Cubs and Rick Wise of the Phils were the only two National League ERA-crown qualifiers in 1968 who had ERAs above 4.00.

Jay Leads Cincy to Pennant

Eight years after the Braves had signed him to a mammoth bonus contract, Joey Jay had yet to mature as a pitcher. His 9-8 record in 1960 at age 25 convinced Milwaukee to package him with Juan Pizzaro, another young hurler of perennial promise but meager output, and ship the pair to Cincinnati on December 15, 1960, for shortstop Roy McMillan. That same day, the Reds sent Pizarro to the White Sox as part of a deal for third baseman Gene Freese, but they kept Jay and threw him into their starting rotation the following spring. Given his first chance to work on a regular basis, Jay in 1961 blossomed into the National League's leading winner with 21 victories. He lost only 10 games, although his ERA actually increased from his 1960 earned run average. He spearheaded the '61 Reds to their first pennant in 21 years. Jay won 21 games again the following year but then stumbled to a 7-18 mark in 1963 and never again was more than a second-line hurler.

Denny McLain explained his philosophy on conditioning: "All that running and exercise can do for you is make you healthy."

1960s PITCHER ASSISTS	
1. Don Drysdale	513
2. Larry Jackson	488
3. Jim Kaat	431
4. Claude Osteen	430
5. Dick Ellsworth	422

Although Roger Craig (above) was with the Mets for only two years, his career respectability as a hurler was nevertheless destroyed. He had a 59-52 record (.532 win percentage) with 14 saves in the 10 seasons he spent in uniforms other than the expansion club's; he was 15-46 with the Mets.

Gene Brabender, with a 13-14 mark and a 4.36 ERA in 202 innings, holds the Seattle Pilots' records for the most wins, most innings, and best ERA by an ERA-crown qualifier.

The 1969 season was the first in National League history that saw as many as five no-hit games.

On April 30, 1967, Steve Barber and Stu Miller of the Orioles tossed the first combined no-hitter in major league history.

Houston's Ken Johnson in 1964 was the first major league hurler to lose a complete-game no-hitter in nine innings.

The 1966 Cubs were the only major league team between 1965 and 1969 to give up as many as five runs per game.

In an 11-inning game with Cleveland on September 15, 1966, the Kansas City A's used seven different pitchers before finally triumphing 1-0.

1960s PITCHER PUTOUTS	
1. Bob Gibson	204
2. Juan Marichal	192
3. Larry Jackson	189
4. Earl Wilson	174
5. Milt Pappas	168

In 1963, the Mets had six pitchers who lost 14 or more games, led by Roger Craig with 22 defeats.

Met pitcher Roger Craig in 1963 suffered nine shutout losses, the most by any NL hurler since 1908.

Roger Craig of the New York Mets in 1963 tied the major league single-season record when he lost 18 consecutive games.

Dennis Ribant, with an 11-9 mark in 1966, was the first Mets pitcher to achieve a winning record.

In 1968, Jim McAndrew of the Mets lost a record four consecutive games in which his team was shut out.

Cincy Pitchers Breathe Cy of Despair

Even though he paced the National League in wins in 1961, the Reds' Joey Jay failed to garner a single first-place vote for the Cy Young Award. His disappointment was shared by every pitcher on his team during the 1960s. Throughout the decade, Cincinnati had a wealth of pitchers who had fine seasons but were always judged to be just a cut below Cy Young status. In fact, the only Reds hurler to receive so much as a single vote for the top pitching honor was Bob Purkey, when he put together a 23-5 season in 1962 and topped the majors with an .821 winning percentage. Other Reds hurlers who were blanked in the Cy Young balloting during the 1960s despite enjoying fine seasons were Sammy Ellis (1965: 22-10, 3.79 ERA), Jim O'Toole (1961: 19-9, 3.10 ERA), and Jim Maloney. In 1963, Maloney's 23-7 record with 265 strikeouts got him nowhere with voters as Sandy Koufax chose that year to go 25-5 with a 1.88 ERA. A case can be made that Maloney was the best pitcher of the era who never got a single vote in his career as his loop's top pitcher.

After tying for the American League lead in wins as a soph in 1960, Jim Perry (above) was little more than a mediocre hurler for the next eight seasons. He revived in 1969 to post the first of back-to-back 20-win seasons with the Twins.

I Must Be In the Front Row

Jim Brosnan, relief pitcher and author, when asked if it bothered him that bullpen seats afford a poor view of the game, responded: "That's the best part of it."

1960s PITCHER CHANCES ACCEPTED	
1. Larry Jackson	677
2. Don Drysdale	645
3. Juan Marichal	596
4. Jim Kaat	567
5. Dick Ellsworth	537

In 1969, the National League batting average jumped seven points and the AL's jumped 16 points after new rules reduced the height of the pitcher's mound and the size of the strike zone.

At age 65, Satchel Paige was the oldest player ever in a major league game when he hurled three scoreless innings for the Kansas City A's against Boston on September 25, 1965.

1960s PITCHER FIELDING AVERAGE	
1. Rick Wise	.994
2. Don Mossi	.993
3. Woodie Fryman	.993
4. Bill Stafford	.988
5. Ralph Terry	.985

Expansion Alters Schedule

When expansion swelled the American League from eight teams to 10 in 1961, and the composition of the National League was likewise altered a year later, the major league schedule was revised for the first time since 1904. After playing a 154-game slate for over half a century, both leagues adopted a 162-game season. Under the old schedule, every team played 22 contests against each of the other seven clubs in its loop. With two new franchises added, the number of contests teams played against their rivals was pared to 18. Expansion thereby made for a longer schedule but shorter series. Instead of customarily playing one another four contests each time they met, teams now usually played only three per meeting. One important casualty was the traditional weekend series, which began with a night game on Friday, followed by a Ladies' Day game on Saturday and then a doubleheader on Sunday.

Don Kessinger discussed Bill Mazeroski: "He was as good as I've ever seen at turning the double play. They called him 'No Hands' because he threw so quickly he never seemed to touch the ball."

1960s CATCHER GAMES	
1. Johnny Roseboro	1,206
2. Tom Haller	990
3. Clay Dalrymple	974
4. Earl Battey	967
5. Elston Howard	961

Above: *Bill Mazeroski is the only player who has yet to make the Hall of Fame despite being generally regarded as the best gloveman ever at his position. Many find his absence incomprehensible.*

Jerry Adair of Baltimore set a record for second sackers by compiling a .994 fielding average in 1964.

Bill Mazeroski of Pittsburgh led all NL second basemen in double plays a record eight straight seasons between 1960 and 1967.

Thanks largely to having to handle knuckleballers Eddie Fisher and Hoyt Wilhelm, catcher J.C. Martin of the White Sox committed a modern-record 33 passed balls in 1965.

"To a pitcher, a base hit is a perfect example of negative feedback."
—Steve Hovley, outfielder and flake

1960s CATCHER FIELDING AVERAGE	
1. Bill Freehan	.994
2. Joe Azcue	.993
3. Elston Howard	.993
4. Randy Hundley	.992
5. Tom Haller	.992

Jim Davenport of the Giants set a record in 1968 with 97 consecutive errorless games at third base.

In 1966, Curt Flood of the Cardinals set a record for outfielders when he had a perfect 1.000 fielding average in 396 chances.

When he handled 568 consecutive chances flawlessly between September 3, 1965, and June 4, 1967, Cardinals gardener Curt Flood set an all-time mark for outfielders.

In 1964, Larry Jackson of the Cubs broke Eppa Rixey's 47-year-old record for pitchers when he handled 109 chances without making an error all season.

Mickey Stanley of the Detroit Tigers was awarded an American League Gold Glove as an outfielder in 1968; In the 1968 World Series, however, he played all seven games of the affair at shortstop.

Above: *Bill White was one of the many 1960s sluggers bred by the Giants who made their marks in rival uniforms.*

Luis Aparicio led the American League in steals a record nine consecutive years, from 1956 to 1964.

Rod Carew tied Pete Reiser's major league record when he stole home successfully seven times in 1969.

New York Yankee second baseman Bobby Richardson ended the 1962 World Series by spearing Willie McCovey's hard line drive, leaving tying and winning runs in scoring position.

I'm the Wanderer

Joe Pepitone, complaining about his move from first base to the outfield, said: "In center field you've got too much time to think about everything but baseball."

"A great catch is like watching girls go by. The last one you see is always the prettiest."
—Bob Gibson

1960s FIRST BASE GAMES	
1. Norm Cash	1,375
2. Bill White	1,265
3. Orlando Cepeda	1,181
4. Ernie Banks	1,177
5. Donn Clendenon	992

The Chicago White Sox led the American League in stolen bases a loop-record 11 consecutive times, from 1951 to 1961.

Cardinal Lou Brock in 1967 set a World Series record by stealing seven bases. Brock tied his record in the 1968 Series with seven steals.

1960s FIRST BASE FIELDING AVERAGE	
1. Wes Parker	.995
2. Joe Adcock	.995
3. Vic Power	.994
4. Ernie Banks	.994
5. Joe Pepitone	.993

On September 1, 1963, Curt Simmons of the Cardinals became the last pitcher to steal home in a major league game.

Gus Triandos retired in 1965 with the record for the most consecutive games without being caught stealing; in his 1,206-game career Triandos was successful in his one and only stolen base attempt.

NL Not Quite Geographic

In 1969, a second wave of expansion, which created two new teams in both major leagues, resulted in each circuit splitting into two six-team divisions rather than balloon to an unwieldy 12-team loop. The schedule remained at 162 games, with clubs playing 18 contests against each of their five division rivals and 12 against each of the six clubs in the other division. To determine the pennant winner, it was decided that the two division champions would play a best three-of-five League Championship Series at the conclusion of the regular season. Only the World Series format was left unchanged by schedule-makers in 1969. The restructuring that was done to divide the two leagues into separate divisions resulted in several quixotic geographical arrangements that may last until the NL again expands in 1993. Atlanta was placed in the National League West as was Cincinnati, while St. Louis and Chicago got spots in the East. The Chicago American League entry meanwhile was sent to the West Division, where it still remains.

In 1964, the New York Yankees tied their own record by winning their fifth consecutive flag in the AL.

In the 1963 fall classic, the Los Angeles Dodgers swept the New York Yankees. It was the first time New York was swept since 1922.

Hodges Transforms Mets

In 1961, Gil Hodges retired after a long career as one of the game's top sluggers to take a dugout post with the Washington Senators. Although Hodges was unable to lift the Senators out of the second division in any of his five seasons at their helm, the New York Mets thought highly enough of his managerial skills to offer Washington pitching prospect Bill Denehy if the Senators would agree to release Hodges from his contract so that he could take over the Mets' reins. It turned out to be the Mets' greatest deal. Denehy never won a game in Washington. Hodges, however, turned around a franchise that had previously been close to a travesty, and brought a pennant to Shea Stadium after only two seasons. After the Miracle Mets' triumph in 1969, Hodges kept the club in contention during the next two years, but not even his genius could overcome a weak offense. Near the end of spring training in 1972, after playing a round of golf, Hodges suffered a fatal heart attack.

Ron Santo set a National League mark for third sackers when he paced the senior loop in assists for seven consecutive seasons, from 1962 to 1968.

The New York Yankees had winning seasons in 39 consecutive years, from 1926 to 1964. The second-longest streak was 18 straight seasons, owned by the Baltimore Orioles from 1968 to 1985.

Above: *Rusty Staub, hurrying to beat this throw to Cubs third sacker Ron Santo, was the Expos' first bona fide star.*

Casey Stengel, after he was fired by the Yankees following the club's 1960 World Series loss, said: "I'll never make the mistake again of being 70 years old."

1960s SECOND BASE GAMES	
1. Bill Mazeroski	1,421
2. Julian Javier	1,330
3. Bobby Richardson	1,075
4. Jerry Lumpe	1,038
5. Tony Taylor	940

The New York Yankees in 1966 stumbled into the American League cellar for the first time since 1912.

The last time the Cleveland Indians finished above .500 two years in a row was in 1965 and '66.

Willie Had Better Hands

Jimmy Breslin wrote about the early Mets: "Having Marv Throneberry play for your team is like having Willie Sutton play for your bank."

The Yankees lost the 1963 and '64 World Series, the first time since 1921 and 1922 that the Bronx Bombers have been beaten twice in a row in fall play.

1960s SECOND BASE FIELDING AVERAGE	
1. Jerry Adair	.986
2. Chuck Schilling	.985
3. Nellie Fox	.985
4. Jerry Lumpe	.984
5. Bill Mazeroski	.983

Cubs Collapse

As the 1960s drew to a close, the Chicago Cubs seemed about to mark their second consecutive decade without a pennant. Then in 1969, in their fourth season under manager Leo Durocher, the Bruins roared out of the starting gate at such a furious pace that it seemed certain they would make their first postseason appearance since 1945. In early August, the Cubs led the second-place Mets by 9½ games. The Bruins then went into a tailspin that left them only 2½ games in front when they faced New York on September 8 in the first of a two-game set. Three days later the Mets were in first place by percentage points, a margin that swelled to eight full games when the season closed. What triggered the Cubs' late-season collapse was the lack of an adequate center fielder, plus some sniping by Durocher that helped to undermine the team's morale.

Ed Kranepool said about his manager on the Mets, Gil Hodges: "You played his way or you didn't play. He molded young players. He was the turning point."

1960s THIRD BASE GAMES	
1. Brooks Robinson	1,576
2. Ron Santo	1,526
3. Clete Boyer	1,253
4. Ken Boyer	1,169
5. Eddie Mathews	1,024

The Pittsburgh Pirates in 1960 won the franchise's first National League pennant since 1927, and first world championship since 1925.

A National League East crown with the 1969 Cubs would have put Leo Durocher (above) on the threshold of managing three different National League teams to pennants.

When the Braves shifted from Milwaukee to Atlanta in 1966, they became the first NL franchise in this century to move twice.

Between 1946 and 1962, the Dodgers played in four NL pennant playoff series in 17 seasons and lost three of them; in 1980 they also lost the only division playoff game in NL history.

In 1960, the New York Yankees ended the season with 15 straight wins and copped the pennant by eight games after leading the AL by just .002 percentage points before their streak started.

1960s THIRD BASE FIELDING AVERAGE	
1. Brooks Robinson	.975
2. Don Wert	.970
3. Clete Boyer	.966
4. Bubba Phillips	.964
5. Jim Davenport	.962

Before the 1968 season, the Athletics moved from Kansas City to Oakland.

In 1960, the Cincinnati Reds set a 20th-century record for the lowest winning percentage (.435) by a team destined to win the pennant the following year. That record was broken by the 1990 Atlanta Braves, who fashioned a .401 winning percentage.

The 1967 Red Sox jumped from ninth place in 1966 to first in '67—the first team to do so in this century.

Amazin'
Richie Ashburn, on playing with 1962 Mets, said: "I don't know what's going on, but I know I've never seen it before."

The Cincinnati Reds in '61 won their first NL pennant since 1940.

The 1962 to '65 New York Mets not only were the last team to lose 100 games for four straight years but set a major league record for the most losses over a four-year period with 452.

Above: *Al Kaline was among the many fine performers whose career stats were curtailed because their peak years coincided with the 1960s hitting drought.*

Ty Cobb in 1960, on why he would only hit .300 against modern pitching, said: "You've got to remember I'm now 73 years old."

1960s SHORTSTOP GAMES

1.	Luis Aparicio	1,482
2.	Leo Cardenas	1,298
3.	Zoilo Versalles	1,212
4.	Maury Wills	1,172
5.	Jim Fregosi	1,143

In 1967, Detroit outfielder Al Kaline won his last of 10 Gold Gloves.

Ashford Breaks Blue Color Bar

In 1966, Emmett Ashford broke a color barrier that had been even more difficult to surmount than the one faced by Jackie Robinson, when Ashford became the first black umpire in major league history. Hired by the American League, Ashford served as a junior loop official for five seasons. Two years after his departure, Art Williams joined the National League arbiters staff as the senior loop's first black umpire and remained on its rolls until 1977. Neither Ashford nor Williams was a particularly outstanding official, lending support to historians who have since written that they were both hired simply because the timing was right. It would be a task, however, for any historian to point to a more qualified candidate who ought to have been hired prior to 1966. With all the documentation there is about the many great Negro League stars who were denied access to the majors because of their color, astonishingly little has been written about early day black umpires.

The San Diego Padres were beaten twice during the 1969 season by scores of 19-0, the modern NL record for the largest score of a shutout game.

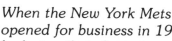

When the New York Mets opened for business in 1962 by losing their first nine games, they tied the National League record for the most consecutive losses at the start of the season.

When the Chicago Cubs won 87 games in 1967, it was the most victories they had achieved in any season since 1945, the last year they won a pennant.

The Phillies set a 20th-century record for the most consecutive losses when they were beaten 23 straight times in 1961.

Manager Casey Stengel was fired after the 1960 World Series loss, despite winning nine world championships in 12 seasons at the helm of the New York Yankees.

1960s OUTFIELD GAMES

1.	Hank Aaron	1,513
2.	Vada Pinson	1,494
3.	Willie Mays	1,464
4.	Curt Flood	1,461
5.	Roberto Clemente	1,443
6.	Billy Williams	1,438
7.	Johnny Callison	1,379
8.	Carl Yastrzemski	1,353
9.	Frank Robinson	1,340
10.	Willie Davis	1,314
11.	Rocky Colavito	1,261
12.	Al Kaline	1,235
13.	Tony Gonzalez	1,216
14.	Lou Brock	1,180
15.	Frank Howard	1,179

Bigs Hire Schools of Umps

In its 1959 edition, the Baseball Register discontinued its annual custom of listing the playing records of umpires along with those of active players, coaches, and managers. The change was made in part because not many umpires by the late 1950s had had careers of any substance as players. Among the few who had, only Ken Burkhart, Ed Sudol, and Frank Secory would still be in blue by the end of the following decade. Others, such as Vinny Smith, Jocko Conlan, and Dusty Boggess all retired during the 1960s. To replace them, the two major leagues drew new recruits from the graduates of the many umpiring schools that sprang up after World War II rather than, as before, from the ranks of former players who had turned to officiating after their retirement. The trend has only increased in recent years. For every former major league player like Bill Kunkel, there are a dozen umpires who never played so much as a single inning professionally.

In 1963, Harmon Killebrew (above) lead the American League in slugging despite batting .258 with just 18 doubles and no triples.

In 1964, Harmon Killebrew played 157 games in the outfield for the Minnesota Twins and collected just one assist, an all-time low for a gardener in 150 or more games.

"The only good thing about playing in Cleveland is you don't have to make road trips there."
—Richie Scheinblum

In 1966, the Cubs set an all-time major league record when they finished in the second division for the 20th straight year.

1960s SHORTSTOP FIELDING AVERAGE	
1. Luis Aparicio	.974
2. Roy McMillan	.972
3. Gene Alley	.970
4. Dal Maxvill	.969
5. Rico Petrocelli	.969

"Old-timers weekends and airplane landings are alike. If you can walk away from them, they're successful."
—Casey Stengel

1960s OUTFIELD PUTOUTS	
1. Curt Flood	3,512
2. Willie Mays	3,457
3. Vada Pinson	3,307
4. Hank Aaron	3,105
5. Willie Davis	2,973
6. Roberto Clemente	2,701
7. Johnny Callison	2,681
8. Carl Yastrzemski	2,608
9. Al Kaline	2,517
10. Billy Williams	2,446
11. Tony Gonzalez	2,356
12. Frank Robinson	2,353
13. Rocky Colavito	2,309
14. Felipe Alou	2,125
15. Lou Brock	2,121

The New York Mets in 1963 lost a big league-record 22 straight games on the road.

The revival of the stolen base as an offensive weapon gave Maury Wills (above) life in the majors. He was nearly 28 before he first won a regular job with the Dodgers.

Jimmy Dykes managed a record six different major league teams without even winning a pennant with any of them.

In 1967, the Mets traded Bill Denehy and $100,000 to Washington in order to obtain Gil Hodges as their manager.

Dodger manager Walter Alston in 1965 won an NL record fourth world championship.

Shortstop Maury Wills of the Los Angeles Dodgers in 1962 swiped a major league record 104 bases.

NL Clubs Recruit Blacks, Latinos

In All-Star play, considered by many to be the best measure of talent in the two rival major leagues, the National League won all but two of the games played between 1961 and 1978. Much of the reason was the greater zeal with which senior loop teams scouted, signed, and developed black and Latin players in the late 1950s and early 1960s. Between 1961 and 1978, only four NL bat titles, one slugging championship, and five home run crowns were won by white players. The huge disparity between the two leagues in their recruitment of black and Latin players was apparent as early as 1961. The AL's top five hitters and sluggers in the first expansion season were all white, but the three top sluggers and three of the five leading hitters in the NL were either black or Latin. No team was more guilty of shortsightedness or suffered harder for it than the New York Yankees. The club's stubborn refusal to stock its farm system with young black and Latin talent, more than anything else, caused the end of its long dominance of the game.

One Small Step

"I'm anxious to see one of the moon-rock samples the astronauts brought back. I'm sure there are a few of my home run balls in that crowd."
—Wilmer Mizell, former congressman and 1950s NL hurler

1960s OUTFIELD FIELDING AVERAGE	
1. Jim Piersall	.993
2. Don Demeter	.991
3. Ted Uhlaender	.991
4. Jim Landis	.990
5. Paul Blair	.989
6. Curt Flood	.989
7. Tommy Harper	.989
8. Vic Davalillo	.987
9. Bill Bruton	.987
10. Tony Gonzalez	.987
11. Ken Berry	.987
12. Gary Geiger	.986
13. Lenny Green	.986
14. Roger Maris	.986
15. Ty Cline	.986

The first team to win both the Most Valuable Player and Cy Young awards in back-to-back seasons was the Los Angeles Dodgers in 1962 and 1963. In 1962, Don Drysdale was the Cy Young Award recipient, and Maury Wills won the MVP trophy. In 1963, Sandy Koufax swept the awards. The first AL team to match this feat was the Brewers. Rollie Fingers swept the awards in 1981 and in 1982 Pete Vuckovich won the Cy Young Award and Robin Yount was the MVP.

In 1960, the Tigers and Indians engineered the only managerial trade in history when Detroit Skipper Jimmy Dykes came to Cleveland in return for Tribe pilot Joe Gordon.

Brosnan, Bouton Bull-Pen Baseball Books

Few of Jim Bouton's teammates in 1969 on the Seattle Pilots and the Houston Astros were aware that he was occupying himself in the bullpen by keeping a journal that would soon appear under the title of *Ball Four*. Bouton's sense of the absurd in the game and his irreverent exposé of the adolescent male egos that were both playing it and running it in 1969 was a joy to read for everyone but his former teammates. *Ball Four* followed in the footsteps of *The Long Season* and *Pennant Race*, two books by Jim Brosnan, a relief pitcher who broke the ground for Bouton nearly a decade earlier. When the first of Brosnan's books appeared, there was general amazement that a baseball player could write both wittily and coherently, to say nothing of the shock that one would actually tell the truth about the game and the men who played it.

When Brooks Robinson and Ken Boyer copped the two league MVP Awards in 1964, it marked the first season that two third sackers had copped both honors.

While serving as a Dodgers coach, Jim Gilliam observed: "There are some great ballplayers, but there aren't any superstars. Superstars you find on the moon."

Above: *Brooks Robinson (left) and Clete Boyer vied all during the 1960s for recognition as the game's best fielding third baseman. Boyer's older brother Ken was also in the running.*

"The charm of baseball is that, dull as it may be on the field, it is endlessly fascinating as a rehash."
—*Jim Murray, sportswriter*

On April 17, 1960, on the eve of the season opening, Cleveland swapped defending home run champion Rocky Colavito to Detroit for defending batting champion Harvey Kuenn.

1960s MANAGER WINS	
1. Walter Alston	878
2. Gene Mauch	698
3. Bill Rigney	658
4. Alvin Dark	640
5. Ralph Houk	610
6. Hank Bauer	594
7. Al Lopez	574
8. Sam Mele	524
9. Gil Hodges	494
10. Danny Murtaugh	456

1960s MANAGER WINNING PERCENTAGE	
1. Herman Franks	.567
2. Al Lopez	.558
3. Red Schoendienst	.554
4. Ralph Houk	.550
5. Chuck Dressen	.548
6. Walter Alston	.546
7. Sam Mele	.546
8. Fred Hutchinson	.545
9. Johnny Keane	.532
10. Dave Bristol	.529

In 1961, Cubs owner William Wrigley decided that the Bruins would be managed by eight coaches, a "College of Coaches."

When the Boston Red Sox leaped from ninth place in 1966 to first in 1967, it represented the biggest gain by a pennant winner since the 1898 and 1899 Brooklyn Superbas.

1960s TEAM WINS		
	WON	LOST
1. Baltimore-AL	911	698
2. San Francisco-NL	902	704
3. New York-AL	887	720
4. St.Louis-NL	884	718
5. Detroit-AL	882	729
6. Los Angeles-NL	878	729
7. Washington-Minnesota-AL	862	747
Wash. 1960-AL	*73*	*81*
Minn.-AL	*789*	*666*
8. Cincinnati-NL	860	742
9. Chicago-AL	852	760
10. Milwaukee-Atlanta-NL	851	753
Milwaukee-NL	*515*	*441*
Atlanta-NL	*336*	*312*
11. Pittsburgh-NL	848	755
12. Cleveland-AL	783	826
13. Boston-AL	764	845
14. Philadelphia-NL	759	843
15. Chicago-NL	735	868
16. Kansas City-Oakland-AL	686	922
KC A's-AL	*516*	*768*
Oakland-AL	*170*	*154*
17. Los Angeles-California-AL	685	770
Los Angeles-AL	*308*	*338*
California-AL	*377*	*432*
18. Wash. 1961-69-AL	607	844
19. Houston-NL	555	739
20. New York Mets-NL	494	799
21. Kansas City Royals-AL	69	93
22. Seattle Pilots-AL	64	98
23. San Diego-NL	52	110
24. Montreal-NL	52	110

The last member of the Cleveland Indians to finish as high as fifth in MVP voting was Luis Tiant, who tied for fifth in the balloting in 1968.

The National League elected to expand to 10 teams in 1961, placing franchises in New York and Houston.

Above: *Gene Mauch and the Phillies seemed certain to win a flag in 1964 but wound up playing the spoiler.*

In 1963, New York Yankee catcher Ellie Howard became the first black player to win the American League MVP.

In 1966, the White Sox allowed an AL record low 2.66 runs per game at home but could finish no better than fourth as Sox hitters batted just .231, the lowest batting average in the majors.

"Open up a ballplayer's head and you know what you'd find? A lot of broads and a jazz band."
—*Mayo Smith, manager and former player*

Ball Four

"You spend a good part of your life gripping a baseball, and in the end it turns out it was the other way around all the time."
—Jim Bouton

Robinson Swap Leaves Cincy Red-Faced

On November 30, 1959, shortly after restrictions on interleague trading were lifted, at least during the off-season, the Baltimore Orioles sent pitchers Billy O'Dell and Billy Loes to the San Francisco Giants for outfielder Jackie Brandt and two other players. The deal was considered a blockbuster when it was first made, but it was soon overshadowed by several other interleague swaps that had much greater repercussions. Among the more significant transactions between the two leagues in the early 1960s was one that took former bat titlist Harvey Kuenn from Cleveland to San Francisco for Johnny Antonelli and Willie Kirkland prior to the 1961 season and one that brought Jim Bunning from Detroit to the Phillies three years later. But probably no interleague deal will ever surpass in impact the December 1965 exchange between Baltimore and Cincinnati that gave the Orioles Frank Robinson for pitcher Milt Pappas and two lesser players. In his initial year with Baltimore, Robinson won the Triple Crown and sparked the Birds to their first AL pennant.

In 1968, the Player Relations Committee and the Players Association hammered out their first "Basic Agreement."

In 1960, Jim Brosnan wrote *The Long Season*, regarded as the best baseball book written by a player.

"You can't get rich sitting on the bench—but I'm giving it a try."
—Phil Linz, highly paid utility infielder

In 1968, Houston beat the Mets 1-0 in 24 innings on April 15, 1968, the longest 1-0 game in major league history.

1960s TEAM WINNING PERCENTAGE	
1. Baltimore-AL	.566
2. San Francisco-NL	.562
3. New York-AL	.552
4. St.Louis-NL	.552
5. Detroit-AL	.547
6. Los Angeles-NL	.546
7. Cincinnati-NL	.537
8. Washington-Minnesota-AL	.536
Washington 1960-AL	*.418*
Minnesota-AL	*.542*
9. Milwaukee-Atlanta-NL	.531
Milwaukee-NL	*.539*
Atlanta-NL	*.519*
10. Pittsburgh-NL	.529
11. Chicago-AL	.529
12. Cleveland-AL	.487
13. Boston-AL	.475
14. Washington 1961-69-AL	.474
15. Philadelphia-NL	.474
16. Los Angeles-California-AL	.471
Los Angeles-AL	*.477*
California-AL	*.466*
17. Chicago-NL	.459
18. Houston-NL	.429
19. Kansas City-Oakland-AL	.427
Kansas City A's-AL	*.402*
Oakland-AL	*.525*
20. Kansas City Royals-AL	.426
21. Seattle Pilots-AL	.395
22. New York Mets-NL	.382
23. San Diego-NL	.321
24. Montreal-NL	.321

Players Flourish in Both Leagues

Previous to the cessation of the ban on interleague trading, it was a rare player who accomplished something of significance in both major leagues during his career. Generally a player was waived from one circuit to the other only when, like Babe Ruth, he seemed near the end of the line, or, like Lew Burdette, before he had established himself. By the mid-1960s, though, many players had been swapped from one circuit to the other while at their peak. In 1963, after joining the Boston Red Sox, former Pirates first baseman Dick Stuart became the first player in history to hit 35 or more homers in a season in each major league. Frank Howard marked the beginning of the 1960s by being named the National League Rookie of the Year and the beginning of the 1970s by pacing the American League in homers and RBI. And in 1970, Jim Bunning became the first hurler in this century to win 100 or more games in each league.

The only athlete to play both pro football and major league baseball during the 1960s was Tom Brown, a member of both the Washington Senators and the NFL Green Bay Packers.

Prior to his death in 1969, John Hollison was the last surviving major league pitcher who threw from inside a rectangular box only 50 feet from home plate.

Above: *Dick Stuart was a minor league slugging great; in 1960, he shared Pittsburgh's first base job with Rocky Nelson, another minor league thumper.*

White Sox owner Bill Veeck in 1960 was the first owner to put player names on the backs of his team's uniforms. He also unveiled the first exploding scoreboard that year.

After topping Cleveland with 27 homers and 93 RBI in 1969, first sacker Tony Horton encountered mental problems the following year and never played again.

It's the Thought That Counts
"I was a bonus baby. I got two autographed baseballs and a scorecard from the 1935 All-Star Game."
—Bob Feller

Carew Cruises to Crown

Ted Williams hit .406 in 1941 and George Brett hovered around the .400 mark for much of the 1980 season before finishing at .390. But Williams, who received tons of walks, had only 456 at bats and Brett, owing to a stint on the disabled list, came to bat officially just 449 times. Since 1930, only once has a player made a serious bid to hit .400 while collecting far more than the minimum number of plate appearances to qualify for a batting title. In 1977, Rod Carew of the Twins sizzled to a .388 mark with 239 hits in 616 at bats. Carew's performance was tarnished somewhat by the fact that 1977 was an expansion year in the American League, with the addition of two new teams in Toronto and Seattle. On the plus side, his .388 figure exceeded the league average of .266 by 122 points, a staggering amount in the current era when few batting titlists outhit the average player in their loop by even a 100 point margin. The following year Carew won his eighth and last batting title with a .333 average.

In 1972, Rod Carew of the Twins was the first batting crown winner to go homerless since Zach Wheat in 1918.

In 1972, Rod Carew (above) won the American League batting title while compiling just 203 total bases, the fewest ever by a batting leader with over 500 at bats. In contrast, Billy Williams, the 1972 National League hitting champ, bagged 348 total bases.

In 1977, the Dodgers became the first team in history with four 30-homer men—Ron Cey, Steve Garvey, Dusty Baker, and Reggie Smith.

Rod Carew received 4 million All-Star votes in 1977 to set a major league record.

Earl Williams of the Braves, a catcher-third baseman, set a rookie record for both catchers and infielders when he crushed 33 home runs in 1971.

1970s GAMES	
1. Pete Rose	1,604
2. Graig Nettles	1,557
3. Sal Bando	1,527
4. Bobby Murcer	1,500
5. Larry Bowa	1,489
6. Carl Yastrzemski	1,479
Bobby Bonds	1,479
8. Tony Perez	1,471
9. Lee May	1,464
10. Amos Otis	1,462
11. Joe Morgan	1,458
12. Reggie Jackson	1,440
13. Al Oliver	1,438
14. George Scott	1,437
15. Johnny Bench	1,435
16. Rusty Staub	1,433
17. Ted Simmons	1,412
18. Ken Singleton	1,405
19. Mark Belanger	1,402
20. Aurelio Rodriguez	1,400
Lou Brock	1,400
22. Thurman Munson	1,397
23. Roy White	1,393
Bob Watson	1,393
25. Willie Montanez	1,373

In 1974, the Chicago White Sox led the American League in home runs for the first time.

"Babe Ruth will always be No. 1. Before I broke his home run record it was the greatest of all. Then I broke it and suddenly the greatest record is Joe DiMaggio's hitting streak."
—Hank Aaron

Giants Taken in Trades

The player who posted the highest single-season home run and RBI totals during the 1970s and the first pitcher to win a Cy Young Award in each league began the 1970s as teammates with the San Francisco Giants. Unfortunately for the Giants, both had moved on to other teams by the time they accomplished their feats, and in return for them the Bay Area club received next to nothing. In 1977, at Cincinnati, George Foster amassed 52 dingers and 149 ribbies. In May of 1971, the future home run and RBI king was shipped to the Reds for pitcher Vern Geishert and shortstop Frank Duffy. Geishert never threw a single pitch in Giants livery; Duffy had time to appear in only 21 games with San Francisco before he was packaged with Gaylord Perry at the end of the 1971 season and tossed Cleveland's way for sore-armed Sam McDowell. Sudden Sam had only nine wins left in him, a mere 170 less than Perry would accumulate in the years ahead along with his two Cy Young trophies. With these two deals the Giants solidified their reputation, begun in the 1960s, for being everyone's patsy in the trade mart.

In 1976, Atlanta left fielder Jim Wynn hit just .207 but nevertheless led the club in runs, RBI, and home runs.

In 1979, Dave Winfield and Gene Tenace combined to hit 54 of the Padres' 93 home runs.

Above: *George Foster was not an instant star after coming to Cincinnati in a 1971 deal with the Giants; his maturation did not really begin until 1975.*

Bobby Bonds set an Angels' club record for the most home runs by a righthanded batter when he clubbed 37 dingers in 1977.

Oakland's Gene Tenace hit back-to-back home runs in the 1972 World Series in his first two fall classic at bats.

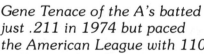

Gene Tenace of the A's batted just .211 in 1974 but paced the American League with 110 walks, as he collected eight more free passes than he did base hits.

Bull Market
"I came to the Braves on business, and I intended to see that business was good as long as I could."
—Hank Aaron

George Foster had only 79 career home runs in nearly 2,000 at bats before he blasted 52 dingers for the Reds in 1977.

After hitting .204 the previous year with just seven homers and 36 RBI, Willie McCovey rebounded in 1977 to bat .280 for the Giants with 28 homers and 86 RBI.

The Dodgers began the 1970s by finishing last in the National League in home runs and ended the decade by pacing the loop with 183 four-baggers in 1979.

1970s RUNS	
1. Pete Rose	1,068
2. Bobby Bonds	1,020
3. Joe Morgan	1,005
4. Amos Otis	861
5. Carl Yastrzemski	845
6. Lou Brock	843
7. Rod Carew	837
8. Reggie Jackson	833
9. Bobby Murcer	816
10. Johnny Bench	792
11. Cesar Cedeno	777
12. Reggie Smith	776
13. Graig Nettles	773
14. Al Oliver	767
15. Sal Bando	759
16. Roy White	752
17. Tony Perez	740
18. Rusty Staub	732
19. Larry Bowa	725
20. George Scott	724
21. Willie Stargell	719
22. Ralph Garr	703
23. Ken Singleton	701
24. Bert Campaneris	700
25. Dave Cash	699

Johnson Fails to Utilize Talent

Fans in every city where Alex Johnson played came out in droves just to watch him take batting practice. In pregame drills, he always looked as if he was ready to go 4-for-4, and some days he actually did. He hit over .300 two years in a row, with the 1968 and '69 Reds. In 1970, Johnson became the only member of the California Angels franchise ever to win an American League batting title, when he hit .329. At the time he was spending his first season in Anaheim after having played for three National League teams. The surly and self-centered Johnson would remain with the Angels for one more year before beginning an odyssey that would take him to four other AL teams in the next five seasons. With each move the quality of his play grew more lackadaisical and his stats declined. After winning the AL bat crown, Johnson never again hit anywhere near .300. He played for seven ballclubs and had a career .288 batting average. But he continued to look great in batting practice.

Stan Musial was the only living member of the 3,000-hit club when Hank Aaron made his 3,000th hit. Musial said: "It was getting awfully lonely. Congratulations, Henry."

In 1973, the Atlanta Braves had three players with at least 40 homers—Dave Johnson (43), Darrell Evans (41), and Hank Aaron (40).

Among the multitude of distinctions Hank Aaron (above) holds is being the first player in major league history to begin and end a career of 20 or more seasons in a Milwaukee uniform.

In 1973, Hank Aaron set a record for the most home runs (40) by a player who collected fewer than 400 at bats.

After hitting 124 homers among them for the Braves in 1973, Hank Aaron, Darrell Evans, and Davey Johnson combined for just 60 four-baggers in 1974.

Fore!

"It took me 17 years to get 3,000 hits in baseball. I did it in one afternoon at the golf course."
—Hank Aaron

1970s HITS	
1. Pete Rose	2,045
2. Rod Carew	1,787
3. Al Oliver	1,686
4. Lou Brock	1,617
5. Bobby Bonds	1,565
6. Tony Perez	1,560
7. Larry Bowa	1,552
8. Ted Simmons	1,550
9. Amos Otis	1,549
10. Bobby Murcer	1,548
11. Ralph Garr	1,546
12. Thurman Munson	1,536
13. Bob Watson	1,507
14. Carl Yastrzemski	1,492
15. Rusty Staub	1,487
16. George Scott	1,475
17. Steve Garvey	1,469
18. Dave Cash	1,464
19. Lee May	1,461
20. Joe Morgan	1,451
21. Graig Nettles	1,441
22. Willie Montanez	1,437
23. Cesar Cedeno	1,422
24. Reggie Jackson	1,410
25. Johnny Bench	1,396

Carty Battles Knee and TB to DH

The National League batting titlist in 1970, Rico Carty of the Atlanta Braves, also never again approached the hitting form he displayed that season. In Carty's case, though, the reason was physical rather than psychological. Tuberculosis compounded by a severe knee injury caused Carty to miss the entire 1971 season and held him to just 82 games the following year. Lacking the mobility to play the outfield any longer, he was then traded by the Braves to Texas in the American League, which had just adopted the designated hitter rule. But Carty's knee was still so shaky that he could not handle even a DH role. Not until late in the 1974 campaign, after being picked up by Cleveland, did he start to regain the form that had made him a .322 career hitter prior to his illness and injury. Carty served as a regular DH for five seasons before retiring in 1979 with a .299 average.

Hank Aaron slugged a major league record 715th career homer on April 8, 1974, off Al Downing of the Dodgers.

In 1974, Hank Aaron defeated Japanese slugger Sadaharu Oh 10-9 in a specially arranged home run contest in Tokyo.

In 1979, the Houston Astros hit just 49 home runs and were led by outfielder Jose Cruz with nine four-baggers.

Above: *Rusty Staub joined Houston as a 19-year-old and left the game as a 41-year-old. He was the second player in baseball to homer before age 20 and after age 40 (after Ty Cobb). Staub was the first player to collect 500 hits for four teams.*

1970s TOTAL BASES	
1. Pete Rose	2,804
2. Bobby Bonds	2,762
3. Tony Perez	2,627
4. Reggie Jackson	2,604
5. Johnny Bench	2,566
6. Al Oliver	2,564
7. Lee May	2,535
8. Bobby Murcer	2,455
9. Graig Nettles	2,441
10. Willie Stargell	2,440
11. Amos Otis	2,418
12. George Scott	2,414
13. Carl Yastrzemski	2,383
14. Ted Simmons	2,370
15. Rod Carew	2,368
16. Rusty Staub	2,358
17. Reggie Smith	2,355
18. Joe Morgan	2,339
19. Bob Watson	2,272
20. Steve Garvey	2,258
21. Cesar Cedeno	2,252
22. Sal Bando	2,228
23. Thurman Munson	2,160
24. Ken Singleton	2,153
25. Willie Montanez	2,139

After signed by the Phils as a free agent, Pete Rose said: "With all the money I'm making, I should be playing two positions."

Giants outfielder Bobby Bonds fanned 189 times in 1970 to set a major league record that still stands.

Giant Bobby Bonds in 1973 just missed becoming the first "40-40" player in major league history, when he hit 39 homers and swiped 43 bases.

In 1978, Giants outfielder Bobby Bonds earned membership in the 30-30 club (30 homers and 30 steals) for a major league record fifth time.

In 1975, Leroy Stanton led the Angels with 14 home runs and was the only player on the club with more than six dingers.

When Willie Horton compiled 29 homers as Seattle's designated hitter in 1979, it marked his highest four-bagger total since 1968.

In 1977, his first year in the National League after being traded to the Braves by Texas, Jeff Burroughs was the senior loop runner-up for the home run crown with 41.

Sanguillen, Simmons Strive for Stick Summit

No catcher has won a batting crown since 1942, but during the 1970s, the National League had two receivers who made a serious bid to end the long drought. In 1970, Manny Sanguillen of the Pirates hit .325 to tie for the second-best average in the loop. Five years later, Sanguillen finished third in the NL bat race with a .328 mark. Four points ahead of him at .332 was Ted Simmons, the Cardinals' switch-hitting back-stopper. He also was in the top five with 193 base hits. Simmons made a second run at the NL hitting title in 1977 before finishing at .318, some 20 points behind champion Dave Parker. Although he never again hit .300 after 1975, Sanguillen retired in 1980 with a .296 career average, the sixth highest mark in history by a receiver. He batted over .300 in four seasons. A string of poor seasons near the end of his career dropped Simmons's average to .285, but he nonetheless remains the top switch-hitting catcher in history. He batted over .300 in seven seasons.

Ted Simmons of the Cardinals set an all-time season record for catchers when he logged 193 hits in 1975.

As a rookie in 1977, Mitchell Page led the Oakland A's in batting (.301) and RBI (75) and was second on the club in homers with 21.

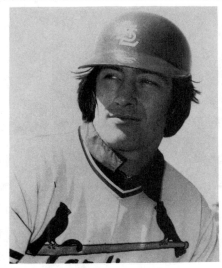

Above: *Ted Simmons was the National League's top offensive-minded catcher during the 1970s.*

The longest hitting streak in the American League during the 1970s was Ron LeFlore's 30-game skein in 1976.

No member of the Houston Astros has ever won the NL batting crown and only one, Cesar Cedeno in 1973, has finished as high as second in hitting.

In 1972, Bobby Murcer (who later became a Yankees broadcaster) paced the American League in runs with 102 and total bases with 314 for the Bronx Bombers.

"The only way I can't hit .300 is if there is something physically wrong with me."
—*Pete Rose*

1970s DOUBLES	
1. Pete Rose	394
2. Al Oliver	320
3. Tony Perez	303
4. Ted Simmons	299
5. Cesar Cedeno	292
6. Amos Otis	286
7. Hal McRae	285
8. Joe Morgan	275
9. Reggie Jackson	270
10. Willie Montanez	266
11. Johnny Bench	264
12. Rusty Staub	263
13. Bobby Bonds	255
14. Willie Stargell	253
15. Chris Chambliss	252
16. Joe Rudi	251
17. Bob Watson	250
18. Steve Garvey	248
19. Carl Yastrzemski	247
Reggie Smith	247
21. Lou Brock	243
22. Rod Carew	241
23. George Scott	239
Garry Maddox	239
25. Bobby Murcer	237

After winning the NL batting title in 1970, Rico Carty was idled all of the following season and was never again able to play regularly except as a designated hitter.

When Rico Carty hit safely in 31 straight games in 1970, it was the longest hit skein by a righthanded hitter in the National League since 1922.

In 1979, Garry Templeton of the Cardinals became the first switch-hitter to collect 100 hits in a season from each side of the plate.

'70s AL Receivers Swing Sweet Sticks

Eighth on the list for the highest career batting average by a catcher is Thurman Munson at .292. The Yankees backstopper finished among the top-five hitters in the American League just once, in 1975, but prior to his death in 1979 he bettered .300 on five occasions, the most by any AL catcher since World War II. Carlton Fisk, while never the hitter for average that Munson was, ranked as the AL's equivalent to Johnny Bench as a slugging receiver during the 1970s. In 1977, his finest all-around season, Fisk stood seventh in the AL when he hit .315 to go with his 26 homers and 102 RBI. The receiver who might have been the AL's best-hitting backstopper of all during the 1970s if not for an injury was Ray Fosse. In 1970, his first full season with Cleveland, Fosse was batting well over .300 before being sent to the disabled list after a bone-crunching All-Star game home-plate collision with Pete Rose. Even though he held his average at .307 in 1970, Fosse was never again able to generate the same power.

Before being killed in a 1979 private plane crash, Thurman Munson (above) was on course to compile some of the best career stats of any catcher in baseball history. At the time of his death, Munson was in the process of learning to play both first base and the outfield in an effort to save his legs.

1970s TRIPLES		
1.	Rod Carew	80
2.	Larry Bowa	74
3.	George Brett	73
4.	Roger Metzger	71
5.	Willie Davis	70
6.	Pete Rose	64
	Ralph Garr	64
8.	Al Oliver	63
9.	Mickey Rivers	61
10.	Lou Brock	56
11.	Don Kessinger	55
12.	Amos Otis	53
	Garry Maddox	53
	Dave Cash	53
15.	Garry Templeton	52
16.	Manny Sanguillen	51
	Dave Parker	51
	Bobby Bonds	51
19.	Jim Rice	49
20.	Joe Morgan	47
	Jose Cruz	47
	Cesar Cedeno	47
23.	Bill Russell	46
	Freddie Patek	46
25.	Cesar Geronimo	45

Terrifying
Willie McCovey, when asked how he'd recommend pitchers pitch to him, responded: "I'd walk me."

In 1979, catcher Brian Downing of the Angels finished third in the American League in batting with a .326 mark.

Catfish Hunter, a team-mate of Reggie Jackson's on both the A's and the Yankees, said that Jackson would "give you the shirt off his back. Of course, he'd call a press conference to announce it."

In 1979, the American League leader in both walks and on-base percentage was catcher Darrell Porter of Kansas City.

Vada Pinson is the only player who retired with more than 2,750 hits and is not at present in the Hall of Fame.

1970s HOME RUNS

1.	Willie Stargell	296
2.	Reggie Jackson	292
3.	Johnny Bench	290
4.	Bobby Bonds	280
5.	Lee May	270
6.	Graig Nettles	252
	Dave Kingman	252
8.	Mike Schmidt	235
9.	Tony Perez	226
10.	Reggie Smith	225
11.	Willie McCovey	207
12.	George Scott	206
13.	Greg Luzinski	204
14.	Carl Yastrzemski	202
15.	George Foster	201
	Hank Aaron	201
17.	Bobby Murcer	198
	John Mayberry	198
19.	Sal Bando	195
20.	Rusty Staub	184
	Darrell Evans	184
22.	Jeff Burroughs	183
23.	Billy Williams	177
24.	Willie Horton	176
25.	Dick Allen	174

Torre! Torre! Torre!

Few players have performed as regulars at three different positions during their careers. Fewer still have posted 100-RBI seasons as regulars at three different positions. Only one, Joe Torre, has achieved it with catcher among his three positions. After two 100-RBI campaigns as a backstopper with the Braves, Torre was swapped to the Cardinals in 1969 and converted to a first baseman. He promptly rang up 101 ribbies. In 1971, the Cards moved Torre to third base and saw him have the finest all-around season of any National League player during the decade when he stroked .363 and added 230 hits and 137 RBI. He also had 24 homers, a .424 on-base average, and a .555 slugging percentage. Torre's monster year earned him the MVP Award by a comfortable margin over slugger Willie Stargell, whose 48 homers led the majors. In his first year at the hot corner, Torre also led all NL third sackers in putouts.

The last player to top the NL in both batting average and slugging average in the same season was Dave Parker of the Pittsburgh Pirates in 1978.

The last NL player to top the major leagues in both batting average and slugging percentage in the same season was Billy Williams of the Cubs in 1972.

Above: *Joe Torre ranks among the finest hitting catchers of all time. He served principally as a backstopper in nine of his 18 seasons and topped 100 RBI in three of them. He had a high of 109 RBI in 1964, when he also hit .321 for the Braves.*

In 1970, seven players in the majors collected 200 or more hits, led by Billy Williams and Pete Rose with 205 each.

Billy Williams of the Chicago Cubs scored the most runs in a single season of any player during the 1970s when he led the National League in 1970 with 137 tallies.

Count Your Lucky Stars

"I don't want to be a hero. I don't want to be a star. It just works out that way."
—Reggie Jackson

Yearling Lynn Wins MVP

Frosh players generally fare poorly in MVP balloting regardless of how sensational their yearling campaigns are. In 1964, when he led the American League in batting and total bases as a rookie, Tony Oliva finished a distant fourth on the MVP list. All leading the majors with 49 homers as a frosh in 1987 brought Mark McGwire was the sixth spot at MVP time. In 1975, however, Fred Lynn of the Red Sox had an inaugural season so sensational that he forced AL writers to break with tradition and vote him the MVP prize. Lynn's credentials included a .331 average (second in the AL), the loop's top slugging average of .566, and 105 RBI (only four behind leader George Scott). In addition, Lynn manned center field, a trouble spot for the Red Sox in 1974, and was instrumental in bringing the AL pennant to Boston. He finished with 326 points in the MVP voting, more than twice the total of runner-up John Mayberry.

"I'd rather hit than have sex."

—Reggie Jackson

In 1970, Chicago Cubs outfielder Billy Williams set an NL record when he played in his 1,117th consecutive game.

In 1975, Dave Cash of the Phillies set a single-season major league record with 699 at bats.

Above: *Fred Lynn foreshadowed his 1975 rookie year by batting .419 with two homers and 10 RBI in 1974 during a 15-game stint with Boston.*

The last player to average 50 or more at bats per strikeout in a season was Dave Cash of the Phils, who fanned just 13 times in 666 at bats in 1976.

In 1972, San Diego Padre Nate Colbert drove home 13 teammates during a doubleheader to break a big league record; he had five homers during the twin bill to tie a major league record.

In 1979, Keith Hernandez of the Cardinals set a National League mark for first basemen by compiling 48 doubles.

1970s RUNS BATTED IN	
1. Johnny Bench	1,013
2. Tony Perez	954
3. Lee May	936
4. Reggie Jackson	922
5. Willie Stargell	906
6. Rusty Staub	860
7. Bobby Bonds	856
8. Carl Yastrzemski	846
9. Bobby Murcer	840
10. Graig Nettles	831
11. Ted Simmons	828
12. Bob Watson	822
13. Al Oliver	812
Sal Bando	812
15. George Scott	802
16. Greg Luzinski	755
17. Amos Otis	753
18. Reggie Smith	750
19. Steve Garvey	736
20. Willie Montanez	730
21. John Mayberry	724
22. Joe Morgan	720
23. Ken Singleton	715
24. Joe Rudi	696
25. Thurman Munson	692

Lynn Wins, but Rice Also Nice

Third in the American League MVP balloting in 1975 was a second rookie. Even more remarkable, he too played for the Red Sox—and right beside center fielder Fred Lynn. In left field for Boston in 1975, replacing incumbent Juan Beniquez, was Jim Rice, a Triple Crown winner the previous year with Pawtucket of the Triple-A International League (.337 average, 25 homers, 97 RBI). Rice was the minor loop's Most Valuable Player. Ironically Lynn also played with Pawtucket in

1974 but did not particularly distinguish himself (.282 average, 21 homers, 68 RBI). It was Rice who was regarded by the Red Sox in the spring of 1975 as their rookie prize, and he in no way disappointed Hub followers. His frosh season was, in fact, the second best of the decade, with a .309 average, 22 home runs, and 102 RBI. Rice's misfortune was that his teammate chose that same year to have one of the best yearling campaigns ever. Rice would become AL MVP in 1978.

1970s STOLEN BASES	
1. Lou Brock	551
2. Joe Morgan	488
3. Cesar Cedeno	427
4. Bobby Bonds	380
5. Davey Lopes	375
6. Freddie Patek	344
7. Bert Campaneris	336
8. Billy North	324
9. Amos Otis	294
Ron LeFlore	294
11. Rod Carew	253
12. Larry Bowa	251
13. Frank Taveras	248
14. Don Baylor	240
15. Mickey Rivers	226
16. Dave Concepcion	220
17. Omar Moreno	217
18. Tommy Harper	200
19. Garry Maddox	193
20. Pat Kelly	192
21. Reggie Jackson	183
22. Jose Cruz	180
Jose Cardenal	180
24. Sandy Alomar	171
25. Ralph Garr	170

In 1978, Boston slugger Jim Rice (above) topped the American League in RBI, homers, triples, hits, total bases, and slugging.

"If I'm hitting, I can hit anyone. If not, my 12-year-old son can get me out."
—Willie Stargell

The last player to collect 400 or more total bases in a season was Boston's Jim Rice, who netted 406 in 1978.

Manny Mota, an NL outfielder from 1962 to 1982, not only holds the record for the most career pinch hits with 150 but also the mark for the highest batting average (.297) among players with at least 100 career pinch hits.

Above: *Hal McRae, loser of the controversial 1976 American League bat title, tagged a Royals' record 54 doubles in 1977.*

The first player to collect 100 career pinch hits in the AL was Gates Brown, who played with Detroit from 1963 to 1975 and retired with 108 pinch safeties.

Jose Morales of the Expos set a major league record that still stands when he rapped 25 pinch hits in 1975.

1970s WALKS		
1.	Joe Morgan	1,071
2.	Carl Yastrzemski	888
	Ken Singleton	888
4.	Darrell Evans	828
5.	Sal Bando	817
6.	Gene Tenace	805
7.	Pete Rose	783
8.	Bobby Murcer	744
9.	Bobby Bonds	738
10.	Jim Wynn	733
11.	John Mayberry	724
12.	Roy White	720
13.	Rusty Staub	709
14.	Mike Schmidt	689
15.	Johnny Bench	687
16.	Reggie Jackson	677
17.	Willie McCovey	660
18.	Graig Nettles	656
19.	Toby Harrah	640
20.	Bobby Grich	628
21.	Reggie Smith	621
22.	Jeff Burroughs	611
23.	Amos Otis	605
24.	Rick Monday	604
25.	Ron Cey	599

Brett Shaves McRae with Gift Hit

In 1910, Nap Lajoie won the American League batting title when rookie St. Louis Browns third baseman Red Corriden was instructed to play deep on the last day of the season and allow Lajoie to bunt at will for hits. Joe DiMaggio nearly won the Pacific Coast League hitting crown in 1935 on a similar gift. No batting chase, nonetheless, in either major league or minor league history was ever decided in a more disputed fashion than the American League race in 1976. George Brett of the Kansas City Royals won out by a single point—.333 to .332—over teammate Hal McRae. Twins outfielder Steve Brye allowed a routine fly ball hit by Brett to fall safely on Brett's final at bat of the season. Brye made only a token disclaimer that he'd deliberately thrown the bat title to Brett. Brye justified his maneuver by maintaining that Brett, a third baseman, was more deserving of the crown, than McRae, a designated hitter who played only 31 games in the field in 1976.

The Giants hoped Bill Madlock (above) would end the hex that plagued hitters in Candlestick Park when they acquired him in 1977. Madlock's best year at the Stick was 1978 when he batted .309. Later he won two more hitting titles with Pittsburgh. The 1992 season ended with the Giants still looking for their first bat leader since moving to San Francisco.

Merv Rettenmund of the Padres set a major league record in 1977 with 86 plate appearances as a pinch hitter.

In 1974, Ed Kranepool of the Mets hit a major league record .486 as a pinch hitter with 17 hits in 35 pinch at bats.

Cardinal outfielder Vic Davalillo in 1970 tied a major league record with 24 pinch hits.

Johnny Bench revealed his hitting success, calling it: "Inner conceit. It's knowing within yourself you can meet any situation."

Madlock Wins Second Crown at Third

Like the AL race, the National League batting chase also went right down to the wire in 1976 before Bill Madlock of the Cubs emerged triumphant on the final day of the season. Madlock, Chicago's third baseman, won by three points over Cincinnati's Ken Griffey. Madlock's .339 mark was down 15 points from his .354 figure the previous year, which brought him the first of what would be four hitting crowns before he finished. His 1976 batting title also made him the first third baseman in major league history to win more than one. Madlock has since been joined in this select company by George Brett and Wade Boggs. When both Madlock and Brett won in 1976, it marked the first season that the batting crown in each major league had been captured by a third sacker. Madlock enjoys yet another distinction. He and Roberto Clemente are the only two righthanded hitters since Rogers Hornsby to win four batting titles.

In 1979, Philadelphia Phillie outfielder Del Unser slugged home runs in three consecutive pinch-hit plate appearances.

In 1974, the Chicago White Sox for the first time in history led the AL in home runs with 135.

In 1974, Pittsburgh's Richie Zisk notched 21 RBI in a 10-game span.

Willie Stargell, when told Dave Parker had called him his idol, said: "That's pretty good, considering that Dave's previous idol was himself."

In 1976, the Cincinnati Reds won their second consecutive world championship despite leaving an NL-record 1,328 men on base.

The 1979 Houston Astros were the last team in the major leagues to hit more triples (52) than home runs (49).

1970s STRIKEOUTS		
1.	Bobby Bonds	1,368
2.	Reggie Jackson	1,247
3.	Lee May	1,148
4.	Willie Stargell	1,100
5.	Dave Kingman	1,095
6.	Tony Perez	1,090
7.	Greg Luzinski	998
8.	George Scott	985
9.	Mike Schmidt	958
10.	Rick Monday	947
11.	Johnny Bench	896
12.	Doug Rader	870
13.	Ken Singleton	857
14.	Gene Tenace	846
15.	Jeff Burroughs	815
16.	Lou Brock	784
17.	Nate Colbert	752
18.	Larry Hisle	748
19.	George Foster	740
20.	Willie Horton	728
21.	Bobby Grich	727
22.	Graig Nettles	717
23.	Dick Allen	705
24.	Jim Wynn	699
25.	Sal Bando	698

Gloveless

In 1973, the 12 American League clubs then in existence, after voting unanimously in favor of the designated-hitter rule, used designated hitters for pitchers for the first time in major league history. The National League disdained the rule and refused to go along with it. Interestingly, however, the notion of a designated hitter was first proposed in 1928 by National League president John Heydler; NL owners were all for it, but the proposal died a quick death when American League moguls roundly vetoed it. The introduction of the DH rule in 1973 immediately gave new life to such players as Tony Oliva, Orlando Cepeda, Frank Robinson, Carlos May, and Tommy Davis, all of whom were too crippled to play regularly in the field. The new position also provided a home for others like Hal McRae, whose fielding was so suspect it made them a liability anywhere but with a bat in their hands.

In 1971, the San Diego Padres became the last team to date to score fewer than 500 runs (486) in a season when a full schedule of games was played.

By fanning 123 times in 1971, Willie Mays set an all-time record for the most strikeouts by a 40-year-old player.

On April 6, 1973, Yankee Ron Blomberg became the first designated hitter to bat in a major league game.

A .248 career batting average will in all likelihood shut the Hall of Fame door to Graig Nettles (above), but there have been few better all-around third basemen. His glove and long-ball bat served the Yankees for 11 seasons and helped the club to cop four pennants during his sojourn.

Prior to 1985, the New York Mets had just one player in their 23-year history who collected as many as 100 RBI in a season—Rusty Staub with 105 in 1975.

Forest For the Trees
John Candelaria, when told by Pirates teammate Dave Parker that he was a vegetarian, asked: "What do you eat, redwoods?"

1970s BATTING AVERAGE	
1. Rod Carew	.343
2. Bill Madlock	.320
3. Dave Parker	.317
4. Pete Rose	.314
5. Manny Mota	.313
6. Jim Rice	.310
7. George Brett	.310
8. Ken Griffey	.310
9. Fred Lynn	.309
10. Ralph Garr	.307
11. Steve Garvey	.304
12. Joe Torre	.303
13. Al Oliver	.303
14. Bob Watson	.301
15. Tony Oliva	.299
16. Bake McBride	.298
17. Greg Gross	.298
18. Lou Brock	.298
19. Ted Simmons	.297
20. Ron LeFlore	.297
21. Manny Sanguillen	.297
22. Cecil Cooper	.296
23. Garry Maddox	.293
24. Rico Carty	.293
25. Mike Hargrove	.292

Kaline Designates 3,000th

In 1973, the Detroit Tigers made Gates Brown their first regular designated hitter. Brown, so indifferent an outfielder that he had previously been employed mostly as a pinch hitter, flopped in his new role, hitting just .236 in 125 games. His failure enabled the Tigers to turn the job over to Al Kaline in 1974 without any qualms. Nearing 3,000 hits, Kaline opted to play one more year in an effort to reach the coveted figure when he was given the DH assignment. By collecting 146 hits in 1974 to put him over the top and allow him to retire with 3,007 lifetime base hits, Kaline became the first player the DH rule permitted to reach a significant career milestone stat that otherwise might have eluded him. There have been numerous others in the years since, including George Brett—whose quest for 3,000 hits has been made possible by the DH rule. Whether career attainments like Kaline's and Brett's should be viewed with a certain amount of cynicism is still a subject of debate.

Curt Gowdy announced about Brooks Robinson: "Brooks is not a fast man, but his arms and legs move very quickly."

In 1971, Enzo Hernandez of the Padres set a record for the fewest RBI by a player with 500 or more at bats when he knocked home just 12 runs in 549 at bats.

Above: *Al Oliver compiled 2,743 hits, 1,326 RBI, and a .303 career batting average over 18 seasons between 1968 and 1985.*

In 1978, Pirates outfielder Omar Moreno fanned 104 times but had just two home runs; he stole 71 bases but hit just .235.

In 1978, Pete Rose became the first switch-hitter to earn his 3,000th career base hit.

In 1974, Cincinnati's Pete Rose made a major league-record 771 plate appearances.

Pete Rose in 1978 set a modern National League record by hitting in 44 consecutive games.

1970s SLUGGING AVERAGE	
1. Willie Stargell	.555
2. Jim Rice	.552
3. Hank Aaron	.527
4. Fred Lynn	.526
5. Dave Parker	.521
6. George Foster	.517
7. Dick Allen	.513
8. Mike Schmidt	.511
9. Reggie Jackson	.508
10. Reggie Smith	.507
11. Dave Kingman	.504
12. Greg Luzinski	.493
13. Johnny Bench	.491
14. Billy Williams	.491
15. Carlton Fisk	.484
16. Bobby Bonds	.483
17. Frank Robinson	.483
18. Willie McCovey	.478
19. Tony Perez	.478
20. Bill Robinson	.476
21. George Brett	.475
22. Andy Thornton	.475
23. Steve Garvey	.468
24. Richie Zisk	.467
25. Cecil Cooper	.467

Cincy's Scoring Apparatus a Hit

When the Cincinnati Reds outscored every other team in the National League by at least 105 runs in 1975, rival NL clubs were hopeful it was just a momentary show of offensive force. But the Reds proceeded to tally 857 runs in 1976, 232 more than any of the other five teams in their division and at least a run a game more than every other team in the National League but the Phillies. The offensive deluge earned Sparky Anderson's Cincinnati club the nickname "The Big Red Machine." Anderson had under his command in the mid-1970s three almost certain Hall of Famers in Joe Morgan, Pete Rose, and Johnny Bench, plus four other players—Tony Perez, Dave Concepcion, George Foster, and Ken Griffey—who would also put up numbers before they retired that merited Cooperstown consideration. The Reds' only regular in 1975 and '76 who was something less than an All-Star was center fielder Cesar Geronimo, but even he was hardly a weak link. In 1975, Geronimo led all National League gardeners in putouts and double plays. The following year he hit .307, joining with Griffey and Foster to give the Reds an all-.300-hitting outfield.

Four of the six key members of the "Big Red Machine" in the mid-1970s were, from left: Tony Perez, Johnny Bench, Joe Morgan, and Pete Rose. Missing are George Foster and Ken Griffey.

1970s ON-BASE AVERAGE	
1. Rod Carew	.411
2. Joe Morgan	.408
3. Mike Hargrove	.404
4. Ken Singleton	.401
5. Pete Rose	.391
6. Bernie Carbo	.390
7. Gene Tenace	.389
8. Carl Yastrzemski	.388
9. Fred Lynn	.387
10. Merv Rettenmund	.384
11. Bill Madlock	.384
12. Greg Gross	.380
13. Dick Allen	.379
14. Frank Robinson	.379
15. Ken Griffey	.379
16. Ron Fairly	.379
17. Reggie Smith	.378
18. Mike Schmidt	.378
19. Boog Powell	.377
20. Willie Stargell	.377
21. Joe Torre	.376
22. Manny Mota	.376
23. Hank Aaron	.376
24. Andy Thornton	.375
25. Billy Williams	.375

Plastic
Dick Allen said about artificial turf: "If a horse can't eat it, then I don't like it."

Melton Dissolves ChiSox Pale Homer History

The Chicago White Sox began the 1971 campaign as the only major league franchise in existence since 1901 that had never had a home run champion. By the end of that season, third baseman Bill Melton had removed that stigma from the Pale Hose. Melton's 33 dingers gave him the American League crown by a margin of one over Detroit's Norm Cash and Reggie Jackson of the A's. Prior to 1971, no White Sox player had ever finished higher than third in the AL home run derby, and only three had ranked that high. The trio were Eddie Robinson in 1951, Jack Fournier in 1914, and Ping Bodie in 1913. In 1951, Gus Zernial had given the Sox a minuscule claim on a home run crown when he won the honor with the A's after beginning the season in Chicago. But Zernial had played only four games before exiting from the Windy City and departed with no home runs. Braggo Roth, on the other hand, hit three of his AL-leading seven homers in 1915 for the Sox before being swapped to Cleveland.

Enzo Hernandez and Don Mason, the Padres two regular keystone performers in 1971, between them accounted for just 23 RBI.

In 1976, both of the Houston Astros keystone operatives, Rob Andrews and Roger Metzger, went homerless for the entire season.

En route to 563 career dingers, Reggie Jackson (above) won four American League home run crowns with three different teams— Oakland, New York, and California. He also paced the junior loop in slugging average in 1976, his lone season with Baltimore.

Reggie Jackson in the 1977 World Series earned the nickname "Mr. October." He had four home runs in four straight official times at bat, including three in game six.

In 1971, Bill Melton became the first member of the Chicago White Sox to lead the AL in home runs; the following year Dick Allen became the second Sox player to do it.

Roger Angell said Joe Morgan "has the conviction that he should affect the outcome of every game he plays in every time he comes up to bat and every time he gets on base."

In 1977, Duane Kuiper hit his only home run in 3,379 at bats in the majors and also topped 200 total bases for the lone time in his 12-year career.

Bobby Knoop retired in 1972 with a .236 career batting average, the lowest in history by a second baseman with 3,000 or more at bats.

The New York Mets gave up on weak-hitting shortstop Tim Foli in 1979, only to see him hit .291 for the Pirates and pace the National League in fewest strikeouts by a batter with 14.

1970s ON-BASE PLUS SLUGGING	
1. Willie Stargell	.932
2. Jim Rice	.914
3. Fred Lynn	.913
4. Hank Aaron	.902
5. Dave Parker	.893
6. Dick Allen	.892
7. Mike Schmidt	.889
8. Reggie Smith	.885
9. Reggie Jackson	.873
10. George Foster	.872
11. Billy Williams	.865
12. Rod Carew	.865
13. Joe Morgan	.864
14. Greg Luzinski	.862
15. Frank Robinson	.862
16. Willie McCovey	.850
17. Andy Thornton	.850
18. Ken Singleton	.849
19. Bill Madlock	.845
20. Johnny Bench	.844
21. Bobby Bonds	.843
22. Carlton Fisk	.843
23. Carl Yastrzemski	.840
24. George Brett	.834
25. Tony Perez	.831

Above: *Willie Stargell holds almost all the Pittsburgh career batting records that do not belong to Honus Wagner. In 21 seasons, spent entirely with the Pirates, Stargell amassed 475 home runs and 1,540 RBI—and also a club-record 1,936 strikeouts.*

Jim Hickman, who had never hit higher than .257 or had more than 57 RBI in eight previous major league seasons, in 1970 hit .315 for the Cubs with 115 RBI.

After hitting .307 for the Cubs in 1971 for his career-best season, Joe Pepitone never again played regularly in the majors.

Tidy Bowl

John Lowenstein revealed how he stays ready when he's a designated hitter: "I flush the john between innings to keep my wrists strong."

Allen Spurs White Sox to First Homer Title

Bill Melton's homer crown in 1971 was considerably facilitated by changes made in the design of Comiskey Park in the late 1960s, shortening the distance to and the height of the outfield walls. The alterations brought a second home run leader to Comiskey immediately on the heels of Melton in the person of Dick Allen. The 1972 American League four-bagger king, Allen hit 37 homers in his first year with the Sox after being acquired over the winter in a deal with the Dodgers. Injured much of the following season, Allen rebounded in 1974 to again pace the AL with 32 round-trippers. Help from Melton and outfielder Ken Henderson, who contributed 21 and 20 homers respectively, enabled the Sox to claim their first-ever team home run crown that season. In 1975, after Allen was traded to the Phillies, the Pale Hose reverted to form and hit just 94 homers, the second-fewest in the AL.

In 1978, designated hitter Leroy Stanton hit a paltry .182 for the Seattle Mariners in 302 at bats.

The Conigliaro brothers, Tony and Billy, hit a sibling record 54 homers for the 1970 Boston Red Sox.

The 1972 season was the only one during the 1970s in which no players in either league managed to compile 200 hits.

"When I was a little boy I wanted to be a baseball player and join the circus. With the Yankees I've accomplished both."
—*Graig Nettles*

In 1976, Dan Driessen of the Cincinnati Reds became the first designated hitter in National League history, as the World Series employed the DH for the first time.

In 1970, Dal Maxvill of the Cardinals set a major league record for the fewest hits by a player in 150 or more games when he compiled just 80 singles in 152 contests.

1970s EXTRA-BASE HITS	
1. Reggie Jackson	586
Bobby Bonds	586
3. Tony Perez	572
Johnny Bench	572
5. Willie Stargell	568
6. Pete Rose	537
7. Al Oliver	527
8. Lee May	514
9. Reggie Smith	511
10. Amos Otis	498
11. Joe Morgan	495
12. Cesar Cedeno	487
13. George Scott	486
14. Ted Simmons	484
15. Graig Nettles	480
16. Rusty Staub	475
17. Bobby Murcer	473
18. Carl Yastrzemski	468
19. Greg Luzinski	458
20. Mike Schmidt	449
21. Sal Bando	440
22. Steve Garvey	439
23. Joe Rudi	435
24. Bob Watson	433
25. Hal McRae	432

Baltimore Four Take 20

In 1971, manager Earl Weaver of the Orioles had the good fortune to establish his pitching rotation on Opening Day and never have to veer from it. Of the Orioles' 158 games (four were postponed and not made up), Weaver's regular rotation of Mike Cuellar, Pat Dobson, Dave McNally, and Jim Palmer started 142. The quartet furthermore made Baltimore the only team other than the 1920 White Sox to exhibit four 20-game winners. McNally led the Orioles with 21 victories and the other three members of the club's Big Four all kicked in an even 20 wins apiece. Oddly, McNally, although the top winner, was idled for part of the season by a sore arm, causing him to make seven fewer starts than any of his compatriots. The Orioles rotation helped Baltimore take the AL team ERA crown by posting a 2.99 earned run average. The 16 games that were not started by the 20-game winning foursome were distributed by Weaver among Grant Jackson (nine), Dave Leonard (six), and Dave Boswell (one).

Ouch
After being hit by a record 50 pitches in 1970, Ron Hunt explained: "Some people give their bodies to science. I give mine to baseball."

After the 1979 season, the Houston Astros signed free-agent pitcher Nolan Ryan for $1 million.

Above: *Jim Palmer won 20 or more games eight times during the 1970s. Physical problems cut into his work time and held him below 20 victories in the other two campaigns.*

St. Louis hurler Bob Gibson won nine consecutive Gold Gloves, from 1965 to 1973.

Tom Seaver of the New York Mets in 1973 became the first pitcher in major league history to win a Cy Young Award without claiming at least 20 victories, as he had 19.

Tom Seaver became the first pitcher to claim his third Cy Young Award when he triumphed in 1975, after previously winning in 1969 and 1973.

The first American League hurler to bag three Cy Young Awards was Jim Palmer, who scored in 1973, 1975, and 1976.

Jim Palmer had eight 20-win years in his career; only two other hurlers in AL history have had as many: Walter Johnson (12) and Lefty Grove (eight).

1970s GAMES PITCHED	
1. Rollie Fingers	640
2. Sparky Lyle	600
3. Pedro Borbon	561
4. Dave LaRoche	543
Darold Knowles	543
6. Tug McGraw	542
7. Mike Marshall	528
8. Dave Giusti	470
9. Paul Lindblad	460
10. Tom Burgmeier	458
11. Clay Carroll	447
12. Al Hrabosky	445
13. Gene Garber	444
14. Grant Jackson	443
15. Randy Moffitt	436
16. John Hiller	426
17. Elias Sosa	423
18. Ron Reed	412
19. Phil Niekro	406
20. Dick Drago	396
Stan Bahnsen	396
22. Skip Lockwood	390
23. Ken Forsch	389
24. Tom Murphy	388
25. Steve Mingori	385

Who'd Start Doubleheader? Wilbur Wood

Wilbur Wood's knuckleball delivery was so effortless that his arm seemed almost indefatigable. A reliever early in his career, he was converted to a starter when it grew apparent to the White Sox that they were not getting full value out of his rubber wing in just a bullpen role. In 1973, Wood was used so extensively by Sox manager Chuck Tanner that Wilbur became the last American League pitcher to date who was both a 20-game winner and a 20-game loser. Wood's 24-20 record was achieved in 48 starts and 359 innings. Two of his starts came on the same day. When Wood took the hill in each game of a doubleheader against the Yankees on July 20, 1973, he gained the distinction of being the last pitcher to start both ends of a twin bill. The Yankees rudely treated Wood on the occasion, though, knocking him out early in each contest and pinning two losses on him for the day.

In a game on April 22, 1970, Tom Seaver of the Mets fanned a major league record 10 San Diego Padres in a row. He went on to tie a major league record by fanning 19 batters during the game.

The record for the highest ERA by a National League Cy Young Award winner is held by St. Louis Cardinal Bob Gibson, with a 3.12 ERA in 1970.

In the early 1970s, Wilbur Wood (above) worked longer hours than any hurler since the dead-ball era.

Nolan Ryan in 1977 became the only pitcher in major league history to average both nine or more strikeouts and six or more walks per nine innings.

When Nolan Ryan notched a 20th-century record 383 strikeouts in 1973, four other American League hurlers registered 214 or more whiffs.

California's Nolan Ryan set a major league record in 1972 by allowing only 5.26 hits per game.

When asked whether he'd rather face Jim Palmer or Tom Seaver, Merv Rettenmund replied: "That's like asking if I'd rather be hung or go to the electric chair."

The AL record for the most wins by a pitcher on a last-place team is held by Nolan Ryan, who logged 22 victories for the cellar-dwelling California Angels in 1974.

In 1973, Nolan Ryan broke Sandy Koufax's old mark of 382 strikeouts in a season when he notched his 383rd strikeout by fanning Rich Reese of the Twins on his last pitch of the campaign.

On June 1, 1975, Angels hurler Nolan Ryan tied Sandy Koufax's record when he tossed his fourth no-hitter.

1970s GAMES STARTED		
1.	Phil Niekro	376
2.	Gaylord Perry	368
3.	Steve Carlton	366
4.	Fergie Jenkins	354
5.	Jim Palmer	352
6.	Bert Blyleven	350
7.	Don Sutton	349
8.	Tom Seaver	345
9.	Nolan Ryan	333
10.	Catfish Hunter	327
	Vida Blue	327
12.	Mike Torrez	313
	Jerry Koosman	313
14.	Rick Wise	303
15.	Jack Billingham	296
16.	Ken Holtzman	294
17.	Jim Kaat	290
18.	Jerry Reuss	287
19.	Paul Splittorff	286
20.	Luis Tiant	285
21.	Tommy John	282
22.	Mickey Lolich	277
	Ross Grimsley	277
24.	Wilbur Wood	276
25.	Rick Reuschel	274
	Dock Ellis	274

Wood, Lolich, Others Prove that Life Starts at 40

Wilbur Wood's 48 starts in 1973 were one less than he made the previous year, when he drew more starting assignments than any hurler since Ed Walsh in 1908. Wood started 42 or more games for five successive seasons between 1971 and 1975 to set a 20th-century record for the most starts (223) over a five-year period. Right behind Wood was Mickey Lolich of the Tigers. Between 1970 and 1974, Lolich logged 208 starts, with a high of 45 in 1971. Phil Niekro, who also started more than 40 games on several occasions during the 1970s, like Wood was a knuckleballer who found the delivery so untaxing he seemed apt to pitch forever. Some of the other hurlers who were able to start 40 games at least a couple of years during this time included: Gaylord Perry, Catfish Hunter, Stan Bahnsen, Steve Carlton, Joe Coleman, Bill Singer, Fergie Jenkins, Dave McNally, and Don Sutton. Lolich, unlike Wood, threw very hard, as well as fairly often. In 1971, while making 45 starts to set a Detroit club record, he also set a Tigers mark for the most strikeouts, with 308 whiffs.

After the 1971 season, Dave McNally (above) had a career record of 135-69. For the remaining four years he pitched he was only 49-50 but still finished with a .607 winning percentage.

1970s COMPLETE GAMES		
1.	Gaylord Perry	197
2.	Fergie Jenkins	184
3.	Jim Palmer	175
4.	Steve Carlton	165
5.	Nolan Ryan	164
6.	Phil Niekro	160
7.	Tom Seaver	147
8.	Bert Blyleven	145
9.	Catfish Hunter	140
10.	Mickey Lolich	133
11.	Vida Blue	124
12.	Luis Tiant	120
13.	Don Sutton	117
14.	Mike Cuellar	115
15.	Wilbur Wood	113
16.	Rick Wise	107
17.	Mike Torrez	100
18.	Ken Holtzman	97
19.	Bob Gibson	89
20.	Andy Messersmith	86
21.	Frank Tanana	85
	Jon Matlack	85
	Jerry Koosman	85
24.	Jerry Reuss	83
25.	Jim Slaton	80
	Dave Goltz	80

In both the 1973 and '74 seasons, Minnesota's Bert Blyleven fanned 507 hitters and averaged more than seven and one-half strikeouts for every nine innings he pitched.

Phil Niekro Wins 287 After 30, 121 After 40

Phil Niekro is the only 300-game winner who began as a relief pitcher. He also is the only 300-game winner who did not reach the majors to stay until he was 26 years old. As a result of his belated arrival and starting out as a relief pitcher, Niekro had only 31 wins in the majors when he turned 30. No one could possibly have predicted then that he was less than a 10th of the way to his career total of 318. Niekro made at least 32 starts in every season during the 1970s. Twice, he led the National League in wins, and on four occasions, he paced the senior loop in losses. In 1979, when he finished at 21-20, Niekro became the only hurler since Jim Whitney in 1881 to top his league in both wins and losses. Interestingly, Whitney labored for the Boston Red Stockings, later to become the Boston Braves, then the Milwaukee Braves, and finally the Atlanta Braves, the team with which Niekro was affiliated in 1979 and for most of his career.

Reggie Jackson said about Tom Seaver: "Blind people come to the park just to listen to him pitch."

In 1972, Milt Pappas of the Cubs became the first pitcher in history to bag 200 career victories without ever winning 20 games in a season.

Above: *Phil Neikro early in his major league career seemed unlikely to earn a pension from the game, let alone 318 victories.*

Mike Marshall set the AL record for most appearances when he totaled 90 for the Minnesota Twins in 1979.

Jim Bibby hurled the first no-hitter for the Washington Senators-Texas Rangers franchise when he beat Oakland 6-0 on July 7, 1973.

On September 2, 1972, Milt Pappas of the Chicago Cubs lost a perfect game by walking the 27th man on a 3-2 pitch. He went on to get the no-hitter.

Tim McCarver said about Steve Carlton: "Carlton does not pitch to the hitter, he pitches through him. The batter hardly exists for Steve. He's playing an elevated game of catch."

In 1979, Phil Niekro of Atlanta and his brother, Joe Niekro of Houston, tied for the National League lead in wins (21).

Jim Barr of the San Francisco Giants retired a major league-record 41 batters in a row over a two-game period.

1970s SAVES		
1.	Rollie Fingers	209
2.	Sparky Lyle	190
3.	Mike Marshall	177
4.	Dave Giusti	140
5.	Tug McGraw	132
6.	Dave LaRoche	122
7.	John Hiller	115
8.	Gene Garber	110
9.	Clay Carroll	106
10.	Bruce Sutter	105
11.	Rich Gossage	101
12.	Terry Forster	100
13.	Darold Knowles	99
14.	Bill Campbell	95
15.	Jim Brewer	92
16.	Al Hrabosky	90
17.	Kent Tekulve	83
	Randy Moffitt	83
19.	Ken Sanders	82
20.	Pedro Borbon	79
21.	Wayne Granger	77
22.	Jim Kern	75
23.	Gary Lavelle	74
24.	Rawly Eastwick	67
25.	Elias Sosa	66
	Skip Lockwood	66

Niekro Induces Batters to Knuckle Under

What saved Phil Niekro from a lifetime in the minor leagues was learning to throw a knuckleball. His mastery of the butterfly pitch was also much of the reason that his early managers in both the minors and the majors could not envision him as a starting pitcher. Most of the knuckleballers who preceded Niekro either settled into careers as firemen, such as Hoyt Wilhelm and Eddie Fisher. Some, such as Gene Bearden and Roger Wolff, bloomed for a season or two as starters only to flounder after batters, catching on that they had no more idea than anyone else where their dipsy-doodles were going, simply waited for them to fall behind in the count and then sat on their fastballs. Niekro was the first pitcher to make his name as a starter on little more than a knuckler. The pitch was so effective for him, however, that his other deliveries often caught batters with their bats on their shoulders in surprise. In 1977, Niekro even snuck past such flamethrowers as J.R. Richard, Steve Carlton, and Tom Seaver to lead the NL in strikeouts.

Sprinkles?

Reggie Jackson said about Nolan Ryan: "Every hitter likes fastballs just like everybody likes ice cream. But you don't like it when somebody's stuffing it into you by the gallon."

The last pitcher to win 25 or more games in a season and fail to receive a Cy Young Award was Mickey Lolich with the 1971 Tigers.

In 1971, Mickey Lolich's 48 starts and 376 innings were the most by any hurler since the dead-ball era.

After his reconstructive elbow surgery, Tommy John said: "When they operated, I told them to put in a Koufax fastball. They did—but it was a Mrs. Koufax fastball."

1970s SHUTOUTS		
1.	Jim Palmer	44
2.	Nolan Ryan	42
3.	Tom Seaver	40
4.	Don Sutton	39
	Bert Blyleven	39
6.	Gaylord Perry	36
7.	Fergie Jenkins	33
8.	Steve Carlton	32
	Vida Blue	32
10.	Catfish Hunter	30
11.	Luis Tiant	28
	Jon Matlack	28
13.	Jack Billingham	27
14.	Phil Niekro	25
	Mike Cuellar	25
16.	Wilbur Wood	24
	Frank Tanana	24
	Andy Messersmith	24
19.	Rick Wise	22
	Jerry Reuss	22
	Rudy May	22
	Ken Holtzman	22
23.	Jim Slaton	21
	Steve Rogers	21
	Burt Hooton	21

For 13 seasons between 1964 and 1976, Mickey Lolich (above) never started fewer than 30 games and four times started over 40. He then opted to retire, only to return two years later as a relief pitcher.

In 1973, John Hiller of the Tigers was 10-5 with a 1.44 ERA, and he set a major league record for saves with 38.

After Bruce Sutter won the 1979 Cy Young Award for the Cubs, he took the club to arbitration and won a $700,000 salary.

In 1974, Mike Marshall of the Dodgers appeared in a major league-record 106 games; that year, he became the first reliever to win a Cy Young Award.

In 1972, Mike Marshall of the Dodgers became the first pitcher to appear in five games during a five-game World Series.

Perrys' Cy Young Awards Fill Family Mantel

Jim Perry retired at the finish of the 1975 season with the satisfaction of knowing that he and his younger brother Gaylord held the record for the most career wins by pitching siblings. Jim had 215 wins, and at that point Gaylord had 216 Ws, beating John, Dad, and Walter Clarkson, who had 385. The younger Perry later extended the record to 529 wins before retiring himself in 1983. The mark was shortlived, however, lasting only until 1987 when it was broken by the Niekro brothers, who finished with 539 wins between them. But to the Perrys belongs a distinction they need not share with any other siblings. In 1970, Jim snagged the American League Cy Young Award. When Gaylord took the same honor two years later, it was the first and to date the only time that a pair of brothers has each received so high a tribute. Later in the decade Gaylord garnered a second Cy Young after he returned to the National League, giving the Perrys another first.

Above: *Gaylord Perry won 314 games in the majors but never appeared in a World Series game. Phil Niekro is the only other 300-game winner in this century to suffer the same fate.*

Cincinnati's Wayne Granger in 1970 set a major league record with 35 saves.

In 1970, when Gaylord Perry tied Bob Gibson for the NL lead in wins and Jim Perry tied two pitchers for the AL lead in wins, it marked the first time that brothers topped their respective leagues in wins.

Padre pitcher Gaylord Perry won the NL Cy Young Award in 1978, becoming the only hurler to win the award in both leagues.

Their Biggest Fan

Cesar Geronimo commented on being the 3,000th strikeout victim of both Nolan Ryan and Bob Gibson: "I was just in the right place at the right time."

John Hiller of the Tigers in 1974 compiled a record 31 decisions as a relief pitcher when he went 17-14.

1970s WINS		
1.	Jim Palmer	186
2.	Gaylord Perry	184
3.	Tom Seaver	178
	Fergie Jenkins	178
	Steve Carlton	178
6.	Catfish Hunter	169
7.	Don Sutton	166
8.	Phil Niekro	164
9.	Nolan Ryan	155
	Vida Blue	155
11.	Bert Blyleven	148
12.	Luis Tiant	142
13.	Wilbur Wood	136
14.	Jack Billingham	135
15.	Mike Torrez	134
16.	Rick Wise	133
	Tommy John	133
18.	Ken Holtzman	126
19.	Jerry Koosman	124
20.	Paul Splittorff	123
21.	Jim Kaat	122
22.	Dock Ellis	121
23.	Mike Cuellar	120
24.	Ross Grimsley	117
25.	Mickey Lolich	115

Perry Pitch Packs Petroleum Jelly

Jim Perry was a fairly straight-forward hurler during his career, but brother Gaylord was another kettle of fish. Enemy batters were certain the younger Perry cheated by throwing a spitter or some kind of spitball and Vaseline ball combination, and he did little to disabuse them of their suspicions. Perry seemed actually to relish the accusations, perhaps because he knew that as long as the flames were fanned it could only give hitters something more to think about. In any case, Gaylord Perry hung up his spikes in 1983 with the issue still unresolved. Did he throw the wet one or didn't he? Had he ever been caught in the act, the rules would have demanded Perry's ejection. But not since 1944, when Nels Potter of the St. Louis Browns was asked to leave the mound in a game against the Yankees, has a hurler been ousted expressly for violating the spitball prohibition.

"Why pitch nine innings when you can get just as famous pitching two?"
—Sparky Lyle

Darold Knowles set an American League record (since tied) when he lost 14 games in relief for Washington in 1970 en route to a 2-14 season.

In 1979, Gene Garber set a record for the most relief losses in a season when he suffered 16 defeats after coming out of the bullpen.

"When you're a winner you're always happy, but if you're happy as a loser you'll always be a loser."
—Mark Fidrych

Hoyt Wilhelm in 1972 retired holding records of: 1,018 career relief appearances, 1,070 total games, 227 career saves, and 350 career relief wins and saves.

On June 23, 1971, Rick Wise of the Philadelphia Phillies no-hit Cincinnati and clobbered two homers.

Above: *Steve Carlton was a dazzling 27-10 in 1972 with a cellar dweller; in 1983, he went 15-16 with a pennant winner.*

1970s INNINGS	
1. Gaylord Perry	2,905.0
2. Phil Niekro	2,881.0
3. Steve Carlton	2,747.0
4. Jim Palmer	2,745.0
5. Fergie Jenkins	2,706.2
6. Tom Seaver	2,652.1
7. Bert Blyleven	2,624.2
8. Don Sutton	2,557.1
9. Nolan Ryan	2,465.0
10. Catfish Hunter	2,399.0
11. Vida Blue	2,398.2
12. Jerry Koosman	2,281.1
13. Wilbur Wood	2,150.1
14. Mike Torrez	2,138.2
15. Rick Wise	2,121.0
16. Mickey Lolich	2,110.0
17. Ken Holtzman	2,073.2
18. Luis Tiant	2,063.0
19. Jack Billingham	2,045.2
20. Jim Kaat	2,004.1
21. Tommy John	1,973.0
22. Jerry Reuss	1,967.0
23. Dave Roberts	1,952.1
24. Joe Coleman	1,937.2
25. Paul Splittorff	1,905.2

In 1972, Steve Carlton had a 27-10 record for the Phillies while the rest of the Phils pitchers had a combined 32-87 record.

In 1972, Steve Carlton of the Phillies tied Sandy Koufax's record, set just six years earlier, for the most wins since 1900 by an NL southpaw when Carlton logged 27 wins.

Steve Carlton set a record for the most consecutive wins by a pitcher on a last-place team when he rang up 15 straight victories for the Phillies in 1972.

John's Surgery Regreases Elbow

In the winter of 1965, Cleveland, desperate since 1960 to get Rocky Colavito back into a Tribe uniform, engineered a three-team deal involving Kansas City and the Chicago White Sox that transferred a young Tribe lefty named Tommy John to the Windy City club. In some respects, the trade to reobtain Colavito proved even more devastating to Cleveland than the one in which he'd been lost, for John proceeded to win more games than any postexpansion southpaw except Steve Carlton. John's career did not really begin to accelerate, though, until he was swapped to the Dodgers in 1972. Even then, he first had to overcome a seemingly impossible obstacle. An elbow injury in 1974 forced him to submit to an experimental surgical procedure that offered only guarded hope he would ever pitch again. After sitting out all of the 1975 campaign while his elbow mended, John returned in 1976 with his pitching wing as good as new. The following year, at age 34, he nailed the first of what would be three 20-win seasons before he retired in 1989 with 288 victories.

1970s STRIKEOUTS	
1. Nolan Ryan	2,678
2. Tom Seaver	2,304
3. Steve Carlton	2,097
4. Bert Blyleven	2,082
5. Gaylord Perry	1,907
6. Phil Niekro	1,866
7. Fergie Jenkins	1,841
8. Don Sutton	1,767
9. Vida Blue	1,600
10. Jerry Koosman	1,587
11. Jim Palmer	1,559
12. Mickey Lolich	1,496
13. J.R. Richard	1,374
14. Andy Messersmith	1,340
15. Joe Coleman	1,319
16. Catfish Hunter	1,309
17. Rudy May	1,238
18. Luis Tiant	1,229
19. Jon Matlack	1,215
20. Fred Norman	1,208
21. Jerry Reuss	1,141
22. Wilbur Wood	1,138
23. Rick Reuschel	1,122
24. Frank Tanana	1,120
25. Rick Wise	1,112
Steve Renko	1,112

Above: *Tommy John won 288 games in 26 seasons. With Cleveland in the mid-1960s, he was rated a distant second by Tribe brass to fellow southpaw prospect Sam McDowell.*

Among the many records Hoyt Wilhelm held when he retired in 1972 is the distinction of being the last pitcher to win at least 100 games in both the major and the minor leagues.

Fergie Jenkins, with 25 victories in 1974, was the last 20-game winner to date for the Texas Rangers.

See Ya
Graig Nettles remarked when Yankees teammate Sparky Lyle was traded to Texas after the 1978 season: "He went from Cy Young to sayonara in a year."

Vida Blue After Big 1971 Campaign

Who is the only 200-game winner in this century whose best season came when he was 22 years old? Who was the first black switch-hitter to win an MVP Award? Who is the only hurler to fan 300 batters in a season but never before or never again in his career fan as many as 200? The answer to all three questions is Vida Blue, and his glorious year came in 1971 when he notched 24 wins, 301 Ks, and a 1.82 ERA while spurring the Philadelphia-Kansas City-Oakland A's franchise to its first postseason appearance in 40 years. Blue actually did not turn 22 until the 1971 campaign was deep into its fourth month. By then he had become the youngest winning pitcher in All-Star game history and brought the American League its first midsummer victory since 1962. When Blue faded somewhat in the second half of the season and the A's failed to beat Baltimore in the League Championship Series, Oakland owner Charlie Finley rebuked his young pitcher's salary demands. After a long and bitter holdout, Blue was ineffective in 1972 and never again matched his early brilliance.

When Lindy McDaniel retired in 1975, he stood second only to Hoyt Wilhelm in career relief wins with 119, a position he still holds.

Vida Blue in 1971 struck out 301 batters in his first full major league season.

Above: *Vida Blue nearly spearheaded the Giants to a division crown in 1978, his first year in San Francisco; it turned out to be his last outstanding season.*

In 1971, Vida Blue of the A's became the first hurler in major league history to strike out at least 300 batters (301) and not lead the league, as Mickey Lolich of the Tigers notched 308 Ks that year.

Tug McGraw said about relief pitching: "Some days you tame the tiger. And some days the tiger has you for lunch."

In 1978, Ron Guidry tied Babe Ruth's American League record for most shutouts in a season by a lefty with nine.

1970s WINNING PERCENTAGE	
1. Don Gullett	.686
2. Jim Palmer	.644
3. Tom Seaver	.638
4. Catfish Hunter	.624
5. Tommy John	.613
6. Gary Nolan	.612
7. Luis Tiant	.607
8. Dennis Eckersley	.606
9. Mike Cuellar	.606
10. Don Sutton	.601
11. Dave McNally	.595
12. Bill Lee	.592
13. J.R. Richard	.591
14. Vida Blue	.587
15. Steve Carlton	.586
16. Dennis Leonard	.584
17. Gaylord Perry	.580
18. Doug Rau	.580
19. Frank Tanana	.580
20. Fergie Jenkins	.578
21. Steve Busby	.575
22. Ed Figueroa	.575
23. Ross Grimsley	.571
24. Bob Gibson	.568
25. Jack Billingham	.567

Guidry Gains Grand Campaign

In the fall of 1976, southpaw Ron Guidry had shown so little evidence of becoming a major league pitcher that he was nearly left unprotected by the Yankees in the expansion draft to stock the new Seattle and Toronto franchises. The following spring, Yankees skipper Billy Martin became so exasperated with Guidry that he said, "Show me somebody you can get out and I'll let you pitch to him." Finally given his chance in relief against the Kansas City Royals, Guidry struggled but managed to post his first major league victory. By the fall of 1978, he was the toast of New York after collecting 25 triumphs, a 1.74 ERA, and an .893 winning percentage, the best ever by a 25-game winner. He led the AL by hurling nine shutouts, yielding 8.6 baserunners per nine innings, and holding batters to a .193 batting average. Like Vida Blue, the southpaw sensation in 1971, Guidry never had another season that approached his 1978 gem, although he remained a fine pitcher for another decade.

1970s EARNED RUN AVERAGE	
1. Jim Palmer	2.58
2. Tom Seaver	2.61
3. Bert Blyleven	2.88
4. Rollie Fingers	2.89
5. Gaylord Perry	2.92
6. Frank Tanana	2.93
7. Andy Messersmith	2.93
8. Jon Matlack	2.97
9. Mike Marshall	2.98
10. Don Wilson	3.01
11. Don Sutton	3.07
12. Vida Blue	3.07
13. Tommy John	3.09
14. Mel Stottlemyre	3.11
15. Don Gullett	3.11
16. Dennis Eckersley	3.12
17. Steve Rogers	3.13
18. Nolan Ryan	3.14
19. Catfish Hunter	3.17
20. Ken Forsch	3.18
21. Steve Carlton	3.18
22. Burt Hooton	3.19
23. Bob Gibson	3.20
24. Al Downing	3.21
25. Gary Nolan	3.22

In 1978, Ron Guidry (above) fashioned perhaps the greatest season in history when he went 25-3.

"Almost every batter guesses a few times a game. This is an advantage for me. Hell, most of the time I don't know what I'm going to throw."
—Sam McDowell, wild and woolly lefty

Ron Guidry of the Yankees set an AL record for lefties in 1978 when he notched 18 strikeouts in a game.

I Agree
"In baseball you're supposed to sit on your ass, spit tobacco, and nod at stupid things."
—Bill Lee, zany pitcher

Hurlers Not Good Buys

The advent of free agency opened the flood gates for disgruntled players to sell their services to the highest bidder. With the advent of the era, pitchers who were looking to make a change often went where the money was, no matter the quality of the team offering it, and the results were sometimes catastrophic. Andy Messersmith, after bagging 19 wins while pitching without a contract for the Dodgers in 1975, signed with the lowly Braves for 1976 and collected just 18 more victories in his career. In 1977, Cleveland, hungering for a staff bulwark, wooed Wayne Garland away from Baltimore where he had been a 20-game winner the previous year. Determined to get their money's worth from their expensive free-agent acquisition, the Indians overworked Garland in 1977 and saw him go down with a torn rotator cuff. Surgery enabled Garland to fulfill his multiyear contract, but in five seasons with Cleveland he won a mere 28 games against 48 losses.

Al Hrabosky explained why he refused to shave off his beard: "How can I intimidate batters if I look like a !*@#$%? golf pro?"

In 1971, pitcher Bob Veale of the Pirates had a 7.04 ERA but nevertheless turned in a perfect 6-0 record.

Above: *Andy Messersmith had moments during the 1970s and even entire seasons when he laid claim to being the game's top pitcher. In 1974, Messersmith went 20-6 for the Dodgers with a 2.59 ERA but lost the Cy Young Award to teammate Mike Marshall.*

The 1975 World Series was the first to feature two teams that lacked a 20-game winner, as Rick Wise led the Red Sox with 19 victories and the Reds had three hurlers with 15 wins apiece.

Range
Ralph Kiner, Mets announcer, described Phillies outfielder Garry Maddox: "Two-thirds of the earth is covered by water; the other one-third is covered by Garry Maddox."

1970s FEWEST WALKS	
1. Fergie Jenkins	1.72
2. Fritz Peterson	1.82
3. Jim Kaat	1.94
4. Gary Nolan	1.98
5. Jim Barr	2.06
6. Randy Jones	2.15
7. Nelson Briles	2.23
8. Bill Hands	2.26
9. Catfish Hunter	2.27
10. Ron Reed	2.28
11. Don Sutton	2.32
12. Gaylord Perry	2.35
13. Mike Caldwell	2.35
14. Rick Wise	2.36
15. Tommy John	2.37
16. Wilbur Wood	2.39
17. Frank Tanana	2.40
18. Ross Grimsley	2.42
19. Jon Matlack	2.42
20. Dick Bosman	2.43
21. Bert Blyleven	2.44
22. Mickey Lolich	2.48
23. Marty Pattin	2.49
24. Rick Reuschel	2.49
25. Bill Lee	2.51

Above: *Kent Tekulve labored 102⅔ or more innings in relief for four straight seasons and culminated his workhorse skein in 1979 by logging three saves for Pittsburgh in the World Series.*

1970s RATIO	
1. Tom Seaver	9.66
2. Catfish Hunter	9.95
3. Don Sutton	9.97
4. Fergie Jenkins	10.06
5. Rollie Fingers	10.27
6. Gaylord Perry	10.28
7. Jim Palmer	10.28
8. Frank Tanana	10.30
9. Gary Nolan	10.34
10. Andy Messersmith	10.44
11. Bert Blyleven	10.44
12. Dennis Eckersley	10.66
13. Don Wilson	10.72
14. Jon Matlack	10.72
15. Vida Blue	10.73
16. Randy Jones	10.83
17. Burt Hooton	10.88
18. Luis Tiant	10.90
19. Marty Pattin	10.94
20. Mike Cuellar	11.01
21. Steve Rogers	11.02
22. Don Gullett	11.05
23. Steve Carlton	11.05
24. Ron Reed	11.06
25. Dave McNally	11.10

When Gaylord Perry's agent approached the makers of Vaseline for a possible endorsement contract, a company representative replied: "We soothe babies' asses, not baseballs."

Jones Loses Dominance After Cy Young Season

Arm and elbow miseries have plagued pitchers since the invention of the curveball in the late 1860s, but never have more hurlers fallen prey to the pitfalls of their profession than in recent times. Steve Stone, the American League Cy Young winner in 1980 on the basis of his 25 victories with the Orioles, threw his last pitch before the following season was out. Another Cy Young recipient whose arm went soon after his triumph was Randy Jones. The sinkerballer went 20-12 with 18 complete games in 1975 for a Padres team that climbed out of the NL West basement for the first time in franchise history. Jones finished second in Cy Young voting. Logging 22 wins for the Padres in 1976 and pacing the National League with 25 complete games earned Jones the NL's top pitching honor the next year, but the price was high. An ailing flipper hounded him for much of the '77 season, sending him to a 6-12 record with just one complete game in 25 starts. Jones rebounded somewhat in 1978 but was never again able to win as often as he lost or to complete more than seven games in a season.

Bryant Denied '73 Cy Young

By all the laws of probability, Ron Bryant ought to have been another pitcher during the 1970s who fizzled after winning a Cy Young Award. In 1973, Bryant won 24 games for the Giants, five more than any other National League hurler. However, Mike Marshall chose that year to shatter the major league record for both the most mound appearances and the most relief innings (he broke both of his own marks in 1974). The other NL East teams also decided that year to let the Mets cop the pennant with a .509 winning percentage. As a result, Bryant finished in the show position in the Cy Young chase, behind Marshall, the place hurler, and Tom Seaver of the Mets, the winner. The writers who voted for Seaver defended their choice by pointing out that although Seaver had just 19 wins, he led the NL in ERA, complete games, and strikeouts, but Bryant's supporters nonetheless felt cheated. After reporting in less than top condition the following spring, Bryant slipped to just three victories in 1974 and never won another game.

1970s PITCHER ASSISTS	
1. Phil Niekro	459
2. Gaylord Perry	445
3. Wilbur Wood	441
4. Tommy John	420
5. Fergie Jenkins	410

The last pitcher to hurl as many as 30 complete games in a season was Catfish Hunter of the New York Yankees in 1975.

Above: *Catfish Hunter led all hurlers in World Series starts during the 1970s with nine but completed only one of them.*

Four Oakland A's hurlers— Vida Blue, Paul Lindlad, Glenn Abbott, and Rollie Fingers—combined to toss a no-hitter on September 28, 1975.

Ken and Bob Forsch were the first brothers in major league history to toss no-hitters. Bob threw his first in 1978, and Ken followed in 1979.

When John Candelaria of Pittsburgh no-hit LA on August 9, 1976, it was the first no-hitter thrown by a Pirates pitcher at home since 1907.

The record for the fewest victories by the leader in wins on a world championship team is 14, set in 1979 by John Candelaria of the Pirates.

Charley Lau, the hitting guru of the Royals and others, said after a particularly rough outing against Phil Niekro: "There are two theories on hitting the knuckleball. Unfortunately neither of them works."

1970s PITCHER PUTOUTS	
1. Fergie Jenkins	236
2. Phil Niekro	219
3. Jim Palmer	215
4. Rick Reuschel	185
5. Gaylord Perry	182

When the A's won three straight world championships between 1972 and 1974, Catfish Hunter was the only Oakland hurler to collect a victory in all three fall classics.

In the 1977 World Series, Mike Torrez hurled two complete-game victories for the Yankees and racked up 15 strikeouts.

In 1978, the Phillies lost the National League Championship Series for the third time in a row. That year, the Royals lost the ALCS for the third time in a row, all to the Yankees.

Let It Roll
"The way to catch a knuckleball is to wait until the ball stops rolling and then pick it up."
—Bob Uecker

Red Sox Regret Letting Lyle Leave

Which team got the better of the deal that sent Tom Seaver to the Reds in 1977 is still an open question, but there is little dispute over who took a reaming in the trade between the Yankees and the Red Sox during spring training in 1972. Ticketed for New York was reliever Sparky Lyle while Boston made ready to welcome first baseman Danny Cater. It seemed a fairly even swap on the surface, but it turned out to be the steal of the decade. After joining the Red Sox, Cater was never again more than a part-time player, whereas Lyle immediately established himself as the American League's premier fireman. Lyle led the loop in saves his first season in the Bronx and repeated his conquest three years later. The following season Lyle became the first AL reliever to win a Cy Young Award. Cater by then had been out of the majors for two years.

The Yankees' uncontested bullpen ace during the early and mid-1970s, Sparky Lyle (above) suddenly lost his magic when he was made to share Bomber relief chores in 1978 with Goose Gossage. The first American League reliever to win a Cy Young Award, Lyle was dealt in 1979 to Texas, where he had his last productive season.

1970s PITCHER CHANCES ACCEPTED	
1. Phil Niekro	678
2. Fergie Jenkins	646
3. Gaylord Perry	627
4. Jim Palmer	618
5. Tom Seaver	543

In the 1975 ALCS, won by the Red Sox over Oakland three games to none, Ken Holtzman was the starting pitcher in two of the A's three losses and became the only starter to register two decisions in a three-game LCS.

In 1973, with the new designated hitter rule in place, the American League posted 167 more complete games than the National League.

Owing to inclement weather that caused a five-day gap between games five and six of the 1975 World Series, Luis Tiant of the Red Sox was able to start three of the first six games of the seven-game set.

"Trying to hit Phil Niekro is like trying to eat Jell-O with chopsticks."
—Bobby Murcer

Yankee Sparky Lyle in 1977 was the first reliever to win the American League Cy Young Award.

1970s PITCHER FIELDING AVERAGE	
1. Gary Nolan	.991
2. Woodie Fryman	.990
3. Joe Niekro	.983
4. Roger Moret	.981
5. Mike Caldwell	.981

On May 31, 1979, Detroit's Pat Underwood made his major league debut against brother Tom of Toronto; Pat beat Tom 1-0.

The Montreal Expos have only had one 20-game winner in their history— Ross Grimsley, who won 20 on the nose in 1978.

After Phil Huffman of the Blue Jays had a 6-18 record and led the American League in losses as a rookie in 1978, he never registered another decision in the majors.

In 1974, the Baltimore Orioles set an AL record when they won five straight games by shutouts.

On August 27, 1977, pitching against the Texas Rangers, Ken Clay of the New York Yankees allowed two inside-the-park home runs on successive pitches, to Toby Harrah and Bump Wills.

You Say Goodbye, and I Say Hello

Billy Martin was a perfect 3-for-3 by the summer of 1975. Three times he had been hired to manage floundering American League teams, and three times he had almost instantly led them either to a division title or else their best showing in years only to be fired before the following season was out when his volatile personality shot away his welcome. Yankees owner George Steinbrenner was convinced that Martin had the right chemistry to restore the Bombers to their pre-1965 supremacy, nonetheless. Hence, Steinbrenner dumped Bill Virdon late in the 1975 season and gave the Yankees dugout post to Martin, thereupon beginning a love-hate relationship between the two that would last until Martin's death in December 1989. As had happened in Minnesota, Detroit, and Texas, Martin quickly hoisted the Yankees into contention and then was fired just as quickly. Steinbrenner, however, proved to be as mercurial as Martin. Between 1975 and 1988, George hired and fired the tempestuous skipper no fewer than five times.

1970s CATCHER GAMES	
1. Ted Simmons	1,305
2. Johnny Bench	1,299
3. Thurman Munson	1,253
4. Manny Sanguillen	973
5. Darrell Porter	893

Billy Martin won his only world championship as manager with the New York Yankees in 1977.

For all the times Billy Martin (above) changed jobs in his 16 seasons as a manager, he never worked a single day in the National League. One can only wonder now what he might have done in the 1970s at the helm of the Phillies or the Giants.

Detroit's Ed Brinkman set a major league fielding average record of .990 for shortstops, including 72 straight errorless games.

Phillie Larry Bowa's .987 fielding average in 1971 set a major league record for shortstops.

After Brooks Robinson made three errors in the Orioles first eight games in 1974, Dave McNally said to the third baseman: "You've gone from being a human vacuum cleaner to a litterbug."

The highest career fielding average by a catcher belongs to Bill Freehan, who retired in 1976 with a .993 mark.

Don Money of the Brewers established a record for third basemen when he registered a .989 fielding average in 1974.

Larry Bowa of the Philadelphia Phillies again took the fielding average record for shortstops in 1979 with a .991 mark.

Luis Aparicio in 1971 won the last of his nine Gold Gloves at shortstop.

Chicago's Chet Lemon in 1977 set an AL record for outfielders with 512 putouts.

1970s CATCHER FIELDING AVERAGE	
1. Jerry Grote	.993
2. Duffy Dyer	.992
3. Bill Freehan	.992
4. Jim Sundberg	.991
5. Johnny Bench	.990

It Takes a Thief

Baseball has had its share of unsavory characters, but the game's magnates have always been loath to take on players they know to have a criminal record. In the 1930s, the Washington Senators sent a shudder through the major league community when they scouted and signed a convict named Alabama Pitts. To the relief of most, Pitts proved unable to hit top-caliber pitching. Ron LeFlore recalled memories of Pitts when he joined the Detroit Tigers in 1974. A product of the Motor City ghetto, LeFlore came to the Bengals only after serving a prison stint for armed robbery that made him a *persona non grata* to most of the other teams in the majors. Tigers skipper Ralph Houk, though, swiftly recognized that the fleet LeFlore was the answer to the club's center field hole. In 1976, LeFlore's second full season, he led the club in hitting with a .316 batting average. Two years later he paced the American League in runs and stolen bases. Convicted of thievery, LeFlore spent nine years in the majors being paid for being a thief, swiping an average of 50 bases a season.

At 5'7" and 150 pounds during his prime, Joe Morgan (above) was the smallest player in big league history to hit more than 250 home runs.

In 1978, Joe Morgan's record streak of 91 consecutive errorless games at second base ended.

Only one second baseman has ever won more than one MVP Award—Joe Morgan, who took the honor in 1975 and repeated in 1976.

Lou Brock commented on stealing: "It's almost like choosing weapons. The runner chooses, the pitcher chooses, you step off three paces, and come out firing."

Short Arm

Mickey Stanley described how he tried to conceal that his arm was shot: "I knew how different my arm was. Maybe others didn't know. I didn't advertise it. Every day when infield was practicing and outfielders were taking their positions, I would not line up in my normal position but about 30 feet in. I did everything I could to keep people from noticing."

1970s FIRST BASE FIELDING AVERAGE	
1. Ed Kranepool	.996
2. Jim Spencer	.996
3. Steve Garvey	.995
4. Carl Yastrzemski	.995
5. Lee May	.994

1970s FIRST BASE GAMES	
1. George Scott	1,297
2. Chris Chambliss	1,252
3. John Mayberry	1,193
4. Tony Perez	1,186
5. Lee May	1,079

Dodger Quartet Consistent

In 1973, the Dodgers moved Steve Garvey from third base to first base to free a spot for rookie hot corner prospect Ron Cey. The following year Garvey, Cey, second baseman Davey Lopes, and shortstop Bill Russell formed an infield unit for Los Angeles that would remain intact a record eight seasons until Steve Sax replaced Lopes in 1982. During that span, the Dodgers won four pennants and two world championships and just once, in 1979, finished lower than second place in their division. Four different All-Star Games saw three of the four on the NL team, but never did all four make it in the same year. Each of the quartet except Russell eventually took advantage of free agency to move on and play elsewhere. Lopes left in 1982 to join the Oakland A's. A year later Garvey signed with the Padres and Cey with the Cubs. Russell remained in Los Angeles, retiring in 1986 after 18 seasons in Dodger blue. His 1,746 games at shortstop are second in Dodgers' annals only to Pee Wee Reese.

1970s SECOND BASE GAMES	
1. Joe Morgan	1,415
2. Dave Cash	1,190
3. Ted Sizemore	1,162
4. Tito Fuentes	1,078
5. Felix Millan	1,077

During the 1970s, Ron Fairly and Ernie Banks both joined the select list of just four players who have participated in 1,000 or more games at two different positions.

Heaven on Earth

"Ninety feet between bases is the nearest to perfection that man has yet achieved."
—Red Smith, sportswriter

The last major league player to post a season fielding average below .900 was third baseman Butch Hobson of Boston in 1978, with an .899 average.

In 1972, Tiger flycatcher Al Kaline's AL record streak of 242 consecutive errorless games in the outfield ended.

"The rhythms of the game are so similar to the patterns of American life. Periods of leisure, interrupted by bursts of frantic activity."
—*Roger Kahn*

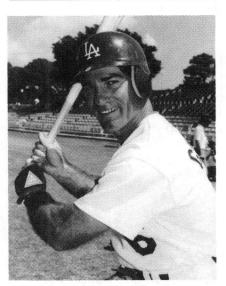

Above: *Steve Garvey had 100 or more RBI five times but never scored 100 runs in a season; the biggest reason was his low walk totals.*

Dale Murphy began his major league career in 1976 as a catcher but was forced to find another position when he developed a mental block about throwing out would-be thieves at second base.

1970s SECOND BASE CHANCES ACCEPTED	
1. Joe Morgan	7,287
2. Dave Cash	6,313
3. Ted Sizemore	6,037
4. Tito Fuentes	5,786
5. Felix Millan	5,437

On September 19, 1972, the Oakland A's used eight different second basemen in a 15-inning game with the White Sox, an all-time single-game record for the most players employed at a position other than pitcher.

When he played his 23rd consecutive season with Baltimore in 1977, Brooks Robinson set the all-time record for playing the most seasons with the same team.

Lou Brock retired after the 1979 season with a major league record for career stolen bases (938).

1970s SECOND BASE FIELDING AVERAGE	
1. Tommy Helms	.985
2. Cookie Rojas	.985
3. Joe Morgan	.985
4. Bobby Grich	.984
5. Dick Green	.983

Dodger Skippers Stay the Course

From its inception in 1884, the Dodgers franchise has displayed extraordinary continuity. Nowhere is it more prominent than in the way the club has treated its managers. Since 1900, the Dodgers have had only 13 different skippers. By contrast, the Giants have had 21, the Pirates 23, the Cards 33, the Phillies 38, the Braves 39, the Cubs 40 (not counting the "College of Coaches"), and the Reds 41. All but one of the Dodgers' 13 different managers since 1900—Harry Lumley, who sat at the reins in 1909—has manned the wheel for at least two full seasons. The three who have enjoyed the greatest longevity are Wilbert Robinson, Walter Alston, and Tommy Lasorda. Alston piloted the club for nearly 23 years, breaking Robinson's record of 18 seasons in 1972. When Alston stepped down voluntarily on September 28, 1976, turning the job over to Lasorda, it forged a chain that reaches back 40 years. Not since Chuck Dressen was relieved of command at the end of the 1953 season have the Dodgers had to resort to firing a manager.

Jeff Torborg exposed the art of catching: "There must be some reason we're the only ones facing the other way."

St. Louis Cardinal outfielder Lou Brock in 1974 broke the major league swipe record by stealing 118 bases.

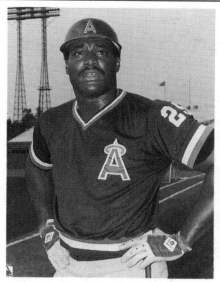

Above: *Don Baylor became primarily a designated hitter after winning the MVP Award in 1979 but was so effective in the role that he played nearly 10 more seasons.*

In 1976, the Oakland A's set a team record with 341 stolen bases.

Davey Lopes of Los Angeles set a major league record in 1975 when he swiped 38 consecutive bases without being caught.

The Oakland A's have turned five triple plays since moving to Oakland in 1968. Wayne Gross was involved in four triple killings, three in one season (1979).

1970s THIRD BASE GAMES	
1. Graig Nettles	1,547
2. Sal Bando	1,449
3. Aurelio Rodriguez	1,389
4. Doug Rader	1,102
5. Ken Reitz	1,086

As a rookie in 1972, Don Baylor of the Orioles swiped 24 bases in 26 attempts to pace the American League with a 92.3 stolen base average.

1970s THIRD BASE FIELDING AVERAGE	
1. Brooks Robinson	.971
2. Rico Petrocelli	.970
3. Don Money	.969
4. Ken Reitz	.968
5. Aurelio Rodriguez	.966

"If there is such a thing as a good loser, then the game is crooked."
—Billy Martin

In 1975, Bob Watson of the Astros scored the millionth run in major league history.

For the second time in Detroit's history, it won a flag by a half-game. In 1972, the first players' strike in major league history ended on April 10; several games were not made up, and Boston lost to the Tigers by a half-game. The first time was in 1908.

In 1976, the New York Yankees garnered their first AL flag since 1964.

In 1975, the Detroit Tigers went winless in 19 straight games, the longest losing skein in the AL since 1943.

Jim Bouton described how he prepared to make a comeback at age 38: "This winter I'm working out every day, throwing at a wall. I'm 11 and 0 against the wall."

1970s SHORTSTOP GAMES	
1. Larry Bowa	1,481
2. Mark Belanger	1,385
3. Bert Campaneris	1,320
4. Freddie Patek	1,306
5. Dave Concepcion	1,303

In 1971, the Baltimore Orioles became the first team since the 1942 to '44 St. Louis Cardinals to win 100 or more games three years in a row.

The first general strike in major league history was a 13-day strike by the players in 1972 that delayed the opening of the season for 10 days.

The Oakland Athletics in 1972 captured the franchise's first American League pennant since 1931 and first world championship since '30.

The Oakland A's in 1974 won their third consecutive world championship, becoming the only franchise other than the New York Yankees to win three in a row.

The average player's salary in 1979 reached the $113,500 mark.

Above: *Johnny Bench caught at least 107 games in every season during the 1970s. By 1979, it had exacted a toll on him. After age 31 he was never again a major offensive force.*

The Milwaukee Brewers are the only major league team to be a member of both divisions in its league while based in the same city; now in the AL East, the Brewers were stationed in the AL West in 1970 and '71, their first two seasons in Milwaukee.

In 1979, the Toronto Blue Jays set an AL record for the most losses since the schedule was lengthened to 162 games when they went down to defeat 109 times.

1970s SHORTSTOP FIELDING AVERAGE	
1. Larry Bowa	.982
2. Mark Belanger	.979
3. Dal Maxvill	.978
4. Frank Duffy	.977
5. Bucky Dent	.976

Cheap Suds Brew Trouble

For the past 30 years, the Cleveland Indians management has tried everything short of summoning Bill Veeck's ghost in a vain effort to boost attendance and revive the fan interest that made the Forest City the envy of the majors in the late 1940s. Most of the promotional stunts have failed miserably and some have even resulted in near disaster. The closest brush with catastrophe came on June 4, 1974, when the club staged a special "10-cent Beer Night" for a game with the Texas Rangers. At a dime a throw, the suds flowed so freely that the crowd raged out of control before the verdict was settled. With the score tied 5-5, fans began pouring out of the stands while the game was in progress and invading the field. Unable to restore order, the umpires forfeited the contest to Texas. On two other occasions during the decade, at Chicago's Comiskey Park in 1979 and at RFK Stadium in 1971 near the end of the Senators' last game in Washington, unruly crowds similarly gave arbiters no choice but to stop the action and declare a forfeit.

The 1973 Mets won the National League pennant with a .509 winning percentage, the lowest ever for a major league flag winner.

After six consecutive last-place finishes in the NL West, the San Diego Padres escaped the division cellar for the first time in 1975.

Cleveland Bottoms Out

Anyone who has followed the plight of the Cleveland Indians since the Tribe won its last pennant in 1954 knows why the club for years has had the most execrable attendance figures in the majors. The last time the Indians played a game after the month of the July in which they had anything significant at stake was in 1959. The last time Cleveland finished more than 10 games above .500 was in 1968. After enjoying more than its share of batting leaders and home run champs in the first half of the century, the Tribe has not had a batting king since Bobby Avila in 1954 and the club's last home run leader was Rocky Colavito, who tied for the top spot in 1959. The last MVP winner? Al Rosen in 1953. The one and only Cy Young celebrant? Gaylord Perry in 1972. Two years after his triumph Perry posted 21 victories, making him the Tribe's last 20-game winner to date.

Above: Amos Otis, holder of many Royals' team marks, was a bargain-basement acquisition from the New York Mets.

Fame and Fortune

Jim Bouton explained why he wrote *Ball Four* while he was still an active player: "I thought if I ever got to be famous or great I'd write a book about it. Unfortunately, I couldn't wait any longer."

On April 10, 1977, Cleveland and Boston combined to score a major league-record 19 runs in one inning.

Punch Line

"Lots of people look up to Billy Martin. That's because he just knocked them down."
—Jim Bouton

Luis Aparicio retired in 1973 with almost every major career fielding record for a shortstop, including the most chances accepted and the most games played at the position.

In 1975, the Pittsburgh Pirates beat the Cubs 22-0; it was the most one-sided shutout in the major leagues since 1901.

"Why am I wasting so much dedication on a mediocre career?"
—Ron Swoboda

1970s OUTFIELD GAMES	
1. Bobby Murcer	1,467
2. Amos Otis	1,422
3. Bobby Bonds	1,386
4. Lou Brock	1,327
5. Reggie Jackson	1,318
6. Ken Singleton	1,310
7. Roy White	1,190
8. Paul Blair	1,189
9. Cesar Cedeno	1,181
10. Al Oliver	1,174
11. Ralph Garr	1,167
12. Cesar Geronimo	1,145
Dusty Baker	1,145
14. Reggie Smith	1,140
15. Greg Luzinski	1,116

Nettles Some Hot Corner Performer

Graig Nettles may be the only player in the past 50 years to play for a team in New York and never get the attention he deserved. Brooks Robinson hauled down all the Gold Gloves at third base in the early 1970s, and in the last half of the decade Mike Schmidt was rated the best slugging third baseman and George Brett the best hitter for average at the hot corner. But as an all-around player, none of the three was superior to Nettles. What hampered him in his quest for recognition was that he never hit much for average. His peak season was .276 in 1978, and he usually finished somewhere around .250. Nettles was in many ways a prototype of the sort of player who performed at third base a century ago. Strong, durable, sure-armed, fearless, and a magnet for balls hit his way, Nettles retired in 1988, second only to Brooks Robinson in career assists and games played at third base.

Earl Weaver's motto was: "Bad ballplayers make good managers." Weaver then said the best part of his game was "the base on balls."

The last major league game ever played in Washington, in 1971, ended in a forfeit when angry Senators fans stormed onto the field in the ninth inning with the Senators leading the Yankees and only one out away from victory.

Above: *Mike Schmidt displays his home run trot. After hitting .196 in 1973 as a rookie, one of the poorest marks ever by a third baseman in over 100 games, the Phils' hot corner operative claimed his first home run crown as a soph. Schmidt won eight four-bagger crowns before he retired.*

On July 30, 1978, the Atlanta Braves suffered the worst loss by a home team in NL history, as they were blown out by the Expos 19-0.

1970s OUTFIELD PUTOUTS	
1. Amos Otis	3,674
2. Garry Maddox	3,020
3. Cesar Cedeno	3,003
4. Bobby Murcer	2,975
5. Bobby Bonds	2,929
6. Paul Blair	2,841
7. Al Oliver	2,760
8. Reggie Jackson	2,756
9. Roy White	2,536
10. Cesar Geronimo	2,532
11. Mickey Rivers	2,486
12. Willie Davis	2,476
13. Reggie Smith	2,460
14. Dusty Baker	2,440
15. Billy North	2,423

1970s OUTFIELD ASSISTS	
1. Bobby Murcer	119
2. Bobby Bonds	106
3. Rusty Staub	97
4. Amos Otis	93
5. Reggie Smith	86
6. Jose Cardenal	85
7. Del Unser	82
8. Reggie Jackson	81
9. Dave Parker	80
Jeff Burroughs	80
11. Dusty Baker	78
12. Ken Singleton	77
Ralph Garr	77
14. Dwight Evans	76
15. Cesar Cedeno	74

Umpire Marty Springstead razzed Earl Weaver: "The way to test a Timex watch would be to strap it to his tongue."

In 1971, the Houston Astros played a major league record 75 one-run games.

In 1977, the Kansas City Royals became the first expansion team in history to top the majors in wins (102).

The Washington franchise moved to Texas in 1972 and was renamed the "Rangers."

My Friend Goose
"I've come to the conclusion that the two most important things in life are good friends and a good bullpen."
—Bob Lemon

Bird's Wing Clipped Career

All through the 1976 season, Mark Fidrych talked to the ball on the mound, and most of the time it obeyed him. At the end of his rookie year, the Tigers righthander had 19 wins, the American League's top ERA of 2.34 and also the AL lead in complete games with 24. Owing largely to Fidrych, Detroit regained respectability in 1976 after losing 102 games the previous year. Nicknamed "The Bird," Fidrych was a near unanimous choice for the AL Rookie of the Year Award. Expected to take his place among the premier pitchers in the game the following season, Fidrych instead encountered arm trouble. For the next four years the Tigers stuck with him in his struggle to pitch again with his rookie elan, but the comeback that never quite materialized finally was abandoned in 1980. Fidrych's 29 career wins rank as the fewest among pitchers who have won an American League Rookie of the Year Award.

After piloting Oakland to two consecutive world championships, Dick Williams (above) resigned in 1973, citing differences with owner Charlie Finley.

The first player from an expansion team to be selected for an MVP Award was Jeff Burroughs of the Texas Rangers in 1974.

In 1970, the expansion Seattle franchise was moved to Milwaukee just prior to the season; the team name changed from "Pilots" to "Brewers."

Tactical Virtuoso

"My best strategy was to sit on the bench and call out specific instructions like, 'C'mon, Boog,' 'Get hold of one, Frank', or 'Let's go, Brooks.'"
—Earl Weaver

The only city that had a major league team in 1901 but no longer has one is Washington, which lost the original Senators in 1961 and the expansion Senators in 1972.

1970s OUTFIELD CHANCES ACCEPTED	
1. Amos Otis	3,767
2. Bobby Murcer	3,094
3. Garry Maddox	3,084
4. Cesar Cedeno	3,077
5. Bobby Bonds	3,035
6. Paul Blair	2,906
7. Reggie Jackson	2,837
8. Al Oliver	2,812
9. Cesar Geronimo	2,605
10. Roy White	2,592
11. Reggie Smith	2,546
Mickey Rivers	2,546
13. Willie Davis	2,531
14. Dusty Baker	2,518
15. Billy North	2,479

Bicentennial Freshmen Flop

The record for the fewest career wins by a pitcher who received a Rookie of the Year Award (18) belongs to Butch Metzger, one of the National League's co-honorees in 1976. Metzger, a reliever with the Padres, shared the prize with Pat Zachry of the Reds. After going 11-4 with 16 saves as a yearling, Metzger collapsed almost at once, collecting only seven more saves and five more wins before departing from the majors a mere two years after his rookie triumph. Zachry likewise never lived up to his frosh billing, finishing in 1985 with a 69-67 career mark. Most of the rest of the rookie crop in 1976 fared little better. Hector Cruz, rated the National League's top frosh regular after he led the Cardinals in home runs and RBI, never again appeared in enough games to be a batting title qualifier. Of the 1976 yearling stars, only receiver Butch Wynegar of the Twins went on to have a productive career.

"Baseball was made for kids, and grownups only screw it up."
—Bob Lemon

The first American League MVP Award winner to wear glasses was Dick Allen of the White Sox in 1972.

Mike Flanagan in 1979 became the third Oriole pitcher to win a Cy Young Award.

Above: *Augie Donatelli wrapped up his 24-year career as a National League arbiter in 1973.*

In 1975, Frank Robinson became the first black manager in major league history, as he was named the manager of Cleveland.

In 1975, Fred Lynn of the Red Sox became the only rookie in major league history to win an MVP Award.

1970s OUTFIELD FIELDING AVERAGE	
1. Pete Rose	.994
2. Ken Berry	.992
3. Joe Rudi	.991
4. Steve Brye	.991
5. Amos Otis	.990
6. Mickey Stanley	.990
7. Bake McBride	.989
8. Dwight Evans	.989
9. Roy White	.989
10. Elliott Maddox	.989
11. Lyman Bostock	.988
12. George Hendrick	.988
13. Cesar Geronimo	.988
14. Mike Lum	.988
15. Paul Blair	.987

Dick Williams in 1973 said of A's owner Charlie Finley: "He has been wonderful to me. I have nothing but the highest regard for him." A year later the deposed manager said: "A man can take just so much of Finley."

1970s MANAGER WINS	
1. Earl Weaver	944
2. Sparky Anderson	919
3. Gene Mauch	771
4. Chuck Tanner	770
5. Billy Martin	719
6. Ralph Houk	697
7. Dick Williams	681
8. Bill Virdon	646
9. Walter Alston	636
10. Danny Ozark	594

The last manager to pilot a team to a division title and 100 or more wins in two consecutive seasons was Danny Ozark with the 1976 and '77 Phillies.

Frank Robinson marked his debut as Cleveland's player-manager and the first black pilot in major league history by homering on Opening Day in 1975.

In 1970, his first full season at the Oakland A's helm, John McNamara piloted the club to 89 wins and the franchise's best record since 1932.

In 1971, Cleveland third baseman Graig Nettles compiled a major league record 412 assists.

1970s MANAGER WINNING PERCENTAGE	
1. Sparky Anderson	.591
2. Earl Weaver	.590
3. Walter Alston	.567
4. Danny Murtaugh	.564
5. Billy Martin	.555
6. Eddie Kasko	.539
7. Danny Ozark	.538
8. Whitey Herzog	.536
9. Chuck Tanner	.527
10. Dick Williams	.523

Gates Brown, an ex-convict who preceded Ron LeFlore on the Tigers, said of high school "I took a little English, a little math, some science, a few hubcaps, and some wheel covers."

In 1977, the Rangers went through three managers and were a game below .500 at 34-35 before turning to Billy Hunter, who guided the club to a sparkling 94-68 finish.

In 1977, Braves owner Ted Turner took over the managerial reins for one game before pressure from commissioner Bowie Kuhn forced him to return them to Dave Bristol.

Pirates first baseman Willie Stargell and Cardinal first baseman Keith Hernandez in 1979 were the first players to finish in a flat tie for a league Most Valuable Player Award.

Staub Gets 500 Hits with Four Teams

Free agency and the corresponding frequency with which players nowadays are traded have made for so much mobility that fans seldom have an opportunity to form the sort of allegiance that a Ted Williams or a Mickey Mantle or a Bob Feller once commanded. At one point during the 1970s, Mike Torrez won 14 or more games five years in a row with five different teams. Rusty Staub meanwhile achieved a distinction that would have seemed impossible prior to expansion. When he made his 500th hit as a member of the Detroit Tigers in 1978, Staub became the first player in history to collect 500 or more hits with four different teams. The clubs that benefited from Staub's bat were the Astros, the Expos, the Mets and, finally, the Tigers. In addition, Staub notched 102 hits with the Texas Rangers in 1980. He completed his 23-year career in 1985 with 2,712 base hits.

High Averages
"It isn't really the stars that are expensive. It's the high cost of mediocrity."
—Bill Veeck

In June 1976, Charlie Finley tried to sell Joe Rudi, Rollie Fingers, and Vida Blue, but commissioner Bowie Kuhn vetoed the deals using the "Best Interest of Baseball" clause of the National Agreement.

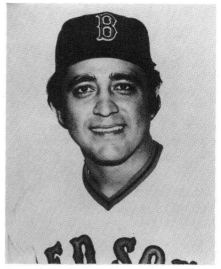

Above: *Mike Torrez won at least 11 games for eight different major league teams. The Red Sox were the chief beneficiaries of his work, receiving 60 of his 185 victories.*

On September 12, 1976, Minnie Minoso (age 54) of the White Sox became the oldest player to get a hit in a major league game.

Willie Stargell of the Pittsburgh Pirates in 1979 became the oldest MVP in history at age 39.

The last manager to steer a club to three consecutive 100-loss seasons is Roy Hartsfield with the 1977 to 1979 Toronto Blue Jays.

Pennies From Heaven
Vida Blue once paid a fine of $250 to Charlie Finley all in coins, saying: "I wanted to make it all in pennies, but they're hard to come by."

Weaver Winds Up Winning

In 1948, his first year in organized baseball, Earl Weaver led all second basemen in the Class-D Illinois State League in putouts and fielding average and also topped the loop in games played. Promoted to St. Joseph in the Class-C Western Association the following year, Weaver hit .282 and was fourth in the circuit in RBI with 102. Year by year Weaver continued to advance up the ladder in the minors, until he got to the Class-AA Texas League. There, for the first time, he found himself in over his head and was forced to drop back a notch to the Class-A Western League. Realizing soon thereafter that the major leagues were out of reach, Weaver did what another scrappy minor league second baseman named Joe McCarthy had done 40 years earlier. He turned to managing. Like McCarthy, Weaver evolved into the most successful major league manager of his era. In his 17 seasons at the Baltimore helm, he bagged four pennants ('69 to '71, 1979) and six division titles ('69 to '71, '73 and '74, 1979). He won the Series in 1970.

No, Thanks

"I'm not sure which is more insulting, being offered in a trade or having it turned down."
—Claude Osteen

The first night game in World Series history was game four of the 1971 World Series, on October 13, 1971, at Pittsburgh.

Above: *Earl Weaver retired in 1982 with a .604 career winning percentage. A subsequent return to the Orioles helm lowered his mark to .583.*

After years of protracted legal battles, girls were finally allowed to play baseball on the Little League level in 1974.

In 1973, the American League adopted the designated hitter rule, allowing a permanent pinch hitter for pitchers.

Former Cleveland slugger Luke Easter was shot to death by two robbers during a payroll holdup outside a Cleveland bank in 1979.

"We will scheme, connive, steal, and do everything possible to win the pennant—except pay big salaries."
—*Bill Veeck, White Sox owner, in the 1970s*

The third "Basic Agreement"—signed in 1973—granted to the players the right to salary arbitration.

In 1971, the Pittsburgh Pirates became the first major league team to wear form-fitting double knit uniforms.

The Los Angeles Dodgers in 1978 were the first team to draw more than 3 million fans in a single season.

1970s TEAM WINS		
	WON	LOST
1. Cincinnati-NL	953	657
2. Baltimore-AL	944	656
3. Pittsburgh-NL	916	695
4. Los Angeles-NL	910	701
5. Boston-AL	895	714
6. New York-AL	892	715
7. Kansas City-AL	851	760
8. Oakland-AL	838	772
9. Philadelphia-NL	812	801
10. Minnesota-AL	812	794
11. St. Louis-NL	800	813
12. San Francisco-NL	794	818
13. Houston-NL	793	817
14. Detroit-AL	789	820
15. Chicago-NL	785	827
16. California-AL	781	831
17. New York Mets-NL	763	850
18. Chicago-AL	752	853
19. Montreal-NL	748	862
20. Washington-Texas-AL	747	860
Washington-AL	*133*	*188*
Texas-AL	*614*	*672*
21. Milwaukee-AL	738	873
22. Cleveland-AL	737	866
23. Atlanta-NL	725	883
24. San Diego-NL	667	942
25. Seattle-AL	187	297
26. Toronto-AL	166	318

Murtaugh Murder on Pirate Foes

Danny Murtaugh was in many ways a near mirror image of Earl Weaver. As Weaver spent his entire major league dugout career with Baltimore, Murtaugh's 15 seasons as a big league pilot all came with one club, Pittsburgh. And, like Weaver, Murtaugh was a scrappy second baseman during his playing days who had more brains than talent. The difference was that Murtaugh got to play in the majors for nearly a full decade. Perhaps the best indication of how he succeeded in finessing his way to the top came in his rookie season of 1941. Even though he played in just 85 games, Murtaugh paced the National League in stolen bases—albeit with a .219 batting average, the lowest in this century by a league leader in pilfered sacks. Time and again, a heart condition forced Murtaugh to surrender his managerial responsibilities, but his dugout expertise was so sorely missed that on each occasion he was begged by the Pirates to return, until at last he succumbed to his ailing heart at the finish of the 1976 season.

The third Basic Agreement in '73 also had a "five-and-10" rule, saying that players in the majors 10 years and with a team for five years can veto any trades.

At the finish of the 1976 season, Tom Gorman retired after serving as a National League umpire for 26 consecutive years.

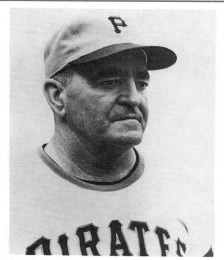

Above: *Danny Murtaugh skippered the Pirates to two pennants and fell short three other times when Pittsburgh faltered in the LCS.*

Roy Howell needed surgery after he was wounded in the arm in a drive-by shooting while deer hunting in the 1972 off-season but recovered to play 11 seasons in the majors.

In 1973, it was made public that Yankee pitchers Mike Kekich and Fritz Peterson swapped wives.

The only "rainout" in Astrodome history occurred on June 15, 1976, when heavy rains prevented fans and the umpires from getting to the dome.

Perfection Plus
"They expect an umpire to be perfect on opening day and to improve as the season goes on."
—Nestor Chylak, umpire

"Isn't it amazing that we're worth so much on the trading block and worth so little when we talk salary with the general manager?"
—Jim Kern, Texas reliever

After pleading guilty in 1974 to 14 felony counts of illegal contributions to Richard Nixon's reelection campaign, Yankees owner George Steinbrenner was fined $15,000 and suspended from baseball for two years.

1970s TEAM WINNING PERCENT-AGE	
1. Cincinnati-NL	.592
2. Baltimore-AL	.590
3. Pittsburgh-NL	.569
4. Los Angeles-NL	.565
5. Boston-AL	.556
6. New York-AL	.555
7. Kansas City-AL	.528
8. Oakland-AL	.520
9. Minnesota-AL	.506
10. Philadelphia-NL	.503
11. St. Louis-NL	.496
12. San Francisco-NL	.493
13. Houston-NL	.493
14. Detroit-AL	.490
15. Chicago-NL	.487
16. California-AL	.484
17. New York Mets-NL	.473
18. Chicago-AL	.469
19. Washington-Texas-AL	.465
Washington-AL	*.414*
Texas-AL	*.477*
20. Montreal-NL	.465
21. Cleveland-AL	.460
22. Milwaukee-AL	.458
23. Atlanta-NL	.451
24. San Diego-NL	.415
25. Seattle-AL	.386
26. Toronto-AL	.343

Chapter 11

1980 to 1993

Robin Yount, Paul Molitor, and Jim Gantner played together from 1978 to 1992 for the Brewers. In that time, they compiled 6,399 base hits, the most ever for a trio of team-mates. The second-top trio was George Brett, Willie Wilson, and Frank White, Royals from 1976 to 1990 who compiled 6,200. Brett, White, and Hal McRae, Royals from 1973 to 1987, are third with 5,804.

The last player to top the majors in both batting average and slugging average in the same season was George Brett of the Kansas City Royals in 1980.

Pill

"George Brett could get good wood on an aspirin."

—Jim Frey

Of all the members of the 3,000-hit club, George Brett (above) reached the coveted pinnacle in the most spectacular fashion. Needing four hits to make an even 3,000, Brett promptly went 4-for-5.

1980-1993 GAMES	
1. Eddie Murray	2,118
2. Ozzie Smith	2,034
3. Robin Yount	2,011
4. Cal Ripken	1,962
Harold Baines	1,962
6. Andre Dawson	1,956
7. Lou Whitaker	1,937
8. Rickey Henderson	1,904
9. Tim Wallach	1,900
10. Dave Winfield	1,895
11. Dale Murphy	1,888
12. Brett Butler	1,834
13. Willie Wilson	1,831
14. Ryne Sandberg	1,822
George Brett	1,822
16. Tim Raines	1,813
17. Alfredo Griffin	1,778
18. Alan Trammell	1,777
19. Wade Boggs	1,768
20. Steve Sax	1,762
21. Paul Molitor	1,751
22. Tony Pena	1,750
23. Gary Gaetti	1,745
24. Chili Davis	1,743
25. Tom Brunansky	1,736

Brett Flirts With .400 Batting Average

In 1979, George Brett became only the second player in American League history to compile 20 or more doubles, triples, and home runs in the same season. The following year, a lengthy stay on the disabled list with a foot injury held him to just 117 games and prevented him from repeating his 1979 achievement. In 1980, however, Brett accomplished something even more remark-able—he hit .390 to post the highest batting average since 1941. In addition, the Kansas City third baseman achieved another rarity by collecting 118 RBI to give him an average of more than one ribbie for every game he played. He also had a .461 on-base percentage and a .664 slugging average. Brett's performance in 1980 earned him both the AL MVP Award and selection as the *Sporting News* Man of the Year. More importantly, it sparked Kansas City to its first pennant and a date with the Phillies in the World Series. Even though Philadelphia prevailed in six games, it was no fault of Brett's. He capped his amazing 1980 campaign by slapping .375 in the fall classic.

Boggs Establishes Batting Mastery

Even after Wade Boggs hit .349 in 108 games as a rookie in 1982, the Boston Red Sox were still not convinced he was for real. With considerable trepidation, they traded incumbent third baseman Carney Lansford to Oakland and installed Boggs at the hot corner in 1983. The Sox' anxiety quickly evaporated after Boggs hit .361 as a sophomore and claimed the American League batting title. At the conclusion of the 1988 season, Boggs had four more batting crowns to his credit and a .356 career average, the highest of any player at a comparable point in his career since Al Simmons in 1931. He batted .361 in 1983, .325 in 1984, .368 in '85, .357 in '86, .363 in '87, and .366 in 1988. That same season, Boggs collected his sixth successive 200-hit season to break Simmons's old AL mark of five. In 1989, Boggs added a 20th-century record seventh straight 200-hit season despite being hounded by a palimony suit that for a time eclipsed all of his on-the-field accomplishments.

Kansas City manager Jim Frey revealed the advice he gave to George Brett about hitting: "I tell him, 'Attaway to hit, George.'"

Only three third basemen in major league history—Bill Madlock, Wade Boggs, and George Brett—have won more than one batting title and all were active during the 1980s.

Above: *Wade Boggs threatened in the late 1980s to compile the highest career batting average of any post-World War II player before tailing off considerably in recent years.*

Wade Boggs's .480 on-base percentage in 1988 was the highest in the majors since Mickey Mantle's .488 in 1962.

The Boston Red Sox hold the American League record for having the most batting titlists with 20; Wade Boggs in 1988 was the team's last champion.

Two of the three top career batting averages of all-time by third basemen belong to Wade Boggs and George Brett.

George Brett in 1990 became the first player in major league history to win batting average titles in three different decades.

When Wade Boggs of Boston led the major leagues with 240 hits in 1985, he totaled the most safeties in the majors since 1930.

Wade Boggs in 1989 collected 200 hits for the 20th-century record seventh consecutive year.

1980-1993 RUNS	
1. Rickey Henderson	1,537
2. Robin Yount	1,254
3. Paul Molitor	1,235
4. Tim Raines	1,210
5. Eddie Murray	1,164
6. Wade Boggs	1,150
7. Ryne Sandberg	1,143
8. Lou Whitaker	1,132
9. Cal Ripken	1,130
10. Brett Butler	1,128
11. Dave Winfield	1,113
12. Dale Murphy	1,070
13. Dwight Evans	1,057
14. Andre Dawson	1,056
15. George Brett	1,051
16. Alan Trammell	1,026
17. Ozzie Smith	1,008
18. Willie Wilson	999
19. Harold Baines	929
20. Tony Gwynn	912
21. Steve Sax	911
22. Kirby Puckett	909
23. Willie Randolph	895
24. Julio Franco	892
25. Brian Downing	889

Gwynn Gives San Diego Batting Champ

As the 1991 season entered its final lap, Tony Gwynn seemed poised to snag his fifth National League batting title. But a knee injury froze his average at .317, two points behind eventual winner Terry Pendleton. Few doubted, however, that Gwynn would rebound from off-season surgery to challenge for more hitting crowns, since he had always been in the running for a decade. His .328 career average at the finish of the 1991 season stood as the highest by any NL performer since Stan Musial retired in 1963. Gwynn ap-peared on the major league scene in 1982, and he won his first batting crown in 1984, getting a .351 average on 213 base hits. His high-water mark came in 1987, when he hit .370, the best average in the senior loop in the past 44 years. The following season the San Diego outfielder garnered a second distinction as his .313 average was the lowest ever to take an NL hitting title. In 1989, Gwynn became the first senior loop performer since Musial in 1952 to nab three consecutive batting crowns.

1980-1993 HITS	
1. Eddie Murray	2,294
2. Robin Yount	2,271
3. Wade Boggs	2,267
4. Paul Molitor	2,162
5. Andre Dawson	2,132
6. Cal Ripken	2,087
7. Ryne Sandberg	2,080
8. George Brett	2,072
9. Harold Baines	2,060
10. Tim Raines	2,050
11. Rickey Henderson	2,043
12. Tony Gwynn	2,039
13. Dave Winfield	2,034
14. Kirby Puckett	1,996
15. Ozzie Smith	1,989
16. Willie Wilson	1,962
17. Brett Butler	1,958
18. Steve Sax	1,943
19. Lou Whitaker	1,932
20. Alan Trammell	1,927
21. Don Mattingly	1,908
22. Dale Murphy	1,844
23. Willie McGee	1,832
24. Tim Wallach	1,800
25. Julio Franco	1,784

Tony Gwynn described his hitting success: "See the ball, hit the ball, run like hell.'

Andres Galarraga of Colorado was the first player on a first-year expansion team to win a bat title, hitting .370 in 1993.

Willie McGee in 1990 became the first major league player to win a batting title without being in the league at the time he won it, because he was traded from St. Louis to Oakland in August.

Above: *Tony Gwynn has won four National League batting titles in the past 10 seasons. Injuries have impeded his quest for a fifth crown in recent years.*

McGee Atypical Two-Time Titlist

Willie McGee ranks as the strangest two-time batting titlist since Mickey Vernon. McGee's first crown came in 1985, when he emerged from nowhere in his fourth season with the Cardinals to stroke .353 and establish a new post-1900 record for a National League switch-hitter. McGee followed his glittering 1985 campaign by sagging to .256 in 1985, a drop of 97 points, the largest in history by a defending senior loop hitting champ. Three years later, he reached a career nadir, hitting just .236 in an injury-plagued season. Then in 1990, he came out of nowhere again to hit .335 and win his second batting crown, albeit the first one ever claimed in absentia. Late in the campaign, McGee was shipped to the American League Oakland A's by the Cardinals, meaning that he was no longer even in the NL at the season's close. He returned to the senior loop prior to the 1991 campaign, however, signing with San Francisco as a free agent.

In 1988, Jose Canseco of the Oakland A's became the first player to steal 40 bases and hit 40 homers in the same season.

On August 17, 1990, Carlton Fisk hit his 329th homer as a catcher—a major league record.

In 1987, Mark McGwire of the A's pounded a rookie record 49 homers.

Pittsburgh's Barry Bonds in 1990 became the first player in major league history to hit .300 with 30 homers, 100 RBI, and 50 stolen bases.

A record four players shared the American League home run crown in the abbreviated 1981 season with 22 circuit clouts apiece.

In the 1987 season, 34 players in the American League alone clouted 25 or more home runs and seven teams had at least four players with 20 or more dingers.

The only player ever to clout 40 homers and steal 40 bases in the same season, Jose Canseco (above) once seemed poised to take his place among the game's all-time greats. He still may.

1980-1993 TOTAL BASES	
1. Eddie Murray	3,831
2. Andre Dawson	3,686
3. Robin Yount	3,557
4. Dave Winfield	3,461
5. Cal Ripken	3,447
6. George Brett	3,383
7. Harold Baines	3,291
8. Dale Murphy	3,281
9. Ryne Sandberg	3,274
10. Paul Molitor	3,194
11. Rickey Henderson	3,144
12. Wade Boggs	3,072
13. Lou Whitaker	3,022
14. Don Mattingly	2,959
15. Tim Raines	2,953
16. Kirby Puckett	2,939
17. Dwight Evans	2,933
18. Tim Wallach	2,891
19. George Bell	2,873
20. Alan Trammell	2,869
21. Kent Hrbek	2,861
22. Joe Carter	2,723
23. Chili Davis	2,712
24. Tony Gwynn	2,709
25. Gary Gaetti	2,704

A Brewers official said about Robin Yount: "When Robin was 20, the fear was that he had none [no fear]. It still is."

Ron Kittle followed his minor league leading 50 home runs for Edmonton of the Pacific Coast League in 1982 by hammering 35 dingers as a White Sox rookie in 1983.

In 1987, Eric Davis of the Reds set a record for the most combined home runs and steals by a 30-30 Club member when he had 37 homers and 50 thefts for a total of 87.

Parker Finds New Life as DH

During the 1980s, the American League continued to be a haven for aging or disabled veterans who could no longer cut it in the field but still had enough offensive pop to serve as a designated hitter. Several, such as Dave Parker, even made the transition a highly profitable one for them. After a mediocre year with the Reds in 1987, Parker was traded to Oakland for Jose Rijo. In 1989, Parker had 22 homers and 97 RBI as the A's designated hitter. He signed that winter as a free agent with the Brewers. Parker's luck ran out in 1991, however, when his .239 average and huge salary made the Blue Jays, his fourth AL team in three seasons, loath to offer him a new contract. Parker's departure left Brian Downing of the Texas Rangers as the oldest reigning DH both in terms of age and longevity in the role. The 1992 season marked the 41-year-old Downing's fifth straight as a designated hitter.

A Los Angeles Times columnist instructed how to conduct a paternity test to determine whether a baby was Steve Garvey's: "If the baby's hair is mussed, it's not Garvey's."

In 1986, when Bert Blyleven of the Twins set a major league record by allowing his 47th homer of the season, the blow was struck by Cleveland's Jay Bell in his first major league at bat.

Above: *Julio Franco for nearly a decade has ranked among the top-hitting middle infielders in recent times. In 1992, injuries ruined his bid to defend his 1991 batting crown.*

Second baseman Julio Franco in 1991 became the first member of the Washington-Texas Rangers franchise to win an AL bat crown when he hit .341.

Rafael Palmeiro, Julio Franco, and Ruben Sierra of the Rangers all notched more than 200 hits in 1991 to tie an AL team record.

On September 20, 1981, Minnesota's Gary Gaetti, Kent Hrbek, and Tim Laudner all homered in their first major league game.

1980-1993 DOUBLES	
1. George Brett	454
2. Wade Boggs	448
3. Robin Yount	439
4. Eddie Murray	399
5. Cal Ripken	395
Andre Dawson	395
7. Don Mattingly	390
8. Paul Molitor	389
9. Tim Wallach	379
10. Dave Winfield	366
11. Lou Whitaker	358
12. Alan Trammell	356
Harold Baines	356
14. Kirby Puckett	343
15. Ryne Sandberg	340
16. Rickey Henderson	338
17. Ozzie Smith	334
18. Dwight Evans	333
19. Tim Raines	331
20. Dave Parker	323
21. Tony Gwynn	316
22. Dale Murphy	315
23. George Bell	308
24. Gary Gaetti	307
Chili Davis	307

Winfield Still Chasing Flies

Dave Winfield celebrated his 18th major league season in 1991 by turning 40 and still taking his regular turn in the outfield. Idled all of the 1989 season by a back ailment, Winfield upon his return in 1990 collected just 475 at bats. In 1991, however, he performed in 150 games with the Angels and slammed 28 home runs. Winfield then joined the Blue Jays prior to the 1992 campaign as a free agent and continued to defy his age. Although finally relegated to the DH role, he batted .290 with 26 homers and 108 RBI. On September 14, 1992, he became the first 40–year–old ever to drive in 100 runs in a season. Winfield helped the Jays to the '92 world title by driving in the winning run in the sixth game of the World Series. Winfield joined the Twins in 1993 and hit a solid .271 with 21 dingers and 76 RBI. On September 16, 1993 Winfield became the 19th player in major league history to collect 3,000 career hits.

1980-1993 TRIPLES		
1.	Willie Wilson	130
2.	Brett Butler	109
3.	Tim Raines	100
4.	Robin Yount	98
5.	Juan Samuel	89
6.	Andy Van Slyke	86
7.	Willie McGee	84
8.	Tony Fernandez	81
9.	Tony Gwynn	78
10.	Mookie Wilson	71
	Paul Molitor	71
12.	Vince Coleman	70
13.	Alfredo Griffin	68
14.	Ryne Sandberg	67
15.	Lloyd Moseby	66
16.	Andre Dawson	65
17.	George Brett	64
18.	Lonnie Smith	58
	Omar Moreno	58
20.	Larry Herndon	56
21.	Mitch Webster	54
	Garry Templeton	54
	Kirby Puckett	54
	Spike Owen	54
25.	Rickey Henderson	53

In the 1992 American League Championship Series, Dave Winfield (above) became the oldest player ever to homer in postseason play.

In 1986, Willie Aikens set a 20th-century record for the highest batting average to lead a professional league when he hit .454 for Puebla of the Mexican League.

Monthly

In 1981, George Steinbrenner reviewed expensive free-agent Dave Winfield after Steinbrenner let Reggie Jackson go as a free agent to the Angels: "I let Mr. October get away and I got Mr. May."

Mike Hargrove set a Cleveland Indians club record in 1980 when he walked 111 times.

Mattingly Mashes Myriad Marks

In 1986, Don Mattingly shattered two all-time New York Yankee franchise marks when he logged 238 hits and rapped 53 doubles. He batted .352 and slugged .573 that year. The following year, his hit totals and slugging figures dropped across the board, but he continued to set records. In 1987, he tied Dale Long's 31-year-old record by homering in eight consecutive games. Next, Mattingly broke Ernie Banks's 32-year-old mark of five grand slams in a season by clubbing six four-ribbie round-trippers. Finally, on July 20, Mattingly tied a major league record for first basemen when he handled 22 chances in a game. For the season, Mattingly compiled 30 home runs and 115 RBI, good totals but hardly awesome. He nevertheless packed two remarkable all-time slugging records into his stats, plus a fielding mark as a bonus. Although just age 26 at the time, Mattingly has not matched any of his 1987 slugging totals in the years since.

A premier hitter early in his career, Don Mattingly (above) has since fallen prey to an ailing back and a poor supporting cast. Mattingly is the only performer to play 10 straight years with the Yankees and never get into a postseason game.

Mike Schmidt of the Philadelphia Phillies in 1980 set a major league record for third basemen with 48 home runs.

The 1982 Brewers set a major league record with 1.57 homers per game on the road.

In 1982, the world champion Cardinals ranked last in the majors in home runs with just 67.

In 1987, the Toronto Blue Jays smacked a major league single-game record 10 homers.

Brotherly Love

"Philadelphia is the only city where you can experience the thrill of victory and the agony of reading about it the next day."
—Mike Schmidt

Toronto outfielder George Bell was the first player in major league history to hit three home runs on Opening Day, in 1988.

The American League record for the most RBI in a season since expansion is held by Don Mattingly with 145 in 1985.

On July 6, 1986, Atlanta's Bob Horner became the first player in this century to hit four homers in a game lost by his team.

Mike Piazza of the Los Angeles Dodgers in 1993 shattered numerous records for a rookie catcher when he cracked 35 home runs with 112 RBI and a .561 slugging average.

1980-1993 HOME RUNS	
1. Eddie Murray	362
2. Dale Murphy	352
3. Andre Dawson	343
4. Dave Winfield	319
5. Mike Schmidt	313
6. Cal Ripken	297
7. Darryl Strawberry	290
8. Kent Hrbek	283
9. Lance Parrish	281
10. Dwight Evans	275
Joe Carter	275
12. Jack Clark	274
13. George Bell	265
14. Tom Brunansky	261
Harold Baines	261
16. Gary Gaetti	245
Jose Canseco	245
18. George Brett	243
19. Jesse Barfield	241
20. Ryne Sandberg	240
21. Carlton Fisk	232
22. Darrell Evans	230
Brian Downing	230
24. Mark McGwire	229
25. Fred McGriff	228

With the hometown Los Angeles Dodgers in 1992, Darryl Strawberry (above) had a disc problem that severely cut his production. It stopped him from collecting at least 26 homers for the first time in his career and helped contribute to the Dodgers' first cellar finish since 1905.

The first member of an expansion team to lead the National League in slugging average was Darryl Strawberry of the Mets in 1988.

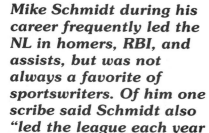

Mike Schmidt during his career frequently led the NL in homers, RBI, and assists, but was not always a favorite of sportswriters. Of him one scribe said Schmidt also "led the league each year in false humility."

Pendleton Arrives to Advance Atlanta

Few in the Mound City mourned when Terry Pendleton left the Cardinals at the end of the 1990 season to sign with the Braves. After a peak of .286 with 96 RBI in 1987, Pendleton had declined steadily thereafter, reaching bottom in 1990 when he hit just .230 with a .280 on-base percentage and a .324 slugging average. In his first season with the Braves, Pendleton posted a batting average that nearly matched his 1990 slugging average as he hit .319 to win the National League batting crown. Moreover, he hoisted his on-base percentage to .363 and his slugging average to .517. Voted both the NL's MVP and Comeback Player of the Year, Pendleton culminated his stunning 1991 season by spurring the Braves from a cellar finish in 1990 to their first pennant since moving to Atlanta. The third sacker in addition became only the third switch-hitter in NL history to seize a batting crown. He backed up his strong 1991 stats with an equally good season in '92 to prove that his stirring comeback was not a fluke.

In 1984, Phillie Mike Schmidt became the first major leaguer to end up in a tie for both his loop's home run and RBI crowns in the same season.

In 1986, Mike Schmidt set a major league record by leading his league in homers for the eighth time, as he clubbed 37.

1980-1993 RUNS BATTED IN	
1. Eddie Murray	1,380
2. Andre Dawson	1,256
3. Dave Winfield	1,247
4. Harold Baines	1,144
5. George Brett	1,135
6. Dale Murphy	1,107
7. Cal Ripken	1,104
8. Robin Yount	1,103
9. Kent Hrbek	1,033
10. George Bell	1,002
11. Dwight Evans	1,001
12. Don Mattingly	999
13. Joe Carter	994
14. Tim Wallach	967
15. Dave Parker	960
16. Jack Clark	933
17. Chili Davis	930
18. Mike Schmidt	929
19. Gary Gaetti	922
20. Lance Parrish	919
21. Lou Whitaker	895
22. Pedro Guerrero	888
23. Tom Brunansky	885
24. Gary Carter	882
25. Ryne Sandberg	881

After enjoying his best year to date in 1991, Cal Ripken (above) suffered his poorest all-around campaign in 1992. His lackluster performance gave fuel to critics who feel his run at Lou Gehrig's "Ironman" record is sapping his offensive skills.

Cal Ripken in 1991 became the first shortstop in AL history to hit .300 with 30 or more homers and 100 or more RBI.

Blame It On Rio

Toby Harrah, Cleveland third baseman, compared baseball statistics to a girl in a bikini: "They both show a lot, but not everything."

Lansford Joins List of High-Average Hot Corner Men

Prior to 1975, only two third basemen—Heinie Zimmerman in 1912 and George Kell in 1949—won major league batting titles. When Bill Madlock of the Chicago Cubs triumphed in 1975, it seemed to set off a chain reaction among third sackers in both leagues. Indeed, since 1975 no fewer than five different hot corner men have grabbed hitting crowns. A sixth, Mike Schmidt, gave it a run in 1981 before finishing at .316, good for fourth in the National League. In the American League that year, third sacker Carney Lansford of Boston joined with Seattle's Tom Paciorek to mark the first season in the junior loop since 1959 that a pair of righthanded hitters finished one-two in the batting race. Lansford's .336 average established a career high that he matched in 1989 when he nearly copped a second hitting crown before finishing behind winner Kirby Puckett of the Twins.

Padres catcher Benito Santiago in 1987 set a rookie record by hitting safely in 34 straight games.

When he paced the National League in batting in 1982 at age 35, Al Oliver became the oldest player in history to win his first batting crown.

Pittsburgh extended its own team record in 1983 when Bill Madlock gave the club its 22nd batting crown winner.

Bill Madlock won the National League batting title in 1981 with just 279 at bats, the fewest since 1879 by a hitting crown winner.

In 1993, the White Sox concluded their all-time record 50th consecutive season without having a batting crown winner; Luke Appling in 1943 was the team's last champ.

1980-1993 STOLEN BASES	
1. Rickey Henderson	1,062
2. Tim Raines	749
3. Vince Coleman	648
4. Willie Wilson	530
5. Ozzie Smith	495
6. Brett Butler	476
7. Steve Sax	444
8. Paul Molitor	371
9. Lonnie Smith	363
10. Juan Samuel	358
11. Gary Pettis	354
12. Otis Nixon	352
13. Mookie Wilson	327
14. Ryne Sandberg	323
15. Gary Redus	322
16. Willie McGee	317
17. Eric Davis	301
18. Dave Collins	291
19. Lloyd Moseby	280
Barry Bonds	280
21. Omar Moreno	270
22. Kirk Gibson	268
23. Tony Gwynn	263
24. Lenny Dykstra	257
25. Von Hayes	253

Armas: Free Swings, Not Free Passes

In 1984, Tony Armas of the Red Sox set a record for the fewest walks by a player with more than 40 home runs when he collected just 32 free passes en route to claiming the American League four-bagger crown with 43 dingers. He retired in 1989 with 251 career homers and 260 career bases on balls. Armas was so impatient at the plate that one must wonder why pitchers ever gave him a decent pitch to hit. In 1983, the slugger set an even more dubious record in his first season with the Hub team after coming to Boston from Oakland. Despite amassing 36 homers and 107 RBI, Armas registered a meager .258 on-base percentage, the lowest ever by an outfielder who had 500 or more at bats. The comparable post-1900 record for an outfielder with more than 400 at bats is held by another contemporary free-swinger, Cory Snyder. Playing for the Indians in 1989, Snyder compiled a .253 on-base percentage when he collected just 23 walks to go with a .215 batting average.

Willie Wilson explained why he refuses to sign autographs: "When I was a little kid, teachers use to punish me by making me sign my name 100 times."

In 1982, Robin Yount became the first shortstop in American League history to top the circuit in total bases (367) and slugging percentage (.578).

Above: *Rickey Henderson will soon challenge the mark for the most career hits by a righty-hitting lefty thrower.*

Rickey Henderson in 1985 scored 146 runs, the most in the majors since 1949.

In 1982, Kansas City Royal Hal McRae led the majors with 133 RBI, setting a record for the most RBI by a designated hitter.

When Rod Carew collected his 3,000th hit in 1985, he was the first infielder since Eddie Collins to attain the 3,000-hit circle.

Carl Yastrzemski was the first American League player to collect 3,000 hits and 400 home runs.

1980-1993 WALKS	
1. Rickey Henderson	1,372
2. Jack Clark	1,091
3. Wade Boggs	1,078
4. Dwight Evans	1,040
5. Tim Raines	1,003
6. Eddie Murray	997
7. Lou Whitaker	982
8. Brett Butler	943
9. Willie Randolph	937
10. Ozzie Smith	908
11. Dale Murphy	899
12. Brian Downing	857
13. George Brett	835
14. Mike Schmidt	818
15. Cal Ripken	817
16. Kent Hrbek	801
17. Dave Winfield	787
18. Robin Yount	783
19. Chili Davis	778
20. Darrell Evans	776
21. Tony Phillips	766
22. Paul Molitor	765
23. Keith Hernandez	756
24. Tom Brunansky	746
25. Barry Bonds	737

Above: *Longevity was one of Dwight Evans's hallmarks. In his 20-year career, he batted .300 just once but nevertheless compiled 2,446 hits and 1,384 RBI. Evans also concluded his playing days among the top 10 in career strikeouts.*

In 1993, the Toronto Blue Jays became the first team since the 1893 Phillies to have its loop's top three batting leaders: John Olerud (.363), Paul Molitor (.332), and Roberto Alomar (.326).

Dave Kingman set records for the most home runs and the most RBI by a player in his final season when he departed after slamming 35 four-baggers and knocking home 94 runs in 1986.

Saddle Up

Johnny Bench explained why he waited so long before he converted to third base: "A catcher and his body are like an outlaw and his horse. He's got to ride that nag until it drops."

Evans Boys Are Closely Related

Darrell and Dwight Evans were not kin, but there are so many parallels between them they might have been brothers. Both were born in the Los Angeles area, both played 20 or more seasons in the majors, and both were effective up to the end of their careers. Both collected more than 1,300 runs, more than 1,300 RBI, and more than 2,200 hits. In addition, each was rated a fine defensive performer who seldom hit much for average but nevertheless compiled outstanding on-base percentages, owing to high walk totals. Darrell led the National League in free passes twice while Dwight topped the American League in walks on three occasions. Last but not least, both were sluggers of the first order. Dwight tied for the American League four-bagger lead in 1981. Four years later, at age 38, Darrell cracked 40 homers to snare the AL crown. The two amassed 799 circuit clouts between them, almost evenly divided—414 for Darrell and 385 for Dwight.

Detroit's Darrell Evans in 1987 set a major league record for players over 40 years old by hitting 34 homers.

Babe Ruth and Dave Kingman are the only two players who were active 10 or more seasons and posted career slugging averages that were more than double their career batting averages.

On September 11, 1985, Pete Rose tallied his 4,192 career hit, breaking Ty Cobb's major league record.

In 1984, Pete Rose set major league records with 100 or more hits for the 22nd consecutive year and playing in his 3,309th game.

Darrell Evans in 1985 became the first hitter to smack 40 or more homers in a season in each league, as he pummeled a major league-leading 40 for Detroit.

1980-1993 STRIKEOUTS	
1. Dale Murphy	1,519
2. Rob Deer	1,379
3. Juan Samuel	1,261
4. Lance Parrish	1,259
5. Jesse Barfield	1,234
6. Chili Davis	1,222
7. Jack Clark	1,181
8. Kirk Gibson	1,152
9. Dwight Evans	1,150
10. Gary Gaetti	1,147
11. Darryl Strawberry	1,138
12. Lloyd Moseby	1,135
13. Tom Brunansky	1,130
14. Dave Winfield	1,107
15. Tim Wallach	1,079
16. Dave Henderson	1,077
17. Harold Baines	1,069
18. Pete Incaviglia	1,061
19. Jose Canseco	1,060
20. Andre Dawson	1,049
21. Danny Tartabull	1,037
22. Ryne Sandberg	1,010
23. Eddie Murray	1,006
24. Willie Wilson	1,003
25. Hubie Brooks	995

Rose's Renown Reduced

Pete Rose retired as a player in 1986 with the career records for the most hits (4,256), the most at bats (14,053), and the most games (3,562). He continued at his post as manager of the Cincinnati Reds for two more seasons and part of a third before a probe into his gambling activities grew so intense in 1989 that he was forced to accept banishment from the game. Compounding Rose's problems was a conviction for income tax evasion that brought a prison sentence. A Hall of Fame committee then rendered a decision in 1991 that no player or official who had been expelled from baseball could have his name put on the Hall of Fame ballot unless he was first reinstated. Since Rose is still under suspension and there are no indications from the commissioner's office that his ouster is likely to be lifted anytime soon, the possibility looms that the holder of the most major career longevity marks may never have a plaque in Cooperstown.

"There's no such thing as bragging. You're either lying or telling the truth."
—Al Oliver

Pete Rose's 4,000th career hit came 21 years to the day after he made his first major league hit.

Pete Rose collected his 3,631st hit, breaking Stan Musial's NL record, in 1981.

Above: *Keith Hernandez (left) and Pete Rose both won numerous awards during the 1970s but were tarnished in the 1980s. Hernandez was implicated in drug investigations while Rose was barred from the game.*

Pete Rose in 1983 was the first first baseman for a pennant winner to not hit a home run since Red Sox first baseman Stuffy McInnis in 1918.

In the 1983 fall classic, Pete Rose, the oldest World Series regular in history at age 42, batted .313 in the Series.

In 1981, Pete Rose of the Phillies led the major leagues in base hits (with 140) to become the only 40-year-old player ever to top both circuits.

1980-1993 BATTING AVERAGE	
1. Wade Boggs	.335
2. Tony Gwynn	.329
3. Kirby Puckett	.318
4. Rod Carew	.314
5. Don Mattingly	.309
6. Mike Greenwell	.307
7. Al Oliver	.307
8. Paul Molitor	.307
9. Mark Grace	.304
10. Ken Griffey	.303
11. George Brett	.302
12. Pedro Guerrero	.300
13. Julio Franco	.300
14. Cecil Cooper	.300
15. John Kruk	.300
16. Will Clark	.299
17. Willie McGee	.298
18. Barry Larkin	.298
19. Tim Raines	.298
20. Lee Lacy	.298
21. Keith Hernandez	.298
22. Roberto Alomar	.297
23. Brian Harper	.297
24. Rafael Palmeiro	.296
25. Mike Easler	.295

Kuenn's Crushers Tear Down the Walls

Harvey Kuenn took over the reins of the staggering Milwaukee Brewers a third of the way into the 1982 season. Kuenn then molded the team into the top slugging and scoring outfit in the majors, so much so that it fairly begged that his crew be dubbed "Harvey's Wallbangers." Leading the Brewers and the American League with 39 homers was Gorman Thomas, followed by Ben Oglivie (34), Cecil Cooper (32), Robin Yount (29), and Ted Simmons (23). Third baseman Paul Molitor nearly gave Milwaukee a record-tying sixth 20-homer man before finishing with 19, and part-time DH Don Money added 16 taters in just 275 at bats. The Brewers parlayed their 216 home runs into 891 tallies, 77 more than any other club in the majors. The Brew Crew's .455 slugging percentage was 22 points better than California's, the second-place club. A mere two years later, with all of the main 1982 Wallbangers except Thomas still on the club, Milwaukee finished last in the AL and compiled both the fewest runs and the fewest homers in the loop.

The Milwaukee Brewers set an American League record for most base hits in a nine-inning game with 31 on August 28, 1992. The Brew Crew tied a modern major league record set by the New York Giants, who had 31 hits on June 9, 1901, against the Cincinnati Reds.

Above: *Paul Molitor has surmounted frequent injuries to post nearly 2,500 career hits.*

Among players with 500 or more career home runs, Reggie Jackson posted the lowest career slugging average (.490).

Reggie Jackson in 1987 retired with a major league career-record 2,597 Ks.

Brewer Paul Molitor in 1982 notched a World Series record five hits in one game.

In 1987, Brewer Paul Molitor got hits in 39 consecutive games, the most in the American League since Joe DiMaggio's 56 in 1941.

1980-1993 SLUGGING AVERAGE	
1. Mike Schmidt	.540
2. Fred McGriff	.531
3. Barry Bonds	.526
4. Ken Griffey	.520
5. Kevin Mitchell	.515
6. Danny Tartabull	.510
7. Mark McGwire	.509
8. Darryl Strawberry	.508
9. Jose Canseco	.507
10. Cecil Fielder	.500
11. Will Clark	.499
12. George Brett	.494
13. Andre Dawson	.492
14. Bob Horner	.486
15. Eddie Murray	.485
16. Dave Winfield	.484
17. Dwight Evans	.484
18. Kent Hrbek	.483
19. Eric Davis	.483
20. Pedro Guerrero	.481
21. Ken Phelps	.480
22. Don Mattingly	.479
23. Kal Daniels	.479
24. Jack Clark	.477
25. Leon Durham	.475

Fielder Returns From Far East, Fires 51

In his first four seasons with the Toronto Blue Jays, first sacker Cecil Fielder displayed good power, but his propensity for striking out kept his average below .250. Few in the Canadian city grieved when he opted to play in Japan for the 1989 campaign. A year in the Far East was evidently all that Fielder needed. He returned from Japan to hammer 51 home runs and silence critics who jeered the Tigers for giving him a two-year $3 million contract. Fielder's four-bagger total was the highest in the American League since the two M&M boys, Roger Maris and Mickey Mantle, both topped the 50 mark in 1961. Big Cecil also led the loop with 132 RBI, thus becoming the first Bengal to top the circuit in both homers and RBI since Hank Greenberg did so in 1946. The first player to use the game in Japan as a launching pad to major league stardom, Fielder claimed his second homer crown in 1991 when he tied Jose Canseco for the AL lead with 44 dingers.

Howard Johnson's 117 RBI in 1991 set a Mets' single season record, breaking the old club mark of 105 shared by Gary Carter and Rusty Staub.

In 1980, Cecil Cooper became the only player since Norm Cash in 1961 to hit .350 or better with at least 25 home runs and 120 RBI.

In 1983, Expo Tim Raines set an NL record when he scored 19.6 percent of his team's runs, as he led the major leagues with 133 runs.

Cecil Cooper of the Brewers was the only American Leaguer to enjoy three seasons of 120 or more RBI during the 1980s.

On September 14, 1987, the Blue Jays hit 10 home runs against the Baltimore Orioles. The O's hit one homer to tie the major league record of 11 home runs by both teams in one game.

1980-1993 ON-BASE AVERAGE

1.	Wade Boggs	.428
2.	Rickey Henderson	.411
3.	John Kruk	.400
4.	Mike Hargrove	.395
5.	Barry Bonds	.394
6.	Jack Clark	.393
7.	Dave Magadan	.393
8.	Fred McGriff	.391
9.	Keith Hernandez	.391
10.	Rod Carew	.391
11.	Tim Raines	.390
12.	Mike Schmidt	.390
13.	Dwight Evans	.386
14.	Kal Daniels	.385
15.	Tony Gwynn	.385
16.	Alvin Davis	.384
17.	Jason Thompson	.384
18.	Toby Harrah	.382
19.	Mark Grace	.381
20.	George Brett	.380
21.	Willie Randolph	.379
22.	Brett Butler	.379
23.	Ken Griffey	.378
24.	Will Clark	.378
25.	Danny Tartabull	.378

Above: Tim Raines ranks as the most savvy base thief in history. Although both his success rate and number of steals have declined in recent years, he continues to excel at a baserunner's first objective, which is scoring runs. Six times in his 15-year career Raines has logged over 100 tallies.

In 1991, the Los Angeles Dodgers became the first team since the 1917 Chicago White Sox to be held hitless twice in a three-game span.

When Kal Daniels led the National League with a .400 on-base percentage in 1988, it was the lowest mark registered by a loop leader since 1968.

Goofball
"Yeah, I was a little nutty. If there'd be some guy on a pogo stick with three girls around him, it would be me."
—pitching flake Dave Rozema

Tigers Swing For Fences

Despite his advancement as a slugger, Cecil Fielder did little in Japan to learn how to cut down his strikeout totals. In 1991, he fanned 151 times to help boost the Tigers to 1,184 Ks, a new American League record. Other heavy contributors to the whiff total were outfielder Rob Deer (175), second-year infielder Travis Fryman (149), and catcher Mickey Tettleton (131). The staggering number of Ks helped result in a .247 team batting average, the lowest in the AL. Nevertheless Detroit scored 817 runs, second in the loop only to Texas, which tallied 829. A circuit-leading 209 home runs and an AL-best 699 walks nearly made the free-swinging Tigers the first team in history to lead its league in runs despite finishing last in batting. Fielder (44 homers), Tettleton (31), Deer (25), Lou Whitaker (24), and Fryman (21) all notched over 20 round-trippers. As it was, the club's offensive production overrode woeful pitching to allow Detroit to finish with an 84-78 record.

Willie Wilson of the Royals in 1980 set a major league record with 705 at bats.

The only Oakland A's player to reach double figures in triples since 1976 is Luis Polonia with 10 in 1987.

Terry Puhl of the Houston Astros set a record with 11 base hits in the 1980 NLCS.

In the 1982 ALCS, Fred Lynn of the losing Angels went 11-for-18 and hit .611 while Angels designated hitter Don Baylor bagged 10 RBI.

The Royals set an American League record in 1980 by leading the loop in triples for the sixth consecutive season.

In 1986, sub outfielder and DH Johnny Grubb of Detroit slugged 13 home runs and had 51 RBI in just 210 at bats.

Cincinnati's Billy Hatcher in 1990 hit an all-time Series record .750 (9-for-12), as he collected seven hits in his first seven at bats.

In an era when most performers with knees like his would have long since turned to designated hitting, Andre Dawson (above) remained a solid every-day player, especially in right field.

In the 1989 NLCS, the two opposing first basemen, Will Clark of the Giants and Mark Grace of the Cubs, collected 24 hits and 16 RBI and hit a combined .649 in the five-game set.

"The key to this game is to do the things that it takes to stay, day in and day out."
—Andre Dawson

Andre Dawson in 1990 became the second player in major league history to compile 2,000 hits, 300 homers, and 300 steals (Willie Mays was the first).

Will the Thrill Fills the Bill

In an era studded with wildly fluctuating team and individual performances, Will Clark of the San Francisco Giants has remained a consistently excellent player at all phases of the game. Other players have posted higher batting averages and slugging totals and outperformed Clark in the field and as a baserunner, but none has exceed his dedication to becoming the best player his skills will allow him to be. In his first major league at bat in 1986, Clark homered against Houston's Nolan Ryan at the Astrodome, giving San Francisco fans the first of many moments that quickly led to him being nicknamed "Will the Thrill." He is a tough, hard-working, and gutsy player. Through the 1993 season, Clark's career has been a model of consistency. His batting averages have ranged between .282 and .333, and he enjoyed a five-year streak in which he posted 90 or more RBI each season.

Hobbled Dodger Kirk Gibson won game one of the 1988 World Series with a pinch-hit homer in the bottom of the ninth.

The Kansas City Royals led off the 1980s by hitting .286 in 1980, the highest team batting average during the decade.

In 1988, there were only 3,180 homers hit in the major leagues—1,278 fewer than in 1987.

Above: *Will Clark went the way of the rest of the San Francisco Giants in 1992. With Kevin Mitchell gone and Matt Williams in a season-long slump, Clark saw his offensive production dip as he registered post-rookie lows in both homers and RBI.*

1980-1993 EXTRA BASE HITS

1.	Andre Dawson	803
2.	Eddie Murray	787
3.	George Brett	761
4.	Robin Yount	754
5.	Dave Winfield	737
6.	Cal Ripken	729
7.	Dale Murphy	700
8.	Harold Baines	663
9.	Dwight Evans	655
10.	Ryne Sandberg	647
11.	Tim Wallach	627
	Paul Molitor	627
13.	Lou Whitaker	618
14.	Don Mattingly	616
15.	Joe Carter	611
16.	Rickey Henderson	610
17.	George Bell	607
18.	Kent Hrbek	602
19.	Tom Brunansky	587
20.	Wade Boggs	583
21.	Gary Gaetti	581
22.	Alan Trammell	566
	Mike Schmidt	566
24.	Dave Parker	564
25.	Kirby Puckett	561

Long Time Comin'

San Francisco first baseman Will Clark was drafted in 1985 and spent his first season in the major leagues in 1986. When the Giants clinched their division in 1987, Will roared: "I've waited so long for this."

In 1985, the Cardinals took the World Series to seven games and nearly won it in six despite tallying just 13 runs in the fray on a .185 batting average.

In 1981, the Padres hit just 32 home runs in 110 games as outfielder Joe Lefebvre led the club with eight dingers.

Dave Henderson's two-out, two-strike, two-run homer in the ninth inning of game five saved the 1986 Red Sox from ALCS elimination, helping Boston to its first AL flag since 1975.

The Cubs hit .303 in the 1989 NLCS, led by Mark Grace at .647, but nevertheless contrived to lose the series to the Giants four games to one.

Joel Youngblood in 1982 got hits for two different teams in two different cities on the same day when he was traded from the Mets to the Expos.

Welch Wins 27

At the onset of the 1990 campaign, Bob Welch of the Oakland A's was 33 years old and had been in the majors for 12 years without ever winning more than 17 games in a season. He had accomplished both 17-win years with the A's in 1988 and '89. Welch proceeded to notch 27 wins in 1990, the most of any American League hurler since 1968 and the most in the majors since Steve Carlton of the Phillies also won 27 in 1972. Welch lost only six for a winning percentage of .818, notching a 2.95 ERA. His career year earned Welch the Cy Young Award and left him only 24 victories short of 200. In addition, he approached the record for the oldest pitcher since the end of the dead-ball era to win 25 or more games in a season. At age 33, Welch fell two years short of Hall of Famer Burleigh Grimes, who was 35 when he snagged 25 wins for the Pirates in 1928. In 1991, Welch returned to earth, winning just 12 of 25 decisions and posting a 4.56 ERA, the highest of his career, as the A's surrendered their three-year lock on the American League throne to Minnesota.

When Bob Welch and Dave Stewart won 49 games between them for the 1990 Oakland A's, they achieved more victories than any two mound teammates since 1965.

Baltimore's Gregg Olson set an AL rookie saves record in 1989 with 27.

Above: *Bob Welch in 1994 stands to perform what was once a rare achievement: winning at least 100 games in each major league.*

Toronto's Dennis Lamp set a single-season record for the most wins by a reliever without a loss when he went 11-0 in 1985.

Bob Welch's 27 wins in 1990 were the most in the major leagues since 1972 and the most in the American League since 1968.

"I'm sick of hearing about J.R. Richard. We all know what he can do with his stuff. He's tremendous. But what I'd like to see is what he could do with my stuff."

—Don Sutton

1980-1993 GAMES PITCHED	
1. Jeff Reardon	851
2. Lee Smith	850
3. Jesse Orosco	696
4. Kent Tekulve	687
5. Dave Righetti	685
6. Craig Lefferts	666
7. Steve Bedrosian	657
8. Larry Andersen	648
9. Dan Quisenberry	642
10. Greg Minton	637
11. Dennis Eckersley	633
12. Greg Harris	620
13. Dave Smith	609
14. Rich Gossage	607
15. Roger McDowell	586
16. Mark Davis	585
17. Willie Hernandez	572
18. Rick Honeycutt	571
19. Mitch Williams	567
20. John Franco	566
21. Ted Power	564
22. Danny Darwin	562
23. Dennis Lamp	553
Tom Henke	553
25. Juan Agosto	543

Rollie Fingers in 1982 became the first pitcher in major league history to collect 300 saves.

Rollie Fingers in 1981 became the first relief pitcher to win both the MVP Award and the Cy Young Award in the same season.

In 1981, Rollie Fingers won or saved 55 percent of Milwaukee's victories.

In 1986, Cardinal yearling Todd Worrell set a major league rookie record with 36 saves.

1980-1993 GAMES STARTED

1.	Jack Morris	464
2.	Bob Welch	429
	Frank Tanana	429
4.	Nolan Ryan	411
5.	Frank Viola	405
6.	Charlie Hough	404
7.	Dave Stieb	391
8.	Mike Moore	390
9.	Dennis Martinez	384
10.	Bill Gullickson	371
11.	Fernando Valenzuela	353
12.	Bruce Hurst	351
13.	Scott Sanderson	349
14.	Rick Sutcliffe	347
15.	Charlie Leibrandt	346
16.	Bert Blyleven	335
17.	Mark Langston	331
18.	Jim Clancy	327
19.	Ron Darling	318
20.	Bob Knepper	313
21.	Dave Stewart	310
	Mike Scott	310
23.	Mike Boddicker	309
24.	Ed Whitson	307
25.	Roger Clemens	301

Polished Stone Becomes Jewel With 25 Gems

As Bob Welch began the 1990s by unexpectedly producing a Cy Young season, so Steve Stone of the Orioles opened the 1980s with an upset win in the Cy Young derby. Like Welch, Stone had never before had a 20-win season when he registered 25 victories in 1980; and also like Welch, Stone was age 33 at the time, just two years short of Burleigh Grimes's record for the oldest 25-game winner since 1920. Stone's best season had been a 15-12 record with the 1977 White Sox. He had been in the bigs since 1971. Stone stood alone in history, however, after arm trouble decked him permanently midway through the 1981 season. He set a new American League mark for the fewest career triumphs subsequent to a 25-win season when he logged just four more victories before he was forced to retire. Stone also became the only hurler other than Sandy Koufax to cop a Cy Young Award in his last full season. Upon leaving the playing field, Stone simply moved upstairs, launching a new career in the broadcast booth.

Gipper
Ronald Reagan told to Gaylord Perry before Perry won his 300th game at age 43: "I just know it's an ugly rumor that you and I are the only two people alive who saw Abner Doubleday throw the first pitch out."

Above: *Orel Hershiser has been the Dodgers' mound mainstay since 1984.*

Orel Hershiser set a major league record in 1988 with 59 consecutive scoreless innings pitched.

White Sox Bobby Thigpen in 1990 shattered the major league save record by 11, as he slammed the door 57 times.

Bobby Thigpen of the White Sox earned either a save or a win in 61 of the 77 games in which he appeared in 1990.

Mike Torrez was the first pitcher in major league history to win 10 or more games in a season for seven different teams.

Underhanded Quiz Passes Test

From day one of his professional career, Dan Quisenberry was bred for a career as a relief pitcher. He nevertheless needed a four and one-half year apprenticeship in the minors before he reached the show. He surfaced with the Kansas City Royals in 1979 at age 26, a rather ripe age for a rookie. Quiz swiftly made up for lost time, however, topping the American League in saves in five of his first six full seasons. In 1983, his unorthodox sidearm-to-underhanded slants gained him a new major league record when he racked up 45 saves in just 69 appearances. Quiz retired in 1990 after hurling in 674 games without ever making a start, but he was still a long way from the record for startless mound appearances in the majors. The previous year, Kent Tekulve had departed after seeing action in 1,050 games, all in relief. Tekulve was furthermore only the second hurler in history to work 1,000 games in the majors.

Like many relief aces in modern times, Dan Quisenberry (above) never started a single game in the majors. He collected 212 of his 244 saves in a six-year period between 1980 and '85.

1980-1993 COMPLETE GAMES	
1. Jack Morris	164
2. Fernando Valenzuela	112
3. Charlie Hough	106
4. Bert Blyleven	97
5. Dave Stieb	96
6. Roger Clemens	91
7. Bruce Hurst	83
8. Mark Langston	75
9. Frank Viola	74
Mike Moore	74
11. Mike Witt	72
12. Dennis Martinez	71
13. Mario Soto	70
14. Bret Saberhagen	69
15. Rick Sutcliffe	67
Dwight Gooden	67
17. Orel Hershiser	64
18. Mike Boddicker	63
19. Scott McGregor	62
20. Rick Langford	61
Jim Clancy	61
22. Frank Tanana	58
Tom Candiotti	58
24. Bob Welch	56
Walt Terrell	56

When Doug Drabek won 22 games for Pittsburgh in 1990, he was the first Pirates pitcher to be a 20-game winner since John Candelaria in 1977.

In 1983, Dan Quisenberry of the Kansas City Royals set a major league record with 45 saves.

"Natural grass is a wonderful thing for little bugs and sinkerball pitchers."
—Dan Quisenberry

Above: Bruce Sutter led the NL in saves five times between 1979 and '84. Arm trouble in 1986 caused him to miss most of that year and all of 1987, but he returned for one last hurrah in 1988.

The Seattle Mariners will begin their 18th season of operation in the majors in 1994 still in search of their first 20-game winner.

The Cincinnati Reds are the only one of the eight NL franchises that have been in existence since 1892 that has never had a 30-game winner.

Cardinal Bruce Sutter in 1984 tied the major league record with 45 saves.

Dan Quisenberry appraised his unorthodox pitching style: "I found a delivery in my flaw."

Stroke Halts Richard's Career

The Houston Astros at first thought J.R. Richard was malingering when he claimed halfway into the 1980 season that he felt too weak and disoriented to take his regular turn on the mound. A thorough physical examination, however, revealed that Richard had a blocked artery. He again started pitching when he suffered a stroke. The Astros top pitcher at the time with a 10-4 mark, Richard was expected to join with expensive free-agent acquisition Nolan Ryan to give the club the most potent strike-out tandem in history. In 1978, Richard had set a franchise record when he bagged 303 strikeouts and then broke his own mark a year later by whiffing 313 enemy hitters. Since he was only 30 in 1980, the Astros were prepared to give him every chance to recover from the effects of his stroke. But Richard's comeback attempt stalled before he could ever again throw a single pitch in the majors. He departed with a .601 career winning percentage and 1,493 strikeouts in 1,606 innings, an average of nearly one per frame.

Are We Having Fun Yet?

"People say baseball players should go out and have fun. No way. To me, baseball is pressure. I always feel it. This is work. The fun is afterwards, when you shake hands."
—Dennis Eckersley

Mike Scott of the Houston Astros, with 306 strikeouts in 1986, was the only NL hurler to notch 300 Ks in a season during the decade of the 1980s.

Mike Scott of the Astros no-hit the San Francisco Giants on September 25, 1986; it was the only no-hitter in NL history to clinch a pennant or division crown.

When he topped the American League with 187 strikeouts in 1980, Cleveland's Len Barker became the only loop leader since expansion to notch fewer than 200 Ks.

1980-1993 SAVES	
1. Lee Smith	401
2. Jeff Reardon	363
3. Dennis Eckersley	272
4. Tom Henke	260
5. Dave Righetti	252
6. Dan Quisenberry	239
7. John Franco	236
8. Dave Smith	216
9. Rich Gossage	208
10. Bobby Thigpen	201
11. Bruce Sutter	195
12. Doug Jones	190
13. Mitch Williams	186
14. Randy Myers	184
Steve Bedrosian	184
16. Bryan Harvey	171
17. Gregg Olson	160
Jeff Montgomery	160
19. Rick Aguilera	156
20. Jay Howell	153
21. Roger McDowell	151
22. Jeff Russell	146
Greg Minton	146
24. Willie Hernandez	140
25. Todd Worrell	134

Astros Lose Promising Young Hurlers

The Astros overcame the loss of J.R. Richard in 1980 to win their division but then faltered in the League Championship Series with Philadelphia. The 'Stros are still in search of their first pennant. Much of the reason for Houston's lengthy fruitless quest can be traced to the fate that has befallen not only Richard but many of its talented young pitchers. Larry Dierker, the club's first mound prize, won his first big league game when he was 18 years old and had a 20-win season in 1969 at age 23. Dierker had several more productive seasons, but he saw his arm run out of steam before he was 30. In 1969, 21-year-old rookie Tom Griffin fanned 200 hitters in just 188 innings but never again collected more than 110 Ks in a season. And Don Wilson, a staff bulwark for several seasons in the early 1970s, committed suicide in January 1975.

Yankee Dave Righetti in 1986 set a major league record with 46 saves.

Above: *Dave Righetti hurled a no-hitter as a starting pitcher before turning exclusively to relief duties in 1984.*

WIN

Famed reliever Mike Marshall had a bad season in 1980 while with the Twins. After some Minnesota fans booed him, he said: "If they worked as hard at their jobs as I do at mine, this country wouldn't have the inflation problem it now has."

En route to a 1-16 record, Anthony Young of the Mets sustained an all-time record 27 straight losses before beating Florida in relief on July 28, 1993. During the skein, Young appeared in 74 games.

Tommy John retired in 1989 with 2,245 career strikeouts, the most of any hurler who never compiled as many as 150 Ks in a season.

Don Sutton in 1985 became the first pitcher in major league history to fan 100 or more hitters in 20 consecutive seasons.

When both Phil Niekro and Tom Seaver won their 300th games in 1985, it marked the first time since 1890 that two hurlers had notched 300 career wins in the same season.

1980-1993 SHUTOUTS	
1. Roger Clemens	35
2. Fernando Valenzuela	31
3. Dave Stieb	29
4. Jack Morris	27
5. Bob Welch	25
6. Orel Hershiser	24
7. Bruce Hurst	23
Dwight Gooden	23
9. Mike Scott	22
10. Bert Blyleven	21
11. Bob Knepper	20
12. Nolan Ryan	19
13. Geoff Zahn	18
Dennis Martinez	18
Charlie Leibrandt	18
Doug Drabek	18
17. Rick Sutcliffe	17
Jerry Reuss	17
Scott McGregor	17
20. Frank Viola	16
John Tudor	16
Bret Saberhagen	16
Steve Rogers	16
Bob Ojeda	16
Mike Moore	16
Mark Langston	16
David Cone	16
Mike Boddicker	16
Tim Belcher	16

On September 10, 1980, Bill Gullickson of the Expos became the first rookie hurler to fan as many as 18 hitters in a game. He mowed down 18 Chicago Cub batters.

I♥NY

"I never could play in New York. The first time I ever came into a game there, I got in the bullpen car and they told me to lock the doors."

—Mike Flanagan

Starter Stieb Stars North of Border

In June 1978, the Toronto Blue Jays selected Dave Stieb in the fifth round of the free-agent draft. Barely a year later, Stieb was a regular member of the Canadian team's starting rotation. By 1980, in only his first full season, he was already the staff leader, a role that he held for 10 years. Shoulder and back trouble idled Stieb for most of the 1991 season after he had become the first pitcher in club history to author a no–hitter the previous year. Stieb nevertheless entered the 1993 season with 174 career wins, all for Toronto, and without the distinction of ever having a 20–win season (he won 16 games six times). He is also known as a fine fielder and perhaps the best–hitting pitcher of the current era, although he has had little chance to show it. Because of the designated hitter rule, Stieb has collected just one at bat in his 14 major league seasons—plus one in the 1981 All–Star Game.

Randy Myers of the Chicago Cubs set the NL record for saves with 53 in '93.

Among the all-time top nine hurlers in career strikeouts, Walter Johnson is the only one who was not active in 1983.

Greg Maddux of the Atlanta Braves led the NL in complete games in 1993 with eight, the lowest total ever by a major league leader.

Above: Lee Smith seems only to grow stronger as he ages. Three times a league leader in saves, Smith passed Jeff Reardon durin the 1993 season to become the all-time save leader. Smith ended the year with 401.

1980-1993 WINS	
1. Jack Morris	223
2. Bob Welch	196
3. Frank Viola	174
4. Dave Stieb	167
5. Charlie Hough	165
6. Roger Clemens	163
7. Dennis Martinez	162
8. Dave Stewart	158
Bill Gullickson	158
10. Nolan Ryan	157
11. Dwight Gooden	154
12. Fernando Valenzuela	149
Frank Tanana	149
14. Rick Sutcliffe	148
15. Mike Moore	145
16. Mark Langston	144
17. Bruce Hurst	143
18. Scott Sanderson	141
19. Charlie Leibrandt	140
20. Bert Blyleven	139
21. Jimmy Key	134
Mike Boddicker	134
23. Danny Darwin	133
24. Orel Hershiser	128
25. Jim Clancy	124

Mariners Lose Moore, Langston

Toronto's sister American League expansion club, Seattle, has also had its share of talented young hurlers selected via the free-agent draft route. Unlike the Blue Jays, who enjoyed Dave Steib's services for 14 years, the Mariners have been unable to satisfy the salary and competitive demands of their youthful mound stars. The M's selected Mark Langston in the third round of the June 1981 draft. Rather than lose him to free agency, Seattle dealt him to Montreal in 1989 after he had led the American League in strikeouts three times as a Mariner. Prior to the 1989 season, Mike Moore, the first player chosen in the same 1981 draft that brought the Mariners Langston, availed himself of the free-agency escape hatch to slip away to Oakland. The Langston swap at least brought Seattle two young quality hurlers, Brian Holman and Randy Johnson, in exchange, but Moore's loss left the Mariners with only an extra draft choice in compensation.

Above: *His first 20-win season since 1986, 1992's success revived Jack Morris's Hall of Fame aspirations despite an ever-swelling career ERA.*

Doctors In the House

Don Sutton after a meeting with Gaylord Perry remarked: "He handed me a tube of Vaseline. I thanked him and gave him a sheet of sandpaper."

Tom Seaver extended his own major league record when he started his 16th consecutive Opening Day game for the White Sox in 1986.

Steve Bedrosian of the Braves established a major league record in 1985 when he started 37 games and completed none of them.

◆ ◆ ◆

In 1981, with the season shortened by a strike to just 109 games, Oakland A's pitchers turned in 60 complete games, the most in the past 10 years.

"Let me put it this way: There's a lot of luck in getting to the majors."
—*Mark Funderburk, who spent most of his career in the minors*

1980-1993 INNINGS

1.	Jack Morris	3,333.1
2.	Charlie Hough	2,920.1
3.	Bob Welch	2,830.2
4.	Frank Tanana	2,777.0
5.	Frank Viola	2,760.2
6.	Dave Stieb	2,715.2
7.	Nolan Ryan	2,694.2
8.	Dennis Martinez	2,621.0
9.	Mike Moore	2,544.2
10.	Fernando Valenzuela	2,534.0
11.	Bill Gullickson	2,443.2
12.	Dave Stewart	2,413.1
13.	Rick Sutcliffe	2,381.1
14.	Bruce Hurst	2,379.1
15.	Bert Blyleven	2,345.1
16.	Mark Langston	2,329.0
17.	Charlie Leibrandt	2,303.2
18.	Danny Darwin	2,284.2
19.	Roger Clemens	2,222.2
20.	Scott Sanderson	2,183.1
	Jim Clancy	2,183.1
22.	Dwight Gooden	2,128.1
23.	Mike Boddicker	2,123.2
24.	Mike Witt	2,108.1
25.	Ron Darling	2,096.1

Gooden Great, Career Has Promise

In 1984, when he was still just 19 years old, Dwight Gooden broke Herb Score's modern rookie strikeout record by fanning 276 hitters in only 218 innings. The following year, at age 20, the Mets' young fireballer, led the NL with 24 wins, a 1.53 ERA, and 268 strikeouts. After Gooden dipped to 17 wins and a mere 200 Ks in 1986, Mets fans speculated on what could be wrong with him and talked as if he were a has-been at 21. Gooden's problem was cocaine usage, which he has since conquered, but in recent years shoulder woes have somewhat stymied him. Nevertheless, Gooden began the 1993 season still short of his 29th birthday but with 142 career wins and a stellar .683 winning percentage. At the time, it was the fifth-best mark in major league history. At a comparable age, Whitey Ford, another frosh sensation who ran into midcareer troubles, had just 43 of his 236 career wins.

When John Tudor in 1985 joined Dwight Gooden (above) by having an ERA under 2.00, it marked the first time since 1972 that two pitchers were under the 2.00 ERA mark. In 1992, Gooden sustained the first losing season in his first nine years.

ChiSox hurler LaMarr Hoyt in 1983 issued 1.07 walks per game, the loop's fewest per game since Tiny Bonham's 0.96 in 1942.

1980-1993 STRIKEOUTS	
1. Nolan Ryan	2,805
2. Jack Morris	2,189
3. Roger Clemens	2,033
4. Mark Langston	2,001
5. Fernando Valenzuela	1,842
6. Dwight Gooden	1,835
7. Frank Viola	1,813
8. Bob Welch	1,795
9. Charlie Hough	1,786
10. Bruce Hurst	1,665
11. Frank Tanana	1,653
12. Bert Blyleven	1,619
13. Dave Stieb	1,590
14. Dave Stewart	1,571
15. Mike Moore	1,541
16. Rick Sutcliffe	1,533
17. Danny Darwin	1,495
18. Jose DeLeon	1,462
19. Sid Fernandez	1,458
20. Steve Carlton	1,453
21. Mike Scott	1,448
22. Dennis Martinez	1,432
23. David Cone	1,418
24. Ron Darling	1,413
25. Floyd Bannister	1,402

"Luck is the by-product of busting your fanny."
—Don Sutton

Rick Langford of the 1980 A's was the last pitcher to hurl at least 25 complete games when he tossed 28.

Mets Mound Masters Crumble

In 1986, Dwight Gooden, though he dipped to just 17 wins, remained the crown jewel in the Mets' pitching staff, regarded by the end of the season as the best and the deepest in recent history. Joining Gooden in the starting rotation were Ron Darling (15-6), Bob Ojeda (18-5), Sid Fernandez (16-6), and Rick Aguilera (10-7). Roger McDowell (14-9, 22 saves) and Jesse Orosco (8-6, 21 saves) anchored the bullpen. Should any of these seven falter, manager Davey Johnson had only to pick up the phone and call for help to the club's well-stocked farm operation, where such trainee hurlers as David Cone and Randy Myers waited in the wings. The following season, though, the Mets' vaunted pitching corps staggered as only Aguilera matched his 1986 win total, and after rallying in 1988, thanks to a 20-3 season from Cone, it began to unravel completely in 1989. The club that seemed poised in 1986 to build a dynasty around its pitching staff has yet to win another pennant.

"When I'm on the road, my greatest ambition is to get a standing boo."
—Al Hrabosky, relief pitcher

In 1990, Toronto Blue Jays pitchers turned in a major league record low six complete games as Todd Stottlemyre led the staff with four complete games and Dave Stieb had the other two.

1980-1993 WINNING PERCENTAGE	
1. Dwight Gooden	.655
2. Roger Clemens	.655
3. John Tudor	.624
4. Jack McDowell	.623
5. Teddy Higuera	.612
6. Ron Guidry	.607
7. Jimmy Key	.606
8. Bob Welch	.601
9. David Cone	.594
10. La Marr Hoyt	.590
11. Tom Glavine	.590
12. Dave Stewart	.581
13. Tom Browning	.580
14. Moose Haas	.579
15. Greg Maddux	.575
16. Jack Morris	.572
17. Bret Saberhagen	.571
18. Orel Hershiser	.571
19. John Smiley	.568
20. Dave Stieb	.568
21. Curt Young	.566
22. Bob Walk	.565
23. Kevin Brown	.563
24. Scott McGregor	.563
25. Mark Portugal	.563

Floyd Bannister in 1982 became the first Mariner to lead the AL in Ks, with 209.

On September 26, 1981, Nolan Ryan tossed his fifth career no-hitter, breaking Sandy Koufax's record of four. Ryan pitched his sixth no-hitter on June 11, 1990. He got his seventh no-hitter on May 1, 1991.

In 1988, Jerry Reuss of the White Sox became the first southpaw to log 200 victories in the majors without ever having a 20-win season.

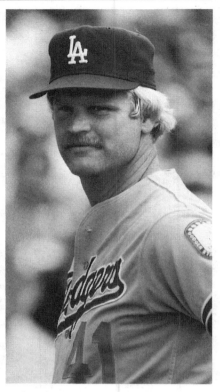

Above: *Jerry Reuss pitched in four decades and won 220 games for eight different major league teams but never collected more than 18 victories in a season. Being a southpaw helped to lengthen his career. Over and over Reuss would be released only to find another team in need of a lefthander.*

Five of the top nine pitchers in career innings pitched were active during the 1980s: Phil Niekro, Nolan Ryan, Gaylord Perry, Don Sutton, and Steve Carlton.

Nolan Ryan of Houston got his 3,000th career strikeout in 1980.

Nolan Ryan and Steve Carlton both surpassed Walter Johnson's career strikeout record of 3,506 in 1983.

1980-1993 EARNED RUN AVERAGE	
1. Dan Quisenberry	2.74
2. Lee Smith	2.91
3. Roger Clemens	2.94
4. Orel Hershiser	2.95
5. Dwight Gooden	3.04
6. John Tudor	3.07
7. Jose Rijo	3.13
8. Dave Dravecky	3.13
9. Jeff Reardon	3.14
10. David Cone	3.14
11. Sid Fernandez	3.15
12. Greg Maddux	3.19
13. Doug Drabek	3.21
14. Nolan Ryan	3.22
15. Bret Saberhagen	3.24
16. Steve Rogers	3.24
17. Steve Bedrosian	3.31
18. Rick Reuschel	3.31
19. Dave Righetti	3.33
20. Mario Soto	3.37
21. Dave Stieb	3.37
22. Jimmy Key	3.37
23. Craig Lefferts	3.39
24. Chuck Finley	3.40
25. Tim Belcher	3.40

After making his first pitching appearance in several weeks for the Orioles, Doyle Alexander divulged: "When I got to the mound, catcher Johnny Oates reminded me that the lower mask was his and the upper one was the umpire's."

When he made his 535th consecutive start with no intervening relief appearances in 1991, Nolan Ryan broke Steve Carlton's record of 534.

Nolan Ryan's 5,000th strikeout victim (in 1989) was Rickey Henderson.

Kingman Tosses 20 Setbacks

In 1979, Phil Niekro of Atlanta became the last National League pitcher to date to lose 20 games in a season. A year later, Brian Kingman became the majors' last 20-game loser when he clocked an 8-20 mark for Oakland, made more remarkable by the fact that the A's finished second in their division with an 83-79 record. Kingman pitched in 211 innings, and he notched a 3.83 ERA (the AL had a 4.03 ERA). Since 1980, no hurler has lost more than 19 games in a season. The last to do it was Tim Leary with the Yankees in 1990, when he finished at 9-19. Once he was perched on the threshold of his 20th loss, Leary was spared the ignominy by being held out of the starting rotation, as had happened to several other 19-game losers earlier in the decade. One of them, Jose DeLeon of Pittsburgh, set a National League record for the lowest winning percentage by a pitcher in 20 or more decisions (.095) when he finished at 2-19 in 1985.

In the mid-1980s, Nolan Ryan (above) looked to be fading. Nevertheless, he continued to mow down hitters through 1993, his 27th season.

A successful comeback from rotator cuff surgery in 1992 rekindled the possibility that Bert Blyleven (above) will join the elite circle of 300-game winners, perhaps even in 1994.

Minnesota's Bert Blyleven in 1986 allowed a major league record 50 home runs.

Vin Scully remembered Burt Hooton: "He's such a quiet person that the night the Dodgers won the World Series [in 1981] he went out and painted the town beige."

When John Tudor of the Cardinals racked up 10 shutouts in 1985, he fell only one short of the modern southpaw record of 11, set in 1963 by Sandy Koufax.

Martin's Starters Amass Complete Games

Despite logging 20 losses in 1980, Brian Kingman turned in 10 complete games. At that he was by far the low man in the A's rotation, as Oakland starters compiled 94 complete games, the most in either major league since 1946 (when Detroit also had 94). Whereas every other American League team fashioned at least 61 complete games in 1946, only the Milwaukee Brewers in 1980, with 48 complete games, registered even half of Oakland's total. The credit was assigned to A's skipper Billy Martin, who believed his young hurlers—Rick Langford, Mike Norris, Matt Keough, Steve McCatty, and Kingman—could only profit from the work. Langford pitched a league-top 290 innings and 28 complete games. Norris had 284 innings pitched and 24 complete games, Keough 250 innings and 20 complete games, and McCatty 222 and 11 complete games. The following year, Martin's strategy paid off in a division title, but the credit given him turned to blame when all of the A's young starters in 1980 were either gone from the majors or reduced to mop-up roles by 1984.

Jose DeLeon of the Pirates set the 20th-century National League record for the lowest winning percentage by a pitcher in a minimum of 20 decisions when he went 2-19 in 1985, for an .095 winning percentage.

1980-1993 FEWEST WALKS	
1. Dan Quisenberry	1.39
2. Dennis Eckersley	1.62
3. Bret Saberhagen	1.78
4. Greg Swindell	1.91
5. La Marr Hoyt	1.92
6. Moose Haas	2.00
7. Jerry Reuss	2.03
8. John Candelaria	2.06
9. Jimmy Key	2.08
10. Bill Wegman	2.12
11. Don Sutton	2.16
12. Bryn Smith	2.17
13. Scott Sanderson	2.18
14. Terry Mulholland	2.19
15. Tommy John	2.19
16. Bill Gullickson	2.20
17. Rick Reuschel	2.24
18. Doyle Alexander	2.26
19. Ron Guidry	2.26
20. Lary Sorensen	2.29
21. Chris Bosio	2.31
22. Scott McGregor	2.32
23. Doug Drabek	2.32
24. Atlee Hammaker	2.34
25. Bert Blyleven	2.34

Fernando Accepts Frequent, Extensive Outings

A contemporary hurler whose career has been hampered by overwork is Fernando Valenzuela. In 1986, the Dodgers southpaw became what may well be the last pitcher to author 20 complete games in a season. The following year he again led the National League in complete games for the third time in the 1980s. Fernando then tumbled to just five wins in 1988 and struggled with injuries and inaffectiveness the rest of his career. From 1982 to '87, though, he pitched at least 250 innings a year, with his high being 285 in '82. Valenzuela was a workhorse from the inception of his career. As a rookie in 1981, he paced the National League in innings, starts, complete games, and strikeouts. The last frosh hurler to approach Valenzuela's performance was the Giants' Bill Voiselle, who in 1944 topped the NL in all of the same departments except complete games. Voiselle too succumbed prematurely to overuse, winning his last game when he was 30.

Tom Lasorda said about his young star pitcher from Mexico, Fernando Valenzuela: "All last year we tried to teach him English, and the only word he learned was 'million.'"

Steve Carlton became the first lefthander to collect 3,000 career strikeouts, in 1981, and the first to collect 4,000, in 1986.

Above: *Fernando Valenzuela paced the National League in innings pitched as a rookie in 1981 and labored over 250 innings in each of his first seven full seasons in the majors. By 1988, although still only 27 years old, overwork had already put him on the decline. After a year in the Mexican League, he made a comeback in 1993.*

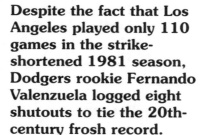

Despite the fact that Los Angeles played only 110 games in the strike-shortened 1981 season, Dodgers rookie Fernando Valenzuela logged eight shutouts to tie the 20th-century frosh record.

Los Angeles Dodger yearling hurler Fernando Valenzuela in 1981 became the first player in major league history to win Rookie of the Year and Cy Young honors in the same year.

1980-1993 RATIO	
1. Sid Fernandez	10.05
2. Roger Clemens	10.11
3. Bret Saberhagen	10.16
4. Dennis Eckersley	10.22
5. Mario Soto	10.46
6. Dwight Gooden	10.52
7. Dan Quisenberry	10.56
8. Don Sutton	10.60
9. Doug Drabek	10.61
10. Nolan Ryan	10.63
11. Jimmy Key	10.67
12. Orel Hershiser	10.69
13. John Tudor	10.70
14. Mike Scott	10.74
15. John Smiley	10.75
16. Jeff Reardon	10.76
17. Tim Belcher	10.82
18. Bryn Smith	10.84
19. Teddy Higuera	10.86
20. Dave Dravecky	10.87
21. David Cone	10.88
22. Pascual Perez	10.93
23. La Marr Hoyt	10.94
24. John Candelaria	10.96
25. Greg Maddux	10.99

Complete Games On Endangered List

When Jack McDowell of the White Sox churned out 15 complete games in 1991, he was the first pitcher in three years to compile that many. Even as McDowell was topping the American League, Tom Glavine of Atlanta and Bruce Hurst of San Diego shared the National League complete-game crown in 1991 with just nine, the first time a loop leader posted fewer than 10. The previous record low of 10 had belonged to Hurst and Tim Belcher of Los Angeles, who tied for the NL lead in 1989. That year, Bret Saberhagen led the AL with 12, despite having the DH rule that protects pitchers from being lifted for pinch-hitters. In 1987, the Cincinnati Reds finished second in their division despite collecting just seven complete games, one short of the loop record low set by the 1977 Padres. The Toronto Blue Jays also finished second in their division in 1990 when they established a new American League negative mark with a mere six complete games. Four of the six belonged to Todd Stottlemyre, and Dave Stieb bagged the other two.

Tom Browning of Cincinnati hurled a perfect game against the Dodgers on September 16, 1988.

The only perfect game to occur on the final day of a season was logged by Mike Witt of the Angels on September 30, 1984.

When Boston met his salary demands, Frank Viola (above) in 1992 became a rare southpaw who chose to make Fenway Park home.

Toronto's Dave Stieb was denied no-hitters in each of two consecutive games by a two-out base hit in the ninth inning in 1988.

Len Barker of Cleveland pitched a perfect game against Toronto on May 15, 1981.

1980-1993 PITCHER PUTOUTS	
1. Jack Morris	354
2. Dave Stieb	255
3. Dan Petry	246
4. Mike Boddicker	245
5. Mike Moore	242

In 1982, Bob Stanley hurled 168⅓ innings in relief to set an American League record.

Tom Browning of the Cincinnati Reds was the last rookie 20-game winner, with a 21-9 mark in 1985.

After failing to win the Cy Young after his second straight 20-win season, Joaquin Andujar complained: "If there was nobody else pitching, they still wouldn't give it to me."

Above: *Durability has been Jeff Reardon's forte. In 1992, durability made him the new career saves record-holder.*

Tanana Tallies 240 Without 20-Win Season

Frank Tanana finished the 1993 campaign with 240 career victories, the most of any pitcher in history who never had a 20-win season. Three years earlier, he had become the first hurler to log 200 wins without ever coming to bat or scoring a run in a major league game. A power pitcher early in his career, Tanana led the American League in strikeouts in 1975 with 269. Four years later, an arm ailment forced him to begin winning with guile rather than speed. He came within one victory of winning 20 in 1976, when he had a 19-10 record for the Angels. His career high point came in 1987, when he blanked Toronto on the last day of the season to clinch the division title for Detroit. In his lone League Championship Series start in 1987, he was bombed by the Twins, however, to further frustrate his bid to pitch in a World Series. Although twice on a division champion, Tanana marked his 21st season in 1993 without ever being a member of a pennant winner.

On August 11, 1991, Wilson Alvarez of the Chicago White Sox threw a no-hitter in his second major league game after having failed to survive the first inning in his first outing.

Good ERA
Jose Rijo, after he filed for a divorce from his wife, said: "My wife, she takes half of everything I make. I give up six runs and three are charged to her."

The 1982 season was the first campaign since 1949 that failed to see a no-hit game in either major league.

On April 23, 1983, Tiger Milt Wilcox missed a perfect game when he gave up a single with two out in the ninth inning.

Rich Gale in 1980 set a Royals record with 11 straight wins.

1980-1993 PITCHER ASSISTS

1. Dennis Martinez		496
2. Fernando Valenzuela		489
3. Charlie Leibrandt		465
4. Dave Stieb		457
5. Charlie Hough		447

The American League record for the most starts in a season without registering a complete game is held by Milt Wilcox of the Tigers with 33 in 1983.

Stewart Takes Trio of 20-Win Seasons

In the 1980s, pitchers, especially in the National League, shared in the wild swings that characterized the entire game. Throughout the decade only one senior loop hurler—Joaquin Andujar in 1984 and 1985—was able to win 20 games in two consecutive seasons. Andujar preceded his first 20-victory campaign, however, by notching just six wins in 1983 and followed his modest skein by winning only 17 more games in his career. Apart from Andujar, only Dwight Gooden managed even to win 40 or more games during any two-year period during the decade. Gooden collected 17 victories as a rookie in 1984 and then bagged 24 wins in his sophomore season for a two-year total of 41. The American League, in contrast, had several hurlers collect 40 or more wins over a two-year span between 1980 and 1989, led by Roger Clemens with 44 in 1986 and '87 and LaMarr Hoyt with 43 in 1982 and '83. Dave Stewart (1987 to 1989) was the only hurler to score 20 wins in three successive seasons during the decade.

Since joining the Red Sox regular rotation in 1986, Roger Clemens (above) has been a model of consistency, winning at least 17 games seven straight seasons.

1980-1993 PITCHER CHANCES ACCEPTED	
1. Dave Stieb	712
2. Jack Morris	702
Dennis Martinez	702
4. Fernando Valenzuela	664
5. Charlie Hough	646

In 1992, Steve Reed set the single-season minor league save record with 43.

Roger Clemens jokingly complained about Nolan Ryan: "If Ryan would act his age, there might be a few records left for me."

In 1991, Roger Clemens tied the AL record for the fewest wins by a starting pitcher who won a Cy Young with 18.

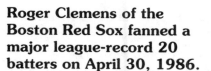

Roger Clemens of the Boston Red Sox fanned a major league-record 20 batters on April 30, 1986.

On September 29, 1986, Greg Maddux of the Cubs and brother Mike of the Phils became the only rookie siblings in major league history to face each other as starting pitchers.

In 1992, the strange even-odd year jinx haunting Bret Saberhagen (above) rendered him of little help to the New York Mets.

On July 1, 1990, Yankee hurler Andy Hawkins no-hit Chicago in a regulation nine-inning game, but lost 4-0.

Sparky Lyle was the first pitcher to play 15 or more full seasons in the majors without ever receiving a starting assignment.

In 1985, Oakland A's pitchers led the majors in complete games and the AL in fewest walks allowed but had only the 11th-best ERA in the AL.

1980-1993 PITCHER FIELDING AVERAGE	
1. Jim Slaton	.994
2. Les Lancaster	.993
3. Larry Gura	.992
4. Jim Acker	.992
5. Rick Rhoden	.991

Bret Saberhagen was, if nothing else, amazingly consistent in his inconsistency from his rookie year in 1984 through the 1991 campaign, his eighth in the majors. As a frosh hurler with Kansas City, he had an undistinguished 10-11 mark that offered no suggestion he would go 20-6 the next year at age 21 to become the youngest Cy Young Award winner ever. He had a 2.87 ERA and allowed only 9.6 baserunners a game. Saberhagen followed his eye-popping soph season with a 7-12 junior year. He then rebounded to 18-10 in 1987. But again the even-year jinx caught up with him as he finished the 1988 season at 14-16. In 1989, Saberhagen won his second Cy Young prize on the coattails of a 23-6 season. He led the league with 12 complete games, 262⅓ innings, and a 2.16 ERA. Hopes were riding high that he would finally stop the every-other-year jinx, only to crash once more in an even year, tumbling to 5-9 in 1990. After Saberhagen went 13-8 in 1991, the Royals, finally convinced that there was more afoot in the even-odd year syndrome than mere coincidence, unloaded him to the Mets prior to the 1992 season.

In 1987, Tom Candiotti, Scott Bailes, and Phil Niekro tied for the Cleveland club lead in wins with just seven apiece. They were the first pitchers in this century to lead a team in wins with just seven.

Willie Wilson said about Roger Clemens: "He struts around out there like 'Hey, man, I'm God. I'm Roger God Clemens, and nobody's going to hit me.'"

In 1984, Tigers reliever Willie Hernandez earned a record 32 saves in his first 32 save opportunities; he won the AL's Cy Young and MVP honors that year.

In 1991, Dennis Eckersley became the first pitcher in major league history to collect both 150 career wins and 150 career saves.

Dennis Eckersley in 1990 saved 48 games, posted a 0.61 ERA, and walked just four batters in 73⅓ innings.

Rick Sutcliffe in 1984 became the only Cy Young winner who began the year with another team. He started the season with a 4-5 record at Cleveland, was traded, and finished at 16-1 with the Cubs.

Gene Nelson, who later pitched for the Oakland A's, posted a 20-3 record in 1980 for Fort Lauderdale of the Florida State League.

Steve Carlton in 1982 set a major league record by winning his fourth Cy Young Award.

Oakland Loses Series, Dynasty Claim

By ending the 1980s with their second straight flag, the Oakland A's became the only team during the decade to cop two consecutive pennants. A third flag in a row followed in 1990, making the club the first since the 1976 to 1978 Yankees to sweep to three straight World Series appearances. Bidding to match the Yankees' two successive world titles in 1977 and '78, the A's instead dropped four straight contests to the Cincinnati Reds in one of the hugest upsets in professional sports history. A similar unexpected and egregious loss to the Dodgers in the 1988 fall classic doomed Oakland's chance to rank among the top dynasties since expansion. Indeed, by winning three straight pennants but emerging with just one World Championship for the effort, the A's invited comparison to the 1969 to 1971 Baltimore Orioles, unquestionably the game's strongest team at the time but ignored in most discussions of dynasties because they too came away from their skein of dominance with but one world title in three tries.

Above: *Outfielder Jose Canseco (left), first baseman Mark McGwire (center), and shortstop Walt Weiss (right) gave the Oakland A's three straight Rookie of the Year Award winners from 1986 to '88.*

The 1984 Tigers won 26 of their first 30 games, and 35 of their first 40—which were the best starts for any major league team this century.

The 1984 Tigers won an AL record 17 straight games on the road.

In 1982, the Atlanta Braves opened the season with 13 consecutive wins, a National League record.

Peter Gammons wrote of the 1986 Series: "When the ball went through Bill Buckner's legs, 41 years of Red Sox history flashed before my eyes."

The 1991 California Angels (81-81) were the first team in major league history to finish in the basement without a losing record.

In 1993, the Oakland A's became the first team since the 1915 Philadelphia A's to finish in the cellar after posting the best record in their loop the previous year. Winners of 96 games in 1992, the A's won 68 in '93.

33⅓
"No matter how good you are you're going to lose a third of your games. No matter how bad you are, you're going to win a third of your games. It's the other third that makes the difference."
—Tom Lasorda

1980-1993 CATCHER CHANCES ACCEPTED	
1. Tony Pena	10,919
2. Gary Carter	9,679
3. Mike Scioscia	9,072
4. Lance Parrish	8,740
5. Bob Boone	7,410

LaRussa Oversees Oakland's Ascent

Many observers felt the Oakland A's had the best talent in the American League West during the mid-1980s but lacked the leadership to go over the top. In 1986, with the season more than half over and the A's lagging in the rear 21 games under .500, the club's brain trust speedily hired Tony LaRussa to bring order to the dugout after he was dumped by the Chicago White Sox. LaRussa—the first successful manager with a law degree since Hughie Jennings—boosted the A's from 21 games below .500 to 10 under by the close of the 1986 season. After bringing the A's home third in 1987, just four games back of division-winning Minnesota, LaRussa then guided the club to three easy division triumphs followed in each case by a mercilessly one-sided League Championship Series win. LaRussa's commanding presence in the dugout coupled with his devotion to detail and skill at choosing coaches to whom he can comfortably delegate responsibility combine to make him one of the most respected American League managers.

Off and Running

Doc Medich said about Rickey Henderson: "He's like a little kid in a train station. You turn your back on him and he's gone."

In 1989, the Detroit Tigers set a franchise record for the most losses in a season when they bowed 103 times.

In 1984, the Philadelphia Phillies set a franchise record when they finished with a .500 or better record for the 10th straight season.

1980-1993 CATCHER GAMES	
1. Tony Pena	1,714
2. Gary Carter	1,488
3. Lance Parrish	1,480
4. Mike Scioscia	1,395
5. Carlton Fisk	1,354

In 1984, the New York Mets finished 18 games above the .500 mark despite being outscored by their opponents 676 runs to 652.

In 1984, the Pirates finished last in the NL East despite achieving an NL-best 3.11 team ERA and allowing the fewest runs in the majors (567).

1980-1993 CATCHER FIELDING AVERAGE	
1. Jim Sundberg	.994
2. Bob Melvin	.993
3. Ron Hassey	.993
4. Mike LaValliere	.992
5. Dave Valle	.992

Carlton Fisk in 1993 set a career record for catchers when he caught his 2,226th game.

◆◇◆◇◆

"There are three types of baseball players—those who make it happen, those who watch it happen, and those who wonder what happens."
—Tom Lasorda

1980-1993 FIRST BASE GAMES	
1. Eddie Murray	2,012
2. Kent Hrbek	1,537
3. Don Mattingly	1,412
4. Pete O'Brien	1,377
5. Keith Hernandez	1,363

At the conclusion of the 1991 season, the only team in the majors to play better than .500 ball both at home and on the road every year since 1985 was Toronto.

In 1991, the Kansas City Royals became the first major league team to occupy a division cellar as late as August while playing better than .500 ball.

Above: *Bob Boone, the record-holder for most games caught; both his father and his son also played in the majors.*

After the 1993 season, Rickey Henderson (above) said his new goal was to break Ty Cobb's career record for runs. He needed 659 more.

Successful Swipe Percentages Soar

When he swiped 96 bases in 1915 to establish the modern preexpansion record, Ty Cobb was caught 38 times, giving him a .716 percentage rate of success. Cobb's ratio, though good for its times, would border on unacceptable in today's game. Rickey Henderson had a .756 success rate in 1982, the year he pilfered 130 bases, the current single-season stolen base record. Henderson also ranks among the top 10 in career stolen base average. First on the list among players who have at least 400 steal attempts is Tim Raines, with an .849 percentage through the 1993 season. Willie Wilson ranks second at .833, and Davey Lopes, who retired with an .830 percentage, is third. Kevin McReynolds in 1988 swiped 21 bases without getting caught. He beat Max Carey's single-season record; in 1922, Carey stole 51 bases and was caught two times. Contemporary players dominate the career stolen-base percentage list to such an extent that the only preexpansion performer among the top 30 is George Case, whose .762 career percentage was first bettered by Luis Aparicio.

Rickey Henderson in 1991 topped Lou Brock's record for career thefts of 938 and finished the season with 994 stolen bases.

In 1982, when Rickey Henderson broke Lou Brock's swipes record with 130, Henderson also set the all-time mark for the most times caught stealing with 42.

Rickey Henderson became the first major league player to swipe at least 100 bases in three different seasons.

1980-1993 FIRST BASE CHANCES ACCEPTED	
1. Eddie Murray	19,112
2. Kent Hrbek	14,166
3. Keith Hernandez	13,320
4. Don Mattingly	13,188
5. Pete O'Brien	12,715

1980-1993 FIRST BASE FIELDING AVERAGE	
1. Steve Garvey	.997
2. Don Mattingly	.996
3. Dan Driessen	.996
4. Mark McGwire	.995
5. Mike Squires	.995

"You look at a guy who's being brave. He's afraid, or he wouldn't be brave. If he isn't afraid, he's stupid."
—*Joe Torre*

In 1993, the Atlanta Braves became the first team in this century to blank an opponent for an entire season when they were a perfect 13-0 versus the Colorado Rockies.

Billy Martin was fired as Yankee manager a record fifth time, in 1988.

In Short, Ripken Long on Iron

If he remains free of injury, Cal Ripken is slated to break Lou Gehrig's record for consecutive games played in 1995. Ripken last failed to appear in a Baltimore Orioles box score on July 1, 1982, during his rookie season. The following year, he obliterated the notion that he might be a victim of the sophomore jinx by hitting .318 with 27 homers and 102 RBI to snare the MVP Award. Ripken's 1983 season was the best all-around hitting season by an American League shortstop since Joe Cronin hit .346 with 13 homers and 126 RBI for Washington in 1930. After dropping to a career-low .250 in 1990, Ripken revived the following year to compile what many consider the best offensive season in history by an American League shortstop. At the All-Star break, he was leading the loop with a .348 average. Even though he subsequently dipped to .323, his 210 hits, 34 homers, 114 RBI, and .566 slugging average all put him high on the list for the best single-season output by a shortstop. For his super season, Ripken was a natural choice to claim his second MVP Award.

"Baseball has been very good to me since I quit trying to play it."
—**Whitey Herzog**

Cal Ripken Sr. of the Orioles in 1987 became the first man to manage two sons in the major leagues—Cal Jr. and Billy.

Above: *Cal Ripken Sr., seated between his sons Billy (left) and Cal Jr., managed both on the 1987 Orioles.*

In 1983, Cal Ripken of the Orioles became the only player ever to play every inning of every regular-season, League Championship Series, and World Series game played by his team.

1980-1993 SECOND BASE GAMES	
1. Lou Whitaker	1,891
2. Steve Sax	1,673
3. Ryne Sandberg	1,666
4. Willie Randolph	1,580
5. Frank White	1,475

When he topped the American League with 60 steals in 1987, the Mariners' Harold Reynolds prevented Rickey Henderson from leading the AL in thefts every season during the 1980s.

Cal Ripken broke Buck Freeman's record for consecutive innings played in 1985, as Iron Cal played 5,342 innings without respite. Ripken's streak (8,243) came to an end in 1987.

"The worst thing about managing is the day you realize you want to win more than the players do."
—*Gene Mauch*

Crunch
"Managing is like holding a dove in your hand. Squeeze too hard and you kill it; not hard enough and it flies away."
—**Tom Lasorda**

Smith Snares a Dozen Glove Awards

In 1993, Ozzie Smith's record streak of 13 consecutive Gold Glove Awards ended, as Jay Bell dethroned the Cardinals' slick-fielding infielder. The skein began in 1980 while Smith was still a member of the Padres. What launched him that year in the voters' eyes were his 621 assists, establishing a new all-time single-season record for shortstops. The acrobatic Smith has since topped the National League in assists seven more times for a total of eight, another major league mark. Although it is hard to prove, the Wizard of Oz lays claim to being history's best glove at shortstop. Even if he were a dead weight on offense, Smith's glove alone would demand that a place be found for him in the lineup, but he is among the better-hitting shortstops of the current era. At the conclusion of 1991 he had a .285 career batting average. Early in the 1992 campaign, he collected both his 2,000th hit and his 500th stolen base. At the end of 1993, Smith stood second only to Luis Aparicio in games played at shortstop.

1980-1993 SECOND BASE FIELDING AVERAGE	
1. Jose Oquendo	.993
2. Ryne Sandberg	.990
3. Tom Herr	.989
4. Jose Lind	.988
5. Scott Fletcher	.988

In 1990, Mark Grace of the Chicago Cubs set an NL record for first basemen when he accumulated 180 assists.

Above: *Ozzie Smith celebrated his 15th season as the major leagues' top all-around shortstop in 1992 by collecting his 2,000th hit. A weak hitter early in his career, Smith has steadily hiked his career batting average since the mid-1980s.*

Larry Bowa retired in 1985 with a major league-record .980 career fielding average at shortstop.

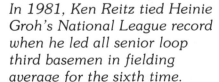

In 1981, Ken Reitz tied Heinie Groh's National League record when he led all senior loop third basemen in fielding average for the sixth time.

Mike Schmidt of the Phillies in 1986 won his last of 10 Gold Gloves, an NL record for third basemen.

Not to Mention Their Curlers

Bob Lemon, while managing the Yankees in 1981, remarked: "Today's players like to play their stereos early because after the game their hair dryers cause static."

Toronto's Tony Fernandez in 1989 made just six errors and set a major league fielding average record for shortstops (.992).

In 1980, Rick Burleson of the Red Sox set a major league record for the most double plays by a shortstop when he was involved in 147 twin kills.

Bobby Grich of the Orioles set a major league record for the highest single-season fielding average by a second baseman in 1985 with a .997 mark.

In 1987, Lou Whitaker and Alan Trammell of the Tigers became the first keystone combo in major league history to play regularly for the same team for 10 consecutive years.

1980-1993 THIRD BASE GAMES	
1. Tim Wallach	1,754
2. Wade Boggs	1,654
3. Gary Gaetti	1,609
4. Carney Lansford	1,446
5. Terry Pendleton	1,375

Super Joe Jinxed, Job Junked

For a Cleveland frosh, being named Rookie of the Year can be more of a curse than a blessing. Only Chris Chambliss, the choice in 1971, has escaped the jinx, largely perhaps because he was traded soon thereafter to the Yankees. Gene Bearden, the American League's top rookie in 1948, and Herb Score, everyone's favorite in 1955, both were unable to capitalize on their early promise. Likewise Sandy Alomar, the AL's top yearling in 1990, was decked the following year by rotator cuff problems and has still not regained his frosh form. No Cleveland rookie toppled more precipitously after bagging freshman honors than Super Joe Charboneau. Two consecutive minor league batting titles earned him a shot at a Tribe outfield post in 1980, and he seized the opportunity to hit .289 with 23 homers and 87 RBI, making him a runaway choice for loop rookie honors. Charboneau played only 70 more games in the majors after 1980. Injuries and a lack of motivation stymied his comeback bids and relegated him to softball.

Joe DiMaggio, upon being named greatest living player at age 66, said: "At my age I'm just glad to be named the greatest living anything."

Steve Garvey's record streak of 193 consecutive errorless games at first base ended in 1985.

Originally a third baseman, Steve Garvey (above) was moved to first base in 1973. That year he also played 10 games in the outfield. After 1973, however, Garvey never played any position but first.

Steve Garvey's NL record streak of 1,207 consecutive games ended in 1983 when he broke his thumb.

In 1984, Steve Garvey of the Padres became the only regular first baseman ever to go errorless for an entire season.

Rookie Ivan Rodriguez of Texas in 1991 caught 88 games at age 19—the most since 1949 by a teenage backstopper.

Cornered

Brewers manager Harvey Kuenn, after the Angels led the ALCS two games to none in 1982, explained: "They had us with the walls to our back."

1980-1993 THIRD BASE FIELDING AVERAGE	
1. Steve Buechele	.968
2. Toby Harrah	.967
3. Carney Lansford	.966
4. Buddy Bell	.966
5. Ken Oberkfell	.965

Manager Dave Bristol addressed his Giants team after a loss: "There'll be two buses leaving the hotel for the park tomorrow. The 2 o'clock bus will be for those of you who need a little extra work. The empty bus will leave at 5 o'clock."

In 1983, Carl Yastrzemski completed his 23rd and final season in a Red Sox uniform to tie Brooks Robinson's record for the most seasons of service with the same team.

Terry Puhl finished his major league career in 1990 with a .993 fielding average, currently the best in history by an outfielder.

Phillie Garry Maddox in 1982 won his last of eight consecutive Gold Gloves as an NL outfielder.

The Boston Red Sox lost game six of the 1986 World Series after leading 5-3 in the 10th inning, as Met Mookie Wilson hit a grounder that dribbled through Bill Buckner's legs to drive in the winning run.

In his 18 years in the majors, Buddy Bell (above) never even came close to seeing postseason action.

In 1981, Buddy Bell of the Rangers set a modern record for third basemen when he totaled 2.93 assists per game, just .03 shy of the all-time mark.

Blink of an Eye
"It's a mere moment in a man's life between an All-Star Game and an old-timer's game."
—Vin Scully, Dodgers broadcaster

In 1988, the Atlanta Braves posted a .338 winning percentage, the franchise's worst since 1935, and won just 54 games, the fewest by any NL team during the 1980s.

The Phillies in 1982 traded Larry Bowa and Ryne Sandberg to the Chicago Cubs for Ivan DeJesus.

Atlanta Ascends From Ashes

In 1890, the Louisville Colonels, spared by Players' League raiders because they had few performers coveted by the rebel loop, won the American Association pennant after finishing dead last the previous year. Almost exactly a century later, the Atlanta Braves became the first major league team to match Louisville's feat. The Braves copped the National League pennant in 1991 after spending the season before in the loop's basement. In 1990, the Braves were 65-97, with a .401 winning percentage. The next season, Atlanta went 94-68 for a .580 win average. Prior to 1991, the two closest parallels in this century to the 1889 and '90 Louisville Colonels were the 1967 Boston Red Sox, who won the AL pennant after finishing only half a game out of the cellar in 1966, and the 1914 and '15 St. Louis Terriers. After finishing last in the first Federal League season, the Terriers in 1915 missed winning the FL flag by a single percentage point, losing out to the Chicago Whales .566 to .565.

Stan Musial assessed the new domed stadiums: "I got started too early in baseball. In air conditioning I could have lasted another 20 years."

1980-1993 SHORTSTOP GAMES	
1. Ozzie Smith	2,008
2. Cal Ripken	1,885
3. Alfredo Griffin	1,687
4. Alan Trammell	1,673
5. Garry Templeton	1,455

"All I ever wanted to be president of was the American League."
—A. Bartlett Giamatti

1980-1993 SHORTSTOP FIELDING AVERAGE	
1. Tony Fernandez	.980
2. Omar Vizquel	.980
3. Ozzie Smith	.979
4. Alan Trammell	.978
5. Cal Ripken	.978

In 1987, the Minnesota Twins set a major league record for the lowest road winning percentage by a pennant winner when they played just .375 ball away from home.

The 1983 White Sox won their division by 20 games, and Chicago was the only team in the American League West to break .500.

In 1993 Sparky Anderson of the Tigers became the first manager since Connie Mack retired in 1950 to manage 24 consecutive seasons in the majors.

The Kansas City Royals in 1980 were the first AL expansion team to win a pennant.

Since the A's moved to Oakland in 1968, no member of the club has won an AL batting title and Carney Lansford, in 1989, was the only Oakland A ever to make a serious bid to win one.

Home Dome Advantage

The Minnesota Twins in a sense matched the Braves' feat in 1991 by rising to the American League pennant following a last-place finish in their division. The Twins did not perform a true worst-to-first leapfrog because their record in 1990 of 74-88 was better than the Yankees (67-95) and the same as the Brewers, meaning that the Twins finished in a tie with Milwaukee as the 12th-best team in the 14-club circuit. To the Twins, however, belongs a distinction that is as remarkable in its own right as the Braves' achievement. When Minnesota beat Atlanta in the World Series, it marked only the second time a team had claimed a fall classic without winning a single game in its opponent's park. The first victorious team to win all four of its Series triumphs on its home ground was none other than the 1987 Twins. Minnesota thus has won two world titles even though it has yet to win a Series game on the road.

Above: *Three key offensive contributors on the 1987 world champion Minnesota Twins were, from left, right fielder Tom Brunansky, center fielder Kirby Puckett, and first baseman Kent Hrbek.*

In 1992, Toronto's Joe Carter was the first player to start at three different positions (left field, first base, and right field) in three straight World Series games.

The Atlanta Braves in 1991 and '92 were the first team to win back-to-back senior loop pennants since the 1977 and 1978 Los Angeles Dodgers.

The '87 World Series marked the first time neither team could win a game on the road.

"All baseball fans can be divided into two groups: those who come to batting practice and the others. Only those in the first category have much chance of amounting to anything."

—Thomas Boswell, sportswriter

In 1987, the Twins set a record for the lowest winning percentage by a world championship team when they went 85-77 to finish with a .525 mark.

Otis Nixon's 72 stolen bases in his drug-suspension-abbreviated 1991 season set a Braves' 20th-century franchise record.

1980-1993 OUTFIELD GAMES	
1. Dale Murphy	1,853
2. Brett Butler	1,795
3. Rickey Henderson	1,792
4. Andre Dawson	1,792
5. Willie Wilson	1,742
6. Tim Raines	1,692
7. Tom Brunansky	1,631
8. Tony Gwynn	1,570
9. Dave Winfield	1,562
10. Willie McGee	1,532
11. Lloyd Moseby	1,529
12. Kirby Puckett	1,492
13. Kevin McReynolds	1,422
14. Chet Lemon	1,402
15. Jesse Barfield	1,387

Mauch Thwarted From Championship Bid

In 1964, Gene Mauch piloted the Philadelphia Phillies to a 6½-game lead in the National League with just 12 contests to play, only to see his club go into a monumental skid that handed the pennant to the St. Louis Cardinals. Eighteen years later, Mauch, still without a flag in 23 seasons as a helmsman, had the 1982 California Angels needing only one win in three games at Milwaukee to claim their first American League pennant. The Angels then dropped all three contests to the Brewers to become the only AL team ever to lose a five-game League Championship Series after leading 2-0 in games. Disappointed again, Mauch felt he finally had a lock on his first pennant when the Angels led the Red Sox 3-1 in games in the 1986 ALCS. The Angels were ahead 5-2 in the ninth inning of game five. California, though, lost that contest 7-6 and then dropped the next two games in Boston to leave Mauch high and dry once again. He managed just one more season before departing after a record 26 years as a skipper without winning a pennant.

Boo!

"Philly fans are so mean that on Easter Sunday, when the players staged an Easter-egg hunt for their kids, the fans booed the kids who didn't find any eggs."
—Bob Uecker

"Fenway Park in Boston is a lyric little bandbox of a ballpark. Everything is painted green and seems in curiously sharp focus, like the inside of an old-fashioned peeping-type Easter egg."
—John Updike, writer

Cardinal Vince Coleman swiped 100 or more bases for a major league record third consecutive season, in 1987.

On September 20, 1992, Phillies second sacker Mickey Morandini completed the first unassisted triple play since 1968.

In 1985, Vince Coleman of the Cardinals stole a rookie record 110 bases.

After the 1988 season was over, the Chicago Cubs had gone 43 years without a pennant to break the old major league record of 42 years held by the St. Louis Browns.

The New York Yankees' .414 winning percentage in 1990 was the team's worst since 1912.

Toronto and Seattle, expansion brothers in 1977 have been the majors' best and worst teams respectively since 1980.

Above: *Vince Coleman paced the NL in stolen bases in each of his first six seasons before leaving the Cardinals to sign with the Mets; the move has been disastrous for him thus far.*

In their last seven World Series appearances—1946, 1964, 1967, 1968, 1982, 1985, and 1987—the St. Louis Cardinals have been forced to go the full seven games on each occasion.

1980-1993 OUTFIELD FIELDING AVERAGE	
1. Brian Downing	.995
2. Dave Gallagher	.993
3. Brett Butler	.992
4. Terry Puhl	.992
5. Gary Roenicke	.990
6. Robin Yount	.990
7. Gerald Young	.990
8. Fred Lynn	.990
9. John Moses	.990
10. Kirby Puckett	.989
11. Henry Cotto	.989
12. Stan Javier	.989
13. Darrin Jackson	.989
14. Paul O'Neill	.989
15. Tim Raines	.988

Hot Stove

"There is no off-season in Chicago. It is only when the teams start playing that the fans lose interest."
—Steve Daley, writer

Bill Veeck in 1981 sold the Chicago White Sox for the second time in his life.

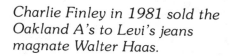

Charlie Finley in 1981 sold the Oakland A's to Levi's jeans magnate Walter Haas.

1980-1993 MANAGER WINS	
1. Tony La Russa	1,175
2. Sparky Anderson	1,162
3. Tom Lasorda	1,148
4. Whitey Herzog	822
Bobby Cox	822
6. Bob Rodgers	768
7. John McNamara	739
8. Jim Leyland	667
9. Davey Johnson	648
10. Joe Torre	643

Prior to the 1982 season, the Yankees traded future two-time bat king Willie McGee to the Cardinals for pitcher Bob Sykes, who never hurled another inning in the majors.

The five players who were drafted who did not have seasoning in the minors include Dave Winfield of San Diego (drafted in June 1973), Bob Horner of Atlanta (June 1978), Pete Incaviglia of Texas (June 1985), Jim Abbott of California (June 1988), and John Olerud of Toronto (June 1989).

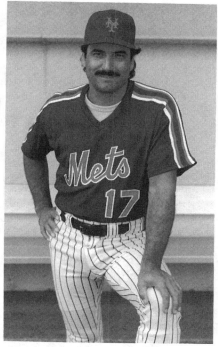

Considered the best-fielding first baseman of the current era, Keith Hernandez (above) also notched over 2,000 hits and a .296 batting average.

Since the start of the free-agent draft in 1965, 16 players have made their professional debuts in the major leagues.

In 1986, for the first time in history, every club in the majors exceeded 1 million in attendance.

1980-1993 MANAGER WINNING PERCENTAGE	
1. Cito Gaston	.575
2. Davey Johnson	.573
3. Bobby Cox	.549
4. Dick Howser	.545
5. Earl Weaver	.545
6. Billy Martin	.541
7. Jimy Williams	.538
8. Tony La Russa	.536
9. Joe Morgan	.535
10. Whitey Herzog	.530

Glovemen Gather at Gateway Bag

First base has traditionally been the province of slow-footed sluggers and murderously inept fielders, such as Dick Stuart ("Doctor Strangeglove") and Zeke Bonura. In recent years, though, first base has become a bastion for some of the slickest glovemen in the game. In 1988, Keith Hernandez of the Mets set a new mark for gateway guardians when he acquired his 11th consecutive Gold Glove. Three years earlier, Bill Buckner, although never a Gold Glove winner, shattered his own all-time record of 161 assists, set in 1983, when he tossed out 184 runners from his first base post. Buckner at one point held both the American League and the National League record for the most assists in a season, but his NL mark fell in 1986 to Sid Bream of the Pirates, who notched 166 assists. Bream's record stood only until 1990 when the Cubs' Mark Grace racked up 180 assists, only four shy of Buckner's all-time mark.

"One of my goals in life was to be surrounded by unpretentious, rich young men. Then I bought the Braves and I was surrounded by 25 of them."
—Ted Turner

In 1981, the Mets swapped Jeff Reardon, who in 1992 broke Rollie Fingers's mark as the all-time saves leader, to the Expos for Ellis Valentine, a backup outfielder.

Skipper Howser Leads KC to Crown

In his senior year at Palm Beach High School in Florida, Dick Howser hit below .200 and was moved to second base because his arm was judged too weak for shortstop. Seven years later, he narrowly missed winning the American League Rookie of the Year Award after he hit .280 and swiped 37 bases while serving at shortstop for the Kansas City A's. Owing to injuries, Howser enjoyed only one other season as a full-time player before retiring to the coaching lines in 1969. After 10 years as a Yankees coach, Howser was given a chance to manage the club in 1980. He responded by taking the Bombers to the AL East title but was fired when New York fell to Kansas City in the League Championship Series. If Howser was underappreciated in New York, though, Kansas City knew his true worth. Hired to replace Whitey Herzog at the Royals' helm in 1981, Howser led Kansas City to the second-half division title. Two more postseason appearances followed in the next four years, including the Royals' first world championship in 1985. But in 1986, during the All-Star break, Howser learned he had an inoperable brain tumor. The Royals have not appeared in postseason play since his death in 1987.

After he found out that umpire Ron Luciano signed to become a sportscaster, Earl Weaver stated: "I hope he takes this job more seriously than he did his last one."

In 1992, Robin Yount (above) became the youngest righthanded hitter to amass 3,000 hits, at age 37.

The Los Angeles Dodgers had four consecutive Rookie of the Year Award winners between 1979 and 1982.

The only city that has had a major league team for at least 30 years in this century but never hosted a World Series game is Houston.

The only major league park to be home to both an AL and an NL champion since World War II is Milwaukee County Stadium.

Ken Griffey Sr. and Ken Griffey Jr. in 1989 became the first father and son in major league history to both be active in the majors at the same time.

Robin Yount in 1989 won his second AL MVP Award and was the first AL player to win the honor twice while playing two different positions.

Hostile
"The old fan used to yell, 'Kill the umpire.' The new fan tries to do it."
—Psychiatrist Arnold Beisser

Above: *Ryne Sandberg is on a pace to break both records for the highest fielding average and the most career home runs by a second baseman.*

1980-1993 TEAM WINNING PERCENTAGE

1.	Toronto-AL	.536
2.	Detroit-AL	.525
3.	New York-AL	.523
4.	Oakland-AL	.521
5.	St.Louis-NL	.521
6.	Montreal-NL	.519
7.	Los Angeles-NL	.519
8.	Boston-AL	.518
9.	Kansas City-AL	.516
10.	Houston-NL	.507
11.	Milwaukee-AL	.507
12.	Chicago-AL	.507
13.	Baltimore-AL	.506
14.	New York Mets-NL	.505
15.	Cincinnati-NL	.501
16.	San Francisco-NL	.500
17.	Philadelphia-NL	.500
18.	Pittsburgh-NL	.497
19.	California-AL	.491
20.	Atlanta-NL	.487
21.	San Diego-NL	.480
22.	Minnesota-AL	.480
23.	Chicago-NL	.477
24.	Texas-AL	.476
25.	Cleveland-AL	.451
26.	Seattle-AL	.442
27.	Colorado-NL	.414
28.	Florida-NL	.395

Sandberg Second to None as Slugger

Observers of the game cannot be blamed for looking askance at the many record errorless skeins and high fielding averages in recent years. Not only are official scorers nowadays loath to charge fielders with miscues on anything less than an egregious error, but players themselves join in the conspiracy to make a mockery of fielding records. Ryne Sandberg, for one, helped protect his record 123-game errorless streak at second base in 1989 and '90 by removing himself from several contests in the late innings. Although historically his fielding mark was sullied, he is still a fine fielder. Also, his offensive output in 1990 left nothing to dispute. By rapping 40 circuit blows, he became the only second baseman since the end of the dead-ball era other than Rogers Hornsby to win a loop home run crown in a season when a full schedule was played. Sandberg also became the first second sacker since Hornsby to be a league leader in total bases by collecting 344 total sacks, the most in the majors.

"When I am right, no one remembers. When I am wrong, no one forgets."
—Doug Harvey, umpire

The Oakland A's swept the San Francisco Giants in the 1989 fall classic, in the most one-sided World Series ever. A massive earthquake in the San Francisco Bay area prior to game three forced a 10-day delay of the World Series.

1980-1993 TEAM WINS

		WON	LOST
1.	Toronto-AL	1,185	1,026
2.	Detroit-AL	1,162	1,052
3.	New York-AL	1,156	1,054
4.	Oakland-AL	1,154	1,061
5.	St.Louis-NL	1,149	1,058
6.	Montreal-NL	1,148	1,062
	Los Angeles-NL	1,148	1,066
8.	Boston-AL	1,146	1,065
9.	Kansas City-AL	1,139	1,068
10.	Houston-NL	1,125	1,092
11.	Milwaukee-AL	1,122	1,090
12.	Chicago-AL	1,119	1,089
13.	Baltimore-AL	1,117	1,091
14.	New York Mets-NL	1,115	1,091
15.	Cincinnati-NL	1,109	1,103
16.	San Francisco-NL	1,108	1,108
17.	Philadelphia-NL	1,105	1,106
18.	Pittsburgh-NL	1,096	1,109
19.	California-AL	1,087	1,127
20.	Atlanta-NL	1,073	1,132
21.	San Diego-NL	1,064	1,151
22.	Minnesota-AL	1,063	1,151
23.	Chicago-NL	1,051	1,151
	Texas-AL	1,051	1,156
25.	Cleveland-AL	996	1,211
26.	Seattle-AL	979	1,235
27.	Colorado-NL	67	95
28.	Florida-NL	64	98

In the strike-shortened 1981 season the Cincinnati Reds had the best overall record in the majors but failed to qualify for postseason play.

The Toronto Blue Jays in 1991 became the charter member of the 4 million home-attendance club. The Blue Jays averaged 49,402 paid attendance a game, with 66 sellouts at the SkyDome. Fans took advantage of the stadium's indoor-outdoor capabilities.

All-Time Leaders

GAMES

1.	Pete Rose	3,562
2.	Carl Yastrzemski	3,308
3.	Hank Aaron	3,298
4.	Ty Cobb	3,035
5.	Stan Musial	3,026
6.	Willie Mays	2,992
7.	Rusty Staub	2,951
8.	Brooks Robinson	2,896
9.	Robin Yount	2,856
10.	Dave Winfield	2,850
11.	Al Kaline	2,834
12.	Eddie Collins	2,826
13.	Reggie Jackson	2,820
14.	Frank Robinson	2,808
15.	Honus Wagner	2,792
16.	Tris Speaker	2,789
17.	Tony Perez	2,777
18.	Mel Ott	2,730
19.	George Brett	2,707
20.	Graig Nettles	2,700
21.	Darrell Evans	2,687
22.	Rabbit Maranville	2,670
23.	Joe Morgan	2,649
24.	Lou Brock	2,616
25.	Dwight Evans	2,606
26.	Luis Aparicio	2,599
27.	Eddie Murray	2,598
28.	Willie McCovey	2,588
29.	Paul Waner	2,549
30.	Ernie Banks	2,528
31.	Cap Anson	2,523
32.	Sam Crawford	2,517
	Bill Buckner	2,517
34.	Babe Ruth	2,503
35.	Carlton Fisk	2,499
36.	Billy Williams	2,488
	Dave Concepcion	2,488
38.	Nap Lajoie	2,480
39.	Max Carey	2,476
40.	Vada Pinson	2,469
	Rod Carew	2,469
42.	Dave Parker	2,466
43.	Ted Simmons	2,456
44.	Bill Dahlen	2,443
45.	Ron Fairly	2,442
46.	Harmon Killebrew	2,435
47.	Roberto Clemente	2,433
48.	Andre Dawson	2,431
49.	Willie Davis	2,429
50.	Luke Appling	2,422
51.	Zack Wheat	2,410
52.	Mickey Vernon	2,409
53.	Buddy Bell	2,405
54.	Mike Schmidt	2,404
	Sam Rice	2,404
56.	Mickey Mantle	2,401
57.	Eddie Mathews	2,391
58.	Jake Beckley	2,386
59.	Bobby Wallace	2,383
60.	Enos Slaughter	2,380
61.	Al Oliver	2,368
	George Davis	2,368
63.	Nellie Fox	2,367
64.	Willie Stargell	2,360
65.	Jose Cruz	2,353
66.	Ozzie Smith	2,349
67.	Brian Downing	2,344
68.	Steve Garvey	2,332
69.	Bert Campaneris	2,328
70.	Frank White	2,324
71.	Charlie Gehringer	2,323
72.	Jimmie Foxx	2,317
73.	Frankie Frisch	2,311
74.	Harry Hooper	2,309
75.	Gary Carter	2,296
76.	Ted Williams	2,292
	Don Baylor	2,292
78.	Goose Goslin	2,287
79.	Jimmy Dykes	2,282
80.	Lave Cross	2,275
81.	Bob Boone	2,264
82.	Chris Speier	2,260
83.	Rogers Hornsby	2,259
84.	Larry Bowa	2,247
85.	Ron Santo	2,243
86.	Fred Clarke	2,242
87.	Doc Cramer	2,239
88.	Red Schoendienst	2,216
89.	Al Simmons	2,215
90.	Lou Whitaker	2,214
91.	Joe Torre	2,209
92.	Willie Randolph	2,202
93.	Tommy Corcoran	2,200
94.	Tony Taylor	2,195
95.	Richie Ashburn	2,189
96.	Bill Russell	2,181
97.	Dale Murphy	2,180
98.	Chris Chambliss	2,175
99.	Joe Judge	2,171
100.	Pee Wee Reese	2,166
	Charlie Grimm	2,166

RUNS

1.	Ty Cobb	2,246
2.	Babe Ruth	2,174
	Hank Aaron	2,174
4.	Pete Rose	2,165
5.	Willie Mays	2,062
6.	Cap Anson	1,996
7.	Stan Musial	1,949
8.	Lou Gehrig	1,888
9.	Tris Speaker	1,882
10.	Mel Ott	1,859
11.	Frank Robinson	1,829
12.	Eddie Collins	1,821
13.	Carl Yastrzemski	1,816
14.	Ted Williams	1,798
15.	Charlie Gehringer	1,774
16.	Jimmie Foxx	1,751
17.	Honus Wagner	1,736
18.	Jim O'Rourke	1,732
19.	Jesse Burkett	1,720
20.	Willie Keeler	1,719
21.	Billy Hamilton	1,690
22.	Bid McPhee	1,678
23.	Mickey Mantle	1,677
24.	Joe Morgan	1,650
25.	Jimmy Ryan	1,642
26.	George Van Haltren	1,639
27.	Robin Yount	1,632
28.	Paul Waner	1,627
29.	Dave Winfield	1,623
30.	Al Kaline	1,622
31.	Roger Connor	1,620
32.	Fred Clarke	1,619
33.	Lou Brock	1,610
34.	Jake Beckley	1,600
35.	Ed Delahanty	1,599
36.	Bill Dahlen	1,589
37.	Rickey Henderson	1,586
38.	George Brett	1,583
39.	Rogers Hornsby	1,579
40.	Hugh Duffy	1,552
41.	Reggie Jackson	1,551
42.	Max Carey	1,545
43.	George Davis	1,539
44.	Frankie Frisch	1,532
45.	Dan Brouthers	1,523
46.	Tom Brown	1,521
47.	Sam Rice	1,514
48.	Eddie Mathews	1,509
49.	Al Simmons	1,507
50.	Mike Schmidt	1,506
51.	Nap Lajoie	1,504
52.	Harry Stovey	1,492
53.	Goose Goslin	1,483
54.	Arlie Latham	1,478
55.	Dwight Evans	1,470
56.	Herman Long	1,455
57.	Harry Hooper	1,429
58.	Dummy Hoy	1,426
59.	Rod Carew	1,424
60.	Joe Kelley	1,421
61.	Eddie Murray	1,420
62.	Roberto Clemente	1,416
63.	Billy Williams	1,410
64.	John Ward	1,408
65.	Mike Griffin	1,405
66.	Paul Molitor	1,396
67.	Sam Crawford	1,391
68.	Joe DiMaggio	1,390
69.	Vada Pinson	1,366
70.	King Kelly	1,357
	Doc Cramer	1,357
72.	Tommy Leach	1,355
73.	Darrell Evans	1,344
74.	Pee Wee Reese	1,338
75.	Luis Aparicio	1,335
76.	Lave Cross	1,333
77.	George Gore	1,327
78.	Richie Ashburn	1,322
79.	Luke Appling	1,319
80.	Patsy Donovan	1,318
81.	Mike Tiernan	1,313
82.	Ernie Banks	1,305

83. Andre Dawson	1,303	
84. Jimmy Sheckard	1,296	
85. Kiki Cuyler	1,295	
86. Harry Heilmann	1,291	
87. Zack Wheat	1,289	
88. Heinie Manush	1,287	
89. George Sisler	1,284	
90. Lou Whitaker	1,283	
Harmon Killebrew	1,283	
92. Donie Bush	1,280	
93. Nellie Fox	1,279	
94. Fred Tenney	1,278	
95. Carlton Fisk	1,276	
96. Tony Perez	1,272	
Dave Parker	1,272	
98. Duke Snider	1,259	
99. Bobby Bonds	1,258	
100. Sam Thompson	1,256	

HITS

1. Pete Rose 4,256
2. Ty Cobb 4,189
3. Hank Aaron 3,771
4. Stan Musial 3,630
5. Tris Speaker 3,514
6. Carl Yastrzemski 3,419
7. Honus Wagner 3,415
   Cap Anson 3,415
9. Eddie Collins 3,312
10. Willie Mays 3,283
11. Nap Lajoie 3,242
12. George Brett 3,154
13. Paul Waner 3,152
14. Robin Yount 3,142
15. Rod Carew 3,053
16. Lou Brock 3,023
17. Dave Winfield 3,014
18. Al Kaline 3,007
19. Roberto Clemente 3,000
20. Sam Rice 2,987
21. Sam Crawford 2,961
22. Frank Robinson 2,943
23. Willie Keeler 2,932
24. Rogers Hornsby 2,930
    Jake Beckley 2,930
26. Al Simmons 2,927
27. Zack Wheat 2,884
28. Frankie Frisch 2,880
29. Mel Ott 2,876
30. Babe Ruth 2,873
31. Jesse Burkett 2,850
32. Brooks Robinson 2,848
33. Charlie Gehringer 2,839
34. Eddie Murray 2,820
35. George Sisler 2,812
36. Vada Pinson 2,757
37. Luke Appling 2,749
38. Al Oliver 2,743
39. Goose Goslin 2,735
40. Tony Perez 2,732
41. Lou Gehrig 2,721
42. Rusty Staub 2,716
43. Bill Buckner 2,715
44. Dave Parker 2,712
45. Billy Williams 2,711
46. Doc Cramer 2,705
47. Luis Aparicio 2,677
48. Fred Clarke 2,672
49. Max Carey 2,665
50. Nellie Fox 2,663
51. Harry Heilmann 2,660
    George Davis 2,660
53. Ted Williams 2,654
54. Jim O'Rourke 2,646

Jimmie Foxx	2,646	
56. Lave Cross	2,645	
57. Andre Dawson	2,630	
58. Rabbit Maranville	2,605	
59. Steve Garvey	2,599	
60. Ed Delahanty	2,597	
61. Reggie Jackson	2,584	
62. Ernie Banks	2,583	
63. Richie Ashburn	2,574	
64. Willie Davis	2,561	
65. George Van Haltren	2,532	
66. Heinie Manush	2,524	
67. Joe Morgan	2,517	
68. Buddy Bell	2,514	
69. Jimmy Ryan	2,502	
70. Mickey Vernon	2,495	
71. Paul Molitor	2,492	
72. Ted Simmons	2,472	
73. Joe Medwick	2,471	
74. Roger Connor	2,467	
75. Harry Hooper	2,466	
76. Lloyd Waner	2,459	
77. Bill Dahlen	2,457	
78. Jim Rice	2,452	
79. Red Schoendienst	2,449	
80. Dwight Evans	2,446	
81. Pie Traynor	2,416	
82. Mickey Mantle	2,415	
83. Stuffy McInnis	2,405	
84. Enos Slaughter	2,383	
85. Edd Roush	2,376	
86. Carlton Fisk	2,356	
87. Joe Judge	2,352	
88. Orlando Cepeda	2,351	
89. Billy Herman	2,345	
90. Joe Torre	2,342	
91. Jake Daubert	2,326	
Dave Concepcion	2,326	
93. Eddie Mathews	2,315	
94. Jim Bottomley	2,313	
95. Bobby Wallace	2,309	
96. Charlie Grimm	2,299	
Kiki Cuyler	2,299	
98. Dan Brouthers	2,296	
99. Joe Cronin	2,285	
100. Hugh Duffy	2,282	

TOTAL BASES

1. Hank Aaron 6,856
2. Stan Musial 6,134
3. Willie Mays 6,066
4. Ty Cobb 5,854
5. Babe Ruth 5,793
6. Pete Rose 5,752
7. Carl Yastrzemski 5,539
8. Frank Robinson 5,373
9. Tris Speaker 5,101
10. Dave Winfield 5,063
11. Lou Gehrig 5,060
12. George Brett 5,044
13. Mel Ott 5,041
14. Jimmie Foxx 4,956
15. Ted Williams 4,884
16. Honus Wagner 4,862
17. Al Kaline 4,852
18. Reggie Jackson 4,834
19. Robin Yount 4,730
20. Rogers Hornsby 4,712
21. Ernie Banks 4,706
22. Eddie Murray 4,699
23. Al Simmons 4,685
24. Billy Williams 4,599
25. Cap Anson 4,577
26. Tony Perez 4,532

27. Andre Dawson	4,529	
28. Mickey Mantle	4,511	
29. Roberto Clemente	4,492	
30. Paul Waner	4,478	
31. Nap Lajoie	4,474	
32. Dave Parker	4,405	
33. Mike Schmidt	4,404	
34. Eddie Mathews	4,349	
35. Sam Crawford	4,328	
36. Goose Goslin	4,325	
37. Brooks Robinson	4,270	
38. Vada Pinson	4,264	
39. Eddie Collins	4,263	
40. Charlie Gehringer	4,257	
41. Lou Brock	4,238	
42. Dwight Evans	4,230	
43. Willie McCovey	4,219	
44. Willie Stargell	4,190	
45. Rusty Staub	4,185	
46. Jake Beckley	4,147	
47. Harmon Killebrew	4,143	
48. Jim Rice	4,129	
49. Zack Wheat	4,100	
50. Al Oliver	4,083	
51. Harry Heilmann	4,053	
52. Carlton Fisk	3,999	
53. Rod Carew	3,998	
54. Joe Morgan	3,962	
55. Orlando Cepeda	3,959	
56. Sam Rice	3,955	
57. Joe DiMaggio	3,948	
58. Steve Garvey	3,941	
59. Frankie Frisch	3,937	
60. George Sisler	3,871	
61. Darrell Evans	3,866	
62. Duke Snider	3,865	
63. Joe Medwick	3,852	
64. Bill Buckner	3,833	
65. Ted Simmons	3,793	
66. Ed Delahanty	3,792	
67. Roger Connor	3,788	
68. Ron Santo	3,779	
Graig Nettles	3,779	
70. Willie Davis	3,778	
71. Jesse Burkett	3,759	
72. Mickey Vernon	3,741	
73. Jim Bottomley	3,737	
74. Dale Murphy	3,733	
75. Fred Clarke	3,674	
76. Heinie Manush	3,665	
77. Paul Molitor	3,662	
78. George Davis	3,656	
79. Buddy Bell	3,654	
80. Johnny Bench	3,644	
81. Yogi Berra	3,643	
82. Jimmy Ryan	3,621	
Johnny Mize	3,621	
84. Max Carey	3,612	
85. Enos Slaughter	3,599	
86. Jim O'Rourke	3,597	
87. Don Baylor	3,571	
88. Willie Keeler	3,562	
89. Joe Torre	3,560	
90. Joe Cronin	3,546	
91. Luke Appling	3,528	
92. Chuck Klein	3,522	
93. Luis Aparicio	3,504	
94. Bob Johnson	3,501	
95. Gary Carter	3,497	
96. Lee May	3,495	
97. Dan Brouthers	3,484	
98. Lave Cross	3,467	
99. Bill Dahlen	3,448	
100. Cal Ripken	3,447	

DOUBLES

1.	Tris Speaker	792
2.	Pete Rose	746
3.	Stan Musial	725
4.	Ty Cobb	724
5.	George Brett	665
6.	Nap Lajoie	657
7.	Carl Yastrzemski	646
8.	Honus Wagner	640
9.	Hank Aaron	624
10.	Paul Waner	605
11.	Robin Yount	583
12.	Cap Anson	582
13.	Charlie Gehringer	574
14.	Harry Heilmann	542
15.	Rogers Hornsby	541
16.	Joe Medwick	540
17.	Al Simmons	539
18.	Lou Gehrig	534
19.	Al Oliver	529
20.	Frank Robinson	528
21.	Dave Parker	526
22.	Ted Williams	525
23.	Willie Mays	523
24.	Ed Delahanty	522
25.	Dave Winfield	520
26.	Joe Cronin	515
27.	Babe Ruth	506
28.	Tony Perez	505
29.	Goose Goslin	500
30.	Rusty Staub	499
31.	Sam Rice	498
	Al Kaline	498
	Bill Buckner	498
34.	Heinie Manush	491
35.	Mickey Vernon	490
	Eddie Murray	490
37.	Mel Ott	488
38.	Billy Herman	486
	Lou Brock	486
40.	Vada Pinson	485
41.	Hal McRae	484
42.	Ted Simmons	483
	Dwight Evans	483
44.	Brooks Robinson	482
45.	Zack Wheat	476
46.	Andre Dawson	473
	Jake Beckley	473
48.	Jim O'Rourke	467
49.	Frankie Frisch	466
50.	Jim Bottomley	465
51.	Reggie Jackson	463
52.	Dan Brouthers	460
53.	Jimmie Foxx	458
	Sam Crawford	458
55.	Jimmy Dykes	453
56.	Jimmy Ryan	451
	George Davis	451
58.	Joe Morgan	449
59.	Wade Boggs	448
60.	Rod Carew	445
61.	George Burns	444
62.	Paul Molitor	442
	Dick Bartell	442
64.	Roger Connor	441
65.	Steve Garvey	440
	Roberto Clemente	440
	Luke Appling	440
68.	Eddie Collins	438
69.	Joe Sewell	436
	Cesar Cedeno	436
71.	Wally Moses	435
72.	Billy Williams	434
73.	Joe Judge	433
74.	Red Schoendienst	427
75.	Keith Hernandez	426
76.	George Sisler	425
	Sherry Magee	425
	Buddy Bell	425
79.	Willie Stargell	423
80.	Carlton Fisk	421
81.	Max Carey	419
82.	Orlando Cepeda	417
83.	Cecil Cooper	415
84.	Enos Slaughter	413
	Bill Dahlen	413
86.	Joe Kuhel	412
87.	Lave Cross	411
88.	Mike Schmidt	408
89.	Frank White	407
	Ben Chapman	407
	Ernie Banks	407
92.	Paul Hines	405
93.	Marty McManus	401
	Earl Averill	401
95.	Gee Walker	399
	Babe Herman	399
97.	Chuck Klein	398
98.	Chet Lemon	396
	Bob Johnson	396
	Gabby Hartnett	396
	Doc Cramer	396

TRIPLES

1.	Sam Crawford	309
2.	Ty Cobb	295
3.	Honus Wagner	252
4.	Jake Beckley	243
5.	Roger Connor	233
6.	Tris Speaker	222
7.	Fred Clarke	220
8.	Dan Brouthers	205
9.	Joe Kelley	194
10.	Paul Waner	191
11.	Bid McPhee	188
12.	Eddie Collins	186
13.	Ed Delahanty	185
14.	Sam Rice	184
15.	Edd Roush	182
	Jesse Burkett	182
17.	Ed Konetchy	181
18.	Buck Ewing	178
19.	Stan Musial	177
	Rabbit Maranville	177
21.	Harry Stovey	174
22.	Goose Goslin	173
23.	Zack Wheat	172
	Tommy Leach	172
25.	Rogers Hornsby	169
26.	Joe Jackson	168
27.	Sherry Magee	166
	Roberto Clemente	166
29.	Jake Daubert	165
30.	Pie Traynor	164
	George Sisler	164
	Elmer Flick	164
33.	Nap Lajoie	163
	Lou Gehrig	163
	George Davis	163
	Bill Dahlen	163
37.	Mike Tiernan	162
38.	George Van Haltren	161
39.	Sam Thompson	160
	Heinie Manush	160
	Harry Hooper	160
42.	Joe Judge	159
	Max Carey	159

HOME RUNS

44.	Ed McKean	158
45.	Jimmy Ryan	157
	Kiki Cuyler	157
47.	Tommy Corcoran	155
48.	Earle Combs	154
49.	Harry Heilmann	151
	Jim Bottomley	151
51.	Al Simmons	149
	Kip Selbach	149
	Jim O'Rourke	149
54.	Enos Slaughter	148
	Wally Pipp	148
56.	Bobby Veach	147
57.	Charlie Gehringer	146
58.	Willie Wilson	145
	Willie Keeler	145
	Harry Davis	145
61.	Bobby Wallace	143
	Cap Anson	143
63.	Lou Brock	141
64.	Willie Mays	140
65.	John Reilly	139
66.	Jimmy Williams	138
	Frankie Frisch	138
	Willie Davis	138
	Tom Brown	138
70.	George Brett	137
71.	Elmer Smith	136
	Jimmy Sheckard	136
	Babe Ruth	136
74.	Pete Rose	135
	Lave Cross	135
76.	Shano Collins	133
77.	George Wood	132
78.	Buck Freeman	131
	Joe DiMaggio	131
80.	Buddy Myer	130
81.	Larry Gardner	129
	Oyster Burns	129
83.	Arky Vaughan	128
	Earl Averill	128
85.	Vada Pinson	127
86.	Robin Yount	126
	Hardy Richardson	126
88.	Jimmie Foxx	125
89.	Frank Schulte	124
	Hal Chase	124
	John Anderson	124
92.	Duke Farrell	123
	Larry Doyle	123
94.	Dummy Hoy	121
95.	Mickey Vernon	120
96.	Fred Pfeffer	119
	Hugh Duffy	119
98.	Lloyd Waner	118
	Chick Stahl	118
	Joe Cronin	118

HOME RUNS

1.	Hank Aaron	755
2.	Babe Ruth	714
3.	Willie Mays	660
4.	Frank Robinson	586
5.	Harmon Killebrew	573
6.	Reggie Jackson	563
7.	Mike Schmidt	548
8.	Mickey Mantle	536
9.	Jimmie Foxx	534
10.	Ted Williams	521
	Willie McCovey	521
12.	Eddie Mathews	512
	Ernie Banks	512
14.	Mel Ott	511
15.	Lou Gehrig	493

16.	Willie Stargell	475
	Stan Musial	475
18.	Dave Winfield	453
19.	Carl Yastrzemski	452
20.	Dave Kingman	442
21.	Eddie Murray	441
22.	Billy Williams	426
23.	Darrell Evans	414
24.	Andre Dawson	412
25.	Duke Snider	407
26.	Al Kaline	399
27.	Dale Murphy	398
28.	Graig Nettles	390
29.	Johnny Bench	389
30.	Dwight Evans	385
31.	Jim Rice	382
	Frank Howard	382
33.	Tony Perez	379
	Orlando Cepeda	379
35.	Norm Cash	377
36.	Carlton Fisk	376
37.	Rocky Colavito	374
38.	Gil Hodges	370
39.	Ralph Kiner	369
40.	Joe DiMaggio	361
41.	Johnny Mize	359
42.	Yogi Berra	358
43.	Lee May	354
44.	Dick Allen	351
45.	George Foster	348
46.	Ron Santo	342
47.	Jack Clark	340
48.	Boog Powell	339
	Dave Parker	339
50.	Don Baylor	338
51.	Joe Adcock	336
52.	Bobby Bonds	332
53.	Hank Greenberg	331
54.	Willie Horton	325
55.	Gary Carter	324
56.	Roy Sievers	318
57.	Lance Parrish	317
	George Brett	317
59.	Ron Cey	316
60.	Reggie Smith	314
61.	Al Simmons	307
	Greg Luzinski	307
63.	Fred Lynn	306
64.	Rogers Hornsby	301
65.	Chuck Klein	300
66.	Cal Ripken	297
67.	Rusty Staub	292
68.	Jim Wynn	291
69.	Darryl Strawberry	290
70.	Hank Sauer	288
	Bob Johnson	288
	Del Ennis	288
73.	Frank Thomas	286
74.	Kent Hrbek	283
75.	Ken Boyer	282
76.	Ted Kluszewski	279
77.	Rudy York	277
78.	Roger Maris	275
	Brian Downing	275
	Joe Carter	275
81.	Steve Garvey	272
82.	George Scott	271
83.	Gorman Thomas	268
	Brooks Robinson	268
	Joe Morgan	268
86.	George Hendrick	267
87.	Vic Wertz	266
88.	George Bell	265
89.	Bobby Thomson	264
90.	Tom Brunansky	261
	Harold Baines	261
92.	Vada Pinson	256
	Larry Parrish	256
	Bob Allison	256
95.	John Mayberry	255
96.	Andy Thornton	253
	Joe Gordon	253
	Larry Doby	253
99.	Joe Torre	252
	Bobby Murcer	252

RUNS BATTED IN

1.	Hank Aaron	2,297
2.	Babe Ruth	2,213
3.	Lou Gehrig	1,995
4.	Cap Anson	1,981
5.	Stan Musial	1,951
6.	Ty Cobb	1,937
7.	Jimmie Foxx	1,922
8.	Willie Mays	1,903
9.	Mel Ott	1,860
10.	Carl Yastrzemski	1,844
11.	Ted Williams	1,839
12.	Al Simmons	1,827
13.	Frank Robinson	1,812
14.	Dave Winfield	1,786
15.	Honus Wagner	1,732
16.	Reggie Jackson	1,702
17.	Eddie Murray	1,662
18.	Tony Perez	1,652
19.	Ernie Banks	1,636
20.	Goose Goslin	1,609
21.	Nap Lajoie	1,599
22.	Mike Schmidt	1,595
	George Brett	1,595
24.	Harmon Killebrew	1,584
	Rogers Hornsby	1,584
26.	Al Kaline	1,583
27.	Jake Beckley	1,575
28.	Willie McCovey	1,555
29.	Willie Stargell	1,540
30.	Harry Heilmann	1,539
31.	Joe DiMaggio	1,537
32.	Tris Speaker	1,529
33.	Sam Crawford	1,525
34.	Mickey Mantle	1,509
35.	Dave Parker	1,493
36.	Andre Dawson	1,492
37.	Billy Williams	1,475
38.	Rusty Staub	1,466
39.	Ed Delahanty	1,464
40.	Eddie Mathews	1,453
41.	Jim Rice	1,451
42.	George Davis	1,437
43.	Yogi Berra	1,430
44.	Charlie Gehringer	1,427
45.	Joe Cronin	1,424
46.	Jim Bottomley	1,422
47.	Robin Yount	1,406
48.	Ted Simmons	1,389
49.	Dwight Evans	1,384
50.	Joe Medwick	1,383
51.	Johnny Bench	1,376
52.	Orlando Cepeda	1,365
53.	Brooks Robinson	1,357
54.	Darrell Evans	1,354
55.	Lave Cross	1,345
56.	Johnny Mize	1,337
57.	Duke Snider	1,333
58.	Ron Santo	1,331
59.	Carlton Fisk	1,330
60.	Al Oliver	1,326
61.	Roger Connor	1,322
62.	Pete Rose	1,314
	Graig Nettles	1,314
64.	Mickey Vernon	1,311
65.	Paul Waner	1,309
66.	Steve Garvey	1,308
67.	Roberto Clemente	1,305
68.	Enos Slaughter	1,304
69.	Hugh Duffy	1,302
70.	Eddie Collins	1,300
71.	Sam Thompson	1,299
72.	Dan Brouthers	1,296
73.	Del Ennis	1,284
74.	Bob Johnson	1,283
75.	Hank Greenberg	1,276
	Don Baylor	1,276
77.	Gil Hodges	1,274
78.	Pie Traynor	1,273
79.	Dale Murphy	1,266
80.	Zack Wheat	1,248
81.	Bobby Doerr	1,247
82.	Lee May	1,244
	Frankie Frisch	1,244
84.	George Foster	1,239
85.	Bill Dahlen	1,233
86.	Gary Carter	1,225
87.	Dave Kingman	1,210
88.	Bill Dickey	1,209
89.	Bill Buckner	1,208
90.	Chuck Klein	1,201
91.	Bob Elliott	1,195
92.	Joe Kelley	1,194
93.	Tony Lazzeri	1,191
94.	Boog Powell	1,187
95.	Joe Torre	1,185
96.	Heinie Manush	1,183
97.	Jack Clark	1,180
98.	Gabby Hartnett	1,179
99.	Vic Wertz	1,178
100.	Sherry Magee	1,176

STOLEN BASES

1.	Rickey Henderson	1,095
2.	Lou Brock	938
3.	Billy Hamilton	912
4.	Ty Cobb	891
5.	Tim Raines	751
6.	Eddie Collins	744
7.	Arlie Latham	739
8.	Max Carey	738
9.	Honus Wagner	722
10.	Joe Morgan	689
11.	Willie Wilson	667
12.	Tom Brown	657
13.	Bert Campaneris	649
14.	Vince Coleman	648
15.	George Davis	616
16.	Dummy Hoy	594
17.	Maury Wills	586
18.	George Van Haltren	583
19.	Hugh Duffy	574
20.	Bid McPhee	568
21.	Ozzie Smith	563
22.	Davey Lopes	557
23.	Cesar Cedeno	550
24.	Bill Dahlen	547
25.	John Ward	540
26.	Herman Long	534
27.	Patsy Donovan	518
28.	Jack Doyle	516
29.	Harry Stovey	509
30.	Fred Clarke	506
	Luis Aparicio	506
32.	Clyde Milan	495
	Willie Keeler	495

34.	Omar Moreno	487	6.	Mel Ott	1,708	80.	Cupid Childs	991
35.	Brett Butler	476	7.	Eddie Yost	1,614	81.	Dale Murphy	986
36.	Mike Griffin	473	8.	Darrell Evans	1,605	82.	Gene Tenace	984
37.	Tommy McCarthy	468	9.	Stan Musial	1,599		Cap Anson	984
38.	Jimmy Sheckard	465	10.	Pete Rose	1,566	84.	Bid McPhee	981
39.	Bobby Bonds	461	11.	Harmon Killebrew	1,559	85.	Earl Torgeson	980
40.	Ron LeFlore	455	12.	Lou Gehrig	1,508		Joe Kuhel	980
	Ed Delahanty	455	13.	Mike Schmidt	1,507	87.	Augie Galan	979
42.	Curt Welch	453	14.	Eddie Collins	1,499	88.	Duke Snider	971
43.	Steve Sax	444	15.	Willie Mays	1,464	89.	Bob Elliott	967
44.	Joe Kelley	443	16.	Jimmie Foxx	1,452	90.	Robin Yount	966
45.	Sherry Magee	441	17.	Eddie Mathews	1,444	91.	Buddy Myer	965
46.	John McGraw	436	18.	Frank Robinson	1,420		Joe Judge	965
47.	Tris Speaker	434	19.	Rickey Henderson	1,406		Mike Hargrove	965
	Paul Molitor	434	20.	Hank Aaron	1,402	94.	Honus Wagner	963
49.	Mike Tiernan	428	21.	Dwight Evans	1,391	95.	Jimmy Dykes	958
50.	Bob Bescher	427	22.	Tris Speaker	1,381	96.	Mickey Vernon	955
51.	Frankie Frisch	419	23.	Reggie Jackson	1,375	97.	Rocky Colavito	951
	Charlie Comiskey	419	24.	Willie McCovey	1,345	98.	Goose Goslin	949
53.	Jimmy Ryan	418	25.	Luke Appling	1,302	99.	Dolph Camilli	947
54.	Tommy Harper	408	26.	Al Kaline	1,277	100.	Gil Hodges	943
55.	Donie Bush	403	27.	Ken Singleton	1,263		Brett Butler	943
56.	Frank Chance	401	28.	Jack Clark	1,262			
57.	Bill Lange	399	29.	Rusty Staub	1,255		**STRIKEOUTS**	
58.	Willie Davis	398	30.	Ty Cobb	1,249	1.	Reggie Jackson	2,597
59.	Sam Mertes	396	31.	Willie Randolph	1,243	2.	Willie Stargell	1,936
60.	Billy North	395	32.	Jim Wynn	1,224	3.	Mike Schmidt	1,883
	Dave Collins	395	33.	Pee Wee Reese	1,210	4.	Tony Perez	1,867
62.	Jesse Burkett	389	34.	Richie Ashburn	1,198	5.	Dave Kingman	1,816
63.	Tommy Corcoran	387	35.	Brian Downing	1,197	6.	Bobby Bonds	1,757
64.	Freddie Patek	385	36.	Eddie Murray	1,187	7.	Dale Murphy	1,748
	Tom Daly	385		Billy Hamilton	1,187	8.	Lou Brock	1,730
66.	Hugh Nicol	383	38.	Charlie Gehringer	1,186	9.	Mickey Mantle	1,710
	George Burns	383	39.	Dave Winfield	1,171	10.	Harmon Killebrew	1,699
68.	Fred Pfeffer	382	40.	Donie Bush	1,158	11.	Dwight Evans	1,697
69.	Walt Wilmot	381	41.	Toby Harrah	1,153	12.	Dave Winfield	1,609
70.	Nap Lajoie	380		Max Bishop	1,153	13.	Lee May	1,570
71.	George Sisler	375	43.	Harry Hooper	1,136	14.	Dick Allen	1,556
	Harry Hooper	375	44.	Jimmy Sheckard	1,135	15.	Willie McCovey	1,550
73.	Jack Glasscock	372	45.	Lou Whitaker	1,125	16.	Dave Parker	1,537
74.	Lonnie Smith	369	46.	Ron Santo	1,108	17.	Frank Robinson	1,532
75.	King Kelly	368	47.	George Brett	1,096	18.	Willie Mays	1,526
76.	Tommy Dowd	366	48.	Stan Hack	1,092	19.	Rick Monday	1,513
	Sam Crawford	366		Lu Blue	1,092	20.	Greg Luzinski	1,495
78.	Hal Chase	363	50.	Paul Waner	1,091	21.	Eddie Mathews	1,487
79.	Tommy Leach	361	51.	Graig Nettles	1,088	22.	Frank Howard	1,460
80.	Fielder Jones	359	52.	Bobby Grich	1,087	23.	Lance Parrish	1,447
	Hughie Jennings	359	53.	Wade Boggs	1,078	24.	Jack Clark	1,441
82.	Juan Samuel	358	54.	Bob Johnson	1,075	25.	Jim Wynn	1,427
83.	Gary Pettis	354	55.	Keith Hernandez	1,070	26.	Jim Rice	1,423
	Buck Ewing	354		Harlond Clift	1,070	27.	George Foster	1,419
85.	Rod Carew	353	57.	Bill Dahlen	1,064	28.	George Scott	1,418
86.	Tommy Tucker	352	58.	Joe Cronin	1,059	29.	Darrell Evans	1,410
	Otis Nixon	352	59.	Ron Fairly	1,052	30.	Andre Dawson	1,398
88.	Sam Rice	351	60.	Billy Williams	1,045	31.	Carl Yastrzemski	1,393
89.	George Case	349	61.	Eddie Joost	1,043	32.	Carlton Fisk	1,386
90.	Paul Radford	346		Norm Cash	1,043	33.	Hank Aaron	1,383
91.	Julio Cruz	343	63.	Roy Thomas	1,042	34.	Rob Deer	1,379
92.	Amos Otis	341	64.	Max Carey	1,040	35.	Larry Parrish	1,359
93.	Willie Mays	338	65.	Rogers Hornsby	1,038	36.	Robin Yount	1,350
	John Anderson	338	66.	Jim Gilliam	1,036	37.	Ron Santo	1,343
95.	Joe Tinker	336	67.	Sal Bando	1,031	38.	Gorman Thomas	1,339
96.	Hub Collins	335	68.	Jesse Burkett	1,029	39.	Babe Ruth	1,330
97.	Kip Selbach	334	69.	Enos Slaughter	1,018	40.	Deron Johnson	1,318
98.	Elmer Flick	330		Rod Carew	1,018	41.	Willie Horton	1,313
99.	Ned Hanlon	329	71.	Ron Cey	1,012	42.	Jimmie Foxx	1,311
	Jose Cardenal	329	72.	Ralph Kiner	1,011	43.	Eddie Murray	1,285
			73.	Dummy Hoy	1,004	44.	Bobby Grich	1,278
	WALKS		74.	Tim Raines	1,003		Johnny Bench	1,278
1.	Babe Ruth	2,056		Miller Huggins	1,003	46.	Claudell Washington	1,266
2.	Ted Williams	2,019	76.	Roger Connor	1,002	47.	Juan Samuel	1,261
3.	Joe Morgan	1,865	77.	Boog Powell	1,001	48.	Ken Singleton	1,246
4.	Carl Yastrzemski	1,845	78.	Eddie Stanky	996	49.	Duke Snider	1,237
5.	Mickey Mantle	1,733	79.	Ozzie Smith	992	50.	Ernie Banks	1,236

51. Ron Cey 1,235	23. Eddie Collins .... .333	97. Jake Beckley .... .308
52. Jesse Barfield 1,234	24. Mike Donlin .... .333	98. Stuffy McInnis .... .307
53. Roberto Clemente 1,230	25. Cap Anson .... .332	99. Joe Vosmik .... .307
54. Boog Powell 1,226	26. Stan Musial .... .331	100. Frank Baker .... .307
55. Chili Davis 1,222	27. Sam Thompson .... .331	
56. Graig Nettles 1,209	28. Heinie Manush .... .330	**SLUGGING AVERAGE**
57. Tony Armas 1,201	29. Tony Gwynn .... .329	1. Babe Ruth .... .690
58. Vada Pinson 1,196	30. Rod Carew .... .328	2. Ted Williams .... .634
59. Dave Concepcion 1,186	31. Honus Wagner .... .327	3. Lou Gehrig .... .632
60. Orlando Cepeda 1,169	32. Tip O'Neill .... .326	4. Jimmie Foxx .... .609
61. Kirk Gibson 1,155	33. Bob Fothergill .... .325	5. Hank Greenberg .... .605
62. Gary Gaetti 1,147	34. Jimmie Foxx .... .325	6. Joe DiMaggio .... .579
63. Pete Rose 1,143	35. Earle Combs .... .325	7. Rogers Hornsby .... .577
64. Bert Campaneris 1,142	36. Joe DiMaggio .... .325	8. Johnny Mize .... .562
65. Donn Clendenon 1,140	37. Babe Herman .... .324	9. Stan Musial .... .559
66. Willie Wilson 1,138	38. Hugh Duffy .... .324	10. Willie Mays .... .557
Darryl Strawberry 1,138	39. Joe Medwick .... .324	11. Mickey Mantle .... .557
68. Gil Hodges 1,137	40. Edd Roush .... .323	12. Hank Aaron .... .555
69. Lloyd Moseby 1,135	41. Sam Rice .... .322	13. Ralph Kiner .... .548
Leo Cardenas 1,135	42. Ross Youngs .... .322	14. Hack Wilson .... .545
Jeff Burroughs 1,135	43. Kiki Cuyler .... .321	15. Chuck Klein .... .543
72. Tom Brunansky 1,130	44. Charlie Gehringer .... .320	16. Duke Snider .... .540
73. Brian Downing 1,127	45. Chuck Klein .... .320	17. Frank Robinson .... .537
74. Bob Bailey 1,126	46. Pie Traynor .... .320	18. Al Simmons .... .535
75. Gary Matthews 1,125	47. Mickey Cochrane .... .320	19. Dick Allen .... .534
76. Fred Lynn 1,116	48. Ken Williams .... .319	20. Earl Averill .... .534
77. Jim Fregosi 1,097	49. Kirby Puckett .... .318	21. Mel Ott .... .533
78. Joe Torre 1,094	50. Earl Averill .... .318	22. Babe Herman .... .532
79. Garry Templeton 1,092	51. Arky Vaughan .... .318	23. Fred McGriff .... .531
80. Norm Cash 1,091	52. Roberto Clemente .... .317	24. Ken Williams .... .530
81. Tony Taylor 1,083	53. Chick Hafey .... .317	25. Willie Stargell .... .529
82. Tommy Harper 1,080	54. Joe Kelley .... .317	26. Mike Schmidt .... .527
83. Tim Wallach 1,079	55. Zack Wheat .... .317	27. Barry Bonds .... .526
84. Dave Henderson 1,077	56. Roger Connor .... .317	28. Chick Hafey .... .526
85. Don Baylor 1,069	57. Lloyd Waner .... .316	29. Hal Trosky .... .522
Harold Baines 1,069	58. Frankie Frisch .... .316	30. Wally Berger .... .522
87. Johnny Callison 1,064	59. Goose Goslin .... .316	31. Harry Heilmann .... .520
88. Pete Incaviglia 1,061	60. George Van Haltren .... .316	32. Dan Brouthers .... .519
89. Jose Canseco 1,060	61. Bibb Falk .... .314	33. Charlie Keller .... .518
90. Joe Adcock 1,059	62. Cecil Travis .... .314	34. Joe Jackson .... .517
91. Doug Rader 1,055	63. Hank Greenberg .... .313	35. Willie McCovey .... .515
92. Billy Williams 1,046	64. Jack Fournier .... .313	36. Ty Cobb .... .512
93. Danny Tartabull 1,037	65. Elmer Flick .... .313	37. Danny Tartabull .... .510
94. Frank White 1,035	66. Bill Dickey .... .313	38. Eddie Mathews .... .509
95. Bob Allison 1,033	67. Dale Mitchell .... .312	39. Jeff Heath .... .509
96. Jose Cruz 1,031	68. Johnny Mize .... .312	40. Harmon Killebrew .... .509
97. Reggie Smith 1,030	69. Joe Sewell .... .312	41. Darryl Strawberry .... .508
98. Rod Carew 1,028	70. Deacon White .... .312	42. Jose Canseco .... .507
99. Darrell Porter 1,025	71. Fred Clarke .... .312	43. Bob Johnson .... .506
100. Chet Lemon 1,024	72. Barney McCosky .... .312	44. Bill Terry .... .506
	73. Bing Miller .... .312	45. Ed Delahanty .... .505
BATTING AVERAGE	74. Hughie Jennings .... .311	46. Sam Thompson .... .505
1. Ty Cobb .... .366	75. Freddy Lindstrom .... .311	47. Joe Medwick .... .505
2. Rogers Hornsby .... .358	76. Jackie Robinson .... .311	48. Jim Rice .... .502
3. Joe Jackson .... .356	77. Baby Doll Jacobson .... .311	49. Tris Speaker .... .500
4. Ed Delahanty .... .346	78. Taffy Wright .... .311	50. Jim Bottomley .... .500
5. Tris Speaker .... .345	79. Rip Radcliff .... .311	51. Goose Goslin .... .500
6. Ted Williams .... .344	80. Jim O'Rourke .... .311	52. Roy Campanella .... .500
7. Billy Hamilton .... .344	81. Ginger Beaumont .... .311	53. Ernie Banks .... .500
8. Dan Brouthers .... .342	82. Mike Tiernan .... .311	54. Orlando Cepeda .... .499
9. Babe Ruth .... .342	83. Denny Lyons .... .310	55. Bob Horner .... .499
10. Harry Heilmann .... .342	84. Luke Appling .... .310	56. Will Clark .... .499
11. Pete Browning .... .341	85. Irish Meusel .... .310	57. Frank Howard .... .499
12. Willie Keeler .... .341	86. Elmer Smith .... .310	58. Ted Kluszewski .... .498
13. Bill Terry .... .341	87. Bobby Veach .... .310	59. Bob Meusel .... .497
14. George Sisler .... .340	88. Jim Bottomley .... .310	60. Hank Sauer .... .496
15. Lou Gehrig .... .340	89. John Stone .... .310	61. Al Rosen .... .495
16. Jesse Burkett .... .338	90. Sam Crawford .... .309	62. Billy Williams .... .492
17. Nap Lajoie .... .338	91. Bob Meusel .... .309	63. Ripper Collins .... .492
18. Riggs Stephenson .... .336	92. Don Mattingly .... .309	64. Dolph Camilli .... .492
19. Wade Boggs .... .335	93. Jack Tobin .... .309	65. Tommy Henrich .... .491
20. Al Simmons .... .334	94. Spud Davis .... .308	66. Larry Doby .... .490
21. John McGraw .... .334	95. Richie Ashburn .... .308	67. Reggie Jackson .... .490
22. Paul Waner .... .333	96. King Kelly .... .308	68. Dick Stuart .... .489

69.	Reggie Smith	.489
70.	Gabby Hartnett	.489
71.	Rocky Colavito	.489
72.	Norm Cash	.488
73.	George Brett	.487
74.	Gil Hodges	.487
75.	Bill Dickey	.486
76.	Roger Connor	.486
77.	Gus Zernial	.486
78.	Joe Adcock	.485
79.	Wally Post	.485
80.	Andre Dawson	.484
81.	Fred Lynn	.484
82.	Kent Hrbek	.483
83.	Jack Fournier	.483
84.	Rudy York	.483
85.	Eric Davis	.483
86.	Eddie Murray	.483
87.	Yogi Berra	.482
88.	Charlie Gehringer	.480
89.	Pedro Guerrero	.480
90.	George Foster	.480
91.	Al Kaline	.480
92.	Don Mattingly	.479
93.	Heinie Manush	.479
94.	Gavvy Cravath	.478
95.	Dave Winfield	.478
96.	Dave Kingman	.478
97.	Mickey Cochrane	.478
98.	Greg Luzinski	.478
99.	Tony Oliva	.476
100.	Roger Maris	.476

ON-BASE AVERAGE

1.	Ted Williams	.483
2.	Babe Ruth	.474
3.	John McGraw	.465
4.	Billy Hamilton	.455
5.	Lou Gehrig	.447
6.	Rogers Hornsby	.434
7.	Ty Cobb	.433
8.	Jimmie Foxx	.428
9.	Tris Speaker	.428
10.	Wade Boggs	.428
11.	Ferris Fain	.425
12.	Eddie Collins	.424
13.	Dan Brouthers	.423
14.	Joe Jackson	.423
15.	Max Bishop	.423
16.	Mickey Mantle	.423
17.	Mickey Cochrane	.419
18.	Stan Musial	.418
19.	Cupid Childs	.416
20.	Jesse Burkett	.415
21.	Mel Ott	.414
22.	Roy Thomas	.414
23.	Hank Greenberg	.412
24.	Ed Delahanty	.412
25.	Charlie Keller	.410
26.	Eddie Stanky	.410
27.	Jackie Robinson	.410
28.	Harry Heilmann	.410
29.	Roy Cullenbine	.408
30.	Rickey Henderson	.408
31.	Denny Lyons	.407
32.	Riggs Stephenson	.407
33.	Joe Cunningham	.406
34.	Arky Vaughan	.406
35.	Paul Waner	.404
36.	Charlie Gehringer	.404
37.	Pete Browning	.403
38.	Lu Blue	.402
39.	Joe Kelley	.401
40.	John Kruk	.400

41.	Mike Hargrove	.400
42.	Luke Appling	.399
43.	Elmer Valo	.399
44.	Ross Youngs	.399
45.	Ralph Kiner	.398
46.	Joe DiMaggio	.398
47.	Elmer Smith	.398
48.	Richie Ashburn	.397
49.	Johnny Mize	.397
50.	Roger Connor	.397
51.	Earle Combs	.397
52.	Joe Morgan	.395
53.	Rod Carew	.395
54.	Hack Wilson	.395
55.	Eddie Yost	.395
56.	Earl Averill	.395
57.	Johnny Pesky	.394
58.	Barry Bonds	.394
59.	Stan Hack	.394
60.	Frank Chance	.394
61.	Ken Williams	.393
62.	Wally Schang	.393
63.	Bob Johnson	.393
64.	Bill Terry	.393
65.	Cap Anson	.392
66.	George Grantham	.392
67.	Frank Robinson	.392
68.	Tip O'Neill	.392
69.	Jack Fournier	.392
70.	Mike Tiernan	.392
71.	Fred McGriff	.391
72.	Minnie Minoso	.391
73.	Joe Sewell	.391
74.	Honus Wagner	.391
75.	Ken Singleton	.391
76.	Gene Tenace	.391
77.	Augie Galan	.390
78.	Hughie Jennings	.390
79.	Harlond Clift	.390
80.	Tim Raines	.390
81.	Joe Cronin	.390
82.	Buddy Myer	.389
83.	Elmer Flick	.389
84.	Bernie Carbo	.389
85.	Dolph Camilli	.388
86.	Mike Griffin	.388
87.	Willie Keeler	.388
88.	Gene Woodling	.388
89.	Keith Hernandez	.388
90.	Larry Doby	.387
91.	Earl Torgeson	.387
92.	Goose Goslin	.387
93.	Willie Mays	.387
94.	Al Rosen	.386
95.	George Gore	.386
96.	Barney McCosky	.386
97.	Kiki Cuyler	.386
98.	Roger Bresnahan	.386
99.	Mike Donlin	.386
100.	Dummy Hoy	.385

ON-BASE PLUS SLUGGING

1.	Babe Ruth	1.163
2.	Ted Williams	1.116
3.	Lou Gehrig	1.080
4.	Jimmie Foxx	1.038
5.	Hank Greenberg	1.017
6.	Rogers Hornsby	1.010
7.	Mickey Mantle	.979
8.	Stan Musial	.977
9.	Joe DiMaggio	.977
10.	Johnny Mize	.959
11.	Mel Ott	.947
12.	Ralph Kiner	.946

13.	Ty Cobb	.945
14.	Willie Mays	.944
15.	Dan Brouthers	.942
16.	Joe Jackson	.940
17.	Hack Wilson	.940
18.	Hank Aaron	.932
19.	Harry Heilmann	.930
20.	Frank Robinson	.929
21.	Earl Averill	.928
22.	Tris Speaker	.928
23.	Charlie Keller	.928
24.	Ken Williams	.924
25.	Fred McGriff	.923
26.	Chuck Klein	.922
27.	Duke Snider	.921
28.	Barry Bonds	.920
29.	Ed Delahanty	.917
30.	Babe Herman	.915
31.	Al Simmons	.915
32.	Dick Allen	.914
33.	Mike Schmidt	.912
34.	Bob Johnson	.899
35.	Bill Terry	.899
36.	Chick Hafey	.898
37.	Mickey Cochrane	.897
38.	Hal Trosky	.892
39.	Willie McCovey	.892
40.	Willie Stargell	.892
41.	Sam Thompson	.888
42.	Eddie Mathews	.888
43.	Danny Tartabull	.887
44.	Billy Hamilton	.887
45.	Harmon Killebrew	.887
46.	Goose Goslin	.887
47.	Charlie Gehringer	.884
48.	Jackie Robinson	.883
49.	Roger Connor	.883
50.	Al Rosen	.882
51.	Wade Boggs	.881
52.	Wally Berger	.881
53.	Dolph Camilli	.880
54.	Riggs Stephenson	.880
55.	Jeff Heath	.879
56.	Paul Waner	.878
57.	Larry Doby	.877
58.	Will Clark	.876
59.	John McGraw	.875
60.	Jack Fournier	.875
61.	Tommy Henrich	.873
62.	Jim Bottomley	.869
63.	Pete Browning	.869
64.	Bill Dickey	.868
65.	Joe Medwick	.867
66.	Darryl Strawberry	.866
67.	Norm Cash	.865
68.	Jesse Burkett	.862
69.	Roy Campanella	.861
70.	George Brett	.861
71.	Kiki Cuyler	.860
72.	Arky Vaughan	.859
73.	Earle Combs	.859
74.	Reggie Smith	.859
75.	Al Kaline	.859
76.	Gabby Hartnett	.858
77.	Jack Clark	.858
78.	Jim Rice	.858
79.	Gavvy Cravath	.858
80.	Joe Cronin	.857
81.	Honus Wagner	.857
82.	Jose Canseco	.856
83.	Billy Williams	.856
84.	Heinie Manush	.856
85.	Pedro Guerrero	.854
86.	Kent Hrbek	.854

87. Mike Tiernan	.854
88. Mike Donlin	.854
89. George Grantham	.854
90. Frank Howard	.853
91. Eddie Collins	.853
92. Bob Meusel	.852
93. Joe Kelley	.852
94. Orlando Cepeda	.852
95. Ripper Collins	.852
96. Ted Kluszewski	.852
97. Rickey Henderson	.851
98. Minnie Minoso	.851
99. Rocky Colavito	.851
100. Eddie Murray	.851

EXTRA-BASE HITS

1. Hank Aaron	1,477
2. Stan Musial	1,377
3. Babe Ruth	1,356
4. Willie Mays	1,323
5. Lou Gehrig	1,190
6. Frank Robinson	1,186
7. Carl Yastrzemski	1,157
8. Ty Cobb	1,136
9. Tris Speaker	1,131
10. George Brett	1,119
11. Ted Williams	1,117
Jimmie Foxx	1,117
13. Reggie Jackson	1,075
14. Mel Ott	1,071
15. Dave Winfield	1,058
16. Pete Rose	1,041
17. Mike Schmidt	1,015
18. Rogers Hornsby	1,011
19. Ernie Banks	1,009
20. Al Simmons	995
21. Honus Wagner	993
22. Andre Dawson	980
23. Al Kaline	972
24. Eddie Murray	964
25. Tony Perez	963
26. Robin Yount	960
27. Willie Stargell	953
28. Mickey Mantle	952
29. Billy Williams	948
30. Dwight Evans	941
31. Dave Parker	940
32. Eddie Mathews	938
33. Goose Goslin	921
34. Willie McCovey	920
35. Paul Waner	909
36. Charlie Gehringer	904
37. Nap Lajoie	903
38. Harmon Killebrew	887
39. Joe DiMaggio	881
40. Harry Heilmann	876
41. Vada Pinson	868
42. Sam Crawford	864
43. Joe Medwick	858
44. Duke Snider	850
45. Roberto Clemente	846
46. Carlton Fisk	844
47. Rusty Staub	838
48. Jim Bottomley	835
49. Jim Rice	834
50. Al Oliver	825
51. Orlando Cepeda	823
Cap Anson	823
53. Brooks Robinson	818
54. Joe Morgan	813
55. Roger Connor	812
56. Johnny Mize	809
57. Ed Delahanty	808
58. Joe Cronin	803

59. Jake Beckley	802
60. Johnny Bench	794
61. Dale Murphy	787
62. Mickey Vernon	782
63. Hank Greenberg	781
64. Zack Wheat	780
65. Bob Johnson	779
Darrell Evans	779
67. Ted Simmons	778
68. Lou Brock	776
69. Ron Santo	774
70. Chuck Klein	772
71. Dan Brouthers	771
72. Earl Averill	767
73. Heinie Manush	761
74. Steve Garvey	755
75. Dick Allen	750
76. Graig Nettles	746
77. Hal McRae	741
78. Fred Lynn	737
79. Reggie Smith	734
80. Don Baylor	732
81. Enos Slaughter	730
82. Cal Ripken	729
83. Yogi Berra	728
84. Jimmy Ryan	726
Gary Carter	726
86. Lee May	725
87. Bill Buckner	721
88. Sam Rice	716
89. Paul Molitor	715
Del Ennis	715
Willie Davis	715
92. Gil Hodges	713
93. Jack Clark	711
94. Frankie Frisch	709
95. Dave Kingman	707
96. Cecil Cooper	703
97. George Foster	702
98. Bobby Bonds	700
99. Gabby Hartnett	696
100. Cesar Cedeno	695

GAMES PITCHED

1. Hoyt Wilhelm	1,070
2. Kent Tekulve	1,050
3. Lindy McDaniel	987
4. Rich Gossage	966
5. Rollie Fingers	944
6. Gene Garber	931
7. Cy Young	906
8. Sparky Lyle	899
9. Jim Kaat	898
10. Don McMahon	874
11. Jeff Reardon	869
12. Phil Niekro	864
13. Lee Smith	850
14. Roy Face	848
15. Charlie Hough	837
16. Tug McGraw	824
17. Nolan Ryan	807
18. Dennis Eckersley	804
19. Walter Johnson	802
20. Gaylord Perry	777
21. Don Sutton	774
22. Darold Knowles	765
23. Tommy John	760
24. Jack Quinn	756
25. Ron Reed	751
26. Warren Spahn	750
27. Gary Lavelle	745
Tom Burgmeier	745
29. Willie Hernandez	744
30. Steve Carlton	741

31. Ron Perranoski	737
32. Ron Kline	736
33. Clay Carroll	731
34. Jesse Orosco	714
35. Johnny Klippstein	711
36. Greg Minton	710
37. Jim Galvin	705
38. Stu Miller	704
39. Joe Niekro	702
40. Bill Campbell	700
41. Bob McClure	698
42. Pete Alexander	696
43. Bob Miller	694
44. Eppa Rixey	692
Grant Jackson	692
Bert Blyleven	692
47. Early Wynn	691
48. Eddie Fisher	690
49. Dave Righetti	688
50. Ted Abernathy	681
51. Robin Roberts	676
52. Dan Quisenberry	674
Waite Hoyt	674
54. Larry Andersen	670
55. Red Faber	669
56. Dave Giusti	668
57. Craig Lefferts	666
58. Fergie Jenkins	664
59. Bruce Sutter	661
60. Steve Bedrosian	657
61. Tom Seaver	656
62. Paul Lindblad	655
63. Wilbur Wood	651
64. Dave LaRoche	647
Sam Jones	647
66. Gerry Staley	640
Dutch Leonard	640
Rick Honeycutt	640
69. Diego Segui	639
Dennis Lamp	639
71. Frank Tanana	638
72. Bob Stanley	637
73. Christy Mathewson	635
74. Charlie Root	632
75. Jim Perry	630
76. Jerry Reuss	628
77. Lew Burdette	626
78. Woodie Fryman	625
Murry Dickson	625
80. Red Ruffing	624
81. Eddie Plank	623
Mike Marshall	623
83. Dick Tidrow	620
Kid Nichols	620
Greg Harris	620
86. Herb Pennock	617
87. Lefty Grove	616
Burleigh Grimes	616
89. Terry Forster	614
90. Jerry Koosman	612
91. Dave Smith	609
92. Al Worthington	602
Bob Friend	602
94. Elias Sosa	601
95. Bobo Newsom	600
John Candelaria	600
97. Tim Keefe	599
98. Ted Lyons	594
99. Pedro Borbon	593
100. Jim Bunning	591

GAMES STARTED

#	Player	GS
1.	Cy Young	815
2.	Nolan Ryan	773
3.	Don Sutton	756
4.	Phil Niekro	716
5.	Steve Carlton	709
6.	Tommy John	700
7.	Gaylord Perry	690
8.	Jim Galvin	689
9.	Bert Blyleven	685
10.	Walter Johnson	666
11.	Warren Spahn	665
12.	Tom Seaver	647
13.	Jim Kaat	625
14.	Frank Tanana	616
15.	Early Wynn	612
16.	Robin Roberts	609
17.	Pete Alexander	599
18.	Fergie Jenkins	594
19.	Tim Keefe	593
20.	Bobby Mathews	568
21.	Kid Nichols	561
22.	Eppa Rixey	552
23.	Christy Mathewson	551
24.	Mickey Welch	549
25.	Jerry Reuss	547
26.	Red Ruffing	536
27.	Rick Reuschel	529
	Eddie Plank	529
29.	Jerry Koosman	527
30.	Jim Palmer	521
31.	Jim Bunning	519
32.	John Clarkson	518
33.	Jack Powell	516
34.	Tony Mullane	504
	Jack Morris	504
36.	Gus Weyhing	503
	Charley Radbourn	503
38.	Joe Niekro	500
39.	Bob Friend	497
40.	Mickey Lolich	496
41.	Burleigh Grimes	495
42.	Claude Osteen	488
43.	Sam Jones	487
44.	Jim McCormick	485
45.	Luis Tiant	484
	Ted Lyons	484
	Bob Feller	484
48.	Bobo Newsom	483
	Red Faber	483
50.	Bob Gibson	482
51.	Dennis Martinez	476
	Catfish Hunter	476
53.	Earl Whitehill	473
	Vida Blue	473
55.	Vic Willis	471
56.	Milt Pappas	465
	Don Drysdale	465
58.	Doyle Alexander	464
59.	Curt Simmons	461
60.	Mike Torrez	458
61.	Juan Marichal	457
	Lefty Grove	457
63.	Rick Wise	455
64.	Bob Welch	454
65.	Jim Perry	447
66.	Paul Derringer	445
67.	Jack Quinn	444
68.	Whitey Ford	438
69.	Mel Harder	433
70.	Billy Pierce	432
71.	Carl Hubbell	431
72.	Larry Jackson	429
73.	George Mullin	428
74.	Amos Rusie	427
75.	Freddie Fitzsimmons	426
76.	Waite Hoyt	423
77.	Bob Forsch	422
78.	Herb Pennock	420
79.	Charlie Hough	419
80.	Bob Knepper	413
81.	Ken Holtzman	410
82.	Tom Zachary	409
	Dave Stieb	409
84.	Wilbur Cooper	408
	Tommy Bond	408
86.	Adonis Terry	406
87.	Frank Viola	405
88.	Camilo Pascual	404
	Lee Meadows	404
	Mike Flanagan	404
91.	Rube Marquard	403
92.	Will White	401
93.	Bucky Walters	398
94.	Jim Whitney	396
	Dave McNally	396
	Charlie Buffinton	396
97.	Al Orth	394
98.	Steve Rogers	393
99.	Paul Splittorff	392
100.	Mike Moore	390

COMPLETE GAMES

#	Player	CG
1.	Cy Young	749
2.	Jim Galvin	646
3.	Tim Keefe	554
4.	Kid Nichols	531
	Walter Johnson	531
6.	Mickey Welch	525
	Bobby Mathews	525
8.	Charley Radbourn	489
9.	John Clarkson	485
10.	Tony Mullane	468
11.	Jim McCormick	466
12.	Gus Weyhing	448
13.	Pete Alexander	437
14.	Christy Mathewson	434
15.	Jack Powell	422
16.	Eddie Plank	410
17.	Will White	394
18.	Amos Rusie	392
19.	Vic Willis	388
20.	Tommy Bond	386
21.	Warren Spahn	382
22.	Jim Whitney	377
23.	Adonis Terry	367
24.	Ted Lyons	356
25.	George Mullin	353
26.	Charlie Buffinton	351
27.	Chick Fraser	342
28.	Clark Griffith	337
29.	Red Ruffing	335
30.	Silver King	329
31.	Al Orth	324
32.	Bill Hutchison	321
33.	Joe McGinnity	314
	Burleigh Grimes	314
35.	Red Donahue	313
36.	Guy Hecker	310
37.	Bill Dinneen	306
38.	Robin Roberts	305
39.	Gaylord Perry	303
40.	George Bradley	302
41.	Ted Breitenstein	300
42.	Lefty Grove	298
	Bob Caruthers	298
44.	Ed Morris	297
	Pink Hawley	297
46.	Mark Baldwin	296
47.	Brickyard Kennedy	293
48.	Early Wynn	290
	Eppa Rixey	290
50.	Bill Donovan	289
51.	Bert Cunningham	286
52.	Al Spalding	281
53.	Sadie McMahon	279
	Bob Feller	279
	Wilbur Cooper	279
56.	Jack Taylor	278
	Jack Stivetts	278
58.	Charlie Getzien	277
59.	Red Faber	273
60.	Mordecai Brown	271
61.	Jouett Meekin	270
	Frank Dwyer	270
63.	Fergie Jenkins	267
64.	Matt Kilroy	264
	Elton Chamberlain	264
66.	Jesse Tannehill	263
67.	Doc White	262
68.	Rube Waddell	261
69.	Carl Hubbell	260
	Red Ehret	260
	Jack Chesbro	260
72.	Larry Corcoran	256
73.	Bob Gibson	255
	Chief Bender	255
75.	Steve Carlton	254
76.	Frank Killen	253
77.	Win Mercer	251
	Paul Derringer	251
79.	Ed Walsh	250
	Sam Jones	250
81.	Stump Weidman	249
	Eddie Cicotte	249
83.	Herb Pennock	247
84.	Bobo Newsom	246
85.	Phil Niekro	245
	Hooks Dauss	245
87.	John Ward	244
	Juan Marichal	244
	Harry Howell	244
90.	Jack Quinn	243
91.	Bucky Walters	242
	Deacon Phillippe	242
	Bert Blyleven	242
94.	Sam Leever	241
95.	Kid Gleason	240
96.	Addie Joss	234
97.	Candy Cummings	233
98.	George Uhle	232
99.	Harry Staley	231
	Tom Seaver	231
	Carl Mays	231

SAVES

#	Player	SV
1.	Lee Smith	401
2.	Jeff Reardon	365
3.	Rollie Fingers	341
4.	Rich Gossage	309
5.	Bruce Sutter	300
6.	Dennis Eckersley	275
7.	Tom Henke	260
8.	Dave Righetti	252
9.	Dan Quisenberry	244
10.	Sparky Lyle	238
11.	John Franco	236
12.	Hoyt Wilhelm	227
13.	Gene Garber	218
14.	Dave Smith	216
15.	Bobby Thigpen	201

16.	Roy Face	193
17.	Doug Jones	190
18.	Mike Marshall	188
19.	Mitch Williams	186
20.	Kent Tekulve	184
	Randy Myers	184
	Steve Bedrosian	184
23.	Tug McGraw	180
24.	Ron Perranoski	179
25.	Lindy McDaniel	172
26.	Bryan Harvey	171
27.	Gregg Olson	160
	Jeff Montgomery	160
29.	Rick Aguilera	156
30.	Stu Miller	154
31.	Don McMahon	153
	Jay Howell	153
33.	Roger McDowell	151
34.	Greg Minton	150
35.	Ted Abernathy	148
36.	Willie Hernandez	147
37.	Jeff Russell	146
38.	Dave Giusti	145
39.	Darold Knowles	143
	Clay Carroll	143
41.	Gary Lavelle	136
42.	Todd Worrell	134
43.	Dan Plesac	133
44.	Bob Stanley	132
	Jim Brewer	132
46.	Jesse Orosco	130
	Ron Davis	130
48.	Mike Henneman	128
	Steve Farr	128
50.	Terry Forster	127
51.	Dave LaRoche	126
	Bill Campbell	126
53.	John Hiller	125
54.	Jack Aker	123
55.	Dick Radatz	122
56.	Duane Ward	121
57.	Tippy Martinez	115
58.	Frank Linzy	111
59.	Al Worthington	110
60.	Fred Gladding	109
61.	Ron Kline	108
	Wayne Granger	108
63.	Johnny Murphy	107
64.	Bill Caudill	106
65.	John Wyatt	103
	Ron Reed	103
67.	Ellis Kinder	102
	Tim Burke	102
	Tom Burgmeier	102
70.	Firpo Marberry	101
71.	Craig Lefferts	100
72.	Joe Hoerner	99
73.	Mike Schooler	98
74.	Tom Niedenfuer	97
	Al Hrabosky	97
76.	Randy Moffitt	96
	Clem Labine	96
	Mark Davis	96
79.	Bob Locker	95
80.	Aurelio Lopez	93
81.	Phil Regan	92
	Tom Hume	92
83.	Bill Henry	90
84.	Donnie Moore	89
85.	Jim Kern	88
	Rob Dibble	88
87.	Cecil Upshaw	86
	Ken Sanders	86
	Jim Gott	86

90.	Joe Sambito	84
91.	Elias Sosa	83
	Claude Raymond	83
	Turk Farrell	83
	Mark Clear	83
95.	Larry Sherry	82
	Don Aase	82
97.	John Wetteland	81
	Eddie Fisher	81
	Doug Bair	81
100.	Eddie Watt	80
	Pedro Borbon	80

SHUTOUTS

1.	Walter Johnson	110
2.	Pete Alexander	90
3.	Christy Mathewson	79
4.	Cy Young	76
5.	Eddie Plank	69
6.	Warren Spahn	63
7.	Tom Seaver	61
	Nolan Ryan	61
9.	Bert Blyleven	60
10.	Don Sutton	58
11.	Ed Walsh	57
	Jim Galvin	57
13.	Bob Gibson	56
14.	Steve Carlton	55
	Mordecai Brown	55
16.	Gaylord Perry	53
	Jim Palmer	53
18.	Juan Marichal	52
19.	Vic Willis	50
	Rube Waddell	50
21.	Early Wynn	49
	Luis Tiant	49
	Fergie Jenkins	49
	Don Drysdale	49
25.	Kid Nichols	48
26.	Jack Powell	46
	Tommy John	46
28.	Doc White	45
	Red Ruffing	45
	Robin Roberts	45
	Phil Niekro	45
	Addie Joss	45
	Whitey Ford	45
34.	Bob Feller	44
	Babe Adams	44
36.	Milt Pappas	43
37.	Bucky Walters	42
	Catfish Hunter	42
	Tommy Bond	42
40.	Mickey Welch	41
	Hippo Vaughn	41
	Mickey Lolich	41
43.	Mel Stottlemyre	40
	Ed Reulbach	40
	Claude Osteen	40
	Sandy Koufax	40
	Larry French	40
	Jim Bunning	40
	Chief Bender	40
50.	Jerry Reuss	39
	Sam Leever	39
	Tim Keefe	39
53.	Nap Rucker	38
	Billy Pierce	38
	Stan Coveleski	38
56.	Steve Rogers	37
	Eppa Rixey	37
	Larry Jackson	37
	John Clarkson	37
	Vida Blue	37

61.	Will White	36
	Curt Simmons	36
	Allie Reynolds	36
	Camilo Pascual	36
	Sam Jones	36
	Carl Hubbell	36
	Bob Friend	36
	Mike Cuellar	36
69.	Charley Radbourn	35
	Herb Pennock	35
	George Mullin	35
	Lefty Grove	35
	Burleigh Grimes	35
	Bill Donovan	35
	Wilbur Cooper	35
	Jack Coombs	35
	Roger Clemens	35
	Eddie Cicotte	35
	Jack Chesbro	35
	Joe Bush	35
81.	Jesse Tannehill	34
	Frank Tanana	34
	Earl Moore	34
	Bill Doak	34
85.	Virgil Trucks	33
	Bob Shawkey	33
	Hal Newhouser	33
	Dave McNally	33
	Jim McCormick	33
	Dutch Leonard	33
	Lefty Leifield	33
	Jerry Koosman	33
	Mort Cooper	33
	Dean Chance	33
	Lew Burdette	33
	Tommy Bridges	33
97.	Jim Perry	32
	Joe McGinnity	32
	Paul Derringer	32
	George Bradley	32

WINS

1.	Cy Young	511
2.	Walter Johnson	417
3.	Christy Mathewson	373
	Pete Alexander	373
5.	Jim Galvin	364
6.	Warren Spahn	363
7.	Kid Nichols	361
8.	Tim Keefe	342
9.	Steve Carlton	329
10.	John Clarkson	328
11.	Eddie Plank	326
12.	Don Sutton	324
	Nolan Ryan	324
14.	Phil Niekro	318
15.	Gaylord Perry	314
16.	Tom Seaver	311
17.	Charley Radbourn	309
18.	Mickey Welch	307
19.	Early Wynn	300
	Lefty Grove	300
21.	Bobby Mathews	297
22.	Tommy John	288
23.	Bert Blyleven	287
24.	Robin Roberts	286
25.	Tony Mullane	284
	Fergie Jenkins	284
27.	Jim Kaat	283
28.	Red Ruffing	273
29.	Burleigh Grimes	270
30.	Jim Palmer	268
31.	Eppa Rixey	266
	Bob Feller	266

33.	Jim McCormick	265
34.	Gus Weyhing	264
35.	Ted Lyons	260
36.	Red Faber	254
37.	Al Spalding	253
	Carl Hubbell	253
39.	Bob Gibson	251
40.	Vic Willis	249
41.	Jack Quinn	247
42.	Joe McGinnity	246
43.	Amos Rusie	245
	Jack Powell	245
45.	Jack Morris	244
46.	Juan Marichal	243
47.	Frank Tanana	240
	Herb Pennock	240
49.	Mordecai Brown	239
50.	Waite Hoyt	237
	Clark Griffith	237
52.	Whitey Ford	236
53.	Tommy Bond	234
54.	Charlie Buffinton	233
55.	Will White	229
	Luis Tiant	229
	Sam Jones	229
58.	George Mullin	228
59.	Catfish Hunter	224
	Jim Bunning	224
61.	Mel Harder	223
	Paul Derringer	223
63.	Jerry Koosman	222
	Hooks Dauss	222
65.	Joe Niekro	221
66.	Jerry Reuss	220
67.	Earl Whitehill	218
	Bob Caruthers	218
69.	Mickey Lolich	217
	Freddie Fitzsimmons	217
71.	Wilbur Cooper	216
72.	Jim Perry	215
	Stan Coveleski	215
74.	Rick Reuschel	214
75.	Chief Bender	212
76.	Billy Pierce	211
	Bobo Newsom	211
	Charlie Hough	211
79.	Jesse Haines	210
80.	Milt Pappas	209
	Don Drysdale	209
	Vida Blue	209
83.	Bob Welch	208
	Dennis Martinez	208
	Eddie Cicotte	208
86.	Hal Newhouser	207
	Carl Mays	207
	Bob Lemon	207
89.	Al Orth	204
	Silver King	204
91.	Jack Stivetts	203
	Lew Burdette	203
93.	Charlie Root	201
	Rube Marquard	201
95.	George Uhle	200
96.	Bucky Walters	198
	Jack Chesbro	198
98.	Dazzy Vance	197
	Adonis Terry	197
	Jesse Tannehill	197
	Bob Friend	197
	Larry French	197

INNINGS

1.	Cy Young	7,355.1
2.	Jim Galvin	6,003.1
3.	Walter Johnson	5,915.0
4.	Phil Niekro	5,404.1
5.	Nolan Ryan	5,386.0
6.	Gaylord Perry	5,350.1
7.	Don Sutton	5,282.1
8.	Warren Spahn	5,243.2
9.	Steve Carlton	5,217.1
10.	Pete Alexander	5,190.0
11.	Kid Nichols	5,056.1
12.	Tim Keefe	5,047.1
13.	Bert Blyleven	4,970.0
14.	Bobby Mathews	4,956.1
15.	Mickey Welch	4,802.0
16.	Tom Seaver	4,782.2
17.	Christy Mathewson	4,780.2
18.	Tommy John	4,710.1
19.	Robin Roberts	4,688.2
20.	Early Wynn	4,564.0
21.	John Clarkson	4,536.1
22.	Charley Radbourn	4,535.1
23.	Tony Mullane	4,531.1
24.	Jim Kaat	4,530.1
25.	Fergie Jenkins	4,500.2
26.	Eddie Plank	4,495.2
27.	Eppa Rixey	4,494.2
28.	Jack Powell	4,389.0
29.	Red Ruffing	4,344.0
30.	Gus Weyhing	4,324.1
31.	Jim McCormick	4,275.2
32.	Frank Tanana	4,188.1
33.	Burleigh Grimes	4,179.2
34.	Ted Lyons	4,161.0
35.	Red Faber	4,086.2
36.	Vic Willis	3,996.0
37.	Jim Palmer	3,948.0
38.	Lefty Grove	3,940.2
39.	Jack Quinn	3,920.1
40.	Bob Gibson	3,884.1
41.	Sam Jones	3,883.0
42.	Jerry Koosman	3,839.1
43.	Bob Feller	3,827.0
44.	Amos Rusie	3,769.2
45.	Waite Hoyt	3,762.1
46.	Jim Bunning	3,760.1
47.	Bobo Newsom	3,759.1
48.	Charlie Hough	3,687.2
49.	George Mullin	3,686.2
50.	Jack Morris	3,682.2
51.	Jerry Reuss	3,669.2
52.	Paul Derringer	3,645.0
53.	Mickey Lolich	3,638.1
54.	Tommy Bond	3,628.2
55.	Bob Friend	3,611.0
56.	Carl Hubbell	3,590.1
57.	Joe Niekro	3,584.0
58.	Herb Pennock	3,571.2
59.	Earl Whitehill	3,564.2
60.	Rick Reuschel	3,548.1
61.	Will White	3,542.2
62.	Adonis Terry	3,514.0
63.	Juan Marichal	3,507.1
64.	Jim Whitney	3,496.1
65.	Luis Tiant	3,486.1
66.	Wilbur Cooper	3,480.0
67.	Claude Osteen	3,460.1
68.	Catfish Hunter	3,449.1
69.	Joe McGinnity	3,441.1
70.	Don Drysdale	3,432.0
71.	Mel Harder	3,426.1
72.	Charlie Buffinton	3,404.0

73.	Hooks Dauss	3,390.2
74.	Clark Griffith	3,385.2
75.	Dennis Martinez	3,384.0
76.	Doyle Alexander	3,367.2
77.	Chick Fraser	3,356.0
78.	Al Orth	3,354.2
79.	Curt Simmons	3,348.1
80.	Vida Blue	3,343.1
81.	Billy Pierce	3,306.2
	Rube Marquard	3,306.2
83.	Jim Perry	3,285.2
84.	Larry Jackson	3,262.2
85.	Freddie Fitzsimmons	3,223.2
86.	Eddie Cicotte	3,223.1
87.	Dolf Luque	3,220.1
88.	Dutch Leonard	3,218.1
89.	Jesse Haines	3,208.2
90.	Red Ames	3,198.0
91.	Charlie Root	3,197.1
92.	Silver King	3,190.2
93.	Milt Pappas	3,186.0
94.	Mordecai Brown	3,172.1
95.	Whitey Ford	3,170.1
96.	Lee Meadows	3,160.2
97.	Larry French	3,152.0
98.	Rick Wise	3,127.0
99.	Tom Zachary	3,126.1
100.	George Uhle	3,119.2

STRIKEOUTS

1.	Nolan Ryan	5,714
2.	Steve Carlton	4,136
3.	Bert Blyleven	3,701
4.	Tom Seaver	3,640
5.	Don Sutton	3,574
6.	Gaylord Perry	3,534
7.	Walter Johnson	3,509
8.	Phil Niekro	3,342
9.	Fergie Jenkins	3,192
10.	Bob Gibson	3,117
11.	Jim Bunning	2,855
12.	Mickey Lolich	2,832
13.	Cy Young	2,803
14.	Frank Tanana	2,773
15.	Warren Spahn	2,583
16.	Bob Feller	2,581
17.	Jerry Koosman	2,556
18.	Tim Keefe	2,545
19.	Christy Mathewson	2,502
20.	Don Drysdale	2,486
21.	Jim Kaat	2,461
22.	Sam McDowell	2,453
23.	Luis Tiant	2,416
24.	Sandy Koufax	2,396
25.	Jack Morris	2,378
26.	Robin Roberts	2,357
27.	Early Wynn	2,334
28.	Rube Waddell	2,316
29.	Juan Marichal	2,303
30.	Charlie Hough	2,297
31.	Lefty Grove	2,266
32.	Eddie Plank	2,246
33.	Tommy John	2,245
34.	Jim Palmer	2,212
35.	Dennis Eckersley	2,198
	Pete Alexander	2,198
37.	Vida Blue	2,175
38.	Camilo Pascual	2,167
39.	Bobo Newsom	2,082
40.	Dazzy Vance	2,045
41.	Roger Clemens	2,033
42.	Rick Reuschel	2,015
43.	Catfish Hunter	2,012
44.	Mark Langston	2,001

45.	Billy Pierce	1,999
46.	Red Ruffing	1,987
47.	John Clarkson	1,978
48.	Whitey Ford	1,956
49.	Amos Rusie	1,934
50.	Bob Welch	1,925
51.	Jerry Reuss	1,907
52.	Kid Nichols	1,868
53.	Mickey Welch	1,850
54.	Fernando Valenzuela	1,842
55.	Dwight Gooden	1,835
56.	Dennis Martinez	1,831
57.	Charley Radbourn	1,830
58.	Frank Viola	1,813
59.	Tony Mullane	1,803
60.	Jim Galvin	1,799
61.	Hal Newhouser	1,796
62.	Ron Guidry	1,778
63.	Rudy May	1,760
64.	Joe Niekro	1,747
65.	Ed Walsh	1,736
66.	Bob Friend	1,734
67.	Milt Pappas	1,728
	Joe Coleman	1,728
69.	Floyd Bannister	1,723
70.	Chief Bender	1,711
71.	Larry Jackson	1,709
72.	Jim McCormick	1,704
73.	Bob Veale	1,703
74.	Red Ames	1,702
75.	Charlie Buffinton	1,700
76.	Curt Simmons	1,697
77.	Carl Hubbell	1,677
78.	Tommy Bridges	1,674
79.	John Candelaria	1,673
80.	Gus Weyhing	1,665
	Bruce Hurst	1,665
82.	Rick Sutcliffe	1,653
83.	Vic Willis	1,651
84.	Rick Wise	1,647
85.	Dave Stieb	1,642
86.	Al Downing	1,639
87.	Mike Cuellar	1,632
88.	Chris Short	1,629
89.	Andy Messersmith	1,625
90.	Steve Rogers	1,621
	Jack Powell	1,621
92.	Ray Sadecki	1,614
93.	Claude Osteen	1,612
94.	Hoyt Wilhelm	1,610
95.	Jim Maloney	1,605
96.	Ken Holtzman	1,601
97.	Rube Marquard	1,593
98.	Woodie Fryman	1,587
99.	Jim Perry	1,576
100.	Harvey Haddix	1,575

WINNING PERCENTAGE

1.	Al Spalding	.796
2.	Dave Foutz	.690
3.	Whitey Ford	.690
4.	Bob Caruthers	.688
5.	Lefty Grove	.680
6.	Vic Raschi	.667
7.	Larry Corcoran	.665
8.	Christy Mathewson	.665
9.	Sam Leever	.660
10.	Sal Maglie	.657
11.	Dick McBride	.656
12.	Dwight Gooden	.655
13.	Sandy Koufax	.655
14.	Roger Clemens	.655
15.	Johnny Allen	.654
16.	Ron Guidry	.651
17.	Lefty Gomez	.649
18.	John Clarkson	.648
19.	Mordecai Brown	.648
20.	Dizzy Dean	.644
21.	Pete Alexander	.642
22.	Jim Palmer	.638
23.	Kid Nichols	.634
24.	Deacon Phillippe	.634
25.	Joe McGinnity	.634
26.	Ed Reulbach	.632
27.	Juan Marichal	.631
28.	Mort Cooper	.631
29.	Allie Reynolds	.630
30.	Jesse Tannehill	.629
31.	Ray Kremer	.627
32.	Firpo Marberry	.627
33.	Eddie Plank	.627
34.	Chief Bender	.625
35.	Don Newcombe	.623
36.	Nig Cuppy	.623
37.	Addie Joss	.623
38.	Fred Goldsmith	.622
39.	Doc Crandall	.622
40.	Carl Mays	.622
41.	Carl Hubbell	.622
42.	Bob Feller	.621
43.	Mel Parnell	.621
44.	John Tudor	.619
45.	Clark Griffith	.619
46.	Bob Lemon	.618
47.	Cy Young	.618
48.	John Ward	.617
49.	Urban Shocker	.615
50.	Jeff Tesreau	.615
51.	Jim Maloney	.615
52.	Lon Warneke	.613
53.	Charley Radbourn	.613
54.	Gary Nolan	.611
55.	Schoolboy Rowe	.610
56.	Carl Erskine	.610
57.	Ed Walsh	.607
58.	Charlie Ferguson	.607
59.	Dave McNally	.607
60.	Hooks Wiltse	.607
61.	Candy Cummings	.607
62.	Jimmy Key	.606
63.	Jack Stivetts	.606
64.	Art Nehf	.605
65.	Charlie Buffinton	.605
66.	Orval Overall	.603
67.	Tim Keefe	.603
68.	Tom Seaver	.603
69.	Stan Coveleski	.602
70.	Preacher Roe	.602
71.	Wes Ferrell	.601
72.	J.R. Richard	.601
73.	Jack Chesbro	.600
74.	Walter Johnson	.599
75.	Freddie Fitzsimmons	.598
76.	Bob Welch	.598
77.	Ed Lopat	.597
78.	Warren Spahn	.597
79.	Herb Pennock	.597
80.	Rip Sewell	.596
81.	Mike Garcia	.594
82.	Mickey Welch	.594
83.	David Cone	.594
84.	Pat Malone	.593
85.	General Crowder	.592
86.	John Candelaria	.592
87.	Harry Brecheen	.591
88.	Jim Bagby	.591
89.	Bob Gibson	.591
90.	Dutch Ruether	.591
91.	Denny McLain	.590
92.	Eddie Rommel	.590
93.	Jack Coombs	.590
94.	Tommy Bond	.589
95.	Tiny Bonham	.589
96.	Mike Cuellar	.587
97.	Bill Bernhard	.586
98.	Jeff Pfeffer	.585
99.	Lew Burdette	.585
100.	Amos Rusie	.585

EARNED RUN AVERAGE

1.	Ed Walsh	1.82
2.	Addie Joss	1.89
3.	Mordecai Brown	2.06
4.	John Ward	2.10
5.	Christy Mathewson	2.13
6.	Al Spalding	2.14
7.	Rube Waddell	2.16
8.	Walter Johnson	2.17
9.	Orval Overall	2.23
10.	Will White	2.28
11.	Ed Reulbach	2.28
12.	Jim Scott	2.30
13.	Tommy Bond	2.31
14.	Eddie Plank	2.35
15.	Larry Corcoran	2.36
16.	George McQuillan	2.38
17.	Eddie Cicotte	2.38
18.	Ed Killian	2.38
19.	Doc White	2.39
20.	George Bradley	2.42
21.	Nap Rucker	2.42
22.	Jeff Tesreau	2.43
23.	Jim McCormick	2.43
24.	Terry Larkin	2.43
25.	Chief Bender	2.46
26.	Hooks Wiltse	2.47
27.	Sam Leever	2.47
28.	Lefty Leifield	2.47
29.	Hippo Vaughn	2.49
30.	Candy Cummings	2.49
31.	Bob Ewing	2.49
32.	Hoyt Wilhelm	2.52
33.	Noodles Hahn	2.55
34.	Pete Alexander	2.56
35.	Slim Sallee	2.56
36.	Deacon Phillippe	2.59
37.	Frank Smith	2.59
38.	Ed Siever	2.60
39.	Bob Rhoads	2.61
40.	Tim Keefe	2.62
41.	Cy Young	2.63
42.	Vic Willis	2.63
43.	Red Ames	2.63
44.	Barney Pelty	2.63
45.	Claude Hendrix	2.65
46.	Joe McGinnity	2.66
47.	Dick Rudolph	2.66
48.	Jack Taylor	2.66
49.	Carl Weilman	2.67
50.	Nick Altrock	2.67
51.	Charlie Ferguson	2.67
52.	Charley Radbourn	2.67
53.	Cy Falkenberg	2.68
54.	Jack Chesbro	2.68
55.	Fred Toney	2.69
56.	Bill Donovan	2.69
57.	Larry Cheney	2.70
58.	Mickey Welch	2.71
59.	Fred Goldsmith	2.73
60.	Harry Howell	2.74
61.	Whitey Ford	2.75
62.	Dummy Taylor	2.75

63.	Howie Camnitz	2.75
64.	Babe Adams	2.76
65.	Dutch Leonard	2.76
66.	Sandy Koufax	2.76
67.	Jeff Pfeffer	2.77
68.	Earl Moore	2.78
69.	George Zettlein	2.78
70.	Jack Coombs	2.78
71.	Jesse Tannehill	2.79
72.	Tully Sparks	2.79
73.	Phil Douglas	2.80
74.	John Clarkson	2.81
75.	Ed Morris	2.82
76.	Ray Fisher	2.82
77.	George Mullin	2.82
78.	Bob Caruthers	2.83
79.	Dave Foutz	2.84
80.	Dick McBride	2.85
81.	Jim Palmer	2.86
82.	Andy Messersmith	2.86
83.	Tom Seaver	2.86
84.	Jim Galvin	2.86
85.	George Winter	2.87
86.	Willie Mitchell	2.88
87.	Bobby Mathews	2.89
88.	Juan Marichal	2.89
89.	Stan Coveleski	2.89
90.	Wilbur Cooper	2.89
91.	Rollie Fingers	2.90
92.	Bob Gibson	2.91
93.	Harry Brecheen	2.92
94.	Carl Mays	2.92
95.	Doc Crandall	2.92
96.	Dean Chance	2.92
97.	Guy Hecker	2.92
98.	Dave Davenport	2.93
99.	Roger Clemens	2.94
100.	Lefty Tyler	2.95

FEWEST WALKS

1.	Al Spalding	0.49
2.	Candy Cummings	0.49
3.	Tommy Bond	0.49
4.	George Bradley	0.60
5.	George Zettlein	0.61
6.	Terry Larkin	0.71
7.	Dick McBride	0.74
8.	John Ward	0.92
9.	Fred Goldsmith	0.96
10.	Bobby Mathews	0.97
11.	Jim Whitney	1.06
12.	Jim Galvin	1.12
13.	Deacon Phillippe	1.25
14.	Will White	1.26
15.	Babe Adams	1.29
16.	Jack Lynch	1.38
17.	Addie Joss	1.41
18.	Cy Young	1.49
19.	Guy Hecker	1.51
20.	Lee Richmond	1.53
21.	Jesse Tannehill	1.56
22.	Jim McCormick	1.58
23.	Christy Mathewson	1.59
24.	Red Lucas	1.61
25.	Nick Altrock	1.62
26.	Pete Alexander	1.65
27.	Jumbo McGinnis	1.65
28.	Tiny Bonham	1.67
29.	Ed Morris	1.67
30.	Noodles Hahn	1.69
31.	Charlie Ferguson	1.72
32.	Fritz Peterson	1.73
33.	Robin Roberts	1.73

34.	Charley Radbourn	1.74
35.	Dick Rudolph	1.77
36.	Al Orth	1.77
37.	Bret Saberhagen	1.78
38.	Stump Weidman	1.78
39.	Pete Donohue	1.80
40.	Jesse Barnes	1.80
41.	Carl Hubbell	1.82
42.	Juan Marichal	1.82
43.	Slim Sallee	1.83
44.	Bill Bernhard	1.83
45.	Lew Burdette	1.84
46.	Curt Davis	1.85
47.	Ed Siever	1.86
48.	Larry Corcoran	1.87
49.	Ed Walsh	1.87
50.	Ken Raffensberger	1.88
51.	Paul Derringer	1.88
52.	Bob Caruthers	1.90
53.	Mordecai Brown	1.91
54.	Bill Swift	1.93
55.	Sherry Smith	1.93
56.	George Suggs	1.93
57.	Henry Boyle	1.94
58.	Watty Clark	1.97
59.	Jack Quinn	1.97
60.	Frank Kitson	1.98
61.	Doc White	1.98
62.	Sam Leever	1.99
63.	Fergie Jenkins	1.99
64.	Jack Taylor	2.00
65.	Vern Law	2.01
66.	Dupee Shaw	2.02
67.	Syl Johnson	2.03
68.	Jim Barr	2.04
69.	Don Newcombe	2.05
70.	George Winter	2.05
71.	Dennis Eckersley	2.05
72.	Clark Griffith	2.06
73.	Dutch Leonard	2.06
74.	Scott Stratton	2.06
75.	Dizzy Dean	2.07
76.	Walter Johnson	2.07
77.	Jimmy Key	2.08
78.	Lary Sorensen	2.08
79.	Hal Brown	2.08
80.	Red Donahue	2.09
81.	Larry Jansen	2.09
82.	Jack Powell	2.09
83.	John Candelaria	2.11
84.	Bill Monbouquette	2.12
85.	Hooks Wiltse	2.12
86.	Joe McGinnity	2.12
87.	Chief Bender	2.12
88.	Art Nehf	2.13
89.	Charlie Getzien	2.13
90.	Ken Johnson	2.14
91.	Jack Chesbro	2.14
92.	Eddie Plank	2.15
93.	Jim Kaat	2.15
94.	Sloppy Thurston	2.15
95.	Phil Douglas	2.17
96.	Eppa Rixey	2.17
97.	Bryn Smith	2.17
98.	Ralph Terry	2.17
99.	Bob Purkey	2.17
100.	Scott McGregor	2.18

RATIO

1.	Addie Joss	8.71
2.	Ed Walsh	9.00
3.	John Ward	9.40
4.	Christy Mathewson	9.53

5.	Walter Johnson	9.55
6.	Mordecai Brown	9.59
7.	George Bradley	9.80
8.	Babe Adams	9.83
9.	Tommy Bond	9.83
10.	Juan Marichal	9.91
11.	Rube Waddell	9.92
12.	Larry Corcoran	9.94
13.	Deacon Phillippe	9.95
14.	Sandy Koufax	9.96
15.	Ed Morris	9.97
16.	Will White	10.00
17.	Chief Bender	10.01
18.	Charlie Ferguson	10.05
19.	Sid Fernandez	10.05
20.	Terry Larkin	10.05
21.	Eddie Plank	10.07
22.	Tom Seaver	10.09
23.	Pete Alexander	10.09
24.	Tim Keefe	10.09
25.	Doc White	10.10
26.	Roger Clemens	10.11
27.	Hoyt Wilhelm	10.12
28.	Bret Saberhagen	10.16
29.	Cy Young	10.17
30.	George McQuillan	10.18
31.	Hooks Wiltse	10.18
32.	Noodles Hahn	10.19
33.	Jim McCormick	10.19
34.	Catfish Hunter	10.21
35.	Nick Altrock	10.27
36.	Sam Leever	10.27
37.	Fergie Jenkins	10.28
38.	Don Sutton	10.28
39.	Andy Messersmith	10.29
40.	Ed Reulbach	10.29
41.	Jeff Tesreau	10.30
42.	Gary Nolan	10.31
43.	Jim Whitney	10.32
44.	Don Drysdale	10.33
45.	Charley Radbourn	10.34
46.	Jack Chesbro	10.35
47.	Barney Pelty	10.35
48.	Tiny Bonham	10.38
49.	Fred Goldsmith	10.38
50.	Dennis Eckersley	10.39
51.	Eddie Cicotte	10.40
52.	Rollie Fingers	10.40
53.	Bob Caruthers	10.42
54.	Dick Rudolph	10.42
55.	Orval Overall	10.45
56.	Denny McLain	10.47
57.	Jumbo McGinnis	10.47
58.	George Winter	10.48
59.	Carl Hubbell	10.49
60.	Frank Smith	10.50
61.	Guy Hecker	10.51
62.	Dwight Gooden	10.52
63.	Robin Roberts	10.53
64.	Slim Sallee	10.53
65.	Nap Rucker	10.57
66.	Dave Foutz	10.60
67.	Bob Ewing	10.60
68.	Jack Taylor	10.61
69.	Jim Bunning	10.61
70.	Doug Drabek	10.61
71.	Jim Scott	10.62
72.	Jim Palmer	10.62
73.	Gaylord Perry	10.63
74.	Ron Guidry	10.65
75.	John Candelaria	10.66
76.	Jimmy Key	10.67
77.	Al Spalding	10.67

78. Mario Soto	10.67
79. Ralph Terry	10.68
80. Jesse Tannehill	10.68
81. Orel Hershiser	10.69
82. Fred Toney	10.69
83. Joe McGinnity	10.69
84. Bob Gibson	10.69
85. Harry Brecheen	10.70
86. Claude Hendrix	10.70
87. Joe Horlen	10.71
88. Jim Galvin	10.72
89. Carl Weilman	10.72
90. Fritz Peterson	10.72
91. Phil Douglas	10.73
92. Eddie Fisher	10.74
93. Warren Spahn	10.75
94. Dupee Shaw	10.76
95. Mike Cuellar	10.77
96. John Tudor	10.78
97. Bert Blyleven	10.78
98. Luis Tiant	10.79
99. Ken Johnson	10.79
100. Hippo Vaughn	10.81

PITCHER PUTOUTS

1. Phil Niekro	386
2. Jack Morris	375
3. Fergie Jenkins	363
4. Gaylord Perry	349
5. Don Sutton	334
6. Tom Seaver	328
Rick Reuschel	328
Tony Mullane	328
9. Jim Galvin	324
10. Robin Roberts	316
11. Chick Fraser	315
12. Kid Nichols	311
13. Jim Palmer	292
14. Juan Marichal	291
Bob Gibson	291
16. Bert Blyleven	287
17. Christy Mathewson	281
18. Walter Johnson	276
19. Vic Willis	271
Dennis Martinez	271
21. Dave Stieb	267
22. Doyle Alexander	264
23. Jim McCormick	263
Bob Lemon	263
25. Jim Kaat	262

PITCHER ASSISTS

1. Cy Young	2,014
2. Christy Mathewson	1,503
3. Pete Alexander	1,419
4. Jim Galvin	1,382
5. Walter Johnson	1,351
6. Burleigh Grimes	1,252
7. George Mullin	1,244
8. Jack Quinn	1,240
9. Ed Walsh	1,208
10. Eppa Rixey	1,195
11. John Clarkson	1,143
12. Carl Mays	1,138
13. Hooks Dauss	1,128
14. Vic Willis	1,124
15. Eddie Plank	1,108
Red Faber	1,108
17. Tim Keefe	1,060
18. Tony Mullane	1,041
19. Kid Nichols	1,031
20. Tommy John	1,028
21. Red Ames	1,000

22. Warren Spahn	999
23. Eddie Cicotte	998
24. Jack Powell	967
25. Harry Howell	965

PITCHER CHANCES ACCEPTED

1. Cy Young	2,243
2. Christy Mathewson	1,784
3. Jim Galvin	1,706
4. Walter Johnson	1,627
5. Pete Alexander	1,608
6. Burleigh Grimes	1,477
7. George Mullin	1,473
8. Ed Walsh	1,441
9. Vic Willis	1,395
10. Jack Quinn	1,379
11. Tony Mullane	1,369
12. John Clarkson	1,364
13. Kid Nichols	1,342
14. Eddie Plank	1,337
15. Eppa Rixey	1,326
16. Tim Keefe	1,320
17. Carl Mays	1,312
18. Tommy John	1,265
19. Phil Niekro	1,264
20. Chick Fraser	1,253
21. Red Faber	1,238
22. Hooks Dauss	1,227
23. Gaylord Perry	1,226
24. Warren Spahn	1,221
25. Doc White	1,194

PITCHER FIELDING AVERAGE

1. Don Mossi	.990
2. Gary Nolan	.990
3. Rick Rhoden	.989
4. Lon Warneke	.988
5. Jim Wilson	.988
6. Woodie Fryman	.988
7. Elmer Riddle	.987
8. Larry Gura	.986
9. Pete Alexander	.985
10. General Crowder	.984
11. Bill Monbouquette	.984
12. Rick Langford	.983
13. Dana Fillingim	.983
14. Willie Hernandez	.983
15. Harry Brecheen	.983
16. Socks Seibold	.982
17. Rick Wise	.982
18. Red Lucas	.981
19. Ron Guidry	.981
20. Jim Gott	.981
21. Chuck Dobson	.981
22. Bob Smith	.981
23. Urban Shocker	.980
24. Al Demaree	.980
25. Dan Petry	.980

CATCHER GAMES

1. Carlton Fisk	2,229
2. Bob Boone	2,225
3. Gary Carter	2,056
4. Jim Sundberg	1,927
5. Al Lopez	1,918
6. Rick Ferrell	1,806
7. Gabby Hartnett	1,793
8. Ted Simmons	1,771
9. Johnny Bench	1,742
10. Ray Schalk	1,727
11. Tony Pena	1,714
12. Lance Parrish	1,713
13. Bill Dickey	1,708

14. Yogi Berra	1,699
15. Rick Dempsey	1,633
16. Jim Hegan	1,629
17. Deacon McGuire	1,611
18. Bill Freehan	1,581
19. Sherm Lollar	1,571
20. Luke Sewell	1,562
21. Ernie Lombardi	1,544
22. Steve O'Neill	1,532
23. Darrell Porter	1,506
24. Rollie Hemsley	1,482
25. Del Crandall	1,479

CATCHER PUTOUTS

1. Gary Carter	11,785
2. Carlton Fisk	11,369
3. Bob Boone	11,260
4. Tony Pena	9,968
5. Bill Freehan	9,941
6. Jim Sundberg	9,767
7. Johnny Roseboro	9,291
8. Johnny Bench	9,249
9. Lance Parrish	9,076
10. Johnny Edwards	8,925
11. Ted Simmons	8,906
12. Yogi Berra	8,738
13. Mike Scioscia	8,335
14. Tim McCarver	8,206
15. Jerry Grote	8,081
16. Bill Dickey	7,965
17. Jim Hegan	7,506
18. Rick Dempsey	7,367
19. Del Crandall	7,352
20. Gabby Hartnett	7,292
21. Rick Ferrell	7,248
22. Ray Schalk	7,168
23. Alan Ashby	7,086
24. Sherm Lollar	7,059
25. Tom Haller	7,012

CATCHER ASSISTS

1. Deacon McGuire	1,859
2. Ray Schalk	1,811
3. Steve O'Neill	1,698
4. Red Dooin	1,590
5. Chief Zimmer	1,580
6. Johnny Kling	1,552
7. Ivey Wingo	1,487
8. Wilbert Robinson	1,454
9. Bill Bergen	1,444
10. Wally Schang	1,420
11. Duke Farrell	1,417
12. George Gibson	1,386
13. Oscar Stanage	1,381
14. Malachi Kittridge	1,363
15. Lou Criger	1,342
16. Frank Snyder	1,332
17. Bill Killefer	1,319
18. Billy Sullivan	1,314
19. John Warner	1,309
20. Pop Snyder	1,295
21. Gabby Hartnett	1,254
22. Bill Rariden	1,231
23. Gary Carter	1,203
24. Roger Bresnahan	1,195
25. Bob Boone	1,174

CATCHER CHANCES ACCEPTED

1. Gary Carter	12,988
2. Bob Boone	12,434
3. Carlton Fisk	12,417
4. Tony Pena	10,919

5. Jim Sundberg 10,774
6. Bill Freehan 10,662
7. Johnny Bench 10,099
8. Lance Parrish 10,000
9. Johnny Roseboro 9,966
10. Ted Simmons 9,821
11. Johnny Edwards 9,628
12. Yogi Berra 9,536
13. Mike Scioscia 9,072
14. Ray Schalk 8,979
15. Bill Dickey 8,919
16. Tim McCarver 8,794
17. Jerry Grote 8,716
18. Deacon McGuire 8,711
19. Gabby Hartnett 8,546
20. Rick Ferrell 8,375
21. Jim Hegan 8,201
22. Rick Dempsey 8,135
23. Del Crandall 8,111
24. Alan Ashby 7,770
25. Al Lopez 7,759

CATCHER FIELDING AVERAGE

1. Bill Freehan .... .993
2. Elston Howard .... .993
3. Ron Hassey .... .993
4. Jim Sundberg .... .993
5. Joe Azcue .... .992
6. Mike LaValliere .... .992
7. Sherm Lollar .... .992
8. Dave Valle .... .992
9. Buddy Rosar .... .992
10. Tom Haller .... .992
11. Johnny Edwards .... .992
12. Jerry Grote .... .991
13. Ernie Whitt .... .991
14. Lance Parrish .... .991
15. Mickey Tettleton .... .991
16. Jim Pagliaroni .... .991
17. Gary Carter .... .991
18. Johnny Bench .... .990
19. Tony Pena .... .990
20. Randy Hundley .... .990
21. Johnny Romano .... .990
22. Rick Cerone .... .990
23. Bruce Benedict .... .990
24. Earl Battey .... .990
25. Tim McCarver .... .990

FIRST BASE GAMES

1. Jake Beckley 2,377
2. Eddie Murray 2,368
3. Mickey Vernon 2,237
4. Lou Gehrig 2,137
5. Charlie Grimm 2,131
6. Joe Judge 2,084
7. Cap Anson 2,082
8. Ed Konetchy 2,073
9. Steve Garvey 2,059
10. Joe Kuhel 2,057
11. Willie McCovey 2,045
12. Keith Hernandez 2,014
13. Jake Daubert 2,002
14. Stuffy McInnis 1,995
15. George Sisler 1,971
16. Chris Chambliss 1,962
17. Norm Cash 1,943
18. Jimmie Foxx 1,919
19. Gil Hodges 1,908
20. Jim Bottomley 1,885
21. Wally Pipp 1,819
22. Hal Chase 1,815
23. Fred Tenney 1,810

24. Tony Perez 1,778
25. George Scott 1,773

FIRST BASE PUTOUTS

1. Jake Beckley 23,709
2. Ed Konetchy 21,361
3. Eddie Murray 20,842
4. Cap Anson 20,794
5. Charlie Grimm 20,711
6. Stuffy McInnis 19,962
7. Mickey Vernon 19,808
8. Jake Daubert 19,634
9. Lou Gehrig 19,510
10. Joe Kuhel 19,386
11. Joe Judge 19,264
12. Steve Garvey 18,844
13. George Sisler 18,837
14. Wally Pipp 18,779
15. Jim Bottomley 18,337
16. Hal Chase 18,185
17. Keith Hernandez 17,909
18. Fred Tenney 17,903
19. Chris Chambliss 17,771
20. Roger Connor 17,605
21. Jimmie Foxx 17,207
22. Willie McCovey 17,170
23. George Burns 16,892
24. Tommy Tucker 16,393
25. Dan Brouthers 16,365

FIRST BASE ASSISTS

1. Eddie Murray 1,828
2. Keith Hernandez 1,682
3. George Sisler 1,529
4. Mickey Vernon 1,448
5. Fred Tenney 1,363
6. Chris Chambliss 1,351
   Bill Buckner 1,351
8. Norm Cash 1,317
9. Jake Beckley 1,315
10. Joe Judge 1,301
11. Ed Konetchy 1,292
12. Gil Hodges 1,281
13. Stuffy McInnis 1,238
14. Willie McCovey 1,222
    Jimmie Foxx 1,222
16. Charlie Grimm 1,214
17. Joe Kuhel 1,163
18. Wally Pipp 1,152
19. George Scott 1,132
20. Jake Daubert 1,128
21. Bill Terry 1,108
22. George Burns 1,094
23. Lou Gehrig 1,087
24. Vic Power 1,078
25. George McQuinn 1,074

FIRST BASE CHANCES ACCEPTED

1. Jake Beckley 25,024
2. Eddie Murray 22,670
3. Ed Konetchy 22,653
4. Charlie Grimm 21,925
5. Cap Anson 21,749
6. Mickey Vernon 21,256
7. Stuffy McInnis 21,200
8. Jake Daubert 20,762
9. Lou Gehrig 20,597
10. Joe Judge 20,565
11. Joe Kuhel 20,549
12. George Sisler 20,366
13. Wally Pipp 19,931
14. Steve Garvey 19,870

15. Keith Hernandez 19,591
16. Fred Tenney 19,266
17. Hal Chase 19,234
18. Jim Bottomley 19,151
19. Chris Chambliss 19,122
20. Roger Connor 18,461
21. Jimmie Foxx 18,429
22. Willie McCovey 18,392
23. George Burns 17,986
24. Tommy Tucker 17,142
25. Bill Terry 17,080

FIRST BASE FIELDING AVERAGE

1. Steve Garvey .... .996
2. Don Mattingly .... .996
3. Wes Parker .... .996
4. Dan Driessen .... .995
5. Mark McGwire .... .995
6. Jim Spencer .... .995
7. Frank McCormick .... .995
8. Mark Grace .... .994
9. Keith Hernandez .... .994
10. Carl Yastrzemski .... .994
11. Vic Power .... .994
12. Pete Rose .... .994
13. Joe Adcock .... .994
14. Kent Hrbek .... .994
15. Greg Brock .... .994
16. Wally Joyner .... .994
17. Pete O'Brien .... .994
18. Rafael Palmeiro .... .994
19. Mike Jorgensen .... .994
20. Ernie Banks .... .994
21. John Mayberry .... .994
22. Lee May .... .994
23. Ed Kranepool .... .994
24. Danny Cater .... .994
25. Chris Chambliss .... .993

SECOND BASE GAMES

1. Eddie Collins 2,650
2. Joe Morgan 2,527
3. Nellie Fox 2,295
4. Charlie Gehringer 2,206
5. Lou Whitaker 2,162
6. Willie Randolph 2,152
7. Frank White 2,150
8. Bid McPhee 2,126
9. Bill Mazeroski 2,094
10. Nap Lajoie 2,035
11. Bobby Doerr 1,852
12. Red Schoendienst 1,834
13. Billy Herman 1,813
14. Bobby Grich 1,765
15. Frankie Frisch 1,762
16. Johnny Evers 1,735
17. Larry Doyle 1,728
18. Del Pratt 1,688
19. Steve Sax 1,673
20. Ryne Sandberg 1,666
21. Kid Gleason 1,583
22. Rogers Hornsby 1,561
23. Julian Javier 1,552
24. Fred Pfeffer 1,537
25. Miller Huggins 1,530

SECOND BASE PUTOUTS

1. Bid McPhee 6,545
2. Eddie Collins 6,526
3. Nellie Fox 6,090
4. Joe Morgan 5,742
5. Nap Lajoie 5,496

6.	Charlie Gehringer	5,369
7.	Bill Mazeroski	4,974
8.	Bobby Doerr	4,928
9.	Willie Randolph	4,859
10.	Billy Herman	4,780
11.	Frank White	4,740
12.	Fred Pfeffer	4,713
13.	Red Schoendienst	4,616
14.	Lou Whitaker	4,527
15.	Frankie Frisch	4,348
16.	Bobby Grich	4,217
17.	Del Pratt	4,069
18.	Kid Gleason	3,883
19.	Cupid Childs	3,859
20.	George Cutshaw	3,762
21.	Johnny Evers	3,758
22.	Lou Bierbauer	3,724
23.	Larry Doyle	3,635
24.	Joe Gordon	3,600
25.	Steve Sax	3,558

SECOND BASE ASSISTS

1.	Eddie Collins	7,630
2.	Charlie Gehringer	7,068
3.	Joe Morgan	6,967
4.	Bid McPhee	6,905
5.	Bill Mazeroski	6,685
6.	Nellie Fox	6,373
7.	Willie Randolph	6,336
8.	Nap Lajoie	6,262
9.	Frank White	6,250
10.	Lou Whitaker	6,244
11.	Frankie Frisch	6,026
12.	Bobby Doerr	5,710
13.	Billy Herman	5,681
14.	Ryne Sandberg	5,443
15.	Bobby Grich	5,381
16.	Red Schoendienst	5,243
17.	Rogers Hornsby	5,166
18.	Hughie Critz	5,138
19.	Johnny Evers	5,124
20.	Fred Pfeffer	5,104
21.	Del Pratt	5,075
22.	Steve Sax	4,785
23.	Kid Gleason	4,768
24.	Joe Gordon	4,706
25.	Manny Trillo	4,699

SECOND BASE CHANCES ACCEPTED

1.	Eddie Collins	14,156
2.	Bid McPhee	13,450
3.	Joe Morgan	12,709
4.	Nellie Fox	12,463
5.	Charlie Gehringer	12,437
6.	Nap Lajoie	11,758
7.	Bill Mazeroski	11,659
8.	Willie Randolph	11,195
9.	Frank White	10,990
10.	Lou Whitaker	10,771
11.	Bobby Doerr	10,638
12.	Billy Herman	10,461
13.	Frankie Frisch	10,374
14.	Red Schoendienst	9,859
15.	Fred Pfeffer	9,817
16.	Bobby Grich	9,598
17.	Del Pratt	9,144
18.	Johnny Evers	8,882
19.	Ryne Sandberg	8,723
20.	Kid Gleason	8,651
21.	Hughie Critz	8,584
22.	Cupid Childs	8,537
23.	Rogers Hornsby	8,372

24.	Steve Sax	8,343
25.	Joe Gordon	8,306

SECOND BASE FIELDING AVERAGE

1.	Ryne Sandberg	.990
2.	Tom Herr	.989
3.	Jose Lind	.988
4.	Rich Dauer	.987
5.	Doug Flynn	.986
6.	Marty Barrett	.986
7.	Jerry Adair	.985
8.	Jim Gantner	.985
9.	Lou Whitaker	.984
10.	Frank White	.984
11.	Bobby Grich	.984
12.	Jerry Lumpe	.984
13.	Cookie Rojas	.984
14.	Dave Cash	.984
15.	Nellie Fox	.984
16.	Duane Kuiper	.983
17.	Tommy Helms	.983
18.	Dick Green	.983
19.	Bill Doran	.983
20.	Red Schoendienst	.983
21.	Jackie Robinson	.983
22.	Bill Mazeroski	.983
23.	Glenn Hubbard	.983
24.	Julio Cruz	.983
25.	Horace Clarke	.983

THIRD BASE GAMES

1.	Brooks Robinson	2,870
2.	Graig Nettles	2,412
3.	Mike Schmidt	2,212
4.	Buddy Bell	2,183
5.	Eddie Mathews	2,181
6.	Ron Santo	2,130
7.	Eddie Yost	2,008
8.	Ron Cey	1,989
9.	Aurelio Rodriguez	1,983
10.	Sal Bando	1,896
11.	Pie Traynor	1,863
12.	Stan Hack	1,836
13.	Ken Boyer	1,785
14.	Pinky Higgins	1,768
15.	Tim Wallach	1,754
16.	Lave Cross	1,721
17.	Carney Lansford	1,720
18.	George Kell	1,692
	George Brett	1,692
20.	Jimmy Collins	1,683
21.	Willie Kamm	1,674
22.	Larry Gardner	1,656
23.	Wade Boggs	1,654
24.	Willie Jones	1,614
25.	Gary Gaetti	1,609

THIRD BASE PUTOUTS

1.	Brooks Robinson	2,697
2.	Jimmy Collins	2,372
3.	Eddie Yost	2,356
4.	Lave Cross	2,306
5.	Pie Traynor	2,289
6.	Billy Nash	2,219
7.	Frank Baker	2,154
8.	Willie Kamm	2,151
9.	Eddie Mathews	2,049
10.	Willie Jones	2,045
11.	Jimmy Austin	2,042
12.	Arlie Latham	1,975
13.	Ron Santo	1,955
14.	Stan Hack	1,944

15.	Graig Nettles	1,898
16.	Pinky Higgins	1,848
17.	George Kell	1,825
18.	Billy Shindle	1,815
19.	Buddy Bell	1,798
20.	Larry Gardner	1,788
21.	Jerry Denny	1,777
	Harlond Clift	1,777
23.	Harry Steinfeldt	1,774
24.	Bill Bradley	1,753
25.	Denny Lyons	1,672

THIRD BASE ASSISTS

1.	Brooks Robinson	6,205
2.	Graig Nettles	5,279
3.	Mike Schmidt	5,045
4.	Buddy Bell	4,925
5.	Ron Santo	4,581
6.	Eddie Mathews	4,322
7.	Aurelio Rodriguez	4,150
8.	Ron Cey	4,018
9.	Sal Bando	3,720
10.	Lave Cross	3,706
11.	Jimmy Collins	3,702
12.	George Brett	3,674
13.	Eddie Yost	3,659
14.	Ken Boyer	3,652
15.	Arlie Latham	3,545
16.	Pie Traynor	3,521
17.	Tim Wallach	3,513
18.	Stan Hack	3,494
19.	Larry Gardner	3,406
20.	Willie Kamm	3,345
21.	Gary Gaetti	3,323
22.	George Kell	3,303
23.	Wade Boggs	3,267
24.	Harlond Clift	3,262
25.	Pinky Higgins	3,258

THIRD BASE CHANCES ACCEPTED

1.	Brooks Robinson	8,902
2.	Graig Nettles	7,177
3.	Buddy Bell	6,723
4.	Mike Schmidt	6,636
5.	Ron Santo	6,536
6.	Eddie Mathews	6,371
7.	Jimmy Collins	6,074
8.	Eddie Yost	6,015
9.	Lave Cross	6,012
10.	Pie Traynor	5,810
11.	Aurelio Rodriguez	5,679
12.	Arlie Latham	5,520
13.	Ron Cey	5,518
14.	Willie Kamm	5,496
15.	Stan Hack	5,438
16.	Sal Bando	5,367
17.	Billy Nash	5,338
18.	Frank Baker	5,309
19.	Ken Boyer	5,219
20.	Larry Gardner	5,194
21.	George Kell	5,128
22.	Pinky Higgins	5,106
23.	George Brett	5,046
24.	Harlond Clift	5,039
25.	Jimmy Austin	4,991

THIRD BASE FIELDING AVERAGE

1.	Brooks Robinson	.971
2.	Rico Petrocelli	.970
3.	Ken Reitz	.970
4.	George Kell	.969

5.	Steve Buechele	.968
6.	Don Money	.968
7.	Don Wert	.968
8.	Hank Majeski	.968
9.	Willie Kamm	.967
10.	Heinie Groh	.967
11.	Carney Lansford	.966
12.	Clete Boyer	.965
13.	Billy Cox	.965
14.	Ken Oberkfell	.965
15.	Ken Keltner	.965
16.	Jim Davenport	.964
17.	Buddy Bell	.964
18.	Aurelio Rodriguez	.964
19.	Gary Gaetti	.963
20.	Chris Sabo	.963
21.	Willie Jones	.963
22.	Toby Harrah	.963
23.	Eric Soderholm	.962
24.	Pinky Whitney	.961
25.	Ron Cey	.961

SHORTSTOP GAMES

1.	Luis Aparicio	2,581
2.	Ozzie Smith	2,322
3.	Larry Bowa	2,222
4.	Luke Appling	2,218
5.	Dave Concepcion	2,178
6.	Rabbit Maranville	2,153
7.	Bill Dahlen	2,132
8.	Bert Campaneris	2,097
9.	Tommy Corcoran	2,073
10.	Roy McMillan	2,028
11.	Pee Wee Reese	2,014
12.	Roger Peckinpaugh	1,982
13.	Alan Trammell	1,973
14.	Garry Templeton	1,964
15.	Don Kessinger	1,955
16.	Mark Belanger	1,942
17.	Chris Speier	1,900
18.	Honus Wagner	1,887
19.	Cal Ripken	1,885
20.	Dick Groat	1,877
21.	Dave Bancroft	1,873
22.	Donie Bush	1,867
23.	Alfredo Griffin	1,861
24.	Joe Cronin	1,843
	Leo Cardenas	1,843

SHORTSTOP PUTOUTS

1.	Rabbit Maranville	5,139
2.	Bill Dahlen	4,850
3.	Dave Bancroft	4,623
4.	Honus Wagner	4,576
5.	Tommy Corcoran	4,550
6.	Luis Aparicio	4,548
7.	Luke Appling	4,398
8.	Herman Long	4,225
9.	Bobby Wallace	4,142
10.	Pee Wee Reese	4,040
11.	Donie Bush	4,038
12.	Monte Cross	3,975
13.	Ozzie Smith	3,965
14.	Roger Peckinpaugh	3,919
15.	Dick Bartell	3,872
16.	Joe Tinker	3,758
17.	Roy McMillan	3,705
18.	Joe Cronin	3,696
19.	Dave Concepcion	3,670
20.	Bert Campaneris	3,608
21.	George McBride	3,585
22.	Mickey Doolan	3,578
23.	Dick Groat	3,505

24.	Garry Templeton	3,393
25.	Everett Scott	3,351

SHORTSTOP ASSISTS

1.	Luis Aparicio	8,016
2.	Ozzie Smith	7,793
3.	Bill Dahlen	7,500
4.	Rabbit Maranville	7,354
5.	Luke Appling	7,218
6.	Tommy Corcoran	7,106
7.	Larry Bowa	6,857
8.	Dave Concepcion	6,594
9.	Dave Bancroft	6,561
10.	Roger Peckinpaugh	6,337
11.	Bobby Wallace	6,303
12.	Don Kessinger	6,212
13.	Roy McMillan	6,191
14.	Bert Campaneris	6,160
15.	Germany Smith	6,154
16.	Herman Long	6,136
17.	Donie Bush	6,119
18.	Honus Wagner	6,041
	Garry Templeton	6,041
20.	Pee Wee Reese	5,891
21.	Joe Tinker	5,848
22.	Joe Cronin	5,814
23.	Dick Groat	5,811
24.	Mark Belanger	5,786
25.	Chris Speier	5,781

SHORTSTOP CHANCES ACCEPTED

1.	Luis Aparicio	12,564
2.	Rabbit Maranville	12,493
3.	Bill Dahlen	12,350
4.	Ozzie Smith	11,758
5.	Tommy Corcoran	11,656
6.	Luke Appling	11,616
7.	Dave Bancroft	11,184
8.	Honus Wagner	10,617
9.	Bobby Wallace	10,445
10.	Herman Long	10,361
11.	Dave Concepcion	10,264
12.	Roger Peckinpaugh	10,256
13.	Larry Bowa	10,171
14.	Donie Bush	10,157
15.	Pee Wee Reese	9,931
16.	Roy McMillan	9,896
17.	Bert Campaneris	9,768
18.	Joe Tinker	9,606
19.	Joe Cronin	9,510
20.	Dick Bartell	9,462
21.	Garry Templeton	9,434
22.	Don Kessinger	9,363
23.	Monte Cross	9,344
24.	Dick Groat	9,316
25.	Germany Smith	8,967

SHORTSTOP FIELDING AVERAGE

1.	Tony Fernandez	.980
2.	Larry Bowa	.980
3.	Ozzie Smith	.979
4.	Cal Ripken	.978
5.	Frank Duffy	.977
6.	Spike Owen	.977
7.	Alan Trammell	.977
8.	Mark Belanger	.977
9.	Dick Schofield	.977
10.	Bucky Dent	.976
11.	Roger Metzger	.976
12.	Ozzie Guillen	.975
13.	Greg Gagne	.973

14.	Tim Foli	.973
15.	Dal Maxvill	.973
16.	Lou Boudreau	.973
17.	Jay Bell	.972
18.	Barry Larkin	.972
19.	Eddie Miller	.972
20.	Luis Aparicio	.972
21.	Roy McMillan	.972
22.	Rafael Belliard	.971
23.	Scott Fletcher	.971
24.	Rick Burleson	.971
25.	Bobby Wine	.971

OUTFIELD GAMES

1.	Ty Cobb	2,935
2.	Willie Mays	2,842
3.	Hank Aaron	2,760
4.	Tris Speaker	2,698
5.	Lou Brock	2,507
6.	Al Kaline	2,488
7.	Dave Winfield	2,468
8.	Max Carey	2,421
9.	Vada Pinson	2,403
10.	Roberto Clemente	2,370
11.	Zack Wheat	2,337
12.	Willie Davis	2,323
13.	Mel Ott	2,313
14.	Sam Crawford	2,299
15.	Paul Waner	2,288
16.	Harry Hooper	2,284
17.	Sam Rice	2,270
18.	Andre Dawson	2,258
19.	Babe Ruth	2,241
20.	Fred Clarke	2,189
21.	Goose Goslin	2,188
22.	Jose Cruz	2,156
23.	Ted Williams	2,151
24.	Dwight Evans	2,146
25.	Al Simmons	2,142
	Doc Cramer	2,142
27.	Frank Robinson	2,132
28.	Richie Ashburn	2,104
29.	Reggie Jackson	2,102
30.	Billy Williams	2,088
31.	Carl Yastrzemski	2,076
32.	Jimmy Sheckard	2,071
33.	Enos Slaughter	2,064
34.	Jesse Burkett	2,053
35.	Willie Keeler	2,039
36.	Willie Wilson	2,021
37.	Mickey Mantle	2,019
38.	Jimmy Ryan	1,943
39.	Amos Otis	1,928
40.	Chet Lemon	1,925
41.	Duke Snider	1,918
42.	Clyde Milan	1,903
43.	Stan Musial	1,890
44.	Rickey Henderson	1,880
	George Foster	1,880
46.	Paul Blair	1,878
47.	Gary Matthews	1,876
48.	Dave Parker	1,867
49.	Sherry Magee	1,861
50.	Dale Murphy	1,853
51.	Joe Medwick	1,852
52.	Edd Roush	1,848
53.	Heinie Manush	1,845
54.	George Burns	1,844
55.	Dusty Baker	1,842
56.	Del Ennis	1,840
57.	George Van Haltren	1,827
58.	Fred Lynn	1,825
59.	Cy Williams	1,818
	Lloyd Waner	1,818

61.	George Hendrick	1,813	58.	Enos Slaughter	3,925	George Burns	197
	Patsy Donovan	1,813	59.	George Burns	3,918	56. Charlie Jamieson	196
63.	Jim Wynn	1,810	60.	Jim Wynn	3,912	57. Carl Yastrzemski	195
64.	Kiki Cuyler	1,807	61.	Bill Bruton	3,905	Willie Mays	195
65.	Dummy Hoy	1,795	62.	Dom DiMaggio	3,859	59. Frank Schulte	194
	Brett Butler	1,795	63.	Jim Piersall	3,851	Chuck Klein	194
67.	Wally Moses	1,792	64.	Heinie Manush	3,841	61. Ross Youngs	192
68.	Tom Brown	1,783	65.	Rick Manning	3,831	62. Kiki Cuyler	191
69.	Jose Cardenal	1,778	66.	George Foster	3,809	63. Tommy Griffith	189
70.	Johnny Callison	1,777	67.	Sherry Magee	3,800	64. Roy Thomas	188
71.	Rocky Colavito	1,774	68.	Dave Parker	3,791	Cy Seymour	188
72.	Fielder Jones	1,770	69.	Bill Virdon	3,777	66. Joe Jackson	183
73.	Bob Johnson	1,769	70.	Lloyd Moseby	3,765	Harry Heilmann	183
74.	Bobby Veach	1,740	71.	Bobby Veach	3,754	68. Billy Hamilton	182
75.	Carl Furillo	1,739	72.	George Hendrick	3,751	69. Chief Wilson	181
			73.	Dode Paskert	3,734	Max Flack	181
			74.	Stan Musial	3,730	71. Mike Mitchell	180
			75.	Jimmy Ryan	3,698	72. Richie Ashburn	178

OUTFIELD PUTOUTS

1.	Willie Mays	7,095			73. Shano Collins	177
2.	Tris Speaker	6,788			74. Red Murray	176
3.	Max Carey	6,363	## OUTFIELD ASSISTS		Sherry Magee	176
4.	Ty Cobb	6,361			Nemo Leibold	176
5.	Richie Ashburn	6,089	1. Tris Speaker	449	Joe Hornung	176
6.	Hank Aaron	5,539	2. Ty Cobb	392	Gavvy Cravath	176
7.	Willie Davis	5,449	3. Jimmy Ryan	375		
8.	Doc Cramer	5,412	4. George Van Haltren	348	## OUTFIELD CHANCES ACCEPTED	
9.	Vada Pinson	5,097	Tom Brown	348		
10.	Andre Dawson	5,077	6. Harry Hooper	344	1. Willie Mays	7,290
11.	Willie Wilson	5,051	7. Max Carey	339	2. Tris Speaker	7,237
12.	Al Kaline	5,035	8. Jimmy Sheckard	307	3. Ty Cobb	6,753
13.	Zack Wheat	4,996	9. Clyde Milan	294	4. Max Carey	6,702
14.	Chet Lemon	4,993	10. Orator Shaffer	289	5. Richie Ashburn	6,267
15.	Al Simmons	4,988	11. King Kelly	285	6. Hank Aaron	5,740
16.	Dave Winfield	4,972	12. Sam Thompson	283	7. Willie Davis	5,592
17.	Amos Otis	4,936	13. Sam Rice	278	8. Doc Cramer	5,584
18.	Paul Waner	4,872	14. Dummy Hoy	273	9. Vada Pinson	5,269
19.	Lloyd Waner	4,860	15. Jesse Burkett	270	10. Andre Dawson	5,231
20.	Goose Goslin	4,793	16. Tommy McCarthy	268	11. Zack Wheat	5,228
21.	Fred Clarke	4,790	Sam Crawford	268	12. Al Kaline	5,205
22.	Sam Rice	4,774	18. Roberto Clemente	266	13. Al Simmons	5,157
23.	Rickey Henderson	4,754	19. Patsy Donovan	264	14. Dave Winfield	5,138
24.	Roberto Clemente	4,696	20. Willie Keeler	258	15. Willie Wilson	5,127
25.	Fred Lynn	4,556	21. Mel Ott	256	16. Paul Waner	5,113
26.	Edd Roush	4,537	22. Fred Clarke	254	17. Chet Lemon	5,108
27.	Brett Butler	4,517	23. Mike Griffin	243	18. Amos Otis	5,062
28.	Joe DiMaggio	4,516	George Gore	243	19. Sam Rice	5,052
29.	Mel Ott	4,511	Ed Delahanty	243	20. Fred Clarke	5,044
30.	Garry Maddox	4,449	26. Paul Waner	241	21. Goose Goslin	5,015
31.	Babe Ruth	4,444	27. Hugh Duffy	240	22. Lloyd Waner	5,011
32.	Mickey Mantle	4,438	28. Zack Wheat	232	23. Roberto Clemente	4,962
33.	Lou Brock	4,394	29. Jimmy Wolf	229	24. Rickey Henderson	4,856
34.	Jose Cruz	4,391	30. Cy Williams	226	25. Mel Ott	4,767
35.	Dwight Evans	4,371	Hugh Nicol	226	26. Edd Roush	4,759
36.	Paul Blair	4,343	32. Fielder Jones	225	27. Fred Lynn	4,670
37.	Sam West	4,300	33. Pop Corkhill	224	28. Joe DiMaggio	4,669
38.	Jimmy Sheckard	4,203	34. Dode Paskert	223	29. Babe Ruth	4,648
39.	Cy Williams	4,180	35. Edd Roush	222	30. Brett Butler	4,620
40.	Ted Williams	4,158	Goose Goslin	222	31. Mickey Mantle	4,555
41.	Cesar Cedeno	4,131	37. Tilly Walker	221	32. Garry Maddox	4,543
42.	Duke Snider	4,099	Paul Hines	221	33. Lou Brock	4,536
43.	Clyde Milan	4,095	39. Paul Radford	217	34. Dwight Evans	4,528
44.	Reggie Jackson	4,062	40. Jim O'Rourke	216	35. Jose Cruz	4,516
45.	Dale Murphy	4,053	41. Joe Kelley	212	36. Jimmy Sheckard	4,510
46.	Kiki Cuyler	4,034	42. Bobby Veach	211	37. Paul Blair	4,454
47.	Curt Flood	4,021	43. Curt Welch	210	38. Sam West	4,451
48.	Bob Johnson	4,003	Duffy Lewis	210	39. Cy Williams	4,406
49.	Wally Moses	4,000	45. Bob Johnson	208	40. Clyde Milan	4,389
50.	Kirby Puckett	3,994	Ned Hanlon	208	41. Harry Hooper	4,325
	Joe Medwick	3,994	Steve Brodie	208	42. Ted Williams	4,298
52.	Harry Hooper	3,981	48. Babe Ruth	204	43. Cesar Cedeno	4,233
53.	Frank Robinson	3,978	49. George Wood	203	44. Dummy Hoy	4,231
54.	Earl Averill	3,969	50. Jack Tobin	202	Jesse Burkett	4,231
55.	Jesse Burkett	3,961	51. John Titus	201	46. Kiki Cuyler	4,225
56.	Dummy Hoy	3,958	Hank Aaron	201		
57.	Carl Yastrzemski	3,941	53. Kip Selbach	197		
			Elmer Flick	197		

47.	Duke Snider	4,222
48.	Bob Johnson	4,211
49.	Reggie Jackson	4,195
50.	Dale Murphy	4,166
51.	Wally Moses	4,147
52.	Carl Yastrzemski	4,136
53.	Curt Flood	4,135
54.	Joe Medwick	4,133
55.	George Burns	4,115
56.	Kirby Puckett	4,114
57.	Frank Robinson	4,113
58.	Earl Averill	4,084
59.	Enos Slaughter	4,077
60.	Jimmy Ryan	4,073
61.	Jim Wynn	4,051
62.	Bill Bruton	4,010
63.	Dom DiMaggio	4,006
64.	Sherry Magee	3,976
65.	Tom Brown	3,971
66.	Bobby Veach	3,965
67.	Dode Paskert	3,957
68.	Jim Piersall	3,946
	Heinie Manush	3,946
70.	Dave Parker	3,934
71.	George Foster	3,928
72.	Rick Manning	3,902
73.	Sam Crawford	3,894
74.	Bill Virdon	3,877
75.	George Hendrick	3,865

OUTFIELD FIELDING AVERAGE

1.	Brian Downing	.995
2.	Terry Puhl	.993
3.	Brett Butler	.992
4.	Pete Rose	.991
5.	Ted Uhlaender	.991
6.	Amos Otis	.991
7.	Joe Rudi	.991
8.	Mickey Stanley	.991
9.	Don Demeter	.990
10.	Robin Yount	.990
11.	Jim Piersall	.990
12.	Jim Landis	.989
13.	Ken Berry	.989
14.	Kirby Puckett	.989
15.	Henry Cotto	.989
16.	Tommy Holmes	.989
17.	Bake McBride	.989
18.	Paul O'Neill	.989
19.	Elliott Maddox	.989
20.	Gene Woodling	.989
21.	Tim Raines	.988
22.	Cesar Geronimo	.988
23.	Fred Lynn	.988
24.	Johnny Cooney	.988
25.	Gary Roenicke	.988
26.	Phil Bradley	.988
27.	Paul Blair	.988
28.	Otis Nixon	.988
29.	Charlie Maxwell	.988
30.	Roy White	.988
31.	Jim Busby	.988
32.	Andy Van Slyke	.988
33.	Bill Sample	.987
34.	Dwayne Murphy	.987
35.	Dwight Evans	.987
36.	Curt Flood	.987
37.	Willie Wilson	.987
38.	Lenny Dykstra	.987
39.	Eddie Milner	.987
40.	Johnny Groth	.987
41.	Tony Gonzalez	.987
42.	Billy Hatcher	.986
43.	Ruppert Jones	.986

44.	Gary Geiger	.986
45.	Tommy Harper	.986
46.	Al Kaline	.986
47.	Kevin McReynolds	.986
48.	Mike Lum	.986
49.	Lee Mazzilli	.986
50.	Tony Gwynn	.986
51.	Vic Davalillo	.986
52.	Al Bumbry	.986
53.	Tony Scott	.986
54.	Ken Griffey	.986
55.	Gary Pettis	.986
56.	Dave Collins	.986
57.	Rick Miller	.986
58.	George Hendrick	.985
59.	Dusty Baker	.985
60.	Barry Bonds	.985
61.	Gus Bell	.985
62.	Rick Manning	.985
63.	Sam Mele	.985
64.	Terry Moore	.985
65.	Cesar Cedeno	.985
66.	Merv Rettenmund	.985
67.	Rowland Office	.985
68.	Ellis Burks	.985
69.	Devon White	.985
70.	Johnny Hopp	.985
71.	Dale Mitchell	.985
72.	Dave Henderson	.985
73.	Al Cowens	.985
74.	Marvell Wynne	.985
75.	Sid Gordon	.985

MANAGER WINS

1.	Connie Mack	3,731
2.	John McGraw	2,763
3.	Bucky Harris	2,157
4.	Joe McCarthy	2,125
5.	Sparky Anderson	2,081
6.	Walter Alston	2,040
7.	Leo Durocher	2,008
8.	Casey Stengel	1,905
9.	Gene Mauch	1,902
10.	Bill McKechnie	1,896
11.	Ralph Houk	1,619
12.	Fred Clarke	1,602
13.	Dick Williams	1,571
14.	Clark Griffith	1,491
15.	Earl Weaver	1,480
16.	Tom Lasorda	1,422
17.	Miller Huggins	1,413
18.	Al Lopez	1,410
19.	Jimmy Dykes	1,406
20.	Wilbert Robinson	1,399
21.	Chuck Tanner	1,352
22.	Ned Hanlon	1,313
23.	Cap Anson	1,296
24.	Charlie Grimm	1,287
25.	Frank Selee	1,284
26.	Whitey Herzog	1,281
27.	Billy Martin	1,253
28.	Bill Rigney	1,239
29.	Joe Cronin	1,236
30.	Harry Wright	1,225
31.	Tony La Russa	1,202
32.	Hughie Jennings	1,184
33.	Lou Boudreau	1,162
34.	John McNamara	1,150
35.	Frankie Frisch	1,138
36.	Danny Murtaugh	1,115
37.	Billy Southworth	1,044
38.	Red Schoendienst	1,041
39.	Steve O'Neill	1,040
40.	Chuck Dressen	1,008

41.	Bill Virdon	995
42.	Alvin Dark	994
43.	Bobby Cox	957
44.	Frank Chance	946
45.	Paul Richards	923
46.	Don Zimmer	885
47.	George Stallings	879
48.	Charlie Comiskey	839
49.	Fred Hutchinson	830
50.	Bill Terry	823

MANAGER WINNING PERCENTAGE

1.	Joe McCarthy	.615
2.	Jim Mutrie	.611
3.	Charlie Comiskey	.608
4.	Frank Selee	.598
5.	Billy Southworth	.597
6.	Frank Chance	.593
7.	John McGraw	.586
8.	Al Lopez	.584
9.	Earl Weaver	.583
10.	Harry Wright	.581
11.	Eddie Dyer	.578
12.	Cap Anson	.578
13.	Fred Clarke	.576
14.	Cito Gaston	.575
15.	Davey Johnson	.573
16.	Monte Ward	.563
17.	Pat Moran	.561
18.	Steve O'Neill	.559
19.	Walter Alston	.558
20.	Miller Huggins	.555
21.	Patsy Tebeau	.555
22.	Bill Terry	.555
23.	Buck Ewing	.553
24.	Billy Martin	.553
25.	Sparky Anderson	.552
26.	Walter Johnson	.550
27.	Jimmy Collins	.548
28.	Charlie Grimm	.547
29.	Sam Mele	.546
30.	Moon Gibson	.546
31.	Dick Howser	.544
32.	Hughie Jennings	.543
33.	Tris Speaker	.543
34.	Leo Durocher	.540
35.	Danny Murtaugh	.540
36.	Fielder Jones	.540
37.	Joe Cronin	.540
38.	Del Baker	.538
39.	Herman Franks	.537
40.	Tony La Russa	.535
41.	Danny Ozark	.533
42.	Whitey Herzog	.532
43.	Johnny Keane	.532
44.	Ned Hanlon	.530
45.	Frank Bancroft	.530
46.	Pie Traynor	.530
47.	Lou Piniella	.527
48.	Bobby Cox	.526
49.	Tom Lasorda	.526
50.	Pete Rose	.525

TEAM WINS

		WON	LOST
1.	**NY/San Fran-NL**	**9,034**	**7,673**
	New York-NL	6,067	4,898
	San Francisco-NL	2,967	2,775
2.	**Chicago-NL**	**8,936**	**8,307**
3.	**Pittsburgh-NL**	**8,426**	**7,852**
4.	**Bos/Mil-Atl-NL**	**8,398**	**8,815**
	Boston-NL	5,118	5,598

	Milwaukee-NL	1,146	890
	Atlanta-NL	2,134	2,327
5.	**Brklyn/LA-NL**	**8,309**	**7,573**
	Brooklyn-NL	5,214	4,926
	Los Angeles-NL	3,095	2,647
6.	**Cincinnati-NL**	**8,043**	**7,857**
7.	**New York-AL**	**7,943**	**6,134**
8.	**St. Louis-NL**	**7,892**	**7,734**
9.	**Philadelphia-NL**	**7,778**	**8,902**
10.	**Detroit-AL**	**7,456**	**6,938**
11.	**Boston-AL**	**7,321**	**7,043**
12.	**Cleveland-AL**	**7,270**	**7,104**
13.	**Chicago-AL**	**7,228**	**7,127**
14.	**Wash/Minn-AL**	**6,887**	**7,476**
	Washington-AL	4,223	4,865
	Minnesota-AL	2,664	2,611
15.	**Phil/KC/Oak-AL**	**6,877**	**7,459**
	Philadelphia-AL	3,886	4,248
	Kansas City A's-AL	829	1,224
	Oakland-AL	2,162	1,987
16.	**St. Louis/Baltimore-AL**	**6,790**	**7,427**
	St. Louis-AL	3,414	4,465
	Baltimore-AL	3,376	2,962
17.	**LA/Cal-AL**	**2,553**	**2,728**
	Los Angeles-AL	308	338
	California-AL	2,245	2,390
18.	**Houston-NL**	**2,473**	**2,648**
19.	**Washington/Texas-AL**	**2,405**	**2,860**
	Washington-AL	740	1,032
	Texas-AL	1,665	1,828
20.	**New York Mets-NL**	**2,372**	**2,740**

21.	**Kansas City-AL**	**2,059**	**1,921**
22.	**Montreal-NL**	**1,948**	**2,034**
23.	**Seattle/Milwaukee-AL**	**1,924**	**2,061**
	Seattle Pilots-AL	64	98
	Milwaukee-AL	1,860	1,963
24.	**San Diego-NL**	**1,783**	**2,203**
25.	**Toronto-AL**	**1,351**	**1,344**
26.	**Seattle-AL**	**1,166**	**1,532**
27.	**Colorado-NL**	**67**	**95**
28.	**Florida-NL**	**64**	**98**

TEAM WINNING PERCENTAGE

1.	**New York-AL**	.564
2.	**NY/San Fran-NL**	.541
	New York-NL	.553
	San Francisco-NL	.517
3.	**Brooklyn/Los Angeles-NL**	.523
	Brooklyn-NL	.514
	Los Angeles-NL	.539
4.	**Chicago-NL**	.518
5.	**Detroit-AL**	.518
6.	**Pittsburgh-NL**	.518
7.	**Kansas City-AL**	.517
8.	**Boston-AL**	.510
9.	**Cincinnati-NL**	.506
10.	**Cleveland-AL**	.506
11.	**St. Louis-NL**	.505
12.	**Chicago-AL**	.504
13.	**Toronto-AL**	.501
14.	**Montreal-NL**	.489

15.	**Boston/Milwaukee-Atlanta-NL**	.488
	Boston-NL	.478
	Milwaukee-NL	.563
	Atlanta-NL	.478
16.	**Los Angeles/California-AL**	.483
	Los Angeles-AL	.477
	California-AL	.484
17.	**Houston-NL**	.483
18.	**Seattle/Milwaukee-AL**	.483
	Seattle Pilots-AL	.395
	Milwaukee-AL	.487
19.	**Philadelphia/KC/Oakland-AL**	.480
	Philadelphia-AL	.478
	Kansas City A's-AL	.404
	Oakland-AL	.521
20.	**Washington/Minnesota-AL**	.479
	Washington-AL	.465
	Minnesota-AL	.505
21.	**St. Louis/Baltimore-AL**	.478
	St. Louis-AL	.433
	Baltimore-AL	.533
22.	**Philadelphia-NL**	.466
23.	**New York Mets-NL**	.464
24.	**Washington/Texas-AL**	.457
	Washington-AL	.418
	Texas-AL	.477
25.	**San Diego-NL**	.447
26.	**Seattle-AL**	.432
27.	**Colorado-NL**	.414
28.	**Florida-NL**	.395

Index

Index